The *De Re Militari* of Vegetius

Vegetius' late Roman text became a well-known and highly respected 'classic' in the Middle Ages, transformed by its readers into the authority on the waging of war. Christopher Allmand analyses the medieval after-life of the *De re militari*, tracing the growing interest in the text from the Carolingian world to the late Middle Ages, suggesting how the written word may have influenced the development of military practice in that period. While emphasising that success depended on a commander's ability to outwit the enemy with a carefully selected, well-trained and disciplined army, the *De re militari* inspired other unexpected develop-ments, such as that of the 'national' army, and helped create a context in which the role of the soldier assumed greater social and political impor-tance. Allmand explores the significance of the text and the changes it brought for those who accepted the implications of its central messages.

CHRISTOPHER ALLMAND is Emeritus Professor of Medieval History at the University of Liverpool. He has published widely on the history of war and medieval society, including *The Hundred Years War: England and France at war c.1300–c.1450* (Cambridge, 1988) and *The New Cambridge Medieval History, Volume VII: c.1415–c.1500* (as editor, Cambridge, 1998).

Frontispiece: A copy of Vegetius' work is presented to a king (*left*), while the importance of training is underlined (*right*). (BL Royal 20 B xi, fo. 3)

The *De Re Militari* of Vegetius

The Reception, Transmission and Legacy of a Roman Text in the Middle Ages

Christopher Allmand

Emeritus Professor of Medieval History,
University of Liverpool

CAMBRIDGE
UNIVERSITY PRESS

 # 72770 2083

CAMBRIDGE UNIVERSITY PRESS
Cambridge, New York, Melbourne, Madrid, Cape Town,
Singapore, São Paulo, Delhi, Tokyo, Mexico City

Cambridge University Press
The Edinburgh Building, Cambridge CB2 8RU, UK

Published in the United States of America by Cambridge University Press,
New York

www.cambridge.org
Information on this title: www.cambridge.org/9781107000278

First published 2011

Printed in the United Kingdom at the University Press, Cambridge

A catalogue record for this publication is available from the British Library

Library of Congress Cataloguing in Publication data
Allmand, C. T.
The De re militari of Vegetius : the reception, transmission and legacy of a
Roman text in the Middle Ages / Christopher Allmand.
p.   cm.
Includes bibliographical references and index.
ISBN 978-1-107-00027-8 (hardback)
1. Military art and science – History – Medieval, 500–1500.   2. Military art
and science – Europe – History.   3. Europe – History, Military.   4. Military
history, Medieval.   5. Vegetius Renatus, Flavius. De re militari.   6. Military
art and science – Rome – Early works to 1800.   7. Rome – Army – Early works
to 1800.   I. Title.
U37.A45   2011
355.020937 – dc23   2011031352

ISBN 978-1-107-00027-8 Hardback

Contents

Figures

Preface

It is now some forty years since I first became aware of the name Vegetius, and of how often I was meeting it in a variety of medieval texts, in particular in those concerned with war. It is getting on for thirty-five years that I first spoke about him and other 'veteres scriptores de re militari' at a meeting at the University of Nottingham. For years, thereafter, I copied down information on odd bits of paper which came to hand. Elsewhere, unbeknown to me, historians of late Antiquity and the Middle Ages were working more scientifically on aspects of his work, the classicists being interested in his sources and contemporary context and relevance, the medievalists rather more in showing the influence of his text upon the practice of war during the long Middle Ages. The past generation has seen a marked growth of interest in Vegetius, witnessed to by new editions and, not least, by translations of his work. Furthermore, the medieval translations of his text have provided not only historians, but philologists and those interested in the development of European vernacular languages, with evidence useful to more than a single discipline. In 1998, Philippe Richardot published the first historical study of Vegetius' text, which helped me in a number of ways as I approached the subject from sometimes rather different directions.

From the start, it seemed important to appreciate how Vegetius' medieval readers had responded to the texts which they read. The limitations of microfilms, however carefully made, soon became obvious to one wanting to read and study such responses, mostly written in the margins of manuscripts. In the end, I handled more than 200 manuscripts of the Latin text and almost 100 of those of vernacular translations. It is pleasant to record that the staff in libraries where it is policy to offer the researcher a film of a manuscript being studied understood the problem, and were willing to modify their practices to help me.

I have been constantly accompanied on my travels by the invaluable *Handlist of extant manuscripts of the De re militari*, published in 1979, a copy of which its author, Charles R. Shrader, kindly gave me many years ago, and which became a well-used and annotated companion. More recently, Dr Shrader's list has to some extent been overtaken by a more complete one drawn up by Michael Reeve, lately Professor of Latin at Cambridge, who has provided the world of scholarship with the second new edition of Vegetius' text to appear in less than ten years. In preparing his edition Professor Reeve consulted almost every known manuscript. I have benefited greatly from his practical experience, and I am deeply grateful to him for help and advice generously offered over a period of years, as I am, too, for his willingness to read and comment on an early version of this study.

I am grateful, too, to colleagues who have invited me to speak on aspects of Vegetius' work at meetings in Bristol, Durham, Edinburgh, Leeds, Liverpool, London, Nottingham, Oxford, Paris, Perth (Western Australia) and York. Long ago Professor R. B. Tate, and more recently Professor Sir Peter Russell, offered me bibliographical help on Iberian matters related to the study of Vegetius; I have three times had the pleasure of addressing groups of Hispanic scholars, and have greatly benefited from hearing their views. Bernard Guenée invited me to address his *séminaire* in Paris many years ago. My thanks also go to Peter Lewis not only for reading some of the pages which appear below, but for giving me the opportunity of speaking more than once to his 'Late Medieval France' seminar, held at All Souls College, Oxford, on Vegetian and related subjects.

Over the years, I have benefited from practical help in tracing manuscripts given me by a number of antiquarian booksellers. Librarians, too numerous to mention by name, in more than a dozen countries have either replied to my enquiries or welcomed me and given me help when I have visited their libraries, which have generally proved to be very agreeable places in which to work. In the spirit of generous co-operation common among scholars Lola Badia, Diane Bornstein, Cecil Clough, Philippe Contamine, Jean Devaux, Frank Fürbeth, John Gillingham, Walter Goffart, Michael C. E. Jones, Rainer Leng, the late Michael Mallett, João Monteiro and Richard and Mary Rouse gave me copies of their published works; Antoni Alomar Canyelles sent me copies of his unpublished transcriptions of the two Catalan translations; and José Manuel Fradejas helped me with problems arising from the Castilian translation, an edition of which he is preparing for publication. Barry Taylor, of the British Library, kindly took an active interest in my work, and was a source of up-to-the-minute bibliographical information from Spain, while my one-time colleague Roger Wright helped me with matters of translation. Sydney Anglo, Christopher Tyerman and Daniel Wakelin each cast a critical eye over a section of my work for me. I am particularly indebted to two good friends, Maurice Keen and Tony Goodman, who both read an early version of this book. I hope to have taken account of the suggestions for improvement which they made.

By making positive suggestions for improvement, pointing out the traps which I had set myself, encouraging me to modify both my opinions and my use of language, the two readers for Cambridge University Press have contributed to making this a better book. I thank them both for their professional approach to the task given them, as I do those members of the Press' staff, Liz Friend-Smith, Chloe Howell, Rosina Di Marzo, Beata Mako and not least Frances Brown, a wonderful copy-editor, who have done so much to transform a text into a book. I alone admit responsibility for what is to be read in the pages which follow.

While pursuing evidence in nearly 100 libraries I received financial assistance from the University of La Sapienzia, Rome, as part of an exchange scheme arranged with the University of Liverpool, for two visits to the Vatican Library. Above all, I am hugely indebted to the Leverhulme Trust for making a generous and greatly appreciated financial contribution towards the costs of this undertaking. I feel that the Trustees must have long ago written off the investment which they made in giving me their support. Belatedly, but no less very sincerely, I thank them for upholding the confidence expressed (I can only suppose!) in my referees' reports regarding my ability to deliver a book. Without that assistance, I could never have contemplated starting upon this journey.

My wife, Bernadette, has helped in innumerable ways to bring this project to a conclusion. The book is dedicated to her, with gratitude.

Abbreviations

AHR	*American Historical Review*
AN	Archives Nationales, Paris
Annales ESC	*Annales: Economies, Sociétés, Civilisations*
Add. Ms.	Additional Manuscript (British Library)
BEC	*Bibliothèque de l'École des Chartes*
BIHR	*Bulletin of the Institute of Historical Research*
BL	British Library, London
BN	Biblioteca Nacional, Madrid
BnF	Bibliothèque nationale de France, Paris
CCCM	*Corpus Christianorum, Continuatio medievalis*
DRM	*De re militari*
DRP	*De regimine principum*
EETS	Early English Text Society
EHR	*English Historical Review*
JMMH	*Journal of Medieval Military History*
JMedH	*Journal of Medieval History*
JWCI	*Journal of the Warburg and Courtauld Insiitutes*
MGH	Monumenta Germaniae Historica
RH	*Revue Historique*
RHistS	Royal Historical Society
RS	Rolls Series
SATF	Société des Anciens Textes Français
SHF	Société de l'Histoire de France
SP	*Siete Partidas*

Introduction

Little is known about Publius Vegetius Renatus. He was probably born in the mid-fourth century AD, possibly in Spain. Although familiar with the language of the army, it is unlikely that he was ever a soldier or had practical military experience. He was, rather, a member of the bureaucratic élite at the imperial court, bearing the title 'Flavius', which identifies him as a public servant, as does the title 'comes', found in one branch of the manuscript tradition. It is likely, however, that he had experience of the recruitment, administration and provisioning of armies, for these receive much of his attention. From the *Mulomedicina*, a work on veterinary medicine which he almost certainly wrote, we learn that he was a much travelled man.[1] From the evidence of the *De re militari*, it appears that he also appreciated literature, as his references to the works of Virgil and Sallust testify. That he was a Christian (writing some three or four generations after Constantine had issued the Edict of Milan in 312) is witnessed to by his references to the Trinity in the *De re militari*.[2]

The discussion regarding the date of composition of the *De re militari* has caused much ink to flow. We cannot be certain about the precise date, as the author does not say for which emperor he was writing, although it must have been between 383 and 450. A recent study of the cultural, literary and historical milieu of, and the language used by Vegetius, has led its author to suggest, that, on the balance of probability, a date in the mid-fifth century was the most likely.[3] Majority opinion, however, still appears to favour a date in the late 380s, and that Vegetius' 'patron' was his fellow Spaniard, Theodosius I 'the Great' (379–395), the first emperor to enforce orthodox Christianity and the last to have charge of a united empire. In any event, in whatever form the text was presented to the imperial authority, the origins of the work lay in a memorandum of

---

[1] The *De re militari* and the *Mulomedicina* are found together in BL Royal 12 C. xxii.
[2] *DRM*, II, 5.
[3] M. B. Charles, *Vegetius in context. Establishing the date of the* Epitoma rei militaris (Stuttgart, 2007).

1

proposals on military reform which Vegetius presented to the emperor. This was well received, and its author was asked to write more. It was from this effort that what came to be known as the *Epitoma rei militaris* or, less formally, as the *De re militari* emerged.

The modern reader should be clear what he can expect to find in Vegetius' work. As an 'art of war', the *De re militari* does not possess the originality which many imagine it to have. Its author (a civilian, in today's language) lacked practical experience of fighting to compile such a work. However, what he could do, and was good at doing, was consider, assimilate and draw practical conclusions of a general kind from earlier Latin military literature, much of it now lost, in which he was well read. Was this likely to produce a masterpiece whose impact would be immediate? No. To his contemporaries, the *De re militari* may have seemed retrospective, if not old fashioned, in its views and attitudes, and it probably made little impression upon them.

The reader is offered a text which is esssentially a work of polemic reflecting what its author regarded as the pressing needs of the time, the effective recruitment, training and organisation of the army, along with the requirement to provide it with the arms and equipment necessary to achieve victory against those threatening the security of the Empire. While it deals, in some respects, with strategic requirements, it does not consider every aspect of war. Little is said about cavalry, precisely because there was little to say;[4] the same could not be said of infantry. And although attention is paid to the defence of towns, there is little advice on how to attack them, perhaps because Rome's main enemies were not town dwellers. This is a work concerned mainly with field armies, and the contribution which these could make to the success of Roman arms.

How was the ruler to learn what he needed to know regarding the 'disciplina armorum'? For Vegetius, the answer lay in the written word. Compiled under a particular set of circumstances, the *De re militari* represented what were, in its author's view, 'systematized remedies', the search for which made him look back unashamedly to the days when the Roman army had carried all before it. A firm believer in the value of the study of past writers on war, whose teachings, both moral and practical, passed down through generations, Vegetius sought to incorporate them into his model. So it is that the reader encounters (at least by name) the historian Sallust, and some of the main military writers of the past who had written in Latin: Cornelius Celsus, Paternus, Cato the Censor and Julius Frontinus. As he formulated his ideas, so he showed where these came from and what had influenced them. He modestly

---

[4] *DRM*, I, 20; III, 26.

played down his contribution which, he insisted, was limited to having selected basic ideas 'dispersed through various authors and books' which he had brought together, 'summarising [them] as if to form an orderly sequence'. Explaining how the Romans had conquered much of the known world, Vegetius emphasised that while it was important to know what had happened, it was more important to learn why and how it had happened. It was in seeking answers to such questions that he reached what he regarded as the root causes of Roman success, and in so doing helped to further the long tradition begun by the Greeks, who had created the science of war passed down through the written word 'later consolidated by the authority of generals'. It does neither text nor author a favour if the work's derivative character is ignored or forgotten. There are few signs of any impact which it may have had in the early years of its life. Although, unlike the *Mulomedicina*, not translated into Greek, the work was known in Constantinople, by then capital of the Empire, when Flavius Eutropius corrected it in 450. It is possible that it was in Constantinople that Cassiodorus came to know it in the mid-sixth century, while about 600 a Greek rendering of twenty-one of the Rules ('Regulae') contained in the *De re militari* (III, 26) was incorporated in the *Strategikon* (VIII.B) associated with the emperor Maurice, although it may be doubted whether his knowledge of Vegetius' text extended any further.

These would be only the first examples of generations to come to use the contents as a mine of information and ideas for works of very different character, some primarily military, others less so. The emphasis of this study will be to see how men in the Middle Ages responded to what Vegetius wrote, what parts of his work they appreciated (and why), and how they used what they learnt from him to influence what they wrote and did centuries after his death. From this Vegetius, a near contemporary of such intellectual giants as Ambrose, Augustine and Jerome, will emerge as a man of both philosophical and practical influence who, although not an original thinker, set out principles which, in later times and circumstances, would have influence extending beyond the military sphere to which they had originally been directed.

The main purpose of the inquiry traced in the pages which follow is to help a modern-day reader appreciate how the contents of the *De re militari* may have been understood when read through the eyes of medieval man, and what effects that understanding may have had, mainly but far from exclusively, upon military practice during the Middle Ages. The inquiry will be divided into three parts. In the first, on the reception of the text, attention will concentrate upon what the surviving manuscripts of the *De re militari* can tell us about the responses of readers to the work, and what they found interesting and useful in it. Some two-thirds of the extant manuscripts bear marginal evidence of such reactions which, when assembled, enables us to understand something of the response of the otherwise anonymous readership to Vegetius' ideas. Was it, for them, largely a historical text, evidence of how a man thought about military affairs in the late fourth century? On the other hand, did it contain ideas and information, about military organisation for instance, which could be useful in a later age and setting? Or should it be read mainly as a moral or philosophical work whose advice and teachings were, in most respects, simply 'basic principles in an unspecific form which could be adapted to serve a great variety of military situations'[5] and, therefore, likely to appeal to all ages? To many others, as the manuscripts reveal, the text was largely a source of philological knowledge, a mine of unfamiliar words and terms which clearly puzzled some while delighting others: 'About that word "accensi", which gave us trouble; I have found it in Vegetius. This was the discovery I wanted to share with you', Erasmus wrote to a correspondent in 1497.[6] The use of the interrogative 'Quid . . . ' in the margins of many manuscripts underlines the sense of questioning which filled the minds of many who read the *De re militari* anticipating the chance of acquiring new knowledge. The medieval manuscripts provide the modern reader with a valuable opportunity of accompanying readers of the period, among them no less a figure than Petrarch, along what was for many a voyage of discovery into the past, and how that past might be related to the present.

Our quest can be furthered by considering two further, closely related matters: what texts were most commonly associated with Vegetius' work, and who were the principal owners of that work? In the cases in which the *De re militari* was linked to another text, whether through being copied by a single scribe or through sharing the binding of a single codex, what associations linked Vegetius' work with others in the minds of its owner? Were they texts which happened to be 'classical'? Or, perhaps, had they a subject, theme or author in common? When the *De re militari* was bound, as it was on several occasions, with the *Strategemata* of Frontinus, we can reasonably assume that the owner's intention was to create a codex of classical writings on war.[7] This was particularly so when the owner may have been of the military class; here, a link between the content of the work and his professional/social interests clearly existed. Rulers,

[5] *Vegetius: Epitome of military science*, trans. N. P. Milner (2nd rev. edn, Liverpool, 1996), xiii.

[6] *The correspondence of Erasmus. Letters 1 to 141, 1484–1500*, ed. W. K. Ferguson, trans. R. A. B. Mynors and D. F. S. Thomson (Toronto, 1974), I, 116.

[7] See below, chapter 4, pp. 56–9.

as Vegetius had emphasised and the Middle Ages were to accept, must know about war; to such as these, the *De re militari* would be useful. But would it be of use or, possibly more important still, of interest to military men alone? Were there elements or underlying messages in Vegetius' work which could appeal to those who had no prima facie interest in its content? The clergy, or at least certain ones of their number, were major owners of the text. What can be learnt from surviving codices and their owners (as far as we know who they were) which will inform us about the reception of the *De re militari* in the Middle Ages?

The section on the transmission, which follows, will attempt to show first, through a consideration of a number of codices copied in the Middle Ages, how Vegetian ideas came to be taken up and passed on through the works of selected medieval authors. These 'particular responses' to Vegetius are largely taken from examples of work which, it can be suggested with confidence, owed at least something to Vegetian thinking and advice. What makes this section both interesting and important is the variety of avenues along which that thought was to travel, and the influence it was to exert. Both John of Salisbury and Giles of Rome, writing in the twelfth and thirteenth centuries, used Vegetius' teaching about the army to bolster a message at times seemingly more political than military, the need to enhance the effective power of the ruler as a force for peace and order in society.[8] The works penned by Guillaume le Breton early in the thirteenth century, and the *Siete Partidas*, compiled half a century later, each underlined the importance of a king taking steps to lead his people against a common enemy; this, too, was both a military and a political message. Towards the end of the Middle Ages the emphasis would be upon the need for military organisation to be placed increasingly in the hands of the ruler, as the advice of both Christine de Pisan and Jean Juvénal des Ursins, and the contents of the Burgundian military ordinances issued by duke Charles the Bold, all show. The trend would be brought to fruition in the work of Machiavelli. Finally, to show that Vegetius offered ideas that could be useful in forms of conflict other than that between armies, the waging of the spiritual war also found itself guided by certain Vegetian principles, set out in the work of the monk Denis the Carthusian.

In this way, Vegetius would influence the ages which came after him. We should not underestimate the debt which the propagation of his ideas would owe to those writers whose works, written centuries later, diffused his ideas for later generations to consider and act upon. Anyone wanting

---

[8] The point is emphasised by F. H. Sherwood, 'Studies in medieval uses of Vegetius' *Epitoma rei militaris*' (PhD diss., University of California, Los Angeles, 1980).

to cite a respected authority could do no better than to make use of, or at least reference to, the *De re militari*, the work, as a number of illuminated manuscripts show, of a sage to whom rulers, in particular, should feel obliged to listen. At the same time, it must be recognised that the Vegetian influence, reflected in a group of texts written between 1465 and 1520, suggests an inspiration in slow decline, yielding to the rapidly changing nature of war.

Together, these serve to underline the variety of texts reflecting the ideas of the Roman writer to be compiled in the Middle Ages. An important practical element in the transmission of Vegetian ideas and principles was to be found in the translations which appeared from the last quarter of the thirteenth century onwards, a process (the breaking of the Latin monopoly) which, by 1500, would bring Vegetius to the notice of readers in six European languages. The story of translation, which should be seen as part of the broader tendency towards the 'vernacularisation' of classical texts at this period, was not always straightforward. For whom was a translation intended, and for what purpose was it made? Translating a work containing so much technical vocabulary into meaningful language created problems for the translator. A rendering which stuck closely to the original (what today we might call a 'crib') might be a difficult task even for a man with a good command of fourth-century Latin. On the other hand, by translating the text freely he might recontextualise it to make a contribution to the development of the military thought and practice of the late Middle Ages through (in effect) the creation of a new work which had something to teach his readers about war in their own time. Yet, if this road were followed, would not those interested in the 'historic' text lose out, for, as the evidence of marginalia makes plain, unfamiliar words and terms interested many readers? As will be seen, translators, some more skilled than others, took different views as to what their task involved. However, their contribution to the dissemination of Vegetian ideas, like the role played by patrons who commissioned the translations, should never be in doubt.

We should appreciate that an understanding of the *De re militari* could be acquired in other ways than these. Although a complete text gave the interested reader the chance to read and interpret the work as he wished, not all had the intention, the time or the opportunity to read the entire text. From early on, collections of excerpts presented readers with the chance to read selections from the work, selections which inevitably restricted the reader's knowledge and, consequently, his appreciation of Vegetius' ideas. Yet by their very nature collections of excerpts could be influential, as being all too easily able to persuade readers that what they read constituted the very essence of Vegetian thinking while, in fact, reflecting mainly the particular interest of the person who had chosen the excerpts, thereby not necessarily offering a true reflection of the work as a whole.

One may ask how far Vegetius, if fancifully brought back to life a thousand years after his death, would have appreciated the scope and use being made of the *De re militari*. He might have been surprised by the degree of authority which had come to be attached to his name ('Vegetius' came to be almost synonyous with 'war'), since he had written for what was, for him, the present. Was the price of reputation the 'decontextualisation' of his work and its original recommendations? Would he have appreciated how his work had been dissected (the creation of collections of excerpts did precisely that) rather than being regarded as a whole? Might he have thought that some were reading too much into his text, and that he was being interpreted in ways he had never intended? What would he have thought about the use of certain crucial words when his text came to be translated into the languages of later times, conditions and circumstances? Was the late-Roman understanding of what an army ('exercitus') was understood, if not shared, by later ages? The number of occasions when the word 'exercitus' is written in the margin of manuscripts suggests an unusually high interest in the Roman concept of the army and of its place and function in society. When Vegetius wrote about selection, how much of this was there (or could there be?) in the Middle Ages? In brief, while at a linguistic level such words and concepts might, to all intents and purposes, be fairly easily understood, at a practical level was there not always the likelihood that, rather like that of Ovid, Vegetius' work had not always been fully understood, or was being used to serve new purposes, not necessarily by some deliberate metamorphosis but, in this instance, more by the effects of the passing of time on everyday vocabulary?

The third section will suggest that Vegetius left the medieval world with elements of a not insignificant military legacy. Some critics may not agree with this, preferring to disparage the banality of much of his work, arguing, for example, that it does not require a Vegetius to tell a commander that he should be well informed about things going on around him, that he must act with caution, and that he should earn the respect of his soldiers by the way he treats them. Is advice claimed to be Vegetian not largely common sense rather than the expression of opinion on the part of a man who, although he had read a lot, had never experienced real fear, while presuming to tell military men what fear was in language which hardly corresponded to that used by modern-day writers with field experience to back them up? For these critics, Vegetius' emphasis on the passing down of experience through the written word underlined his 'bookish' rather than his 'hands-on' experience of war. For such reasons, it is argued, his teachings did not merit the regard generally accorded to them in the Middle Ages.

In spite of such reservations, it will be argued that a reading of the *De re militari* by men of the Middle Ages did leave something of a legacy. This assumed different forms. Certainly the army (and those who fought in it) might emerge enhanced in the eyes of society as a result of what Vegetius wrote about it. Following the teaching of John of Salisbury and of Giles of Rome (among others), the army slowly developed into a 'statist' force, the 'hand' ('manus') used by the ruler to fulfil his obligation to protect his people, even if it was sometimes abused by him for his own advantage. Similarly the 'miles', whether knight or soldier, assumed an enhanced position in society partly as a result of descriptions of him as the protector of society and the public good.

The Vegetian canon also attributed great practical importance to leadership. The gradual move from command exercised by virtue of social rank to that based on authority delegated by the ruler to those who had proved their military worth would be an important one. The emphasis which the text placed on a reasoned approach to the waging of war would also become increasingly widespread. The importance of the triumph of the mind over physical strength, based, as Vegetius had emphasised, upon a proper assessment of the current military situation, would be seen as increasingly significant as time passed by.

The evidence of a work's legacy is not always easy to pin down in precise terms. But an examination of the relationship between important aspects of Vegetian thinking and certain historically recognised developments in, for instance, military practice and procedure can lead to the recognition that the *De re militari* inspired future practitioners of the art of war. The marked interest in certain themes among the readers of the text strongly suggests that, in returning time and again to those same themes (illustrated here, for instance, by a recurring interest in matters of provisioning and logistics), they were creating a de facto legacy for some of the ideas offered and often insisted upon by Vegetius. In so far as men read the *De re militari* for examples of good practice (which might well extend to a search for examples of effective military organisation, as described mainly in Book II) from which they might seek inspiration useful in their own day, we are entitled to see this as recognition that readers were ready to acknowledge that the *De re militari* constituted a legacy to be drawn upon by men who lived centuries after it was written. This evidence only confirms the fact that the history of Vegetius' text in the Middle Ages was no ordinary one. 'Few classical texts can boast as many Carolingian witnesses as the *Epitoma*, or so wide a spread either on the map or over the centuries, or vernacular translations at so early a date.'[9] What follows is an attempt to show and underline the truth of that statement.

[9] M. D. Reeve, 'The transmission of Vegetius's *Epitoma rei militaris*', *Aevum*, 74 (2000), 250.

Part I

The medieval reception

1   General remarks on the manuscripts

How should we describe the process of the medieval reception of the *De re militari* from the manuscripts which have survived into our own time? How was the text read and understood? A manuscript, of course, will not talk about its life, about those who have owned, read or merely handled it. Yet, if examined closely, its folios can reveal a good deal about the use to which it has been put, whether it has been much read or has simply taken up space on a shelf, not to speak of its contents which have been either appreciated or criticised by past readers.

Of the 200 or more Latin manuscripts examined, about a third show little or no evidence of having prompted their readers to leave evidence of their labours; sometimes the folios remain uncannily clean. Are we then to conclude that these texts will have played little part in the transmission of Vegetius' ideas? Others bear the marks of having been read, sometimes closely, and of having encouraged readers to respond by marking the folios in different ways. It is these manuscripts, the remaining two-thirds of the total, which provide us with the material upon which to form judgements regarding the interest provoked by the *De re militari* in the Middle Ages.

The personality and interests of the reader, along with the age in which he lives, will determine why a text is read, and how its contents are appreciated and understood. Different people, of different backgrounds and levels of knowledge or education, will look for and discover different things in this, or any, text. Knowledge of what might be found in the *De re militari* spread largely through clerical circles, for it was in those communities that men who read Latin lived. We know that the clergy were among the first guardians of Vegetius' work and teaching, probably because, from early Christian times, the lives of monks and soldiers, both governed by discipline and obedience to authority, were seen as having much in common.[1] The fact that the text, as well as the notes and

---

[1] The text was 'l'equivalente militare della regola di S. Benedetto' (quoted in A. A. Settia, *De re militari. Pratica e teoria nella guerra medievale* (Rome, 2008), 41. See E. Manning, 'La

comments on it, were, until a late date, written in Latin is a strong indication of this. This is backed up by the facts of ownership as we know them from the texts themselves. Many copies were made for monastic communities for inclusion in their libraries, thereby underlining the fact that until the fourteenth century owners, not to say readers, were largely members of the clerical or, at least, the formally educated class. This tends to be confirmed by the existence of examples written in heavily abbreviated script, sometimes in a cramped hand, often set out in narrow columns. Only those accustomed to reading such texts could have benefited from the experience. Once again, the finger points at a clerical or well-educated readership.

What treatment was meted out to the manuscripts by their readers? From the start it is important to understand that the margins contain words, marks, signs, even small drawings executed, in many cases, by more than a single hand, sometimes over a period of centuries. A few examples will emphasise this. A line down the side of a passage is clearly intended to reflect the interest of the reader who drew it. Passages dealt with in this way could be quite lengthy, sometimes as long as a whole chapter. More often, however, a passage or form of words deemed worthy of notice or remembrance was very much shorter, a line or less, or perhaps two or three consecutive lines. Common, too, was the use of other ways of drawing the attention to a particular passage of a future reader, who might be the same or an altogether different person. A capital 'N', or 'Nota', was used throughout the period, but was perhaps more common in the central Middle Ages. Examples of a hand with long fingers extended to point to a particular line or sentence are commonly found. Occasionally the content of a sentence or group of sentences might be summed up in a drawing, such as that of a Roman soldier or a military formation, as the contents of a passage demanded.[2] These, and other signs (sometimes, and surely not without significance, a monk's head)[3] drew attention to individual passages. It was not uncommon for readers to indicate their own appreciation of a text already well marked by earlier readers, showing the interest which the passage had provoked in several readers, perhaps over a long period of time. It can be of considerable interest to know that a text deemed worthy of note in one century interested another reader a century or two (or perhaps more) later.

---

signification de "militare–militia–miles" dans la règle de Saint Benoît', *Revue bénédictine*, 72 (1962), 135–8.

[2] Bern, Burgerbibl. 280, fo. 50; Leiden, Univ. Periz. F. 17, fos. 121v, 122v–124.

[3] London, BL Harley 2667, fos. 5v, 11v, 12. Manuscripts with several drawings include BL Add. Ms 21,242, and Vatican, Chigi. H. vii 238.

Alas, too few copyists gave details about the date when their work was done, so that palaeographical evidence is often of crucial importance in dating a manuscript. Even when this is expertly done, some elasticity must be given to the dating proposed. Difficult as this is, putting a date to marginal comments is often infinitely more difficult. Occasionally, luck may be on one's side. A word or words in the margin may be in the hand of the scribe; in which case it becomes doubly important to arrive at an accurate dating of the manuscript. Sometimes an 'N' may be stylistically close to another in the text itself, or may be datable by its own style, perhaps to the estimated date of the text, perhaps later. But with regard to the huge number of simple markings, it is more often than not almost impossible to judge their date accurately. They may be contemporary – or nearly so – with the manuscript: sometimes one senses that they may have been copied by the copyist along with the text itself.[4] At the same time, we should remember that texts might sometimes be read centuries after they were copied, so that comments are not necessarily contemporary with the text. In such cases, the palaeographical evidence is often clearer and more explicit.

How, then, can one date a note, even approximately? For self-evident reasons, it cannot be older than the manuscript on which it is found; hence the great importance of narrowing down the date of the copying of the text itself. Very occasionally this is helped by reference made to a databable event or person in a note which provides a *terminus post quem*. Such precise information is very helpful in the otherwise often difficult task of according even an approximate date to a marginal scribble.

The method employed here in noting the highlighted passages in the manuscripts examined has been simple, hardly scientific, at times even crude. I have inspected these postils (most of them hardly worthy of the term) and noted their relationship with the text, and where they impinge upon it. Occasionally, I have concluded that the marginalia were contemporary with the text. The later the copy, the less margin of error there is for the dating of notes and comments. However, my inability to date these scribblings with complete confidence has meant that it has not always proved possible to assert that the highlighting of a passage was done at a particular period, thereby making it difficult to show as clearly as I would have liked how different passages of the *De re militari* may have appealed to different readers at different times in the Middle Ages.

---

[4] Salamanca, Univ. 2137, has marginal annotations in the copyist's hand indicating author-ities, and cross-references to other chapters within the work. Cross-referencing is also to be found in, for example, Madrid, BN 9245, and Trento, Com. W 3154.

None the less, for a substantial number of individual passages it has proved possible to suggest either that they always (or normally) constituted the most (or least) appreciated part of the *De re militari* or, as in some cases, that the fortunes of particular chapters or passages fluctuated with the passing of centuries. In spite of the difficulties encountered, it is evident that an examination of the texts can tell us something, sometimes important, about how different centuries, with different interests and preoccupations, looked to and reacted to the ideas and proposals which Vegetius had set out at the end of the fourth century.

2 Analysis of the manuscripts

This chapter is intended to introduce the reader to, and concentrate his attention upon, a particular view of Vegetius' work, that taken by those largely unknown persons who read his text in the period between the ninth and the fifteenth centuries. Today, writing in the margins of books not owned by the reader is normally frowned upon. In earlier times, readers were less afraid to express themselves, whether it was to record, with an excitement or pleasure which can sometimes still be felt, a discovery just made, to correct or question a text, or to draw attention to an important idea well expressed. To the historian, such comments, some conveyed as small drawings, are a godsend, since they often represent the spontaneous reaction of readers to the text before them.

In this chapter, an attempt will be made to utilise the examination of some 200 or more Latin manuscripts of the *De re militari* to see, among other things, what parts of the text interested readers, and whether they thought Vegetius' ideas were applicable to their own day, and (although this has proved difficult) to judge whether conditions and circumstances in the readers' own times made some passages or sections of the work more interesting or relevant to them than others. It is clear that interest in different parts of the text varied with the times at which they were read. This we learn from focusing on the marginalia found in the surviving manuscripts, marginalia which are key witnesses with valuable things to reveal as we try to understand how the text of the *De re militari* may have been understood and appreciated by its medieval readers.

Book I

From the very first line of Book I, Vegetius set out the fundamental point of his credo: skill and training rather than numbers or inordinate bravery bring success, a message which, according to the evidence of surviving manuscripts, was to be increasingly regarded as fundamental as the Middle Ages progressed. How could the Romans, Vegetius asked in a frequently noted passage, have dominated the world if not through discipline, order and training?[1] Success in war was based largely upon what had been done to prepare for it; conversely, defeat often resulted from a failure to anticipate future action. It was an early expression of the idea that the victory achieved at Waterloo had really been won on the playing fields of Eton.

Vegetius' approach emphasised that future success lay in making use of the experience which the past could offer. His argument emphasised the central role which the army had played in creating and defending the dominion which Rome had exercised over the world. Fundamental was his understanding of what an army, and its constituent parts, consisted of. From the start he showed a willingness to put certain questions up for consideration, and to work out the answers analytically. The army, of course, consisted of its personnel. That, however, was not sufficient. The personnel had to be men of high quality, with proven qualifications based on experience. In order to achieve a high level of professional attainment, the army required that recruits be carefully selected, instructed in the arts of war, brought to and maintained at a high degree of physical fitness by regular training, and prepared for the eventualities of war, points which showed all the signs of having been carefully noted by readers. It was, however, when Vegetius stressed that a good understanding of the science of war increased men's courage ('audacia'), and their training made them less afraid to fight,[2] that he emphasised the point with which he had begun (but was now more convincing), that small but well-trained forces were more effective than those which, for lack of preparation, exposed themselves unnecessarily to the enemy. These concluding lines of chapter 1 were marked enthusiastically by readers; notes in a ninth-century manuscript may well be contemporary with the text itself.[3]

However, it was legitimate to ask what sort of men might advantageously be trained as recruits. Vegetius would give his answer over the course of several chapters. Of these, chapter 2, which dealt with the regions of the world which produced the best soldiers (he was mainly concerned with the effects of climate upon personality), and chapter 5 (on the ideal height of the recruit) scarcely troubled the notice of

---

[1] When, in the mid-fifteenth century, Ghillebert de Lannoy wrote in praise of Roman discipline which had given the Empire dominion over the world ('la discipline de chevalerie, aigrement tenue et gardee, [qui] enfanta a l'empire de Romme la monarchie du monde') he was surely expressing Vegetius' statement (*DRM*, I, 1) in his own words. See M. Vale, *War and chivalry. Warfare and aristocratic culture in England, France and Burgundy at the end of the Middle Ages* (London, 1981), 16, n. 7.

[2] The point was taken up in so many words by Sir John Fortescue in the fifteenth century. See *On the laws and governance of England* (ed. and trans. S. Lockwood, Cambridge, 1997), 78 (ch. liv).

[3] Escorial, L. iii. 33, fo. 3.

medieval readers, more interested to learn about other factors. In chapter 3, for instance, Vegetius discussed whether townsmen or countrymen made better soldiers. His unequivocal statement that the superiority of the countryman could never be doubted, and his reasons for preferring that group, drew a good deal of attention. One reader interpreted this as meaning that townsmen should be called to arms only as an extreme measure ('urbani nisi cogente necessitate ad arma non sunt vocandi').[4] When called upon to do so, however, they must adopt the more moderate diet and habits of countrymen, learn to live under canvas, and keep away from the attractions of towns while undergoing training. The farmer, like Quintus Cincinnatus, who turned soldier was the ideal to look to. Those unaccustomed to the life of luxury feared death less than those who were.[5] They were better soldiers for it.

What was there about these ideas which provoked the understanding of men living centuries later, as the response of readers clearly shows? As already noted, most early copies of Vegetius' work were to be found in the hands of churchmen, who were among the leaders of the movements to bring peace out of internecine rivalries between secular lords so common from the tenth to the twelfth centuries. Much of what Vegetius had written would also have appealed in particular to monks who, intent upon a life of asceticism, would have been impressed by the self-denying ordinance of the new recruit (were he an urban dweller) to abandon the life of luxury for one of rigour and self-discipline. We should also see this chapter in the context of the criticism, often made from the twelfth century onwards, of the knight who, by giving himself over to soft beds, sleep, wine and women, abandoned the rigours of his calling. There were clear similarities between the roads which led to sanctity and those which enabled men to become good soldiers, those of self-discipline and constant training being but two of them. At the root of both lay a certain disregard of self and life. It was the final statement in chapter 3 to this effect which drew the attention of readers of more than fifty manuscripts, almost a quarter of all surviving Latin texts of Vegetius' work.

The considerable and increasing interest aroused among readers by the ideas expressed in chapter 7, in which Vegetius discussed the trades from which recruits should be chosen or rejected, is of some significance. Vegetius made clear his views regarding the kind of men whom the army needed to recruit, as well as those who should never be allowed to serve. Not all, he taught, were acceptable, for at issue was nothing less than the safety of the state.[6] Vegetius had therefore emphasised that the ideal

---

[4] London, Lambeth Palace, 752, fo. 30v.   [5] Rome, Casanatense, 512, fo. 4.
[6] One reader of BL Harley 2475 urged that men be tested before being selected (fo. 221v).

recruit should not only be endowed with appropriate physical characteristics; he also needed the moral qualities which Vegetius associated with
'breeding' ('genus').[7] This last point, however it was understood, drew
much approval from readers, particularly in the fourteenth and fifteenth
centuries, the age which we associate with the 'Age of Chivalry'.[8] In the
fifteenth century, however, we can also detect a marked shift of interest
towards those passages which referred to the role of the army in protecting the needs of the state, with an emphasis upon the importance
of ensuring the selection of the best candidates for the army.[9] Both the
understanding of the army as an instrument for the achievement of peace
and social stability, and the development of permanent forces in a number of European countries and territories in the fifteenth century, may
lie behind the increase in interest in this chapter of Vegetius' work.

A further question regarding recruits needed to be asked: the optimum
age at which they should be introduced to the military life. Interest
in chapter 4 increased throughout the period. The passage regarding
speed of movement which, when properly developed, gave confidence
and courage to the soldier, was marked in many manuscripts,[10] as was
a reference to Sallust's teaching that the youth should be introduced to
camp life as soon as possible, so as to be taught the various aspects of
the art of war. It was preferable for a young man to regret not yet being
old enough to serve than that he should regret being already too old.[11]
An enthusiastic recruit, once properly trained, would relish war, not fear
it.[12]

In chapter 6 Vegetius chose to argue that the military potential of a
young man could be judged by looking at his face and eyes, as well as
at his limbs.[13] The point, although important, aroused little reaction.[14]
However, the lines which followed, taken from Virgil describing two
kinds of bee, the one 'active', the other 'shaggy and inert',[15] was marked
by many readers, particularly in the fifteenth century. Vegetius knew his

---

[7] Or, as one reader commented, 'fortitudo corporis et sapientia animi' (Turin, Reale,
Saluzzo 15, fo. 3). Vegetius would ask for intellectual qualities in *DRM*, II, 19.

[8] 'Honestas et verecundia militem ornant' (Lambeth, 752, fo. 31v).

[9] A number of manuscripts of the time underlined the importance of *DRM*, I, 7, emphasising the factors which made a good soldier ('que faciunt militem ydoneum'), as a
reader wrote in the margin of BnF lat. 5697, fo. 252v.

[10] Lambach, Stiftsbibl. Chart. 20, fo. 323; Vienna, Nationalbibl. 313, fo. 4; BnF lat. 7234,
fo. 3v; Vatican, Reg. lat. 1880, fo. 3v; Holkham, 398, fos. 2, 13v.

[11] Florence, Laur. Plut. 89, inf. 28, fo. 84v; Kraków, Jagiell. 1952, p. 5; BL Harley 2551, fo.
4; Naples, Naz. V. A. 22, fo. 3v; Ravenna, Class. 140, fo. 3v; San Daniele, Guarneriana,
50, fo. 100v.

[12] Padua, Cap. B. 47, fo. 53; BnF lat. 7384, fo. 5v; Vienna, Nationalbibl. 313, fo. 4v.

[13] 'De physonomia militis' (Padua, Sem. 26, fo. 2).

[14] See, none the less, BnF lat. 7469, fo. 6.   [15] *Georgics*, 4. 92–94.

authors, and could quote them wittily, too. His remarks on the physical characteristics to be sought in a recruit,[16] ending with the clear advice that strength should be preferred to size, was noted by an ever-increasing number of readers who were responding (as they did elsewhere) to the aphoristic character of the writer's conclusions. We may note here the increasing pleasure of readers on finding references to the works of the classical authors, in this case Virgil, a pleasure which Vegetius had consciously tried to create for his earliest readers. We should also note the growing recognition of the importance of proper recruitment methods and standards, and an implied acceptance of Vegetius' teaching, set out in these chapters, that society could afford to recruit only the best among those who offered themselves for military service. Setting standards for selection was another way of stressing that rejection of the unsuitable was as important as acceptance of those who met the standards set.

The second and much longer part of Book I (chapters 8–28) is devoted to the training of the young soldiers recruited in the earlier chapters. Much interest was to be expressed in chapter 20; its length and the variety of points upon which it touched may have been responsible for this. Of particular interest to readers was the long section which described and discussed the arms and armour used by Roman soldiers in earlier times, in particular the growth of the bad practice of not training in armour, finding it heavy to bear (for lack of training, as Vegetius was quick to point out), and eventually the rejection of the protection it offered, negligence which had led to Rome's defeat. We may perhaps see here a reflection of the need for the development and use of body armour by all ranks in the closing centuries of the Middle Ages. Well known is the change from mail to plate, itself a reaction to developments in both contemporary weaponry and metallurgy, which was occurring by the early fourteenth century. The evidence of the marginalia accompanying this chapter of the *De re militari* can be read as suggesting that it reflected a growing understanding of the need for foot soldiers to wear some armour, and of the importance for all to enjoy the benefits of protection to both head and body. Vegetius had emphasised the danger presented by Gothic archers, and the damage which they could inflict: 'archers are greatly dominant' ('sagitarii multum prevalent'), one commentator added in a manuscript copied in Paris soon after the battle of Poitiers (1356).[17] Perhaps the author of that note was thinking of the successes achieved by archers in the wars of his day. Nor, in considering the effects of arms upon soldiers'

---

[16] 'Optima tyronis forma et descriptio' (Lambeth Palace, 752, fo. 31); 'Signa quibus optimus tiro dignoscetur' (Vienna, Nationalbibl. 313, fo. 5v).
[17] BnF lat. 7469, fo. 13v.

bodies, had Vegetius ignored the effects upon their minds. The best-protected, he had written, fought most effectively. By reducing the fear of being wounded, the soldier was given courage and, by implication, confidence too.[18]

The needs of self-defence were further emphasised in other passages in this chapter. In one which received much attention, Vegetius recalled that the infantry army had been called a wall ('murus') in times past, not least because the legions standing in rank shone in their shields, armour and weapons, provoking the comment (probably of the fifteenth century) that 'the army was said to be a wall' ('exercitus dicebatur murus').[19] The image was to reappear in the text of one of the military ordinances of Charles, duke of Burgundy, dated 1473.[20] As described in Vegetius' work, the use of armour had the triple function of protecting the foot soldiers themselves, acting as a wall between the enemy and the second or third ranks of the Roman army, as well as being a psychological barrier against the oncoming enemy, who would be deterred by the brightness of the armour. It was an idea to which Vegetius would return.

It is evident that late medieval writers saw in chapter 20 valuable ideas applicable to their own day. The physical and psychological advantage of wearing armour could scarcely be denied.[21] The interest in it may well reflect the development, in fourteenth-century England for example, of archers properly protected by padded jacks, or aketons, and helmets, while miniatures show scenes of archers in action wearing protective armour to their arms, legs and heads, as well as to their torsos.[22] The chapter was also regarded as an interesting mixture of the kind of general, practical and psychological advice to be found in many parts of the work.

Considerable attention was also given to chapter 8. This emphasised that not all accepted for training would or should be allowed to complete it. Did the recruit have the necessary speed of movement ('velocitas'), already referred to in chapter 4,[23] and intelligence to enable him to master the discipline of arms? Did he have the confidence expected of the good soldier? If not, he should be rejected. In war, quality was more important than numbers.

---

[18] See below, pp. 310–14, for the use of armour.   [19] Naples, Naz. V. A. 19, fo. 4.

[20] C. Allmand, 'Did the *De re militari* of Vegetius influence the military ordinances of Charles the Bold?', *Publication du Centre européen d'études bourguignonnes (XIVe–XVIe s.)*, 41 (2001), 139.

[21] Florence, Laur. Plut. 89 inf. 28, fo. 92; BL Harley 3859, fo. 6v; Royal 12 B. xxi, fo. 86; Paris, Maz. 3732, fo. 40; BnF Smith-Lesouëf 13, fo. 10; lat. 7384, fo. 11v; Ravenna, Class. 140, fo. 10v.

[22] M. Prestwich, *Armies and warfare in the Middle Ages. The English experience* (New Haven and London, 1996), 134.

[23] BnF lat. 7234, fo. 3v; 'velocitas et robur' (Padua, Sem. 26, fo. 2v).

The recruit, therefore, must go through a vigorous training, which should be carried out daily.[24] But who, when the tradition of military knowledge was in sharp decline as the result of years of peace, could teach what he himself had not learned? Those wanting to know should turn to the histories and other books to find out. However, they should be interested not only in what happened in past wars; it was necessary to understand how and, above all, why Romans had acted as they did in the past, in other words to learn what the 'disciplina militaris' really was.[25] To achieve this, the historians and other writers of the past, not least Julius Frontinus, should be read.[26] Vegetius offered the reader only summaries of what his predecessors had written.

By far the most popular passage in this chapter was that which stressed the importance of quality over numbers; attention was drawn to it in about a quarter of the surviving Latin manuscripts.[27] Other passages emphasised that the Roman military system might be learned from the reading of books, the stress laid on experience reflecting the importance attached to named authorities by the medieval mind ready, as it often was, to trust those authorities who had written in the past.

With its contents drawn to readers' attention almost more than any other chapter in Book I, chapter 13 bore several important messages. Outwardly about the special training ('armatura') carried out by certain soldiers led by special instructors ('doctores armorum'), the emphasis was to be turned towards Vegetius' favourite theme, which was, too, the directing theme of this section of Book I: training, and the benefits which it conferred. As seen by the Middle Ages, these were threefold: the enemy was deterred not by gold but by the respect due to a well-prepared army;[28] well-exercised troops were less likely than others to make irremediable mistakes, to lack courage and flee; at the same time, the state benefited from having a copious supply of trained men upon whom it could rely. While all these points were appreciated from the twelfth century onwards, it was the number of fifteenth-century manuscripts in particular, noting

---

[24] In Vatican, Ottob. lat. 1437, fo. 4, a reader has added the words 'Ab ortu solis usque ad occasum' ('from the rising of the sun to its setting'), citing Psalm 112 sung at the Church's evening service of Vespers. It is a witty comment of this kind which makes one think that the clergy may have viewed the soldier's formation in the same light as they saw their own. A full-page illumination in New York, Morgan, M 364, fo. 3, shows recruits wrestling or practising archery, while others practise combat on horseback.

[25] Naples, Naz. V. A. 22, fo. 5; BnF lat. 7384, fo. 7.

[26] *Inter al.*, BL Harley 2551, fo. 6; Royal 12 B. xxi, fo. 82v; New York, Morgan, M 364, fo. 8v; San Daniele, Guarneriana, 50, fo. 102; Göteborg, Univ. lat. 22, fo. 4v.

[27] A clerical readership, above all, will not have failed to recall the passages in Maccabees (I, 4: 8–9) which emphasised that an army should not fear the enemy's superior numbers.

[28] See the finger pointing at this passage in BL Royal 12 C. xxii, fo. 10.

the advantages which an army conferred upon a state and its welfare, which showed a marked increase of interest in the idea at the end of the Middle Ages.

Readers also gave attention to chapter 9. Examination of the manuscripts reveals much about the approach of readers to its contents. The first section, which extols the military virtues of marching in step,[29] keeping rank and training in order to achieve these skills, receives surprisingly little attention. On the other hand, a short sentence on the dangers incurred by a divided army, which follows immediately, becomes, in the manuscripts of the fourteenth and fifteenth centuries, by far the most marked passage in the chapter. The need for the recruit to learn to run and jump,[30] and the advantages of taking the enemy by surprise, thereby causing alarm among his ranks, are noted; one learned reader would later remark that this passage had been cited by Peter of Blois.[31] The chapter's popular concluding lines contain references to the Roman historian Sallust, describing the training in running and jumping undertaken by Pompey with his army which enabled him to defeat Sertorius in Spain.[32]

The regular increase between the twelfth and the fifteenth centuries in the number of manuscripts in which readers noted these lines may reflect two things. One is the way readers grasped the point that victory was the outcome of a conscious effort undertaken by a commander to train his soldiers, with the implication of this for the present day. The second was the increase of interest in the names of classical writers and soldiers as these appeared in the text, reflecting, in this case, the interest among readers in the history, people and ideas of the classical past. What this chapter (and it is not alone) illustrates is that it is often the generalisations about war, whose formulation was one of Vegetius' special characteristics (although one not appreciated by all his critics, particularly modern ones), which caught the eyes of readers before being marked or noted in the manuscripts. It may often appear that it is the timeless, unspecific elements of Vegetius' proposals which won him the greatest appreciation in the centuries to come.

Finally, we should consider chapter 28, described by one annotator inspired by the formal heading as an 'adhortacio rei militaris', by another

---

[29] Florence, Laur. S. Croce, Plut. 24, sin. 6, fo. 2v.

[30] BnF lat. 7230, fo. 5v; Prague, Nat. Lib. 2369, fo. 67; Rimini, Gambalunga, SC. 33, fo. 63; Vienna, Nationalbibl. 313, fo. 8.

[31] Venice, Marc. 4435, fo. 369.

[32] Milan, Ambros. D 2 sup., fo. 5; R 6 sup., fo. 4v; Naples, Naz. V. A. 21, fo. 3v; Venice, Marc. Z. lat. 463, fo. 147v; Vienna, Nationalbibl. 313, fo. 8; Wrocław, Bibl. Uniw. Rehd. 10, fo. 29; Göteborg, Univ. lat. 22, fo. 5v.

more as an 'epilogatio predictorum'.[33] In truth, the chapter was a bit of each: it looked both forwards and backwards. Vegetius was anxious to emphasise that his work was based essentially on the evidence of past texts, and that he was only summarising what he had found in these; in so doing he was, of course, stressing the completion of the task which he had set himself earlier. But the Middle Ages seem also to have understood his message for the future: by following his teaching, men could help to settle their own destinies, as the nations and tribes mentioned by Vegetius had done. It was not simply defeat at the hands of an enemy which had brought Rome low; rather, her decline was more the result of years of peace ('quid faciat longeva securitas pacis')[34] which had led men to cease practising the arts of war. However, Rome had picked herself up, and by providing a regular flow of recruits had given herself a new lease of life. It was cheaper to train one's own men than to hire them from another state.[35]

The chapter was above all a call to revive Rome's fortunes through an understanding and practical application of the arts of war. The message, as evidenced by the attention given to the passage claiming that martial energy was not dead, and was capable of being revived if young men were constantly recruited and trained, was much noticed, particularly in the fourteenth and fifteenth centuries. There was an important message to be learned here. The commonly encountered attitude that victory and defeat were in the hands of God (or of Dame Fortune), an attitude which all too easily led to a fatalistic acceptance of the outcome of war, was under challenge. Vegetius was stressing that victory would go to the side better prepared, better trained, better adapted to the circumstances of locality, conditions and time. The emphasis on the mental condition of the soldier as he went into battle (the theme would re-emerge later) was essential to the Vegetian view that the outcome of battle depended largely upon the state of preparedness, both mental and physical, of the armies involved. This was underlined by the recurring message that, well prepared, a small force would overcome a larger but poorly trained one.

---

[33] Florence, Moreniana, Frullani 24, fo. 19v; BnF lat. 5691, fo. 24v.

[34] Göteborg, Univ. lat. 22, fo. 10v; Rome, Casanatense, 512, fo. 17v; Rimini, Gambalunga, SC. 33, fo. 69; Kraków, Jagiell. 1952, p. 18; Paris, Maz. 3732, fo. 41; Wolfenbüttel, Gud. lat. 15, fo. 2v; BL Harley 2551, fo. 14v. In Europe, one may recall, the thirteenth century had been one of relative peace.

[35] A widely appreciated view which, as one reader of a late fourteenth-/early fifteenth-century manuscript noted, applied to those responsible for the wars waged by the kingdom of France (Naples, Naz. V. A. 19, fo. 5v). In some manuscripts 'vilius' ('cheaper') was replaced by 'utilius ('more useful')', a reading which still made some sense of Vegetius' assertion.

Vegetius' punch-line to both book and chapter, that it cost less to train a native army than to hire one from outside, set the seal on what he had been teaching.[36] He had emphasised more than once[37] the need for the state, its people and their material interests to be defended. Who would be responsible for this? The call would have struck a chord with those (clergy) familiar with Christ's teaching regarding the unreliability of the hireling shepherd who ran away at the approach of the wolf. It would have done so, particularly after 1300, with those who were coming to regard national armies as the defenders of the legal and territorial interests of the emerging nation states. Although this was not happening all over Europe, states (the great kingdoms as much as the city states of the Italian peninsula) were turning more and more to armies drawn from their own populations rather than relying, other than in the case of specialist troops, upon mercenaries from outside.[38] This was also the age which witnessed the development of state taxation on an unprecedented scale, taxation raised mainly to meet the ever-increasing costs of war. That the statement regarding money being better spent paying native soldiers, rather than foreign mercenaries, should have touched a nerve among readers of the fourteenth and fifteenth centuries in particular causes no surprise.

Book II

The differences between the first two books of the *De re militari* are considerable. While much of Book I had been fairly general in character, stressing the importance of proper selection and training, Book II would be given over mainly to a consideration of the structures of the Roman army, both as they had been and as they might be. It is not surprising, therefore, that interest in Book II would not be as great as it had been in Book I.[39] Many manuscripts bear few or no signs of the responses of readers in their margins.

Yet interest in military administration did develop towards the end of the Middle Ages. To some, interest in things Roman might be greater in the declining years of the period than a few centuries earlier. It is evident that the growing Renaissance interest in the classical past is reflected in many of the notes and comments entered in the texts of Book II. That interest, however, is not necessarily practical or inspired by the wish to apply lessons learnt from the past to the contemporary world.

---

[36] The passage was marked in some thirty-five manuscripts.   [37] *DRM*, I, Praef, 13.

[38] As implied in the comment in Naples, Naz. V. A. 19, fo. 5v.

[39] On this lack of interest in Book II, see D. Wakelin, *Humanism, reading and English literature, 1430–1530* (Oxford, 2007), 86, n. 70.

Rather, it was what we may call scholarly. For instance, curiosity in the meaning of unfamiliar words and terms is reflected in the marginalia of the fourteenth century onwards. Book II of the *De re militari* was treated by many as a valuable source of information, clearly set out, regarding certain historical aspects of the Roman past. For these, it was a valuable source to be plundered, as indeed it often was. If the clean manuscripts suggest that many readers were not inspired to gloss their texts because of the book's apparent lack of relevance to their lives and interests, equally we may see in the nature of the texts which did attract attention a measure of curiosity in the largely historical nature of the book's contents. Closer inspection, however, reveals that in spite of his intention to describe, in some detail, the workings of the Roman army (what may be called, rather loosely, the antiquarian interest) Vegetius found it difficult to break away from some of the basic messages and underlying ideas set out in Book I, in which, it now becomes apparent, he believed with conviction.

Like Book I, Book II may be informally divided into sections. The first consists of chapters 1 to 3, on the armed forces. The interest accorded by late medieval readers to his discussion of the origins of the word 'army' ('exercitus') reflects not merely an interest in philology and etymology, but a questioning of the practical role of the army in society. If the Latin word for army emerges from the verb to 'exercise' ('exerceo': 'exercitum', thus men who are 'exercised' or 'trained'), Vegetius also emphasised that the legion ('legio') was derived from the verb ('legere') to 'select' (thus men who are chosen), subtly underlining the first and fundamental message of Book I, that the army consisted of men first selected and then trained. In a passage which drew a good deal of attention, Vegetius reminded his readers of the importance of a largely infantry army, at once more versatile than one dominated by cavalry and, returning to a point made in Book I, 28, cheaper to maintain as well. The benefit to a state of having such an army was clearly understood. Citing Virgil that he was writing about arms and men ('armis . . . et viris') Vegetius was again emphasising the importance of men which he had stressed in Book I. From the markings in manuscripts, it becomes evident that there were readers who recognised the elements of continuity in Vegetius' thinking, and who welcomed the ideas which he was conveying.

In the first section, parts of chapter 3 had much appeal, particularly in the late Middle Ages. In a much noted passage, Vegetius had played down the value of brave deeds whose memory (and influence?) did not last, before going on to stress that only what was done for the benefit of the common good ('pro utilitate reipublicae') possessed lasting value. Did this attention reflect a realisation that Vegetius' teaching appeared to be at odds with ideas and practices reflected in much chivalric literature, in which notable actions per se received prominence? After all, Jean Froissart had written, in the famous 'Preface' to his *Chroniques*, that such actions should be recorded for the sake of the example which they gave to future generations. Vegetius was changing the emphasis. As he put it, the memory of fine deeds was limited to a single age; it was to actions which brought benefit to the public good that eternal remembrance should be given. The implication of this is clear. The common good is best defended not by individual action, but by the communal action of the army.

Writing in chapter 2 to the heading 'The differences between legions and "auxilia"', Vegetius pointed out that differences within the army hindered victory, a view with which his readers readily agreed. They appreciated, too, that an army composed of men originating from many parts, and following different military traditions, could not learn to act together without rigorous training carried out in common. Two things were required. One was the need for daily training upon which the army's success was to depend. The other, new at this stage, but with a great future before it, stressed the need for the army to act with one mind, a principle underlined in the emphasis given to a further imperative, that an army should have but a single leader. In this way, trained and led to win, it would become the effective defensive arm of the state.

The following eleven chapters – almost half of Book II – were given over to the formation and structure of the legion. Most were concerned with matters such as numbers, the grades and titles of personnel, along with their duties and responsibilities, information which bore little relevance to war as practised in the greater part of the Middle Ages. A small number of chapters, however, hid remarks by Vegetius, or descriptions of practices within the Roman army, which encouraged a response. Chapter 5, for instance, discussed the formation of the legion. Much of this short chapter contained material which, in practice, was of greater interest and significance than the rather bland title to the chapter might suggest. Having noted that, once selected and trained, the best candidates were formed into legions by order of the emperor (perhaps surprisingly, few noted the last point that an army came into being as the result of a decision taken by a ruler, thus emphasising its very existence and its dependence upon him), Vegetius went on to stress the formalisation of their relationship through the oaths which they took to obey and serve him.

The number of manuscripts marked at this chapter increased with every passing century. What did readers find of note here? The formation of the legion from soldiers who had submitted to a training course of four months or more, all this on the orders of the emperor, 'second to God on earth', caused (for once) little comment. Much more surprising was the fact that Vegetius was a Christian, and that the oath was taken in the name of the Trinity.[40] The considerable attention given to what followed is also significant, bordering as it does on what we would today term political thought. When the soldier swore to serve the emperor (or ruler) he was also undertaking to serve God through him who ruled by God's authority.[41] As a result, it was understood that the soldier looked to the ruler as the ultimate source of authority whom he must never betray. Furthermore, he must always be ready to fight to the death for the good of the state.

The interest taken by medieval readers in the statements – and their implications – made in this chapter is both interesting and important. At one level they may have been interpreted, in a world in which the power of the Holy Roman Emperor in Europe was in decline, as a justification for kings and princes to assume charge over the nation states developing in western Europe at this period. Achieving this placed certain responsibilities upon their shoulders, of which the defence of national interests, using force if necessary, was one. In the Roman tradition, it was seen as the responsibility of men drawn from among the ruler's own subjects to constitute the army, the body increasingly regarded as a force for peace able to deter or fight off an enemy.[42] As the position and responsibilities of the army were increasingly defined and justified, so the pivotal role played by the individual soldier reached new heights. He was now coming to be regarded as a force for stability (although it must be accepted that both reality and opinion often contradicted this), trained and prepared to oppose the ruler's enemies, ready to fight for the good of the country. The duties imposed upon the army by Vegetius had the almost inevitable effect of elevating its role in any society's affairs to a level not experienced since the days described in the *De re militari*.

The text of chapter 14, in which Vegetius went on to discuss the legionary cavalry, would also interest medieval readers. A passage setting out the criteria for choosing a centurion was coming to be recognised as one with a bearing on a subject open to lively debate in the fourteenth century and later: what qualities made a good leader? By criticising undue

---

[40] 'Hic notum quod Vegetius fuit Christianus' (Florence, Laur. S. Croce, Plut. 20, sin. 9, fo. 112v); 'Iuratio . . . per Christum et Spiritum Sanctum' (Bern, Burgerbibl. 280, fo. 18).

[41] 'Nota formam sacramenti militaris' (Novara, Cap. Duomo, XCV, fo. 9). In BnF Smith-Lesouëf 13, fo. 16, the capital D of the chapter's first word shows a hand with armour on the arm placed on a book to take the oath.

[42] 'No one dares challenge or harm one whom he realises will win if he fights' (*DRM*, III, Praef. See also IV, 31).

influence in the securing of promotion,[43] Vegetius had both implicitly and explicitly opposed promotion on grounds other than merit. A centurion, he took it for granted, was a man of strength and stature; he was also a man of skill, able to fight with different weapons, accustomed to using his shield effectively, alert and agile, ready to lead his men in training and to see to their interests. In brief, he was a man who understood arms and their use as well as men and their needs. Such a man as this earned promotion to a position of responsibility and command because of the physical and mental skills which he possessed, and the moral authority he had won for himself. In a society in which the right to exercise authority or leadership depended largely upon birth and status, such a message was bound to cause disquiet. Some, however, saw that the best interests of their states depended upon placing the most competent and the most experienced in positions of command, a change which Vegetius' text may have helped to encourage.

Another passage in the same chapter was to be noticed by many readers. One of the centurion's responsibilities was to ensure that his soldiers were properly clothed and shod, and that their arms were burnished and as bright as the light.[44] Such a practice was important to keep a soldier active and his weapons in good working order. Inattentiveness quickly led to slovenly action and even disaster. The need to maintain both discipline and morale was regarded as most important. Not to be forgotten, either, was Vegetius' appreciation of the effect to be made upon the enemy by psychological factors. Fear he recognised as an important element in wartime, one from which real advantage might be derived. An army of well-drilled, well-protected soldiers, whose arms shone in the sun (it was clearly a man of Mediterranean climes who wrote this) would make an adverse impact upon any enemy facing it. As the large number of marginal marks at this point in chapter 14 show, men of later ages also appreciated the significance of Vegetius' foray into the psychology of the soldier facing the enemy.

Little attention was paid to the content of chapter 7 other than to the passage referring to the importance of the chain of command. However, Vegetius also considered the titles and grades of the legion's officers that provided examples of a technical vocabulary which, being unfamiliar, had to be noted and explained. 'Quid . . . quid . . . quid' enquired readers, perhaps puzzled, yet encouraged, by technical words which, not encountered before, prevented them making sense of the text. In this,

---

[43] See DRM, II, 1, 2, 3.
[44] 'Armorum splendor' (Rome, Casanatense, 512, fo. 26). Today's equivalent might be the polishing of the toe caps of a soldier's boots and the brasses on his belt.

and in many chapters of Book II, marginal notes reflect an interest in the details and intricacies of Roman military organisation. It is plain that there was little in what readers found in chapter 7 that would be of practical use to them in the organisation of their own forces. The interest, whose deepest intensity is found, not surprisingly, in the manuscripts of the Renaissance period, lay much more in a genuine wish to appreciate the workings of the Roman legion and in a scholarly interest in the vocabulary used.[45] The significance of chapter 7 (and of others in Book II, as well as of many in Book IV) is that it reflects another aspect of the *De re militari* which we cannot ignore: its importance as a source of knowledge regarding Roman military organisation and life which drew those, perhaps of more scholarly than military bent, towards Vegetius' text. Many different types of reader (we have already noted the sympathy for the text shown by the clergy) found something to interest or stimulate them in this work.

Response to chapter 6, concerned with numbers in the cohorts and legions, may have been spread more broadly;[46] interest in Vegetius' vocabulary was already clearly discernible. However, the evidence suggests that the main interest in this chapter lay in a short passage regarding the responsibilities of the front cohort for protecting the eagle which served as a distinctive sign of the legion. A number of manuscripts have an eagle, sometimes crowned,[47] drawn in the margin, while in others, the word 'aquila' is found. This evidence probably went beyond an interest in Roman practice. The development of heraldry, the greater use of pennants and banners as signs of unity among those who rallied to them, were characteristic of the practice of war from the thirteenth century onwards. The retinues of French and English armies needed some distinguishing marks for men to tell them apart. If the Roman soldier owed an allegiance to the cohort and the legion, the late medieval army would use what were essentially developments and refinements of Roman practice to keep soldiers close to their commanders and fighting alongside others in the same unit. In late fifteenth-century Burgundy an attempt to use the personal banners of leaders to keep ducal forces together in the confusion of battle reflects the influence of the use of the eagle upon certain military developments in the Middle Ages.[48]

---

[45] Both the 'decanus' and the 'centurio' appeared in Burgundian ducal ordinances in the late fifteenth century (Allmand, 'Did the *De re militari* . . . ?', 141); Francis I would introduce 'legions' into the French army in 1534 (Vale, *War and chivalry*, 164).

[46] 'De numero militum unius legionis' (Vicenza, Bertoliana, 295, fo. 6v).

[47] Naples, Naz. V. A. 19, fo. 6v.

[48] Allmand, 'Did the *De re militari* . . . ?', 141. On ensigns and standards, see Vale, *War and chivalry*, 148–9.

Four chapters, 15 to 18, constitute a consideration of the battle order of the ancient legion. The first three chapters created only limited interest among medieval readers. Unfamiliar words and their meanings provoked more response than did the contents, particularly in chapters 15 and 16. In chapter 17 Vegetius moved closer to a discussion of tactics. The need to draw an enemy attack upon a well-trained 'wall of iron', by sending forward lightly armed troops, was noted in some fifteenth-century manuscripts. Since the 'wall' must be ready to bear the brunt of the enemy's attack with javelins and swords, it was essential that it remained intact, even in the event of defeat. In chapter 18, the 'best chapter' in the view of one reader,[49] Vegetius managed to mix a hugely popular aphorism, 'everything is difficult before you try it', with the view, once more widely appreciated, that if suitably trained men are put in charge of the army, then a force ready for war can soon be brought together. The use of skills properly learned through long training can achieve anything, although, Vegetius added, the expense must not be spared. In this way, by bringing together old principles and new ideas, the safety of the state will be assured. To all this Vegetius added the point that the legion must never flee, just as it ought never to pursue. Such words of practical wisdom won approval from readers right through the centuries.

In a final group of chapters, 19–25, Vegetius turned to the administration of the legion. Part of that administration was the training of the soldiers who constituted it. Chapter 23 gave Vegetius the chance to return to the need for regular training by both recruits and veterans. It was exercise, he noted to the approval of later readers, which enabled the art of war to be transmitted; he finished with the typically Vegetian statement that an unexercised veteran always remains a raw recruit. There followed a long programme of training needed to turn that recruit into the full legionary: the emphasis on rapid action; the use of particular weapons; the toughening of the physique; target practice for archers – all these formed part of it. Most were noted by readers as significant in the creation of an effective army. One may add, however, that although one important canon in Roman military practice, the need to keep rank and follow ensigns in mock battles, was scarcely noted in the manuscripts, it would be influential among those who later wrote on good military practice, and whose work reflected Vegetian teaching. None the less, Vegetius' conclusions that the well trained were eager for battle, and that skill was more useful than strength, won the acknowledgement of readers. They could scarcely deny Vegetius' statement that it was military

---

[49] 'optimum capitulum' (Trento, Com. W 3154, fo. 12v).

training which distinguished the soldier from the civilian.[50] In the short chapter (24) which followed, Vegetius reasoned that all forms of art, not merely the military one, flourished only when time and effort were given to their practice. If the actor developed skills through daily routine, soldiers, upon whom the safety of the state depended, should do the same; such was the way to victory. Training, too, had the further advantage of raising the soldier in the esteem of the emperor, who could advance or promote him. Thus the soldier was fighting for himself and his reputation, as well as for the common liberty. Whether he succeeded or not would depend on how much practice he did. In judging the acceptability of the argument, we may note that the contents of this chapter found favour with readers, if lines drawn in the margins are anything to go by. We may also note that the aphorism (regarding the training which divides the civil from the military) with which the chapter ends was one of the most popular in the entire work. Once again Vegetius is seen to place the soldier in society, according him a position which is one both of honour and, above all, of wide-ranging responsibility.

Book III

Already emerging from the earlier books, and now developed as a major theme in chapter 3, was the important idea of preparation seen as the anticipation of events and, above all, of requirements. Centrally placed in the chapter, central indeed to the whole argument, was a passage underlining the importance of preparing weapons and defences (which might include repairs) well before the need for these became apparent. Vegetius had also emphasised that provisions should be collected for the longest siege while, by denying the enemy access to animals and every kind of provisions, everything should be done to make life difficult for him. A miniature showing a soldier eating out of a bowl, painted within the initial 'O' of the chapter's opening word ('Ordo'), illustrates that the message had been understood well enough.[51] Had not Vegetius already stated, at the beginning of the chapter, that victory was more often achieved by starving the enemy to surrender/death than by defeating him in battle, and that hunger held out more terrible consequences than did the sword? The importance of provisioning and logistics in time of war, eased by measures taken in time of peace, was thus drawn to the attention of society's leaders. Only in this way could war be fought with confidence.

---

[50] Rimini, Gambalunga, SC. 33, fo. 79v; Naples, Naz. V. A. 19, fo. 9; Rome, Casanatense, 512, fo. 31, all carry favourable comments on the effects of training.

[51] BnF Smith-Lesouëf 13, fo. 29. See below, pp. 204–5.

And if the money required to buy food and provisions was insufficient, then the ruler should have the right to compel the purchase of such goods for the public good, which could allow no shortages.

This was a chapter containing a well-appreciated message: it concerned the need to look ahead, to assess likely requirements and whether they could be met, and to act accordingly. Foresight, or the anticipation of needs in the event of a difficult campaign, was now being emphasised. The material support to be given to an army should occupy much time in preparation. The gains were obvious; an army at war far from home had to rely more on its own supply line, while the risks of having to live off the country were thus reduced. Not surprisingly, these ideas were met with interest in the age which witnessed an increase in the number of wars fought in foreign lands. The recognition of the importance of provisioning or logistics is reflected both in the chronicle accounts of wars and campaigns, and in the records of contemporary military administration, a forgotten aspect of war whose importance has been recently emphasised by historians. Not least has been the significance, social and economic, accorded to the development of purveyance, or the compulsory purchase of provisions as recommended by Vegetius, a practice which developed in time of financial difficulty, and which was on the increase from the thirteenth century onwards.[52]

In chapter 4 Vegetius would advance ideas about the properly trained soldier and leadership which evoked considerable response. Discussing the subject of mutiny, he emphasised the need to prepare and train soldiers for war, which they would come to prefer to other forms of life if that training was properly carried out. Punishment might quell a few mutineers and deter others,[53] but no soldier, he argued in a well-appreciated passage, would consider mutiny if he possessed the confidence and skills required to fight. Mutineers feared war; good soldiers, ready to use their skills, did not. The successful commander, then, was the one who led by training his men thoroughly. Well prepared for war, they would not act against his authority.

By far the most consistently noted chapter in Book III was chapter 6, which advised caution in the vicinity of the enemy. But, as so often with

---

[52] See, for example, H. J. Hewitt, *The organization of war under Edward III, 1338–62* (Manchester and New York, 1966), ch. 3; R. A. Newhall, *The English conquest of Normandy 1416–1424. A study in fifteenth-century warfare* (New Haven and Oxford, 1924), ch. 6; M. E. Mallett, *Mercenaries and their masters. Warfare in Renaissance Italy* (London, 1974), ch. 6.

[53] See the miniature in BnF Smith-Lesouëf 13, fo. 30, depicting a man with a sword striking another who is blindfolded, probably suggesting the punishment meted out to mutineers. See below, p. 205.

this text, Vegetius embellished the subject considerably by developing other, related points. Two stood out in the interest they provoked. One was the absolute necessity to act with secrecy – and not only when the enemy was close by.[54] The other was the importance for the commander to be well informed, in particular when the army was on the move, for this was the time of greatest danger. Vegetius favoured the use of itineraries and maps, and the gathering of information from local people (although care had to be taken regarding whom to trust), as well as from scouts and spies. The aim was to avoid being surprised by the unexpected which, Vegetius emphasised, could lead to panic. For much the same reason he strongly advised that the army should keep together, and not allow itself to become too dispersed; the baggage, too, should be kept under control.[55] Such a state of physical preparedness should be accompanied by the army being mentally prepared for any eventuality. It was thus the commander's task to keep himself informed about what was going on around him. In that way enemy attacks, particularly ambushes, could be anticipated and dealt with.

The second group of chapters 8–13, is mainly concerned with different battle strategies. In chapter 9,[56] the most popular assertion made by Vegetius was that hunger kills from within without a blow being struck, in effect a restatement, although from a different perspective, of the claims regarding the importance of provisioning and starvation made in chapter 3. Emerging, too, as a major point of emphasis was the role to be played by the commander, whose qualities must enable him to make the right decisions between alternatives put before him.[57] Faced with the choice of fighting at once or delaying the action, he had to weigh the psychological effects of delay upon his troops, and the possibility that they could desert. Another well-supported passage referred to the need for the commander to maintain the hopes of his soldiers. Morale, and how it could be sustained, was regarded as crucial, and Vegetius' statement that no hesitant army should be led into battle, since loyalty was less common in adversity, was widely appreciated.[58] In such a situation the need for the commander to address his troops so as to raise their morale

---

[54] 'Solus dux sciat quo itur, non hostes' (Trento, Com. W 3154, fo. 19).

[55] 'Notum quod accidit quando exercitus inordinate procedunt et ambulant' (Milan, Ambros. G 83 sup., fo. 15v).

[56] In Venice, Marc. 3347, fo. 24, this has a wavy line down the entire length of the chapter.

[57] Emphasised in a note 'Nota pulcerime in toto isto capitulo que ante conflictum consciderare debeat dux belli' (Novara, Cap. Duomo, XCV, fo. 19v).

[58] BL Harley 2475, fo. 244, lists in the margin a series of questions to be answered by leaders about to fight. See also BnF lat. 5697, fo. 272v.

was regarded as an imperative.[59] Appreciation of Vegetius' discussion of the qualities of good leadership emerged clearly from the manuscripts.[60] A sensible commander would listen to others and take advice on crucial situations; at the same time it would be up to him to make decisions, taking care to keep them secret. He should also avoid open confrontations unless the outlook were very good: raids and ambushes from hidden places were more effective; and he should never fail to find out as much as he could about the enemy's intentions and the state of his morale, comparing it with that of his own army. Last, we may note the interest given by Vegetius to the greater versatility enjoyed by the infantry over cavalry, a point increasingly accepted with the advance of the Middle Ages. 'See how infantry make the better soldiers' ('nota quod pedestres milicia melior'), commented one reader, while another added 'there is strength in infantry' ('in peditibus robur'), as if he were composing a motto for a regiment of foot.[61]

In chapter 10 Vegetius, asking what a commander should do with an inexperienced army, gave himself the opportunity to discuss the psychology of the soldier about to fight. The sight of death could cause fear, even panic, among those who had not witnessed it before, so the moment of attack must be well chosen. Stressing the adverse effects of fear upon an army, in a much marked passage Vegetius insisted that it was easier to train a new army than to reanimate one which had experienced fear.[62] Thus, as in the previous chapter, the need for confidence-building was emphasised, this being best achieved by adopting an aggressive attitude towards the enemy. At the same time, the enemy could be weakened if dissension were sown among his ranks; nothing is more effective than self-destruction.[63] As for the general, he must get to know his soldiers, recalling that they were individuals as well as men who constituted the army. The need for training, abandoned in the years of peace, must be actively revived and the written works of former leaders must be studied. In this way the army, which preserved liberty, the provinces and the Empire, would be successful again.

---

[59] 'Crescit animus exercitus cum princeps aliquid fortiter gesserit' (Leipzig, Univ. Rep. I. fol. 18, fo. 279, and Trento, Com. W 3154, fo. 22).

[60] Particularly in the Novara and Leipzig manuscripts cited in notes 70 and 72.

[61] Naples, Naz. V. A. 19, fo. 5v; Vatican, Ottob. lat. 1964, fo. 41v. 'A major advance in the military history of the central Middle Ages is the attention that is now given to the once-despised infantry' (N. Housley, 'Recent scholarship on crusading and medieval warfare, 1095–1291: convergence and divergence', in *War, government and aristocracy in the British Isles, c.1150–1500. Essays in honour of Michael Prestwich*, ed. C. Given-Wilson, A. Kettle and L. Scales (Woodbridge, 2008), 203).

[62] *DRM*, III, 10. See, for example, BL Harley 3859, fo. 22v.

[63] See Trento, Com. W 3154, fo. 23.

In chapter 12, whose perceived importance is suggested by notable marginalia,[64] Vegetius developed yet further what we have termed the psychology of the soldier. On the day of the battle[65] it was the commander's duty to find out as best he could how his forces felt about the coming encounter. Their features, he wrote, could betray their inner feelings. While most men feared battle, the sight of the enemy could be sweet to the inexperienced, and the general must act with care. Vegetius advised him that, since what is known does not frighten, an army should be given a good view of the enemy before the battle began. Once again Vegetius emphasised that the army's confidence could be increased by words from its leader, words of encouragement as well as those to arouse feelings of hatred or anger towards the enemy.

In the final, and longest, group of chapters, concerned with battle tactics and strategies, four chapters stand out as having been of greatest interest to medieval readers. In two of these, 14 and 18, concerned respectively with drawing up the battle line and the positions to be taken up by the commanders themselves, much of the interest lay in the unfamiliar vocabulary employed by the author. To the question 'what is a battle line?' ('quid acies, quid frons?') the Valladolid manuscript gave the clearest answer: 'it is an army drawn up for battle' ('acies dicitur exercitus instructus').[66] Like many others, the readers of this fifteenth-century manuscript, probably Italian in origin, were interested in the occasionally unfamiliar language encountered in the text. In parts of Book III, linguistic interests sometimes overtook historical or military ones. While it is tempting to imagine that different approaches to the text reflect different readers, we should beware of assuming that this was necessarily the case. The hand which reflects an interest in vocabulary or philology can also draw attention to points which, if categorised, could be labelled 'historical' or 'military'. None the less, it is clear that the late manuscripts show a markedly greater tendency towards comments of a philological character. The doubts regarding the true meaning of technical words make it easier for us to understand why translators found support for rendering into vernacular languages a text which many must have considered, at least in parts, unusually difficult to understand.

Like those on chapter 14, comments on chapter 18 were largely concerned with words (as a number of manuscripts, mostly Italian, clearly show). Attentive readers were ready to notice other things, too. Some manuscripts dating from the twelfth century onwards drew attention to

---

[64] See, for example, Venice, Marc. Z. lat. 463, fo. 183.
[65] 'Dies pugne' (Florence, Moreniana, Frullani 24, fo. 51v).
[66] Trento, Com. W 3154, fo. 24v; Valladolid, Santa Cruz, 384, fo. 46.

Vegetius' insistence that leaders should do everything possible to confuse the enemy before encountering him.[67] Once confused, he should then be frightened: the war cry, uttered not too early but, for maximum effect, at the critical moment when the forces impacted upon each other, was a means of terrifying the enemy.[68] At the same time everything should be done to help one's own men gain the psychological advantage. It was important to be on the field before the enemy, since it was discouraging to take the field before an army already in place and waiting; there could be little doubt which side held the initiative and which felt the more vulnerable in this situation.[69] As he had done before, Vegetius insisted that generals should make the most of opportunities given to them: at best, the enemy might be caught unprepared; at worst, he would be fought on equal terms.

Two chapters towards the end of the book attracted the attention of their readers. Chapter 21, marked in its entirety in one manuscript,[70] and much of it in a number of others, advised that if the enemy were defeated, he should be given the opportunity to escape.[71] Two short complementary passages, noting that desperate men will stand and fight to the last, were heavily scored in many manuscripts.[72] As Vegetius pointed out, most thought it best to surround the enemy so as to leave him no means of escape. In reality, however, men prefer to die in company, taking others with them. So, citing Scipio, he advocated giving a defeated enemy the chance to escape.[73] Knowing that such an opportunity existed, not only did the enemy become less desperate, he also sought it out and, in so doing, ceased to face his opponent, thus making him easier to kill. The wide approval of readers of Virgil's paradox,[74] preserved in one manuscript group, that 'the only hope of safety for the defeated is to expect no safety', reflects how Vegetius' message had been accepted.

---

[67] E.g. Escorial, O. iii. 9, fo. 58v; Phillipps, 16370, fo. 27; Milan, Ambros. D 2 sup., fos. 34–34v.

[68] See M. Keen, 'Richard II's ordinances of war of 1385', in *Rulers and ruled in late medieval England. Essays presented to Gerald Harriss*, ed. R. E. Archer and S. Walker (London and Rio Grande, 1995), 46.

[69] 'Nota bonas cautelas' (Naples, Naz. V. A. 19, fo. 15v). In modern football, both teams usually come on to the pitch together.

[70] Novara, Cap. Duomo, XCV, fo. 24.

[71] 'Nota viam hostibus qui refugiant minime claudamus' (Vienna, Nationalbibl. 313, fo. 84v).

[72] 'Desperatio facit audaciam' (Rome, Casanatense, 512, fo. 60); 'Non est bonum semper hostibus aditus fugiendi tollere quia cum desperant audaciam resumunt' (Trento, Com. W 3154, fo. 28).

[73] This was a conventional piece of advice found in both Latin and Greek literature concerned with war.

[74] Virgil, *Aeneid*, 2, 354.

As an antidote to the lesson of the previous chapter, allowing the enemy to flee, came Vegetius' advice on how an army should carry out a retreat. Once again, it made demands upon the leadership. It was widely appreciated that the effect on morale of too early a retreat in battle, open to interpretation as an act of despair, could be disastrous by leading to panic and a disordered flight. On the other hand a well-organised retreat could appear to both sides as part of a wider plan. A strong element of deceit was involved in an ordered retreat, which, best carried out at night,[75] should be completed by the setting up of ambushes to deter or prevent pursuit by the enemy.

There was much interest in this chapter, particularly in the late Middle Ages. It is significant that no comment appears anywhere suggesting that a retreat is anything other than honourable. The subject is presented by Vegetius in purely military terms, and nowhere is there any attempt, in the margins of manuscripts, to regard it otherwise. Rather, it is seen as an example of good leadership and proper discipline within the army that a retreat can be carried out successfully, without loss, the army thus surviving to fight another day.

Chapter 26 brought Book III to a close. Unlike its predecessors, the chapter consisted of thirty-three 'Rules of war' or, as the author preferred to call it, an 'art of victory', summing up many of the points made earlier, sometimes in Books I and II but mainly in Book III. Consisting chiefly of pithy résumés (mostly of only a single line or two) of points made earlier, the format proved popular and drew much attention from readers, who may have seen in it a form of summary of the many principles set out and developed earlier in the work.

The importance of this chapter in the minds of its readers is reflected in the many marginalia found in the manuscripts. The entire chapter is marked by a line in four,[76] while two others[77] have 'note it all' ('nota totum') in fifteenth-century hands in the margin, reflecting something of the interest in the rules expressed by readers of the late period. An examination of the attention accorded to each rule reveals some interesting facts. One is the frequent correspondence, in the same manuscript, between the interest shown by readers in a rule and the chapter (often in Book III) where the matter has already been discussed at length. Most notable of these is Rule 6, which emphasises opportunity ('occasio') in war, a concept which appears a dozen times in ten chapters, including

---

[75] 'Recedere de nocte bonum est' (Trento, Com. W 3154, fo. 28).

[76] Milan, Ambros. G 83 sup., fos. 23v–24v; Naples, Naz. V. A. 22, fo. 43; Ravenna, Class. 140, fos. 51v–52v; Venice, Marc. Z. lat. 463, fos. 194–195v.

[77] Bern, Burgerbibl. 280, fo. 49v; Bologna, Coll. di Spagna, 147, fo. 86v.

the much appreciated chapters 6, 9, 10 and 22. Furthermore, the theme is clearly reflected in other rules. Rule 5, for instance, insists that the best plans are those which the enemy does not know about, but that they should be based on discussion (Rule 29) and on the possession of information regarding the enemy's intention from scouts and spies; Rule 11 emphasises the advantage to be gained from terrain, while Rule 15 underlines the importance of surprise. Rule 4, which stresses that famine, raids and terror are usually more effective than battle, not only finds support from Rule 32, but refers back directly to the importance of denying the enemy food (found in the much appreciated chapters 3 and 9 of Book III) while underlining the importance of planned provisioning contained in Rule 17. Vegetius' understanding of the role played by psychology in preparing the army, both individuals and units, for war is to be found in Rules 3 and 14, which, in their turn, refer to chapters 6, 9, 10 and 12, the first three of which are noted as being among the most highly estimated in Book III.

The 'Rules of war' allow us to note the place which courage ('virtus', 'audacia') occupies in Vegetius' thinking. This attribute, he tells his readers, does not come naturally to most men (Rule 12); none the less, it can be achieved through work and training (Rules 12 and 13), which create the confidence essential to courage, the logic being that the unprepared should never be led into battle (Rule 3). Courage, Vegetius argues, is more important than numbers (Rule 10). Yet, as he points out in other rules, it is not everything. The lie of the land will determine whether battle should be sought or shunned, what troops should be used, and what formations they will assume; thus 'terrain is often of more influence than courage' (Rule 11). Above all he insists that opportunity is usually of greater value than courage (Rule 6). Vegetius' contribution was to stress that conditions and circumstances, and the advantage to which they might be turned, could be decisive factors in battle.

What emerges from this analysis is that while Vegetius spent much time and space describing different forms of battle tactics and strategies, and accorded a number of his rules to these aspects of war,[78] what interested his medieval readers (as emphasised by the correspondence between the most noted chapters and the rules to which they were linked) was the emphasis on training, readiness to seize opportunities, and the importance to be attached to logistics and provisioning, all summed up in the advantage to be reaped by the soldier who is trained to defeat the enemy by any means other than by direct action itself. It has even been suggested that these rules have a life apart, as if they were a kind

---

[78] *DRM*, III, 14–25 and III, 26, Rules 18 to 24.

of 'Vegetius Minor', expressing the essence of the thought of the man who exercised considerable authority in military matters at the end of the Middle Ages.[79]

Book IV

The relatively small number of marginalia found in Book IV of the *De re militari* suggests that this part of the work had rather less appeal to men of the Middle Ages, a surprising fact given the growing military significance of siege warfare, dealt with in Book IV, chapters 1–30. Over all, the number of manuscripts bearing no marginalia in Book IV is about 40 per cent, some 84 out of the 205 manuscripts examined. However, jumping to conclusions from figures alone would be wrong, for Book IV does contain important and interesting evidence. Etymologists, for example, will have had a field day. What is difficult to gauge is whether the matter ended there; was there not a genuine interest in the arms and weapons used by Roman armies as well? Probably so, and we should see the interest in words and their meanings as evidence of a broader attempt to understand the Roman past and how Roman armies won so many successes against those who stood against them.

The emphasis in this book is on the practical. A rapid look at the first group of chapters (1–6) will illustrate this. The passage which attracts the most attention is found in chapter 6 where Vegetius, having described how thick cloaks and goats' hair mats are hung before battlements to absorb the impact of arrows, explains that this is done since arrows do not pass through material that yields and swings! At the same time other measures, mostly of a defensive nature, are underlined. It is clear from the start that medieval readers were more interested in what Vegetius had to say about defence than in anything else. This view is supported by the two other chapters, 4 and 1, which attracted the most attention from readers. Chapter 4 is concerned with the defence of town gates through the use of the portcullis and the bastion. The words used, 'cataracta' and 'propugnaculum', attract much attention, sometimes in the form of an explanation into a modern vernacular term: 'iron portcullises which we call serrazinesca in the vernacular' ('cataracta ferrea quam vulgo la serrazinesca appellamus'),[80] or, even more graphically, into a

---

[79] 'Ces *Regulae* ont une vie à part, on dirait qu'elles composent une sorte de "Vegetius Minor"' (L. Löfstedt, 'Végèce au moyen âge: motifs et modifications des traducteurs et des copistes', in *Homenaje a Álvaro Galmés de Fuentes* (Madrid, 1985), I, 498–9).

[80] Göteborg, Univ. lat. 22, fo. 43v. For a similar example of rendering into the vernacular, taken from the translation of Jean de Meun, see Löfstedt, 'Végèce au moyen âge', p. 493.

plan of a bastion.[81] Like chapters 4 and 6, chapter 1 is about defence, the emphasis being a general observation on man's ability to protect cities built on plains without nature's defences being of assistance to him.

In the second group of chapters (7–11) two stand out as being the most noticed by medieval readers. They share with each other, and with the three already discussed, an interest in aspects of siege warfare. In chapter 9, as he had already done in earlier books, Vegetius warned against shortages which might occur, in this case against an insufficiency of sinews required for the use of catapults and torsion engines. Emphasising that in an emergency human hair could be used as a substitute, Vegetius recalled the story how, when the Capitol had been under siege, and the Roman engines had broken down for lack of sinews, the women had nobly saved the day by cutting their hair, an act which demonstrated their wish to live in freedom rather than submit to the enslavement of the enemy. The story had much appeal, being marked or commented upon in thirty out of thirty-six manuscripts which drew attention to chapter 9 in any way.[82]

In chapter 7 Vegetius returned to one of his recurrent themes, the absolute necessity of being well prepared in time of war. The theme also had its place in the 'Rules of war': in Rules 4 and 32 Vegetius had insisted on the importance of being able to defeat an enemy through starvation. He now emphasised the need for those defending a town or castle to ensure that they did not fall victims to famine, one way by which an enemy might compel surrender. If men ate frugally in times of plenty, they would never be in danger of starving. None the less, provisions should be collected and distributed carefully by responsible persons, while every opportunity should be taken to grow food in both public and private places. The possibility of excluding those unfit to fight from a besieged city was also a passage noted by many readers. Events at Rouen, besieged by an English army in the winter of 1418–19, show

---

[81] As in Vatican, Chigi. H. vii 238, fo. 83, inserted by a later hand on this thirteenth-century manuscript, which also has a small drawing to show how walls should be constructed at angles for effective defence.

[82] 'Dive femine romane' (Vatican, Ottob. lat. 1964, fo. 64v). The person who wrote 'uxores adtulere crines maritis pugnantibus' (Naples, Naz. V. A. 22, fo. 47v) may have been trying to emphasise the point, also made in Vegetius' text, that defence was not the work of men alone. The same idea may have been behind the comment 'Crines sociarum pro funiculis balistarum utiles' (Florence, Laur. Plut. 89, inf. 41, fo. 127). On the same theme, see BnF lat. 7233, fo. 44v. A comment of a different kind was made in Venice, Marc. Z. lat. 463, fo. 200: 'Nota de pudicissimis foeminis romanorum'; while an illuminated capital letter 'N' shows a woman cutting her hair (BnF Smith-Lesouëf 13, fo. 55v). See below, pp. 206–7.

how the defenders were sometimes forced by a shortage of provisions to act in this apparently inhumane fashion.[83]

The emphasis placed upon defence, rather than on attack, is carried over into some parts of the long third group of chapters (11–30) noted by readers. Here four chapters, 26, 21, 25 and 22, stand out, three emphasising the needs of defence. The interest taken in the contents of chapter 26 is clearly reflected in the marking of this chapter in manuscripts of every century from the ninth to the fifteenth, the only case of this being done in Book IV. As in chapter 9, in which he had emphasised the role of women in saving the Capitol, so in this chapter Vegetius used the story of the same Capitol being saved by geese whose cackling had awoken the defenders, unaware of the danger they were in. Vegetius was making the important point that no garrison should be misled into thinking that danger was past when the enemy withdrew; having created a false sense of security among defenders, he could easily return at night and capture a town. Vegetius recommended that both dogs and geese should be kept to warn of approaching danger. How remarkable it was that one bird should have saved the people who would one day conquer the whole world![84] For this reason, therefore, once an enemy had withdrawn, small huts should be erected on the walls and towers in which those guarding the town might shelter from the elements. The theme of defence was maintained in chapters 22 and 25. In the first, interest fell on three kinds of weapon, the 'ballista' (a frame-mounted, torsion-powered bolt-projector), the 'onager' (or mangonel),[85] and the 'scorpio' or 'manuballista' (a kind of crossbow), which, along with slings and heavy stones, could be used effectively in a defensive situation. In the second, Vegetius emphasised the role which all citizens should play in resistance, presented as a common responsibility, a miniature in one manuscript showing a soldier and a civilian confronting each other.[86]

Only in chapter 21 were the challenges experienced by the attacker seriously faced by medieval readers. This chapter dealt with the dangerous process of assault upon the wall of a town and, in greater detail, with the use of siege towers[87] and the methods they provided of forcing an

---

[83] *The Brut or The Chronicles of England*, ed F. W. D. Brie, (2 vols, EETS, London, 1906–8), II, 402.

[84] One reader of Naples, Naz. V. A. 19, drew a goose in the margin (fo. 21); a bird also appears at this point in BnF lat 15076, fo. 159v.

[85] 'Onager sit manganus iuxta vulgare' (Milan, Ambros. G 83 sup., fo. 28).

[86] BnF Smith-Lesouëf 13. fo. 60v. The full-page illumination in New York, Morgan, M 364, fo. 91, shows defence by townspeople, including women, who throw stones on their attackers. In Milan, Ambros. R 6 sup., fo. 49, the text is accompanied by both 'Nota' and a pointing finger.

[87] 'Turres ambulantes' (BnF lat. 5719, fo. 62).

entry into a city: the 'sambuca' (drawbridge), the 'exostra' (crane) and the 'tolleno' (swing beam).[88] This part of the text was still being commented upon in fifteenth-century manuscripts. One wonders how much of what it described was, by that date, of greater antiquarian or scholarly interest than practical value.[89]

The last fifteen chapters (31–46) of Book IV were given over to ships and naval warfare. In some seventeen manuscripts, the earliest of which, Escorial, L. iii. 33, is ninth century, these chapters, renumbered, become Book V. The justification for this change must lie in the very different nature of the matter discussed and the material presented. Nowhere else in the entire work is the sea mentioned or naval affairs considered. Such a change would justify the new subject matter being accorded the status of a book on its own. There is a sense that in the last two centuries of the Middle Ages there occurred a development in the appreciation of what the final section of the work contained. This impression is confirmed by the interest shown in the two aphoristic statements made in chapter 31, which, although far from original, nevertheless had important general points to make. The first concerned the Roman practice of keeping fleets ever in readiness, for, as Vegetius put it, those known to be able to retaliate will not be attacked. The second emphasised that, in the winning of sea battles, speed was more important than courage; this came very close to Rule 6, which had stressed that opportunity was usually of greater value than bravery. Some fifteen manuscripts show evidence that readers appreciated both these typical Vegetian expressions of opinion. What is of interest here is the greater emphasis being placed upon the need to provide and maintain permanent naval forces, for service (in Italy, for instance) on both sea and rivers.[90] This interest in what may at first appear a rather trite generalisation advocating permanent naval forces is, in some respect, recognition that such forces were useful, indeed increasingly important, in the defence of national interests. In the Mediterranean context, navies, already important for such powers as Venice and Genoa, would find their role and responsibilities increased in Pisa, Aragon and the kingdom of Naples.[91] In northern waters, Castile,

---

[88] Vatican, Chigi. H. vii. 238, fo. 85, has a drawing of one reader's impression of a *tolleno*.

[89] The popularity of Valturio's *De re militari*, published in 1472, would suggest that interest in machines was widespread. See P. Richardot, 'La reception de Végèce dans l'Italie de la Renaissance: entre humanisme et culture technique', *Studi umanistici Piceni*, 15 (1995), 195–214.

[90] Vegetius had referred to river boats, used on the Danube, in the concluding lines of the work. On their use by Venice, see M. E. Mallett and J. R. Hale, *The military organization of a Renaissance State. Venice c.1400 to 1617* (Cambridge, 1984), 96–100.

[91] See, for example, A. Ryder, *The kingdom of Naples under Alfonso the Magnanimous. The making of a modern state* (Oxford, 1976), ch. 9 ('Naval forces').

France, England and Burgundy, as well as in the Baltic kingdoms, naval power was coming to assume growing importance; rulers found themselves obliged to build and maintain fleets on a more permanent basis, although in England Henry VI let the fleet created by his father fall into disrepair, thus provoking a strong call for renewal later in the century. Likewise shipyards for building and maintenance, such as Rouen and Southampton, came into being. Above all, it was seen that fleets should come under the control of rulers, who appointed the admirals to lead them.

The significance of chapter 33 should not be passed over without comment. Here Vegetius recounted how the common name ('liburnae') given to ships of war was derived from the model provided by the Liburni, whose vessels, found to be best in war, came to be copied by others.[92] Important here is the message that such ships were specially designed for the purpose. All too often in the Middle Ages merchant ships were commandeered and recommissioned to meet the needs of war. By the fourteenth century the building of ships specifically intended to serve as warships ('naves bellicae') was becoming more common; and as the fifteenth century passed into the sixteenth, so the building of special ships, constructed and used for that purpose alone, became more general.

How far may interest in a chapter advocating that states should have their own warships ever at the ready have been influential in encouraging development in that direction? However that question is answered, the possible role of Book IV in encouraging the expansion of fleets intended for war at sea is suggested by reactions to the content of chapters 34–37, which make up the next group in this book whose overall concern was shipbuilding. While Vegetius had chapters on the best time of the year to cut wood,[93] and how it should be preserved, readers showed particular interest in chapters 34 and 37. In the first, Vegetius emphasised the need to build warships with the very best materials and with the greatest care: bronze nails, although more expensive than iron ones, were worth the extra cost. Vegetius was clearly suggesting that those responsible for building warships should act with the longer term in mind. In chapter 37 he discussed the size of warships, both large and small, including the 'scouting skiffs' ('scaphae exploratoriae')[94] to be used either to intercept enemy convoys or to keep a watch on enemy movements and intentions.[95] States, he was arguing, should have the means of fighting at sea always at

---

[92] 'Liburna dicitur navis velox' (Berlin, Staatsbibl. lat. oct. 3, fo. 46).
[93] 'Quo tempore cedendae arbores' (Florence, Laur. Plut. 45. 21, fo. 71).
[94] 'Scapha est navis exploratoria' (Naples, Naz. V. A. 21, fo. 33v).
[95] As he had done when discussing war on land, Vegetius again emphasised the need to have good knowledge of what the enemy was doing and planning. See *DRM*, III, 6.

their disposal, and ships designed for fighting should be built to last. The only surprise is that Vegetius wrote nothing about the training that sailors (or were they to be soldiers fighting at sea?) should receive. The point is not academic. We may notice the comments of one reader who was surprised to see the word 'miles' describing those who fought at sea: 'Nota pugnantes mari milites vocari' and 'Nota nautae dicuntur milites.'[96] Did Vegetius intend a distinction between 'nauta' (whose function was to sail a vessel) and 'miles' (whose task was to fight on board)? In giving the impression that their functions were separate, Vegetius may have surprised, even confused, a reader in a later age.[97] We should remember, however, that in the late fourteenth century English warships (among others) were manned by sailors (or rowers) and that the fighting was done, primarily, by soldiers. Some confusion there may have been, but there can be little doubt that what Vegetius taught in this group of chapters aroused interest in the declining years of the Middle Ages.

Chapters 38–43 were devoted to the art of navigation. In chapter 38 Vegetius showed the first signs of his awareness of the dangers of war at sea, when weather could do more harm than battles. Men should study the weather, as carelessness could cost lives. Vegetius' interest in the winds was reflected in the reactions of readers to this group of chapters. Perhaps they were encouraged by his dictum that those who bothered to study the winds seldom suffered shipwreck.

More interesting would be some reactions to two of the closing chapters of the work (44–46) which centred on naval warfare. In chapter 44 two themes were picked up by readers. One was the variety of weapons and missiles which could be used in a sea fight. The other, linked to the need to provide soldiers with adequate body armour and shields (a theme already discussed in I, 20), was the great danger of meeting death in a battle fought at sea, death which might come by water or by fire, by steel or by stones, the unburied bodies of such men then being eaten by the fish. Such deaths were not only painful, they were undignified.

The final chapter (46) gave some ideas how a battle should be managed, how it was better to secure the open water, while discussing the weapons and engines which could be used to render the enemy's craft useless, by either battering them, cutting down their sails or disabling their rudders.

---

[96] Vatican, Reg. lat. 1512, fos. 47, 48; 'naute vel milites' (BnF lat. 7470, fo. 108).

[97] We may note what may have been the surprise of a fifteenth-century reader to find the word 'miles' used in the very text which elicited the second quotation cited above (Oxford, Bodl. Laud lat. 56, fo. 51v).

3   A particular response to the *De re militari* . . . and its influence

The manuscript now Vatican, Vat. lat. 2193, copied in Italy (possibly at Verona) in the second quarter of the fourteenth century, written in two columns on both sides of the folio, also contains the *Strategemata* of Frontinus and a number of other works by, among others, Apuleius, Cicero and Palladius. Part of the papal library since the mid-fifteenth century, it is a manuscript of the greatest interest and significance to us as, moving from the general and the anonymous, we seek to understand how a particular known reader responded to the ideas and urgings of the *De re militari*. For here, written on the copy which he owned, we have the glosses of a single person, no less than one of the great European scholars and thinkers of his time, Francesco Petrarch.[1]

Book I was to provide Petrarch with references to many famous names from classical antiquity: writers such as Virgil (one of his favourites), Homer, Sallust and Cato; historical figures such as Cincinnatus, Pompey and Scipio Africanus; while his interest in historical topography and the identification of ancient place names[2] is reflected in the notice of Illyricum.

Study of the passages in the *De re militari* marked or commented upon in the margins reflect a more profound understanding of Vegetius' work and its relevance to the world of the fourteenth century. While it was a book from which to learn how to defend the interests of Rome in particular, its value to Petrarch and his contemporaries was the way it showed how the interests of states could also be defended in their own day. The emphasis in the proem on the value of knowledge (in this case represented by the 'disciplina' or 'ars armorum', 'skill' as we might say today) and what it could achieve appealed to Petrarch as an important branch of human experience. Knowledge dispels fear and increases courage; it was as a part of that experience that Petrarch noted what Vegetius had

---

[1] See C. Tristano, 'Le postille del Petrarca nel Vat. Lat. 2193', *Italia medioevale e umanistica*, 17 (1974), 366.

[2] P. de Nolhac, *Pétrarque et l'humanisme* (2nd edn, 2 vols., Paris, 1907), I, 149; II, 29.

to say about fear. There is a good time, the years of youth, when men should be selected to learn the art of war, so that they shall never regret not having done so. Defeat has been the result of poor selection, and peace has brought neglect of good practice. The effects upon the state are much to be regretted.

Petrarch then showed his appreciation of further points in the work. Quality was more important in battle than numbers. Knowledge was a factor which helped to create that quality. So, as Vegetius argued, the ancient authorities must be consulted to learn what it was that the soldier needed to know, both to put it into practice and to pass it on to others. Petrarch accepted the crucial need for training, before remarking on the different kinds of skills the soldier should develop. Accepting Vegetius' advice that heavy weapons should be used in training so that the soldier's confidence would be increased when he found those used in battle were lighter, Petrarch added that this did not happen in war alone, but in other activities as well,[3] as if underlining that training for war was but one aspect of the broader human experience.

It was in the final chapters that Petrarch resumed the essentials of Vegetius' argument in Book I. He noted what Vegetius had written concerning the peace achieved under the Roman Empire, while recognising that peace might lead to a decline in training and an inability to respond to a threat, such as occurred at the time of the Second Punic War. Rome's fortunes could only be restored when men returned to study military science ('usum exercitiumque militare'). At this point Petrarch added a note that after his victory it was said that Hannibal was weakened by doing only the minimum of training, preferring the delights of leisure afforded him in Campania: 'Nota est ystoria', Petrarch added in warning.[4] Whatever the costs, however, it was better to have one's own soldiers than to rely on mercenaries.

Petrarch's marginal annotations of Book II would be a little more numerous than those he had made to Book I. The long section (chapters 4–18), concerned mainly with the structure of the legion and the order of battle, elicited two responses from Petrarch. Like so many other readers, he approved of the oath[5] given by soldiers to the emperor, and through him to God; this was a further step towards acknowledging the honourable character of the soldier's calling, whch demanded that he obey his superiors. It was with approval, too, that he noted the importance of the role as trainers of soldiers played by the prefects of the legions

---

[3] 'Non in militari tantum, sed in actu quolibet notandum' (Vatican, Vat. lat. 2193, fo. 103).

[4] *Ibid.* fo. 104v.   [5] 'Iuramentum milicie' (*ibid.* fo. 105v).

and the tribunes responsible for their daily supervision as members of the legions. He appreciated the text's emphasis on high standards and twice (in chapters 12 and 14) drew attention to passages in which Vegetius had emphasised the positive effect of brightly shining armour upon the enemy.[6] He also underlined the legion's standard ('aquila') and the cohort's 'dragon' ('draco') in two further passages. Was this an interest in the Roman past? More probably a reflection of the importance which the standard had assumed as a rallying point in his own time?

Noting the Roman achievement of creating the legion ('altitudo Romani in constitutione legionum') and stressing that infantry and cavalry were two quite different arms ('equites a peditibus discrepant'), Petrarch commented on Vegetius' statement, made in the important chapter (23) on the training of soldiers, that it was not experience which transmitted the art of war, but continued exercise, without which even a veteran was but a raw recruit: this was a fact, he wrote in the margin, not limited to the soldiery, but was applicable to others, too ('notabile dictum de arte militari quod de omnibus aliis rectissime dici potest'). His interest in training ('usus') suggests that he appreciated Vegetius' insistence that speed of movement ('velocitas') could only be achieved through constant practice: what had been done in this way (he was now thinking of the use of slings) would be well done on the battlefield; nor would the habit of daily labour in time of peace appear excessive in time of war. On Vegetius' comment that a well-trained soldier desired war, while one inadequately prepared feared it, Petrarch added his view that practice produced more than strength alone ('usum amplius prodesse quam vires'). Comments and marked passages in chapter 23 show Petrarch to have been in sympathy with such ideas.[7]

Petrarch was interested in Book II for another reason. The technical nature of its content presented him (as the wider manuscript evidence suggests that it presented other readers, too) with the opportunity to encounter new words and meanings with which he was unfamiliar. Marginalia underline Petrarch's interest in the etymology of words. The marginal comment 'x cohortes in legione' tells its own tale, while Petrarch's ability to create his own cross-references (suggestive of careful reading) is to be observed in his comment 'in c[apitul]o "Sciendum"' (II, 6) found at the beginning of II, 12, where he had drawn attention to

---

[6] 'Attende' and 'splendor armorum' (*ibid.* fos. 106, 106v). Two centuries later, the Byzantine emperor Maurice would break with classical tradition by advising against shining weapons being in evidence before battle (Maurice's Strategikon, trans. G. T. Dennis (Philadelphia, 1984), 75).

[7] *Ibid.* fos. 107, 107v.

the number of cohorts in a legion. One senses a reader at home in the text, ready to learn from it.[8]

Like many both before and after him, Petrarch found much to interest him in the longer Book III, the number of passages marked or annotated in any way numbering some 147.[9] This, then, as it was for many, was the book to whose content Petrarch responded most enthusiastically. Vegetius' fundamental belief in the value of transmitting the principles of military science through the written word (as the Spartans had done) appealed to him: 'laus rei militaris . . . ingens Lacedemoniorum laus in hac arte', he wrote in the margin of the chapter's proem. When, later in the same proem, Vegetius wrote his famous passage regarding the need to prepare for war in order to secure peace, and that none will challenge a likely winner, Petrarch marked the margin of the manuscript. He also accepted Vegetius' point, supported with examples, that over-large armies could be self-defeating: 'numerositas nimia exercitus pernitiosa. Et adde Pompeii exemplum in Thesalia, teste Floro'. And he warned generals ('Attende') to be careful not to have more auxiliaries (the growing number of mercenaries of Petrarch's day) than Roman citizens in the camp.[10]

Vegetius' concern for the health of soldiers also met a response from Petrarch. Noting that it was hard to fight both war and disease, he accepted what the Roman had written regarding the contribution of exercise to the achievement of victory: 'exercitium corporis quidem salutare et ad victoriam efficax', he commented.[11] Exercise was, of course, part of, if not synonymous with, training. Doing military exercises killed two birds with one stone.

Petrarch appreciated the chapters (*DRM*, III, 9–13) which recommended the proactive strategy of anticipation, based on the commander being kept well informed about conditions and situations as much as on his own confidence that his men were ready for what might happen. A commander who ignored such matters fought on unequal terms. The remaining chapters (14–26) were concerned with the strategies and tactics of war. Once again there were plenty of opportunities for Petrarch to find examples of unusual technical words, in particular in chapters 14, 18 and 19. Next to Vegetius' complex discussion (chapter 15) on formations and the space to be allowed to each soldier, Petrarch noted that close order between men is better than large gaps: 'densitas tutior

---

[8] *Ibid.* fos. 105–106.
[9] Comparable figures being sixty for Book I, sixty-seven for Book II and seventy-six for Book IV.
[10] Vatican, Vat. lat. 2193, fos. 108–108v; *DRM*, III, 1.
[11] Vatican, Vat. lat. 2193, fo. 108v.

raritate'. He saw the point, made in chapter 17, that soldiers, once in their ranks, should not be moved ('Nam de loco movendum sed aliunde supplendum'), pointing out that the instruction had been ignored by the leaders of Bologna and had brought disaster on themselves at a time when he, Petrarch, had been studying in the city ('Observantia non commutandi ordines sub tempus pugne, que, neglecta a ducibus Bononiensium, magnam illi populo cladem intulit, me ibi tunc puero in literarum studiis agente'), a reference to the battle of Zappolino won by Azo Visconti on 15 November 1325.[12] Petrarch understood the importance and value of being the first army to draw up a battle line ('anticipanda aciei instructio'), mainly as a means of boosting the confidence of its soldiers, and recognised that there was an optimum moment when the battle cry should be given.[13] On the other hand, Vegetius had several times written of the need to avoid a tendency towards over-confidence; three marginal annotations show that Petrarch had not ignored this advice.

By contrast with Book III, the annotations of Book IV are disappointing, in both number and interest. Most are little more than a word or two drawing attention to terms, frequently weapons or technical instruments of war, such as the way to measure the height of a wall ('mensura muri'), or to an individual from Roman history ('Manlius' [Capitolinus]). Chapters 31–46, which are mainly concerned with the sea and naval warfare, appear to have interested Petrarch rather more. A note on Vegetius' reference to the bases of the Roman fleets (Misenum and Ravenna) underlined Petrarch's sense of topography, his ability to provide references to works of literature and history (on this occasion to Suetonius) and his appreciation of the active role played by the fleets in the defence of Rome and its interests (chapter 31). What Vegetius had written about the sun and the moon, the seasons (and how their physical effects are felt), the winds, the good and the bad times for sailors to venture out to sea, factors affecting the weather which were beyond human knowledge, all these drew Petrarch's attention. At a later date he appears to have returned to the manuscript and marked chapter 35 (on the best time to cut timber for boats), but it was the single word 'luna' which he wrote in the margin. Was he trying to work out what effects the moon had upon the inhabitants of earth and upon their activities? Later he also marked the concluding three chapters on war at sea. What impressed him most was the cruelty of this form of war. None the less (and here he returned to one of Vegetius' basic lessons), the general

---

[12] *Ibid.* fos. 111–112v. See de Nolhac, *Pétrarque et l'humanisme*, I, 36, n. 1; II, 101.
[13] 'Clamor quando tollendus' (Vatican, Vat. lat. 2193, fo. 112v).

must be ever ready to use the opportunities presented by Fortune to his advantage.[14]

What emerges from this consideration of Petrarch's annotations is that he had appreciated many of the moral points made by Vegetius regarding the role of the army in society, the part to be played by soldiers and those commanding them, and the basic lessons to be learned in order to make the recruit, specially chosen for his qualities of mind and physique, into an effective member of the state's defensive shield. Behind this, too, lay a further important conclusion: the end to which knowledge (or experience) can lead when its lessons are properly applied. Victory in war is not achieved through numbers but stems largely from using the benefits of sustained experience. So the existing body of knowledge on the art of waging war should be passed down from one generation to the next, using the medium of the written word. The importance of that word was inestimable, conveying authority and prestige upon those who made it available.

Consideration of the passages glossed by Petrarch indicates that he appreciated that those who fought wars – however well trained and, in theory, ready for anything – were also men of flesh and blood who feared wounds and death, and who might be inclined to run away if they lost confidence in their leaders. The passages which emphasised the qualities required by those appointed to lead, set out principally in *DRM*, III, underline both Petrarch's humanity and his respect for the text inherited from the Roman past.

It is one thing to follow Petrarch as he read the *De re militari*, and to note his reactions to various parts of the text. It is another to suggest that some of those readings may have found their way into his own work. Yet, although he did not specifically say so, it is likely that points gleaned from Vegetius were, consciously or not, transferred into at least one of Petrarch's works, the epic poem *Africa*, which he began to think about in 1333.

This long poem, describing the culmination of the struggle between Rome and Carthage in the Second Punic War, with its emphasis on the personalities of Scipio Africanus and Hannibal, reached its climax in Book 7 with the description of the battle of Zama (202 BC), which almost certainly contains elements inspired by Petrarch's reading of the *De re militari*. These would influence the poem at different levels and in different ways. At the most sublime is Petrarch's emphasis (which he could have learned about from writers other than Vegetius) on the response of men to the need to defend their country and to secure their

---

[14] *Ibid.* fos. 116v, 117.

liberty: Scipio's efforts were aimed at defeating Hannibal and securing the liberation of both Rome and of Italy as a whole from the Carthaginian yoke. In Vegetius' work, Petrarch would have found texts supporting his ambition to secure that freedom, as well as instruction in the best methods to achieve it.

Examination of Petrarch's manuscript strongly suggests that ideas, principles and the recommendations urged by Vegetius upon his readers were worked into the *Africa*. The defence of country as a priority, and the reputation accorded by later generations to those who sacrificed themselves at the altar of that cause, was a theme introduced early on, and which would reappear later.[15] As Vegetius had noted in a passage marked in Petrarch's manuscript, granted the nobility of the cause, it was one to which only the best types of citizen could be allowed to devote themselves.[16] The theme would find its place in the *Africa*, where, later, Petrarch described it as a responsibility, both vital and honourable, that could not be placed in the hands of every man.[17] In so writing, he was underlining Vegetius' vision of the soldier as the protector of the state and its liberty.[18]

The soldier's calling was, therefore, one which only society's best could fulfil satisfactorily. Once trained, the soldier was anxious to get on with the work for which he had been trained. Vegetius had warned the commander to resist the pressure to fight which might come from the well-prepared, but as yet inexperienced young soldiers with little practical knowledge of war. This passage is marked in Petrarch's copy of the *De re militari*, to which Petrarch added the comment 'the advice of the inexperienced should not be heeded' ('non curanda inexpertorum iudicia').[19] It is not surprising, therefore, to find him telling the reader of the *Africa* that on the day of the battle of Zama 'the youthful veterans / of Rome, all clamorous for combat, fill / the centre'. In this case the line is more than a literary technique to build up expectation; it is quite likely to have been a throwback to Vegetius.

A number of other passages in the poem suggest that Vegetian influence upon Petrarch, whether he was fully conscious of it or not, was a live one. While it is difficult to prove this beyond doubt, it can be argued that in a number of instances we know that Petrarch was struck by what Vegetius had written, and that, since Petrarch himself used the same

---

[15] *Africa*, 22/806–11; 176/1318–20.
[16] *DRM*, I, 7; Vatican, Vat. lat. 2193, fo. 102v.   [17] *Africa*, 22/806–8; 153/448–50.
[18] *DRM*, II, 24; Vatican, Vat. lat. 2193, fo. 107v; *Africa*, 168/1018–21. See also *DRM*, III, 1, marked on fo. 108v, which in general terms could have inspired the *Africa*, 173/1210–14.
[19] Vatican, Vat. lat. 2193, fo. 111.

information, opinion or form of words to make the point elsewhere, it is likely that this constituted an appropriation from Vegetius. As we have seen above, the Roman writer emphasised the human characteristics of his soldiers who, if open to fear, anxiety, even despair, were equally ready to react to good news or encouragement. Prior to the battle of Zama, described in Book 7 of the *Africa*, Scipio addressed his men in an effort to boost their confidence. This passage reflects the urgings of Vegetius in *DRM*, III, 12, which, as Petrarch's manuscript shows, had made a considerable impression upon him. Thus we find Vegetius' concern regarding the anxieties of his soldiers, and his recommendation that commanders do their utmost to lift spirits, both drawing marginal comments from Petrarch, as well as being reflected in the passage from the *Africa* just cited, down to the last detail which sees Scipio putting into practice Vegetius' advice to remind his soldiers of successes over the enemy recorded in the past.[20] Likewise we see reflected in the *Africa* the hatred of the enemy which Vegetius had recommended his generals to stir up among his men in a passage which had earned a note in Petrarch's manuscript.[21]

Other links between the *De re militari* and the *Africa* can be suggested. Unusual comments or allusions shared by texts are a fair indication that one has appropriated material from the other. Recalling that Scipio Africanus used to recommend that fleeing soldiers should be allowed to make good their escape, Vegetius had emphasised that those who feared that there was no escape for them would gladly fight so as to take as many of the enemy as possible to their deaths with them, an observation noted in Vegetius and expressed faithfully, if more poetically, by Petrarch.[22] The juxtapositioning of sun, dust and wind as elements often encountered by the soldier smacks not so much of the dust mentioned more than once by Livy but rather of Vegetius' warning that they may be dangerous factors in a situation of conflict, the passage in Petrarch's manuscript being duly annotated 'sol, pulvis et ventus' in the margin. Less controversial will be the statement made by Petrarch, when describing the armies which opposed each other at Zama, that the Roman army was more homogeneous than the Carthaginian one, drawn as it was from many lands and peoples. Although the point is made by Livy, we may also remind ourselves that, in writing this, Petrarch may have recalled Vegetius' view that

---

[20] *DRM*, III, 12; Vatican, Vat. lat. 2193, fo. 111; *Africa*, 168/1008–28. Livy, greatly admired by Petrarch, recorded several instances of generals' speeches before battle.

[21] *DRM*, III, 12; Vatican, Vat. lat. 2193, fo. 111; *Africa*, 175/1274ff.

[22] *DRM*, III, 21; Vatican, Vat. lat. 2193, fo. 113; *Africa*, 11/387. Vegetius may have taken this point from Frontinus, *Strategemata*, II, vi and IV, vii, 16. So, too, may Petrarch, whose codex included the work of Frontinus.

those who fought in different ways would not achieve victory as quickly as those who had trained in the same military tradition.[23]

Can one in any meaningful sense pinpoint Petrarch's interest in the *De re militari*? No more than the author whose work he was reading may Petrarch be called a military man. Rather, his interest was both literary and, in a sense, practical as well; Petrarch had an interest in knowledge of many (or any) kinds, and Vegetius' work presented this enquiring personality with the opportunity of finding out about, and commenting on, the way armies were organised and wars were fought in the past, while at the same time noting the timeless remarks which Vegetius had made about the effective conduct of war. Petrarch was also a patriot living in mid-fourteenth-century Italy, a man who saw in the *De re militari* a text which could convey a powerful political message about the use of properly organised force and authorised military leadership in the world of his day. His interest in the notion of the army may not have been unusual in the Italy of his time; but it was certainly fostered by the work which he had read and annotated with such care, a work which encouraged him when it came to writing his *Africa*, enabling him to draw on practical details and ideas which he had found in reading it.

[23] *DRM*, II, 2; Vatican, Vat. lat. 2193, fo. 105; *Africa*, 171/1111–38. See above, p. 28.

4   Bedfellows

Consideration mainly of the manuscripts themselves, but also of information gleaned from wills and inventories, can reveal much about other texts with which the *De re militari* was closely associated in the Middle Ages, thus adding to our understanding of the way the work was regarded by its owners and readers. If the copying of a text is always deliberate, the accompanying text(s) given to it within a single codex, or 'bed', may not always be so. It can, none the less, often indicate how that text was regarded, and the (sometimes new) context within which its owners saw it. Although some 20 per cent of manuscripts are of the *De re militari* on its own, codices containing more than a single text can help us appreciate individual works through the eyes of the person who arranged them with particular bedfellows.

No surprise will be caused by the revelation that the text with which the *De re militari* is, by a very large margin, most frequently bound is the *Strategemata* of Julius Frontinus. Compiled in the first century AD, this comprised a collection of 'exempla' of military stratagems derived from both Greek and Roman historical sources, arranged under headings into four books, to support a work of military theory (also probably called *De re militari*) now lost. It cannot be determined whether Vegetius was familiar with this work, or depended on another for his knowledge of it. Frontinus is referred to twice in the *De re militari*,[1] the relevant passages often bearing his name in the margins of manuscripts.[2] The *Strategemata* proved to be a popular work in the Middle Ages; well over 100 manuscripts are known to have survived, including collections of excerpts and translations into at least three languages.[3]

---

[1] *DRM*, I, 8; II, 3. See *Vegetius: Epitome*, trans. Milner, xix–xxiii.

[2] E.g., Florence, Laur. Plut. 45. 21; Lund, Univ. 8; Naples, Naz. V. A. 22, to cite only fifteenth-century examples.

[3] See C. Allmand, 'A Roman text on war. The *Strategemata* of Frontinus in the Middle Ages', in *Soldiers, nobles and gentlemen. Essays in honour of Maurice Keen*, ed. P. Coss and C. Tyerman (Woodbridge, 2009), 153–68.

Copies of the work made before the twelfth century are rare. The first two to combine the *De re militari* and the *Strategemata* are from that century; one is almost complete, while the other offers only selections ('dicta et exempla') from Frontinus' text.[4] None the less, the combination was to grow more popular with time, rising rapidly in the fourteenth century, and reaching its flowering in the fifteenth century, when more than twenty 'combined' manuscripts were copied, including one containing the French translation of both works.[5]

Perhaps the most striking factor to emerge from the evidence of the combined manuscripts is the high proportion copied in Italy and owned by persons living on the peninsula. Of the eight fourteenth-century examples containing the works of both Vegetius and Frontinus, some six were of Italian origin; in the following century the figure would be eleven out of some seventeen, two of the others probably being French and one German. Who owned these manuscripts is seldom clear. As we have seen, Petrarch stands out as a notable owner of both texts, while others included a lawyer, Luca da Cantarelli, from Reggio, who added marginalia before bequeathing it, 'for the good of my soul', to a religious community in Venice in 1428,[6] and the papal library under Nicholas V in 1455.[7] Another was bought in Bologna in June 1451 by Gaspar Volaterranus, Cardinal Bessarion's secretary.[8] In England, in June 1414, John Neuton, an important book collector and a former treasurer of York Minster, bequeathed such a text to Peterhouse, Cambridge,[9] while in France Jean Budé, likewise a well-known collector who commissioned manuscripts from several scribes in the 1480s, and father of the famous humanist, Guillaume Budé, would also own a copy.[10]

The linking of the works of Vegetius and Frontinus suggests a conscious attempt to bring books related to war together under a single cover. This is particularly apparent in a few special cases. The most notable is the manuscript which includes two late Carolingian copies of texts relating to war, the *Book of Maccabees* and the *De re militari*, to which was added, perhaps in the fifteenth century, a collection of excerpts from the

---

[4] Oxford, Lincoln, lat. 100; Vatican, Pal. lat. 1571.
[5] Paris, Arsenal, 2693.   [6] Vatican, Borg. lat. 411.
[7] This text, Vatican, Vat. lat. 1860, is known to have been borrowed by one P. de Grassis in 1485 (E. Pellegrin, *Les manuscrits classiques latins de la Bibliothèque Vaticane* (Paris, 1975–), III, 439).
[8] Vatican, Vat. lat. 7227.
[9] *Testamenta Eboracensia*, ed. J. Raine (Surtees Society 106, Durham, 1902), I, 370; now Cambridge, Peterhouse, 196.
[10] Palma de Mallorca, March-Servera, B96–V3–3; Sotheby's, *Sale of the Bibliotheca Phillippica*, N.S. Medieval X (26 November 1975), 65–6.

Strategemata of Frontinus.[11] The binding of these three texts together at this late date cannot have been other than deliberate. Vegetius' well-read text has many marginalia, most of them dating from the twelfth to the fifteenth centuries, some explaining, in words, the meanings of unfamiliar terms,[12] others, such as the various formations mentioned in Book III, being expressed in drawings to help the reader visualise them easily.[13] These would appear to be intended not only to give life to the meanings of words through the use of more familiar vocabulary or drawings, but also to make the contents of the work more relevant to the modern reader. Not the least remarkable feature of this fine manuscript is the fifteenth-century glossary ('registrum sive tabula libri Vegecii de re militari'), with references to book and chapter, followed by a 'vocabularius' of words, with definitions of their meanings in Latin. A little later one finds a glossary of military terms ('vocabula rariora super Frontones [*sic*] de re bellica'), a table of themes, and another in which important military themes are treated ('in qua tractantur quaedam valde utilia et necessaria ad opus bellicum').[14] Altogether, these factors clearly point to a codex intended for consultation when military matters were under consideration.

Other forms of combination of works relating to war were also made. Turin, Bibl. Reale, Saluzzo 3, contains not only the works of Vegetius and Frontinus, but also the so-called *De re militari* of Modestus; Leiden, Voss. lat. F. 59 has these and the pseudo-Aristotelian *Secretum Secretorum*, all in the same hand; while BnF lat. 6106, copied in Dalmatia in 1435, includes Vegetius, Frontinus and five books by Caesar. Vatican, Reg. lat. 1880, a de luxe manuscript, includes Vegetius, *De re militari*, the *Strategicus* of Onasander (only recently, *c.*1453, translated from the Greek), and the *De instruendis aciebus* of Aelian. Both Wrocław, Bibl. Uniw. Rehd. 10, and Berlin, Staatsbibl. lat. oct. 141, contain the works of Vegetius, Frontinus and Aelian, while Paris, Mazarine, 3732, has these three, with the text of Modestus added. Three manuscripts, Naples, Bibl. Naz. V. A. 21, Milan, Ambros. I, 108 sup. and Vibo Valencia, Capialbi 38, include a *De bellis*, taken from Book XVIII of Isidore's *Etymologiae*, beginning 'There are four kinds of war . . . '. It is surely reasonable to view these codices as attempts to create specialised collections of military texts, which appear to have been largely formed for Italian owners or copied by Italian scribes.

---

[11] Leiden, Univ. Periz. F. 17.
[12] E.g., 'sarisa est longa lancea' (*ibid.* fo. 127v).   [13] *Ibid.* fos. 121v–124.
[14] *Ibid.* fos. 150–163v; fos. 164–169v; fos. 182–185v; fos. 186–189; fo. 190.

It is noticeable that of the eight manuscripts described by Michael Reeve[15] as forming the 'Mazarine group' four, including a thirteenth-century manuscript,[16] should have included Frontinus' *Strategemata*. It appears that in these cases the copyists were instructed to copy both the *De re militari* and the *Strategemata*, thus uniting in a single volume the two outstanding Latin military texts inherited from the Roman world. The closeness of the relationship could be expressed in different ways. In a number of copies of the 'combined' texts, both are written in the same hand.[17] In three other cases[18] the second text (that of Frontinus in the case of the first two, that of Vegetius in the third) begins on the verso side of the folio on which the first had finished, strongly suggesting that the two texts were seen as a pair, each complementing the other. With the evidence just cited of manuscripts containing three military texts, we come to the conclusion that, in Italy at least, such collections were becoming popular (or, simply, more fashionable?) in the second half of the fifteenth century. It was probably no coincidence that in 1487 Eucharius Silber printed a volume in Rome containing the works of Vegetius, Frontinus, Aelian and Modestus. The production of these 'multi-text' volumes for the market appears to have been catching on in Italy in the last years of the fifteenth century.

Twelfth- and thirteenth-century manuscripts of the *De re militari* are found with the *De re rustica* of Vegetius' near contemporary, Palladius. However, this particular combination of practical works would later become rare.[19] Another work associated with the *De re militari* was the *De architectura* of the Roman engineer and architect Vitruvius, a text destined to have much influence on Renaissance architecture; it is found bound with the *De re militari* in a few instances, largely because it contained, in Book X, a consideration of machines, both civil and military.[20] Cicero

[15] Reeve, 'Transmission', 315.   [16] Paris, Maz. 3732.
[17] E.g., The Hague, Konink. 78 F. 4; Leiden, Univ. BPL 128, and Voss. lat. F 59 (this last with four texts, as indicated above, all in the same hand); Vatican, Urb. lat. 1221; Valladolid, Santa Cruz, 384. The same probably applies to Rimini, Gambalunga, SC. 33, and Wrocław, Bibl. Uniw. Rehd. 10.
[18] Paris, Maz. 3732; Vatican, Vat. lat. 4494; BnF lat. 6106.
[19] BL Add. Ms 38,818; Vatican, Reg. lat. 1274, Reg. lat. 1286, Urb. lat. 1362; Escorial, O. iii. 9; Florence, Laur., S. Croce, Plut. 24, sin 6; Milan, Ambros., B 91. sup.; BnF lat. 5719. In Vatican, Chigi. H. vii 238, both texts are written in the same hand. The combination is to be found in a catalogue of the Norman abbey of Le Bec in the twelfth century (Reeve, 'Transmission', 268). Petrarch's manuscript of Vegetius and Frontinus (Vatican, Vat. lat. 2193), copied in northern Italy between 1330 and 1340, also included Palladius.
[20] BL Cotton, Cleo. D. i; Add. Ms 38,818; Harley 3859; Vienna, Nationalbibl. 310; Venice, Marc. Z. lat. 463, this last probably by a single scribe for Cardinal Bessarion.

was sometimes, but irregularly, linked to the *De re militari*, mainly in the fifteenth century,[21] while among the work of historians most frequently found was that of Sallust, twice cited in Vegetius' text.[22]

Linked, as we have seen, to works from the classical past, the *De re militari* was increasingly associated with works written in the Middle Ages. Two such, each indebted to Vegetius, found a natural place alongside the *De re militari*. One was John of Salisbury's *Policraticus*, found with manuscripts of the fourteenth and fifteenth centuries.[23] The other, more important, consisted of the various manifestations of Giles of Rome's *De regimine principum*, written in the late thirteenth century. Both these medieval writers relied upon Vegetius for their knowledge of military affairs At the same time, the act of bringing their respective works together reflected the gradual politicisation of the *De re militari*, an important part of its metamorphosis from being primarily, or solely, a text of military significance into one with increasingly important political messages to convey.[24] Indeed, it is legitimate to ask whether Vegetius composed his work with only military considerations in mind. Whatever the answer given, it requires little prescience to understand that the organisation of war carries political implications. Nor does it require much exegesis to appreciate that Vegetius' recommendation that emperors (for whom read kings, princes, even republics) with armies manned by soldiers who swore obedience to them would lead to the growth of both the military and the political power of those rulers. As John of Salisbury was to write, the army was the king's hand, his 'manus'. Surely this was Vegetius being gradually drawn into the political sphere. The creation of codices including the works of Vegetius with those of either John of Salisbury or Giles of Rome should cause us little surprise.

See L. D. Reynolds (ed.), *Texts and transmission. A survey of the Latin classics* (Oxford, 1983), xxxii.

[21] BnF lat. 7231; BL Add. Ms. 21,242; Harley 2475; Montpellier, Bibl. Méd. 133; Florence, Laur. Plut. 89, inf. 41; Leipzig, Univ. Rep. I, fol. 18; Prague, Nat. Lib. 2369; Trier, Stadtbibl. 1083; Kraków, Jagiell, 1952 and 2120; Warsaw, Bibl. Narodowa, II 8076. In the twelfth-century copy (Montpellier, Bibl. Méd. 133, fo. 66v) the text of the *De re militari* follows on immediately after the conclusion of Cicero's *De officiis* and *De amicitia*.

[22] BL Add. Ms 21,242, Harley 2475 and 3859; Florence, Laur. Plut. 89, inf. 41 and Plut. 53. 12; Leipzig, Univ. Rep. I, fol. 18; Leiden, Univ. BPL 19; Prague, Nat. Lib. 2369; Trier, Stadtbibl. 1083.

[23] Vatican, Vat. lat 4497; The Hague, Konink. 78 F. 4. The second manuscript, copied in the fifteenth century, also includes Frontinus' *Strategemata*, all three texts being written in a single hand.

[24] The *De re militari* interpreted chiefly as a military text has been underlined by Shrader ('The ownership and distribution of manuscripts of the *De re militari* of Flavius Vegetius Renatus before the year 1300' (PhD diss., Columbia University, 1976)), while its politicisation receives greater emphasis from Sherwood ('Studies').

Of the eleven manuscripts of the English translation known to have been owned in England at this time, four consisted of the *De re militari* alone, the others being bound with, or in some cases copied with, other texts. The most notable bedfellow was John Lydgate's *The Book of Governance of Kings and Princes* (with five examples), while the finest manuscript was that which consisted of the English translations of the works of both Vegetius and Giles of Rome, an expensively produced text on vellum written in one hand throughout, creating a manuscript of the highest quality.[25] Significantly, copies of the Latin texts of both Vegetius and Giles, included in Oxford, Balliol College 146A, were written in the same hand, while BL Royal 12 B. xxi, which includes the *De re militari* and the *De regimine principum* (the latter in an abridged form), also shares the same hand throughout. A composite manuscript belonging to Reading Abbey contained works, including those of Vegetius and Giles, in different hands, while another was in the library of Canterbury College, Oxford, by 1501.[26]

Of the two principal translations of the *De re militari* made into French, one by Jean de Meun, the other by Jean de Vignay, about half stand alone.[27] Of the Meun versions combined with another work, one has Honoré Bouvet's *L'arbre des batailles*, another Frontinus' *Strategemata*, while two others have 'le livre nommé l'ordre de [la] chevalerie', probably a translation of Ramon Lull's *Llibre de l'Orde de Cavalleria*, which may have been linked to the French Vegetius through the translator's use of the word 'chevalerie' into the title.[28] Two manuscripts of Vignay's translation are bound with the text (or parts) of Giles' *De regimine principum*, translated by Henri de Gauchi in 1282;[29] one with a translation of Xenophon's *Cyropaedia*;[30] and another with William Caxton's imprint of Christine de

---

[25] Oxford, Bodl. Digby 233.

[26] Oxford, Bodl. Auct. F. 3. 3 and F. 3. 2; C. F. Briggs, *Giles of Rome's* De regimine principum *in England. Reading and writing politics at court and university, c.1275–c.1525* (Cambridge, 1999), 166.

[27] The proportions are about two-thirds for Meun's translation, and one-third for that of Vignay.

[28] Bern, Burgerbibl. 280A (Bouvet); The Hague, Konink. 73 J 22 (Frontinus); Paris, Arsenal, 2915; Turin, Arch. di Stato, Jb II 19 (Lull).

[29] Vatican, Rossi. 457; Cambridge, Univ. Lib. Ee II 17. In addition, Jean, duke of Berry may have owned a fourteenth-century Latin collection which included excerpts from both Vegetius and Giles (BnF lat. 6476), while it is reasonable to think that another collection (BnF nouv. acq. fr. 3074), which includes excerpts from both writers in French, originated in France. Jean Budé owned both a *De re militari* and an abridgement of the *De regimine principum*. Excerpts from Vegetius along with Giles' text (and much else) are to be found in Rein, Stiftsbibl. 205; Lambach, Stiftsbibl. Chart. 20; Prague, Nat. Lib. 2369.

[30] BL Royal 17 E v.

Pisan's *Fais d'armes*, itself founded on Vignay's translation.[31] The quality of the copies is generally high. Most of the Vignay manuscripts have either an illuminated presentation scene or illuminations within the text itself; some have both.[32] Much the same may be said about the larger number of copies of Meun's translation, which includes some fine manuscripts, many with miniatures and/or presentation scenes.[33]

At the same time it appears that Vegetius' original purpose in writing was being subjected to fundamental change by the inclusion of his work, alongside others, in a dossier of works intended to create support for a crusade in the first quarter of the fourteenth century.[34] Paris, BnF lat. 7470 and Vatican, Reg. lat. 1512 both contain a text of Vegetius, a little modified to suit its new purpose, joined to other, fairly recently written works to build up support for a planned crusading venture to the Holy Land. A French version of this dossier[35] was also created at much the same time. In this case the person who envisaged it clearly appreciated the influence which the inclusion of the *De re militari*, by this date *the military authority of the time*, could have upon the dossier's persuasive powers.

[31] Cambridge, Magdalene, PL 1938, later owned by Samuel Pepys.
[32] See below, p. 152.
[33] E.g. The Hague, Konink. 73 J 22; BL Royal 20 B xv; Paris, Arsenal, 2916.
[34] See M. and R. Rouse, 'Context and reception: a crusading collection of Charles IV of France', in *Courtly arts and the art of courtliness*, ed. K. Busby and C. Kleinhenz (Cambridge, 2006), 105–78. See below, pp. 113–15.
[35] BnF fr. 1260.

5   Owners and their texts

It is important to appreciate who owned manuscripts of the *De re militari* in the Middle Ages, and the reasons why they may have wished to do so. Individual owners are revealed by a number of different sources. Wills record texts belonging to particular individuals, as do inventories of goods drawn up after death. Library catalogues, on the other hand, often list the manuscripts owned by institutions, religious or educational, or by rulers who succeed one another through inheritance. Almost by definition, catalogues are concerned with collections of texts, often gathered over a long period of time. These seldom tell us about the tastes and interests of individuals in the way that a will, a very personal document, can do. They are more likely to reveal what the users of a particular library, the monks who constituted an established community for example, found interesting and useful over the generations it took to create the collection. Nor will they betray what individual readers thought of a particular text, except what they sometimes wrote, anonymously, in the margins. Yet such institutional copies are important for the way they may have ensured both the physical safety and a greater knowledge and appreciation of a particular text than of one held in a private library.

However, some manuscripts, particularly later ones, do reveal who copied them, and for whom, while the date (in particular) and place are often recorded. Very occasionally, too, we are even let into the secret of how much a manuscript cost its owner.[1] Other, more general, factors can help in our search. Palaeographical evidence is often valuable. Occasionally an individual hand may be recognised and, when compared with other examples, can lead to the identification of a scribe. Styles of writing and illumination can reveal both dates and the broad geographical origins of the scribe and artist. Whether the text is written on parchment or paper is another indication of date, while watermarks may enable one to attach a date and an indication of geographical origins to a manuscript.

---

[1] E.g. BL Harley 2551 and 2667; Vatican, Vat. lat. 7227; Oxford, Bodl. Douce 147.

No more than books today, manuscripts were not always read by those who owned them; owning a book did not make a man read it. In turn, those who read them out of interest were not always their owners. Not all readers annotated manuscripts, so that an unmarked manuscript should not imply lack of appreciation of its content on the part of its readers, who may not have been its owners. As for manuscripts in libraries, there was, in theory, no limit to the numbers who might read and be influenced by them. Here we may ask who were most likely to be the owners of the *De re militari*. By considering (a) its subject matter (in this instance, war) and (b) the language in which it was written (Latin), we may take the first step towards seeing which persons or groups may have had an interest in possessing their own copies of Vegetius' work. In so doing, we should bear in mind that possesssion of a manuscript would normally have required the availability of a text from which a copy could be made, along with that of the skills of a scribe, and, if necessary, the means to pay for the copying to be done.

From the evidence of catalogues of surviving manuscripts and, occasionally, of the works of men who used them, it is clear that well on into its history the *De re militari* was largely owned by ecclesiastical communities, which formed the chief centres of learning and culture in medieval Europe. Until the twelfth century, ownership of the text was to be dominated by such communities (institutional ownership), although examples of senior ecclesiastics of the non-monastic world possessing the text (private ownership) are also found. This was not simply a case of such communities acting as transmitters of classical culture into a later age. The presence of the *De re militari* in monastic libraries reflected the fact that it could be regarded as an allegory of the monk's struggle against sin to be won through rigorous training and constant practice, discipline and a life of order, lived out in a spirit of obedience to rules and to a superior.[2] For religious communities, it set out a pattern of life which, if followed, could lead to spiritual victory and the attainment of the eternal destiny which formed the purpose of their lives. There are echoes, too, of the *De re militari* forming a link between the monk and the world around him in the correspondence of Alcuin (c.800), who was deeply aware of the spiritual struggle which the bishop must face as he led the Christian body towards its destiny in the next world.[3]

---

[2] Orderic Vitalis, *Historia ecclesiastica*, ed. M. Chibnall (Oxford, 1980), I, 38.

[3] Reeve, 'Transmission', 250; C. Veyrard-Cosme, 'Réflexion politique et pratique du pouvoir dans l'œuvre d'Alcuin', in *Penser le pouvoir au moyen âge (VIIIe–XVe siècle). Études offertes à Françoise Autrand*, ed. D. Boutet and J. Verger (Paris, 2000), 409–10.

Manuscripts owned by monastic institutions and bishops were responsible for much of the sustained interest in Vegetius' work. The earliest evidence of those possessing Vegetius' text, found either in library catalogues or in manuscripts themselves (and sometimes in both), points to the monks of those religious houses, often endowed with their own scriptoria for copying, which blossomed from the ninth century onwards, thereby creating the chief centres of learning in medieval Europe. Yet even a century earlier, in the distant fastness of Northumbria, the monk Bede (d.735) could cite Vegetius, as references found in his *Ecclesiastical history of the English people* and other works indicate.[4] Whether there was a copy of the *De re militari* at Monkwearmouth or Jarrow, we do not know. We cannot tell, therefore, whether Bede had access to a text or simply a collection of excerpts, although at such an early date it may have been the complete text. In the centuries that followed, the owners of the work continued to be, more often than not, monastic communities. It is not surprising, then, that between the ninth and the thirteenth centuries, some of the greatest monastic libraries owned copies of the *De re militari*. Two surviving ninth-century manuscripts were in the library of the monastery of Saint-Denis, outside Paris; another, written at Fleury, was to be found in the library there.[5] In the following century, the list would grow longer. Vegetius' text would be owned by the monasteries of Reichenau, St Peter's, Ghent, Noailles and Freising,[6] while the eleventh century would see manuscripts in other monastic houses, notably St Augustine's, Canterbury, St Martial, Limoges, and Corvey.[7]

The twelfth century, a time which witnessed a marked rise in interest in the *De re militari*, saw other religious institutions acquire copies of it. In Italy, the great Benedictine foundation of Monte Cassino had a manuscript copied by no less a person than Peter the Deacon,[8] while in France copies were owned by the communities of Le Bec-Hellouin and Saint-Evroult in Normandy, at Angers and Limoges further south, and by Saint-Amand and Corbie in the north-east of the

---

[4] C. W. Jones, 'Bede and Vegetius', *The Classical Review*, 46 (1932), 248–9; Reeve, 'Transmission', 249–50.

[5] BnF lat. 6503 and 7230 (Saint-Denis); Bern, Burgerbibl. 280 (Fleury). See B. Bischoff, *Manuscripts and libraries in the age of Charlemagne*, trans. M. Gorman (Cambridge, 1994), p. 144.

[6] Leiden, Univ. Periz. F. 17 (Reichenau); Escorial, L. iii. 33 (Ghent); BnF lat. 7230A (Noailles); Munich, Staatsbibl. CLM. 6368 (Freising). Catalogues reveal copies in the monastic libraries of Lorsch, Murbach, St Gallen, Einsiedeln and Lobbes at this period.

[7] BL Cotton, Cleo. D. i (Canterbury); BnF lat. 7231 (Limoges); Vatican, Pal. lat. 909 (Corvey).

[8] Monte Cassino, Bibl. dell'Abbazia, 361.

country.[9] In England, Christ Church, Canterbury probably possessed more than one manuscript, another was copied for the monastic library at Malmesbury,[10] while St Albans abbey owned a copy by 1235.[11]

Leading members of the secular clergy, bishops and cathedral chapters were also acquiring manuscripts of the work. From early times such men, often counsellors to kings and princes, had an interest in the *De re militari*. When called upon to offer advice on military affairs Freculf, bishop of Lisieux and chancellor of the West Frankish kingdom, revised the text of the *De re militari* before presenting it to Charles the Bald in 840; he probably envisaged it as providing answers to current military problems raised by the growing threat of the Norsemen, not least to his own flock, for whom, as bishop, he was regarded as having responsibilities which went beyond mere pastoral care. Hartgar, bishop of Liège and a contemporary of Hrabanus Maurus, also possessed a copy, while a manuscript belonged to Dido, bishop of Laon, and to his cathedral in the closing years of the ninth century. The second millennium would soon come to witness more episcopal than monastic libraries owning the *De re militari*.[12] By the twelfth century, there were copies in cathedral libraries as far apart as Lincoln, whose holdings otherwise consisted almost entirely of theology and some canon law,[13] Bamberg and Chartres, while in the thirteenth century manuscripts would be found in those of Winchester and Amiens.[14]

No less a figure than Thomas Becket had both a practical and a symbolic importance in the transmission of the *De re militari*. As the owner of a manuscript, he is of interest to us both as a man with practical experience of government under Henry II of England, and as a friend of John of Salisbury, who was to give Vegetius' work a new lease of life and a considerable boost to its influence and authority when he incorporated parts of its teaching into his *Policraticus*. Not least we may note that, on his death, Becket bequeathed his manuscript to the monastic community

---

[9] M. Manitius, *Handschriften antiker Autoren in mittelalterlichen Bibliothekskatalogen* (Leipzig, 1935), 202.

[10] Oxford, Lincoln, lat. 100.

[11] R. Thomson, *Manuscripts from St. Albans Abbey, 1066–1235* (Woodbridge, 1982), 77.

[12] Shrader, 'Ownership and distribution', 37.

[13] 'Vegentium [*sic*], de re militari, cum Eutropio, de rebus romanis, in uno coopertorio, quod Magister Gerardus, canonicus, reddidit de novo pro Boetio, de consolatione, quem perdiderat.' The manuscript (or was it another?) had lost its first folio by 1422 (R. M. Woolley, *Catalogue of the manuscripts of Lincoln cathedral chapter library* (Oxford, 1927), vi, xiii).

[14] Shrader, 'Ownership and distribution', 359 (Bamberg); Migne, *Patrologia Latina*, 199, p. 12 (Chartres); Leiden, Univ. Voss. lat. F 93 (Winchester); Shrader, 'Ownership and distribution', 363 (Amiens).

of Christ Church, Canterbury,[15] making it one of possibly three copies to be found there and so, by transforming it from private into community ownership, making it available to a wider readership. It was probably from one of these that prior Henry of Eastry copied the 'Rules of war' (*DRM*, III, 26) a century and a half later?[16]

Both complete texts and collections of excerpts also came to form the basis of many secular libraries. Louis the German, his brother Charles the Bald, and Odo of Francia Occidentalis each possessed a manuscript of the *De re militari*, while Eberhard, margrave of Friuli, owner of a fine library and active in the military field, had a copy given to him by Hartgar, bishop of Liège. The will of Eccard, count of Macon (d. *c.*876), reveals that he owned a small book, 'de arte militari', almost certainly that of Vegetius, which, with others, suggests that the educated nobleman was not necessarily exceptional.[17] King Alfonso V of Castile possessed a copy in the early eleventh century.[18] However, the jury is still out over the question whether his contemporary Fulk Nerra, count of Anjou, had access to a text and, if so, whether his strategies and tactics reflected its teachings; nor is it unanimous about the veracity of the story, recorded by a chronicler, that Geoffrey Plantagenet, father of Henry II, king of England, had a text which he allegedly consulted at the siege of Montreuil-Bellay *c.*1150.[19] However, the possibility that the link between the counts of Anjou and the kings of England in the twelfth century may have led to the *De re militari* being better known in England at that time is not implausible.

The number of surviving manuscripts suggests that the *De re militari* was increasing in popularity during the thirteenth century. It is not easy, however, to attach precise claims to ownership of many of these. Yet, by looking beyond the evidence provided by the manuscripts themselves, as we shall do later in this study, we see that several developments occurred in the thirteenth century which suggest that Vegetian influence was accruing. One was the use made of his work, principally by

---

[15] A. J. Duggan, 'Classical quotations and allusions in the correspondence of Thomas Becket: an investigation of their sources', *Viator*, 32 (2001), 2, 21.

[16] T. L. Hogan, 'The memorandum book of Henry of Eastry, prior of Christ Church Canterbury' (unpublished PhD diss., University of London, 1966), 980–3. John Palmer kindly passed this reference on to me more than thirty years ago.

[17] P. Riché, 'Les bibliothèques de trois aristocrats laïcs carolingiens', *Le moyen âge*, 69 (1963), 103; R. McKitterick, *The Carolingians and the written word* (Cambridge, 1989), 245–8.

[18] Manitius, *Handschriften*, 204.

[19] B. S. Bachrach, 'The practical use of Vegetius' *De re militari* during the early Middle Ages', *The Historian*, 47 (1985), 239–55; repr. in B. S. Bachrach, *Warfare and military organization in pre-crusade Europe* (Aldershot and Burlington, VT, 2002).

members of the new orders of friars, men such as the Dominican Vincent of Beauvais and the Franciscan John of Wales, who garnered quotations and excerpts from the *De re militari*, many of them extensive, into their encyclopaedic works. These served as sources of knowledge for the clergy, in particular for members of the flourishing preaching orders, as they sought illustrative materials ('exempla') for their sermons.[20] It was from the Carmelite community at Avignon that Pope John XXII (1316–34) purchased a Latin manuscript in July 1317.[21] In England, the Austin friars at York possessed three copies of the *De re militari* around the year 1372, while in Italy, in the fourteenth century, the Franciscans at Santa Croce, Florence owned two manuscripts of the work.[22] In 1403 there was also a poor copy in the library of the order's convent in Cologne.[23]

Ownership of, and access to, the text may also have helped to advance the military education of rulers according to Roman ideas and practices ('imitatio imperii'). The apparent popularity of the *De re militari* has impressed historians of the Carolingian 'renaissance' who have seen in the numbers of the text and the status of their owners evidence of the importance of book learning in conveying practical wisdom ('sapientia utilis') regarding subjects such as law, agriculture and, in this case, war from one age to another. On the other hand, scholarly opinion concerning the practical application of those ideas upon military practice in western Europe in the second half of the first millennium is sharply divided. To some, there was only minimal change in Roman practice and military organisation which continued, essentially unaltered, until at least the ninth century; to others, the age witnessed significant change. Blood has been drawn, but no outright winner has yet been declared.[24]

Far from demeaning the intelligence of young, often royal or princely, commanders-to-be, the system of learning of the experiences of others through the medium of the text inculcated the learner with the bases of skills he might be called upon to practise later on. As Christine de Pisan

---

[20] Examples of Vegetius being cited by John of Wales, and by the Italian Austin friar Michele da Massa Marittima, are cited in B. Smalley, *English friars and Antiquity in the early fourteenth century* (Oxford, 1960), 53, 84, 101–2, 217, 269–70. See also J. T. Welter, *L'exemplum dans la littérature religieuse et didactique du moyen âge* (Paris and Toulouse, 1927).

[21] Vatican, Vat. lat. 4497.

[22] K. W. Humphreys (ed.), *The friars' libraries* (London, 1990), 48, 51, 115; now Florence, Laur. S. Croce, Plut. 20, sin. 9 and Plut. 24, sin. 6.

[23] 'Sed est volumen satis incorrectum, sicut patet legenti' (Erfurt, Univ. CA 2° 5).

[24] On this see R. Abels and S. Morillo, 'A lying legacy? A preliminary discussion of images of antiquity and altered reality in medieval military history', *JMMH*, 3 (2005), 1–13, and the detailed reply by B. S. Bachrach, '"A lying legacy" revisited: the Abels-Morillo defense of discontinuity', *JMMH*, 5 (2007), 153–93.

would point out centuries later, it was impossible to learn a science or art without a knowledge of its basics. Those who aspired to command should not be afraid to learn them. The *De re militari* would provide a text of value for the military education of medieval rulers, for whom the ability to lead in war was of such great concern.[25]

In addition, Vegetius' teachings came to be better known through the influence exerted by the *De regimine principum* of Giles of Rome, which reflected Vegetian teaching in its discussion of military matters. The influence of this thirteenth-century best-seller would be extended through the translations made into seven languages during the next century or so, an influence from which Vegetius was also likely to benefit. Here, we should also note the translations of the *De re militari* itself made into Anglo-Norman, French and Italian in the second half of the century. The first of these was probably owned by King Edward I of England, while Jean de Brienne, count of Eu, and Jean de Châlon-Arlay, both men of military experience, had separate translations made for them by Jean de Meun and Jean Priorat.[26] An age which witnessed men, both rulers and soldiers, increasingly concerned about the use of force, by whom it could be legitimately used, and to what ends, as well as by developments in military practice, could call upon the *De re militari* as a source of ideas and experience which would help it resolve a variety of problems that emerged during the century.

By the fourteenth century the reputation of the *De re militari*, albeit sometimes disguised by encyclopaedists and translators, was entering its heyday; the text could be found in the libraries of an increasingly broad and interested ownership. Latin manuscripts are known to have belonged to three popes in the late fourteenth century,[27] while in the fifteenth century they entered the papal library founded by Nicholas V (1447–55).[28] Among high-ranking secular clergy who owned copies of the *De re militari* were Jean de Dormans, cardinal-bishop of Beauvais and chancellor to King Charles V of France, a ruler particularly sympathetic to the use and influence of works emanating from the classical past,[29] and Cardinal Domenico Capranica, whose possession of the *De re militari* is

---

[25] *Le livre des fais et bonnes meurs du sage roy Charles V par Christine de Pisan*, ed. S. Solente (2 vols., SHF, Paris, 1936–40), I, 189–90.

[26] For Giles' use of Vegetius, see below, pp. 105–11; for the translations, pp. 152–68.

[27] Urban V (1362–70), Gregory XI (1370–78) and the 'anti-Pope' Benedict XIII, elected in 1394.

[28] Vatican, Vat. lat. 1860; Pellegrin, *Manuscrits classiques*, III, 437–40. See also *La bibliothèque pontificale à Avignon et à Peñiscola pendant le Grand Schisme d'Occident, et sa dispersion*, ed. M.-H. Jullien de Pommerol and J. Monfrin (2 vols., Rome, 1991).

[29] Dormans owned two copies in 1373 (P. Richardot, *Végèce et la culture militaire au moyen âge (Ve–XVe siècles)* (Paris, 1998), 196.

recorded in his will drawn up in 1458.[30] Among the bishops we may note the Castilian Diego de Anaya Maldonad, who purchased a number of classical works, including that of Vegetius, in northern Italy while returning home from the Council of Constance in 1418,[31] and the bishop of Trento, who owned a manuscript copied at Basel in 1437 at the time of the Council being held in that city.[32]

A further significant group of owners of the fourteenth and fifteenth centuries consisted of kings and princes, men who, like the emperor to whom Vegetius had originally addressed his work, bore responsibilities for both political and military affairs. In 1347, a copy of the *De re militari*, along with a *De regimine principum* (probably that of Giles of Rome), was among the purchases made in Paris for the court of Savoy.[33] About 1390 Philippe de Mézières would advise King Charles VI of France not to read frivolous literature but rather what was appropriate to one with responsibilities for government ('pour ton gouvernement et ton peuple'), significantly the work of Giles of Rome, along with those of Livy, Valerius Maximus, Vegetius and others. Only a few years later, in 1417, Jean Gerson would recommend that the Dauphin be given the *De re militari* to study.[34] Both advisers must have been aware that Vegetius' text had things to offer its readers at more than one level. They could, quite properly, study it for what it had to teach about war. However, by then, it may have been to the teachings of an increasingly politicised Vegetius that many were turning to understand Roman ideas regarding the place and function of the army in society. The text suggested questions which rulers, and rulers-to-be, could profitably ponder, with a view to possible application in their own day.

Some might prefer to read their Vegetius straight. The rulers of Aragon, Joan I (1387–96), his brother and successor Martí I (1396–1410), Alfonso V, king of Aragon and Naples (1416–58) and his son, Ferrante

---

[30] See A. V. Antonovics, 'The library of Cardinal Domenico Capranica', in *Cultural aspects of the Italian Renaissance*, ed. C. H. Clough (Manchester and New York, 1976), 145.

[31] A. Hobson, 'Manuscripts captured at Vitoria', in *ibid*. 490, 496, n. 28.

[32] Trento, Com. W 3154. This manuscript was one of a number, including Augsburg, Staats-u.-Stadtbibl., 161 and Madrid, BN 9245, copied at Basel during the council. The links between these manuscripts, BL Harley 2475 and Leipzig, Univ. Rep. I. fol. 18, are complex, since they involve some copying of marginalia from one manuscript to another. It would be interesting to know the circumstances surrounding their making: were they copied to order or bought from stock? See Reeve, 'Transmission', 258, 260, 293.

[33] S. Edmunds, 'The medieval library of Savoy', *Scriptorium*, 25 (1971), 256, probably now Turin, Arch. di Stato, Jb II 19.

[34] Philippe de Mézières, *Le songe du vieil pèlerin*, ed. G. W. Coopland (2 vols., Cambridge, 1969), II, 74, 381; Jean Gerson, *Œuvres complètes. II. L'œuvre épistolaire*, ed. P. Glorieux (Paris, 1960), 212–13.

(1458–94), would all own copies of the *De re militari*. Was it merely coincidence that Catalan translations pre-dated Castilian ones, and that there was an interest in other classical texts on the theme of war at the Neapolitan court in the mid-fifteenth century?[35] Isabelle of Castile, under whose rule the Moors would be expelled by military means from Spain, probably owned a copy of the Castilian translation.[36] The text was high in the popularity ratings among the princes and rulers of Italy: the Visconti of Milan, the Malatesta of Rimini, Borso d'Este, duke of Ferrara, the Orsini family, the Montefeltro of Urbino and the Medici of Florence all owned one or more manuscripts of the *De re militari*.[37] Not a few of these would become part of the booty taken at the time of the French invasions about 1500, thus passing into French royal collections.[38] The removal of rich libraries by the leaders of victorious armies strongly suggests that their contents had become valuable status symbols, which could do their new owners no harm in their own country.

No English king, other than Edward I[39] and Edward III,[40] is known to have possessed Vegetius' text before Richard III, who had a copy of the English translation made for himself or perhaps for his son by early 1484,[41] although Henry VI is reported to have studied 'Vegetius in his book, Teachings on military matters' ('Vegetiu[m] in Libro suo "De dogmatibus rei militaris"'), after the battle of Blore Heath in September 1459.[42] Later, Henry VII would approach Vegetian ideas indirectly through the translation which he ordered William Caxton to make and

---

[35] Manitius, *Handschriften*, 204; J. M. Torrents (ed.), 'Inventari dels bens mobles del rey Martí d'Aragó', *Revue hispanique*, 12 (1905), 429; Oxford, Bodl. Canon. class. lat. 274. See S. C. Hughes, 'Soldiers and gentlemen: the rise of the duel in Renaissance Italy', *JMMH*, 5 (2007), 106.

[36] Escorial, &.ii.18.

[37] BnF lat. 5691, 7233 (Visconti); Cesena, Malatestiana, S XIX 5 (Malatesta); Manitius, *Handschriften*, 204 (Este); Berlin, Staatsbibl. lat. oct. 141 and Vatican, Arch. Cap. S. Pietro, H 33 (Orsini); Vatican, Urb. lat, 456, 939, 1221, 1362 (Montefeltro); Florence, Laur. Plut. 45. 20; BL Royal, 12 C. xxii (Medici).

[38] See M. G. A. Ottolenghi, 'La biblioteca dei Visconti et degli Sforza: gli inventari del 1488 e del 1490', *Studi Petrarcheschi*, n.s. 8 (1991), 1–238.

[39] See below, pp. 152–3.

[40] J. Vale, *Edward III and chivalry. Chivalric society and its context 1270–1350* (Woodbridge, 1982), 50.

[41] BL Royal 18 A. xii. See A. E. Sutton and L. Visser-Fuchs, *Richard III's books* (Stroud, 1997), esp. 78 and 282–3. The text bears 'no signs of use or annotations'.

[42] A. E. Goodman, *The Wars of the Roses. Military activity and English society, 1452–97* (London, 1981), 29, 124 and 236, n. 51, citing John Whethamstede, *Registra quorundam abbatum monasterii S. Albani*, ed. H. T. Riley (RS, London, 1872), I, 338–9. Would an attentive reading before the battle have helped the king avoid the defeat which he suffered on this occasion? May the answer lie in which version he was reading: the Latin text, the translation into English of 1408 or what was, in the autumn of 1459, the very recently produced rendering into verse? For these, see below, pp. 185–93.

print of Christine de Pisan's *Fais d'armes*, parts of which were based on the *De re militari*, so that 'euery gentylman born to armes & all manere men of were, captayns, souldiours, vytayllers & all other shold haue knowlege how they ought to behaue theym in the fayttes of warre & of bataylles'.[43] Catalogues of the English royal library in 1535 show that Henry VIII had four manuscripts of Vegetius' work, three in Latin and one in French, this last in the translation of Jean de Vignay having probably belonged to Charles the Bold, duke of Burgundy.[44]

Evidence regarding the English scene indicates that Vegetius was attractive not only to members of the high nobility but also to those of the lesser nobility and gentry, some of whom had followed active military careers in the fifteenth century. We are informed about the owners of about half the eleven surviving manuscripts of the English translation, a higher proportion than in the case of the French ones. Sir Thomas Berkeley, who commissioned the first English translation completed in 1408, stemmed from a family with a background of literary patronage, and was an important figure in the socio-political world of the west of England in the early fifteenth century;[45] Sir John Fastolf, KG, was to have a long and largely distinguished career in the wars fought in France in the reigns of Henry V and Henry VI;[46] while Sir John II Paston was a major landowner with experience of war.[47]

Regarding the ownership of French translations, too little is known. One of a small handful to leave his mark on a manuscript was Jacques Bauchant, *sergent du roi* in the *prévôté* of Saint-Quentin, north-east of Paris, a known translator and collector encouraged by the king, Charles V. Like a good collector, Bauchant recorded the costs of his purchases; he bought the Meun translation of Vegetius at Noyon in March

---

[43] *The book of fayttes of armes and of chyualrye*, trans. W. Caxton, ed. A. T. P. Byles (EETS, London, 1932), 291.

[44] BL Royal 17 E. v. See *The libraries of King Henry VIII*, ed. J. P. Carley (London, 2000), 18, 51, 217, 221.

[45] *The earliest English translation of Vegetius' De re militari*, ed. G. A. Lester (Heidelberg, 1988), 24–5.

[46] *Royal Commission on Historical Manuscripts*, 8th report (London, 1881), 268a.

[47] BL Lansdowne 285. Other owners of the *De re militari* who came from a similar background included Sir Robert Chalons of Devon (Oxford, Bodl. Douce, 291); Sir Robert Roos (Cambridge, Univ. Lib. Ee II 17); Sir Nicholas de Saint Lo (BL Add. Ms 14,408); and Sir John Astley (New York, Morgan, M 775). On the broader background, see R. L. Radulescu, *The gentry context for Malory's Morte Darthur* (Cambridge, 2003), ch. 2: 'The political interests of the gentry and their "Grete Bokes"', esp. 41, 43–4, 47, 49, and R. Radulescu and A. Truelove, *Gentry culture in late medieval England* (Manchester, 2005), 109–10. See also C. Nall, 'Perceptions of financial mismanagement and the English diagnosis of defeat', in *The fifteenth century. VII. Conflicts, consequences and the crown in the late Middle Ages*, ed. L. Clark (Woodbridge and Rochester, NY, 2007), 122–3.

1367, paying three gold florins for it.[48] Some ten copies of the same translation found their way into the royal library in the Louvre between the years 1373 and 1424.[49] On Bauchant's death, probably about 1396, part of his library was acquired by Louis, duke of Orléans. In 1427 the library at Blois of his eldest son and successor, Charles, included two copies of Vegetius' work in French; one, in Meun's translation, may have been that formerly owned by Bauchant.[50] A fine copy of Vignay's translation was owned by Jean, duke of Bourbon; by 1416 it had entered the famous library of Jean, duke of Berry, who also possessed a Latin manuscript. The Latin text was later given to the Sainte-Chapelle in Paris, while the French translation would be confiscated in 1523 from the ducal collection by King Francis I for the benefit of his new library at Fontainebleau, then under the charge of Guillaume Budé.[51] In Burgundy, Duke Philip the Good left two French translations at the time of his death in 1467,[52] and another copy may have been owned by his son, Charles, who was probably inspired by it as he instigated military reform and development in the 1470s.[53] No one can fail to notice how texts of Vegetius, like those of many other authors, moved from one library to another, all the while extending the possibility that they might be read by persons ready to be influenced by their contents.

In Spain the marquis of Santillane (d.1458), a life-long soldier, owned a copy of the Castilian translation.[54] Strong interest in Vegetius in Catalonian royal circles, noted above, is reinforced by evidence of ownership of the text by two noble Valencian families, the first that of Mateu Florimon, baron of Vilamarxant, who possessed two Latin manuscripts, one

[48] L. Delisle, *Le cabinet des manuscrits de la Bibliothèque Nationale* (3 vols., Paris, 1868–81), I, 40; BnF. fr. 2063, fo. 107.

[49] Delisle, *Cabinet*, III, 153–4. Two kings, Charles VII in 1437 and Louis XII in 1499, also owned Latin manuscripts. (Shrader, 'Ownership and distribution', 185; Oxford, Bodl. Laud lat. 56).

[50] Le Roux de Lincy, 'La bibliothèque de Charles d'Orléans à son château de Blois en 1427', *BEC*, 5 (1843–44), 59–82. The manuscript was recorded as being 'à recouvrer', perhaps a sign of use?

[51] Delisle, *Cabinet*, III, 186; BnF fr. 1229; P. Meyer, 'Les anciens traducteurs français de Végèce, et en particulier Jean de Vignai', *Romania*, 25 (1896), 410–11. What appears to be a list of books 'en francois escriptz a la main', probably available (whether from stock or on order is not clear) from a bookseller in Tours in the late fifteenth century, carries a number of military texts, including *Le Jouvencel*, the *Strategemes* of Frontinus, *Végèce de chevalerie*, the *Le rosier des guerres*, the *L'arbre des batailles* of Honoré Bouvet, and *L'ordre de chevalerie*, as well as *L'art de chevalerie* (Vegetius) in print. (BnF fr. 2912, fos. 78–82. I am grateful to Godfried Croenen for drawing my attention to this source).

[52] Brussels, Bibl. royale, 11,048, 11,195.

[53] See Allmand, 'Did the *De re militari . . . ?*', and D. Gallet-Guerne, *Vasque de Lucène et la Cyropédie à la cour de Bourgogne (1470)* (Geneva, 1974). The matter is discussed at greater length below, pp. 132–7.

[54] M. Schiff, *La bibliothèque du marquis de Santillane* (Paris, 1905), 75.

on parchment, the other on paper, in 1485; the second that of Maties Marcader, who also owned two Latin copies, one manuscript, the other in print.[55] At the other end of Europe, we have evidence of a Latin text, probably copied in Poland by Filippo Buonaccorsi, and owned, about 1470, by Prince Casimir, the son of King Casimir IV, which was destined to become a much glossed and annotated manuscript.[56]

The appeal of the text to the growing humanist intelligentsia of the fourteenth century was to be considerable. Not only Petrarch but, after him, Coluccio Salutati, the humanist chancellor of Florence at the end of the century, probably owned a copy which has come down to us.[57] They would be only among the first of a long line of humanists, from many European countries, who owned, read and annotated texts, expressing their delight at the discoveries, historical, philosophical and philological, which they were enabled to make. It is probably no coincidence that a substantial proportion of surviving manuscripts are fourteenth- or fifteenth-century Italian in origin, and that, through their marginalia, many should bear clear witness to the broad humanistic interests of those who owned and read them.

In the fifteenth century the number of owners all over Europe with humanistic interests grew. In January 1417 Bartolomeo da Montepulciani made a copy of the *De re militari* which he and Poggio Bracciolini had discovered at St Gallen.[58] In Italy, Cardinal Bessarion possessed a manuscript, as did his secretary, Gaspar Volaterranus.[59] Curiously, the copy owned by Humfrey, duke of Gloucester, patron of humanistic learning in England, was not the Latin text but Vignay's French translation made a century or more earlier.[60] In France, a number of men with a legal background, all in the royal service, are found as the owners of Vegetius' text: Jean Le Bègue, who enjoyed a long career first as a royal secretary and then as clerk (*greffier*) of the Chambre des Comptes in Paris from the late fourteenth to the mid-fifteenth century;[61] Nicolas de Baye, clerk to the *Parlement* of Paris during part of the same period;[62] and the ecclesiastic Simon de Plumetot, *conseiller* in the same *Parlement*, who had a large

[55] A. I. Alomar i Canyelles, 'La versió catalana de l' "Epitoma rei militaris" de Vegeci: introducció i transcripció del manuscrit del segle XV de la "Biblioteca Bartomeu March"' (diss., Palma de Mallorca, 1985), 29–30.

[56] Berlin, Staatsbibl. lat. oct. 3.   [57] Bologna, Com. A. 146.

[58] J. A. Wisman, 'Flavius Renatus Vegetius', *Catalogus translationum et commentariorum. Medieval and Renaissance Latin translations and commentaries*, VI, eds. F. E. Ganz, V. Brown and P. O. Kristeller (Washington, DC, 1986), 176.

[59] Venice, Marc. Z. lat. 463; Vatican, Vat. lat. 7227.

[60] Cambridge, Univ. Lib. Ee II 17.   [61] BnF lat. 7470.

[62] *Journal de Nicolas de Baye, greffier du parlement de Paris 1400–1417*, ed. A. Tuetey (SHF, Paris, 1888), II, lxxxix (item 120).

library incorporating the works of several classical authors, including Vegetius and Frontinus.[63] Plumetot had a very long and friendly relationship
with the abbey of Saint-Victor in Paris which, in 1514, recorded the possession of two Latin manuscripts of the *De re militari*. One of these had
previously belonged to Jean de Francoville;[64] the other may have been
the gift made to the abbey by Plumetot.

Plumetot probably also knew another luminary of humanism in northern France in the third to sixth decades of the fifteenth century, Zano da
Castiglione, bishop of Lisieux (1424–32) and then of Bayeux (1432–59),
who corresponded with Humfrey of Gloucester on scholarly matters.
While at Bayeux, Castiglione was joined by a group of fellow Italians
who left their mark upon the membership of the cathedral clergy and on
the capitular library. Among the volumes in that library in the 1480s was
a copy of the *De re militari*, bound with, among others, the *Policraticus* of
John of Salisbury. These probably owed their presence there to the group
encouraged by Bishop Castiglione.[65]

Humanistic sympathies flourished elsewhere in France. Three
fifteenth-century manuscripts of the same collection of excerpts from
the *De re militari* draw us to Tours and to its cathedral clergy. This collection, *Florilegium quodam sacrum et profanum*, includes excerpts from a
large and varied number of sources, the Bible, works of classical authors
and Church fathers, medieval theology, and both Roman and canon law.
One manuscript, probably the earliest,[66] would one day become part
of the library of Borgo San Bernadino, near Piacenza. The other two
may have belonged to members of the Fumée family, a leading clan in
fifteenth-century Tours. Both manuscripts are probably French in origin. One was owned by Lucas Fumée, canon of Tours, in the very first
years of the sixteenth century; the other may well have been copied by
Lucas Fumée who called himself both canon of Tours and prior of Saint-
Martin-lès-Bourges.[67] It is perhaps no coincidence that a manuscript of
the work should have been in the library of Saint-Martin-de-Tours in the
fourteenth century?[68]

[63] G. Ouy, 'Simon de Plumetot (1371–1443) et sa bibliothèque', in *Miscellanea codicologica
F. Masai dicata MCMLXXIX*, ed. P. Cockshaw, M.-C. Garani and P. Jodogne (Ghent,
1979), II, 373, 376.

[64] BnF lat. 15076; Reeve, 'Transmission', 261.

[65] He owned a manuscript which included the *De re militari* (J. Vielliard (ed.), *Le registre
de prêt de la bibliothèque de la Sorbonne (1402–1536)* (Paris, 2000), 690, n. 2).

[66] Oxford, Bodl, Add. C. 12.

[67] Vatican, Reg. lat. 358 (described by Pellegrin, *Manuscrits classiques*, II, I, 68–71); Blickling Hall, 6849, esp. fo. 83v.

[68] L. Delisle, *Notice sur les manuscrits disparus de la bibliothèque de Tours pendant la première
moitié du XIXe siècle* (Paris, 1883), 120.

Munich, Bayerische Staatsbibliothek, lat. 522, is a large manuscript of great interest, consisting of a variety of items by Roman authors, including Vegetius, some writings of Petrarch and Leonardo Bruni, and other Latin orations composed by notable figures of its owner's day. That owner was Hartmann Schedel, a physician from Nuremberg who had studied in Padua, and was destined to become a leading light in the German Renaissance. Perhaps it was in Italy that he acquired his humanistic interests, which were strong enough to make him into the copyist of the texts bound in this manuscript, work which he completed between 1466 and 1468. In another part of Europe, the island of Mallorca, a remarkably fertile centre of culture at this period, the sale of sixty-eight books, mainly of theology and Roman and canon law, which had belonged to Antoni de Collel, bishop of Mallorca from 1349 to 1363, also included '1 librum vocatum Vegetius, de re militari', this manuscript fetching '1 lib'.[69] Later Ferran Valenti, a lawyer and humanist who translated Cicero and kept in close touch with developments on the Italian mainland, not least through meetings which he attended at the court of Naples, owned a *De re militari* which may have encouraged his interest in the study of arms.[70]

In the Low Countries, we find that the canons of St Martin, Louvain owned a Latin manuscript in the fourteenth century,[71] while, by 1460, the collegiate church of St Paul at Liège possessed a text which, along with a *De regimine principum*, was listed among the 'libri morales'.[72] Copies of the French translations by both Jean de Meun and Jean de Vignay were in the library of the dukes of Burgundy by the middle of the fifteenth century,[73] while a leading member of the Burgundian nobility, Philippe de Croy, count of Chimay, owned a French Vegetius[74] as well as copies of Honoré Bouvet's *Arbre des batailles*, Christine de Pisan's *Fais*

[69] D. Williman, *Bibliothèques ecclésiastiques au temps de la papauté d'Avignon* (Paris, 1980), I, 215. For other clergy possessing the *De re militari* at this period, see *ibid.* I, 119, 125, 230; and II, ed. M. Jullien de Pommerol and J. Monfrin (Paris, 2001), 136, 139; *La bibliothèque de l'abbaye de Clairvaux du XIIe au XVIIIe siècle*, ed. A. Vernet (Paris, 1979), I, 361.

[70] J. N. Hillgarth, *Readers and books in Majorca, 1229–1550* (2 vols., Paris, 1991), I, 122; II, 529.

[71] Now BL Harley, 2667.

[72] O. J. Thimister, 'La bibliothèque de l'église collégiale de Saint Paul à Liège en 1460', *Bulletin de l'Institut archéologique liégeois*, 14 (1878), 161. The collection also included an 'antiquum quondam librum cum ymaginibus et figuris in papiro, incipientem: Militaris scientia' (*ibid.* 167).

[73] Brussels, Bibl. royale, 11,048, 11,195; BL Royal 17 E. v. See B. Schnerb, *L'Etat bourguignon, 1363–1477* (Paris, 1999), 346–58.

[74] The anonymous translation now Brussels, Bibl. royale, 11046. See below, p. 166 and n. 50.

d'armes, and a book of the rules of duelling specially made for him.[75] Was it the influence of the court, or his more intellectual leanings, which led Guillaume Hugonet, at one time chancellor of Burgundy, to own a copy of Vegetius?[76] Others of similar mind who possessed the work were Willem Pauwels, lawyer and secretary to the city of Antwerp, who left his considerable collection to form the nucleus of the city's library. When the books were handed over, the copy of the *De re militari* was retained on loan ('titulo commodati'), by Jean de Helmale, the donor's son-in-law. One would like to know what Helmale's special interest in this text was.[77] Two better-known figures owned the *De re militari*. As his name on a manuscript testifies, one was Jerome Busleiden, humanist, book collector and friend of Erasmus, who founded the Collegium Trilingue at Louvain for the teaching of Latin, Greek and Hebrew.[78] About 1500, Jean Lemaire de Belges also possessed a copy; in his case, however, it was not a manuscript, but a copy of the 1487 imprint produced in Rome by Eucharius Silber.[79] The influence of the printed book was beginning to be felt.

Unlike the *De regimine principum* of Giles of Rome, the *De re militari* never became a text formally studied in the schools, although in the last years of the Middle Ages copies could be found in several university libraries.[80] At Oxford, thanks to the liberality of Thomas Gascoigne, Balliol College joined Lincoln College as the owner of a Latin Vegetius, while a copy, probably made in the mid-fourteenth century, bound with the *De regimine principum* of Giles of Rome, and perhaps at Oxford for its entire existence, would later enter the library of Canterbury College by 1501.[81] In 1414, Peterhouse, Cambridge benefited from the gift of

[75] J. Devaux, 'Une seigneur lettré à la cour de Bourgogne. Philippe de Croy, comte de Chimay', in *Liber amicorum Raphael de Smedt*, ed. A. Tourneux (Louvain, 2001), IV, 20; *La bibliothèque de Marguerite d'Autriche*, ed. M. Debae (Louvain and Paris, 1995), 285.

[76] See Vale, *War and chivalry*, 18; A. and W. Paravicini, 'L'arsenal intellectuel d'un homme de pouvoir. Les livres de Guillaume Hugonet, chancelier de Bourgogne', in *Penser le pouvoir au moyen âge (VIIIe–XVe siècle). Etudes offertes à Françoise Autrand*, ed. D. Boutet and J. Verger (Paris, 2000), 282, 307.

[77] A. Derolez and B. Victor (eds.), *Corpus catalogorum Belgii. The medieval booklists of the Southern Low Countries* (Brussels, 1999), III, 192. At the end of the century the library of Jean Adorne, probably of Bruges, contained two copies of the *De re militari*, one in Latin, ('latino'), the other in French ('walsche') (*ibid.* I, 25).

[78] New Haven, Yale Univ. Lib., Marston, 102, fo. 74v.

[79] G. Doutrepont, *Jean Lemaire de Belges et la renaissance* (Brussels, 1934), 135.

[80] The work was regarded not as a work 'de faculté' but as one of 'érudition' (G. Beaujouan, *Les manuscrits scientifiques médiévaux de l'université de Salamanque et des ses 'colegios mayores'* (Bordeaux, 1962), 31). The copyist of Salamanca, Univ. 2137 certainly knew the work of Giles of Rome. See, for example, fo. 10v.

[81] Oxford, Balliol 146A; Briggs, *Giles of Rome's De regimine principum*, 165–6, now Oxford, Bodl. Auct. F. 3. 2.

the combined text of Vegetius and Frontinus bequeathed to it by John Neuton.[82] A century later Roger Lupton, once provost of Eton College and a canonist by training, would give a Vegetius manuscript to the school library.[83] On the European mainland, a number of university libraries came to own texts of the *De re militari*. A copy could be consulted at the university of Prague by about 1370. In Germany, there were copies at the university of Heidelberg after 1396, while Amplonius de Berka gave three Latin manuscripts[84] to the Collegium Amplonianum which he founded in Erfurt at about this time. In Paris, the Collège des Lombards already possessed a very old manuscript by the end of the fourteenth century, while the Collège de Montaigu, where Erasmus would one day study, owned a copy by about 1463.[85] The manuscript bought by Bishop Diego de Anaya in Italy in 1418 would be donated to the Colegio Mayor de San Bartolomé in Salamanca, which he had founded at the beginning of the fifteenth century.[86]

Lest it be thought that an interest in books and the waging of war were not natural soul-mates, we should remember the small number of Italian *condottieri* known to have possessed copies of Vegetius' work. The best known of the group was Federigo da Montefeltro, who became duke of Urbino, and whose library contained what are now Vatican, Urb. lat. 939 and 1221. Not far behind him must come Francesco Sforza, who, on assuming power in Milan, inherited a fine library, which included Vegetius' work. There were others, too. Later on we shall encounter Braccio da Montone ('Fortebraccio'), who became ruler of Perugia after a successful career as a *condottiere*: he commissioned a copy of the *De re militari* which, it is argued, played a part in forming his style as a leader of men.[87] Another was Antonio da Marsciano, son-in-law to the great *condottiere* Erasmo da Narni (Gattamelata), who had a library with a marked military bias, including the works of Vegetius and Frontinus and other classical military historians. The array is impressive. Yet whether this conscious classicism always brought them the success which, in theory, it should have done in the world of their day was put in doubt by at least some of their contemporaries.[88]

---

[82] *Testamenta Eboracensia*, I, 370. See above, p. 57.   [83] Eton College Lib., 131.
[84] Manitius, *Handschriften*, 202; P. Lehmann (ed.), *Mittelalterliche Bibliothekskataloge Deutschlands und der Schweiz. II. Bistum Mainz, Erfurt* (Munich, 1928), 45–6. Erfurt, Univ. CA 2° 5 and 4° 393, are survivors of those texts.
[85] Bern, Burgerbibl. 280; Giessen, Univ. 1256.
[86] Salamanca, Univ. 2137; Beaujouan, *Manuscrits scientifiques*, 20.
[87] See below, pp. 170–2.
[88] M. Mallett, 'Some notes on a fifteenth-century *condottiere* and his library: Count Antonio da Marsciano', in *Cultural aspects*, ed. Clough, 202, 208, 210.

Evidence suggests that the *De re militari* was a text which came to be of increasing interest to heralds, whose everyday involvement in war provides an easy and ready explanation why this should have been so. Two manuscripts of the 1408 English translation would grace the libraries of heralds. One belonged to William Bruges and his son, John Smert, the first two Garter Kings of Arms.[89] The other, part of a volume containing the *Grete Boke* or *Boke off Knyghthod* begun for Sir John II Paston about 1468, and including a miscellany of descriptions of pageantry, jousts, tourneys and ordinances governing judicial combat, as well as the *De re militari* and the *Governance of Kings* of John Lydgate, would be owned by a succession of distinguished heralds in the sixteenth century.[90] The selection of excerpts and ideas from the *De re militari*, which also owed much to the *De regimine principum* of Giles of Rome, compiled in the dying years of the fifteenth century by the Scottish herald Adam Loutfut, was intended for Sir William Cumming, Marchemont Herald. The French manuscript which would one day belong to Samuel Pepys includes an illumination of a herald, bearing the arms of France and England, presenting Vegetius' text to a seated emperor or king.[91] In BnF lat. 5697 we find a variety of texts, including the *De re militari*, followed on the verso of its last folio by the *De insignibus et armis* of Bartolus da Sassoferrato; Bern 280A contains a number of works in addition to Meun's translation, one of which is concerned with heralds; and the copy of Vignay's translation, owned by Humfrey of Gloucester, would come into the hands of William Le Neve, a leading herald of the reign of King Charles I of England. By that time, the early seventeenth century, Vegetius' work, while still being printed and still influential on many points, was increasingly becoming part of a 'historical' culture in whose development and propaganda heralds played an important role.

Manuscripts, as we have seen, did not necessarily remain either where they were copied or with their original owners. They travelled, were inherited, bought, removed as loot by victorious armies, or taken away for copying (and not always returned). A way of observing, if not easily measuring, interest in Vegetius' text is to look at the geographical origins of those which, later, may have travelled. The Italian peninsula was, without a doubt, the area in which, from the ninth to the fifteenth century, the most copies of the *De re militari* were made. While, as far as we can judge, numbers may have been in single figures up to and including the thirteenth century, those took a big jump in the fourteenth and another in the

---

[89] Oxford, Bodl. Douce 291.
[90] BL Lansdowne 285; *Earliest English translation*, ed. Lester, 18.
[91] Cambridge, Magdalene, PL 1938, fo. 1.

fifteenth century. The silver medal for production must go to France and the Low Countries, their figures being boosted by the number of copies of translations into French which have survived. Third place is occupied by England, which, like Italy and France, witnessed a sharp increase in the number of manuscripts produced in the fourteenth century, a number further boosted by the copies of the early fifteenth-century English translation made before 1500. German-speaking lands, which had done well in the tenth century, produced fewer manuscripts until the fifteenth century, when production rose quite sharply. As we shall see, printed editions of the *De re militari* in both Latin and the vernacular also came from Germany. The production of Latin manuscripts in Castile does not appear to have been particularly high. On the other hand, Catalan interest is reflected in two translations[92] and in the ownership of Latin texts encouraged, perhaps, by links with the Neapolitan court and, through it, with the wider scene of Renaissance Italy. In eastern Europe, the influence of the Renaissance would be seen in the fifteenth century with copies of Vegetius' work being brought from Italy and copied within Poland by Italian scribes.

---

[92] See below, pp. 175–9.

Part II

The transmission

How were the contents and, in particular, the ideas of the *De re militari* transmitted down the ages? By suggesting how ideas, founded on a consideration of human experience and given expression by Vegetius, were incorporated into their works by some ten writers among whom there was no shared agenda but who all clearly felt that Vegetian ideas had a certain contemporary resonance, we may see how the *De re militari* was able to make its presence felt in what they wrote on a number of subjects with a bearing on war. In this process, the text remained a fundamental factor, and the uses made of it will form the backbone of the story. The importance of this work was that it opened people's minds not only to ways which might bring success in war, and who should be responsible for fighting it, but to other matters such as the importance of military organisation and military institutions, including the very notion of the national army itself. Some readers may be surprised by the way in which ideas and theories, developed from and fed upon the content of Vegetius' work, would encourage developments in fields which did not appear to be, first and foremost, military in character. By means of ten short sections, it is hoped to build up a picture of how this process was developed between the twelfth century and the Renaissance three to four centuries later.

Choices are perforce arbitrary. Yet it is not surprising that a number of the authors to be considered should have been, broadly speaking, French, or at least closely connected to the culture, political as well as military, of France. At least two were Italians, one a Spaniard, another a native of the Low Countries. In time, they range from the twelfth century (1), through the thirteenth (3), the fourteenth (1) and the fifteenth (4) to the early sixteenth century (1). Between them, these authors were responsible for a variety of works, each the product of particular historical circumstances, which would influence both the kind of text in which Vegetian ideas might be reflected and, consequently, the form in which they would be expressed. Thus, at least six of the works to be considered were conceived with a broadly didactic purpose (the *De re militari* was also of that category), and in the case of the writings of John of Salisbury and Giles of Rome, works concerned with political philosophy. One was a chronicle; others (excluding sets of military ordinances) formed part of a new late fifteenth-century development, the handbook on the art of war based on a mixture of ancient wisdom and the author's personal experiences. Propaganda for the crusade, a legal code and, not least, evidence of how Vegetius' text was taken up enthusiastically by at least one religious writer together underline both the number and the variety of works which can be shown to have been indebted, in some way, to the *De re militari*.

The extent of a writer's influence can be judged, if not measured scientifically, by the way his readers react to the ideas and advice which come from his pen. If, falling like seeds onto fertile ground, those ideas are noted, discussed and then applied to new situations, those applications will act as ways of measuring the receptivity of the soil, or, put differently, of explaining the popularity of the *De re militari* in the Middle Ages. The interest which Vegetius' work created is, in large measure, reflected in the reactions of those who read the text. It is, therefore, important for historians to consider the marginalia and notes added to the manuscripts by earlier readers. Such notes can help us appreciate how those readers related the text to their own interests and, often, to some of the wider preoccupations of their times.

In the section which follows, aspects of Vegetius' ongoing influence will be observed through a consideration of how ideas found in the *De re militari* were interpreted, recycled, and developed for contemporary use. In the process, some would be modified and built into very different kinds of work, others put into practice more or less as they stood. The pages that follow will demonstrate examples of each of these.

John of Salisbury, *Policraticus*

In 1159 John of Salisbury, then in the service of Thomas Becket, completed his *Policraticus*, which was dedicated to his patron. The work, part critique of contemporary society, part a book of instruction on the duties and responsibilities of the ruler who held power to direct, owed much to its author's experiences and his view of the world around him, the world seen from Canterbury, but one which took in both the political scene in England under Stephen and Henry II and that of Sicily under Roger II.[1] Yet for John it was not sufficient to criticise aspects of contemporary life

---

[1] H. Liebeschütz, *Medieval humanism in the life and writings of John of Salisbury* (London, 1950), 45.

to which he was opposed. His work contains a strong, positive message of reform, whose creative aspect its author developed from his wide reading of both sacred and secular literature, assimilated or adapted as the need might require, as well as from his observation of the political world around him. True to his ambition to write a work which related ideas and practices taken from the past to the world and to the problems of his day, John wrote against the many abuses of power which his contemporaries endured. His ruler, he argued, should work against the violence of the age in order to create a more just society, expressed in the Roman word 'res publica', which summed up not a social system but the peace in which society must live in order to prosper. The willingness to fight, based on confidence acquired from knowledge, was one way of preserving that peace.

In Book VI of the *Policraticus*, part of a growing didactic literature on kingship, government and society, John turned his attention to war and to those whose task (or calling?) it was to direct or fight it. The text shows that, in addition to a wide selection of classical authors (he preferred those of late Antiquity),[2] he cited or assimilated passages which came to him from either the *Strategemata* of Frontinus or the *De re militari* of Vegetius, copies of whose works he possessed.[3] In one passage he refers familiarly to 'our Renatus' ('Renatus noster'),[4] as if he were on terms of familiarity with the man who was giving him much to consider. Vegetius, indeed, became one of three main planks of the developments which John was urging in his work. Although he appeared to use the *De re militari* eclectically, selecting what suited his case, it would be unfair to argue that he had failed to grasp the main arguments contained in Vegetius' work. The moral and practical messages concerning war, as well as wider political ones which emerge from John's discussions, owe much to proposals put forward by Vegetius nearly eight centuries earlier.

In Book VI, chapter 2, with Vegetius at his side, John approached his discussion of military affairs from several points of view. In the process of setting out the responsibilities of kingship, he underlined Vegetius' view that it was important for a prince to have knowledge to be used for the good of his subjects.[5] While emphasising the value of legal knowledge, he stressed the importance that a ruler should attach to securing military knowledge, too, since this would help him fulfil the responsibility attributed to Roman emperors, the defence of their people, a task to be

---

[2] H. Liebeschütz, 'John of Salisbury and the "Pseudo-Plutarch"', *JWCI*, 6 (1943), 38, n. 2.

[3] Duggan, 'Classical quotations and allusions', 14.

[4] *Policraticus*, VI, 3.   [5] *DRM*, I, Praef.

achieved through the creation of the 'armed hand' ('armata manus') used by society to protect itself.[6] That hand, part of the body of which the ruler was the head, the Church the soul and the ordinary people the feet, must be created from men specially selected and trained for their suitability for war. Here, John picked up another of Vegetius' messages: only certain people were suited to fight. John added a list of occupations largely taken from Vegetius, whose preference for countrymen over townsmen he also followed, citing Vegetius in saying that those with less acquaintance with the good life, having less to lose, had less fear of death.[7]

Vegetius was appealed to again, albeit indirectly, in the short chapter 3, in which John, as his friend Peter of Blois would also do, sketched an unflattering picture of the soldier (probably the mercenary) of his day, more ready to cut a dashing figure before a credulous society than to face the real dangers of war. Returning, unscathed, from war, he delighted in tales of bravado and individual exploits which all too easily become tradition: he took the highest place at the feast and avoided all work and exercise, in which he was at variance with the recommendations made by Vegetius. Here we can observe John distancing himself from the image of the soldier who sought attention from a society ready to recognise and praise individual heroism. The contribution of the soldier should be judged only by the way in which it helped to further the public good through his service.

Having shown what the soldier should not be, John now turned, in chapter 4, to consider the matter more positively. Emphasising the practical education which the soldier should receive, he cited with approval the example of Augustus, who, anxious that his adopted sons should not benefit from their association with him, had them trained so that they would achieve anything only through their own skills and merits ('nisi per virtutem') acquired through education and practice. This enabled him to introduce a whole range of activities important in the training of the soldier: running, jumping, swimming, the use of both the edge and the point of the sword, a list taken from a number of passages in the *De re militari*.[8]

In chapter 5 John widened the discussion to include the 'professio' of arms, declaring it to be both praiseworthy and necessary. Claiming that it was founded by God, he placed it on a par with the priesthood, the latter being concerned with matters eternal, the former with the good of this world ('ad defensionem rei publicae'). The kind of men whom he had described in chapter 3 were not true soldiers, since they

---

[6] Society also had an unarmed hand, the law and justice (*Policraticus* VI, 1).
[7] *DRM*, I, 7; I, 3.   [8] *Ibid.* I, 9, 10, 12.

had not satisfied two important conditions: they had not been selected (as priests were selected), nor had they taken an oath to the properly constituted authority.[9] On selection, he quoted from a lengthy passage from Vegetius which stressed that the wellbeing of the commonwealth relied upon the selection of high-calibre recruits possessing both the physical and the moral qualities required to achieve this. But whereas Vegetius had claimed that birth ('genus') and character ('mores') should be considered in making a choice between young men, John omitted consideration of birth, replacing it with strength ('vires') as a requirement of the successful soldier; probity ('honestas') and modesty ('verecundia') remain as desirable characteristics in both texts. Men endowed with such virtues were not likely to run away. He went on to assert that only those who had shown themselves capable of assimilating the 'armorum disciplinam' should be allowed to undertake training; those failing to do so should be rejected.[10] Quality counted for more than numbers, and the training of recruits was the responsibility of the leader ('dux'). Only when they had shown themselves to be complete soldiers should these men be allowed to take the oath.

In chapter 7, John argued that, in early days, the military oath had been mainly one of allegiance or simply a promise made between soldiers not to run away, thus betraying their unit. But Vegetius, he claimed, had raised it to something higher: the soldier now swore in the name of God and of his Christ and the Holy Spirit to serve loyally.[11] John went on to add that all those exercising authority lawfully should be obeyed faithfully, since they derived their power from God. Soldiers must obey the prince in all matters, even to the point of suffering death for the sake of the 'res publica' which they had been recruited and trained to protect. On swearing the oath, each soldier was given his belt, a mark that the course of preparation was over. So, John argued, selection and the oath-taking, the beginning and the completion of the process of training, combined to create the soldier, since without selection no man could be enlisted or take the oath, and without the oath none could assume the status of soldier ('nomen militis') which, alone, entitled him to fight.

Later, in chapter 19, John returned to the position he wanted to accord to the 'miles' in society, essentially (as the chapter heading indicated) one of honour, rightfully awarded to a select band whose responsibility it was to ensure the defence of their country ('patria').[12] It was the honour due,

---

[9] Matters considered in *Ibid*. I, 1–7, and II, 5.
[10] *Ibid*. I, 7, 8.   [11] *Ibid*. II, 5.
[12] See J. E. Lendon, *Empire of honour. The art of government in the Roman world* (Oxford, 1997), ch. 5 ('The Roman army').

too, to those who had allowed their valour ('virtus') to be developed by training, making them capable of fulfilling their duties. Yet again, John returned to the theme of the skills, learned by the recruit, to be used to ensure peace. Men should read the works of Cato the Censor and Cornelius Celsus (both mentioned in the *De re militari*[13] but not available to John and his contemporaries), as well, of course, as those of Vegetius himself, from whom, John admitted, he had borrowed heavily. Citing a number of points from the Vegetian canon, he ended by emphasising that practice and training, as much in war as in the other arts (an idea taken from Vegetius), were vital for success.[14]

It is not sufficient, however, simply to note that John of Salisbury cited Vegetius on a number of occasions. We must try to appreciate how, if at all, he made use of Vegetius' text to develop and support his own ideas, perhaps along new lines. In short, as we get further and further away from Vegetius' own time, what impact were his ideas to have upon military developments of later ages? John made use of the *De re militari* to provide him with ideas which could be incorporated, sometimes as they came, at other times in a developed form, into his own work. From Frontinus' *Strategemata* he took examples to illustrate points made by Vegetius. Hans Liebeschütz wrote that John turned to ancient writers to enable him 'to throw the cloak of classical antiquity over his discussion of contemporary political problems'.[15] Does this colourful judgement go far enough?

John completed the *Policraticus* when Henry II had been on the throne of England some five years. His adult life, as a student in Paris and later in the service of the Church at Canterbury, had coincided with the period of the 'Anarchy' of Stephen's reign, which had witnessed a marked decline in the authority of the crown which it would be Henry II's destiny to halt and reverse. As we see from the text, two factors struck John. One was the fact that the court, which owed much to Henry's wife, Eleanor of Aquitaine, encouraged a way of life at variance with the one that Vegetius (among others) had taught should be followed, and which went against the spirit of moderation which John advocated in his work. The other criticism was the emphasis placed by John upon the failure of the king's troops to contain the Welsh, whose endeavours were a challenge both to the royal authority and to John's 'patria' itself. It was to the rescue of both the royal authority and the common good that John hoped to come. Using the written word, he planned to sow the seed of a big idea, that the king should have available to him an army which would look to

---

[13] For example, in *DRM*, I, 8.
[14] The essential message of *ibid.* I, 8–28.   [15] Liebeschütz, 'Pseudo-Plutarch', 35.

him for leadership and command (as the army of the Roman Empire had looked to the emperor) and which would regard the protection of the 'res publica' as the first of its duties and responsibilities. Together, the king and the army were to assume charge of the physical defence of the public interest.

The idea of the army as society's means of defence, responsible under the ruler for the common good, owed a good deal to Robert Pullen, one of John's teachers in Paris, who had emphasised the duty of the king to defend civil society.[16] In John's view, the period of civil conflict in Stephen's reign had underlined the nature of that duty. The theme assumes great importance in Book VI of the *Policraticus*. It is here that we have the context for the use made by John of some of the basic ideas contained in Vegetius' work. Along with advances made by the law, 'which, for John, was the apotheosis of order',[17] the use of armed force is given a special role in the attainment and maintenance of social peace by the royal authority. If this plan were to work, the army must be both effective and, consequently, respected. Vegetius' insistence on a rigorous process of selection for those wishing to enter the army formed a key part of John's plans, too. Vegetius had had much to say regarding the preparation and training of the recruit; this was to be a vital part of John's vision of the effectiveness of the soldier, for what use was there in employing an ineffective soldier?[18] We can safely say that John was not simply incorporating long passages of the *De re militari* into the *Policraticus* as illustrative matter for his own text; he was using the persuasive powers of the acknowledged authority in military matters to launch something much more significant.

That much, at least, is likely. Exactly what John was envisaging is less easy to discern. Can we say, for example, that he was consciously laying down a blueprint for something which, in time, could become the 'national' or 'statist' army? Probably not. Yet the emphasis, inspired by Vegetius, upon military developments carried out under the authority of the ruler ('princeps') could well be interpreted as John encouraging rulers to consider that major step forward. In time, the effects could be considerable. The means of strengthening the defence of a society through the creation of military institutions would be set up; the power of the ruler would be enhanced at the expense of the

---

[16] *Ibid.* 33.
[17] W. Ullmann, 'John of Salisbury's *Policraticus* in the later Middle Ages', in *Geschichtsschreibung und geistiges Leben im Mittelalter*, ed. K. Hauck and H. Mordek (Cologne, 1978), 535.
[18] *DRM*, I, 7.

aristocracy; and the right to make war would ultimately rest with the ruler alone.[19]

Were there links between the ideas expressed by John of Salisbury and near-contemporary military developments? That the cause of powerful monarchy was advanced considerably in both England and France during the second half of the twelfth century is undeniable: the long age of private warfare might not yet be over, but it was certainly on the wane, as the right of the ruler alone to decide to fight a war (a war thus considered 'just') became more widely accepted. Under Henry II the employment of professional soldiers by the crown to further its war aims in France assumed greater importance. These men may have been in receipt of standard armament provided by the king; the Pipe Rolls bear references to shields and weapons being provided for them. They certainly possessed sufficient cohesion and solidarity to fight in battle and to deter enemy attacks, and appear to have impressed contemporaries, if not always for the best of reasons.[20] In 1181 Henry II went further by issuing his Assize of Arms, proclaiming that all freemen should be ready to bear certain specified arms in the service of the king, and at his command. Freemen, to include townsmen, were to swear what arms they would have with which to serve the king and the kingdom; such arms were never to be sold or otherwise disposed of, nor were they ever to be confiscated by the freeman's lord. Those responsible for having arms were to declare them formally to properly authorised officers, whereupon the list of them would be read back to them in public session, and they would swear to maintain them for the good of the kingdom. A final clause insisted that freemen alone should be received 'ad sacramentum armorum'.[21] In King John's reign a clause of the Ten Articles (which derived from the reign of William I) reminded all freemen of their obligation to take an active role in national defence, while another ordered all such, of whatever rank, to be constantly ready and prepared with arms and horses to fulfil their service to the crown. In 1242, steps would be taken to reiterate the obligations of the king's subjects to assist in the keeping of domestic peace through the keeping of arms, while in clause 6 of the Statute of Winchester of 1285 Edward I restated that every man between the ages of fifteen and sixty should have arms in his house with which to defend

---

[19] In his *Decretum* (1140) Gratian had already emphasised that it was its use by a recognised public authority (such as a king) which gave the use of force its true legitimacy.

[20] J. Boussard, 'Les mercenaires au XIIe siècle. Henri II Plantagenet et les origines de l'armée de métier', *BEC*, 106 (1945–46), 194, 200, n. 31.

[21] W. Stubbs (ed.), *Select charters and other illustrations of English constitutional history from the earliest times to the reign of Edward the First* (9th edn, Oxford, 1913), 183–4, cc. 3, 4, 9, 12.

the peace according to the ancient assize ('eit en sa mesun armure pur la pees garder solum la aunciene assise') depending upon the lands and goods which he held.[22]

On the other side of the Channel the French king was being obliged to take a leaf out of his English counterpart's book. Historians have emphasised important developments in French military organisation and thinking which took place during the second half of the twelfth century, above all how the emphasis was placed more and more upon the royal army, led by the king or his nominated lieutenant. Henceforth, the military history of France was to be increasingly associated with the history of her kings.[23] As Guillaume le Breton wrote in the *Philippidos*, war was now being fought 'for the honour of king and kingdom' ('pro regni et regis honore'). It is suggestive of changing times and priorities that he appears to have put the public obligation upon the shoulders of the royal army, led by the king or his lieutenant. From now on, king and army were to be more closely associated.

An advocate of strong monarchy, John of Salisbury used the *De re militari* to float proposals which had less to do with war itself than with the means of achieving effective royal government, of which keeping the peace was an essential element. He regarded the law and armed force as the two bastions, or pillars, of a peaceful society ruled by the king. In his view, the army was to be seen as the institution which, working with the king, would bolster the power and increasingly centralised authority of the royal office. Following Vegetius, the army would play an important role in establishing and maintaining the royal authority; it was through loyal service to the king that the soldier proved himself a faithful follower of Christ and an effective guardian of the good of society. From this time onwards, Vegetius' work would seldom be regarded simply as a mine of purely military wisdom. Not the least of John's contributions was to set Vegetius' text off on a long journey which would also give it a role, occasionally a significant role, in the development of both political and social ideas and practices in the centuries to come. It was in large measure due to the particular use made of it by John of Salisbury in the *Policraticus* that the *De re militari* was to be influential in ways which went beyond those which its title may have suggested, and which helped define the spheres of both activity and thought to which Vegetius' work would be called to contribute in the future.

[22] *Ibid.* 362–5, 463–9.
[23] P. Contamine (ed.), *Histoire militaire de la France. I. Des origines à 1715* (Paris, 1992), 77.

Guillaume le Breton

The historical works of Guillaume le Breton, chaplain to Philip II (Augustus), king of France, in the early years of the thirteenth century, demonstrate the influence which Vegetius' text could have on another kind of writer, this time a recorder of events with 'a marked penchant towards things of war'.[24] It should be emphasised that nowhere did le Breton cite Vegetius directly, nor even refer to him as a source or inspiration. It could, therefore, be argued that the similarities between what the two men wrote may be little more than fortuitous coincidence. However, a closer look at the evidence suggests that this was not the case, and that le Breton's work contains strong echoes of Vegetian thought and expression.

It was one of Vegetius' main intentions to help create an effective army which would fight to achieve victory. In both his *Chronique* and, more specifically, in the *Philippidos*, le Breton underlined the use of some of the good practices, such as the acquisition of skills and the regular practice of these, encouraged by Vegetius. Speed of movement (to upset the enemy) was referred to in the works of both men,[25] while the ability to jump onto a horse was reflected in the action of the king himself.[26] Members of the royal army used their skills as swimmers at the siege of Château-Gaillard, reminding us that Vegetius had emphasised how useful it was for soldiers to be able to swim.[27] Likewise, as Vegetius emphasised that a commander should be kept well informed of what was going on around him, so le Breton referred to the use of spies in both his works.[28] The use of musical instruments, in this case brass instruments used to help co-ordinate large troop movements, found in Vegetius' work, also occurred in the same context in that of le Breton.[29]

The use of particular battle formations, the 'wedge' ('cuneus') and the circle, described by Vegetius in a discussion of the advantages of specific formations to meet particular situations, reappeared in both of le Breton's works.[30] Above all, the emphasis placed upon orderliness in the ranks of the royal army reminded the reader of le Breton's admiration for Roman practice which he could have learned from Vegetius: the need for men

---

[24] *Œuvres de Rigord et de Guillaume le Breton, historiens de Philippe Auguste*, ed. H. F. Delaborde (2 vols., SHF, Paris, 1882–85), vol. I, lxxv. Hereafter *Ph.*

[25] *DRM*, I, 4; *Ph.*, V, 33–50.   [26] *DRM*, I, 18; *Ph.*, XI, 303.

[27] *DRM*, I, 10; *Ph.*, VII, 99, 337.

[28] *DRM*, III, 6; *Chronique*, 261 ('vispiliones'); *Ph.*, I, 632: III, 259.

[29] *DRM*, III, 5; 'bucinna' in *Ph.*, II, 613: XI, 63; 'tuba' in *Chronique*, 271, 273, and *Ph.*, III, 333; 'lituus' in *Ph.*, XII, 13.

[30] *DRM*, I, 26; III, 18, 19; *Chronique*, 279, 280, 282; *Ph.*, VIII, 717.

to fight close to one another;[31] the need, too, for each to know his place and under which leader he should be serving.[32]

A major theme running through the *De re militari* was its author's insistence that the successful leader should be constantly looking ahead, anticipating needs, showing awareness of the enemy's plans and actions. This was the quality which the Middle Ages came to term 'prudence', and would be found in several passages of le Breton's work which, in their turn, matched others found in the work of Vegetius. His repeated insistence that the commander should anticipate his need of provisions and armaments, collected in advance to meet emergencies such as long sieges, is reflected in the way that le Breton emphasised, on more than one occasion, how leaders should take steps to insure against such eventualities.[33] At the siege of Château-Gaillard, the English commander expelled civilians from the fortress in order to preserve his food supplies. This passage found its inspiration in the work of Vegetius, in which he noted that such steps were often taken in the past to conserve food for those engaged in the vital work of defence.[34]

Another subject to arouse interest among medieval readers was that of the armour worn by soldiers. A number of texts in le Breton's history referred to armour as the iron protector of the human limbs which they covered; the role of the shield against the effects of violence was emphasised both by him and by Vegetius. Even the fallen, if wearing full armour, were protected as they lay on the ground. Not surprisingly, therefore, le Breton could claim that many 'moderns' were more careful to cover themselves with armour than men had been in ancient times when, 'as we read', many thousands would die on a single day, while elsewhere he could write of 'the thickness of the armour by which men of our time are completely protected'.[35]

The reader who studies both the fourth book of the *De re militari* and the *Philippidos* may be led to conclude that Vegetius did indeed inspire le Breton. This was particularly the case in his descriptions of sieges, details of which harked back to the Vegetian model. The siege of Boves was one such example. The emphasis placed upon the active defence of the walls with a hail of stones and other projectiles corresponded to Vegetius'

---

[31] *DRM*, I, 9; III, 14, 15: *Ph.*, XI, 179.   [32] *DRM*, II, 13; *Ph.*, II, 411–12, 600–4.

[33] *DRM*, III, 1, 3, 9, 26 (Rules 17, 32); *Ph.*, I, 595–600; II, 292–3; IV, 440–4.

[34] *Ph.*, VII, 468–86; *DRM*, IV, 7. See Frontinus, *Strategemata*, III, iv, 5.

[35] *Ph.*, XI, 116–32; 'Armorum densitas quibus milites nostri temporis impenetrabiliter muniuntur' (*Chronique*, 284). See R. Mitchell, 'Archery *versus* mail: experimental archaeology and the value of historical context', *JMMH*, 4 (2006), 18–28 for a recent discussion of the subject.

text,[36] while the measures used by the attacking force, particularly the undermining of the wall and the burning of inflammable material within the mine, also reflected the *De re militari*.[37] The description of the great siege of Château-Gaillard, with its details on the use of mobile towers, may have been inspired by the *De re militari*, as may have been that of the defence of their town by the people of Lille.[38] Even the doleful judgement regretting the lack of proper burial for men killed in conflict at sea, whose bodies are eaten by fish, may well have come to le Breton from Vegetius, who made a similar comment.[39]

As already noticed, very characteristic of the work of Vegetius were those passages reflecting his awareness of the soldier as a human being liable to experience human emotions and reactions in particular situations. Le Breton presented King Richard I urging his elite troops, of whom Vegetius had written in his description of the legion, to greater things, a passage which recalled Vegetius' teaching that everything appeared difficult until it was attempted. Le Breton also accepted that an army's success would stem more from its 'spirit' than from its numbers, both writers agreeing on the importance of 'virtus'.[40]

Like Vegetius, le Breton emphasised the importance of taking the emotions of the participants into consideration when describing the activities of war. Vegetius had argued that indignation and anger were two such which might be used by the skilful commander to provoke hostility towards the enemy among his own men; le Breton would say that the French were encouraged by their king to fight for their own good by arousing their indignation against threats made by the enemy.[41] Following Vegetius, too, le Breton wrote that desperation gave men strength to fight boldly when, for lack of means of escape, death had become inevitable. And where Vegetius had cited Virgil that 'the only hope of safety for the defeated is to expect no safety', le Breton was to report an instance of the French king hurrying to bring succour to his allies so hard pressed by the enemy that they had scarcely any hope of being saved.[42]

In suggesting how much le Breton may have been inspired, both directly and indirectly, by the *De re militari* we may note a number of

---

[36] *DRM*, IV, 8; *Ph.*, II, 313–16.   [37] *DRM*, IV, 24; *Ph.*, 327–49.

[38] *DRM*, IV, 17; *Ph.*, VII, 656–61 (Gaillard); IV, 9, 25 (Lille).

[39] *DRM*, IV, 44; *Ph.*, 30–1. The source may have been Ovid, *Tristia*, I, ii, 53–6.

[40] *DRM*, I, 8: *Ph.*, V, 408.

[41] *DRM*, III, 12; *Ph.*, III, 323–6. Both authors use the word 'indignatio'.

[42] 'una salus victis nullam sperare salutem' (*DRM*, III, 21); 'ut pressis spes jam sit nulla salutis' (*Ph.*, IX, 635).

passages in the *Philippidos* which emphasised that the wars of Philip II
were fought for the sake of the kingdom and the king ('pro regni et regis
honore').[43] While making allowances for changes of meaning and terminology, if we translate 'res publica' in Vegetius by 'patria et rex' ('king and
country') in le Breton, we may argue that the thirteenth-century writer
saw the part played by war and the army in a way not so very different
from that envisaged by Vegetius eight centuries or so earlier.[44] For Vegetius, the army was an instrument used to defend the 'res publica', and
war was the chief means by which peace, achieved through deterrence
or victory in battle, was maintained.[45] In the eyes of le Breton, the reign
of Philip II was a period during which the king (Vegetius' emperor) used
war not only as a means of securing glory for himself and his people, but
also as the most effective way of destroying the opposition (including the
English) who stood in the way of his vision of a country united under the
crown. The achievement of this provided both the theme and the story
of the *Philippidos*. The siege of Château-Gaillard was a famous episode,
but the process was not to be completed until the forces ranged against
France had been routed at the battle of Bouvines in 1214, a victory which
constituted Philip's crowning glory, for thereafter peace was to follow:
'he who wants peace prepares for war'. The new kind of army, dependent upon the crown, was the instrument by which the process had been
achieved.

A comparison of le Breton's texts with the *De re militari* leads to the
conclusion that the author, a man of the court and a eulogiser of the
king, was seeking to make two different points, both, however, based on
Vegetian concepts. First that, by the early thirteenth century, the army
in France was becoming an instrument of monarchy used to subdue and
defeat the enemies of what was regarded by supporters of Capetian rule
as the common good maintained by the monarchy. Secondly, le Breton
created an image of an army, fighting under royal command, defending
the good of society, and doing so successfully through the proper appreciation and use, by its leaders, of proven Roman military methods and
practices which, carefully followed, helped the royal army overcome its
enemies. Applying the lessons of John of Salisbury's discussion of the
role of the army in a monarchy, and, in addition, taking to heart some of
the practical lessons of fighting set out by Vegetius, le Breton had added

---

[43] *Ph.*, X, 792.
[44] See, for example, *Ph.*, VII, 105; X, 792; XI, 67. The idea of men born as 'Frenchmen'
is conveyed by the use of the word 'natalis', one born in France (*Ph.*, XII, 99) who
belonged to the king's people ('ipsius populi', *Ph.*, XII, 62).
[45] *DRM*, III, Praef.

a further dimension to the use to which the *De re militari* was being put by the early thirteenth century.[46]

The *Siete Partidas* of Alfonso X

We have seen how two writers of the mid-twelfth and early thirteenth centuries, composing very different kinds of texts, incorporated teachings from the *De re militari* into their work. After England and France, let us now turn to Spain to consider the *Siete Partidas*, a form of law code in which were set out the rules which Alfonso X, king of Castile from 1252 to 1284, and those who worked with him, sought to apply to the government of the Church, the administration of the kingdom and the army, the law, the merchant community and the lower classes of society. It is a text in which may be found the influence of a number of cultures and intellectual disciplines, and a variety of legal systems ranging from the written (civil and canon law) to the traditional, unwritten customs of different parts of the Iberian peninsula. The text also draws upon the wisdom of the classical world, the 'ancients' as they are often referred to. One such was Vegetius.

Our author is referred to only once by name, as a *sabio*, a 'wise man' or expert, a man with know-how.[47] Yet the influence of Vegetius on the 'Secunda Partida' (from which all references cited are taken), in particular on 'titles' (chapters) xviii to xxiv, which are concerned with different aspects of war, is ever present. Indeed, setting out to show that a king should emulate David and Solomon, both of them learned and wise, the compilers (of v, 16) may also have had at the back of their minds Vegetius' teaching that a ruler's learning should benefit all his subjects.[48] The statement set out an ideal; at the same time it gave a character to the whole work by underlining the written word as a source of worldly wisdom which could be used to the advantage of a king's subjects. Vegetius had taught the value of knowledge gained from such a source; in the *Siete Partidas* Alfonso was doing much the same. It was the assumption upon which the entire didactic canon (including 'Mirrors for Princes') had been, and would continue to be, based.

The text of the *Partidas* left the reader in little doubt about the power attributable to the king. Yet one of the interesting aspects of the titles devoted to war was to see how king and subjects were linked in mutual

[46] J. M. A. Beer (*A medieval Caesar* (Geneva, 1976), 72, 74, 81–2, 143) underlines the significance of the appearance, in 1213, of *Li fet des Romains*, with its emphasis on Caesar's military achievement of conquest through war, and on the fighting spirit of the 'Gauls', arguing that Philip II was to be equated with Caesar.

[47] *Siete Partidas* (hereafter *SP*), II, xxi, 2.   [48] *DRM*, I, Praef.

obligation to one another: he providing for the defence of his people, they obliged to serve him in wartime wherever he might order, in a castle, on the frontier, in the army.[49] Castles, for example, must be preserved and defended for the good of the king and of the kingdom.[50] King and people each had a mutual responsibility to ensure the protection of the other. If a king were threatened with rebellion, his loyal subjects must come quickly to his help; if the country as a whole were attacked, the king was responsible for organising and leading its defence, and all should come to assist him, their lord. Defeat would be felt by both king and people, so that men must be ready to fight 'because the loss would be common to all', the strong implication being that 'no one can avoid joining the army'. In the case of the king launching an attack upon enemy territory, the people were to be summoned as an army, provided that they were given time to gather their arms and provisions; failure to do this would be seen as desertion, bringing dishonour upon the king. Above all, knights should be ready to die for their lord and 'for the common benefit of their country'.[51] Theirs was indeed a public service.

The readiness to fight was to be seen in the fulfilment of a responsibility on the part of both ruler and ruled to act effectively in defence of a good held in common. It was this sense of responsibility, in particular a failure to fulfil it, that made punishment the logical and reasonable consequence of that failure. Men had more than a duty merely to turn up and be present when a war was fought. Each, according to his place in society, was responsible for preparing himself for the military tasks ahead. Training was not only the best way of making a military force efficient; it was also a recognition of the common responsibility of defence, and the way to meet the challenge of preparing oneself for the task of helping society defend itself. From this followed the emphasis placed by Alfonso (following Vegetius and, perhaps, others) on the need to learn from the written word; from this, too, followed the list of penalties and punishments to be imposed upon those who, through some negligence, were unable to fulfil the military role expected of them. Two things may be noticed. One is that none, whether commander or rank and file, was exempted from the threat of punishment. The other is that the punishment exacted would be judged in proportion to the loss or injury it was considered to have caused.[52]

---

[49] *SP*, II, xiii, 16.   [50] *Ibid.* II, xvii, 1.   [51] *Ibid.* II, xix, 3–9; xxi, 21.

[52] 'The king should punish those who do not practise these exercises in proportion to the damage which results from their negligence, which does not include any injury sustained personally as a result of that negligence' (*ibid.* xxiii, 8).

The *Partidas* leaves one in no doubt that all authority, including military authority, rested with the king, the people's natural lord. The call to arms was an inalienable aspect of his sovereignty.[53] In practice, however, it must be shared with others. Military commanders, including admirals, were appointed by the king on the advice of twelve senior commanders.[54] This simple statement tells us a good deal. It emphasises the fact that those appointed were, in a real sense, the recipients of power delegated by the king; the admiral, for instance, was said to exercise royal power at sea.[55] These men were truly the lieutenants, in the full sense of the word, of the king, each appointed to act with his authority. The text describes the ceremony of appointment (or commissioning, as we would say), a ceremony which reminds one of a similar one to be instituted, under the same classical influence, by Charles, duke of Burgundy, two centuries later.[56] The king was seen as taking his responsibilities seriously; he delegated his military authority to persons whose professional qualifications had been guaranteed by senior and experienced commanders (today's referees). Society could rest calmly when its defence was in the hands of such men.

The recognition to be awarded to the development of professional skills was also seen in the manner in which promotion, within both army and navy, was observed.[57] The matter had been discussed by Vegetius, who saw it as an incentive which encouraged men to work in a number of branches of the army, thereby gaining broad experience of the service.[58] Once again, the man who sought promotion must have the support of twelve senior witnesses testifying to his understanding of war, and that he was strong, active and loyal. If successful, the man, newly raised to higher rank, would be presented to the king, from whom he would receive a pennon enabling those placed under his command to identify him. The very formality of the process presupposes a military system both organised along certain lines and ready to recognise that promotion was accorded on the basis of experience and merit, founded on the qualities of skill, virtue and leadership. The influence of Vegetius, hovering here and there, is underlined by the contents of xxiii, 11, a discussion of the benefits of good leadership, a matter to which the 'ancients', including Vegetius, attributed the highest importance.

---

[53] J. F. O'Callaghan, 'War (and peace) in the law codes of Alfonso X', in *Crusaders, condottieri and cannon. Medieval warfare in societies around the Mediterranean*, ed. D. J. Kagay and L. J. A. Villalon (Leiden and Boston, 2003), 16, 14.

[54] *SP*, II, xxii, 2; xxiv, 4.   [55] *Ibid.* xxiv, 3.

[56] See below, pp. 133–4; Allmand, 'Did the *De re militari*...?', 139–40.

[57] *SP*, II, xxii, 5, 6; xxiv, 4.   [58] *DRM*, II, 21.

Much of Book III of the *De re militari* had been devoted to a consideration of the qualities required of the good commander, and how thoughtful leadership could achieve victory with the minimum of effort and human loss. Such an approach was clearly reflected in the *Partidas*. The Alfonsian commander was not afraid to use his mind: 'it is certainly just that a man should make use of all his mental resources in the protection of a place which depends upon his loyalty'.[59] To do this, however, he needed to be supplied with information, without which planning could not be carried out effectively. The reader was then reminded of the importance of the commander having up-to-date information regarding the enemy, his intentions and the conditions in which he found himself, so that plans might be made accordingly. The direct influence of Vegetius is immediately perceptible: his insistence upon taking advantage of an unwary enemy, and his emphasis on the use of spies, were strongly reflected in the *Partidas*.[60] Here, the practical aspects of 'prudence' were given recognition. Be informed of what your enemy is doing, act accordingly and in a way that shows that you are prepared, and none will dare attack you.[61]

Linked to the effort to deter enemy aggression was the use of psychological warfare, encouraged by Vegetius both to weaken resistance and to instil a sense of confidence in one's own men. Such an approach was also found in the *Partidas*, in which encouragement given to achieving maximum material harm was linked to the unseen but significant effects this could have upon the morale of combatants. Other, more subtle methods could be used to influence an enemy. For instance, the sight of a large number of siege engines, in particular if it were seen that those who had them knew how to use them, would have an effect upon the determination of a garrison or citizenry to resist; horses, when not carrying a load, should be ridden to give the enemy the impression that an army was better provided for than might appear; the enemy should never know the extent of one's losses, as this would only encourage him.[62] Likewise, a good defensive site gave a sense of security and increased confidence; while Vegetius' recommendation that troops should be reassured in times of special difficulty was reflected in more than one passage

---

[59] *SP*, II, xviii, 14.

[60] *Ibid.* xxi, 6. The importance accorded to spies in the *Partidas* is underlined by the compilers' insistence that they be properly rewarded for the important and dangerous work which they do, something Vegetius had not referred to (*ibid.* xxvi, 11).

[61] *Ibid.* xviii, 13; xx, 8; xxiii, 3. The theme of preparation or anticipation is to be found in the following *Partidas*: xxi, 2, 17, 20; xxii, 1, 7; xxiii, 3–4, 6–10, 17–27, 29–30.

[62] *Ibid.* xxiii, 22; xviii, 14; xxiii, 3. See Frontinus, *Strategemata*, II, iv and III, xv on such measures.

in the *Partidas*.[63] The general should do everything which he thought would give his men self-reliance and resolution to succeed, making a particular effort to encourage those likely to be timorous in the presence of the enemy.[64]

Title xxiii, one of the longest in the second *Partida*, included thirty laws. Its subject was war itself, boldly announced in its title: 'On war, and on the things which need to be done' ('De la guerra et de las cosas necesarias que pertenescen a ella'). It considered half a dozen or so themes, normally in laws grouped together. In addition to these, a single over-arching theme can be discerned: the insistence on prudence, or readiness, which was referred to, sometimes directly, at other times obliquely, time and again.

First, however, what of the themes which emerged from these laws? The main one was, without doubt, the role to be played by commanders, a subject which had already dominated the previous title (xxii) and which, in this title, lay behind laws 4 to 8. We should note that most, if not all, of these laws included recommendations owing their inspiration to the *De re militari*. Law 5, for instance, suggested that in mid-thirteenth-century Spain commands were normally accorded to men of lineage. However, anxious to have an army which would produce results, Alfonso X tried to play down lineage as the essential requirement for advancement in royal armies in favour of men of prudence who had learned to take orders and proved their worth as men of experience. Leadership consists of more than courage: 'a general should not be selected except on account of his prudence and great talents for command'. Law 6 required a general to be a man of reflection, who considered the military problems facing him, and acted accordingly. Vegetius' teaching was clearly being referred to here. The observations in law 7 regarding the advantages to be gained from securing the support of nature if an army were outnumbered, or the need to turn nature (such as the sun's rays) to advantage, could have been inspired by the *De re militari*.[65] The absolute necessity for all soldiers, infantry and cavalry, to have regular practice in the use of arms and in fighting in armour was seen as the prime responsibility of commanders. Yet again this can be traced back to a number of passages in Vegetius.[66] In law 10, praise is lavished upon those who secured useful information regarding the enemy. The need for soldiers to learn to obey orders given by their leaders was then emphasised, consideration of both these matters reflecting part of the content of *De re militari*, III, 9. The conveying of these orders by signal and the need to change the code if this were to

[63] *DRM*, III, 10; see also, for example, *SP*, II, xxii, 1; xxiii, 5, 22.
[64] *SP*, II, xxiii, 22.   [65] *DRM*, III, 9, 14.   [66] E.g., *ibid.* I, 18; II, 23, 24; III, 9.

be understood by the enemy was clearly influenced by the same text, *DRM*, III, 5.[67]

In law 11, the command forming the link between the general and his army was likened to a rudder giving direction to a ship, direction which all strove to make effective. Laws 12 to 14 underlined how devices (pennons and standards) were both a sign of authority and a means of conveying commands silently within the army, commands which, emanating from authority, should be obeyed. This group of laws, too, owed something to Vegetius, for whom the pennon was a sign of a group's unity, keeping men together, providing them with both a rallying point and leadership. Once again, the passage in the *Partidas* is dependent upon a number of chapters (not all that closely related) in the *De re militari*.

Three further laws (19–21) are concerned with the way that encampments should be located and guarded. A comparison between these laws and the *De re militari* reveals ideas common to both which went beyond the possibility of coincidence. In Vegetius' text the building of camps was an essential part of the recruit's training,[68] the importance of which had probably come to the fore again in Spain as the process of *reconquista* moved forward. Its significance, work to be given over to experts, is understood. The aim in creating a camp was to provide shelter and security for an army on campaign. Various ways of defending it, by placing it within an encirclement of carts[69] or building a ditch around it to keep animals in and the enemy out, were suggested.[70] The site had to be well chosen for the access it must give to provisions, water and wood, as well as fodder for the horses: at the same time it must not present the enemy with any advantage.[71] The shape of the camp, round, oblong or square, should depend on the lie of the land; in all circumstances it must be properly guarded both day and night.[72]

Partida 21 carried a heading which stated its purpose clearly: 'Concerning knights . . . '. It was, in its own right, an important section of the work, offering an insight into how the order of knighthood was regarded at the moment which had witnessed a great reduction of Moorish power on the Iberian peninsula through the force of arms. Not unnaturally, it described knighthood, its obligations and rewards in terms of the recent wars and the successes of Fernando III, who had initiated the process of creating the *Partidas*. The background to the text was thus an increasingly united country, a developing sense of nationhood, and a growing

---

[67] See J. F. Verbruggen, *The art of warfare in western Europe during the Middle Ages. From the eighth century to 1340* (Amsterdam, New York and Oxford, 1977), 292–3.
[68] *DRM*, I, 21.   [69] *DRM*, III, 10: law 19.   [70] *DRM*, I, 25: law 21.
[71] *DRM*, III, 8: law 19.   [72] *DRM*, III, 8: laws 20 and 21.

sense of the common good, all served by the knighthood of Spain, whose defence was its main *raison d'être*. The knight of the *Partidas* was a man with a clear public function to perform.

Following tradition, the text divided the population into three groups, each with a part to play in supporting or sustaining the world, through prayer, through the cultivation of the earth and through the protection of its people. Of these, the third group was seen as the most important, giving status and position to those who assumed responsibility for the defence of their fellow men. These were the 'milites', chosen only in the ratio of one to a thousand ('mille'), an exclusive group whose members had been selected, on account of their attributes, to become knights. The influence of Vegetius is apparent here. In the *De re militari* he underlined the significance of the commander's role in the defence of 'the wealth of landowners, the protection of cities, the lives of soldiers and the glory of the state', a role which could be fulfilled only by the army and the soldiers who made it up.[73] Selection, as we have seen, was the basic principle upon which Vegetius founded his army. The role of the ruler, and of those appointed by him, in carrying out this task was one of crucial importance. The *Partida* then described some of the qualities required of the knight, who must endure hardship, possess the appropriate physical characteristics to fulfil the tasks ahead, and be ready to acquire military skills through practice. All these qualifications could be found in the *De re militari*.[74]

Of the virtues called for in law 4, 'prudence' ('cordura'), 'fortitude' ('fortaleza'), 'moderation' ('mesura') and 'justice' ('justicia'), the first three formed the qualities of the ideal soldier described in the Vegetian system. The emphasis placed on intelligence, or prudence (and on the use made of it by knights in laws 5 and 6), owed much to Vegetius. Fortitude or courage, 'audacia' in Vegetius' text, featured prominently,[75] while moderation, which we may interpret as discipline or order, was a fundamental part of the Vegetian canon, affecting all aspects of military life. Likewise, the means of winning victory formed the core of laws 6, 8 and 10, with the emphasis placed on intelligence ('prudence' again),

---

[73] *DRM*, III, 10. See also I, 7.

[74] Endurance, *DRM*, I. 20; III, 4; the physical characteristics, *DRM*, I, 6; the readiness to acquire skills through training and practice, *DRM*, II, 23; III, 4. For the use made of the *Partidas* by Pere III ('the Ceremonious') of Aragon (d.1387) and, in particular, how knighthood was regarded in his *Tractat*, see D. A. Cohen, 'Secular pragmatism and thinking about war in some court writings of Pere III *el Ceremoniós*', in *Crusaders, condottieri and cannon*, ed. Kagay and Villalon, pp. 19–55. 'The quest here is for effective warriors and nothing else' (p. 42).

[75] See *DRM*, I, 1, 20.

dexterity with arms, astuteness of mind and, finally, skill with horses, all owing much to a text which had stressed the importance of skills achieved through training and constant practice, and the use in war of cunning and experience.

In the eyes of the thirteenth-century compilers, however, such skills, largely acquired, were not sufficient. The prospective knight required something more, something innate and moral: a sense of shame, which would deter him from doing anything dishonourable, such as betraying his lord or deserting the army. This characteristic, honour under another name, was readily recognised as an essential part of the chivalric ethos of the Middle Ages, closely associated with the noble, military class. Yet the concept went back at least as far as Vegetius, to take it no further. Early in the *De re militari* he had written of the need for new recruits, upon whom the defence of the country relied, to be of outstanding breeding and morals.[76] Decent birth ('honestas') made a suitable soldier, whom a sense of shame ('verecundia') prevented from taking flight. This text must have been in the minds of those who drew up this *Partida* with its emphasis upon the sense of honour which the 'miles' should possess, a sense which none the less stressed the public responsibility borne by the soldier/knight as much in the thirteenth as in the fourth century, a responsibility newly underlined in the text of the *Partidas*.

Loyalty was also an essential characteristic of knighthood: first, the knight was the designated protector of society; secondly, it was necessary to preserve the honour of his lineage; and thirdly, it prevented him doing anything of which he might be ashamed.[77] The theme would reappear. In law 14 it was stated that the knight should not fear to suffer death on account of his religion, or in defence of his natural lord (the king) or his country ('por su senor natural . . . por su tierra'). Later (law 21) it would be stated that the knight should not hesitate to die for his lord, whether to avert misfortune and disgrace from him, or to help him in the task of extending his dominions and honour, or for the benefit of his country ('por comunal de su tierra').

The similarities between this passage and that in the *De re militari* in which the new soldier made his promises to serve loyally were striking.[78] The final law (25) of this title returned to the theme of loyalty by emphasising that desertion was a valid reason for stripping a knight of membership of his order. The theme of desertion, regarded as treachery towards

---

[76] 'et genere . . . et moribus debet excellere' (*ibid.* I, 7).   [77] *SP*, II, xxi, 9.

[78] E. H. Kantorowicz, *The king's two bodies. A study in medieval political theology* (Princeton, 1957), 236ff.

lord and the common welfare, was referred to a number of times in the *De re militari*,[79] a fact strongly suggestive that Vegetius' work lay behind sentiments expressed in a different context centuries later. Certain moral values did not change.

What are the elements common to both the *De re militari* and *Partidas*, II, 21? In both texts, selection, with its implication that not all are suited to the arduous, socially responsible role of being a soldier/knight set out both by Vegetius (who wrote of the 'rejected', or 'repudiandi') and by the authors of the *Partidas*,[80] gave soldiers/knights a privileged position in society, but one which they had to live up to. Both texts drew a picture of men who protected society against any enemy who wished it ill; in both, soldiers/knights were committed to the service of the ruler, whom they promised to obey in all matters. An initiation ceremony, at which the soldier or squire was admitted to the higher rank, was common to both texts, as indeed it was to be in the Catalan text, the *Llibre de l'Ordo de Cavalleria*, written by Ramon Lull not many years after the *Partidas*. The Christian nature of this ceremony in both texts made the evidence in the *De re militari* an important example for the more elaborate ceremony of conferring knighthood, including the taking of the oath, developed in later times. Soldier and knight shared certain qualities or characteristics: the martial, the intellectual and the moral receive consideration in both texts.

The *Siete Partidas* witnessed a further blossoming of Vegetian influence, both moral and practical. The defensive needs of the country were emphasised as being a common responsibility carried out under the monarch and those appointed to act in his name. For the first time, the qualities and characteristics of the good leader were discussed in detail, both Vegetius and the compilers of the *Partidas* favouring the thoughtful commander who, while seeking to outwit his enemy, also had his soldiers' interests in mind. On their part, soldiers must obey the orders they received, and should learn to work together, so forming a unified army. Nor was knighthood forgotten, the emphasis being placed upon its overriding function of providing protection for the people under the leadership of the crown. The existence of an army composed of such men constituted the best means of maintaining peace. The fulfilment of that task was both an honour and a responsibility.

---

[79] *DRM*, I, 4; II, 3, 5, 20; III, 6, 9. See also C. Allmand, 'Le problème de la désertion en France, en Angleterre et en Bourgogne à la fin du moyen âge', in *Guerre, pouvoir et noblesse au moyen âge. Mélanges en l'honneur de Philippe Contamine*, ed. J. Paviot and J. Verger (Paris, 2000), 31–41.

[80] *DRM*, I, 7, 8; *SP*, II, xxi, 12.

Giles of Rome, *De regimine principum*

In mid-thirteenth-century Spain, the study of the *De re militari* had led to it exercising considerable influence upon military thinking, in particular on the place and role of the army in Hispanic society, as it fought to regain the initiative against Moorish forces. Elsewhere, it was the Aristotelian revival of the same period, chiefly associated with Thomas Aquinas and the friars, which encouraged men to think more deeply about society, its nature, form, purpose and needs, and how the common good might best be achieved. In that process Vegetius was to play a role which further extended and enhanced his reputation as the chief thinker on military affairs known to the Middle Ages.

It was between 1275 and 1277 that Giles of Rome (Aegidius Romanus), Augustinian hermit and later archbishop of Bourges, wrote his *De regimine principum* for the young man destined to become King Philip IV of France in 1285. It was no coincidence that the second half of the century should see the composition of what would be Giles' highly influential work. Strongly Aristotelian in inspiration and character, it was to prove a very popular work in its Latin form, while, through translations, it would further extend its influence upon men's thinking regarding the duties and obligations of kingship, offering a view of government seen as increasingly active in many aspects of social existence.[81]

To the student of the development of political thought in the late Middle Ages, Giles is an important thinker, who marked the point reached by men of the late thirteenth century regarding the development of the state, its *raison d'être* and functions, as well as the role to be accorded to the ruler in contemporary society. There can be little doubt about the power which Giles accorded to the prince; at the same time that prince, as the 'director populi', gave 'direction' to his people, rather as an archer ('est quasi sagittator quidam') fired arrows (his 'populus') in the direction he wanted them to go. One such might be to mount the defence of the state against exterior enemies who threatened it.[82] In some passages Vegetius' name, accompanied by a quotation from the *De re militari*, appeared in the text, while in others ideas or statements indebted to Vegetius were also to be found.[83]

---

[81] *Aegidii Columnae Romani... De regimine principum Libri III* (Rome, 1607; repr. Aalen, 1967). Hereafter *DRP*. See C. F. Briggs, *Giles of Rome's* De regimine principum. Translations into seven languages would appear in the next century or so.

[82] *DRP*, III, ii, 8: p. 471.

[83] Vegetius is cited by name in *DRP*, I, ii, 14 and III, i, 12; ideas owing much to him in I, ii, 13 and 14.

In the *De regimine principum*, III, iii, Giles turned his attention to the theme of war and the army. The heading described what the author sought to do: 'In which is discussed how a state or kingdom should be ruled in time of war.' The title of the first chapter attacked the matter head on: 'What is military service, and what is it for?' ('Quid est militia et ad quae est instituta?'), the question echoing another similar one, 'What is an army?' ('Quid est exercitus'), found at III, i in the margins of many manuscripts of the *De re militari*.[84] Behind much of what was written by Giles in answer to his question lay ideas attributable to Vegetius. Military service, Giles wrote interpreting the Latin author, may be said to be prudence, or a certain type of prudence.[85] In modern parlance, an army might be termed an insurance policy, an investment whose return was safety and the promise of defence in time of war. As with the law, it was with the common good, its maintenance and protection, that the army was primarily concerned. It was therefore right that none should have a wider knowledge of war than the prince, whose learning might be of benefit to the common good.[86] That good would be defended by the army, trained to act according to the prince's orders in the ways and manners of war. Since the army consisted of those made responsible for the good of the state, it was right that only the very best be chosen, the experts ('doctores') in their own branch of knowledge. So none should be allowed to serve as a soldier unless he showed his loyalty to the state or kingdom, could demonstrate his skill, and was ready to act as his ruler ordered him.[87]

Although Giles might at first appear to be keeping close to what Vegetius had written, he was far from being a slavish follower of the Roman writer. While he cited Vegetius by name[88] on some nineteen occasions in *De regimine principum*, III, iii, more often than not (and increasingly so as the book progressed) Giles preferred to consider Vegetius' ideas in his own way and then express them in his own language. This makes it difficult to trace exact parallels between the texts of the two writers. None the less a search, in this case not for passages which have been borrowed, but rather for important ideas or themes considered by the Roman writer, reveals that Giles knew Vegetius' text well enough to recognise that

---

[84] 'Qu'est ce qu'une armée?' echoes Philippe Contamine in his preface to *Construire l'armée française. Textes fondateurs des institutions militaires. I. De la France des premiers Valois à la fin du règne de François Ier*, ed. V. Bessey (Turnhout, 2006), 5.

[85] 'Sciendum igitur militiam esse quandam prudentiam, sive quandam speciem prudentiae' (*DRP*, III, iii, 1; p. 555).

[86] *DRM*, I, Praef.   [87] *DRP*, III, iii, 1: pp. 555–9.

[88] 'ut patet per Vegetium in "De re militari"' (p. 555); 'recitat enim Vegetius' (p. 572); or 'ideo ait Vegetius' (p. 591).

certain parts of it were of importance to him and to the men of his day, and was then able to reduce a passage of some length (and, sometimes, complexity) to relatively few words, which he then incorporated, with understanding, as an expression of his own thought.

Having already shown in III, iii, 1 that since the state relied upon the army for its defence, and the army must be composed of men of high military capability, it was reasonable that in the following chapters Giles should place emphasis upon the skills and personal qualities of the soldier, and upon the methods used to recruit and train him. The qualities required were essentially three in number. The prospective soldier must possess energy for fighting ('strenuitas bellandi') as well as a thoughtful approach to war ('prudentia erga bella'). He must also have courage ('animositas'), a quality which enabled him to undertake fighting without fear of death, an idea which, earlier in the work, Giles had associated with Vegetius.[89] The hardships of the military life were then underlined but, curiously enough, no reference was made to what Vegetius had written on that subject. When he came to discuss whether townsmen, nobles or countrymen were the best fighters, Giles (like Vegetius) came down in favour of countrymen, doubtless for reasons he had already developed, that such men were more accustomed to bearing burdens, which enabled them to fight while wearing heavy armour.[90] On the other hand, honour (associated with the nobility) would deter men from fleeing before the enemy. Giles probably had *De re militari*, I, 7 in mind when he wrote this passage. Likewise, when reminding his readers that thoughtfulness ('prudentia') was as important as energy ('strenuitas'), Giles was falling back on a fundamental Vegetian message: the mind was as important as muscle in securing victory.

In chapter 6 Giles again quoted Vegetius on the need for the soldier to train and practise. This aspect of 'prudence' had been responsible for Roman victories over Spaniards, Greeks and Africans. Training, which should include running and jumping, removed fear and gave confidence, while also frightening the enemy (just as Vegetius had written).[91] Such training should be undertaken by both infantry and cavalry ('pedites' and 'milites') who, Giles noted in an interesting and perhaps significant aside, might be called upon to fight on foot.[92] Continuing the theme of training in chapter 7, Giles recommended that soldiers be given practice in the use of a variety of arms, as well as in swimming. It is at this point that we observe him, in spite of twice referring to Vegetius as an authority

---

[89] *DRP*, III, i, 12.　　[90] *DRM*, I, 3; *DRP*, III, iii, 4.　　[91] *DRM*, I, 1, 9.
[92] 'si contingat eos pedestres esse' (*DRP*, III, iii, 6).

to draw upon, beginning to express his ideas and recommendations in his words, rather than restating Vegetius' teachings as his own.

In the long central section (chapters 8–15) of the *De regimine principum*, which occupies about a third of III, iii, Giles considered principally two matters: the proper functioning of the army and, significantly, the role of the general, or 'dux' (Vegetius' term), in war. He concerned himself first (chapter 8) with the basics of survival: the need for the army to be able to defend itself adequately against attack through the building of proper defences on carefully chosen sites, and the need to provide satisfactory access to water supplies.[93] Great care must be taken over such matters for, as Vegetius, citing Cato, had written, mistakes made at war cannot be remedied.[94] Chapter 9 contained many reflections of Vegetian ideas, but they are not always easy to pin down, being mixed up and not presented in the order used by Vegetius. What is more significant is that Giles had clearly understood that soldiers must be treated as human beings with feelings of fear and confidence, which made the task of the 'dux' in taking these factors into account before entering a conflict a difficult but highly important one. Indeed, almost the entire section was concerned with the practicalities of leadership, dealing with both the physical conditions of war and the psychological reactions of those involved in it. With the exception of chapter 13, in which Giles emphasised the importance of Vegetius' recommendation that the point of the sword was more effective than its edge,[95] a relevant comment on the effectiveness of the sword against the changing defences set up against it in the second half of the thirteenth century, these central chapters of the *De regimine principum* would be strongly influenced by aspects of the recurring theme of leadership and its attendant problems, which feature so strongly in Books I and (above all) III of the *De re militari*.[96] For instance, in chapters 14 and 15 Giles emphasised two points made by Vegetius. One concerned the need for the *dux* to be kept well informed about the enemy's intentions and movements; the other was for the army to be kept together in both advance and retreat. The use by Giles, in consecutive chapters of the *De regimine principum*, of ideas originally contained in different books of the *De re militari* suggests the ability on his part to use the older work as a source to be plundered while giving

---

[93] Here he takes the points made in *DRM*, I, 21–5, and III, 15.
[94] *DRM*, I, 13. Giles quotes Vegetius here. Earlier (*DRP*, III, i, 12) he had expressed in his own words what looks very much like the same passage.
[95] *DRM*, I, 12.
[96] It is significant that the influence of *DRM*, Book II, is very slight indeed. This corresponds to the relative lack of response shown to much of its contents, up to this time, reflected in the marginalia of manuscripts, already noted above.

him the opportunity of writing a work of his own more appropriate to the needs of his time.

This is underlined by the character of much of the remainder of the work (chapters 16–22), given over to a subject, siege warfare, to which Vegetius had devoted two-thirds of his final book. We may note two things. One is that there was only a single direct reference (in chapter 21) to Vegetius as an authority. The second is that, notwithstanding this reluctance to admit the presence of his Roman mentor in much of what he wrote, Giles relied on information from twenty out of the thirty of Vegetius' chapters, nine of these being cited more than once, while using the information and ideas for his own purpose. We should recall that, by the time Giles was writing, sieges had become a vital part of the way war was fought in both western Europe and the Middle East. The development of siege and counter-siege techniques during the late twelfth and thirteenth centuries was amply justified by and reflected in the space which Giles devoted to the subject. So we find advice given to attackers on how to conduct sieges and what weapons to use, in particular machines and movable towers. Defenders were also given advice: the building of angular walls was encouraged, as were the digging and maintenance of good defensive ditches, the use of machines on the walls, and the all-important provisioning of defensive structures with weapons, as well as food and water. As Giles showed, much Vegetian teaching regarding siege warfare was, with relatively slight modification, still relevant in his own day.

In the final chapter (23) Giles turned briefly to the subject of war at sea. Vegetius was cited once as the authority on a matter, the best time of year to cut wood destined for ship-building.[97] Once again, however, closer inspection enables one to see Giles using the work of Vegetius on at least eight other occasions to provide him with ideas and information, if not with the authority of his name. So Vegetius' ideas on the use of heavy armour by those involved in fighting ('pugnantes', the word suggesting that Giles was uncertain as to whether fighting was done by soldiers or sailors); the use of vases filled with pitch for throwing on to enemy ships; the need to push the enemy ever closer to the shore, while keeping one's own ships in deep water; tricks to deceive and alarm the enemy, and the methods used to immobilise his ships, inspired points made by Giles.[98] The very brevity of the consideration given by Giles to naval affairs strongly suggests that he had neither personal experience nor knowledge of these, nor any real appreciation of the part to be played by naval forces

---

[97] *DRM*, IV, 36.   [98] *Ibid.* IV, 44–6.

in a wider war. That was still to come. A short chapter, therefore, causes no surprise.

None the less, what Giles wrote on waging war was, for its time, important. As already shown, he used and quoted Vegetius as an authoritative source of ideas which, once absorbed, would be incorporated into his work. The impression given is that although it can be shown that he used Vegetian ideas right through those parts of the *De regimine principum* which discussed aspects of war, he acknowledged his debt to his Roman model less and less as his work progressed. We may take it as a sign that Giles was anxious to use Vegetius in a form which he would decide upon to suit his own authorial needs. If Vegetius could sometimes be used as an authority whose standing depended to a large degree upon his classical associations, he could be used more often and more successfully still when he was quietly fitted into Giles' own, late thirteenth-century, discussion regarding war and its role in contemporary society.

For, as Giles was writing, the idea of the royal army based on new premises, advocated by John of Salisbury, described in action by Guillaume le Breton, established as legal principles in Alfonsine Castile, was becoming a reality in certain kingdoms of Europe.[99] It is not surprising that matters discussed by Giles, in particular the role of the army as the defender of the public good under the control of the ruler (who thus gained a quasi-monopoly of military power and activity), should have incorporated ideas taken from Vegetius, who provided him with material relevant and valuable to his discussion.[100] Giles did not regard Vegetius' work as being simply of antiquarian interest. His aim was to try to extract from a classical treatise essential factors which could be useful for his time, and perhaps all time. It was his ability to appreciate this, and his skill in incorporating Vegetian ideas into his own text largely in his own words, which make Giles' use of Vegetius particularly important.[101]

Two further points should be made. Written by a man of the Parisian schools, the *De regimine principum* quickly became a 'texte de faculté', a text for students which the *De re militari*, composed for an altogether different readership at a much earlier date, neither was nor ever would be. In this way, through the incorporation of many of its ideas into the

---

[99] J. Krynen, 'Idéologie et royauté', in *Saint-Denis et la royauté. Études offertes à Bernard Guenée*, ed. F. Autrand, C. Gauvard and J.-M. Moeglin (Paris, 1999), 613.

[100] Norman Housley has emphasised the growth of central control over war during the thirteenth century ('European warfare, *c.* 1200–1320', in *Medieval warfare. A history*, ed. M. Keen (Oxford, 1999), 131, 134). The growing control by the 'state' of the army and the power which it wielded for the public benefit is now seen as part of the growth of the *état moderne* from the thirteenth century onwards.

[101] Sherwood, 'Studies', p. 249.

body of the *De regimine principum*, Vegetius' text would make a further contribution to the discussion concerning the legal and organised use of force by the ruler in the achievement of good government, a major theme in John of Salisbury's *Policraticus*. If John and, now, Giles of Rome recognised the value of what Vegetius had taught for the advancement of their theses, he, in his turn, will have benefited greatly from the publicity of wider readership which they, and the other university-trained men who wrote on government in the years that followed, will have been able to give him. There can be little doubt that the fame earned by Vegetius, and the wide reputation which his work and ideas enjoyed in fourteenth- and fifteenth-century Europe, among both intellectuals and many members of the nobility, owed a great deal to those for whom he had provided ideas and information on the army and the fighting of war, and who carried and extended his reputation more widely than his text, on its own, might ever have done.

We may see this in the evidence provided for us by the contents of a commonplace book written, *c.*1400, by one Guillaume Saignet, who served the French crown as a diplomat for many years before his death in 1441.[102] A man of legal training, Saignet read Giles' work, and decided to copy extracts from it into a book of his own. Not really interested in the work's theoretical aspect ('notions abstraites'), he preferred to copy what was 'concret' and 'utilitaire'. This drew him to the contents of Book III of the *De regimine principum*, in particular to those passages which emphasised the importance of the army. Here he copied extracts from Giles, some of which were citations from Vegetius, or were at least inspired by him. The creation of an army was seen as an act of prudence; one day it would have to defend the general good, or 'bonum commune'. He then went on to copy what Giles had written about (among other things) the way to choose good soldiers; what a soldier should be able to do and how he should be trained; how useful the foot soldier had become; what qualities the commander should demonstrate; and the need for the army to be provided with arms, horses and provisions. He finished off his work with the words: 'These are the more notable ideas set out in the book *De regimine principum* which I have put in writing for memory's sake (Expliciunt conclusiones notabiliores libri nuncupati De regimine principum, quas causa memorie hic redegi). G. Sanheti.' The content of his notes shows that he realised very well that much of what he had copied was owed to Vegetius: 'secundum Vegecium *De re militari*', he wrote at one point.[103] It is difficult not to believe that, like Saignet, others will have

[102] N. Pons, 'Guillaume Saignet, lecteur de Gilles de Rome', *BEC*, 163 (2005), 435–80.
[103] *Ibid.* 477.

owed their knowledge of Vegetius and his work to an intermediary text, in this case one of the best-known political works of the Middle Ages, which could be read in Latin or in one of several languages into which it was translated, thus ensuring the transmission of Vegetian inspiration to a wide public far beyond the schools from which it had emanated.

The literature of crusade

We know that the age of crusades, often regarded as having ended with the fall of Acre in 1291, continued, if not in traditional form, for much longer. A small group of manuscripts of the *De re militari*, associated with the late crusades, the oldest probably copied in France in the 1320s, has recently received scholarly attention.[104] Its chief cause of interest is that Vegetius' work appears to have been copied specifically with the intention of giving support to a revival of crusading activity at a time when the kings of France were planning such an enterprise towards the end of the first quarter of the fourteenth century, planning which led to the compilation of a collection of texts to encourage would-be crusaders.

In BnF lat. 7470, the head of the family of codices which, in the early fifteenth century, would belong to and be annotated (if only slightly) by the French humanist Jean Le Bègue, the *De re militari* is divided into five, rather than the normal four, books. It also includes five illuminations, four of them showing a king, bearing the arms of France and Navarre, leading some knights to war, the fifth depicting a king, again with knights, on board a ship, the illuminations corresponding to the five books of the *De re militari*, whose fifth book (more usually Book IV, chapters 31–46) was concerned with war at sea. It should be noted that each manuscript in this group gives the text five books, thereby giving greater emphasis to what Vegetius had taught regarding the preparation of ships for naval war, a not unreasonable emphasis if the text was to be associated with crusading activity, most of which would take place either at sea or overseas.

To the five books of the *De re militari* the compiler added other matter related to the crusade. One was a small collection of excerpts: *Possumus ad presens*, taken largely from the pseudo-Aristotelian *Secretum Secretorum*, and concerned particularly with naval warfare. This was followed by four texts on the theme of crusade: the *Informacio brevis* of Guillaume Durand, bishop of Mende from 1296 to 1330; the

---

[104] C. Tyerman, 'Philip V of France, the assemblies of 1319–20 and the crusade', *BIHR*, 57 (1984), 28; Tyerman, 'Sed nihil fecit? The last Capetians and the recovery of the Holy Land', in *War and government in the Middle Ages*, ed. J. Gillingham and J. C. Holt (Cambridge and Totowa, 1984), 179–80; Reeve, 'Transmission', 294–97; Rouse and Rouse, 'Context and reception', 105–78.

De preparatoriis circa passagium faciendum, written after 1320; the *Informatio alia* of Garcías de Ayerbe, bishop of León, written between 1317 and 1332; and the *De statu Saracenorum* of the Dominican friar William of Tripoli, written in 1271. These were followed by two tracts composed by Foulques Villaret, Master-General of the Hospitallers, on how the Holy Land could be conquered and retained under Christian control.

These codices, it is argued, did not come together by chance, but were assembled for a purpose, the creation of a dossier compiled to encourage support for the crusade. Commissioned, perhaps, by Pope John XXII (who had a copy of Vegetius' work at Avignon)[105] for presentation to Charles IV, king of France, and, it is suggested, collected under the direction of Guillaume Durand (who, as his text shows, knew the *De re militari*), the content of the dossier, including Vegetius' work, was intended to be seen as a whole. This gave the *De re militari* a new form of existence, indeed a new purpose, as part of a broadly based codex compiled with the aim of persuading the French crown to play an active role in a future crusading enterprise.[106] The unity of the dossier, copied by a single scribe (Peter of Beverley) and illuminated by a single artist (the Wymondswold Master), adds to the sense that the presentation of the dossier reflects the wish of a single mind to make a persuasive case for crusading activity.[107]

As recently demonstrated, the Latin version received at the court of Charles IV was very soon translated into French.[108] All three surviving texts use the translation of the *De re militari* completed by Jean de Meun in 1284, dividing the work into five books. Paris, Bibl. Ste-Geneviève 1654 includes the texts of Guillaume Durand, Garcías de Ayerbe and the Master-General of the Hospitallers; however, neither the *De re militari* nor the tract of William of Tripoli is found in this codex.[109] Bern, Burgerbibliothek 280A, on the other hand, which probably dates from the third quarter of the fifteenth century, thereby suggesting that interest in crusading activity was not yet dead, includes Meun's translation of Vegetius, the tract of William of Tripoli, and the first of the two Hospitaller texts, all copied by a single scribe. In what remains of Vegetius' prologue, the text is brought up to date through the substitution of reference to the contemporary world rather than to Rome and its people, while Meun's spelling and vocabulary, now two centuries old, have been modernised, once again giving the reader the impression of a work with contemporary relevance. The codex also includes Mandeville's *Voyage en*

---

[105] Now Vatican, Vat. lat. 4497.
[106] Rouse and Rouse, 'Context and reception', 113–18.
[107] *Ibid.* 120–1.   [108] *Ibid.* 126–37, 149–61.   [109] *Ibid.* 127, 149–56.

Terre Sainte, Honoré Bouvet's *L'arbre des batailles*, and a work of heraldry, all in French.

Like the manuscript just described, BnF fr. 12,360 dates from the third quarter of the fifteenth century. Including the *De re militari* in Meun's translation, the tracts by Guillaume Durand and William of Tripoli, with part of that by Garcías de Ayerbe, in addition to sections of the first and the entire second Hospitaller tract, it forms the most complete translation into French of the Latin codex compiled for the court of Charles IV, *c*.1323–24.[110] The perceived integration of Vegetius' text into a dossier on the crusade is neatly emphasised on the label added to the manuscript's front cover, 'Vegetius on chivalry and the crusade' ('[V]egece de [la] chevalerie [et] le passage d'oultre [mer]'),[111] which emphasises the recreation of the entire dossier in French, although the order in which the various texts had originally appeared in the Latin was not reproduced in the French version.[112]

Vatican, Reg. lat. 1512, a copy or 'twin' of Paris, BnF lat. 7470, is almost certainly Parisian in origin, probably written between 1323 and 1328 for a member of the royal court. The five illuminations, also by the Wymondswold Master who worked on lat. 7470, depict scenes very similar to those in the other manuscript. The Vatican codex begins 'In the name of the holy and undivided Trinity' ('In nomine sancte et individue Trinitatis'), a formula which suggests a copyist with a notarial training. It contains the *De re militari* in five books, along with the excerpts beginning 'Possumus ad presens'.[113] These two manuscripts are linked in a further, significant way. In Book I, there are some ten instances of the same passage being marked in both manuscripts, which makes it likely that when the text was copied certain marginalia were copied, too. In Book II, although there are fewer annotations, the proportion (almost half) shared by the manuscripts is still high. In Book III, however, while the number of annotations in common is low, in Books IV and V that number is almost identical. If, as suggested, the copyist was a man of notarial training, did he extend his brief to copying not only the text but the existing marginalia as well? These show greater critical interest in Books II, IV and V than is commonly found at this time. The emphasis on siege warfare and on war at sea, found in Books IV and V respectively, hints at the nature of the military venture that was foreseen; a crusade, led by the king of France (strongly suggested by the evidence in the illuminations), would fit the bill. Vegetius' text is followed by a short work on waging war at sea, with an illumination showing the French king in a boat locked to one belonging to the enemy, a drawing of a crossbowman having been added

---

[110] *Ibid.* 134.   [111] *Ibid.* 59–61.   [112] *Ibid.* 34–5.   [113] *Ibid.* 123–6, 144–8.

in the margin. The emphasis placed on the use of fire and sulphur; on the need for archers whose arrows would cut holes in the enemy's sails, thus immobilising him, and on the advantage of having strong sailors is reminiscent of certain passages in the *De re militari*.

Elements of a further member of the textual family, Naples, Biblioteca Nazionale, V. A. 19, link it to the group we are considering. Its references to the French Midi increase the likelihood that, as Michael Reeve has suggested, 'the text of the family was assembled at Avignon', seat of the papacy and very much part of that region of France which experienced war at the hands of either the *routiers* or English armies in the mid-fourteenth century.[114] The manuscript's annotations and drawings, in several hands, show every sign of reflecting contemporary situations and conditions. Next to the recommendation to train soldiers regularly to avoid dependence on foreign mercenaries, someone has written 'Note the remarks made against those waging war in France' ('Nota mirabile verbum contra agentes bella regni Francie'),[115] a finger pointing accusingly at the text in question, which the reader has chosen to apply critically to the prevalence of mercenary activity in France at the time. Indeed, the manuscript reflects many observations and not a little criticism of the way war was fought in that country in the middle years of the fourteenth century. Vegetius' preference for foot soldiers is noted with evident approval, as is the practice of making soldiers swear an oath to their leaders. Similarly Vegetius' critical comments on the large armies of the past are well received. The recommendation that armies should have with them canoes, hollowed out of single trunks, to facilitate river crossings, merits a drawing, as does a reference to cities or walled forts.[116] The strength of an army, whether it lies in infantry or in cavalry, should reflect the terrain on which an encounter is likely to take place: 'Note the statement regarding the people of Nîmes and Lunel' ('Nota contra illos de Nemanso et Lunello'), states a marginal note, perhaps written by the scribe himself, while another note refers to the 'ducem Encastrie', perhaps a reference to the activities of Henry of Derby, duke of Lancaster, in the Midi in the 1350s. It is likely that the text was in southern France, perhaps at Avignon, in the second half of the fourteenth century, its readers regarding many of Vegetius' comments as reflecting the uncertain conditions of the world in which they lived at that time.

What its links with BnF lat. 7470 and Vatican, Reg. lat. 1512 were is not entirely clear. Yet, like these two, it presents the *De re militari* in five

---

[114] Reeve, 'Transmission', 296.   [115] Naples, Naz., V. A. 19, fo. 5v.
[116] Canoes might have been useful in the fast-flowing rivers of the mountainous region of central southern France.

books, the last being given the heading 'Orders for war at sea' ('Precepta belli navalis'). Furthermore, it shares with BnF lat. 7470 an extended and idiosyncratic version of the 'Rules of war', increased from the standard number of thirty-three rules to fifty-four through the addition of short extracts, some of them modified, taken from the text itself. They also share some marginalia, some word for word. Considered together, these strongly suggest a common origin.

Written in the fifteenth century, Glasgow University Library, Gen. 6, 'French and unattractive',[117] may derive perhaps from BnF lat. 7470, perhaps copied from it while that manuscript was in the possession of Jean Le Bègue or of one of the Parisian institutions to which he bequeathed his books. Like the others in this group, this version of the *De re militari* contains five books. The codex also includes three of the tracts which follow Vegetius in the Parisian manuscript: *Possumus ad presens*, the *Informacio brevis* of Guillaume Durand and the *Informacio alia* of Garcías de Ayerbe, all recognised crusading texts. The loss of the first half or so of Book I of the *De re militari*, which might have given us more contemporary information regarding this manuscript, is to be regretted.

A further, late fourteenth-century manuscript, Leiden, Voss. lat. F. 59, probably northern Italian, begins with Frontinus, adds Modestus (sheltering under the name of Cicero) and includes Vegetius in five books. Like the manuscripts in Paris, the Vatican, Naples and Glasgow, it contains the text of the crusading tract *Possumus ad presens*.

Of particular interest in the context of crusade is BnF lat. 7242, a codex of northern Italian origin, which, while in no way connected textually with the group just considered, contains not only Frontinus and Vegetius but also the *Liber recuperationis terre sancte* of the Franciscan Fidenzio da Padova, dedicated to Pope Nicholas IV (1288–92), and the curious allegory *De re bellica spirituali* of the Augustinian hermit Bartolomeo da Urbino, written perhaps a generation or so later. This very fine manuscript is written in the same hand throughout, with the art work in similar style, thus emphasising the striking unity of the different parts of a text which once belonged to the Visconti collection, part of which was brought to Paris by Louis XII of France in 1500.[118]

The illuminations are clearly intended to underline the military character of the volume's contents. A soldier offers a book to a scholar, who is seated, thus underlining the message that the art of war can be taught through the written word. Knights on horseback come to meet a king

---

[117] Reeve, 'Transmission', 295.
[118] See E. Pellegrin, *La bibliothèque des Visconti et des Sforza, ducs de Milan, au XVe siècle* (Paris, 1955).

or prince standing at the top of some steps; he carries a book in his left hand as a symbol of his learning (a theme emphasised by Vegetius). At the beginning of Book II we find a depiction of a mounted knight bearing an ensign of a white cross on a red background; at Book III is a small initial of a soldier looking upwards, hands held up in prayer; while Book IV shows two knights on foot, with swords, along with a soldier carrying a shield. At IV, 31 (the point where Book IV turns to consider naval war) an initial letter 'P'[raecepto] shows the bow of a boat with an oarsman, behind whom stands a knight or soldier, once again bearing the arms of a white cross on a red background.[119] Probably on account of the richness of its character, the text itself has been scarcely touched at all. On folios 50v and 51 a small number of marginalia suggest some interest in Roman military organisation, but nothing more.

In this context, the *Liber recuperationis terre sancte* merits serious consideration. Addressed to the pope in the form of a plan for the recovery of the Holy Land, it reflected the writer's personal experience of conflict between Christian and Muslim forces. The task ahead, he emphasised, would not be easy; the enemy had skilful archers, who practised their skills 'from infancy into old age'. Their horsemen, too, were accustomed to fighting with a sword, and they were superior to Christians when it came to war at sea. With his own eyes the author had observed how well ordered the enemy's forces were. Christians would have to maintain a continuous war on both land and sea; they would require skill, determination and shrewdness of character, in addition to numbers (cavalry in particular), if they were to defeat the enemy. That they must be 'skilled in war' suggests a writer who might have read Vegetius, since he then explained what their experience ('peritia') should mean in practice. Soldiers should be properly armed ('decenter armati'), referring to the adequate provision of both arms and protective armour; they must be trained to fight together ('bene ordinati'); and they should all work with a common purpose ('ad unionem dispositi'). Such advice bore the hallmark of a writer aware of points raised by Vegetius: the need for proper protection for the soldier; the practice required to act in a disciplined manner; the difficulties to be encountered if there were no unity of purpose among the troops, for 'where there is no order, there is only confusion' ('ubi non est ordo, ibi est confusio').

The author made a number of other points which, although supported by texts taken from the Scriptures, may well owe their inspiration to Vegetius. One, to which he returned a number of times, was the need for the Christian army to act as a single body, in spite of the diversity

---

[119] BnF lat. 7242, fos. 1 (Frontinus), 41v, 48v, 56, 72, 79 (Vegetius).

of its origins. This was a difficulty which Vegetius had recognised, and which was reflected in Petrarch's description of the problems faced by Hannibal when he encountered the Roman army at Zama. It explains the author's reiterated recommendation that the army should have a unity of command, which must be the responsibility of one man, whose qualities as a leader were set out in chapters 49–57, and referred to in chapters 23, 48 and 92. More than once, too, the recommendation was made (and it was one based on both the work of Vegetius and growing contemporary experience) that cavalry should be trained and ready to fight with infantry among its numbers: 'cavalry should always have crossbowmen or archers among them . . . the Christian cavalry must take care not to forsake their archers' ('semper debent equites habere ballistarios vel sagittarios multos secum inmixtos . . . Caveant etiam equites Xristiani ne ipsi deserant pedites suos'). Archers, if they were present in sufficient number, might also be employed as units acting on their own. The author recommended that Christian foot soldiers learn the skills of archery, and that they be properly protected, with either 'arma' (?shields) or 'vestimenta' (?aketons), from the effects of enemy archery.

The text also considered the need for proper defences and fortifications. Leaders were urged to build these in places to which supplies could be brought, and which had access to plenty of water. This was said to be done by the Muslims; it was also central to Vegetius' advice on how and where to build camps. The defence of the camp was also considered: ditches should be dug, the watch carefully kept, and arms stored close by, always at the ready. The Tatars were said to do these things; the advice certainly corresponded to that offered by Vegetius. The author emphasises that spies should be constantly maintained to inform Christian leaders what the Muslims were doing: chapter 33 is given over to the subject; the importance of being well informed about the enemy's movements had received much emphasis from Vegetius. In chapter 87 the author told his readers about the skills and weaknesses of the Muslim army. It was as though he was a spy preparing those on his own side regarding what they might expect from the enemy.

Finally there was advice to give on war at sea, on ships (in this case on galleys) and on the keeping of the sea. One has a sense that the author had taken some of the main points in Vegetius' work and used them for his own purposes. Towards the end he returned to a crucial matter: in an army composed of different elements, it was necessary to have one good leader in overall charge ('presidentia unius boni capitis semper necessaria'). Leadership was vital, as Vegetius had insisted. Man should not rely on God to do the difficult work for him. Half a century later, Honoré Bouvet would express very much the same idea: 'although the

King of France may have a good cause against the King of England, yet he must not trust in God without doing what in him lies, by diligence, and by taking good counsel, to overcome the enemy. When he has done what he can, wisely and discreetly, then for the rest that lies beyond his power he must put his whole hope in God.'[120]

The final text in the manuscript, *De re bellica spirituali*, a discussion of war at an allegorical level, included quotations from a number of classical and medieval writers: Vegetius, Valerius Maximus, Sallust, Lucan, Cato, Frontinus, Augustine and Giles of Rome. Near the beginning of the work the author named Vegetius, whom he then cited with references, as the source of the statement that it was valuable to be familiar with ('scire') the art of war since men would not trouble those whom they knew to be worldly-wise regarding fighting ('in pugna sagaces'). Who could doubt that the cause of liberty was actively advanced by familiarity with the arts of war? This was why the Spartans and the Romans taught their young men to fight, a point which the author backed up approvingly with a quotation from Valerius Maximus on peace. Claiming that the achievement of peace depended not on numbers but on the skills of the army, he argued that, as peace grew, so did respect for the 'disciplina militaris' which had brought it about, and for the soldier who practised it. Echoing Vegetius, he asked what could be better for the common good than a good soldier or a good judge? Proper selection procedures and training played a vital part in creating such a man.

At this point the author referred unashamedly to the arguments contained early in the *De re militari* regarding the physical qualities and factors likely to make a good soldier. But he soon returned to his underlying theme of the soldier's contribution to society. 'As Vegetius taught in his first book, ch. 13, the best, most stable society has many trained soldiers at hand: it is fear of our arms, not wealth and riches, which earns the respect of the enemy, and deters him from attacking.' Trained soldiers would achieve victory quickly and (an interesting and significant argument) this will save money, an idea to be repeated shortly afterwards. In a further passage calculated to support this line of thought he cited Vegetius to the effect that it cost less to train one's own men than to hire foreign mercenaries.

The attributes and skills of the good soldier were the chief preoccupation of the writer at this point. Although he cited Valerius Maximus, Frontinus and Livy, it was Vegetius who gave direction to what he was emphasising: the speed needed to surprise and outwit the enemy; the

---

[120] *L'arbre des batailles d'Honoré Bonet*, ed. E. Nys (Brussels and Leipzig, 1883), IV, 49, p. 144; *The Tree of Battles of Honoré Bonet*, trans. G. W. Coopland (Liverpool, 1949), 155.

physical training, reflected in running, jumping and carrying of burdens, along with the skills required to use a variety of weapons, including the valuable art of swimming, whose importance was underlined by a story recorded by Valerius Maximus, and the value of the horsemen, who relied much on careful training – all these texts were of a piece in justifying the careful selection and preparation of the soldier for war. Citing Vegetius once again, the author reminded the reader that the safety of the state depended on the army. Its size was of little importance; a small force of well-trained men, fighting on behalf of all, could achieve remarkable things. Properly prepared and motivated, the army stood for the good of society, above all for its freedom.

It is evident that the author, Bartolomeo da Urbino, knew Vegetius' text well, jumping with confidence from one part of it to another, picking up themes and weaving strands, his approach leading to a good overall understanding of the main elements of Vegetian thought, while underlining the fact that Vegetius' text was more than a collection of memorable sayings. On a limited yet significant scale, Bartolomeo did Vegetius a considerable service. Unlike many of the passages noted in the margins of manuscripts of the complete text of the *De re militari*, those chosen by this author concentrated on the positive contribution of the army and the soldier to society, and so were given a unity which those simply marked in manuscript marginalia so often lacked. This was the work of someone who had grasped the nature of Vegetius' main themes, and whose reading had enabled him to locate texts important to them, thereby giving certain ideas greater significance in relation to both the text and the military needs of his own day, as he perceived them.

In spite of the work's tendency towards repetition, the reader is impressed by certain of its characteristics. An important one is the way the author, clearly well versed in the military literature of the ancient world, made use of quotations from Frontinus and Valerius Maximus (in particular) in his attempt to underline points best illustrated from the ancient writers. Whereas Fidenzio da Padova, a churchman like him, supported his views with copious quotations from the Bible, Bartolomeo da Urbino cited only the best classical authors when looking for supporting textual evidence. This had the effect of making his argument more credible, bolstered as it was by the evidence of history. So, in the search for an effective army, the emphasis was placed on the need for leadership and on the necessity (discussed at far greater length) of choosing good soldiers and of training them well. The manner in which this was done, by bringing together complementary passages from different parts of the *De re militari*, showed the author's familiarity with and understanding of the text's main themes, and of the way they interacted with increasing effectiveness as the work progressed, in particular when supported by the evidence of other classical writers. It is evident that Vegetius was being edited and, to an extent, rewritten to serve the purposes of a later age.

Christine de Pisan

We may now turn to consider parts of the *oeuvre* of Christine de Pisan, one of the most notable and prolific writers living in France in the first quarter of the fifteenth century when she earned both a living and a reputation writing to satisfy the demands of royal and noble patrons. Christine lived at a time both of civil discord and of outright war between France and England. Reacting to the inherent instability of French society in her day, she was prompted to write in many forms on a wide variety of subjects, and in so doing contributed to the intellectual discussion, much of it encouraged by royal and noble patrons, regarding the best way to achieve peace and re-establish effective monarchical rule in France. Not surprisingly, her search for and advocacy of peace obliged her to turn her attention to war, a subject on which, she admitted, it was unlikely that a woman would express herself in writing.

Born in Italy, the daughter of an astrologer who had come to work at the court of France, at that time ruled by Charles V (1364–80), Christine grew up French in her cultural and political attitudes. Yet she was profoundly influenced by the revival of classical learning which emanated from the land of her birth, so that she is now classed among the early humanists who worked and flourished at the French court in the dying years of the fourteenth and the first decades of the fifteenth century. The ancient world, the message implicitly and explicitly stated in much of what Christine wrote, had much to offer French society as it passed through some of the most difficult years of its recent history.

The attention which Christine gave to war was prompted by further factors. One was her firm belief in the effectiveness of the written word as a means of preparing those entering the profession of arms before they encountered the reality towards which their calling would take them: 'it is right to know about knowledge in its written form, which makes men want to learn how things work out in practice' ('est chose pertinent à sçavoir la science escripre, qui les induise avec l'experience à sçavoir la practique'). She recognised that all, whatever art they practised, had once been beginners, knowing little or nothing about their particular profession. It was to instruct them that she was writing, thus enabling them to acquire some theoretical knowledge before moving on to become practical masters of the art ('maistres d'ycelle art'). And even the most experienced could not carry all that they needed to know in their minds.

A book in which information and advice was stored would help them recall good practice. And if accused of offering nothing new, she claimed to provide the bricks with which a sound military structure could be built. Men should not be worried that this was being written by a woman. It was not the messenger, but the message, based on experience, that was important.[121]

Compelled to discuss war, Christine, like many others both before and after her, turned to Vegetius for inspiration and instruction. Three of her works in particular, written over the years 1404–10, give an insight into the use Christine made of Vegetian teachings. The *Livre des fais et bonnes meurs du sage roy Charles V*, written in 1404 at the request of Philip, duke of Burgundy, the late king's brother, was not only the study of the subject's rule but an attempt, too, by using examples, to set out the ideals of both kingship and 'chevalerie'. As befitted a biography of a king in whose reign the fortunes of France in its conflict against England had been greatly revived, it was right that the success should be both recorded and accounted for. Christine had little difficulty in explaining that revival. She depicted Charles V as a king who, because of uncertain health, took no active part in war, but none the less proved himself to be a fine leader. Such an image of an inspiring ruler fitted in well with the ideas of Vegetius' analysis of the characteristics and qualities of effective leadership. The picture of Charles which emerged was of a man with a deep sense of responsibility towards his people – the very Christian image of the shepherd and his flock recorded, notably, in St John's gospel[122] – aware that his armies required the best possible leadership in war, and of his obligation to find the right people to provide it, as well as of the need to encourage order and discipline in war in a country in which the military virtues (at least the Roman ones) were not widely practised.

Emphasis upon the requirements of leadership enabled Christine to lay stress on the achievements of Bertrand du Guesclin, whom Charles V named constable of France in 1370. The appointment could be related to Vegetian principles in a number of ways. While underlining the kingdom's need for leadership of the very highest quality, it was seen as the justified reward given to a soldier who had risen through his practice of the military skills and virtues. Furthermore, in showing that, once appointed, the constable had chosen men with care 'from among both the nobility and the less exalted sort, as seemed right to him' ('tant de gentilz hommes comme de ce qu'il lui convenoit de gent de commune'), it stressed the Vegetian principle that an army should include men of a variety of backgrounds and experience working together. In the context of the transmission of

---

[121] *Charles V*, I, 190–2.   [122] Jn, 10.

Vegetius' ideas, the form and content of *Charles V* is of some interest. In a number of instances Christine used the main theme of a chapter to introduce the reader to Vegetius' ideas on the matter. Thus, to the account of how du Guesclin was elected constable were added, seamlessly, principles to be followed when considering the choice of new war leaders, principles taken not directly from the *De re militari* but from the *Livre du regime des princes*, the French translation of Giles of Rome's *De regimine principum*, which closely reflected Vegetius' ideas on the matter.[123] In the following chapter, having described the celebrations which accompanied this promotion, Christine recalled how du Guesclin had selected his soldiers with great care, ensuring that they were drawn from occupations accustomed to hard, physical labour and those, such as butchers, not afraid to see blood spilled. Christine rarely quoted Vegetius directly; rather, his ideas were transmitted by proxy. In chapter XXXVI, having briefly reported how Philip of Burgundy had captured some towns near Calais, Christine went on to discuss matters of defence, including a series of instructions on the best ways of self-defence taken from Giles,[124] who had paraphrased the first nine chapters (omitting chapter 6) of Book IV of the *De re militari*, more or less in the order in which Vegetius had written them. Likewise, chapter XXXIII, which began by drawing the reader's attention to the recovery of much of Guyenne by French forces largely through the capture of castles, led directly to a discussion of ways in which opposing forces might confront each other: in the field, in the assault on a castle, in active defence by the garrison, and in war at sea.

Here we witness a small but not insignificant change in the way Vegetian ideas and teaching were being applied. Christine was not necessarily using these at first hand. Rather, her use of them as they had been made to bolster and illustrate the work of Giles of Rome, a text more concerned with political practice than with war per se, should remind the reader that what Christine passed on in the way of Vegetian inspiration had already been filtered by Giles, although he still gave her clear résumés of what Vegetius had advised.

Written probably some two years later, in 1406, the *Livre du corps de policie* also reflected something of the condition and perceived needs of the time. Based on the model of the mirror for princes, it owed much to the *Policraticus* of John of Salisbury, in particular in the manner in which the body politic was depicted, the arms and hands being used to describe society's military caste. The direct references to Vegetius appear to be only some five in number; yet, once again, there are passages suggestive of his thinking. As in *Charles V*, Christine was concerned to

---

[123] *Charles V*, I, 184–7.   [124] *DRP*, III, 20.

provide France with the best possible army. She cited Vegetius to the effect that men accustomed to hard work would usually do well bearing arms, an idea which she had already expressed in the earlier work. At the same time, in a wide-ranging discussion on leadership (a subject she had treated before) she referred a number of times (although only once *nominatim*) to the *De re militari* when she urged good military leaders to be both wise and ready to receive advice regarding their work.[125] In the *Livre de policie*, II, 9, Christine dealt with the desirable characteristics of soldiers and their leaders, concentrating on the virtues which make men noble. They should love arms and the practice of them; they must be bold and never run away or fear to suffer death for the general good of all ('pour le bien de leur prince et la garde de leur pays et de la chose publique'); they should be able to give encouragement and confidence to one another; their oath of loyalty must be maintained at all times; they should love honour above all worldly things; and they should be wise and subtle ('saiges et cauteleux') in all their dealings with arms and with the enemy. Such characteristics, as described in this early fifteenth-century text, reflected the general tenor of Vegetius' proposals.

It was in the *Livre des fais d'armes et de chevalerie*, a work in four parts on the art of war and the military law written in 1410, that Christine made the greatest use of Vegetius, probably using the translation made by Jean de Vignay. The *De re militari* dominates Book I; in Book II it shares the honours with Frontinus, whose *Strategemata* was known to Christine through the commentary which accompanied the translation by Simon de Hesdin, and completed by Nicolas de Gonesse, of Valerius Maximus' *Facta et dicta memorabilia*, in particular Book VI; while Books III and IV were based on the *Arbre des batailles* of Honoré Bouvet, written *c.*1389. As in most of her works (and notably so in *Charles V*) Christine showed herself to be in tune with some of the major political issues of her day. Writing at a time when France was split into factions over basic issues of good rule and government, divisions which had led to the assassination of Louis of Orléans in 1407 and debate over tyrannicide, her work reflected great concern for the need to re-establish order and the observance of the law in French society through the exercise of royal authority. In this, the proper regulation of armed force would have its part to play.

It is evident that Christine had much sympathy for Vegetius' view that, if written down, the achievements of the past would last for ever to the advantage of the common good. Her use of Vegetius was therefore based both on the intrinsic value of what he had written (from which, she

---

[125] *Le livre du corps de policie*, ed. R. H. Lucas (Geneva and Paris, 1967), I, 22; II, 9, both reflecting *DRM*, III, 6, 9, 26.

clearly felt, her generation had much to learn) and on her determination to convey his authoritative ideas and teachings to future generations, albeit in a modified form. This could be done in two ways. One was the use which she made, particularly in Book I of the *Fais d'armes*, of ideas drawn from the first three books of the *De re militari*. This book showed Christine's ability to use Vegetius' teachings but in such a way that she created her own work and her own message.[126] Book II of the *Fais d'armes* demonstrated the use of the other modification, namely the author basing herself solely on Book IV of the *De re militari* as she dealt first with Vegetius' material on siege warfare more or less in the order in which he had set it out and then, all too briefly, with the last chapters of that book concerned with naval warfare. Whereas in her consideration of siege warfare Christine had material to add to bring her presentation up to date, her short consideration of war at sea lacked originality and conviction.

Even when writing to a great extent of Book I of the *Fais d'armes*, Christine returned to themes already discussed in *Charles V* and, in some cases, in the *Livre du corps de policie*. As Vegetius had done, so Christine warned against fortune in war, insisting that conflict and battle, above all things, must be conducted with good judgement, adding her favourite caution, taken from Vegetius (in this instance citing Cato), that mistakes made in battle cannot be rectified.[127] The pursuit of this line of thought caused Christine to repeat that, in spite of certain advantages to be gained from their doing so in cases such as the suppression of rebellion, when their personal authority was in question, kings should not play an active part in war. Instead, they should appoint others to assume their military responsibilities. As in *Charles V*, this led to a discussion of the factors influencing the choice of the deputy called, in this instance, the constable.[128] Her concern was the importance of selecting a leader fit to occupy military office with extensive responsibilities. In so doing, she emphasised the qualifications, including practical experience of war, which he should have. Acting under direct royal authority, the constable (in particular) must be responsible, according to the oath of fealty he had taken, for preparing the defences of the country, ensuring that its army

---

[126] This last point emerges from F. Le Saux, 'War and knighthood in Christine de Pizan's *Livre des faits d'armes et de chevallerie*', in *Writing war. Medieval literary responses to warfare*, ed. C. Saunders, F. Le Saux and N. Thomas (Cambridge, 2004). See also the remarks of Wakelin, *Humanism, reading and English literature*, 82–3.

[127] *DRM*, I, 13. This idea occurs in both the *Fais d'armes*, I, 7, and the *Livre du corps de policie*, II, 9, where the need for a reasoned approach to war is also advocated, part of the intellectualisation of war which Christine wished to encourage (Le Saux, 'War and knighthood', 97).

[128] Largely in *Fais d'armes*, I, 7.

was well led, with an established chain of command. He had obligations, too, to ensure the wellbeing of the army: it is remarkable how, following Vegetius, Christine emphasised the responsibilities of the *dux* for the good of individual soldiers and their particular needs. Another group of chapters dealt with the need for society as a whole to acquire at least a minimum of military skills. Christine argued that young noblemen must be properly trained to serve their king in war; this was the education of a nobility facing up to its responsibilities to the king and society as a whole. In the following chapter, she urged that military skills be also taught to the common people. Vegetius, she argued, made no distinction between social groups, so his ideas should be applied to all who shared the obligations of defence. So it was that she moved the discussion towards the training of archers and slingers, who should be given time to practise the skills they required.

Further chapters dealt with the practicalities of waging campaigns, including the use of stratagems and surprise urged by Vegetius.[129] The acquisition of information regarding the enemy was, as ever, given emphasis, for it was this which enabled the commander to act with prudence. Various troop movements, including retreats, were dealt with: battle formations and the particular attention to be given to soldiers as conflict became imminent were duly emphasised, as was the need to plan the provision of reliable food supplies. In every case the inspiration of the *De re militari* was evident.

As already indicated, the nature of Book II of the *Fais d'armes* was rather different, with Vegetius, almost the sole authority cited in Book I, sharing the limelight with Frontinus. At chapter 14, however, he began to come more into his own with a series of chapters dealing with aspects of siege warfare: first three[130] on the building and provisioning of castles; followed by two[131] on aspects of how to press a siege 'according to Vegetius'; finally, four[132] on aspects of defence. In these chapters, little attempt was made to resume what Vegetius had written in the final book of the *De re militari* concerning siege warfare, one chapter following another in the original order, interspersed with the odd chapter on recent practice.[133] Such updating was mainly concerned with the development of modern techniques and, in particular, weaponry, and the possibilities which these

---

[129] On this matter, see D. Whetham, *Just wars and moral victories. Surprise, deception and the normative framework of European war in the later Middle Ages* (Leiden and Boston, 2009), 136–49.

[130] *Fais d'armes*, II, 14, 15, 17.   [131] *Ibid.* II, 20, 35.

[132] *Ibid.* II, 36–9.   [133] E.g., *ibid.* II, 16, 21, 22.

had opened up. The outcome was a work which mixed the old with the new, in which the greatest emphasis was placed on the 'constants' of war: the influence (good as well as bad) which human activity had upon success or failure; the need for order and discipline, vital manifestations of 'the Roman culture of restraint'; the necessity of promoting only the very best to positions of responsibility in the army; and the eternal need for vigilance and forethought in a battle of minds as well as of bodies. When we might have expected to find much on physical skills and prowess, as well as on the glamour of war, the absence of vocabulary giving that emphasis underlines the fact that this was intended as a work which was building upon the (by now) increasingly strong intellectual approach to war. Christine's knight knew not only how to use weapons effectively. More important, and more significantly, he knew 'when and in what manner he should do so'.[134] These, among other features and characteristics, were what an intelligent woman, well read in the classics, anxious to prove their relevance to conditions and circumstances in her own time, had found in the work of Vegetius.

Christine wrote principally for her own day; the problems for which she proposed solutions were of that time. In different works she discussed different problems, but the three texts considered had much in common, for they shared a single aim: the restoration of peace and order in France under the rule and guidance of the monarchy. They underlined the way that the *De re militari* was yet again being used to bolster and justify the use of the ruler's military power at a time of division within his country. Solutions to the problems caused by the ineffectiveness of monarchy under Charles VI, king since 1380, could be sought in examples taken from the inspiring life of his father, the much admired Charles V. The monarchy must reassert itself, not least by the way the war against England should be conducted. If the king did not lead in person, then he must appoint lieutenants who merited confidence to act in his name; he must be ready, too, to seek and accept advice, for, in the end, victories were achieved not by luck but by judgement and experience. In the work of Christine we have a further example of the politicisation of Vegetius' text, a process begun by John of Salisbury, continued by Alfonso X and by Giles of Rome, and now carried on by Christine. War could never be studied in a vacuum; it had to be seen against a much wider background, as a means of achieving an end which was not always primarily, or simply, a military one.

---

[134] Le Saux, 'War and knighthood', p. 97.

Jean Juvénal des Ursins

The political works of Jean Juvénal des Ursins (1388–1473), bishop of Beauvais and Laon and, finally, archbishop of Reims, adviser to two kings of France, Charles VII (to whom these works were addressed) and Louis XI, contain many ideas regarding military practice and the creation of the royal army which may be attributed to the broad inspiration of ancient Rome in general and to Vegetius in particular. Exercising his first episcopal charge at a time when France was at war with England, and over a see whose territory straddled the boundary dividing French rule from that usurped by the English, the new bishop's view of society was to be coloured by division among his flock, the almost total failure of the French royal authority to exercise power and, as a result, a world dominated by violence visited upon persons and property by the soldiers of both sides.

The plight of France, seen in microcosm in the diocese of Beauvais and the surrounding country, was set out most graphically in the text of *Loquar in tribulatione*, probably written as an address intended for the meeting of the Estates of France planned for Bourges early in 1440, but which never took place. Recent attempts at peacemaking had proved fruitless. Juvénal feared for the ability of the French people to preserve their unity if peace were to come through the road of negotiation; the spectrum of continued civil division and disorder was ever present. On the other hand, war would unite the people and enable the king to reassert his authority over the soldiers serving him. By waging war with strategy, peace and order would be achieved: 'if you are looking for a lasting peace, be ready to make war; and if you are hoping for victory, then prepare your soldiers well' ('se voulez avoir bonne paix et la desirez, preparés vous a faire bonne guerre, et se voulez avoir victoire, garnissez bien voz gens de guerre').[135]

Although a loyal supporter of the Valois monarchy, Juvénal had a certain admiration for the relative degree of order found in areas controlled by the English. For reasons which are significant, he was not afraid to praise the enemy's military system. The English, he maintained, obeyed their leaders; they were united and skilled in arms; they had a cavalry capable of dealing a quick blow to their enemy before retreating; their infantry, too, could do the same, being ready to work and to die together. Recent military events had demonstrated the effectiveness and spirit of the English army. What could the French offer in opposition? Numbers,

---

[135] *Écrits politiques de Jean Juvénal des Ursins*, ed. P. S. Lewis (3 vols., SHF, Paris, 1978–92), vol. I, 395–8, 408.

certainly, but whether they were such good fighters was doubtful. Brave men, certainly, but the English had these, too. The French, it was generally said, were good at pillaging and robbing the people, the English more skilful in the various arts of war ('a faire guerre en toutes manieres'). The king, Juvénal told him, should not boast of being stronger than his enemies. If he thought that strength decided the outcome of wars, the Bible should make him think otherwise (Paralipomenon, II, 25, 8). Rather, as Vegetius taught, victory came to those with skill acquired and maintained through practice. It was this, not strength, which distinguished the soldier from the civilian. For this reason, the enemy, powerful and accustomed to submitting his men to daily training, should be feared. It was no good, he added, sending men unsuited for war ('pas du mestier') to attack the English. They lacked the necessary 'courage' and will to be victorious.[136]

Returning to the theme of division within France, Juvénal was able to emphasise the lack of what he termed 'la discipline de chevallerie', which must be based on a willingness to obey a single leader and his subordinates, whom the king would appoint. This would be the means of achieving the degree of unity which constituted the strength of the enemy. The Romans, he emphasised, had relied upon discipline and a sense of obedience; today's men would obey neither the king nor his constable. Citing Vegetius on the oath taken by the new 'miles' to obey, and to be ready to die for the common good, Juvénal wrote that the term 'milites' should now be applicable to all who fought ('se doyvent entendre toutes gens de guerre'), who must obey their leaders and be willing to die for the good of society. Without this discipline, there could be no progress.[137]

In this discussion Juvénal cited the ideas of Vegetius some four or five times. When he returned to the theme of military force a dozen or so years later, he drew even more on the Roman's thinking. In 1452, by which time his treatise *Verba mea* had been written, the situation in France had changed. The *francs-archers* had been created, as had the *compagnies d'ordonnance*, all under the command of the crown. Indeed, it might be said that the king, having risen to the challenge of *Loquar in tribulatione*, had created the nucleus of a royal army, which had expelled the English from Normandy. However, peace was not yet fully achieved, and the need to defend the common good still remained.

In a long section of *Verba mea*, Juvénal discussed the army which France needed. In the light of the adverse criticisms made in *Loquar in tribulatione*, it was clear that there were still many problems to be faced. From

---

[136] *Ibid.* I, 401–3; II, 237–9.   [137] *Ibid.* I, 410–11.

what part of society should the army be drawn? Juvénal favoured no particular group: all could contribute, provided that they were suitable. Such
Vegetian ideas were followed by others. Success depended upon having
an army drawn from men maintained in a state of constant training, since
skill, which resulted from such training, told over strength.[138] It also provided men with experience. Juvénal's main problem was that of finding
captains who would be obeyed, for he needed to draw these from among
those practised in war. Once again, he showed himself influenced by
Vegetius: promotion to positions of responsibility and command would
come to those who had varied experience behind them; as a qualifica-
tion, birth should be less important. In all events, the choice of leaders
had to be very carefully made; nothing could be more Vegetian than this
advice.[139] Regarding the objection that war was not for 'le peuple commun' (but, by implication, for the superior classes), Juvénal insisted that
during his time as bishop of Beauvais he had known men from humble
backgrounds experienced in war who often did as well as others because
they were accustomed to the hard life, a passage clearly reflecting passages in Book I of the *De re militari*,[140] a point which Juvénal himself
recognised. Misquoting Valerius Maximus for Vegetius, he listed trades
(e.g., carpenters, masons) recommended by Vegetius for their physical
strength, adding that they, too, had a place in the army, as the king had
recognised when he had drawn many into the new force of *francs-archers*
created in 1439. What counted was not so much who constituted an army
as how well its members were trained. Again citing Valerius for Vegetius,
he reassured his readers that a country with a well-trained army was a
fortunate one.[141] Even pages who accompanied their masters and simply
observed how things should be done received a good training.[142]

Although Juvénal recognised that those of knightly background would
have had greater experience in the use of arms, his remarks on
'chevalerye' were to apply to all, of whatever status. There were, of course,
'diverses chevaleries': Juvénal was addressing the 'moyenne', the middle-
rankers of the army, those who were knights. Their position, he told them
citing the *Policraticus* of John of Salisbury, was one of both honour and
hard work, a notion based on the *De re militari*.[143] Knights and nobility
constituted the kingdom's hands, to protect the body and defend the
head, the royal person. Through the *Policraticus*, he again cited Vegetius
to the effect that on the proper selection of knights depended the entire
state. So the very greatest care must be taken to choose suitable men, as
the demands made of them would be considerable.

---

[138] *Ibid*, II, 237; I, 403.   [139] *DRM*, I, 7.   [140] *Ibid*. I, 3, in particular.
[141] *Ibid*. I, 13.   [142] *Écrits*, II, 236–40.   [143] *DRM*, I, 7; *Policraticus*, VI, 8.

It followed from this that training was as important for Juvénal as it had been for Vegetius, who was cited more than once to underline the point.[144] Training was the best way of maintaining discipline on the battlefield; it also increased loyalty and gave confidence to an army.[145] It led to the development of obedience, which Juvénal had noted as being one of the characteristics which the French army lacked. He cited Vegetius on the need for recruits to practise advancing in line when ordered to do so, and he praised those commanders who taught their men to obey through the routine of training rather than out of fear of punishment.[146]

This brings us to leadership, as important for Juvénal as it had been for Vegetius. The personality of the leader, along with his ability to inspire by both word and example, remained crucial; the king was recommended to dismiss those who did not come up to a high inspirational standard. Facing the old dilemma of whether or not the king should go to war in person, Juvénal, aware that King John II had been taken prisoner at Poitiers in 1356, agreed that he should not. After all, King Charles V, while not fighting in person, had won a great reputation through his 'understanding, moderation and courage' ('sens, prudence et couraige'). The king, Juvénal argued, should use reliable deputies ('bons executeurs') such as the notable captains, Bertrand du Guesclin, Olivier de Clisson and Louis de Sancerre, all constables of France. Significant here is the manner in which Juvénal presumed that it was the king's right and duty to take charge of the army; his responsibility, too, to appoint deputies to act in his name. In the manner advocated by Vegetius, leadership was increasingly exercised by commission, by royal command.[147]

Significant, too, are the things which Juvénal wrote about the way war should be fought. Vegetius had insisted that everything should be done to defeat the enemy with the least physical effort and risk, by using information obtained by spies, and ensuring that nothing was done to give the enemy an advantage. His insistence on the cerebral qualities required of a commander was taken up and developed by Juvénal. The need to surprise an enemy by attacking him from a hidden position; the need, too, to sow division among his members, emphasising the effectiveness of self-destruction, and the imperative of not allowing the enemy to strike the first blow, were all referred to by Juvénal.[148] Such bits of advice from Vegetius were among those offered in the

---

[144] *Écrits*, II, 237, 250, looking back to *DRM*, I, 1.   [145] *Écrits*, I, 408.
[146] *Ibid.* II, 253, citing *DRM*, I, 26. See, too, *DRM*, III, 4, on the need for 'tough' training.
[147] *Écrits*, II, 226–8. See below, 'Statist army', on this matter.
[148] *Ibid.* II, 255–6, 229, citing *DRM*, III, 9, 10.

hope of bringing victory to the king's armies, thereby restoring peace to France.

Finally, with the English now having only a foothold in France, what was to be done about the army? Should it be retained at great cost to the people, or disbanded as no longer required?[149] Although recognising that if they did not maintain their training, soldiers would not be effective in any future emergency, Juvénal none the less appeared to accept the Roman notion that soldiers did not have to serve full time; it was legitimate for a soldier to perform some other manual occupation as well, a point implied in the acceptance of the idea[150] that men with such skills and those accustomed to bearing heavy burdens made very acceptable soldiers. These skills enabled them to earn a living when their services as soldiers were not required. However, the leisure accorded to part-time soldiers would give men the chance to lead lives of idleness and dissipation, failing to maintain their training in arms, to the detriment of the poor. How to reconcile the need to keep men trained and exercised, while letting them return home when their sevices were not needed, was a problem which would also face Jean de Bueil when he came to write his *Jouvencel* a few years later. The difficulty seemed insoluble.[151]

The Burgundian military ordinances, *c*.1470

The rise and fall of the Valois duchy of Burgundy, a process central to the history of western Europe between 1360 and 1480, was closely linked to the duchy's military history and, not least, to the interest of the last duke, Charles the Bold (d.1477), in the Roman military writers and the practical lessons he hoped to learn from them. The duke shared these interests with many. The libraries of members of the Burgundian and Flemish nobility reflected the advice offered, for instance, by Ghillebert de Lannoy in his *Enseignements paternels* (1440) that noblemen should seek to emulate the exemplars of antiquity. A generation later Philippe de Commynes would virtually repeat Lannoy's call when he claimed that it was through reading the ancient histories, and what they had to teach, that man acquired wisdom.[152]

Such advice was particularly apt for a ruler. Reading the ancients could be compared to receiving the counsel which Vegetius thought every commander should seek from those more experienced than he. The process of

---

[149] 'Se l'ordonnance des gens d'armes se doit continuer, ou non' (*Écrits*, II, 261).
[150] Strongly supported in *DRM*, I, 7.
[151] See C. Allmand, 'Entre honneur et bien commun: le témoignage du *Jouvencel* au XVe siècle', *RH*, 301 (1999), 477–8.
[152] Vale, *War and chivalry*, ch. 1.

encouraging the translation of classical and humanistic works had already begun during the reign of Duke Philip the Good (1419–67) and, under his son Charles, it would be developed in a positively didactic direction.[153] By 1467, the Burgundian court possessed two copies of Jean de Vignay's French translation of the *De re militari*,[154] while Duke Charles may also have owned the copy found in the English royal library at Richmond by 1535.[155] This manuscript, dated about 1470, also contains the French translation made on Charles' orders by the Portuguese, Vasco de Lucena, of Poggio Braccliolini's translation into Latin of Xenophon's *Cyropaedia*, a Greek book of instruction for princes in which the military upbringing of the ruler is given prominence. This work placed great emphasis on training and exercise, while some of the technical vocabulary used by Lucena would re-emerge in the series of military ordinances to be issued by the ducal court in the coming years.

It is not surprising, then, that Duke Charles should have used more than a single text when seeking inspiration and instruction on military matters. At the same time, it is evident that the ideas of Vegetius carried much weight. Referring to the qualifications and powers of the leaders of the ducal army, the military ordinances ('Ordonnances sur le fait et conduicte des gens de guerre') issued late in 1473, and, we are informed, very much the work of Charles himself, stated that each of its companies should be led and governed by men respected for their knowledge of and experience in arms ('regie, conduicte et gouvernée par homme de bonne auctorité . . . sage, prudent et expert en armes').[156] Such language, with its emphasis on the value of practical experience, reflected closely the ideal of leadership described by Vegetius. The emphasis was now on the benefits of practice and merit rather than on social rank and position.

Even more significant was the basis upon which the authority exercised by the army's leaders ('conduictiers') was founded. Vegetius had emphasised the dependence of commanders upon the imperial authority which appointed them, accepted their oaths of loyalty, and acted as the person to whom they were responsible. The iconography of one manuscript containing the text of the ordinance of 1473 shows the duke, surrounded by members of the Order of the Golden Fleece and ducal councillors, handing down copies of the ordinance to two newly appointed captains, and his baton of office to a third;[157] in the other, one captain receives a bound copy of the ordinance, whose text emphasised the ducal authority

---

[153] *Ibid.* pp. 16–17.   [154] Brussels, Bibl. royale, 11,048, 11,195.
[155] BL Royal 17 E v.   [156] BL Add. Ms 36,619, fo. 4v.
[157] *Ibid.* fo. 5; see *The Renaissance. The triumph of Flemish manuscript painting in Europe*, ed. T. Kren and S. McKendrick (Los Angeles, 2003), p. 252.

and the subordinate role of the individual captain receiving a commission to act on the duke's behalf, while a second is given his baton.[158] The ducal authority was further underlined by the fact that appointments were made annually, for a year at a time, at the end of which they required renewal for a further year: 'le quel conduictier se renouvellera d'an en an sans ce qu'il puest estre continué plus longuement d'une annee à la fois'. On 1 January every year those who had acted in the duke's name for the past twelve months were to resign their commissions, either in person or by proxy, each surrendering his 'baston' according to the terms of the ordinance. Nor was a commission automatically renewed. Indeed, encouragement was given to others to apply for high military office in the ducal army. The duke would make his choice ('fera . . . son election des conduictiers'), the appointments would be formally announced, and the commissioning ('institution') of those chosen by ducal authority duly carried out.[159] We should note the formal manner in which the procedures for the appointment of 'conduictiers' are set out. There was, too, the assertion of the ducal claim, based on his responsibility to defend his lands and people, to appoint as leaders of his army men whose competence could be recognised.[160]

[158] BnF fr. 23,963, fo. 2, reproduced in M. H. Keen (ed.), *Medieval warfare. A history* (Oxford, 1999), 285.

[159] BL Add. Ms 36,619, fos. 4v–6. In 1475 Philippe de Mazerolles was paid for having prepared this luxury copy, and twenty other formal copies, of the *ordonnance*, some of which, including BnF fr. 23,963 referred to above, still survive (see A. de Schryver, 'Philippe de Mazerolles: le livre d'heures noir et les manuscrits d'ordonnances militaires de Charles le Téméraire', *Revue de l'art*, 126 (1999), 59–67). See also R. Sablonier, 'État et structures militaires dans la Confédération [suisse] autour des années 1480', in *Cinq-centième anniversaire de la bataille de Nancy [1477]*, plate opposite 352; Vale, *War and chivalry*, 173; R. Vaughan, *Charles the Bold. The last Valois duke of Burgundy* (London, 1973), 204–5. It is of interest in this context to note part of Laurent de Premierfait's second translation of Boccaccio's *De Casibus*, made c.1409, in which he describes the triumph accorded to a general who has secured a victory. In the procession 'il tient en sa main ung baston et au bout dessus doivent estre peintes les armes du souverain seigneur pour qui l'en a combattu', the emphasis being on the 'baston' as a sign of authority granted by the 'seigneur' in whose name the army had fought. See A. D. Hedeman, 'Making the past present: visual translation of Jean Lebègue's "twin" manuscripts of Sallust', in *Patrons, authors and workshops. Books and book production in Paris around 1400*, ed. G. Croenen and P. Ainsworth (Louvain, Paris and Dudley, MA, 2006), 195, app. 4, citing BnF fr. 131, fos. 109v–110.

[160] *DRM*, I, 1–7; II, 12, 21. The mid-fifteenth-century English text 'The III consideracions right necesserye to the good governaunce of a prince', a translation of a French text written a century earlier, encouraged the ruler to appoint 'able and convenient persoones . . . [as] capiteyns of the werres and of the oost . . . soo that every Prince, by the good advise of his true counseill, shuld be well assured of his good and convenient officers for the conduit of his werres, as well upon the lande as upon the see' (*Four English political tracts of the later Middle Ages*, ed. J.-P. Genet (RHistS, London, 1977), 208).

When it came to dealing with those of lower rank, similarities of procedure could also be found. Just as prospective captains did, so too the rank and file offered themselves and their services for acceptance by the duke. An ordinance issued in 1471 stated that those wishing to serve in the army should apply before a specified date. It was from those considered suitable ('ydoines et souffisans', a phrase implying the possibility of rejection) that the selection was made.[161] Those accepted were then drafted to serve under the command of 'conduictiers', themselves appointed by the duke. These took the recruits into the countryside ('aux champs'), demonstrated the use of formations and tactics, and gave them practice in the use of arms, in retreating in an orderly manner, as well as other exercises. Those destined to be archers were trained in the control of horses and in fighting in the company of pikemen who, at a signal, knelt so that the archers could shoot over their heads.[162] Such a movement, and others, was carried out successfully only by dint of regular training. Once learned, these skills could be passed on to others. Had not Vegetius argued that it was impossible to teach others what one had not learned oneself?

Further evidence of practical influence was to be found in the emphasis placed on the use of the trumpet to co-ordinate the movement of companies. Vegetius had shown how the trumpet and other musical instruments could summon troops to action and then regulate their movements. In the ordinance of 1473 Duke Charles described how formal troop movements should be carried out 'a un signe', often the sound of the trumpet, so that the formations advanced together, 'uniement de front'.[163] Both order and the sense of membership of a particular company with its own commander were to be served through the use of the password (the 'tessera' of Vegetius), regularly changed and known only to members of that company, a measure ordered in 1471. Unity would also be maintained by the decision, announced in the ordinance of 1473, that commanders should carry material insignia enabling men to locate their leaders in the confusion of battle. Further, so as to encourage men to keep close to those with whom they had trained, the ensigns were to be numbered, that of the first squadron with a 'C', the second with a 'CC', the third with 'CCC', and so on. In this way it was intended that companies should maintain their unity, making them more effective on the battlefield.[164] These ordinances, and that of 1473 in particular,

---

[161] Vegetius twice used the word 'idoneus' ('suitable') in *DRM*, I, 7.
[162] BL Add. Ms 36,619, fos. 30v–32; cf. *DRM*, II, 12, 22.
[163] *DRM*, II, 22; BL Add. Ms 36,619, fos. 10v–11, 31–31v.
[164] *Ibid.* fos. 11, 12v–13v; *DRM*, II, 13, 23. Anne Curry has emphasised that it was only with the Burgundian forces of the 1460s and 1470s that there was a real development of

constituted a landmark in the attempts of rulers to control their armies both on the field and off it.[165] Vegetius, for instance, had faced the problem; the Burgundians now did the same, limiting the numbers who might legally be absent on a given day.[166] Those who failed to seek leave and absented themselves without permission were to be sought out, arrested and punished. The efficiency of the army could not be compromised, so soldiers were encouraged to report the absence of their fellows.

If we take the words of the ducal councillor, Guillaume de Rochefort, uttered at a ceremonial inauguration late in 1475, as reflecting the ideas of his master, then we understand how much importance Duke Charles attached to the 'arte militare', 'military skill and the virtue of loyal and obedient soldiers directed towards the strength and stability of the state'. Charles, indeed, planned to create what was virtually a new army of permanent paid companies of volunteers, based on an application of his wide reading of classical sources, but influenced, no doubt, by recent military developments in France and in the Swiss Confederation.[167]

The spirit of Vegetius is apparent in many of the formal military ordinances issued by the duke. Almost uniquely, the passages of the *De re militari* which influenced them will have been found in Book II of the work, whose contents (concerned mainly with the administration and proper functioning of the army) had hitherto not raised undue interest. The organisation and chain of command, cemented by the oath taken, ultimately by all ranks, to obey orders; the numerical composition of the early companies; the insistence upon the possession of proper, well-kept equipment, including armour[168] by soldiers according to rank; the provision of special officers to deal with the army's personnel and financial affairs,[169] all were subjects found in the ordinance issued in July 1471, while the ordinance of 1473 referred to the 'logeur',[170] the officer in charge of finding lodgings for the army, perhaps inspired by the quartermaster described by Vegetius. The strengthening of the oath 'to be true and loyal to our said lord . . . and to serve him against all', as set out in the ordinance of 1472, bore a close resemblance to the oath taken by new soldiers in the *De re militari*. So the army, whose task was to assure 'the defence of ourselves, land and people' ('garde, seurté et defence de notre

---

some of the essentials of modern warfare, such as the issue of ordinances, and insistence upon drilling and exercises – a new chapter in the history of the late medieval soldier. See her review of Keen (ed.), *Medieval warfare* in *War in Society*, 9 (2002), 219–21.

[165] C. Brusten, 'Les compagnies d'ordonnance dans l'armée bourguignonne', in *Grandson, 1476*, ed. D. Reichel (Lausanne, 1976), 112–69.

[166] *DRM*, II, 19; BL Add. Ms 36,619, fos. 20–21v.

[167] Vaughan, *Charles the Bold*, 205, 211.   [168] *DRM*, II, 12, 14, 20.

[169] Dealt with by the 'librarii' (*ibid.* II, 7).   [170] BL Add. Ms 36,619, fo. 13v.

personne, estat, pais, seigneuries et subgez'), was developed at a turning point in the military history of Europe, according to legislation which, although it looked backwards for much of its inspiration, 'was applied to every sixteenth-century army, and thus influenced the military history of the entire European continent in early modern times'.[171]

Denis the Carthusian

Copies of the *De re militari* could be found in the libraries of a number of Carthusian communities at the end of the Middle Ages.[172] From the evidence of his writings, in which he showed practical appreciation of the teachings of both Vegetius and Giles of Rome, we learn that the monk Denis, of the Carthusian foundation at Roermond, a prolific and popular spiritual writer of the fifteenth century, made good use of ideas contained in Vegetius' work. In his tract *De vita et regimine principum, III*, Denis drew upon it to make a number of points. The wellbeing of a community must be defended against external aggression by an armed force ('militia') which had the further task of dealing with those trying to incite treasonable action or who oppressed society's poor, a statement reflecting more than a little the traditional *raison d'être* of knighthood.[173] The waging of war, a dangerous activity, should be left to those trained and experienced in its ways. Such should include not only soldiers and knights; princes and kings, too, had a duty to know how to fight for the common good, as this had been set out by Giles (in the *De regimine principum*) and, before him, by Vegetius. All should share a desire for justice and the good of society, for which they must be prepared to die.[174] This set Denis off on the fundamental matter of training, essential if victory was to be achieved.[175]

While implying criticism of those who did not admit that victories came from God, or who would not recognise the wisdom and justice of God in the outcome of battles, Denis none the less insisted that man must fight and do all in human power to achieve victory. To do less was to tempt God into making decisions. In other words, while recognising the overriding 'providence and justice' of God expressed in the outcome

---

[171] Vaughan, *Charles the Bold*, 205.

[172] See, for example, Vatican, Pal. lat. 1573; Basel, Univ. F. V. 6 (excerpts only).

[173] *Doctoris ecstatici D. Dionysii Cartusiani opera omnia. Opera minora V* (Tournai, 1909), 475.

[174] 'paratum esse mori pro equitate et communi utilitate', p. 476, stemming from *DRM*, II, 5.

[175] 'ut omnia in bellicis actibus faciant ordinate et caute, secundum doctrinam libri praeallegati', i.e., the *De regimine principum*.

of battles, those fighting must always do everything possible to influence or dictate those outcomes.[176] It was therefore logical that he should write approvingly of what both Giles of Rome and, through him, Vegetius had urged in terms of training for battle, of preparing men both physically and mentally for war, of approaching a conflict with proper care and attention ('prudentia' and 'cautela'), and of not relying on numbers alone to secure victory. With regard to the last, there were ample biblical texts to show that small armies could defeat larger ones. But whereas victories against the odds might suggest divine intervention, a reading of Vegetius showed that an over-large force was a danger to itself. Furthermore, as Denis pointed out, the logistical problems of providing food, water and other necessities for a large army could not be ignored. The Vegetian model was the best.

As a major spiritual writer, Denis was also concerned with the salvation of souls ('salus animarum'), to which, he commented, neither Vegetius nor Giles had made any reference. Man, he argued, was engaged in a spiritual contest with the forces of evil. In this respect, his text bore a message very similar to that of Alfonso de San Cristóbal, the Castilian translator of the *De re militari*, who had introduced a strong religious commentary to his translation.[177] In the *De vita militiarum*, Denis referred to the spiritual character of a knight's arms needed to defend his spirit, not his body: 'arma militiae nostrae non carnalia sunt sed spiritualia'.[178] The most effective was perseverance ('fortitudo'), which, in Christian tradition, was high on the list of spiritual virtues; but he strongly advocated the practice of 'prudentia', 'cautela' and 'discretio', added by Vegetius as necessary characteristics of the fighting man, and most useful both in resolving worldly conflicts and, by implication, in defeating the wiles of the spiritual foe.[179]

Denis' support for the teachings of Vegetius was never wholehearted. The ambiguity of his position in relation to 'war' or 'battle', temporal one moment, spiritual the next, made it difficult for him to accept all that Vegetius taught and recommended. It is clear that he saw the *De re militari* as we may imagine the clergy of an earlier age had seen it: it taught men how to ready themselves for the fight, to order and discipline their lives, and to approach conflict against a spiritual enemy with forethought. We have suggested that it was such a reading of Vegetius' text which made it popular among the clergy from the time of its

---

[176] 'in proelio tota spes ponenda est in Deo, et Victoria exspectanda ab eo, attamen facere debet homo pugnaturus quidquid per suam industriam atque potentiam licite facere potest' (*Opera minora V*, 478).
[177] See below, pp. 181–2.   [178] II Cor. 10, 4.   [179] *Opera minora V*, 571–2.

reception into medieval western tradition in the Carolingian era right up to the Reformation. Denis only accentuated such a generalisation. There was much that he agreed with in the *De re militari*. At the same time he warned against following Vegetius' text too closely. He was unhappy, for example, about the encouragement given to a policy of sowing discord among the enemy as a means of dividing and defeating them. To Denis, action aimed at deliberately dividing an army against itself went against Christian charity. Likewise, the use of deception and trickery in a situation of war, recommended by Vegetius, needed to be thought about carefully before being practised. Deception, the conscious telling of falsehoods by one man to another so as to deceive him, was sinful, and should not be permitted. On the other hand, the withholding of information regarding future plans and intentions, and being economical with the truth with the deliberate intention of creating doubt or, eventually, causing deception, was legitimate.[180] What do these misgivings amount to? They may be seen as the possible objections to particular practices voiced by one with no practical experience of the conduct of war, yet who possessed a profound sense of sin and a highly developed moral and theological conscience. They may also express a last ditch effort to defend (albeit without great conviction) a traditional 'knightly' approach to war which demanded truthfulness on all sides, at a time when the need to secure a clear outcome in war was becoming increasingly important. The emphasis placed by Vegetius on the role of the mind and intelligence in securing that outcome meant, almost inevitably, that deception would play an important part in battle. Indeed, was there ever a time when it had not done so? None the less, Denis' apparent acceptance that his moral misgivings would have little or no practical influence is an important sign of the times, a sign, perhaps, that certain basic Vegetian teachings had finally won through.

Machiavelli

The number of surviving manuscripts suggests that the *De re militari* was a widely read text on the Italian peninsula during the fourteenth and fifteenth centuries. We should now enquire whether its popularity led to it having influence upon the military scene in that part of Europe during those two centuries and the early years of the one which followed.

The rise of city states and the development of republican ideas in the thirteenth century had led to an appreciation of the needs of self-defence to be met through the application of the Roman ideal of the native militia.

---

[180] *Ibid.* 487.

By the early fourteenth century, however, that militia, generally unpopular and often malfunctioning, was coming to be regarded as outmoded. In the circumstances, men turned to professional mercenaries, led by *condottieri*, to ensure their defence. By the end of the century that system, too, had been discredited; mercenaries were seen as expensive and unreliable; many thought that states were finding themselves too dependent upon them. In short, they constituted a growing danger to the stability of those very states which they were paid to defend.[181]

It was the discrediting of the *condottieri* system which helped to keep the flame of Roman republican ideals alive, particularly among intellectuals, although it was pointed out that militias were seldom the equals of the better-trained and more professional *condottieri*. Humanists emphasised, however, how Plato and Aristotle had been opposed to the purchase of military service from outside. Plato, it was noted, had favoured a home-grown army, selected and then properly trained to provide the state with protection by an exclusively military caste. Aristotle, likewise, favoured an army – a militia – of citizens, but on what we might today call a part-time basis. Later, Vegetius had opposed the employment of mercenaries, while the drift of the argument of the *De re militari* had been towards the provision of defence from within a society, largely but not exclusively by men drawn from its rural areas.

It was here, through Vegetius and his heirs in the thirteenth and fourteenth centuries, that the influence of the ancient world upon the practicalities of military service would be felt. The militia system had failed. So had reliance on the *condottieri*, whose rapacity had turned them from protectors of Italian society into its enemies. In the *Africa*, Petrarch had extolled the virtues of Scipio's militia (or Roman army) which had defeated Hannibal's paid mercenaries at Zama.[182] When Leonardo Bruni wrote his *De militia* in 1422, he was expressing the view of learned opinion that full civic responsibility could only be met effectively through a system of defence founded on the application of ideals inherited from the ancient world, principally from republican Rome. Not all, however, agreed with this. The ideal of citizens defending their homeland, families and properties might fulfil a deep human sense of responsibility. Yet it had to be realised that war was dangerous, its outcome often

---

[181] F. Gilbert, 'Machiavelli: the renaissance of the art of war', in *Makers of modern strategy from Machiavelli to the nuclear age*, ed. P. Paret (Oxford, 1986), 19. See also the old, but still useful, work of L. Arthur Burd, 'Le fonti letterarie di Machiavelli nell' "Arte della Guerra"' (*Atti della R. Accademia dei Lincei, Anno CCXCIII*, Ser. 5, Classe di scienze morali, storiche e philologiche (Rome, 1897), 187–261).

[182] C. C. Bayley, *War and society in renaissance Florence. The 'De militia' of Leonardo Bruni* (Toronto, 1961), 185.

uncertain, the possibility of disaster ever present. Should society not recognise this, and place responsibility for defence on mercenaries, who accepted the risks and consequences of war in which they took part? Such was the view expressed by Stefano Porcari, *capitano del popolo* in Florence in 1427. A few years later, in his *De republica*, Tito Livio dei Frulovisi proposed another point of view, that since the regime of the *condottieri* was to be deplored, individual societies (city states) should recruit permanent armies from within, thus creating a force properly trained and ever on the alert.[183] Opinion was clearly divided. Flavio Biondo, an advocate of following Roman precedent to the letter, argued strongly against a paid force; it was the decision to award pay which had let the *condottieri* in,[184] and which had created a division between the members of the militia and those whom they protected. The reward for good service should not be financial; it was the enduring honour ('gloria solidissima') earned within a man's own society, and the knowledge that his fellow citizens had been protected from dangers besetting them, that constituted the militia man's true reward.

The debate, sketched here in only the broadest outlines, was to a certain extent brought to a temporary close by the establishment of peace on the peninsula in 1454, peace which would endure, more or less, until the invasion of Italy by the French in 1494. During those four decades soldiers were used principally to reflect the magnificence of princes who ruled in Italy.[185] It was the invasion, and the long period of internal conflict that followed, which encouraged further debate regarding the practical needs of defence and the role of the soldier in contemporary Italian society. Of those involved in the debate none was more important than Niccolò Machiavelli, who wrote as a keen student of Roman history and culture, as the author of works concerned with the wider political implications of war, and as the man responsible for Florentine military administration over a period of years. Machiavelli was certainly experienced; he was also committed. He believed strongly in the importance and value of Roman models, which should be maintained and copied in his own time. He believed, too, in the close links between war and politics. Above all, he believed that the state, or civil government, needed an armed force to sustain it and to make it effective. To Machiavelli, the form which that armed force should take, and how it might function most effectively, were more than mere academic questions; they were

---

[183] *Ibid.* 204–5.   [184] *Ibid.* 224–5.
[185] C. H. Clough, 'Chivalry and magnificence in the golden age of the Italian Renaissance', in *Chivalry in the Renaissance*, ed. S. Anglo (Woodbridge and Rochester, NY, 1990), 25–47.

live issues because on their successful resolution depended the future of Florence and the greater Italian peninsula. 'Any principality that does not have its own army', he wrote, 'cannot be secure.'[186]

As Vegetius had begun, so did Machiavelli. Each saw the wisdom and experience of the past as a source of knowledge and inspiration which could help the world of his own time.[187] Writing in the tradition of much classical literature, Machiavelli argued that a ruler must be interested in war, for very practical reasons. 'A ruler who does not understand military matters', he wrote, 'cannot be highly regarded by his soldiers, and he cannot trust them.'[188] The lack of trust between rulers and soldiers weakened the state; this could be avoided if the ruler were seen to have a knowledge of military affairs. While the emphasis in the *De re militari* was rather different, the effect of having a ruler ignorant of such matters was the same. Vegetius and Machiavelli would have agreed about that.

How much further would that agreement have gone? Since Machiavelli was widely read in classical literature, not least in history, many of his ideas may have come from that reading. It is not difficult to see several of Vegetius' recommendations reflected in the Florentine's work, although Vegetius was never credited as his source by Machiavelli, who preferred phrases such as 'some authors who have written on this subject' or 'the opinion of ancient authors' to cover his tracks.[189] However, his argument in favour of a well-trained force and what it might achieve, found in Book II of the *Art of War* (*Arte della Guerra*), was a clear reflection of several consecutive chapters of Book I of the *De re militari*. It was from Vegetius that Machiavelli borrowed the passage in which he described an efficient army as a deterrent to an enemy, before going on to describe some of the skills it should be taught.[190] On the following page Machiavelli repeated Vegetius' dictum that soldiers should learn to swim, as not all rivers might be crossed by a bridge; at the same time (following Vegetius) he referred to the recruits in Rome refreshing themselves after exercise by swimming in the Tiber, and to the Roman practice of having wooden horses which soldiers could use in various exercises.[191]

It is not difficult, therefore, to find passages in the *Art of War* which clearly reflect Vegetius' text. At a more general, but equally telling level it soon emerges how much Machiavelli came to stress some of the Roman's main ideas. The importance attached by Vegetius to selection and to the

---

[186] *The Prince* [*Il Principe*], ch. xiii. See the *Discourses of Niccolò Machiavelli*, ed. L. J. Walker (London, 1950), vol. I, 21; *The art of war*, ed. N. Wood (Indianapolis, 1965), 4, 30, 81; *DRM*, II, 24; III, 3, 10.
[187] *DRM*, Prefaces to Bks I–III; *The Prince*, ch. xiv.   [188] *The Prince*, ch. xiv.
[189] *Art of war*, pp. 33, 108.   [190] *DRM*, III, Praef. (end); I, 13–16; *Art of war*, 57–9.
[191] *DRM*, I, 10; *Art of war*, 57–9.

qualities, physical and moral, demanded of the potential recruit would reappear in the *Art of War*.[192] The need for proper training received the same emphasis as that given it by Vegetius.[193] When Vegetius pointed out the advantages of ranks keeping in close formation (something which Machiavelli admired about the Swiss) and that this was achievable through continuous practice, Machiavelli said the same.[194] It was probably from Vegetius that Machiavelli learned the importance of the practical experience of mock or sham battles, which extended to the infantry benefits which had been largely gained by those who rode at tournaments, benefits already recognised in Venice and at the Burgundian court. The emphasis was constantly on the need to be prepared. As befitted good sense, Vegetius had underlined the importance of not allowing peace to lessen degrees of preparedness. He had recognised the dangers of peacetime, when men all too easily got out of practice. Machiavelli accepted the inference, which he applied to his own day.[195]

Further themes found in the *De re militari* were to make their reappearance in Machiavelli's works. One was the importance of leadership in war, and the qualities and skills which the commander must demonstrate. Another was the need for an army, although divided into units under the immediate charge of a hierarchy of officers, to be ultimately under that of a single general, as Vegetius had emphasised.[196] Since he assumed responsibility, the general should be ready to seek and accept advice from experienced persons around him;[197] he must be able to communicate with his troops both by word of mouth and by a system of signals, failing which he would not be able to convey his orders to them.[198] As Vegetius had done, Machiavelli emphasised the virtues of foresight and planning, and the need to be ahead of events as they occurred: 'Nothing becomes a general more than to anticipate the enemy's plans', he wrote.[199] This gave Machiavelli the opportunity to stress the need for the commander to be aware of the enemy's intentions, a point previously underscored by Vegetius. Here, it has been suggested, Machiavelli the politician and Machiavelli the military theorist merge: 'The necessity of foresight, planning and preparation for the future constitutes a

---

[192] *DRM*, I, 4–7; *Art of war*, 26, 34. Machiavelli helped in person to select and train recruits (Gilbert, 'Machiavelli', 20).
[193] German cities, Machiavelli pointed out (*The Prince*, ch. x), were always ready for war, and insisted on regular exercises for those committed to their defence.
[194] *DRM*, I, 19; *Art of war*, 56–7, 61–3.
[195] *DRM*, I, 28; II, 22, 23; III, 5; *The Prince*, ch. xiv; *Art of war*, 19; Gilbert, 'Machiavelli', 25.
[196] *DRM*, III, 18; *Art of war*, 74; *Discourses* [*Discorsi*], III, 15.
[197] *DRM*, III, 9; *Art of war*, 129.   [198] *DRM*, III, 5, 9; *Art of war*, 107, 127–8, 165.
[199] *Discourses*, III, 18.

favourite political theme . . . that emphasises the need for expert advice and the gathering of intelligence . . . the estimate of factors and the rational calculation of the objective.'[200] Much of this could equally well be applied to Machiavelli's advice on the best way of achieving victory: if the commander was to be the only one in command, he must fulfil his role effectively. This was underlined by Machiavelli's updating of Vegetius' advice that a general should take steps to learn about the nature of the country through which he and his army were about to advance. Vegetius had emphasised the advantage to be gained from having accurate geographical knowledge of terrain being made available to the general. The point was taken up by Machiavelli when, in *The Prince* (*Il Principe*), he stressed the importance of a leader being able to 'read' a landscape, a facility which would bring clear military advantages, and which could best be achieved through frequent engagement in hunting.[201]

Just as Vegetius, in keeping with many writers of the classical era who had described war, drew attention to the psychological aspects of conflict, so Machiavelli did the same. Following Vegetius, he argued that it was better not to oblige an enemy facing defeat to fight to the death, thereby showing his awareness of the effects of desperation upon the psyche of the defeated soldier.[202] As became the author of *The Prince*, Machiavelli emphasised the need to outwit the enemy, and thus secure a military advantage at little or no physical cost; his view 'that it is a glorious thing to use fraud in the conduct of war'[203] recalls passages in the *De re militari* which encourage the use of deceit or surprise to overcome the enemy. It was probably from this model that Machiavelli learned to appreciate the effect of fear upon an army, fear which could arise from seeing the unfamiliar or hearing sounds and cries which caused perturbation among a force which, about to go into action, was perhaps already nervous about what was likely to happen.[204] Vegetius had strongly emphasised the need to prepare soldiers to face the realities of war with confidence: 'Never lead a hesitant and frightened army into a pitched

---

[200] *Art of war*, lxiii.

[201] *DRM*, III, 6; *Art of war*, 143; *The Prince*, ch. xiv. The wording in the passage in the *Arte della guerra* [*Art of war*] is close to that used by Vegetius, suggesting the dependence of Machiavelli upon his Roman model.

[202] *Ibid.* III, 21; *Discourses*, III, 12. Machiavelli also accepted Vegetius' teaching that, having got into a town, an attacking force should leave the gates open to encourage the inhabitants to escape safely rather than offer further resistance (*DRM*, IV, 25; *Art of war*, 193).

[203] *Discourses*, III, 40; *DRM*, III, 22. He was probably also influenced in this matter by the *Strategemata* of Frontinus, a text he knew well (N. Wood, 'Frontinus as a possible source for Machiavelli's method', *Journal of the History of Ideas*, 28 (1967), 243–8).

[204] *DRM*, III, 13; *Art of war*, 46; *Discourses*, III, 14.

battle', he had written. In this, too, he would be followed by Machiavelli. Both writers emphasised the need, as part of the skills of communication expected of him, for every general to be able to encourage his men before battle by means of a harangue.[205] The advice given by Vegetius that an army should be told to hold the enemy in contempt was very close to the advice offered by Machiavelli on the same issue.[206] Confidence was also the attribute of the well-armed and well-protected soldier. Not only were those lacking armour more likely to be killed or wounded; their lack of protection also greatly diminished their effectiveness, for, as Vegetius had written, 'a man who does not fear wounds because he has his head and chest protected must acquire sharper courage for battle'. The importance which Machiavelli attributed to good arms and armour in his appreciation of both ancient and recent warfare indicates that he had understood both the military and the psychological advantages of soldiers having adequate protection.[207]

We have noted how, swimming against the tide, Charles the Bold had taken practical interest in the content of Book II of the *De re militari*, in which Vegetius had set out details of the formation and organisation of the Roman legion. Machiavelli was to encourage the development of this renewed interest. In Books II and III of the *Art of War* he tried to recreate much of what Vegetius had written, mainly in Book II of his work, on the Roman military system using detailed descriptions of Roman methods and practices which he regarded as superior to those of the Middle Ages.[208] He turned his attention to arms and armour; to the formation of military units and battle formations. His insistence on the importance of drill and discipline was to be vital not only for his own day (as the Swiss showed) but also for that of future generations, forming as they did the basis of major developments which could be taken yet further with the use of newly invented weaponry. The military handbook of the future would not be complete without diagrams setting out formations to meet different contingencies. The appearance of Aelian in some of the early printed editions makes this point clear.

Book IV of the *De re militari*, mainly concerned with matters of the attack and defence of fortified towns, was to inform Machiavelli's ideas and provide him with material incorporated into Book VII of the *Art of War*.[209] Although noting, as Vegetius had done, that nature provided

---

[205] *Ibid.* III, 9, 12, 18, 25; *Art of war*, 128; *Discourses*, III, 14, 33.
[206] *DRM*, III, 12; *Art of war*, pp. 127, 129.
[207] *DRM*, I, 20. Machiavelli's discussion of armour can be found at the beginning of Book II of the *Art of war*.
[208] Intro. to *Art of war*, xxxiii; Gilbert, 'Machiavelli', 23.
[209] Particularly *DRM*, IV, 3–5, 7, 21–2, 24, 26, 28.

certain kinds of defence, he did not follow Vegetius' ideas slavishly. The discovery of the effects of gunpowder, and its use in undermining what had hitherto been stable physical platforms upon which to build the fortifications of towns and castles, made him realise that much of what Vegetius had written needed to be brought up to date. Thus he modified Vegetius' teaching regarding the building of walls, while his general approach to physical defences suggests that he was able to distance himself from his sources, and to use them only as they applied to the conditions and weaponry of his own day. On the other hand, by reproducing, with few changes and without acknowledgement,[210] the 'Rules of war' which Vegetius had set out in the closing chapter of Book III of the *De re militari*, he recognised the unchanging character of much of the advice that most of these rules contained, which made their inclusion appropriate at this moment in time.[211] On the matter of war at sea, discussed by Vegetius in the closing chapters of Book IV of the *De re militari*, Machiavelli was to say nothing. It is likely that he found Vegetius' treatment of naval warfare unsatisfactory and, in all probability, irrelevant. The subject was best left alone.

Machiavelli was influenced to write about war by the circumstances in which Italy found itself in his day. 'War is the most essential activity of political life', he was to write.[212] His contribution reflected his admiration for Roman models, one of which, Vegetius' *De re militari*, gave him much food for thought.[213] Not the least part of his debt to Vegetius was the central position occupied by the soldier in Machiavelli's thinking. For both men, the soldier was a foundation of the state: for Vegetius, as the defender of the people's liberties, property and wealth; for Machiavelli, through the role played by the army in establishing and maintaining proper government. Yet, again following Vegetius, Machiavelli did not see the army simply as an instrument to be used by a ruler for political purposes. The army was very much more than a military machine made up of armed men; it was an organisation of human beings who reacted (as human beings do) in particular ways to particular circumstances. Vegetius had been anxious to make all commanders realise that they would get the best out of their men if they recognised, for example, that a well-trained army was an army confident and ready to fight, whereas an ill-trained force was easily demoralised or frightened, and was thus likely

---

[210] S. Anglo, *Machiavelli – The first century. Studies in enthusiasm, hostility and irrelevance* (Oxford, 2005), 484, n. 14.
[211] *Art of war*, 202–4.   [212] Gilbert, 'Machiavelli', 24.
[213] Anglo, *Machiavelli*, 34–5. His overdependence on the Romans prompted Francesco Guicciardini to criticise his 'blind zeal for the Romans'; later in the century other writers would do the same. On this see *ibid.* 30–41.

to fight badly, or even desert. In all such matters Machiavelli appears to have found himself in agreement with his Roman model.[214]

It was in this way that Machiavelli began to build what some critics have termed his 'science' of war. In so doing, he underlined his debt to Vegetius. Both writers recognised that the successful leader was the one who created situations requiring a response, the proactive rather than the reactive. Hence the need, as both writers pointed out, for the leader to be well informed, since this enabled him to see ahead, to seize the initiative and impose his own will upon a situation, leaving his rival with no choice but to react to a situation in whose development he had had little or no say. It was foresight and the use to which it was put that often dictated the outcome of battles between armies which, in other respects, appeared equally matched. War between armies might be won on the battlefield. But it was what went on in the minds of commanders, and their ability to translate thoughts into preparation off the battlefield, which often decided the superiority of one side over the other.

Machiavelli viewed war, and the organisation responsible for fighting it, in a very broad socio-political context. No society could exist with confidence without a sense of security and the means of defending itself. The army, therefore, existed as an essential and central part of the state which was its master, and in whose defence it found its justification. For this reason it was natural that the form which the army should take, and who should make up its numbers, should be subject to debate. But of one thing Machiavelli was certain. The soldier was important because he provided, and supported, the very foundations of the state: peace and security. For this reason, the army must be drawn from the state's citizens, whose protection, as the Italian experience of *condottieri* had shown, was too important (not to say too expensive) to be placed in the hands of others.

---

[214] *Ibid.* 522.

7   Translations

Translations were intended to transmit a work, in this case one originally written in Latin, to a wider public and into a later age. Rendering it into another language made it more specifically part of the culture of that age, although a more or less 'straight' translation retained its attachment to the time of its origins more easily than did one which incorporated adaptions made by the translator, whose task was, therefore, a pivotal one. He had the power to make a work both more widely accessible and better known to those unable, for whatever reason, to read the original. He could try to produce a metaphrase, a translation which stuck as closely as possible to the original. That could be a difficult task, requiring exceptional skills on the part of the translator. An alternative was an adaptation of some sort. One such might be a paraphrase, a free rendering of the original which, while keeping to the original meaning, omitted complex or obscure passages, or those which, in the translator's judgement, had little meaning for readers in his day. A second form of adaptation was to embellish the original by adding material to fill out or illustrate points made by the author so that these might be better appreciated by later readers, thus giving the original text a certain sense of modernity, and making its content more relevant to the thought and circumstances of later times. In this case, the translator was interpreting a work from a former age for readers living in his own age, and doing so in terms of the values which that age might attribute to it. The difficulties presented by the translator's position are summed up in the different words used to convey the nature of his work. It is interesting to observe the number of words used, in French for instance, to convey what translators thought they were doing: 'translater' was there, but so were 'convertir', 'expliquer', 'transferer' and 'transporter', while a translator might be described as a 'translateur' or an 'interpréteur', both words conveying different shades of meaning regarding the function of translation. In French the verb 'traduire' would come into use only in the sixteenth century.[1]

---

[1] F. Bérier, 'La traduction en français', in *La littérature française aux XIVe et XVe siècles*, ed. D. Poirion (Heidelberg, 1988), 239–41.

This would have a variety of effects, depending on the nature of the text. Thus a philosophical work might be treated differently from one concerned with the practicalities of life, war in particular. In a work of this kind, there was bound to be a rupture created by the change which had occurred over a period of some nine centuries. Yet, of its very nature, a translation was essentially a work which underlined interest in the past and the continuity of human thought and practice. For that reason, it must reflect what the past and the present had in common, using appropriate language to convey this. Strict accuracy of translation might appear to be desirable, but could not always be achieved. Nor was it always called for. In the case of a practical work, in particular, there would be passages, sometimes long ones, which were open to various forms of adaptation, paraphrase or, sometimes, omission. Illustrative material, in particular when taken from historical examples, could often be replaced by more recent examples which held greater meaning for the new readership, who would regard the translation as bringing the original text up to date for their own time. In the same way, romances, which were reworkings of old tales and legends, would be modernised to make them acceptable to their readers, to whose experience and knowledge of war writers wished to relate their works of fiction.[2]

Much modern scholarship would hold that the medieval translator, making the most of his author's reputation, sought to adapt the original, domesticating and contextualising it for new conditions, cultures and readers.[3] It would reject the idea, expressed in the Italian phrase 'traduttore: traditore', that translation was an act of treason. Translation made a text better known; in the case of a practical work it might extend its usefulness in both space and time. Translation, however, was not simply providing a way of looking into the past and its ideas and practices. While a work such as the *De re militari* might certainly do that, it must also move things on.

The translator had to judge his own day, what his contemporaries were willing to read, and what they wanted to know. In this respect, his work required the adaptation of a text taken from a past culture for the interest and use of readers brought up in another. The task of the modern

---

[2] M. Murrin, *History and warfare in Renaissance epic* (Chicago and London, 1994)), 53, 83, citing Malory as an example.

[3] 'Writers of the Middle Ages did not hesitate to present Vegetius' precepts in a totally medievalized setting' (D. Bornstein, *Mirrors of courtesy* (Hamden, Conn., 1975), 30). See R. Ellis and R. Tixier (eds.), *The medieval translator. Traduire au moyen âge*, ed. (Turnhout, 1996), 2–3; R. Ellis (ed.), *The medieval translator. The theory and practice of translation in the Middle Ages* (Cambridge, 1989), 2. See also comments in C. Nall, 'William Worcester reads Alain Chartier: *Le quadrilogue invectif* and its English readers', in *Chartier in Europe*, ed. E. Cayley and A. Kinch (Cambridge, 2008), 142.

critic/historian is to appreciate how the translator viewed the original text before him, and what he thought needed doing to make it readable by those living in his own time. His approach to his task would be influenced by the answers he might give to such questions. Too many classical or moral allusions, the use of outdated language, the apparent irrelevance of parts of a text to modern times might not be acceptable. When the translator rendered the Latin chronicle of William of Tyre into thirteenth-century French, he often omitted passages which attributed Christian defeats to the results of sin ('peccatis nostris exigentibus'), which may indicate that such explanations no longer satisfied readers, knights and prospective crusaders, of his day. At the same time he was not averse to adding information, gleaned perhaps from oral sources, to expand his text.[4]

Those translating Vegetius' work would be trying to create a military manual suitable for their own time and society, thus encouraging a wider appreciation of what Vegetius had been aiming to teach. What was that? The word(s) chosen to render two crucial words, 'res militaris', into the vernacular languages gives us a clue to the appreciation which translators had of the work as a whole. While 'chevalerie', 'cavalleria', 'knyghthode' and 'Ritterschaft' were all used, it was a 'chivalry' undergoing change and development as men became increasingly aware, through their reading of historians such as Caesar and Livy, of what the Roman military virtues had been, and what they had achieved.[5] It seems that the translators did not mean 'chivalry' to be understood principally in an ethical or social sense. If they used the word it was because, for the earliest among them at any rate, 'chevalerie' represented 'no more than a body of heavily armed horsemen, a collective of "chevaliers"'; in more modern language, 'an army', a fair translation considering what Vegetius' text contained. But, as is well known, 'chevalerie' could mean a number of things. A glance at the ways 'res militaris' was rendered by Jean de Meun in 1284 and by Jean de Vignay a generation or so later strongly suggests an understanding of the phrase which would make 'On the skills of war' (or 'How to wage war') an acceptable way of translating the Latin title. Similarly, those described as 'rei militaris periti' became 'those who knew about fighting',

[4] B. Hamilton, 'The Old French translation of William of Tyre as an historical source', in *The experience of crusading. II. Defining the crusader*, ed. P. Edbury and J. Phillips (Cambridge, 2003), 93–112.
[5] On the difficulties of creating an exact definition of 'chivalry', see M. Keen, *Chivalry* (New Haven and London, 1984), 2, and G. S. Burgess, 'The term "chevalerie" in twelfth-century French', in *Medieval codicology, iconography, litterature, and translation. Studies for Keith Val Sinclair*, ed. P. R. Monks and D. D. R. Owen (Leiden, New York and Cologne, 1994), 343–58.

or 'experts in arms' ('cil qui d'armes ont esté sages' or 'li sages d'armes'), a view reflected in the translation 'l'usage et diversité de chevalerie' of Vignay, which hints strongly at the number of military skills which the fighting man should acquire. Above all there was emerging a recognition of the strength to be derived from training and discipline, from the military advantages to be achieved from planning and preparation, and from the growth of what could be regarded as the first signs of military professionalism when these were placed at the service of society.[6] So it was that the phrase 'art de feyt d'armes', used in Catalan as the equivalent of *De re militari*, was an attempt to present Vegetius' work as being about the skills of war, while the phrases 'mester d'armes' and 'mester de cavalleria', both found in the second Catalan translation, carried implications of 'professional' skills which the text regarded as requirement for success in war. In the same way, the use of 'ordenança de la cavalleria', found in the same text, had the meaning of military rules, and could be interpreted as 'how to command (or organise, or lead) a military unit'.[7] A further title given to the work, *Epitome/Liber institutionum rei militaris* might be rendered as the 'Summary of/Handbook on war' or, in modern parlance, 'The A to Z of fighting war'. In brief, the translators envisaged a more up-to-date kind of 'chivalry', increasingly reflecting the influence of Roman teaching and example, whose development they were out to encourage.

What success did they have? The difficulties of providing even a readable text would be considerable. To try to do more created yet further problems. Jean de Vignay might claim to have produced a metaphrase, a work all too hopefully 'rendered into French word for word from the Latin' ('translatee en francois mot a mot selonc le latin').[8] Granted the practical and technical nature of the original, was such a straight translation possible, once allowance had been made for changes in the meanings (or even the disappearance) of Latin words over almost a millennium? How far should a translator depart from or modify a text to convey its meaning to readers living centuries after the original had been written? In short, was the translation intended to play a practical role in the new environment, social, intellectual and, above all, military, for which it was being prepared? Was it, in effect, to be a new work? Could it avoid becoming so? The point is debatable. The claim of Vegetius to be considered the author of a translation was not questioned. The view of him as an authority, which gave his work such standing, would ensure that. Yet the

---

[6] Keen, *Chivalry*, 111–13.
[7] Roger Wright helped me with some of the subtleties of this language.
[8] *Li livres Flave Vegece de la chose de chevalerie*, ed. L. Löfstedt (Helsinki, 1982), 128.

way in which the translator was sometimes given prominence in the presentation miniature (emphasising the work as *his*) should be noted, while some printers substituted their own prefaces for those of the translated author, an approach which signified a similar attitude to the matter of what we might today call 'credits'.

The task was by no means easy. Since Vegetius had written in the late fourth century much had happened to the way war was fought. Armies were now differently constituted; many weapons had changed and developed, as had, too, the use made of them; others had gone out of use altogether. The same was true about those who fought in war, the place and rank which they occupied in society, and the way they saw themselves and were seen by the world around them. In order to create a meaningful guide on how to fight war in the late thirteenth century, the translator would have had to recognise these changes and to adapt the text to 'contemporise antiquity'. So even if the resulting translation were not always, strictly speaking, accurate, it had to be sufficiently in tune with contemporary ideals, not least social ideals, to enable it to serve as an adaptation of Vegetius' text in a manner which made it relevant to the preconceptions and practices of the day. The process of achieving *volgarizzamento* did not imply that the newly created text could be an accurate rendering, to the very letter, of the original.[9]

France

The first translation of the *De re militari* into a vernacular language was almost certainly that made into the Anglo-Norman dialect of French by one Master Richard, perhaps as early as 1254–56, more probably at the later date of 1271–72. Opinions regarding the date are divided. Lewis Thorpe, who first drew attention to the unique manuscript, argued from aspects of the internal evidence in favour of the later date, a time when the Prince Edward, later King Edward I of England, was on crusade in the Holy Land, accompanied by his queen, Eleanor, a cultured woman who might easily have commissioned the translation of Vegetius' work.[10] His argument failed to convince Dominica Legge, who argued that in 1272 Edward was a soldier of maturity and experience, not the young man, surrounded by equally young companions, who appeared in one of

---

[9] See C. Dionisotti, 'Tradizione classica e volgarizzamento', *Italia medioevale e umanistica*, 1 (1958), 430.

[10] Cambridge, Fitzwilliam Mus., Marlay Add. 1; L. Thorpe, 'Mastre Richard, a thirteenth-century translator of the "De re militari" of Vegetius', *Scriptorium*, 6 (1952), 39–50, M. Prestwich, *Edward I* (New Haven and London, 1988), 123.

the manuscript's two illuminations. It was more likely, she thought, that a work such as the *De re militari* would be more appropriately offered to one on the threshold of a military career, for instance at the moment when he accepted the responsibilities of knighthood. In the case of Edward, that event had occurred in 1254 when he had married Eleanor, half-sister of Alfonso X, king of Castile, known for his practical interest in the *De re militari* and for his incorporation of many points from its teaching into the *Siete Partidas*. This argument was undermined by the recognition of a reference in the Anglo-Norman text to an event which took place at Kenilworth on 1 August 1265.[11] This restored the balance of the argument to 1271–72, before Edward became king, and to the patronage of Queen Eleanor, perhaps inspired by the attention paid to the *De re militari* at the Castilian court. Little help can be obtained from the two illuminations, the second of which appears to have been added later. It is unlikely that much progress can be made in resolving these issues. The broad dating will have to stand.

Written in a heavy gothic hand of the second half of the thirteenth century, the translation (bound with a copy of the Latin text which, from internal evidence, was not the one from which the translation was made) largely follows the original, at least until the fourth and final book is reached. Unlike Jean de Meun a decade or so later, Master Richard took relatively few liberties with the text. Thorpe described his basic working method as the achievement of 'accuracy where accuracy [was] worthwhile, and bland omission where Prince Edward could get no practical profit from such accuracy'.[12] Such comment appeared to take it for granted that the translation was intended to instruct the prince in the finer aspects of war which had brought the Romans such success. While the fact that the text was some 900 years old could not be hidden, its contents were none the less not regarded as totally out of date in the mid to late thirteenth century.

A number of points suggest this. The evidence gleaned from surviving Latin manuscripts, already surveyed, strongly suggests that certain parts of the *De re militari* aroused greater interest in readers than did others, probably because of their perceived relevance to later ages. The translator of a practical work such as this was likely to be aware of this fact, since it would give him a measure of freedom from the need to produce a translation which stuck slavishly to the original, interest in which would

---

[11] M. D. Legge, 'The Lord Edward's Vegetius', *Scriptorium*, 7 (1953), 262–5; L. Thorpe, 'Mastre Richard at the skirmish of Kenilworth, *ibid.* 120–1.
[12] Thorpe, 'Mastre Richard, a thirteenth-century translator', 44.

be largely, if not solely, antiquarian.[13] Much of Master Richard's translation is a reasonably straightforward rendering of Vegetius' work, granted that vital words and phrases are turned into a language acceptable to a late thirteenth-century military readership. So, for example, Vegetius' sentence 'This is a matter on which the safety of the entire state depends, that recruits be levied who are outstanding both in physique and moral quality ('Et hoc est in quo totius reipublicae salus vertitur, ut tirones non tantum corporibus sed etiam animis praestantissimi deligantur') is rendered by Master Richard as 'E fet a savoir ke le bachelerie a ki om comande la terre a defendre, et a ki om comande laventure de la bataille, doit estre de noble linage.'[14] The 'respublica' is rendered simply as 'la terre', but the use of 'bachelerie' conveys the sense of the young soldier, or 'tiro'. The man 'de noble linage' sums up, rather than translates literally, the phrase 'non tantum corporibus sed etiam animis praestantissimi', while reinforcing the idea that the fulfilment of such a duty falls on the noble class. In addition, the translation of 'to whom is committed the outcome of battle' ('et a ki om comande laventure de la bataille'), while going beyond the original Latin text, does not harm our understanding of the meaning of the sentence as a whole.

The evident importance to the translator of producing a reasonably up-to-the-minute vernacular version of the *De re militari* can be seen in a number of ways. One was the use of omission, which might take several forms. It was probably a conscious decision on the translator's part to omit the names of leading Romans and other figures from the classical past, whose inclusion would have added little or nothing to the understanding of the text by a late thirteenth-century readership. Omission of whole passages was sometimes sanctioned, perhaps on the grounds that, as above, they might have obfuscated the meaning; or was it that the translator had difficulties which he chose to pass over, as in the case of the passage which involved a number of Greek words?[15] Sometimes, as in II, 10, difficult vocabulary, often of a technical nature, was replaced by very inclusive language lacking specificity. A further way of shortening the translation was the conscious use of paraphrasing. When the translator wrote 'As the author says . . . ' ('Ore dit li auctor . . . '), he was effectively announcing the résumé of a longer passage. Book IV experienced much cutting: chapters 1 to 6 were presented to the reader without a break, as were chapters 15 to 22, 24 to 29, 32 to 36 and 43 to 46.

---

[13] Problems, such as anachronism, relating to aspects of medieval translation are discussed by Beer, *A medieval Caesar*, esp. ch. 5.

[14] Cambridge, Fitzwilliam Mus., Marlay Add. 1, fo. 6v.   [15] *Ibid.* fo. 187; *DRM*, IV, 40.

At times the translator liked to place himself between the author and the reader. The chapter headings were sometimes expanded to announce to the reader what the subject of the chapter would be: 'In the chapter the author says . . . ' ('En cel chapitre dit lauteur . . . '), or 'In this chapter eleven the author teaches us how . . . ' ('En cest unzime chapitre aprent li auctors coment . . . '), the words 'En . . . comment' not being found in the original Latin. The general effect of chapters beginning 'This chapter shows/teaches/discusses . . . ' ('Ce chapitre demonstre/aprent/traite . . . ') was to move the reader a step further away from the orginal author, although this was probably not the translator's intention.

Shortening the translation was not the only way of reshaping the text. This could be expanded with the good intention of remedying the translator's perception that the meaning would not be readily understood as it was, and that some explanation of unusual terms and ideas was needed. Thus the reference to the centurion in I, 26 is followed by 'the centurion is leader of one hundred knights' ('le centurion ki est mestre de cent chivalers'); the siege-shed known as a 'testudo' ('tortoise') was explained with the gloss 'the name of an animal which always holds its head forward and then brings it back within itself' ('le noun de une beste ke touz iourz met sa teste avant e puis le retrait e est enclos'); while the mysterious 'mantelets' ('musculi') are explained as 'mussel, after a sea creature' ('apelez muschel apres une beste de la mer').[16] References to Gaul or to the Gauls, the translator appeared to think, required additional information. So the geographical extent of the land of the Gauls had to be explained to readers, while, to avoid confusion, the 'Galli' were translated as the 'Franceis', and the phrase 'intra Gallias' became 'within the lands of the French' ('de denz les terres des Franceis'), the tribe of the 'Cimbri' emerging as the people of Burgundy ('Borgoyne').[17] Thorpe called such additions, a little unkindly, 'spurious modernity'.[18] In the case of this translation, at least, was it not simply an attempt to use names and terms familiar to the reader, thus making his experience of the text more meaningful and worthwhile?[19]

How should one interpret the two illuminations, one occupying a full folio, the other only half, which impress by their realism? In one, a venerable figure, clearly intended to be 'Vegece, le philosophe de Rome', tells

---

[16] *Ibid.* fos. 16v, 77v, 78.
[17] *Ibid.* fos. 3, 20v, 54v. Whenever Jean Lebègue saw the word 'Galli' translated as 'Français', he protested vigorously (G. Ouy, 'Jean Lebègue (1368–1457), auteur, copiste et bibliophile', in *Patrons, authors and workshops*, ed. Croenen and Ainsworth, 159–60).
[18] Thorpe, 'Mastre Richard, a thirteenth-century translator', 44. See Löfstedt, 'Végèce au moyen âge', 493–4.
[19] See Beer, *A medieval Caesar*, 73, 84 on this matter.

the prince and a group of young knights, dressed not as Romans but in contemporary military dress, to listen to him if they wish to learn about the experience of war. The emphasis is upon knowledge, a favourite theme of Vegetius' work, in which he reiterates time and again how possession of it enables an army and its commander to face conflict with confidence. Knowledge is also seen as wisdom, as the fruit of experience, both of which contribute to the defeat of the enemy. The second illumination, probably added, depicts a fight at sea, so doing something towards making up for the lack of attention given to the final third of Book IV, concerned with naval warfare. Here, once again, the scene depicted is modern, not drawing upon the past. It is clear evidence of the way in which every attempt has been made by both translator and illustrator to complement each other's work, and to give it bearing upon the subject of war in late thirteenth-century western Europe.

Jean de Meun

Before turning his attention to Vegetius, Jean de Meun, who completed the text of the *Roman de la rose*, begun a generation earlier by Guillaume de Lorris, had already translated works by Boethius, Aelred of Rievaulx, and Heloise and Abelard. His translation of the *De re militari* was dedicated to and probably commissioned by Jean de Brienne, count of Eu, son of a crusader who had died in 1270, and grandson of Jean de Brienne, king of Jerusalem (d.1237). It is likely that the work was done to commemorate the knighting and marriage, in the summer of 1284, of the heir to the French throne, the young prince Philip, himself son and grandson of crusaders, before long to become King Philip IV. The illuminations to the early manuscripts emphasise the training of the new knight, a theme at the heart of the text and appropriate for a translation made to record the reception of a royal prince into the order of knighthood. It is right to underline here the long history of the involvement of the counts of Eu in crusading warfare, as well as the fact that the Anglo-Norman translation, discussed above, may have been commissioned for a future English king, himself a crusader. We have already examined the relationship between Vegetius' text and crusading activity at this period.[20]

Meun was primarily intent upon producing a work which, like the original, would have practical lessons to teach those who read it. To achieve this, he used language which his contemporaries would

---

[20] See above, pp. 112–21. See also R. and M. Rouse, 'Early manuscripts of Jean de Meun's translation of Vegetius', in *The medieval book. Glosses from friends and colleagues of Christopher de Hamel*, ed. J. H. Marrow, R. A. Linenthal and W. Noel (Houten, 2010), 59–74.

understand while remaining, as far as possible, faithful to the original or, at least, to its spirit, even if a construction involving a participle or an ablative absolute came to be rendered into a clause with a finite verb.[21] Since all language is, to an extent, a time capsule, Meun's role was to interpret Vegetius' thought in a language familiar to men of the late thirteenth century. Occasionally, he would make mistakes which went beyond mere misunderstanding of the meanings of words and terms; but such occasions were relatively rare. Generally speaking, Meun managed to create a work which reflected the original with reasonable accuracy. His most recent editor writes that the translation reads easily, being clear without being too literal, thereby updating the master's teaching to make it applicable to his own age. It was for that reason that the word 'miles' was translated as 'chevalier', because, for Meun, the 'normal' soldier was a mounted soldier.[22]

Let us look briefly to see how this was done. Meun himself added to the text in one instance. Later, after 1300, twenty or so further examples were added to his text, many of them anachronistic to the original Latin, but whose relative modernity was more in keeping with the new work which he was creating.[23] When a classical example was offered, an explanatory note might be added for those who would not otherwise have appreciated its appropriateness, thereby making it easier to understand. It is likely that these elaborations were made to Meun's text at a later date. Some references, such as those to the battle of Bouvines and to the great losses incurred there by the Flemings, to the death of Conradin, to the crusade of Louis IX in Tunisia (in which Jean de Brienne took part) or to the recent wars in Aragon,[24] may have been made at the suggestion of Jean de Brienne or, possibly, at that of the recipient of the translation, King Philip IV himself. They thus came to be included in copies which would emanate from the court. Others, however, some of which were references to events in ancient history,[25] some to stories in the Old Testament, others still taken from the early thirteenth-century *Li Fet des Romains*, referring to events of very recent times ('en cest darrain aage', 'au iour d'ui', 'au tens qui ore est' or 'en noz tens'),[26] indicate how Meun was making Vegetius' text up to date by adding examples taken from the contemporary world. We may note that a number of the additions were

---

[21] See Löfstedt, 'Végèce au moyen âge', 493–6.
[22] *Li abregemenz noble honme Vegesce Flave René des establissemenz apartenanz a chevalerie, traduction par Jean de Meun*, ed. L. Löfstedt (Helsinki, 1977), 8; Beer, *A medieval Caesar*, 93.
[23] Meun, ed. Löfstedt, 11.   [24] *Ibid.* III, 14; II, 17; III, 2.
[25] *Ibid.* I, 5; I, 9; III, 1–3; III, 6–7; III, 9; IV, 45.
[26] *Ibid.* I, 21; I, 8; II, 14; II, 18; II, 17.

not simply intended as historical examples; they were made to bring to the notice of readers instances of military theory or practice which could be of use to them because they illustrated actual events and developments, such as the tourney as an opportunity for fighting men to hone and practise their skills.[27]

It may be noted, however, that Meun was not always as careful as he might have been in his use of military vocabulary, notably in the use of a single word to convey the meaning of a number of others. As his recent editor has pointed out, the word 'bataille' is used to translate seven different Latin words, of which three appear in a single chapter (III, 14). He was also prone to sometimes using very inclusive language, such as 'and other things' ('et autres choses'), to avoid having to describe in detail various forms of missile-throwing machines. It was a difficulty which the translator of an old text containing a specialised vocabulary had to confront. It would have required someone with a particular knowledge of ancient armaments to do justice to the original.[28]

The evidence of the illuminations contained in some of the surviving manuscripts tends to support this view of the text. Many manuscripts contain no illustrative matter. A few have scenes of an emperor or king receiving the text from the author/translator. Some go further than this. Two show a knight practising with a lance against a tree or pile, or mounting a horse;[29] another depicts a mounted group breaking out of a town, confronting another; while a fourth shows some eight knights standing close to a king who is dictating to a clerk, as well as a scene showing mounted knights. There is no attempt to show Romans prac- tising for war. Unanimously modern in the scenes that they show, the illuminations underline the view that the Middle Ages had in a real sense adopted the *De re militari* as its own, complementing the process begun by the translations.

Forced to confront problems arising out of the changing meanings of words and terms, Meun will soon have had to ask how far he should place himself between Vegetius' text and the medieval reader. These problems took on different forms, and thus produced a variety of solutions. Much of Book I was centred upon the recruit, selected before being put through a course of preparation prior to acceptance as a trained soldier, the procedure transforming the 'tiro' into a 'miles'. In some cases Meun translated 'tiro[nes]' as 'new' or 'young' knights ('noviaus' or 'iuenes chevaliers'), in both instances maintaining the sense of them as novices.[30] On most occasions, however, the 'tiro' became simply a 'chevalier'; it is

---

[27] *Ibid.* I, 8. See Löfstedt edition, 10–13.   [28] Meun, ed. Löfstedt, 8.
[29] BL, Royal 20 B xi; Sloane 2430.   [30] Meun, ed. Löfstedt, 68, 73.

here that the problems began. To men of the late thirteenth century a 'chevalier' was a knight, a word implying birth and breeding and an honourable status in society. It implied, too, a potentially active role in war, which involved a specific way of fighting, using specific weapons and doing so in a way which was honourable and, as we would say, chivalric.

Meun thus used the single word 'chevalier' to translate both 'miles', the trained soldier, and 'tiro', the aspirant, one word where the Latin had used two. One wonders whether confusion was sown in the minds of his readers, not least because only a small proportion of the Roman army fought on horseback, whereas a 'chevalier' would normally fight from the saddle. In order to raise the social standing of the 'miles', who, before military training, might have been a blacksmith or a butcher, to that which Meun's contemporaries would have required as necessary for the knight, the translator was forced to take indirect action. The sword ('gladius'), very much the symbol of the knight's practical skill and prowess in battle, as well as of his social standing, was normally rendered as 'épee' (as it would be in a knightly context in French), whereas the same 'gladius' wielded by a man of lesser rank was normally translated as 'glaive', the 'épee' symbolising the knight's superior position in society.[31] The knight was also associated with certain virtues (observable in both literary and historical texts alike) which made of him a man who merited honour and respect because of the moral, physical and practical qualities reflected in his actions. Therefore, in order to make the Vegetian 'miles' look more like the medieval 'chevalier', Meun resorted to the use of recognisable chivalric attributes which, in adjectival form, were added to the 'chevalier' to make him stand out from the crowd. So the descriptive 'strenuus' ('active') was translated as 'brave' or 'good' ('preux' or 'bons'), the superlative 'strenuissimi' as 'most courageous and brave'(' plus vaillans et plus preux'), all words intended to underline the virtue of the 'chevalier'.[32] Confronted with a system which appeared to promote men to rank within the army on a basis of experience and merit, Meun was obliged to admit that distinction between men in his time depended not only on such factors but on the important ones of birth and upbringing with which certain military attributes were largely associated.

---

[31] See *ibid.* I, 11 (p. 79); R. G. B. Mongeau, 'Jean de Meun's translation of military terminology in Vegetius' "Epitoma rei militaris"' (PhD diss., Fordham Univ., 1981), 122–3, 137, 158.

[32] Meun, ed. Löfstedt, I, 2: p. 70; II, 6: p. 98; I, 8: p. 75; Mongeau, 'Jean de Meun's translation', 21, 39–40, 58–60, 85.

Jean Priorat

Between 1284 and 1290 at the latest, Jean Priorat of Besançon rendered Meun's translation into verse, dedicating the 11,370 octosyllabic verses to Jean de Châlon-Arlay, who had probably commissioned them. Châlon-Arlay was uncle to John, count of Burgundy, who had served on a French expedition into Aragon in 1285, an expedition in which Priorat himself had taken part, giving him some small experience of active warfare. It may, indeed, have been the defeat of a French fleet off Rosas on 16 September 1285 which made him add lines to his verse which criticised those who led unprepared forces into conflict.[33]

It should be emphasised that Priorat's work was not, in a strict sense, a translation; he worked only to versify Meun's French prose text, but did so keeping as close as he could to both the sense and the language used. It is likely that Priorat's text reflects the earliest version of Meun's translation, which has not survived. This would account for the twenty or more passages in (later) manuscripts of Meun's translation which have come down to us, but are not included in either Vegetius' original Latin text or in Priorat's verse; likewise all manuscripts of the Meun translation have gaps not found in Priorat's versification.[34]

However, Priorat was no slavish follower of Meun. In his rendering of the prologue to Book I, for instance, he greatly extended Meun's translation. As later translations into other languages would show, Priorat was not the last to take certain liberties with the prologues. Elsewhere, too, he parted from Meun's text to make smaller additions of his own. On rare occasions, too, he also omitted a passage of Meun's translation.

Meun's tendency to use certain words to underline noble or knightly conduct or attitudes was continued by Priorat, whose descriptions of knights were sometimes given improved status. So the simple 'miles' in Vegetius, rendered 'li chevalier' by Meun, became 'bon chevalier d'elite' in Priorat;[35] Vegetius' 'strenuus bellator' was translated as 'the good fighter' ('le bon bateilleur') by Meun, and as 'brave and experienced fighter' ('bataillours prouz et saiges') by Priorat.[36] At the same time Vegetius' original superlative, 'strenuissimi', rendered as 'les plus vaillanz et les plus preuz' in Meun's version, was presented as 'the boldest, the most daring, the most courageous and most hard-working' ('les plus

---

[33] Jean Priorat, *Li abrejance de l'ordre de chevalerie, mis en vers de la traduction de Végèce de Jean de Meun par Jean Priorat*, ed. U. Robert (SATF, Paris, 1897), lines 10,497–10,506.
[34] Meun, ed. Löfstedt, 11–13.
[35] *DRM*, II, 2; Meun, ed. Löfstedt, 95, line 13; Priorat, ed. Robert, line 2216.
[36] *DRM*, I, 4; Meun, ed. Löfstedt, 72, line 7; Priorat, ed. Robert, line 480.

1 In two scenes the author is shown presenting aspects of his teaching:
cavalry advancing in good order; training in the use of swords; soldiers
mounting horses. (BnF fr. 1604, fo. 2)

hardiz, les plus vaillanz, les plus prouz, les plus travaillanz') in order to
meet the demands of Priorat's verse.[37]

Can we make any judgement regarding the influence which this translation may have had upon its readers? We should note that it is known
today in only a single manuscript, albeit one of high quality, with elaborate illuminations on five folios (see Frontispiece and Figures 1, 2 and
3).[38] All relate to the part of the text close to which they appear; all, too,
relate to war at the end of the thirteenth century, with training at the
pile, knights performing various activities, an attack upon a castle with
different weapons, and an armed sea vessel.[39] It may be noted, too, that
there are no readers' marginalia on this manuscript, which remains in
very good condition. Whether or not this was ever other than a unique
manuscript or is the only one of a number, probably small, to survive, it
is unlikely that the influence of the verse rendering was ever very extensive. This argument is strengthened by the fact that the manuscript was
written in a language which reflected the dialect of Franche-Comté, a

[37] DRM, I, 8: Meun, ed. Löfstedt, 75, lines 9–10; Priorat, ed. Robert, lines 743–4.
[38] BnF fr. 1604.
[39] Li abrejance de l'ordre de chevalerie, mis en vers de la traduction de Végèce de Jean de Meun
par Jean Priorat, ed. Robert, xiii, n. 2.

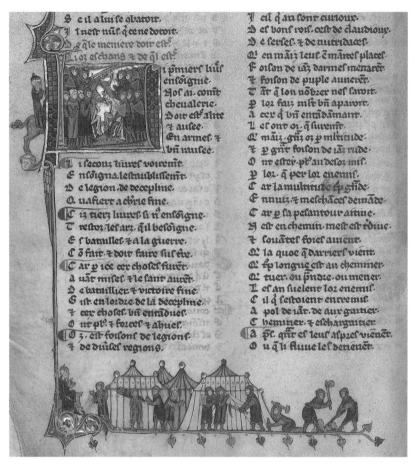

2 In two scenes, Vegetius is shown giving instruction: how armies may be drawn up, and how a camp should be built. (BnF fr. 1604, fo. 27v)

factor likely to diminish rather than extend its readership and, hence, its authority and influence. Bearing in mind, too, the important fact that this was a verse rendering, with all the drawbacks which that form involved, the evidence fails to support an argument that Priorat's version will have enhanced the reputation of the *De re militari* as a major text on the theory and practice of war.

Jean de Vignay

The Norman, Jean de Vignay, completed a second prose translation about 1320. In the course of time, working for Jeanne de Bourgogne,

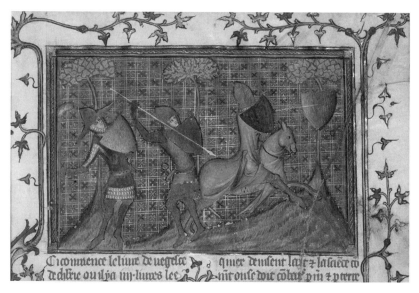

3 Three soldiers, a slinger, a spearman and a mounted knight, practise against a target. (BnF fr. 1229, fo. 5)

wife of King Philip VI of France, he would become quite a practised, if never an outstanding translator. This, one of his first contributions to the art, is not regarded as one of his most successful.[40] More so than Jean de Meun, whose skills in the use of language were far superior, Vignay strove to give a reasonably close translation of the original Latin. But his lack of flair, combined perhaps with a lack of sense of the power of language, could only produce a translation lacking subtlety which hardly did justice to the original.

Like the work of his predecessors, that of Jean de Vignay, whose sufficient knowledge of Latin has been put in doubt,[41] included its fair share of mistranslations, free translations and omissions, as well as passages abridged for one reason or another. If he found abstract, philosophical passages difficult, he was not always sure-footed, either, with his translation of technical language, sometimes adding 'that is to say' ('c'est a dire') or an equivalent to unfamiliar words or particular meanings. To elucidate a meaning, he also employed circumlocutions or two similar

---

[40] C. Knowles, 'Jean de Vignay, un traducteur du XIVe siècle', *Romania*, 75 (1954), 357.
[41] *Li livres Flave Vegece de la chose de chevalerie par Jean de Vignay*, ed. L. Löfstedt (Helsinki, 1989), 5.

words.[42] Furthermore, his translation contained a number of additions to Vegetius' text. Most of these were small, generally not as long or intrusive as those in the translations of Meun or Priorat, being mainly short explanatory sentences (some only clause length) providing readers with snippets of information about place or personal names or, in one case (IV, 7), adding a maxim which had been borrowed, in this case in rather different words, from further back in the translation. This reflects the translator's feeling of a need to provide assistance in helping the reader fully understand the text before him.

In only a single passage did Vignay allow himself the luxury of a serious departure from the original. This was when, at the very beginning of the work, he indulged in a lengthy 'prologue' in which he set out the reasons for making his translation. Human memory being unreliable, he wrote, the ancients developed the practice of committing to writing various branches of knowledge and experience, from which future generations might benefit. After the Greek philosophers, men had turned their attention to matters of government, both the kind imposed through the use of force and that achieved through reason and discussion. Following Vegetius, Vignay argued that such matters were the concern of princes and noblemen who ruled over people committed to their care. There must be no lack of leadership; nor should the people be involved in dangerous conflicts without proper knowledge of what was expected of them. Much had been written on such matters in many books, but where was that information to be found? One such place was in Vegetius' *De la chose de chevalerie*. But this text, being in Latin, a language not normally understood by the military class, ran the risk of being ignored and forgotten. Faced with this possibility, Vignay now undertook to make an accurate translation.[43]

Textual evidence suggests that Vignay had a copy of Meun's translation with him as he worked on certain passages; he may have consulted it when hesitating over difficult passages or military terms which he did not fully understand. However, his confidence in Meun was not always justified. When Meun incorrectly translated 'cuneus' ('wedge') in Vegetius as 'berçueil', Vignay followed him. His translation was later taken up by Christine de Pisan ('bersueil') and through her was to enter the English language ('berseull') when she, in her turn, was translated by William Caxton at the end of the fifteenth century. Similarly, when a

---

[42] C. Buridant, 'Vers un lexique de Jean de Vignay, traducteur: contribution à l'essor de la traduction au XIVe siècle', in *The dawn of the written vernacular in western Europe*, ed. M. Goyens and W. Verbeke (Louvain, 2003), 303–12.

[43] 'n'est pas communement entenduz des chevaliers ... la pure verité de la letre' (Vignay, ed. Löfstedt, p. 38).

part of Meun's translation of one of Vegetius' 'Rules of war' (*DRM*, III, 26) was incorrectly taken up by Vignay, it was later to emerge in Pisan's text and, later still, in that of Caxton.[44]

While there is mention of patronage behind this translation,[45] there is no suggestion that another was needed at the time. Vignay's appeal to his readers to point out mistakes may have been more than a translator's modesty. Should we deduce from it that this was perhaps a novice's translation of a work previously rendered into French (although in a form of the language already disappearing) and which did not require another translation, thus giving Vignay the chance to cut his teeth on a text already available to those wishing to read it? The number of surviving manuscripts suggests that Meun's translation would remain the more popular of the two.[46]

Unlike their Latin equivalents, few vernacular manuscripts contain marginalia, which suggests that they were not intended as, or did not become, working copies; or, perhaps, that the excitement of discovery was largely lacking in a text written in a familiar language.[47] The richness of several manuscripts further supports this impression. Four manuscripts contain illuminations depicting variants of the classic presentation scene involving author or translator offering work to prince or patron.[48] Another shows what appears to be a sage (wearing academic dress?), addressing a king and two courtiers.[49] Various war scenes are depicted, most having a bearing on the text: knights and archers in action, or resistance to attackers scaling a wall. Such standard subjects were appropriate to a translation of the *De re militari*, although those in

---

[44] C. Knowles, 'A 14th century imitator of Jean de Meun: Jean de Vignay's translation of the *De re militari* of Vegetius', *Studies in Philology*, 53 (1956), 454–8.

[45] Vignay claimed to have worked 'sanz nule presumpcion, par commandement' (Vignay, ed. Löfstedt, p. 38).

[46] Was this partly due to the ongoing debate on the *Roman de la rose*, which Meun had helped to translate, and which gave him the advantage of already being known in the literary world? Of the surviving manuscripts, some twenty-five are of Meun's translation, about ten that of Vignay.

[47] One has the original Latin passages written in the margin close to a small number of short passages (Cambridge, Univ. Lib., Ee. II. 17, fos. 17v, 18), while the notes in another reflect a reader's interest in pre-battle strategy and in battle itself (Cambridge, Magdalene, PL 1938, fos. 43–50). In themselves, none of these may be considered significant. Only the attempt by a later reader to modernise the spelling of the early fourteenth-century example, 'sustient' with an 'o' inserted to make 'soustient' (Löfstedt edn, 79, line 65) suggests a wish to make access to the text easier for those reading it later.

[48] Brussels, Bibl. royale, 11,195, fos. 4, 18v; Cambridge, Magdalene, PL 1938, fo. 1; BL Royal 17 E v, fo. 7; BnF fr. 1229, fo. 5.

[49] Vatican, Rossi. 457, fo. 135v.

Vatican, Rossi 457, for example, bear little evident relation to the passage in the text close to which they appear.

These are not the only French translations to exist. Another, made in 1380, perhaps as an attempt to supply a French version of the *De re militari* at a time of high military activity in the country, survives in two copies.[50] Both manuscripts can be dated to the early years of the fifteenth century. The Turin copy is a fine manuscript on vellum, bearing much rich decoration. In addition to Vegetius' work it includes the text of the verse translation of the 'Rules of war', perhaps the work of Philippe de Vitri.[51] The translation, other than that of Book II, is described by its modern editor as 'très libre'; it includes its fair share of doublets (the use of two words to explain an unfamiliar term) and the use of 'c'est à dire', while also containing small additions and omissions, as well as abridgements, particularly to Book IV. The words 'miles' and 'tiro' are usually rendered as 'chevalier', although the term 'batailleur' is also sometimes used.[52]

In the Turin manuscript, at the beginning of the Prologue to Book I (fo. 5) is a large illumination showing a seated figure, dressed in a red robe and black cap, handing out two volumes, to left and to right, to the leaders of two groups of armed knights. One leader wears a gold crown, while a knight holds his golden helm. The other leader has no headgear, only a golden breastplate. At the back is a lectern, upon which lies an open book. The symbolism seems clear. The seated figure represents Vegetius, who is distributing copies of his work on military affairs to a king and to a representative knight who will fight with him.[53] The books contain details of the military wisdom which each will require; the importance of the written word is underlined by the open book on the lectern, available for all to read. It is a scene which, with variations, had been and was to be repeated on other manuscripts, both Latin and vernacular.

A further text, described as a 'translation and adaptation' ('Übersetzung und Bearbeitung') in the modern catalogue, and lacking some of its parts, is currently Wolfenbüttel, Herzog-August-Bibliothek, Blankenburg 111, fos. 1–47v.[54] The text is written in a clear, fourteenth-century gothic minuscule. Of two miniatures, one (fo. 10) shows a king, crowned and seated, with the author, along with four men in

---

[50] Brussels, Bibl. royale, 11,046, fos. 1–75; Turin, Bibl. Reale, Saluzzo, 188, fos. 1–66.

[51] This view was put in serious doubt by Löfstedt, 'Végèce au moyen âge', 498.

[52] See A. Camus, 'Notice d'une traduction française de Végèce faite en 1380', *Romania*, 25 (1896), 393–400, and the 'Introduction' to *Le livre de l'art de chevalerie de Vegese. Traduction anonyme de 1380*, ed. L. Löfstedt *et al.* (Helsinki, 1989).

[53] See *Livre de l'art de chevalerie*, ed. Löfstedt, 10–11.

[54] H. Butzmann, *Die Blankenburger Handschriften* (Frankfurt-am-Main, 1966), 118.

contemporary dress, approaching him; the other (fo. 19) depicts a knight on horseback followed by eight other riders, all wearing helms. Although the chapters of Book IV are numbered continuously to the end, the text is divided into five books: 'Ci fenist li quart livres et commence li quint livre', as if the translator wished to give emphasis to the chapters related to war at sea.[55]

The varied vocabulary used by the translator is of interest. He renders 'tiro[nes]' in at least three ways: 'tirons/tyrons', 'sergens' and 'iuvencaus'. Generally, Meun had chosen to translate the word as 'chevalier'. Vignay had also used 'chevalier', or sometimes 'iovencaus', 'combatierres', or even 'aprentiz d'armes', such indecision making it scarcely surprising that he frequently used a form of circumlocution which enabled him to avoid the word altogether. The anonymous translator's use of 'sergens' marks something new, but it should be recognised that the term was used as part of a growing everyday military vocabulary, and was to be found in the works of the chroniclers in the middle years of the fourteenth century.

The contentious word 'miles' had normally been rendered as 'chevalier' by both Meun and Vignay. The later, anonymous translators, however, preferred a wider choice of words: 'tirons', with its strong suggestion of the 'new' soldier; 'homes d'armes', which would become the term used for the well-armed man who might fight either on foot or in the saddle; 'compaignons', which came to take on a popular sense of the soldier, one of a group, as was implied in the term; while 'chevetaines' carried with it the sense of a man in command, a man who (unlike the 'compaignons') stood out from the rest. Also used were two descriptive phrases: 'men of the army' ('homes de l'ost') and 'those who have to fight' ('gens qui doivent combatre'), in both cases the emphasis being on men whose task it was, indeed, to fight. This hierarchy of terms used to render a single Latin word may cause us to wonder whether the translators had really understood what 'miles' might mean, and whether their inconsistency underlined this fact. Should we not also consider the possibility that we, in our day, may rely too much on precise translations of technical terms? We should remember that 'miles' was, in medieval times, a particularly difficult word for which to provide an exact and immediately recognisable equivalent. What was the translator trying to do: to provide a literal rendering of the Latin (was that ever possible?), or to create a new text in updated, explanatory language? It is evident that most of our translators recognised the difficulty which faced them. Interestingly, the word chosen to translate the Latin 'miles', when referring to a man about

---

[55] Reeve, 'Transmission', 338.

to be executed for a serious demeanour, is revealing. Both Meun and Vignay had continued in the use of 'chevalier'; the last translator, however, as if sensing or fearing that execution would bring dishonour upon a 'chevalier', chose to use the simple word 'home' ('man'). Was this a tacit and belated recognition of the respect which the Middle Ages liked to give to its 'chevaliers'? Was it difficult to give a degraded military man facing death as a criminal any more respect than to call him by what he indoubtedly was: an 'home'?

Italy

By the end of the fifteenth century, the Italian peninsula was to witness the production of four full translations of the *De re militari*, in addition to what has come down to us as a translation of the work's first book, the survival of which should not exclude the possibility that a further complete translation once existed.[56]

The first, into Tuscan, completed by Bono Giamboni before 1292, has left us six manuscripts. Broadly contemporary with those of Master Richard and Jean de Meun, the translation was the product of a time which was coming to appreciate the intellectual nature of the study of war, now assuming a specialist character of its own.[57] Like Meun, Giamboni was the translator of other works into the vernacular. On this occasion he worked to the order of Messer Manetto della Scala, who, we must assume, appreciated the didactic nature of the work whose readership he planned to extend.[58]

The translation which, possibly because it is into Italian, appears to keep closer to the Latin than that completed by Meun, enjoys a certain momentum. When Vegetius intruded himself into his text with the use of the first person singular of the verb, Giamboni did the same.[59] While this suggests that he took care with certain types of detail, he did not allow himself to be ruled by the need to make a word for word translation. As others were doing and would do, he made subtle – and not so subtle – cuts in the Latin text. Perhaps fearful of including names which he thought might mean little to his readers, Giamboni sometimes omitted personal or place names. The familiar problem of how to translate the language of Roman weaponry was sometimes resolved by bypassing the

---

[56] The texts are usefully listed in G. Vaccaro, 'Glossario di un volgarizzamento di Vegezio', *Studi di lessicografia italiana*, 24 (2007), 133–4.

[57] A. Murray, *Reason and society in the Middle Ages* (Oxford, 1978), 124.

[58] *Di Vegezio Flavio, Dell' arte della Guerra, libri IV. Volgarizzamento di Bono Giamboni*, ed. F. Fontani (Florence, 1815), x.

[59] E.g., *ibid.* 21.

difficulty altogether.[60] The careless translation of 'Joviani' as 'Giovani' ('i Marziobarbuli e Giovani') strongly suggests that the translator had not fully grasped the meaning of the passage.[61] At times whole sentences are summed up in a short passage. Giamboni may have felt it unnecessary to translate them in full or, perhaps, he was simply uneasy about his understanding of them.[62] On other occasions the translation was very free, ideas and explanations being offered by the translator himself.[63]

None the less, while not satisfying those with a preference for a more exact translation of the Latin text, Giamboni's work brought an influential, practical work, whose reputation had been rising rapidly in the second half of the thirteenth century, to the notice of readers increasingly anxious to have classical works available to them in the vernacular. It was probably not Giamboni's wish to create a new work with immediate practical utility; his odd comments and additions hardly suggest that this was his intention. Rather, what he probably aimed at was making available an Italian version of the Latin which was reasonably accurate, free of undue historical baggage which might not be fully appreciated, largely free, too, of his own additions and references to relatively recent events such as are found in the translation of Jean de Meun.

A second translation, done anonymously in the late fourteenth or early fifteenth century, known in only a single surviving manuscript and copied in humanistic script on vellum, probably emanated from northern Italy.[64] This 'Epythoma delli institute dell'arte militare' would one day belong to Carolus Franciscus Cena; it bears a bookplate bearing the name of Conti della Trinità and an unidentified coat of arms. In this manuscript of quality, the text begins with a large capital letter, ten lines high, enclosing a man (probably a king) in armour. It is unfortunate there is no indication of who was responsible for what was, perhaps, the most satisfying of the Italian translations. Facing the same text and difficulties as his predecessors, the anonymous translator coped better than some with the many problems which confronted him. His text reads well, probably because he appears to have had a clearer idea than had his predecessor of the meaning of what Vegetius had written.

Two things stand out. One is the general flow of the language used. The second is the degree of accuracy brought to the work of translation, which is seldom interrupted by the need to explain words and phrases. Generally speaking, it remains faithful to the original, subtracting little, adding (or 'improving' the text) even less. Omissions do not come often, and when they do, they are usually small, sometimes causing the reader to wonder

---

[60] *Ibid.* I, 20 (p. 28); II, 17 (p. 60).   [61] *Ibid.* I, 17 (p. 24).   [62] *Ibid.* III, 26 (p. 146).
[63] *Ibid.* III, 26 (p. 142).   [64] Harvard, Houghton Lib. Italian 68, fos. 1–51.

whether an omission may not be the result of the scribe's inattentiveness or lack of concentration rather than the deliberate choice of the translator himself. Who, for instance, was responsible for the curious omission of 'Christ and the Holy Spirit' in the oath taken by the newly fledged 'miles'? On the other hand, the omission of a translation of the clause 'quos galiarios vocant' was probably deliberate, but whether to spare the translator's blushes or because, understandably, he felt that it added little to the text, is not clear.[65]

While there were occasions when the technical language defeated him, and the use of Latinisms became necessary ('Martiobarbuli' and 'triarii', for example, are left unchanged),[66] the translator is often more successful in finding a modern term because he appears to have understood what the original meant, thus making his rendering smoother and easier to read. The occasional use of the extension, or a second explanatory word which might be clearer to a reader than a single word, can also be found.[67] This translation is also more generally respectful of proper names, few of which are omitted. Granted what was done by others, it is unlikely that this was simply chance. More likely it was that the translator expected names in the text to mean something to his readers.

The translator sometimes tried to bring the text up to date by adding material to make it so. When he rendered Vegetius' statement that an army's strength depended largely on its infantry (III, 9) as 'in li pedoni *a questo nostro tempo* sta maximamente la fortessa de lo exercito', he added words '*in our own time*' not found in the Latin. Did the translator do this because he thought that they were implied in Vegetius' original, or in the hope of emphasising the importance of infantry in the context of his own day? The likelihood that he was updating the translation must remain a strong possibility. Although he was generally faithful to his original, the translator did not allow a comment such as that made by Vegetius regarding the importance of infantry to escape him. His use of words such as 'capitani' ('duces'), and 'soldati' ('milites') suggests that this translation, through the use of contemporary language, was intended to have resonance in his own day.

Another translation, the third, is found in two surviving manuscripts.[68] Completed on 27 March 1417, it was the work of Master Venanzo de Bruschino da Camerino, who made it at the request ('ad instantia,

---

[65] *DRM*, I, 10. We should perhaps sympathise with the translator; the most recent English translation renders this clause 'whom they call *galearii*', a clear sign of problems faced by those wishing to translate a technical term into a modern language (*Vegetius: Epitome*, trans. Milner, 12).

[66] *DRM*, I. 17; I, 20.   [67] 'Signum' is rendered as 'signe & bandiera' in II, 13.

[68] Naples, Bibl. Oratoriana, CF. II. 23; Florence, Naz. nuov. acq., 291.

commendamento e piacere') of the Perugian nobleman and captain Braccio da Montone (d.1424), who had been, for a time some years earlier, Captain-General of the Church and, after his victory at S. Egidio in 1416, master of Perugia. The language of the dedication, 'to my most magnanimous, gracious and in matters concerning war in our day most notable leader' ('mio magnanimo e . . . graciose e nei fatti dellarme ai tempi nostri singular conductieri'), is that of indebtedness, hardly surprisingly as Bruschino was chancellor of Perugia at the time. The two manuscripts are very different in character. The 'Neapolitan' one, perhaps the presentation copy, was clearly a product of quality; it carries the heraldic crest of the Narducci di Toscana on folio 1. By contrast, the 'Florentine' manuscript is an unpretentious copy written later on paper.

The translation was a competent one. In his attempt to modernise place names the translator sometimes made mistakes; in some places he omitted (or forgot?) names; in others, he added them. But he appears to have had a reasonable understanding of the meaning of the many technical words in Vegetius' text, or at least to have introduced realistic contemporary language when dealing with them. The translation, however, is long. In marked contrast with the original, Bruschino wrote in a style which, at times, came close to being wordy. Doubtless well intentioned, he used extensions to open up points made in the text, an approach which sometimes altered the character of the work. This is seen, in its most excessive form, in his rendering of some of the briefest of the 'Rules of war' (*DRM*, III, 26), where one rule of five words became sixteen and another of six words grew into seventeen words, their original pithiness and consequent impression upon the reader being much diminished. Sometimes Bruschino felt the need to add information or names, or to elaborate upon these (such as the Balearic Islands); at other times he gave a modern rendering of a place or region which he felt his readers might not know or recognise, thus slightly altering the text and, on occasions, adding to already existing confusion. It is ironical that the man who so extended the length of Vegetius' text should have referred to it as 'the little book', or 'el libretto'.[69]

What effect did this translation have upon the man who ordered it to be made for him? On this occasion we may be able to trace a link between recommendations made by Vegetius and their application by a particular captain, in this case the translator's patron, who, it has been argued, had a distinctive style of warfare which would be inherited by others who were to influence warfare in Italy in the fifteenth century. If 'the strength

---

[69] Note, however, that Vegetius twice referred to his work as an *opusculum*. On this translation see Reeve, 'Transmission', 341–2.

of Montone's method lay, as did that of [Muzio Attendolo] Sforza, in being able to control troops on the battlefield', then he was a man who would have felt at ease reading the *De re militari* and its insistence upon the need for discipline when confronting the enemy, discipline achieved through firm control by the commander. Montone would have agreed with such well-known Vegetian recommendations as the organised (i.e., 'planned and practised') use of formations, which in his case involved men fighting in rotation to give them all a rest, a manoeuvre unachievable without practice; the use of speed in manoeuvres (how often Vegetius had recommended 'velocitas'!), which represented daring, practice and, not least, confidence; and the provision of drinking water, as Montone provided it, to refresh his army in the battle of S. Egidio, fought on a hot summer's day in 1416.[70]

Once in charge of Perugia, Montone organised the militia, holding jousts to encourage a military spirit. The army which he created consisted increasingly of men from the region, and 'began to look almost like a national army'. He also experimented with the so-called 'sword and buckler' infantry, lightly armed and agile troops, equipped for hand-to-hand fighting.[71] While the idea of these probably originated in Spain, and may have come to Italy through the Aragonese presence in Naples, it should also be said that the style of warfare corresponded with much that Vegetius had recommended. Above all, it strongly suggests that the man who commissioned Bruschino's translation had a real and practical interest in military ideas, that he understood the far-reaching implications of many of them, and that he was ready to apply them, with effect, to the military needs and conditions of his own time.[72]

Nothing, other than the very little the text can tell us, is known regarding the origins, inspiration or authorship of the anonymous translation of the first book of the *De re militari* which has survived in a single fifteenth-century manuscript.[73] Was this all that was translated, or was there originally more that is now lost, unrecognised or destroyed? The text itself gives hints regarding certain matters. The translator began by referring to 'my' ('mio') prologue, which he had completed 'in the name of Christ' ('in lo nome de Xristo'), which could indicate that he was a man of the cloth, a suggestion supported by his addition of two references to the work of Isidore of Seville.[74] Elsewhere, his knowledge of

---

[70] Mallett, *Mercenaries and their masters*, 66, 71–2.   [71] *Ibid.* 72, 155.

[72] On Muzio Sforza, and his military style, see *ibid.* 68–9. On Braccio's interest in commissioning this translation, see Settia, *De re militari*, 44.

[73] Naples, Naz. IX C 24, fos. 63v–69v.

[74] *L'ars militaris di Flavio Vegezio Renato: volgarizzamento del libro primo da un codice della Nazionale di Napoli inedito*, ed. G. Tria (Naples, 1887), 16–17.

ancient history is demonstrated by the way he added names not found in the Latin text which he was translating (that of Octavian to a list of emperors, for example), and information regarding the duration of peace between Rome and Carthage.[75] However, much of his translation was rather free, some of it bearing little resemblance to the Latin original.

The possible clerical character of the translator suggests itself in the effort made to explain Vegetius' name, Renatus. Quoting Christ: 'Unless a man be re-born of water and the Holy Spirit ... ('Nisi quis renatus [re-natus] fuerit ex aqua et spiritu sancto ... '), he added that this was a name which the Romans held in great esteem. Then, following the Greek etymology of the word 'Ephithoma', he described briefly what is taught/contained/shown/recounted in each book: 'Lo primo libro insegnia (edocet) ... Lo secundo libro contene (continet) ... Lo terzo libro expone (exponit) ... Lo quarto libro raconta (enumerat) ... '. The list of chapter headings, which is not complete, follows.[76]

The translation is the work of one confident that he knows what the Latin text he has before him means. However, this can in no sense be regarded as a straight translation; there are all too evident omissions as well as additions, and the language at times lacks directness, circumlocutions being not uncommon, perhaps the result of the south-eastern dialect in which it is written. The translator was anxious that some references or allusions might pass the reader by: for instance, he tried to give not only weights, but distances, too, in a language which would be understood by his readers.[77] Several times he made use of the formula 'that is ... '('zo e ... ') to explain difficult or unfamiliar terms: 'a field of Mars, that is to say a battlefield' ('uno campo marcio, zo e de la battaglia');[78] 'bowmen, that is archers and crossbowmen ('sagitarij, zo e a dire arcieri e balistreri'); 'a stake, that is to say a post' ('pali, zo e legnie').[79] The translator was fully aware of his duty of explaining, where he could, words which might mean little or nothing to his readers. That was not the same, however, as creating a new text whose teachings would be applicable to his own day.

In these respects, then, the aim of the translator appears to have been to anticipate the many unfamiliar, technical and even confusing words that readers would not fully understand. That such words did exist is easily proved by the manuscript evidence of the Latin text, which, as we have seen, shows the marginalia as testimony of an interested but sometimes puzzled readership baffled by unfamiliar words and expressions it

---

[75] *Ibid.* 33–4.   [76] *Ibid.* 9–10.   [77] *Ibid.* 27, 33, chs. 19, 27.
[78] Here the translator failed to see that the reference was to the Campus Martius in Rome.
[79] *Ibid.* 21, 24, 31, chs. 10, 15, 24.

could not fully understand. Here the not infrequent use of 'that is...'
('quid est....') is important since it may justify the efforts of translators
to explain a vocabulary no longer in current use, and which was impeding
a proper and intelligent understanding of Vegetius' text. It is not unreasonable to envisage attempts by the translator to provide an extended
meaning of a word as his response to a 'quid est...' found in a margin of
the particular manuscript from which he was working. Explaining a term
is not the same as trying to make a text relevant to a new age. What was
being attempted here – and elsewhere – was often no more than making
a text, hitherto known only in Latin, accessible to a modern readership,
just as today footnotes explain to their readers the meaning of words
which have fallen out of use, and whose sense is seized upon by those
who have an interest either in words, or in the subject being discussed,
or in both.

A fourth, anonymous translation,[80] probably from the area around
Siena, exists in only a single known manuscript, quite unpretentious in
character. The manuscript contains four works, *Della doctrina dal parlare*
by the humanist Brunetto Latini; Aristotle's *Ethics*; the *Secretum secretorum*; and the *De re militari*, all in Italian. The translation is clear and keeps
reasonably close to the original. The text is not without small omissions.
As was the case with Giamboni, some Roman names are omitted from the
translation. Some place names are modernised, not always successfully;
while it is legitimate to translate the Roman Capitol as 'Campidollio', and
'Misenum' as Naples, and reasonable to render the 'Thessali' as 'quelle
de Soloniche', Diocletian is certainly not Domitian. Some passages were
abridged; IV, 9 is a case in point. Others, by contrast, were extended, and
names tentatively added. All in all, however, this would have provided
a useful translation, in spite of the fact that the translator appears not
to have been fully conversant with either the nomenclature or even the
nature of much ancient weaponry, which he frequently rendered with
little alteration to the Latin original.[81]

---

[80] Florence, Naz. II ii 72, fos. 82v–131.
[81] I was unable to see another manuscript of 'un brieve tractato di Vigetio Flavio', preserved
in a private library, Vibo Valentia, Bibl. Capialbi 39. See *Inventari dei manoscritti delle
biblioteche d'Italia*, ed. G. Mazzatinti, VII (Forlì, 1897; repr. 1996, 204). Bibl. Borja,
Sant Cugat del Vallès, Ms Fons E, Varia, includes parts of a manuscript of an Italian
translation of the *De re militari*. See J. A. Iglesias i Fonseca, 'Minima palaeographica: un
codex humanístic de l'Eneida de Virgili a Sant Cugat del Vallès (Barcelona)', *Butlletí de
la Reial Acadèmia de Bones Lletres de Barcelona*, 48 (2002), 570, n. 4. I have not been able
to establish whether these are parts of a known translation, or an altogether different
one. I thank Dr Antoni Alomar for alerting me to this reference, and Professor Iglesias,
of the Universitat Autònoma de Barcelona, who plans a study of the manuscript, for
sharing information about it.

Iberia

With its several languages, Iberia was to make its own contribution to the translation and propagation of the *De re militari*. Strangely, the search for medieval manuscripts of the Latin text in Portugal has so far proved fruitless. Of a Portuguese translation, possibly made by the Infante, Don Pedro, in the 1430s, there are hints, but no text has ever been found.[82] On the other hand, recent research suggests that Portuguese military practice in the late Middle Ages may have been influenced by Vegetian ideas.[83] Until clear evidence is produced, however, the situation must remain uncertain and unsatisfactory.[84]

In Castile the influence of Vegetius is to be observed in the *Partidas* of Alfonso X, composed about 1270. At this relatively early date that influence can only have been transmitted to the Castilian court through the Latin text. It would be a further century or more, probably about 1400, before a translation of the *De re militari* into Castilian would be made.

Catalonia, however, would produce two translations, each of which has survived in a single manuscript. The first of these is today incomplete, having lost the first fourteen chapters and three other later ones of Book I, as well as lacking the last nine chapters of Book IV. As a result, we are possibly deprived of information regarding the background to the translation, the name of the translator and, perhaps, that of his patron, and, not least, the date of the translation.[85] In general, this appears to keep quite close to the Latin original, although some passages are rendered fairly freely into Catalan, and the reader will have no difficulty in locating omissions.[86] Surprising, perhaps, for a Catalan translator was the omission of the passage in I, 16 which referred in the Latin to the inhabitants of the Balearic Islands having been the earliest to use the sling, a weapon which they wielded to great effect. By contrast, the second Catalan translation not only included the passage, but embellished

---

[82] A. A. Nascimento, 'La réception des auteurs classiques dans l'espace culturel portugais: une question ouverte', in *The classical tradition in the Middle Ages and the Renaissance. Proceedings of the first European Science Workshop on 'The reception of classical texts'*, ed. C. Leonardi and B. Munk Olsen (Spoleto, 1995), 52; Reeve, 'Transmission', 342–3; J. G. Monteiro, 'A cultura militar de nobreza na primeira metade de quatrocentos. Fontes e modelos literários', *Revista de história das ideias*, 19 (1997/98), 206–10. Vegetius will have been known in Portugal through the work of John of Salisbury and, in particular, that of Giles of Rome.

[83] See the important study by J. G. Monteiro, *A guerra em Portugal nos finais da idade media* (Lisbon, 1998).

[84] See P. Russell, 'Terá havido uma tradução medieval portuguesa do *Epitoma rei militaris* de Vegécio?', *Euphrosyne. Revista de filologia clássica*, n.s. 29 (2001), 247–56.

[85] Madrid, Bibl. Zabálburu, 1655.   [86] E.g., II, 6 and 22; III, Praef., and IV, 7.

it, too.[87] Passages dealing with the etymology of terms, a characteristic of Vegetius, who liked his readers to understand the origins of words, were normally omitted by the translator; perhaps he felt that his readers would not be interested in such matters. On the other hand, on those occasions when Vegetius introduced the first or second person ('I...' or 'you...') the translator maintained the accuracy of the passage, and did not change it by verbal circumlocution. He also maintained the sense of immediacy which the passage contained. Loose translations suggesting that the translator had misunderstood the text are to be found, but not often. When it came to the point of lengthening a passage in order to introduce the explanation of a word or term, this translator showed himself much more restrained than his French or Italian counterparts had been.

What manner of vocabulary did this translator use? As we have observed with the French translations, the Latin 'tiro' could be rendered in several ways: 'aquells qui deuen esser homens d'armes'; 'jovens'; 'elets a feyt d'armes'; 'cavaller'; 'aquells qui deuen esser caval[lers]'; and 'los novells'.[88] Except when using 'cavallers', the translator managed to preserve the sense of the recruit or the soldier who, in training, was not yet fully fledged. The 'miles' (the 'commissioned' soldier of the *De re militari*) usually emerged as a 'cavaller'; however, the 'equites' were also 'cavallers', while soldiers fighting on foot, 'pedestris exercitus' or 'pedites', were transformed into 'peons'.[89] The translations of 'res militaris' are interesting and varied: 'feyt de cavalleria' and 'doctrina de cavalleria'; 'art de feyt d'armes'; 'cavalleria'; and 'feyt d'armes' (this last putting one in mind of Christine de Pisan's *Fais d'armes*).[90] 'Battala' was doubtless readily understood when used to translate 'bellum', 'certamen', 'conflictus' and 'acies'. This sense may have reflected the influence of the French 'bataille', meaning a company of soldiers (an 'acies', no doubt), although it would also be translated as 'companya' and 'escales' in this text.[91]

The second translation, happily, survives in better condition.[92] It informs the reader that it is entitled 'Del mester darmes e dela art de

---

[87] Cf. Bibl. Zabálburu, 1655, fo. 1, and Palma, Bibl. March Servera, B96–V3–2, fo. 8v: 'en les illes de Spanya qui Beleares foren nomenades e era se appellen Malorqua e Manorqua e Yviça'. In the 1280s, Gil de Zamora had drawn attention to the passage in the *De re militari* which refers to the Balearics, 'nunc Maiorice sive Regnum Maioricarum noviter, secundum aliquos apellatur' (*De preconiis Hispanie*, ed. M. de Castro y Castro (Madrid, 1955), 226).

[88] I, 16; I, 19; I, 20; I, 21; I, 28; III, 12.

[89] 'Miles' = 'cavaller' at I, 20, 26; II, 8, 9, 15, etc.: 'equites' = 'cavallers' at I, 27; II, 6; III, 16: 'pedites' = 'peons' at I, 20; II, 6.

[90] I, 28; III, Praef.; III, 2; III, 6.   [91] II, 6, 15.

[92] Now Palma, Bibl. March Servera, B96–V3–2., formerly Phillipps Ms 16380.

cavalleria', and is the work of Jacme Castellà, who translated ('torna') it out of French. Castellà's language suggests that, like his fellow translators, Antoni Canals and the well-known Francesc Eiximenis, he was a Valencian. Certainly he was a man of the court, who frequented that of King Joan and Violant de Bar, whom he served and under whose patronage he carried out his work.[93]

Which French text was Castellà translating? In spite of what the compilers of the sale catalogue claimed in 1972, internal evidence and comparison with the texts of Jean de Meun and others rule these out, while the one which Castellà may have used has disappeared. As already observed, Meun was not averse to adding whole passages of his own, sometimes by way of comment, other times to provide examples, digressions not encountered in Castellà's text. Perhaps more significantly, Castellà included small but telling details to his version, details not in Meun but certainly in the original Latin. It appears likely, therefore, that Castellà had a Latin text before him as he worked. Sometimes, indeed, one wonders whether he was not translating the Latin, rather than the French.[94]

How does this translation compare with the earlier one already discussed? On the whole it appears less true to the original than the first. Castellà, one surmises, had chosen the route of providing a text which, while reasonably accurate, would sometimes emphasise only the broad sense of the original. He adapted, largely by omitting what he regarded as relatively insignificant phrases or words, and even names. Sometimes he went further, occasionally resorting to paraphrase. Yet he was also prepared to elaborate. In a passage (noted above) in which Vegetius referred to the Balearic Islands, which the first translator had rendered simply, and a little limply, as the 'isolas', Castellà was bolder, spelling them out by name: Mallorca, Menorca and Ibiza. Difficulties with the text were dealt with in a number of ways. Circumlocution, already used by Meun, was one. Another, likewise found in the French texts, was to ignore a list of technical words and substitute a single, inclusive one in their place. In Book IV, in particular, confronted with the common, practical problem that his language did not have exact equivalents for certain arms and machines of war, Castellà chose to call these 'diverses enginys', a method of escape from a dilemma which others had already used, and would use again.

A brief consideration of some of the words and terms used to act as equivalents of a Latin word can again be constructive. 'Tiro[nes]'

[93] L. Badia, 'Frontí i Vegeci, mestres de cavalleria en Català als segles XIV i XV', *Boletín de la Real Academia de Buenas Letras de Barcelona*, 39 (1983–84), 209–10.
[94] *Ibid.* 210–11. See Reeve, 'Transmission', 338–40.

was translated as 'young knights' ('jovens cavallers'), sometimes as simply 'jovens' and, increasingly as the translation progressed, simply as 'tirons'.[95] 'Miles/milites' ('knight' or 'soldier') was presented in almost every case as 'cavallers' but also as 'gent'.[96] 'Equites' ('cavalry') had rather more equivalents, of which the most obvious was 'cavallers'. But the word could also be expressed as 'los de cavall'; 'la gent de cavall'; and 'homens a cavall'.[97] 'Acies' (a battle line) was rendered either as 'escala' or 'scala', or as 'batalla'.[98] We have already noticed how a single word in Catalan might be regarded as the equivalent of a number in Latin. 'Batalla' is found to have four meanings in Latin: 'bellum'; 'pugna'; 'conflictus'; as well as 'acies',[99] whereas 'host' could mean both 'exercitus' and 'castra' ('army' and 'camp'),[100] this last also being translated by the seemingly more appropriate word 'lo camp'.[101] As for the term 'res militaris', this was rendered in at least three different ways: 'mester ['the art'] d'armes'; 'mester de cavalleria'; and, hardly surprisingly, 'la art de cavalleria'.[102] Although not by much, all three versions are different from those used by the first translator.

In one important respect Castellà did both the text and later critics a service. By making it clear what he understood the word 'cavalleria' to mean, he did two things. He showed how far Vegetius' text was about practical factors which brought victory in war. He showed, too, that the reader of the Middle Ages should accept that 'cavallers' might mean 'soldiers', not knights who sought honour or dignity by wearing golden spurs (as he put it in his introduction) but in the more hard-headed sense of men who did the fighting, whether on horseback or on foot. He appeared to be distancing himself from the notion that 'cavalleria' was something which belonged to the romances. His concern was for the real world.

This approach is underlined by a glance at the marginal comments made by readers of the manuscripts. Two characteristics of these may be highlighted. One is the use of the words 'antigua' and 'antigament' in a number of the marginalia, thereby emphasising the wisdom and the practices of the ancients which the text brought to their notice. The second was the stress given in many of the marginalia to practical matters that should concern those preparing for war: the importance of the use of proper armour; the numbers making up the formations; how men should ready themselves for battle; the places to be occupied by commanders on

---

[95] *Tiro[nes]:* I, 2; I, 15; I, 3.   [96] Miles/milites: II, 6; III, 26.
[97] Equites: II, 14; I, 10; II, 23; I, 25; II, 1; III,16; II, 6, 14.   [98] Acies: II, 6; III, 19.
[99] Batalla: I, 20; III, 14; III, 21; III, 19.   [100] Host: II, 6, 8.   [101] Castra: I, 22.
[102] I, 28; II, 1; III, 6. See Badia, 201, n. 22.

the battlefield. It was the practical issues which, the manuscript evidence suggests, interested readers. A few references to recent or contemporary military events emphasise the perceived link between past practices described in the text and actions which had taken place recently.[103] These underline yet further the relevance of the text to the contemporary world.

The closing years of the fourteenth century and the early years of the fifteenth century were generally a very productive period for translators, in both Catalonia and Castile. The second Catalan translation was of this period, when developments in the readership of classical works were already beginning to occur, particularly among the military class ('militares viri'), the nobility and those responsible for the government of the day. Under discussion ('el debat de las armas y las letras') was the running of the state, and the final effort to complete the *reconquista*, in particular the role to be played in the process by the nobility. The role and influence of the 'courtly' nobility was to be challenged by the lay, 'chivalric' nobility, anxious to emphasise a view of chivalry as service of the 'res publica' based on and inspired by Roman models. In this process, translations into the languages of Iberia of classical literature, not least the *De re militari* and works in the vernacular, such as the *Quadrilogue invectif* of Alain Chartier, which reflected many of its ideas, had their part to play.[104]

The single translation into Castilian, six copies of which have survived to this day, was made by the Dominican friar Alfonso de San Cristóbal, probably at the bidding of King Enrique III, at the turn of the fourteenth and fifteenth centuries.[105] In his own words he aimed above all at clarity ('lo mas claramente que yo pudiere'), and at making his translation into a readable one, so important for a text of a didactic nature.[106] Yet

---

[103] IV, 7, 9.

[104] J. N. H. Lawrance, 'The spread of lay literacy in late medieval Castile', *Journal of Hispanic Studies*, 62 (1985), 80–4; see also C. Pascual-Argente, 'From *Invectivo to Inventivo*: reading Chartier's *Quadrilogue invectif* in fifteenth-century Castile', in *Chartier in Europe*, ed. Cayley and Kinch, 119–33.

[105] Madrid, Real Bibl., II/569; Escorial, & ii. 18 and P. i. 23; Santander, Bibl. Menéndez y Pelayo, 94; BnF Esp. 211, 295. The Santander manuscript has been digitalised, and can be viewed online. See M. I. Hernández González (ed.), *En la teoría y en la práctica de la traducción. La experiencia de los traductores castellanos a la luz de sus textos (siglos XIV–XVI)* (Salamanca, 1998), 18–21. See also P. Russell, 'De nuevo sobre la traduccion medieval castellana de Vegecio *Epitoma de rei militaris* [sic], in *Essays on medieval translation in the Iberian peninsula*, ed. T. Martinez Romero and R. Recio (Castello, 2001), 325, 333.

[106] Lawrance ('Spread of lay literacy', 82–3) stresses the importance of rubrics, in which the brief Latin chapter headings are replaced by a much longer version such as 'El (sesto) capitulo fabla (muestra) como (quando)...' intended to assist the reader understand the text.

it may have been this wish to achieve clarity which caused the translator's style, in the words of a modern critic, to become 'thin, wooden and repetitious'.[107] Although a good Latinist, San Cristóbal was not the first to discover that the lack of precise synonyms would cause him difficulties. He was not very confident, for example, of how to translate the word 'tiro', which, at first, he rendered as 'tiron', but later changed to 'mancebo'. Like others, too, he wanted to disguise his lack of a technical vocabulary, so that the 'diverses engynis' of the second Catalan translation became, in his work, 'instrumentos', the equivalent of 'machina', 'artifices' and 'vineas'.[108] Generally speaking, however, he seems to have been a little more consistent in his choice of words and terms used to render a single word in Latin: 'milites' became 'cavalleros', while 'equites' was turned into either 'omes de cavallo' or 'los de cavallo'. The phrase 'res militaris', of key importance in a work of this title, was, like Castellà's Catalan translation, rendered in three ways: 'ordenança de la cavalleria', 'la cavalleria' and 'el uso de la cavalleria'.[109]

Attention has been drawn to San Cristóbal's translation of II, 5, which concerns the 'passing out' ceremony of the newly qualified 'miles'.[110] The version presented marks a considerable departure from the original, both in detail and in the general direction which the translation gives to what Vegetius had written. When San Cristóbal translates 'Romana respublica' as 'tierra', the reader notes the use of the word, particularly resonant in Spain, to mean 'earth' or 'country' in a moral sense perfectly understandable to his contemporaries but a little different from that of the Latin original.[111] Just as often, however, he renders 'res publica' as 'comunidat', giving the sense of a people engaged in a common enterprise and destiny.[112] The political and social resonance of contemporary language could not be avoided.

However, what makes this translation stand out in both an Iberian and a broader European context is that, having translated the work, San Cristóbal appended to each chapter of Book I, and to a number of others in later books, a series of explanatory glosses, originally written in the margins but later included in the text itself, some being longer than the chapter to which they related. In many instances they allowed San

---

[107] Russell, 'De nuevo', 336.   [108] *DRM*, II, 11, 25; IV, 18.
[109] *Ibid.* I, 28; II, 1, 6. See also J. M. Fradejas, 'El modelo latino de la versión castellana medieval de *Epitoma rei militaris* de Vegecio', *Estudios humanísticos. Filología*, 32 (2010), 47–55.
[110] Russell, 'De nuevo', 328–29.
[111] Elsewhere San Cristóbal used the word 'tierra' again to translate 'res publica' (II, 3, 5); once he rendered it as 'reyno e la tierra' (II, 24).
[112] *DRM*, I, 3; II, 4; III, 3, 26; IV, Praef.

Cristóbal to summarise the chapter's main arguments as he understood them ('En este capitulo glosa & pone Vegecio tres cosas...'), which he then set out point by point ('la primera cosa...la segunda cosa...la tercera cosa...) as a person accustomed to preaching or teaching might do, while adding his own summary or comments. Thus the gloss to I, 1 emphasised the importance which the Romans attached to proper preparation for war; how highly Vegetius regarded experience as a factor in war; how, in his attempt to achieve victory, a commander must be prepared to use cunning; and how he looked to have at his disposal both the mature advice of veterans and the confidence and strength of young soldiers. In some, by referring to earlier and later chapters,[113] San Cristóbal showed that he had read (and probably already translated) the entire work, and had appreciated the broader message into which his comments on a particular chapter might be put. He had clearly understood, and was enthusiastic about, Vegetius' basic message that the training in skills, the 'ars militaris' or 'arte in la batalla', was of fundamental importance in securing victory. The way in which he made references to the battles fought against the Moors at Úbeda, Alarcos and Alange suggests that he regarded Vegetius' text as being relevant to the reality of war in his own age.

If his glosses were often not much more than a summary of a chapter,[114] San Cristóbal nonetheless showed himself to be a man of considerable learning. He was well versed in the contents of both the Old and the New Testaments; his liking for the story of Judas Maccabeus earned his approval of Vegetius' doctrine that victory did not depend on numbers alone, although not quite in the way that Vegetius had intended it.[115] He could cite Aristotle, with references to the *Metaphysics*, and a number of the major Christian commentators such as Gregory, Bernard and Aquinas; he also had some knowledge of Roman history[116] and of some Roman authors, particularly, and in this case most appropriately, the *Strategemata* of Frontinus 'el sabio', whom he referred to on a number of occasions.[117]

However, as if these comments were not sufficient, a second San Cristóbal (as it were) was to impose himself further upon the text. This was no longer the translator helping the reader understand Vegetius' original meaning and its contribution to military thought and good practice. It was now the turn of the friar-theologian who saw in the *De re militari* a

---

[113] In I, 6 he looks forward to I, 8; in II, 23, he looks back to things written in I, 9 and 15, while in I, 19 he refers briefly ('sumariamente') to points made in earlier chapters.
[114] E.g., I, 26.   [115] See the glosses to III, 17, 22 and 24.
[116] E.g., I, 27.   [117] In the glosses to I, 11, 21; III, 12.

text which, interpreted as spiritual allegory, might encourage the reader to ponder another kind of war, the conflict between the forces of good and evil. So Book I, already provided with glosses on the text itself, was given a second set (one for each chapter), many beginning 'Spiritually speaking' ('Spiritualmente fablando'), in which, in turn, appeared a range of names taken from the Bible, mostly the Old Testament. What was the aim and purpose of such glosses?[118] Are we in the presence of a Vegetius 'moralised' as Ovid was 'moralised? The word 'moralidad' appears a number of times in the glosses to one of the Escorial manuscripts.[119] San Cristóbal seems to have placed himself in the tradition of clergy who, like Alcuin or Denis the Carthusian, saw the *De re militari* as a text with lessons for those wishing to discipline themselves for the spritual struggle to come. We have already referred to the fact that military discipline might have an appeal to those who wished to practise spiritual discipline, and that this could account for the interest in the *De re militari* shown by many clergy. San Cristóbal, it seems, was trying to interpret some of the lessons regarding war taught by Vegetius as valid for those preparing for a war of the spirit.[120] There were, he reminded his patron, the king of Castile, and his readers, two kinds of war: between 'enemies of this world' ('enemigos corporales') and against those who were 'spiritual enemies' ('enemigos spirituales'). All faithful catholics should prepare themselves to wage the second. They could do this by training which would make them effective opponents of the forces of evil. Vegetius' overall message, that victory would come to those ever ready and trained, had clearly won San Cristóbal's approval; he had already stressed it in his glosses on the text. So, just as men prepared themselves for the battles in this world, so they should resort to the 'arte de cavallera' when engaging in 'las batallas spirituales'. San Cristóbal's remarks on I, 20 (in which Vegetius had written of the soldier's need to provide himself with adequate armour) stressed the importance of the shield in battle, the Church's sacramental shield providing the Christian with the defence needed to avoid the dangers of sin.[121]

---

[118] See J. M. Fradejas, 'Las glosas de San Cristóbal a la versión castellana de la *Epitoma rei militaris*', *Incipit*, 29 (2009), 85–100; J. S. Ruggieri, 'Un Vegezio "a lo divino" nel ms. escurialense & II 18', *Cultura neolatina*, 18 (1958), 207–15; Russell, 'De nuevo', 335.

[119] Escorial, &. ii. 18, fos. 12v, 14, 23, 28v, 35.

[120] A century earlier, the Italian jurist Giovanni da Legnano, composing his *Tractatus de bello*, had referred to the 'bellum spirituale' (chs. iii–viii) and the 'bellum corporale' (chs. ix seq.) See above (pp. 137–9) for the 'spiritual' use made of the text by Denis the Carthusian.

[121] Denis the Carthusian would also comment on this chapter.

Vegetius would be presented to Castilian readers in yet other forms. When San Cristóbal was at work on the *De re militari* about 1400, he was producing what would be the only translation to be made into Castilian in the Middle Ages. This was to be taken up and used as the basis for *El libro de la guerra*, until some years ago attributed to Don Enrique de Villena, the translator of both the *Aeneid* and the *Divine Comedy* into Castilian, who died in 1434.[122] It has now been demonstrated how this work, far from original, is a compilation of a prologue and thirty-six chapters which rely heavily on San Cristóbal's translation of the *De re militari*, four chapters being taken from Book I, nine from Book II and twenty-four from Book III.[123]

In relation to the *De re militari* it is possible to see the results of the compiler's choice of chapters in two ways: what he included or, conversely, what he omitted from the original. Little was selected from Book I, while Book IV, for example, contributed nothing. Indeed the main thrust of the book was ignored: nothing was said about its first theme, recruitment; and of the second, training, only four chapters, all related to the placement and defence of camps, were discussed.[124] As for the nine chapters of Book II which were included, these were all concerned with the structure of the ancient legion, the numbers of soldiers who made it up, and the responsibilities of its officers. This particular selection (nine out of twenty-five chapters in the *De re militari*) certainly gives a sense of what Book II was about. But the emphasis was on 'historical' chapters which showed how the legion was organised in the past. It would need some imagination to adapt the information for use in a contemporary context.

It was Book III which dominated the *Libro de la guerra*. Its influence should be seen in relation to the very brief statement with which the author introduced his work. 'I write' ('escribo'), he told the readers, for the benefit of all, but in particular for knights and others responsible for good government, so that in battles they may know how to attack and how to defend and, in so doing, earn rewards, honour and glory. The

---

[122] Schiff, *La bibliothèque du marquis de Santillane*, xxxi. The *Libro* was first edited by Lucas de Torre in the *Revue hispanique*, 38 (1916), 497–531. It has recently been re-edited: '*Libro de la guerra*'. *Compendio castigliano del 'De re militari' di Flavio Vegezio Renato*, ed. I. Scoma (Messina, 2004); M. E. Roca Barea (ed.), 'El *Libro de la guerra* y la traducción de Vegecio por Fray Alfonso de San Cristóbal', *Anuario de estudios medievales*, 37 (1) (2007), 267–304.

[123] T. G. Rolán and P. Saquero Suarez-Somonte (eds.), 'El *Epitoma rei militaris* de Flavio Vegecio traducido al castellano en el siglo XV. Edicion de los "Dichos de Séneca en el Acto de la Caballería" de Alfonso de Cartagena', *Miscelánea medieval murciana*, 14 (1987–88), 103–50.

[124] Chapters 2–5, corresponding to *DRM*, I, 22–5.

last words suggest that he was addressing those who regarded war as a means of bringing personal advantage (material reward and reputation) to themselves. On the other hand the first part showed that he appreciated that the waging of war was the responsibility of society's leaders, and that it was by following this approach that they would win honour among their own people. In other words, this text was one of those reflecting a view, developing since the twelfth century, which emphasised the public duty and obligations of the military class to society, to its wellbeing and defence. Since he drew heavily on Book III of the *De re militari*, the author was also implying that society should welcome the existence of the army, which was its means of self-defence. He would therefore show how it was to be established, in what conditions, and how it could successfully fulfil its task.

The first chapter of the *Libro* was based on *DRM*, III, 1 and, as such, was a discussion of the nature of an army and its size.[125] It was significant that the author had placed the army at the very forefront of his work, thus giving it the prominence which Vegetius had already attributed to the Roman army: the task of defending the state. There then followed, somewhat out of place, four chapters taken from *DRM*, II, 2–5, on encampments and the ways of defending them. Then came six chapters from Book III: the first two (6–7), on measures to make an army function smoothly (the army's health and the proper provision of supplies), were followed by four (8–11) concerned with practical military problems such as the crossing of rivers and, again, the laying out of a camp.

At this point the *Libro* took on nine chapters (12–20) from *DRM*, II, 3–11 (but not in numerical order) concerned with the structure of the legion, its numbers, its commanders and their duties. This was a very historical section, but one which none the less had lessons applicable to contemporary military organisation and structures. The remainder of the *Libro* (21–36) was entirely gleaned from *DRM*, III, so that by the time the end had been reached, parts of all but three of that book's chapters had been incorporated into it. Since two of these (III, 23, 24) concerned the use of camels and elephants, their omission could be excused. More surprising was the omission of III, 16, which dealt with the deployment of cavalry. The reason for such an omission is difficult to discern. Was it because Vegetius may have appeared to be suggesting that the cavalry had a role secondary to the infantry, and that in certain circumstances it should fight in tandem with the infantry, a view not likely to appeal to the 'caballeros' to whom this work was principally addressed? We cannot

---

[125] On the dependence of the *Libro* on the *DRM*, see Roca Barea, 'El *Libro de la guerra*', 276–7.

tell. What is evident, however, is that Vegetius' teaching on the need for proper pre-battle strategy, which involved planning and responding to situations and conditions, was emphasised, as were the battle tactics and strategies which he advocated.[126]

The text has very rightly been described as based on San Cristóbal's translation of the *De re militari*. It was, indeed, recognition of this fact which finally argued against the authorship of Don Enrique de Villena. None the less, much of the language used was not that of either Vegetius or San Cristóbal. While at times following this translation fairly closely, the author frequently allowed whole phrases to disappear or to be written in a new order, while commonly using a mixture of the translator's language and his own. In chapter 17, for example, San Cristóbal's translation of *DRM*, II, 7 was very much shortened; Vegetius' introductory words were omitted, and all that was left was a series of instructions. With only one exception, found in chapter 1, all historical names and references were omitted, thus at a stroke removing the advice from its historical setting, and changing it into a set of what were sometimes rather bald instructions. In this text, something essential had been removed from Vegetius' original, of which only a skeleton remained.

England

The first English translation of the *De re militari* was completed late in the year 1408 by an unknown person, perhaps John Walton, working at the behest of Sir Thomas Berkeley, an active soldier whose family had previously supported men of letters, notably John Trevisa, well known for his translations, not least that of the *De regimine principum* of Giles of Rome.[127] What does the translator's treatment of the text tell us about how he viewed it?

He certainly demonstrated no interest in 'the dangerous glitter of antiquity'; it was clearly not his prime intention to restore the fortunes of the text. Rather, since he claimed to underline the value of 'infourmacion', it is more likely that he was encouraged to think in terms of a translation which might be of practical use to his patron, now approaching the end of an active military career in the service of the crown. It was also to provide reading for those whose fighting careers were already over, and for the young just beginning theirs.[128] It is likely that those in the Berkeley circle

---

[126] Does it reflect the rise of the Spanish foot soldier in the late fifteenth century?

[127] Lester, *Earliest English translation*, 23–8; R. Hanna, 'Sir Thomas Berkeley and his patronage', *Speculum*, 64 (1989), 878–916.

[128] Lester, *Earliest English translation*, 23; Wakelin, *Humanism, reading and English literature*, 11.

already knew Vegetius' work, perhaps through a French translation, and that it was felt that an English one, so far lacking, would be of use and interest to a wider group whose main (or sole) language was English. For such, a reasonably accurate translation, which none the less bore signs of modernity, might be the most acceptable.

As we now know, however, translators had difficulties with certain passages of Vegetius' text. We should recall that a translator depended upon the accuracy of the manuscript before him, and that all contained misspellings, omissions and other errors introduced by their scribes. Since it was not always clear what Vegetius had meant, it was sometimes difficult to render his entire text in a manner comprehensible in another language. Like others, the Berkeley translator made mistakes, more particularly when translating the prologues and epilogues, whose style and vocabulary were more complex than many of the shorter, technical passages. Admitting to having 'grete difficulte to Englisshe the names of officeris' in the Roman army,[129] and wishing to avoid difficulties and undue repetition, the translator was occasionally driven to 'passe over' certain passages which rendered his task, as he saw it, impossible. If spite of cutting Vegetius' text here and there, the translator's wordy style, which often contrasted with the conciseness of the original Latin, combined with his wish to shed light on difficult words and passages, was to produce a greatly extended English text. All too often he allowed his use of doublets to take over. On other occasions his anxiety to ensure that his readers had fully understood him took on other forms. As others had done, he used the formula 'that is to say' to introduce the explanation of a word which he felt was needed.[130] Digressions, too, were not uncommon. In three widely separated passages Isidore was cited anachronistically, suggesting that the translator was a man of some learning.[131] His intelligent reading may also have encouraged him to note passages in different parts of the text with factors in common, but which were not in Vegetius' original.[132] For reasons such as these, the English translation was extended to more than twice the length of the work whose place it took. It was a far from literal rendering of the Latin original. For reasons which we can only guess, the text had been adapted to the new age.

Yet, in spite of a well-known passage referring to the artillery used by the English armies of his day[133] and of his probable awareness that

---

[129] Lester, *Earliest English translation*, 83, lines 18–19. See the editor's comments on 33–4.
[130] The example given by Lester (*Earliest English translation*, 31, 49, line 15) 'cotidianlich, that is to sey day after day', for the simple Latin *cotidiano*, illustrates the translator's habit.
[131] *DRM*, I, 3; I, 13; III, 6.   [132] Lester, *Earliest English translation*, 32.
[133] *Ibid.* 173, lines 3–9.

with the 'newe craft of werres'[134] currently available Vegetius' text was no longer adequate as a manual of war, the translator made little effort to bring it up to date. Far from omitting or paraphrasing the chapters on camels or elephants, he extended both of them. Many Latin terms with little evident contemporary relevance were maintained unexplained.[135] By using such latinisms, the translator may have been admitting that he did not know what they meant. On the other hand there are hints that his text would be applicable to his day. His admission that it was sometimes difficult to find exact equivalents for the titles of Roman officers suggests that his approach to translation was not wholly historical. Whether intentionally or not, he used words and phrases which were nothing less than medieval: 'princes, dukes, erles, and barouns' were suddenly, and unnecessarily, introduced into the prologue to Book III. In this translation, the 'miles' became a 'knight', while the 'tiro' was often rendered as a 'newe chosen knight' or a 'newe werriour', not yet a fully trained and invested soldier. When, in an introductory paragraph added by him, the translator referred to Vegetius' text as being concerned to teach 'knighthod and of chiualrye', he was using clear medieval language which appeared to imply more than simply 'soldiery', although he used 'chiualrye' as the equivalent of 'res militaris',[136] just as French translations had used the phrase 'De la chevalerie' to translate the same Latin term.[137]

The passing of about half a century would witness the making of a second English translation, this one, like that of Jean Priorat in France, in verse.[138] It gives us a text which, in spite of the not wholly satisfactory nature of the 1408 version, makes that text look like simplicity itself. The problems arising out of the 1459/60 version are considerable. Can one, in all truth, even after making allowances permitted to a translator, call it a translation? Is it not a new work, not that of a translator but of an author?[139] And who was he? Only recently has it been argued that the anonymous translator was quite possibly John Neele rather than Robert Parker, who has until now held the field.[140] How his text may be classified remains a difficult question to answer. Nor are we helped by being told that the use of rhyme royal created 'Vegetius translate/Into Balade'.[141]

[134] *Ibid.* 189, line 26.   [135] E.g., agger, exostre, pale, sambuke.
[136] Lester, *Earliest English translation*, 47, lines 3–4; 77, line 15.
[137] See Whetham, *Just wars and moral victories*, 149–53.
[138] 'a brilliant verse translation' (D. Wakelin, 'The occasion, author and readers of *Knyghthode and bataile*', *Medium Aevum*, 73 (2004), 260). Aspects of this work are discussed by Whetham, *Just wars and moral victories*, 153–61.
[139] On this, see the pertinent remarks of Catherine Nall, 'Perceptions of financial mismanagement', 120–1, 135.
[140] Wakelin, 'The occasion', 265–7.   [141] *Knyghthode and bataile*, 3, lines 52–3.

Could this be seriously equated to the text which Vegetius had written a millennium earlier?

As a literal translation of the *De re militari, Knyghthode and bataile* failed on many counts. Its verse form militated against accuracy; the repeated need to meet the demands of rhyme and metre would cause even the most skilled translator grave difficulties.[142] Putting such problems aside, the question must be asked whether the translator had ever planned a genuine work of translation, accurate as far as possible in both word and spirit. The answer must surely be that he had not. What we have before us fails even the most elementary tests. Mistranslations abound; additions and omissions are common, so that one finds among the editors' notes entries such as '[lines] 1251–1306 = Veg. III, 5'; 'corresponds to Veg.'; 'not in Veg.'; or 'This poetical line has no counterpart in Veg.' Equally serious is the way the translator sometimes played with the order of Vegetius' chapters, using or omitting them altogether in order to create a new work of his own. What emerges from this 'pruning and reordering' is, at best, 'essentially a selective and adaptive translation', a politically committed piece of writing which one should not hesitate to call a paraphrase.[143]

Encouragement for this idea is received from factors within the text itself. Containing, as it does, a number of references to contemporary events and personalities, the strongly anti-Yorkist work begins to assume something of the nature of a tract created to reflect, and probably to influence, the political climate of the time, a period of civil tension in England, with the Lancastrian throne of Henry VI under threat from Yorkist opponents. To be properly understood, the work should be seen as part of a wider tradition of political verse read by the leaders of Lancastrian England and, in particular, one written in the context of the uneasy situation resulting from the civil disputes of the time.[144] It is a call for action by the translator, a scholar and a 'person [i.e., parson/priest] of Caleys', initially a supporter of the Lancastrian dynasty who was to change allegiance for favour at the Yorkist court after the successful seizure of the throne by Edward IV in 1461.[145]

By 1460, *Knyghthode and bataile* had already become caught up in an agenda with strong political overtones. Of the three surviving copies, one was read by members of the powerful and influential Hastings family.

---

[142] See, for example, the notes to lines 1364 and 2296.

[143] Wakelin, 'The occasion', 260–1.

[144] *Ibid.* 261–2, and Nall, 'Perceptions of financial mismanagement'.

[145] Wakelin, 'The occasion', 265–6. This change of sides may account for two later manuscripts of the work bearing the name of the new king, Edward IV, references to the Lancastrian dynasty having been omitted.

Another was owned by a member of the Hatteclyff family;[146] William Hatteclyff served in Calais under William, Lord Hastings, before becoming secretary to Edward IV.[147] Those who read these copies were probably of humanistic sympathies, readers of the classics, the successors to the Lancastrian humanists such as William Waynflete, founder of Magdalen College, Oxford, and Sir John Fortescue, the chief justice and author of political tracts, who had had influence at court until the dynastic changes of 1461. What they had in common, and shared with French and Italian humanists and others, was an interest in and concern for the common weal. This was a subject which, under the label 'res publica', had been raised many times by Vegetius. It was into such a context that the latest version of the *De re militari* was now being placed.[148] What concerns or interests might it help meet? It was a work which was to place great emphasis upon the crown's achievement of reconciling various groups, upon 'Vnitee . . . /In Trinitee', the trinity being not merely divine but human, the traditional three groupings in society, 'The Clergys and Knyghthode/And Comynaltee', existing in accord under the crown.[149] In this context there is significance in marginalia found in three copies of the 1408 translation, all made in the middle years of the fifteenth century, drawing attention to the military advantages to be gained from creating division among the enemy, while warning of the dire effects which civil strife could cause a society not founded upon unity. What had begun as mainly military advice was now being given emphasis with very strong social and political overtones.[150]

A major theme of this work is the importance given by the author to the role played by armed force in the process of achieving the 'salus populi'. 'Knyghthode and bataile', or the 'ars bellica', increases men's liberties by ensuring that the crown is held in respect by every subject, while rebels, who threaten the unity of the country, are 'chastised' before being brought back into the fold.[151] What is required is a ruler with power to overcome these divisions. The good of the entire land and of each estate depends upon the king. He must have an army, properly trained, upon which he can count. Apart from the battle of St Albans, there has

---

[146] The letters ATTE – (part of Hatteclyff) are still discernible on BL Cotton, Titus A xxiii, fo. 56v.

[147] Wakelin, 'The occasion', 267.

[148] Wakelin, *Humanism, reading and English literature*, 19–22.

[149] See *Knyghthode and bataile*, 1–2, lines 17–32.

[150] See Cambridge, Univ. Lib., Add. 8706, fo. 60; Oxford, Bodl. Douce, 291, fo. 72; and Oxford, Magdalen, lat. 30, fo. 68v, which draw attention to the passage: 'for striff [and] debate in a comynalte is to here enmyes an hasty helpinge and to hemselue a sodeyn destroyeng' (*DRM*, III, 10; Lester, *Earliest English translation*, 131, lines 8–14).

[151] *Knyghthode and bataile*, lines 2014–20, 2836–39, 2880, 2917–23.

been no war in England for sixty years. Men must be made to train, to prepare themselves for war so that 'exercise/Of werre may in peax revyue & rise'.[152]

Early in the work the author refers to the opposing forces of good and evil which ensure that 'Mankyndys lyfe is mylitatioun' – a very Hobbesian sentiment. Influenced by Satan, man is beset by 'bataile and discord' which make him wish for liberty and safety, in a word, for peace.[153] If God's army can fight evil using the sword of the word, so equally can man achieve freedom and safety through the service of a human army which, properly used, is immediately shown to be a positive instrument for good, not the negative one all too often presented.

The author therefore presents armed force as an instrument of liberty and safety:

> Certeyn it is, that knyghthode & bataile
> So stronge is it, that therby libertee
> Receyued is with encreste and availe;
> Therby the Croune is hol in Maiestee
> And vche personne in his dignitee,
> The Citesens, and alle men shal be
> If I gouerne wel, in libertee.

From this statement it emerges that the writer is a firm believer in monarchy, in that institution's responsibility and ability to maintain the peace between its subjects, and to put down opposititon to itself, to the advantage of all. The effective rule of law is the best guarantor of peace and liberty. So the king is the one to whom men look to protect the land and interests of 'everych Estate'; if he rules well, all will enjoy freedom. To this end soldiers should be chosen and trained to fight to create what the writer calls 'A myghti choyce of men on hors & foote'.[154]

The same was true of safety. Civil conflict meant that the security of both humans and their property was put at risk. The effective rule of the king, backed up by the army, could bring about a political and social environment in which people felt safe.[155] This was an important aspect of social peace, particularly sought after and desired in years of doubt and fear caused by the dynastic conflict which England experienced in the 1450s. If the solution were to be a military one, how was it to be achieved? To anyone seeking to discover how the problem had been faced in the

---

[152] *Ibid.* lines 1690–1.   [153] *Ibid.* lines 96, 140.   [154] *Ibid.* lines 1629–35, 1924.

[155] John Watts (*Henry VI and the politics of kingship* (Cambridge, 1996), 351–2) has emphasised how it was thought that the acceptance of the royal authority would lead to peace, with its implication of 'oneheed', order, unity and common weal. See Wakelin, 'The occasion', 262, n. 10.

past, and how, consequently, it might be resolved today, the *De re militari* had an answer: 'He redeth, and fro poynt to poynt he secheth/How hath be doon, and what is now to done.' Those giving the lead, the author had little doubt, were the knights, whom he compared to the gems reflecting the stars, which represented the angels of God's army. Just as the Roman army 'Hath in the firste cohors an excellence/Of noble blood, manhode and sapience', so the 'knyghthode an ordir is, the premynent', ready to obey God or to die, 'and as magnificent/As can be thought, exiled al envye'.[156] The author clearly believed in hierarchies, doubtless partly based on skill and achievement. For in keeping with the Roman view, a hierarchy was only worthy of respect if it successfully carried out the role assigned to it.

However, in themselves knights were not enough. The author was led on by some of Vegetius' fundamental ideas, not least his teaching that an army had a positive and beneficial role to play in society. The army which he envisaged was not solely or primarily a 'chivalric' army, composed largely of knights. By 1460 such a force could no longer have been assembled. In any event, the author did not wish to return to those days (if they ever existed) when the army was largely composed of men of rank. His approach was more practical and realistic. Vegetius had convinced him that a proper army consisted of men 'on hors, o[n] fote, or on the see', men of differing skills and backgrounds who had been selected to serve for 'professional' reasons, 'werreours to worthe wise & bolde' who merited to be received 'to that honour as to be werreourys'.[157] The sense of diversity in the army is further encouraged by the clear support which the writer gave to archers and even to the humble slingers, whose skills, Vegetius had emphasised, developed from much practice, and whose stones could do great harm even to men in armour.[158] His picture of social harmony in the army was underlined when the author recommended that 'The Chiualers and werreourys alle' should learn the skills of mounting horses fully armed. Taking his cue from the real world, the writer no longer saw the horse as the preserve of 'knyghthode' alone.[159]

If the ordinary soldier, the 'werreour', was accorded much respect by this author, the reason must be that, having read Vegetius, he had come to realise (i) that the soldier was properly trained to fight and (ii) that he had given an oath, similar to that given by the newly dubbed knight, to

---

[156] *Knyghthode and bataile*, lines 81–2, 145–51, 710–11, 131–4.
[157] *Ibid.* lines 644, 173, 166–72, 180, 188.
[158] 'That archery is grete vtilitee, / It nedeth not to telle eny that here is' (*ibid.* lines 446–7). The entire passage of lines 432 -73 is important.
[159] *Ibid.* lines 474–80; *DRM*, I, 18.

obey God and those holding authority from Him. The soldier was closely associated in this work with the obedience due to the king, which lay at the heart of the concept of liberty outlined earlier.[160] He was thus seen as an instrument of peace and stability in society, a man whose leaders were appointed by the duly constituted authority (in England, the king) through service to whom 'both knyght & comynere' rendered service to God.[161]

By tradition, the 'knyght' was better trained and prepared for war than was the 'comynere'. The author used his text to advance the esteem in which the latter should be held by showing how, if well selected and properly trained, he could contribute greatly to an army's success, and how that contribution should be seen as service to God, to the ruler and to the entire community. Reconsidering the twin benefits of 'safety' and 'liberty', both the product of peace in society, the writer stated that the king recognised that he had a duty to lead society towards that peace. How else was he to achieve this other than through the service of the army, which it was his to raise and command for that purpose? Indeed the king knew that he was at fault if he failed to do this.[162] As for safety, we find this associated with the language which the author used when dealing with the navy and conflict at sea. Storms at sea were metaphors for political turbulence. The translation abandoned its original character and became a commentary on events of the day, the king being depicted not as a military leader with experience of the affairs of war, but rather as 'The Maister Marynere, the gouernour,/He knoweth euery cooste in his viage/And port saluz.'[163] In other words, he was a man worthy to be entrusted with the ship (of state) and its crew (the people), a man in whom to have confidence to reach land – and safe harbour. The author, who knew the port of Calais, wrote with feeling about the involvement of ships and sailors. Like their counterparts on land, they had a role to play in bringing the ship of state into port. Like the 'duke' who controlled the movements of land armies, the 'maister marynere' knew the geogaphy of the sea and the stars, and the movements of the oceans.[164] To him, port was a place of refuge. In the uncertain days of 1460, Calais was a personal safe haven for the author, who was caught up in the breakdown of loyalties and its dire results. The term 'port saluz' appears three times,

---

[160] *Ibid.* lines 684–90. 'Fro mylitaunce that thei shal neuer fle/Ner voyde deth, but rather deth desire/For themperour, and wele of his Empire' (lines 702–4; *DRM*, II, 5).
[161] *Knyghthode and bataile* lines 691–7, esp. 696.
[162] *Ibid.* lines 1636–42.   [163] *Ibid.* lines 2791–3.
[164] 'He knoweth euery rok and euery race,/The swolewys & the starrys, sonde & sholde,/And where is deep ynough his foo to chace/And chese a feeld he can, bataile to holde' (*ibid.* lines 2798–2801; *DRM*, IV, 43).

and serves as a metaphor for the safety of the country, just as freedom had done. If liberty was a concept, safety was its physical embodiment.

Here is evidence that the author's main theme, the good of all 'estates' which make up a community, should be seen in the communal determination to shoulder that responsibility under the orders of the king through the services of an army representing all interests, not merely the knighthood. With his emphasis on quality, on respect given as reward for achievement, Vegetius had shown the way to a concept of an army founded on far from traditional lines. In the England of 1460, military developments in France, which bore some similarity to what was described in this work, were known and discussed among those interested in or concerned with the relationship between the growth of the king's army and the development of a state purporting to represent the public good. It is notable that the author wished his work to be read by those whom he called 'werreouris'. It was they whom he appeared to see as the men of the future.

Responding to different aims, the two English versions of the *De re militari* were to show very different characteristics. The first may be seen as the product of a period which witnessed war in Wales and may have seen the resumption of conflict with France looming on the not too distant horizon; England should be prepared. It was an attempt to provide a version much of it reasonably close to the original Latin, while at the same time allowing the translator to bring the language, in so far as he was able, up to date. Half a century later, the second version constituted something rather different. In this case, accuracy of translation was never intended, and prose became verse, the *De re militari* providing the outline of a political and social message intended to be understood by a reader concerned with events and issues as they developed in England in the late 1450s. It was further evidence of the fact that the influence of Vegetius' text, transcending the purely military, could be extended in other, related directions.

Germany

The recent identification of what is now regarded as the first full translation of the *De re militari* into German (Seitenstetten, Stiftsbliothek 65), made probably in 1438 by an anonymous translator at the faculty of arts of the university of Vienna,[165] greatly extends our perception of the appreciation of Vegetius' work in the German-speaking area. Granted its

---

[165] See the work of Johann Seffner, also of Vienna, carried out some forty years earlier, discussed below, p. 230.

origins in that faculty, it is likely that interest in the work was historical rather than moral.[166] Like the earlier German versions of selections
of Vegetius' text, this translation was carried out for Duke Albrecht V,
who died, as King of the Romans, in 1439. While keeping close to the
Latin original, the text is not always a literal rendering of it. A composite list of chapter headings replaced one presented book by book.[167]
Names of historical characters were introduced while, as in the case of
translations into other languages, some were omitted. In I, 13 the text
suddenly changed from the third person into the first person singular,
while in II, 3 the reverse was to be observed. Several long marginal notes,
and other shorter ones, referring mainly to Book I, suggested interest in
what Vegetius had written.[168] References to the Bible and biblical figures,
to Aristotle, to persons and events in Roman history are indicative of a
reader educated in arts subjects. There was, furthermore, an attempt to
bring the translation up to date, to make its content contemporary. Above
all, two major additions to the German text may be noted. One was the
encouragement given to the use of archery, and in particular to the use
of crossbows. The other was the use of wrestling as a means of keeping
military personnel fit and ready to fight.[169] This was added, the translator tells us, because Vegetius had said nothing about such activity.[170]
What was evidently regarded as part of the contemporary *Ritterspiel* had
to be drawn to the attention of readers. Was wrestling a regular part of
a soldier's training in the mid-fifteenth century? From this evidence it
looks as if some thought it was or, at least, that it should be.

The appearance, as a form of supplement, of what was in essence a
short discourse emphasised two things. First, the importance attached
by the translator to fitness in its own right. By achieving it, the knight
(or soldier) was enabled to fulfil his obligations to society as well as
possible. That important part of Vegetius' recurring message had been

---

[166] F. Fürbeth, 'Zur deutschsprachigen Rezeption der "Epitoma rei militaris" des Vegetius
im Mittelalter', in *Die Wahrnehmung und Darstellung des Krieges im Mittelalter und in der
frühen Neuzeit*, ed. H. Brunner (Wiesbaden, 2000), 157.
[167] See Reeve, 'Transmission', 282.
[168] I thank Frank Fürbeth for providing me with a transcript of these notes.
[169] F. Fürbeth, '*Des Vegecii kurcze red von der Ritterschafft*. Die "Epitoma rei militaris" in
der Übersetzung des Ludwig Hohenwang', in *Flavius Vegetius Renatus, Von der Ritterschaft. Aus dem Lateinischen übertragen von Ludwig Hohenwang, in der Ausgabe Augsburg,
Johann Wiener, 1475/76* (Monumenta xylographica et typographica 6, Munich, 2002),
13; Fürbeth, 'Die "Epitoma rei militaris" des Vegetius. Zwischen ritterliche Ausbildung und gelehrt-humanistischer Lektüre. Zu einer weiteren unbekannten deutschen
Übersetzung aus der Wiener Artistenfakultät', *Beiträge zur Geschichte der deutschen
Sprache und Literatur*, 124 (2002), 319–22.
[170] 'von dem auch Vegecius nichcz geseczt hat . . . ' cited by Fürbeth, 'Vegetius, Publius
Flavius', *Die deutsche Literatur des Mittelalters Verfasserlexikon*, 11(5) (2004), 1608.

clearly understood. Second was the need for the same man to practise regularly in the use of weapons, whether swords or knives. What becomes apparent in this translation is the emphasis given to weapons not normally associated with the knightly class ('unritterlich'). The text appears to be consciously attempting to swing the emphasis away from a noble approach to war in favour of a more popular one. It is a text which both encourages and reflects change already occurring, helping to make better known techniques, such as both the offensive and the defensive use of the 'wagen', which would be incorporated into works on war later in the fifteenth and sixteenth centuries.[171]

Already known to scholars was the translation made by Ludwig Hohenwang no later than 1475, in which year it was printed at Augsburg. Born in Elchingen, near Ulm, about 1440, Hohenwang had studied at the recently founded university of Basel in 1461, later becoming a printer in Augsburg. It is likely that he became interested in the classics while studying at Basel. The translation was dedicated to Count Johann, Graf of Lupfen and Landgrave of Stielingen, a member of a well-known family of bibliophiles, who owned humanistic works. It is significant that Count Johann was also known as something of a soldier.[172]

In his introduction Hohenwang described his work as 'a brief introduction to chivalry' ('kurcze vorred von der Ritterschaft'). He was enough of a scholar, as well as being a practical man, to appreciate some of the problems which faced the translator of a work written more than a millennium earlier. It is possible that Hohenwang made his translation from the first printed Latin edition, that of Nicolaus Ketelaer, made in 1473–74, although it is more likely that he worked from a manuscript.[173] The success of his translation can be measured by the fact that, in the late nineteenth century, Max Jähns took the translator to be an old soldier, 'einen erfahrenen Kriegsmann'.[174]

Hohenwang appreciated that his translation might present difficulties to some of his readers. In his search for synonyms, in particular with regard to a text with an unusually high number of technical/historical words, he faced many problems. None the less, his translation, written in a clear style, follows the Latin original without major deviation. Among his achievements is to have been the first to use comprehensible German

[171] Fürbeth, 'Die "Epitoma rei militaris"', 332.
[172] Fürbeth, 'Des Vegecii', 14–16.   [173] Reeve, 'Transmission', 344, n. 194.
[174] E. K. Heller, 'Ludwig Hohenwang's "Von der Ritterschaft". An evaluation, and a survey of his military and naval terms', in In honorem Lawrence Marsden Price. Contributions by his colleagues and by his former students. Univ. of California Publications in Modern Philology, 36, vi (1952), 178. H. Weichardt, Ludwig Hohenwang, ein Übersetzer des 15 Jahrhunderts (Neudamm, 1933), 108, n. 1.

equivalents for many unfamiliar and, by now, outdated military terms occurring in the Latin text. However, that he was compelled to retain some, mainly technical, Latin words and phrases is hardly surprising. These obliged him to add an occasional 'that is a . . . ' ('Dass ist ein . . . '), as other translators had done before him.[175] He appreciated, too, that there were readers who might wish to accompany him, as it were, on the journey of translation. For these, in a manner reminiscent of the English verse translation completed only a few years earlier, he added an alpha-betical glossary of words and terms. For the first twenty or more of these he explained what the Latin word meant in German: 'aries ist ain wider' ('"aries" is a ram'); 'dux ist ain herezog' ('"dux" is a count'). However, at the second word under the letter 'f' ('fundibulatores') he changed his method. While continuing to provide definitions (albeit briefer ones now), he chose to add references to book and chapter to ease the reader's path as he sought the passage in which the word appeared, much as had been done by the English verse translator. This undoubtedly added to the scholarly value of the glossary, which enabled interested readers, par-ticularly those with philological interests, to seek out and find the context in which a word or term appeared.

One cannot but ask why this was not done for the twenty-three words ('acies' to 'ferentari') for which textual references were not given. Are we to suppose that Hohenwang originally envisaged a translation for those who understood little or no Latin, but later changed his mind, providing references for difficult or unusual terms as well? The evidence of the Latin manuscripts makes it clear that a genuine interest in words and their meaning existed among many readers. Yet one implication of the change cannot be ignored. References to the use of words would be useful only to those persons who also had access to the Latin text, whether manuscript or, by now, also in print. Was Hohenwang trying to provide a German text of use to the person with an insufficient knowledge of Latin to read the original, but with an interest (perhaps a professional one) in military matters, alongside a critical apparatus (the glossary with its references) with which to appeal to the more scholarly minded who wanted easy access to selected words in the original Latin? Was he trying to provide for different kinds of readers within the scope of a single volume? It seems likely.

[175] See above, pp. 163, 166, 173–4, 186.

8 Texts, drawings and illuminations

Both our perception of the understanding of Vegetius' text achieved by readers in the Middle Ages, and the methods used to foster that understanding, may be enhanced by an examination of the drawings and illuminations found in some surviving manuscripts. Sketches added in the margins are normally related to the passage in which they appear. In seeking either to summarise or to emphasise its contents, or to explain, visually, the meaning of a word (often a technical term), they underline the importance attached to a particular passage by immediately attracting the reader's eye to it. They may be classified into broad groups. One represented military formations, such as squares, wedges and circles,[1] the way in which an army might be conceived in diagrammatic form;[2] or how the battle line should be drawn up.[3] A second, smaller group consisted of those which contained drawings of weapons in the margins, the drawings normally being attempts to illustrate references in the text close to which they were to be found: the sword, to be used for thrusting rather than for slashing; the simple bow and arrow; the sling; the stones to be used in defence of a wall; two weapons of aggression, Greek fire ('ignis grecus') and the swing-beam ('tolleno').[4] In another manuscript the drawing of a rat underlined the need for hygiene as a way of keeping the army healthy, while the story of the Roman matrons cutting their hair to supply the city's broken tension engines is depicted in the drawing of two women in the margin.[5]

Attention has been drawn above to some of the practical problems faced by the translators (or modernisers) of Vegetius' text, and how their

---

[1] BL Cotton, Cleo. D. i, fo. 91; BnF lat. 5691, fo. 24v; Vatican, Pal. lat. 1572, fo. 48.
[2] Madrid, BN 9245, fo. 11; BL Harley 2475, fos. 228, 230, 232v; Trento, Com. W 3154, fo. 10.
[3] BL Add. Ms 21,242, fo. 22v.
[4] BnF lat. 7384, fo. 8v (sword), fo. 9 (bow and arrow), fo. 9v (sling); Bern, Burgerbibl., 280, fo. 9v (bow and arrow); Laon, Bibl. Mun. 428, fo. 60 (stones for building); Vatican, Chigi. H. vii 238, fos. 84v, 85 (Greek fire and swing beam (tollenon)). This last manuscript also has drawings of important architectural features (fo. 83).
[5] Escorial, F. iv. 28, fo. 26; Vatican, Pal. lat. 1573, fo. 46v.

solutions can serve as indications of how the text was regarded, and of its importance and significance to their own age and culture. Worthy of attention, too, since they help us understand how the work was interpreted by those who created and illuminated new copies (both Latin and vernacular) were a number of manuscripts enriched with illuminations ranging from full folio size to tiny vignettes incorporated into large capital letters. By the way they 'visualise' how aspects or, indeed, the entire content of the work may have been understood by the artist or the patron at whose bidding he worked, illuminations in a text have much to reveal about the approach taken by those who created them. Illuminations are, therefore, important for what they indicate were regarded as key features of the work. The *De re militari* read as a guide to the duties of knighthood, for instance, is strongly suggested by the mounted knight in armour, with helm, draped in red, bearing a sword, incorporated into the capital letter 'A' of its very first word, 'Antiquis', in the fourteenth-century manuscript copied in Italy and destined to be owned by Petrarch; while another rich manuscript, copied in the mid-fifteenth century on the orders of Alfonso V, king of Aragon, contains a full-folio illumination of a knight on horseback.[6]

A fine manuscript made in Italy at about the same time, and which also contains the works of Onasander and Aelian, shows a half-length figure reading a book: another has a figure, who appears to be teaching, incorporated in the letter 'A' of 'Antiquis'.[7] Although expressed differently, the emphasis in both manuscripts is on the didactic nature of the work, and on Vegetius' well-known insistence that the traditions and good practices of former times can be conveyed, as here, through the written word.

The didactic nature of the *De re militari* is underlined in a number of texts which depict the 'philosopher' ('el sabio', Vegetius himself) teaching an audience about war. The earliest of these, dated *c.*1270, shows him, seated, addressing a group of men, who, out of respect for him, remain standing.[8] The words used, 'Come to me, you knights, who wish to learn about chivalry' ('Venez a moy, senurs chevalers, qui volez aver honur de chevalerie'), indicate that the text was intended for the military class. Yet none is dressed in military attire; each wears a long cloak which may be intended to depict them as men of the council chamber, who must be well-informed about military affairs so as to advise their lord to the best

---

[6] Vatican, Vat. lat. 2193, fo. 102; Oxford, Bodl. Canon. class. lat. 274, fo. 1v.
[7] Vatican, Reg. lat. 1880, fo. 1; Vicenza, Bertoliana, 295, fo. 1.
[8] Cambridge, Fitzwilliam Mus. Marlay Add. 1; reproduced in Prestwich, *Armies and warfare*, 184.

effect. At the whim of the artist, a different emphasis could be introduced into such a scene. A fine French manuscript of the early fifteenth century has a miniature showing a teacher, seated in the chair of authority, reading from a book to an emperor (who holds a drawn sword) and to a group of knights. In this case the knights are dressed to fight, ready to support their lord as he prepares to fulfil his obligation to defend his people.[9] The link between knowledge gleaned from a book and the purpose to which it is put is made clear in both manuscripts; the manner in which Vegetius' audience is presented suggests a particular emphasis which the owner, through the artist's work, wished to place upon the text. The importance of this message is further underlined in another manuscript showing a ruler mounted on a white horse, surrounded by soldiers, emphasising the responsibility of the ruler to lead his army against the enemy as the most effective way of securing the good of his people (see Figures 4 and 5).[10]

In two further cases, manuscripts have much to tell us about the reception of other parts of Vegetius' teaching. New York, Morgan, M 364, has five illuminations, one of which, a battle scene involving mounted men bearing lances and swords, with one or two foot soldiers, is unexceptional for a manuscript of the second half of the fifteenth century. Four others, however, bear greater relation to the practical teaching expounded by Vegetius. The paramount importance of training and preparation is summed up in a scene showing four men engaged in wrestling (an activity not actually mentioned by Vegetius) to make themselves mentally and physically fit, and in archery (regarded as most important by Vegetius); while armed knights practise the art of mounted combat. Another point made by Vegetius is underlined in a second illumination depicting two commanders ('duces') issuing orders to their soldiers; one, mounted on a small horse, appears to be encouraging his men, while the other, on foot, holds a baton or scroll (if the first, his staff of office; if the second, his written instructions, or 'tessera'). These are the men appointed by their prince to lead his army in time of war, command which they exercise by virtue of authority given to them by the prince – hence the baton (see Figure 6).[11] Also set out, and intended to accompany Book IV, was the scene depicting the attack and defence of a walled town, in which the attackers use ladders (as well as three bombards and a handgun, neither found, of course, in Vegetius' text, which is none the less acknowledged

[9] Oxford, Bodl. Laud lat. 56, fo. 1. See O. Pächt and J. J. G. Alexander (eds.), *Illuminated manuscripts in the Bodleian Library, Oxford*, I (Oxford, 1966), 52 (no. 660), and pl. LI.

[10] BnF lat. 7470, fos. 15, 32v, 50v, 88v; Naples, Naz. V. A. 22, fo. 1.

[11] New York, Morgan, M 364, fos. 3, 22v. See above, pp. 133–4.

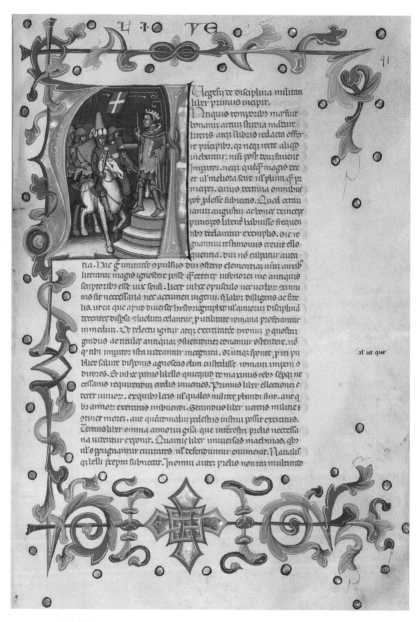

4 A king prepares to lead an army. The text in his hand underlines the importance which Vegetius attached to a ruler being well informed on military matters. (BnF lat. 7242, fo. 41)

5 A French king leads his army to war. (BnF lat. 7470, fo. 15)

as having contemporary relevance) and the defenders employ long poles, stones (thrown by women, perhaps to show the defence being organised on a communal scale) and crossbows (IV, 8). It is clear that the illuminations added to this copy of the *De re militari* were intended to reflect

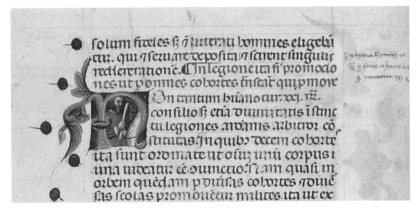

6 An officer on horseback holds what is probably a baton, symbol of his promotion to command. (BnF Smith-Lesouëf 13, fo. 23v)

things said by Vegetius in the text, and that they were inspired by an appreciative reading of it.

Most interesting is a fine manuscript copied in Italy with vignettes attributed to Niccolò da Bologna, the leading Bolognese illuminator of the late fourteenth century.[12] We may call upon one of its most distinctive features, the illuminated capital letter of the first word of every chapter, as evidence to further our understanding of how the *De re militari* was received at the time of the manuscript's making. Almost certainly executed to order, these 'explanatory' vignettes emphasise, in most instances, something of interest or importance in each chapter which they embellish, underlining the perceived significance of part or, in some cases, of the entire chapter to which they relate. When, as happens, those same chapters draw annotations to their margins, we may be reasonably certain that they were regarded as being of more than ordinary interest to the artist and his patron, as well as to readers of the manuscript.

Introducing the work, two small vignettes, depicting both scholar and soldier, recall what has been remarked upon before: the philosophical, yet practical, character of the *De re militari*. Most of the vignettes found in Book I reflect its subject matter with reasonable accuracy. For instance, the soldier carrying shield and sword fits perfectly into the context.[13] More unusual, and consequently more interesting, is a series of vignettes underlining some of the main points made by Vegetius elsewhere in

[12] BnF Smith-Lesouëf 13. See *Inventaire sommaire des manuscrits anciens de la bibliothèque Smith-Lesouëf à Nogent-sur-Marne* (Paris, 1930), 5.
[13] *Ibid.* fo. 3 (*DRM*, I, 1).

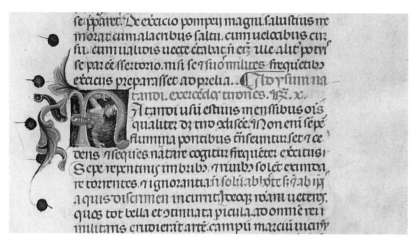

7 Vegetius' recommendation that soldiers should be able to swim is emphasised in this vignette. (BnF Smith-Lesouëf 13, fo. 6)

Book I. A prospective recruit is shown being measured for size by a man with something which resembles a plumb line;[14] a vignette of a man catching a fish reminds the reader that Vegetius had recommended that fishermen (among others) should not be accepted in the army; while the final part of the recruiting process, tattooing in Vegetius' text, is shown as a man signing on in a more modern fashion.[15] The process of training, which occupies a significant part of Book I, is also drawn to the reader's attention. The swimmer placed at the head of the chapter, emphasising the need for soldiers to learn to swim, makes his point clearly; while another vignette shows a man holding a sling ready for use (see Figures 7 and 8).[16] Chapters 21 to 24, three of which begin with the word 'castra' or 'castrorum', all have a vignette showing a medieval castle or tower. In spite of the change in the meaning of 'castra' (no longer 'camp' but 'castle'), the emphasis placed by the vignettes on the essentially defensive nature and attributes of the castle, and its ability to provide safety within its walls, reflects the skills required of the soldier as a camp-builder set out by Vegetius in the late chapters of Book I. The fact that the vignettes receive the support of marginal annotations in chapters 21 and 22 further justifies the choice of them as a means of stressing the importance of these chapters to readers of the late Middle Ages.

---

[14] *Ibid.* fo. 4 (*DRM*, I, 5).
[15] *Ibid.* fos. 4v, 5 (*DRM*, I, 7, 8).   [16] *Ibid.* fos. 6, 8 (*DRM*, I, 10, 16).

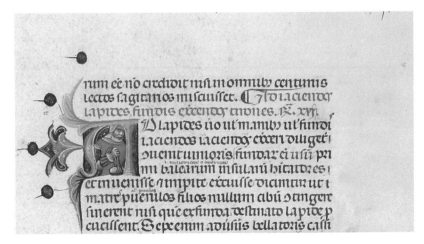

8 A slinger ready for action. (BnF Smith-Lesouëf 13, fo. 8)

In Book II, mainly concerned with the legion, a vignette depicts an arm encased in armour, the hand placed on a book in the act of taking an oath. As in many manuscripts, this part of Vegetius' text describing Roman practice was significant enough in the eyes of medieval readers to receive both pictorial representation and marginal annotation.[17] This was followed by a picture of a man holding an eagle ('aquila'), which, as the marginal 'Nota' also indicates, was an important symbol and rallying point for members of the legion.[18] The key role played by legionaries in the front line of battle was to be underlined with a vignette of a soldier, while another soldier, holding a *saccus*, or purse, was responsible for keeping half of each soldier's pay, thus forcing him to save and deterring him from deserting, for, as the annotated text here pointed out, 'most men, the poor in particular, spend as much as they can get'.[19] A man observed holding a pen and ink pot (?), ready to write, further underlined Vegetius' ideal that soldiers should be literate.[20]

Generally speaking, the vignettes accompanying Book III show less originality than some of those relating to earlier books. None the less they illustrate some its important points A soldier eating from a bowl (or perhaps he is guarding the bowl's contents) draws attention to one of Vegetius' recurring themes: the importance of ensuring adequate supplies

---

[17] *Ibid.* fo. 16 (*DRM*, II, 5); 'Nota de juribus militum' and 'Nota de juramento militis id est prestandum'.

[18] *Ibid.* fo. 16 (*DRM*, II, 6).   [19] *Ibid.* fo. 21v (*DRM*, II, 17); fo. 23 (*DRM*, II, 20).

[20] *Ibid.* fo. 21v (*DRM*, II, 19).

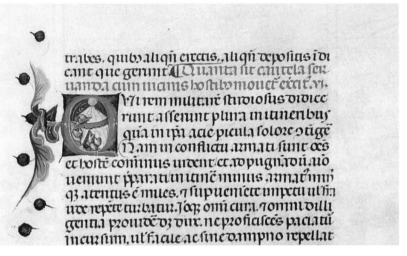

9 A spy peeps surreptitiously into a tent. (BnF Smith-Lesouëf 13, fo. 32)

of food and water for both men and animals, and the effect that a shortage of these, ending in starvation, could have upon a campaign.[21] The scene depicting a man striking another, kneeling and blindfolded, with a sword, is clearly intended to reflect the 'medicine of iron' ('ferri medicina'), or the execution of a trouble-maker or mutineer, which Vegetius judged to be necessary when all other measures had failed. A man dressed as a soldier appearing to be about to peep surreptitiously into a tent underlines Vegetius' warning about spies (see Figure 9).[22] Another man depicted holding his ample beard (reflecting age and wisdom) indicates to the reader that the commander ('dux') should be a man of experience and reflection who considers matters before giving his orders and directions[23] (see Figure 10), while Vegetius' warning of the adverse effects of the sun (he also adds wind and dust) upon men's ability to fight is suggested by the picture of the soldier shielding his eyes from the bright light.[24]

A large illumination drives home the lesson that the artist and his patron have picked out the needs of defence as a major theme in Book IV. Here a man, apparently knitting, prepares some kind of headgear; provisions for a town are delivered by both boat and donkey; and the town's walls are strengthened and put into a state of readiness

---

[21] *Ibid.* fo. 29 (*DRM*, III, 3).   [22] *Ibid.* fos. 30, 32 (*DRM*, III, 4, 6).
[23] *Ibid.* fos. 36v, 40v (*DRM*, III, 9, 13).   [24] *Ibid.* fo. 41 (*DRM*, III, 14).

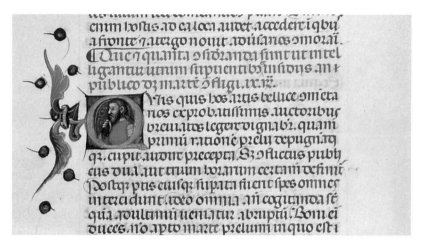

10 A commander ponders the possibilities before him. The importance of leaders acting thoughtfully was emphasised by Vegetius. (BnF Smith-Lesouëf 13, fo. 36v)

11 Supplies are brought to a walled town about to be besieged, while its defences are strengthened. The artist has conveyed successfully the urgency of the situation. (BnF Smith-Lesouëf 13, fo. 52v)

(see Figure 11).[25] This central theme is taken up elsewhere: a man carries a barrel (perhaps containing beer or salted fish) on his shoulder; the wall appears in several vignettes; a woman cuts her hair to supply the

[25] *Ibid.* fo. 52v.

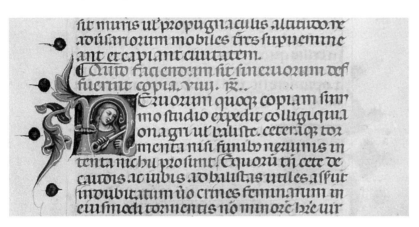

12 A woman cuts her hair to provide sinews for a broken-down torsion engine. (BnF Smith-Lesouëf 13, fo. 55v)

tension engine; a man boils water to obtain salt, which is running short; a mobile tower is set on fire; while the defensive theme is again underlined by a number of vignettes depicting a town with its gates closed (see Figure 12).[26] Nor is the theme of attack forgotten. A variety of siege engines is presented: the ram, the 'vinea' ('vines' or mantlet, shown as grapes on a bush), the wheels of a mobile tower, are shown pictorially.[27] Yet, in accordance with Vegetius' text, defence is given greater emphasis than attack in the vignettes accompanying this book.

In what ways may the illustrations in this text add to our understanding and appreciation of how it was received and regarded? The small drawings reflect what were spontaneous reactions of readers to the text, probably drawn more or less as they read it, in some cases with the intention of enabling later readers to visualise an unfamiliar technical vocabulary. Vignettes, of their nature, were very different. They, too, may have been intended to illuminate the text's meaning, but, as suggested above, this was not always easy or, in some cases, possible. Essentially, the vignettes, which may represent a measure of co-operation between patron and artist, reflect an attempt to add a dimension to a text whose content, probably already known to the patron (and, possibly, also to the artist) from a reading of another manuscript, was considered as one which had so much personal meaning to him that, in the case of this manuscript, he chose to pay an artist of high standing to paint the vignettes intended to

---

[26] *Ibid.* fo. 53 (barrel); fos. 53, 53v, 55 (wall); fo. 55v (woman's hair); fo. 56 (boiling water); fo. 58 (fire); fos. 61, 61v (closed gates).
[27] *Ibid.* fos. 56v–57v (*DRM*, IV, 14, 15, 17).

enhance the quality of his text. The artistic costs underline what possession of a finely illuminated text meant to the patron. As such, it constitutes
evidence of the esteem in which Vegetius' work could be held in northern
Italy in the fourteenth century.

Whose inspiration the vignettes were, we cannot tell. The illumination
occupying about a quarter of the folio placed at the head of Book IV
contains a number of 'simultaneous' scenes which, whether considered
singly or together, underline the theme of preparedness, the state in which
any town or castle must be to defend itself successfully against attack.
The juxtapositioning of images underlining different aspects of the same
theme indicates that much thought had gone into the composition of
the illuminations. Both in this instance and elsewhere we find evidence
of what is nothing less than a subtle reading and understanding of the
text and its messages. This manuscript falls into the category of those
whose illustrations are so closely related to the text that we may say
with confidence that they were intended to fulfil an explanatory, visual
function, the illustration complementing and underlining the significance
of the message carried by the text itself.[28]

The practical difficulties facing the artist were considerable. He had to
paint some 130 vignettes, each about 2×2 cm (although a small number
were allowed to overflow into the margin) within the initial letter of every
chapter's first word, each tiny picture intended to reflect, more or less
clearly, something about the chapter, perhaps a particularly significant
theme or word within it. The first, enlarged, vignette shows a man wearing what appears to be academic dress; we understand him to be the
'philosopher', Vegetius himself, presented in the now familiar manner to
underline the philosophical and didactic nature of the work which follows. While there can be little doubt whom this figure represents, much
less evident is the message carried in the vignette showing two (talking)
heads; it requires reference to the text to appreciate that this picture is
probably of one man interviewing or assessing the other, underlining the
point that recruits must be chosen with the greatest care. Likewise it
requires the text to tell the reader that the soldier holding a sword, point
down, in front of him, is learning to wound or kill with a thrust or stab
rather than with a slash of his weapon, in the manner recommended by
Vegetius.[29]

[28] P. Porter, 'The ways of war in medieval manuscript illumination: tracing and assessing
the evidence', in *Armies, chivalry and warfare in medieval Britain and France*, ed. M.
Strickland (Stamford, 1998), 102–5.
[29] BnF Smith-Lesouëf 13, fos. 3v, 6v; *DRM*, I, 4, 12.

In the case of Book II the problems faced by the artist were accentuated by the book's content and character, which consists, in essence, of a lengthy description of the composition and organisation of the Roman army and its legions. Pity the artist faced with the problem of differentiating pictorially between a long list of holders of military office and their responsibilities as described in Vegetius' text. The sequence of a cardinal with his red hat, a soldier bearing a standard, a bishop, carrying a crozier, blessing, and a man who could be a judge scarcely appears to reflect the content of the text, except the blacksmith, who represents the work done under the Prefect of Engineers ('Prefectus fabrorum').[30] A cardinal and a bishop are surely out of place here. Is the clue to their presence to be found in the text, which refers to 'the Greater Tribune appointed by the sacred letter of the emperor'? In other words, are they intended to represent the most senior of the officers appointed by the emperor (or, in this case, by the pope)? Is the artist looking upon the list of office-holders as a hierarchy whose members obey their superiors, with the cardinal at its head, the bishop a little further down as the prefect of the legion, and the tribune of the soldiers as a man dressed in robes, perhaps those of a judge (if that is what he is) representing the discipline which the army required of its members, acting the role of the marshal, then emerging as the chief disciplinary officer in many armies? Right or wrong, these suggested explanations only serve to underline the difficulties of interpretation to be experienced both by the artist and by those viewing his work. None the less it appears as if the artist was trying to convey an emphasis upon the powers of certain office-holders, firmly established in the language of hierarchy, which the reader would understand.

The artist faced further problems in Book III. One was the length of a number of chapters, which made it hard to express their essence pictorially. Another was the emphasis placed, in some cases, upon moral, in others upon practical, aspects of waging war. In neither case could a chapter be successfully reduced to a small vignette. It requires consultation of the text to appreciate that the vignette showing a man dressed in what appear to be academic robes and holding what could be a bottle of urine was probably intended to be a doctor of medicine, since the chapter was concerned with the need to keep the army healthy.[31] The significance of the position occupied, and the practical role played by the 'dux' as commander (as both planner of campaigns and leader in battle),

---

[30] *Ibid.* fo. 17: *DRM*, II, 7 (cardinal); fo. 17v: *DRM*, II, 8 (soldier); fo. 18: *DRM*, II, 9 (bishop); fo. 19: *DRM*, II 12 (judge); fo. 19: *DRM*, II, 11 (blacksmith).
[31] *Ibid.* fo. 28v; *DRM*, III, 2.

is reflected in the vignette of the 'thoughtful' man, who discusses before giving his orders, and the man who, with drawn sword, leads his men into action.[32]

By contrast, the chapters of Book IV are normally short, sometimes very short. In addition, many have a content which could be expressed pictorially. The miniature at the head of the book conveys, successfully, the importance of preparation for effective defence; this combines the twin themes of preparation and anticipation, which permeate the *De re militari*, with the particular needs of a community soon to come under siege. Several vignettes emphasise aspects of defence: the provision of food in advance; the digging of defensive ditches; the perfecting of mural defences; and a man looking over a wall against which (according to the text) ladders are being placed.[33] All these are reasonably static scenes illustrating aspects of siege warfare, the theme being firmly underlined by three vignettes of a man in a town or castle with its gates firmly closed.[34] The enemy, it appears, has failed to break down the defences. Preparation has paid off.

The final part of Book IV is concerned with war at sea. A man reading from a roll is probably intended to accompany the references to the instructions governing naval warfare. Ship-building is suggested by a man wielding a hammer, while a man shown felling trees reminds the reader that Vegetius had specific recommendations to make on the felling of trees for timber.[35] The importance of the seasons and, above all, of the weather, to the seafarer is three times underlined with vignettes depicting the seasons and men observing what the stars will tell them about meteorological conditions.[36] Boats, mostly small sailing boats, some with a man on board, feature prominently in the art work of this part of the manuscript; these are possibly the river patrol boats to which Vegetius made reference in the concluding lines of his work.

Yet, in another sense, the illuminations, irrespective of size, provide us with crucial information on the attitude of the artist (and/or patron) towards the text, and whether it was regarded as historical or, alternatively, as in any sense contemporary. Was this manuscript intended as a monument to fourth-century Roman military thought and practice, or were its ideas and recommendations to be regarded as relevant to men living in the land and time of Dante or Petrarch? The answer cannot

---

[32] *Ibid.* fo. 36: *DRM*, III, 9; fo. 40v: *DRM*, III, 13; fo. 43v: *DRM*, III, 18.
[33] *Ibid.* fo. 53: *DRM*, IV, 1; fo. 54: *DRM*, IV, 5; fo. 55: *DRM*, IV, 8; fo. 59: *DRM*, IV, 21.
[34] *Ibid.* fos. 61, 61v: *DRM*, IV, 27–9.
[35] *Ibid.* fo. 62v: *DRM*, IV, 31; fo. 63: *DRM*, IV, 34; fo. 63v: *DRM*, IV, 35.
[36] *Ibid.* fos. 65–6: *DRM*, IV, 39–41.

really be in doubt. This is 'conscious medievalism'. Men are dressed (even if it is usually only their head and shoulders which are shown) in the costume of the day, often brightly coloured. The soldiers' armour and shields, although often a little nondescript, are essentially medieval. The pictorial description of the 'castrum'/'castra' is not that of a fortified encampment as set out in the text. 'Castra' are now medieval castles built of stone, with drawbridges and moats. In short, this is a text intended to be applied to the contemporary world and to what can be learned from the past which is useful for that time. It is an example, found elsewhere, of 'making the past present' through the process of visual translation, the updating and enhancement of the value and authority to be attributed to an ancient text through the use of modern illustrative material. However small, however inadequate, this material shows clearly that the artist and his patron regarded the contents of the work as being valuable and useful to men of their own time.[37]

Like the evidence showing the dilemmas faced by translators of the *De re militari* as they prepared it for life in the brave new medieval world, the contribution offered by the work of illuminators shows how another group of men may have understood and appreciated some of the work's key features. That it was clearly recognised as having contemporary relevance is seen in the unexpected (but perhaps not wholly unjustified) appearance of a gun in one instance. As was the case with the translations, the illuminations went through the process of 'medievalisation' and 'contemporisation'. At the same time, they remained largely true to the work's broad message. Where, given the period, one might have expected an emphasis on the role of the knight, the ordinary soldier was now given considerable prominence. Consideration of the theme of training and preparation did not show scenes of the tourney or cavalry charges, all too easily associated with the knightly approach to war; rather, it gave greater (because unexpected) emphasis to the man of lesser rank wrestling and training in the skills required for war. The message was as clear as when Vegetius had delivered it a millennium earlier: training was an obligation

---

[37] The fifteenth-century French humanist Jean Le Bègue was to leave instructions for a manuscript of Sallust to be illustrated with men wearing 'modern' rather then 'ancient' dress. See the remarks made on this subject by Anne Hedeman ('Making the past present', 178, n. 6, 185–6) in which she discusses 'visual translation', the modernising of an old text through the use of 'modern' illustrations, rather than 'literal translation', illustrating a Roman scene with men dressed in togas. It has more to do with the attitude of 'amplification' of translation than has the 'literal' approach. On this matter see also M. W. Driver, 'Medievalizing the classical past in Pierpont Morgan MS M 876', in *Middle English poetry: texts and traditions. Essays in honour of Derek Pearsall*, ed. A. J. Minnis (York, 2001), 211–39.

to be undertaken by all. In the same way the obligation to take part in communal defence was a common one, undertaken even by women. War was an activity which could involve all groups within a society, since it was the means of defending the common good against those who might undermine it.

9 Excerpts

Latin

A manuscript listing twenty-five excerpts from the *De re militari* selected by Sedulius Scotus, an Irish scholar who settled in Liège in the mid-ninth century, represents the first known collection of excerpts taken from Vegetius' work to survive to this day.[1] Two things strike the reader at once. One is the generous proportion (60 per cent) of excerpts taken from Book III, setting an early trend for the relatively high level of interest in that book, already remarked upon. The other, related to the first, is the high proportion (20 per cent in this case) of excerpts taken from Book IV, leaving the opening books I and II with only 20 per cent between them. It may also be noted that all but two of the excerpts feature regularly (and sometimes prominently) in collections made at later dates.

What encouraged Sedulius, by no stretch of the imagination a soldier, to copy excerpts from this work? Close examination reveals that by simply omitting a word (often no more than a conjunction) or by making statements of fact or opinion more concise, he was able to remove the excerpt from its context and transform it into a statement of almost proverbial character and authority which could then stand on its own. It is not surprising, then, that four excerpts should have been taken from Book III, 26, the so-called 'Rules of war', in which Vegetius had already set out in the language of the maxim some important principles of his thinking.

Sedulius made some use of the excerpts thus copied in his own writings. In his *Liber de rectoribus christianis* he twice quoted (more or less accurately) texts which he had copied out earlier. It would be wrong, however, to think that Sedulius was in any meaningful sense a military thinker. Emphasis has been placed on his essentially non-military motives in copying excerpts from the *De re militari*. Although he had interests in

---

[1] Details in *Collectaneum miscellaneum*, ed. Simpson, 144–6; see Sherwood, 'Studies', 85–111.

the ancient world, Sedulius used Vegetius' text as a source of statements and opinions which could be altered to suit his own need, to make a moral point, to further a rhetorical purpose, or to create maxims. Only a small proportion of the passages excerpted bore a genuine military message. Sedulius lived in an age which believed that victory was granted by God; it was not man's purpose to interfere with divine judgements. Can it be said, then, that in taking this attitude he had failed to see the potential which lay in the *De re militari* with its emphasis upon results depending in large measure upon human preparation and effort?

In the middle years of the ninth century, *c.*856, Hrabanus Maurus, abbot of Fulda and later archbishop of Mainz, compiled his short tract, *De procinctu Romanae miliciae*, which he dedicated to Lothar II, king of Lotharingia. The work, which occupies fewer than ten pages in the printed edition, is a form of epitome of the *De re militari*, with supplementary material added. It was compiled, as Hrabanus wrote in his letter of dedication,[2] to enable the king to become more knowledgeable than his subjects in matters concerning war, as was right that he should be. He included only material which was appropriate to the way war was fought in his own day, *tempore moderno*. To further this aim, he put together certain excerpts from Vegetius' work on the training of young soldiers; for it was clear that not numbers but ingenuity and exercise, along with God's help, would bring victory.

These excerpts were to consist of a rewriting, normally incorporating sections in Vegetius' own words, of some sixteen of Book I's twenty-eight chapters, the same treatment being accorded to a mere two chapters of Book II. Hrabanus recognised that the Roman Empire, as Vegetius had claimed, had been founded on the army, and on the quality of its trained soldiers. How was this done? Climate was taken into account when recruiting soldiers; they must be chosen according to their physique and trained while still young; the professions from which suitable soldiers might come were listed, as were those regarded as unsuitable, just as in the *De re militari*. In the following chapters Hrabanus discussed various forms of training, using Vegetius' text, but cutting and adapting it as he felt necessary. He emphasised the need for soldiers to advance in proper formation so as to attack the enemy as a single force. Learning to jump was necessary, as this caused alarm among the enemy, while swimming was encouraged, as was practice in the use of the sword, which was most effectively used when thrust into a body. The javelin was regarded by Hrabanus as an important weapon in war, in spite of the develement of cavalry at this period: practice in archery should be encouraged, for, as

---

[2] Sherwood, 'Studies', 114; Reeve, 'Transmission', 271–2.

could be shown, archers had an important role to play in battle. Slingers had their place in the army which Hrabanus envisaged; they, too, should train. Those who threw 'plumbatae', or lead-weighted darts, also found approval, since their weapons caused severe wounds among the enemy. Finally, Hrabanus underlined the need for training in mounting horses by jumping onto them, not using a stirrup as a means of doing this. Such training should be carried out indoors in specially constructed buildings in winter time, as Vegetius had taught.

Hrabanus' attention to Book II of the *De re militari* was limited to two chapters, 23 and 24, which formed the last two chapters of his own text. Chapter 23 he called a 'recapitulatio', which is what Vegetius' lengthy chapter, in many respects, was. He urged that training be given in the use of all kinds of arms, so that none of the skills needed to wield them effectively should be lost. It may be noted that the skills to which he referred were used by infantry; how appropriate were these in the ninth century, when the cavalry were beginning to assume a dominant position in the armies of the time? In his final chapter Hrabanus praised the skills of the art of war, ending (as Vegetius had done) with praise of the 'miles' who fought to defend his own liberty, the life of his king, and the good of his 'patria' and faith. In brief, he appeared to give his blessing to the fighting man's calling.

Why did Hrabanus stop here? From the start he had promised only excerpts; he was not planning a summary of the *De re militari* as a whole. There were whole chapters in Book I which, he may have felt, had little to offer a mid-ninth-century king. A comparison with what his near contemporary, Sedulius Scotus, felt able to emphasise is instructive. As we have seen, Sedulius had chosen to place heavy emphasis on Book III by selecting the majority of his excerpts from that book; Hrabanus, on the other hand, ignored its contents altogether. By contrast, a very large proportion of his fifteen chapters were versions of chapters from Book I, from which Sedulius had chosen only a few excerpts. And whereas Sedulius had had some interest in Book IV, Hrabanus had none.

We must, of course, allow for the fact that Sedulius had been choosing excerpts to copy, whereas Hrabanus was taking whole chapters at a time and re-forming them, sometimes allowing illustrative matter taken from the Old Testament to replace examples from Roman history which Vegetius had favoured, doubtless to suit his own didactic purpose. That Hrabanus went little further than the end of Book I may have been because he did not have a complete text to hand, but this is unlikely. It is more probable that he felt that the core part of his message was contained in Book I, and in the first two-thirds or so in particular, a perfectly tenable view. By returning to Book II, chapter 23, he drove home the point that selection and, above all, training, were the crucial factors in creating a victorious army, and, by introducing the word 'precauentes' at the end of chapter VII, he showed how important it was for those going to war to be forewarned, and to act accordingly.

In creating his little text of extracts from Vegetius' work, Hrabanus indicated that he thought that the Roman way of making war had much to teach his contemporaries how to meet the military threats confronting them. Modern historical scholarship has not been unanimous regarding men's appreciation of Roman influence upon military developments in the Carolingian era and in the century or two which followed. While there are those who see a marked level of continuity over the centuries, symbolised by the work of Hrabanus Maurus, others do not regard Roman influence as either so pronounced or so effective. Other than in general terms, Hrabanus' *De procinctu* may have had little practical influence outside the walls of the monastery where it was written. Nor should we jump to the conclusion that, because Vegetian ideas were not always followed, war was not fought in an orderly fashion. Rather, did the popularity of the *De re militari* not rest mainly upon the fact that it represented an antiquarian past, reflecting a desire on the part of Hrabanus and his readers to acquire some practical knowledge and experience of an age now fast disappearing? The debate has still some way to run.[3]

Later, two of the thirteenth century's leading encyclopaedists, the friars Vincent of Beauvais and John of Wales (Wallensis), would make use of the *De re militari* in their discussions of military matters. In Vincent's *Speculum doctrinale* many of Vegetius' teachings were subsumed into a huge encyclopaedic compilation bringing together human knowledge. In Book VII, chapter 24, Vincent touched upon military matters. He referred to the 'milites' as the hands of the 'res publica'. No one could become a 'miles' unless he had been chosen and had taken an oath, a reference both to contemporary practice and, beyond that, to what Vegetius and John of Salisbury had written on the matter. In Book XI, Vincent's indebtedness to Vegetius became fully apparent. Starting at chapter 33, he discussed various arms and the words used to describe them. At chapter 38 ('De scientia militari') he began to summarise the content of the *De re militari*, presenting the reader with an abbreviated form of the work. Some chapters he omitted altogether; elsewhere, he amalgamated elements of several chapters to create new ones, for which

[3] See B. S. and D. Bachrach, 'Saxon military revolution, 912–973: myth and reality', *Early Medieval Europe*, 15 (2007), 209; G. Halsall, *Warfare and society in the Barbarian West, 450–900* (London, 2003), 145. See also Abels and Morillo, 'A lying legacy?', 1–13, and Bachrach, '"A lying legacy" revisited', 153–93.

he provided his own headings; others still he left almost untouched. Little attempt was made to produce anything new or original. That was not Vincent's purpose, which was to gather knowledge rather than interpret it to form a new synthesis. He preferred to provide a sure source of information about Roman ideas and military practices. None the less, the fact that much of what he recorded was still appropriate to his own day undoubtedly helped to make his work more popular, while extending men's appreciation of Vegetian ideas.

A little later John of Wales became 'convinced that much in the Roman army merited the attention of his contemporaries'.[4] Collections of excerpts, increasingly drawn under subject headings in alphabetical order for ease of consultation by preachers searching for illustrative materials to liven their sermons, grew considerably in the thirteenth century. One popular compilation was the *Manipulus florum* of Thomas of Ireland (Hibernicus). In this case direct reference to the work of Vegetius, one of the thirty-eight authors whose writings he cited, may be found under the following headings: 'bellum' (17); 'consilium' (1); 'exercitatio' (1); 'militia' (12); 'presumptio' (1); and 'venia' (1). To John Bromyard, the English Dominican who compiled his *Summa praedicantium* as a tool for preachers about 1360, the images of war which it contained might be useful in more than one sort of combat, not least that faced by the soul ('in bello spirituali').[5] Like many, he drew on the *De re militari*, twice citing Vegetius by name. He quoted John of Salisbury's dictum that three factors made the Roman army victorious: confidence, skill and training ('fides, scientia et exercitium'). Like John of Wales, he wrote that the status and deeds of the soldier were worthy of praise. He emphasised, however, that the soldier must not be allowed to become soft; he should always be vigilant, a characteristic which would help him in the struggle against the devil. To ensure that only those most suited were chosen to become knights, Bromyard (like Vegetius) named those who should not be recruited: 'people in business should not fight' ('negotiatores ne militent'), he pronounced, since the new knight would have to be ready to surrender his life for the general wellbeing. Indeed, the very purpose of having an army was to ensure the defence of both the Church and the public good. It was with evident approval that he cited Peter of Blois' advice that knights should swear to stand by the need to defend that good; that they would not flee the battlefield; and that they should prefer

---

[4] J. Swanson, *John of Wales. A study of the works and ideas of a thirteenth-century friar* (Cambridge, 1989), 93.
[5] See parallels with Alcuin, Denis the Carthusian and Alfonso de San Cristóbal.

the public good to their own lives, a statement which owed more than a little to the *De re militari*, II, 5.[6]

The use to which a work might be put, particularly by the clergy, is put before us in the form of a table ('tabula') of the *De re militari* composed by the Benedictine theologian Jean de Fayt, abbot of St Bavo in Ghent, in the late fourteenth century. Sufficiently a man of the world to recognise that secular literature might include moral teachings and ideas useful for the clergy, Fayt appears to have been adept at drawing up tables of classical works to make them more accessible to a wider readership. As a young man he had completed one such for Aristotle's *Moralia*; later, he followed with one for Boethius' *De consolatione philosophiae*, the manuscript of which also contains his table for the *De re militari* in a fourteenth-century hand.[7]

This compilation consists of an alphabetical series of excerpts, under the heading of a word, together with reference to book and chapter. It begins 'acies', and is followed by 'arma', 'ars', 'audacia', 'auxilium'... along with entries under most letters. Not unnaturally, the military element is strong: thus 'bellum', 'castra', 'exercitus', 'militaris ars', 'obsidio', 'sagittarius' and 'velites' all find their place. The table also reflects some of Vegetius' strengths, such as his emphasis on both the moral and the physical benefits of 'consilium' ('advice'), 'fortitudo corporis' ('physical courage'), 'scientia' ('skill') and 'velocitas' ('speed'), all factors which can contribute to success, while 'lassitudo' ('tiredness') and 'metus' ('fear') tend to lead to defeat. In this respect, he appears to have read Vegetius carefully, and to have respected what he had read. What may have been his purpose in creating such a table? The alphabetisation of the excerpts under words and terms which Vegetius used suggests that, as he had done for Aristotle and Boethius, Jean de Fayt was trying to make available something of the moral and practical character of the *De re militari* to teachers and preachers who lacked the full text or had no time or wish to read it. That he had created what would be regarded, in modern terms, as a 'subject' rather than a 'name' index hints strongly at what his purpose was.

By the twelfth century, at the latest, collections of excerpts from the *De re militari* had begun to appear, collections which were probably not always made for the purpose of wide dissemination at some future date.

---

[6] *Summa praedicantium, sub* 'bellum' and 'militia'. See also Whetham, *Just wars and moral victories*, 125–6.

[7] *Tabula super Vegecium de re militari* (Vienna, Nat. Bibl. 4364, fos. 104–118). Another copy can be found in Valenciennes, Bibl-Médiathèque 400 (383), fos. 131v–140. See *Catalogue général des manuscrits des bibliothèques publiques de France. Départements: XXV (Poitiers:Valenciennes)* (Paris, 1894), 365.

The aims and circumstances which influenced or dictated the choice of excerpts is not normally known. To some, Vegetius was simply an author who wrote things which, for one reason or another, were worth noting down and preserving. Others read him with an eye to the creation of a collection of *obiter dicta* taken from the literature of past times. Those who marked a passage for future reference were likely to have been the owners of the manuscripts concerned. By contrast, those who created collections of excerpts by copying them were probably those to whom access to a text, which may have belonged to a private owner or a library, was limited by time or availability. In any event, by creating forms of secondary texts they were helping to disseminate many of Vegetius' ideas. The role of collections in propagating these ideas should not be underestimated.

It is difficult, if not impossible, to say with confidence what factors guided or motivated readers in their choice of passages. How were the collections of excerpts, which varied greatly in size, viewed by those who made them? The terms used to describe their collections tell us something, but by no means everything. Were they interested in producing summaries, however that word might be interpreted, of Vegetius' original? The term 'digesta' was used by the compiler of Florence, Laur., Redi. 151, for what was scarcely a 'digest' as we think of one, since whole sequences of chapters were omitted. Perhaps more honest, although vaguer, was the use of the word 'varia', found in Paris, BnF lat. 7695A, while 'abstractiones' (Venice, Marc. lat. VI 164), 'flores excerpti' (Oxford, Bodl. Add. C.12), 'flores delecti' (Vatican, Vat. lat. 5114) or 'manipulus florum' (Madrid, BN 234) all give the impression of being selections made according to either the whim or the interests of a particular individual. While a proper 'epitoma' or 'digesta' suggests the intention of producing a balanced summary, a collection of 'varia' or a 'flores excerpti' may tell us more, precisely because no attempt is made to summarise the whole work; rather passages are selected from it, preserving only those considered worthy of remembrance, for whatever reasons, by the compiler of the collection.

It is important to recognise that there could be a difference between the effect achieved by a passage to which attention had been drawn in the margin and the very same passage copied into a collection along with others taken from the same work. The first process was simple; it only required marking the manuscript in some way to emphasise agreement with, or recognition of the importance of, an idea or conclusion expressed by the author. Significantly, it left the passage intact within the context of the work in which its author had originally envisaged it, a context which might influence the way in which it was read and understood. While excerpts might be chosen with some underlying idea in mind (thus giving them a thematic unity), the process of creating collections removed the excerpts so chosen from their original contexts. At best, they might be inserted into a collection, set out alphabetically under a particular heading, such as 'bellum', 'exercitus' or 'militia'. At worst, they could only stand alone, their chances of making an impact depending largely on whether they possessed some epigrammatic quality, perhaps summarising an idea or principle in a few words. Vegetius' style possessed such a quality, the ability to create concise summaries in this way. This undoubtedly led to an appreciation of him as an author whose work fitted in well with the medieval practice of creating collections of excerpts. What Vegetius, like many writers, may have lost by being too often known through excerpts from his work was that many readers will not have been able to place his opinions within the broader context of the complete work. Too much emphasis is often placed on the trenchant nature of many of his statements, the wider context in which these should be read being disregarded. For this reason (if for no other) he is too often said to lack depth. If ever there was a writer who needed to be read properly, it was Vegetius.

Once created according to the interests of a particular individual, a collection of excerpts, like a complete text, could be copied again and again. One such, perhaps the first, made in Montpellier about 1132, and now Berlin, Staatsbibl. lat. qu. 198, was to form the basis of copies made much later.[8] Unlike other selections which consist of a number of passages, more often than not short, these are long, including complete chapters. Copies of this text would be made at the end of the Middle Ages: Oxford, Bodl. Canon. class. lat. 268 was written on paper probably about 1400; Leiden, Univ. Voss. lat. O. 54 was copied in Rhodes in 1440, and shows signs of Italian ownership; while Paris, BnF lat. 7243 (owned by the Visconti family), Vatican, Urb. lat. 456 (which belonged to Guidantonio da Montefeltro (d.1443)) and Paris, BnF lat. 10,784 are also of this period.[9] We should not exclude the possibility that other copies, of which we know nothing, were also made in the intervening years.

Another collection, Oxford, Bodl. Add. C. 12, probably copied at the beginning of the fifteenth century, was owned by the monastery of Borgo San Bernardini, near Piacenza. Unusually, it refers to five books making up the De re militari. Two copies of this set are known, Vatican, Reg. lat. 358 and Blickling Hall, 6849; both are French, and both contain the same

---

[8] The excerpts from the De re militari occupy fos. 232–59 of what is otherwise a medical manuscript.

[9] Together, they constitute the 'Omnes artes' group. See Reeve, 'Transmission', 270.

collection of 'flores'.[10] In addition, they share the same owner, or at least two owners from the same family, that of Fumée, from the French town of Tours. The family was a distinguished one in that city, a recognised centre of humanistic interests, and it is possible that the first owner, Lucas Fumée, a canon of Tours, may have travelled in Italy. One of the manuscripts was to pass into the hands of another member of the same family with the same name, probably in the early sixteenth century.[11]

How may we judge the level of appreciation which such collections created? If imitation is the highest form of flattery, then the copying of selections may be regarded as both approval of the process of creating such collections and appreciation of their contents. But we may perhaps go further by asking, for example, whether any effort was devoted to the expensive task of decorating manuscripts to give them added visual value. It must be admitted that all too few collections received such attention. Perhaps they were not regarded as deserving the cost of artistic adornment.

Signs of active use constitute a better way of judging their value to their owners/readers. In the oldest of them fingers point excitedly to many passages, while another, copied in Paris in 1171, was to be liberally decorated with the sign 'No[ta]' in the margins, particularly in regard to excerpts taken from Book III.[12] Oxford, Bodl. Can. class. lat. 268 is enlivened by a series of small drawings, mostly swords, but also including a crossbow opposite the word 'sagitta' in IV, 30. Words written in the margin, 'fortitudo' ('bravery'), 'audacia' ('boldness'), 'terror' ('fear'), 'honestas' ('honour') or 'exercitium' ('training'),[13] were intended to draw attention to passages which a reader regarded as interesting or important. Furthermore, as the majority of these words suggest, readers were interested in the importance attached by Vegetius to both the moral and the physical strengths which the soldier must develop; the inclusion of 'terror' underlined the internal enemy latent within every soldier, so emphasising the importance placed by Vegetius upon the contribution of leadership in preparing an army for battle. We may also note the emphasis placed upon attributes such as 'fortitudo', a word whose meaning could be readily understood in a moral or religious context, as well as in a military one.

One manuscript, Dublin, Trinity College 632, contains a collection of excerpts of great variety, including a culling of classical authors, of whom

[10] *Ibid.*, 255, n. 30.
[11] I am grateful to Bernard Chevalier for giving me information regarding members of the family of Fumée.
[12] Berlin, Staatsbibl. lat. qu. 198, and BnF lat. 8314.
[13] Vatican, Reg. lat. 358; Erfurt, Univ. CA 4° 393.

Vegetius is one. The collection of excerpts from the *De re militari*, probably written in East Anglia in the second half of the fifteenth century, is
not large, but contains some interesting and, at times, entertaining comments. Marginalia include a fair number of 'Nota' or the more emphatic
'Nota bene' against passages recommending quality over numbers, the
need for constant training, and a reminder that armour not only protects
the body but gives courage to the wearer. Most attention, however, is
given to Book III, to the matters of health, logistics, the movement of an
army in the presence of the enemy, how best to treat a newly recruited
army unaccustomed to fighting, all matters which formed part of the
responsibilities of the 'dux', whose 'sapiencia' ('good sense') features in
the margin. The commentator's sense of humour emerges when Vegetius
reminds his readers of the importance of speed, which he regards as
more important than courage; opposite this statement the words 'Nota
contra tardos' ('Against slowcoaches'!) have been added. The contemporary relevance of the excerpts to one reader is found in two references
to (presumably recent) events: opposite the concluding sentence to I,
28 (it costs less to train one's men than to employ foreign mercenaries)
the words 'Contra regem Armenie' ('against the king of Armenia') have
been written (fo. 128v), while next to the statement 'armies are more
often destroyed by starvation than by battle' (III, 3) the words 'de werra
Scottorum' ('on the Scottish war') are added (fo. 128v). What these
comments refer to is not clear,[14] but the reader was trying to relate the
lessons of the text to the world which he, and presumably other readers,
knew about.

As most excerpts from the *De re militari* are embedded in collections
which can only be described as mixed, the search for patterns of con-
sistency tends to lead nowhere. It is interesting, however, to observe
the link, remarked upon earlier, between the *De re militari* and the *De
regimine principum* of Giles of Rome. Excerpts from both, written in the
same fourteenth-century hand, are found in BnF lat. 6476. One known
owner was Jean, duke of Berry, which may make the collection French; it
could account for the interest in such pressing issues as the need to secure
peace, maintain order and rid society of violence.[15] In another collection,
excerpts from the *De regimine principum* citing Vegetius and emphasising
the need to make a proper choice of soldiers are followed immediately
in mid-line by excerpts from the *De re militari*, which are themselves followed by a discussion of what constitutes good rule in which Vegetius

---

[14] Tony Goodman has suggested that this may refer to the scorched earth policy often
adopted by the Scots in their wars against the English.
[15] BnF lat. 6476, fos. 109–109v.

is again cited.[16] As elsewhere, Vegetius' work was being taken to bolster and enlarge a discussion on the need for, and best forms of, government centred around the work of Giles of Rome.

A general overview of collections of excerpts made from Book I suggests a lively interest in its proem and, with the exception of chapter 5, in its early chapters, which are primarily concerned with recruitment. The remaining long section on training (chs. 8–28) aroused rather less interest. There were, however, notable exceptions. It was well understood that, having recruited only the best, the army must learn to act as a body or face defeat (ch. 9); there was clear appreciation of the good fortune enjoyed by a state which benefited from the protection provided by a trained army (ch. 13); while the information on the armour used by the ancients (ch. 24) proved of interest principally to those who copied their excerpts between the twelfth and the fourteenth centuries. Generally speaking, however, the number of excerpts taken from Book I declined as the years progressed; the earlier the collection, the more numerous they were likely to be.[17]

It will be recalled that marginalia in copies of the full text of the De re militari reflected little interest in the details of the structure and administration of the Roman legion included in Book II. The evidence offered by the choice of excerpts by and large supports this view. There was interest in the book's first three chapters on the character of Roman armed forces; but even that declined sharply in the fifteenth century. Only when the oath-taking ceremony transformed the recruit into a fully fledged soldier, when Vegetius referred to the psychological effects which shining arms and armour might have upon the enemy, or when the text left the particulars of battle order and administration to remind the reader of the vital role to be played by the training of soldiers and the encouragement given to regular exercises, did Book II provide texts copied by readers. While excerpts from this book were made in large numbers in the twelfth and thirteenth centuries, it was rare thereafter to find much interest in what it had to offer.[18]

The marginalia emphasised the fact that Book III, mainly concerned with the preparation and fighting of campaigns, constituted that part of the De re militari which provoked the greatest level of interest among its readers, an impression underlined by the number of excerpts taken from

[16] BnF nouv. acq. lat. 3074, fos. 37v–38.
[17] Exceptions are Venice, Marc. lat. VI 164, and BL Royal 12 E xxi.
[18] Exceptions can be found in Erfurt, Univ. CA 4° 393, and Göteborg, Univ. lat. 22. It should also be emphasised, however, that the evidence of marginalia in late medieval manuscripts suggests greater interest in what Book II had to advise than had generally been the case before.

Book III found in different collections. Once again, it is in certain of the early ones that most are to be found; it is notable that some fifteenth-century collections contained nothing from this book.

Of the first eight chapters, concerned mainly with practical aspects of an army's existence and survival, those which showed how to act when the enemy was close at hand, and which dealt with the need to keep an army properly fed and supplied, drew the most attention; only advice on how to cross large rivers appears to have been ignored. However, guidance offered on how to deal with the enemy and, above all, how to lead an army, perhaps largely composed of men nervous of what might happen, scored heavily, as did, too, advice on how to draw up the battle line and where the commander should place himself in relation to it. The need to provide the enemy, hemmed in and desperate, with a means of escape was quite frequently noted. The rules of war, succinct summaries of important points raised in the text, provided a rich seam to be dug and copied for future consideration. The list given here corresponds very much with that drawn up in our earlier consideration of the evidence provided by the marginalia. Essentially they are points taken from Vegetius' teaching which emphasised the need for the commander to fight on his terms, and to impose himself upon the enemy. In that way, victory could be achieved.

Of the final book, concerned mainly with siege warfare and war at sea, there is little to say. About half the collections of excerpts ignore its contents altogether. Among those which do not, however, a few contribute a sizeable number of excerpts, including a handful with evident interest in matters maritime, underlying the very 'personal' character of these collections. Attention is also paid to siege warfare, particularly in defensive measures associated with it. Generally speaking, however, interest in the contents of Book IV merited only limited attention from those creating collections of excerpts of Vegetius' teaching.

Finally, attention should be drawn to the so-called *Libellus de vocabulo rei militaris*, purportedly addressed to the emperor Tacitus, and compiled by one who called himself (or, perhaps, was given the name of) Modestus. Who this figure was and when he lived is a mystery; it is possible that he never existed. All that can be said with certainty is that he lived after AD 450.[19] The date of the compilation of the text, 'simply a patchwork of excerpts from Vegetius, most of them taken from the second book and none from the fourth', is obscure. It may go back to the ninth century; in favour of such an argument is the fact that both Sedulius Scotus and

---

[19] M. D. Reeve, 'Modestus, *scriptor rei militaris*', in *La tradition vive. Mélanges d'histoire des textes en l'honneur de Louis Holtz*, ed. P. Lardet, *Bibliologia*, 20 (2003), 427.

Hrabanus Maurus were assembling their compilations of excerpts from the *De re militari* at this period. It is very likely that the original pre-dated the twelfth-century Montpellier manuscript of Vegetius' work, and one manuscript tradition, at least, appears to have been written by someone familiar with John of Salisbury's *Policraticus*, completed in 1159.[20]

The excerpts selected, and the main line of thought to emerge from that selection, are substantially different from those conveyed in the collections of Sedulius and Hrabanus. Of twenty-three 'chapters', fourteen were based on excerpts copied from Book II, whose contents was generally given little attention until the late Middle Ages. Book I provided the source for two chapters, as Book III did for seven. Book IV was ignored.

Excerpts from Book II, then, dominated the work. Six of the fourteen chapters to which it contributed were included in full. The compiler was concerned with several matters, most of them by now very familiar. The army, as described, consisted of recruits who must learn to fight together; the core of the army was the legion, commanded by hierarchies of men appointed by the emperor, and chosen on the grounds of merit and hard work. Discipline was maintained by imperial officers. Attention was then directed to battles and to the need for soldiers to be able to recognise both their leaders and others alongside whom they were fighting, emphasising the need for unity and discipline in time of action. Much attention was given to the battle array, and to making the army function effectively against the enemy, not least through its ability to respond to orders conveyed by signals. It is significant that the compiler, having created chapter XI out of *DRM*, II, 15, deliberately followed this up in chapter XII with excerpts from III, 14, two of Vegetius' chapters linked by their subject matter, the drawing up of battle lines, before resuming with an excerpt from II, 16. This was no accident, but an attempt to give some kind of form to what might otherwise appear to be a disparate collection of excerpts.

As we have noted, the text consists of six complete chapters copied, more or less exactly, from the *De re militari*, chapters which were interspersed with shorter excerpts from the work. The thirty-one known surviving manuscripts were mostly copied in Italy in the fourteenth and fifteenth centuries at a period when interest in Book II was finally beginning to grow.[21] It was probably this development of interest in the practical application of the 'scientia militaris' which led to the printing of the work, first in 1471, when it was given the title *De disciplina militari*, sometimes also given to Vegetius' work, and then in 1474, this time with the title *De re militari*. From 1487, when it joined Vegetius, Frontinus and Aelian

---

[20] *Ibid.* 431, 422.   [21] *Ibid.* 418.

under one cover, it became known as the *Libellus de vocabulo rei militaris*, doubtless to avoid confusion with Vegetius' better-known work. Its attribution to Cicero in 1471 would be challenged in the 1474 edition. Was this attribution due to Pomponio Leto, head of the Roman academy, about 1470? Who compiled the text, when and where, are questions still unanswered.[22] But its popularity as a text in the early age of print cannot be in doubt. It would even be translated into Italian by the humanist Cristoforo Landino (d.1492), holder of public office in Florence and a known defender of the principle of translation, under the title 'Delle ordinanze de' Romani'. A copy, probably made in the sixteenth century, can be seen in the manuscript collections of the British Library.[23]

French

By contrast with the collections of excerpts in Latin, those in French, although the most numerous among those in the vernacular, are still few in number. Interest, indeed, must largely rest on a group of four manuscripts, each of which contains two items: *Des stratagemes de guerre*, being the translation of the *Strategemata* of Frontinus made by Jean de Rouvroy c.1426, followed, in two cases, by a glossary of words/terms 'which cannot be translated literally without causing difficulty ('lesquelx ne se peuent bonnement translater de mot a mot sans obscureté'); secondly, a relatively brief text, 'Aucuns notables extraiz', taken from the *De re militari* of Vegetius. Whether the same Latin collection of which this may have been a translation ever existed is not known; if it did, I have not found it. There is doubt whether the most reliable of the four surviving manuscripts was itself the original manuscript. As for the translation, it is possible that the collection was originally made – and translated – by Rouvroy himself; similarities in the language used in both the translation of Frontinus and the 'Extraiz' hint at the work of a single mind.[24] The only firm thing we can say about the 'Extraiz' is that the manuscripts all date from the mid-fifteenth century at the earliest, a fact established by the date of the translation of Frontinus and supported by the palaeographical evidence.We should not forget that here are four examples of something rather new, namely vernacular versions of both Frontinus' work and a 'reduced' Vegetius under the same cover. The second of these, our chief concern here, consisted of a collection of excerpts, not chosen at

[22] The idea that this is a genuine work of antiquity persists among some scholars.
[23] BL Add. Ms 24,216, fos. 12–16v.
[24] L. Löfstedt, 'Aucuns notables extraitz du Livre de Végèce', *Neuphilologische Mitteilungen*, 83 (1982), 297.

random but illustrating some of the main themes of Vegetius' thought as expounded almost exclusively in Books I–III of his work, followed by an exposé of most of his general 'Rules of war'. This sense of sharing not only content but form, too, adds to the theory that one person, Rouvroy, may have been responsible for both works.

The 'Extraitz' from the *De re militari* are divided into two parts. The first consists of some sixty-five excerpts set out, with one exception (an excerpt from the first of the 'Rules of war'), in the order in which they appear in the text.[25] The translations are such that in only a case or two is it difficult to find the source in the original. Like most translations, the French is sometimes a fairly free rendering of the Latin; misreadings can be found; additions, too, are usually incorporated with the intention of making the excerpts' meaning clearer; the use of doublets was also commonly used, presumably for the purpose of giving the reader a better understanding of the original text.

The 'Extraiz' provide a reasonable résumé of the first three books of the *De re militari*. The work's didactic nature is emphasised by the implied advice for the modern state to follow Rome's example of having an army and a ruler with interests and concerns in military matters. Then follows emphasis on some of Vegetius' fundamental points. Training and the skills which it develops, rather than numbers, lead to victory; hence the importance attached to training in peacetime, since a long period of inactivity will lead to neglect and the need to employ foreign soldiers, at a cost. Fundamental to all this lies the importance of selecting the right kind of recruits, who, since they will become the defenders of the state, must have both good physical characteristics and sound moral qualities. In the language of the day, they should, if possible, be 'men of good breeding' ('gentilzhommes . . . excellens en bonnes meurs'), as Vegetius' text described them.[26] By learning military skills they would provide the state with an army which would deter prospective attackers. The chapter ends with the need to promote good military practice, not least the provision of proper armour, which gives confidence to fighting men.

Following the same train of thought it is scarcely surprising that, as so often before, Book II provoked little interest since its concern was to describe a system of military organisation and administration which hardly corresponded with the social assumptions and structures of modern times. None the less, the selection of excerpts from this book underlined some points made earlier. Cato was cited for his view that war was

---

[25] Eighteen from Book I; eight from Book II; thirty-seven from Book III; two from Book IV.

[26] *DRM*, I, 7.

a discipline which could be developed by men who wrote down their ideas for consideration by later ages, not least by rulers, who could thus become successful leaders in war. The role of the 'miles' (here the 'gens d'armes') as the trained recruit who swore to obey and serve his ruler was not unnaturally emphasised by a selector of excerpts in mid-fifteenth-century France; this was Vegetius at his most topical. But neither should the reader be allowed to forget other important lessons, not least the psychological effect caused by an army in shining armour, repeated in a later book. Behind all success, as Vegetius would never tire of repeating, lay the need for regular training. Only this could ensure a state of proper preparation when the need arose.

The selection of what were regarded as key passages underlined one characteristic of the *De re militari*, namely the way in which parts of each book emphasised some of the important points made in a previous book or books. The famous statement that the search for peace required preparation for war, made in the preface to Book III, and supporting a similar statement made in Book I, could hardly be omitted. The *pax Romana* had depended on the ability to wage war successfully. Again, we find support for the small army, relying on Roman citizens rather than on those from outside. Yet again, the accent was on training, now including a recognition that the health of the soldier could not be ignored. The emphasis was on a vision of the army primarily as a functioning organisation, ready to fight, and on the position and responsibilities of the man who commanded it. The links between the army and its leaders had to be set out; a proper system of signals, whereby orders could be transmitted in battle, had to be established. The best way to defeat the enemy was to avoid confronting him in battle, and to concentrate on covert warfare, on ambushes and other means of creating alarm and surprise. It was the commander's task to discuss possibilities, to plan strategies, and to encourage his soldiers. Leaders had to be good judges of the state of mind of their troops, and be able to raise their courage so as not to lead apprehensive soldiers into battle. Although it was normal for men to experience fear, there were ways of guarding against it, and of taking the initiative by raising the soldiers' morale. Above all, the enemy should not be despised. A defeated army had often destroyed another to which it had seemingly lost a battle. The text here went beyond Vegetius by warning against conceit of what successes might be won. The outcome of battles often went against those who should have won.

A few folios contained in a miscellany of historical and heraldic texts dating from the fifteenth century may serve to complement the excerpts found in the 'extraiz' just considered.[27] The text was not simply a

[27] BnF fr. 5930, fos. 6v–11.

selection from the *De re militari*, but a restatement of some of Vegetius' basic teaching centred upon a battle against the enemy. Following Vegetius, the emphasis was upon creating an ordered force that would fight with discipline, its ranks neither too close nor too far apart, for both had dangerous consequences. The infantry and cavalry must fight together, the best in the front, the weakest at the rear. They could be placed in a variable number of groups, the idea being to create uncertainty among the enemy. The place of battle should be chosen to suit one's advantage, and the enemy encouraged to make the first attack, the benefit being that the enemy would be out of breath and no longer in disciplined ranks when the armies made physical contact. This could only be of advantage to those defending.

Much of the remainder of the text contained familiar Vegetian doctrine. Emphasis was placed upon the need for the commander to be kept informed about the enemy's position and the morale of his troops. The commander should try to time his attack around the moment when the enemy was not ready, when his horses were tired after a long day, and his soldiers were seeking lodgings. This brought to the fore the value of surprise, based on information provided by spies, as a factor of importance in war. Other principles appear, too. One was the inestimable contribution of seasoned captains, experienced through long service in all aspects of war and battles ('sages et bons capitaines qui sagement ont demené leur vie en guerre et aussi en bataille').[28] The value of courage should be recognised by placing the bravest and most daring ('les plus preux et hardis') where the thick of the action was likely to be, while morale should be maintained by men whose task it was to give hope to those taking part ('donn[er] courage et . . . bon espoir').[29] What emerged from the text was the compiler's recognition that the relationship between commander and men should be an active one: he should tell them what needed to be done, not hiding the dangers which might be encountered. Taking his men into his confidence in this way, he should also give demonstrations in the use of weapons so that his men might learn how to use them effectively. Using ideas drawn from various parts of Vegetius' text, the commander was creating an effective bond between his men and himself, thus adding to their confidence as they prepared to face the enemy.

German

On the evidence of surviving manuscripts, some fourteen copies of the *De re militari* had been produced in the German language area before

[28] *Ibid.* fo. 9v.   [29] *Ibid.* fo. 10.

c.1400,[30] the number more than doubling to thirty-four within a century. On this evidence alone it becomes clear that considerable interest in Vegetius' work existed in these areas of Europe during the fifteenth century. The evidence is supported by what is now known of the development of vernacular versions of the *De re militari* produced at that time. Thanks to the researches of Frank Fürbeth, we are far better informed on the subject than we were only a few years ago.

It was about 1400 that Johann Seffner, dean of the faculty of canon law at the university of Vienna, wrote his short piece of instruction, *Lehre vom Krieg*, which, in the modern edition, takes up less than seven pages.[31] On three occasions he referred to Vegetius as having written about chivalry ('der von der ritterschafft hat gescriben'),[32] while also making use of several Old Testament books and the writings of Cicero, Ambrose and Isidore. About a dozen short passages, some freely adapted, had been shown to have had their origins in the *De re militari* which, the author announced, formed the basis of his work. The excerpts, mostly taken from Book III, referred to such matters as the use of reserves in battle, procedures for retreating, the conveying of orders by signals, and the morale of fighting men. The author was concerned about, and hoped to learn from, the defeat suffered by Duke Leopold III of Austria at the hands of the Swiss at Sempach in July 1386, an event which witnessed the victory of infantry over the feudal nobility fighting for the duke, a 'disorderly conflict' ('ungeordnete streitt') as Seffner termed it. Not surprisingly, since Leopold was killed in action, the author recommended that commanders should, if possible, avoid direct participation in battles; the argument was not a new one. In all events, Seffner could not help placing responsibility for the defeat upon Leopold's shoulders. It was the failings of commanders such as he that Seffner wished to remedy.[33]

Within about two decades, around 1415, the *De re militari* would once more form the source and basis of a work of significance, *Der Ritterspiegel*, or 'Mirror of Knighthood', written by Johannes Rothe. Its 4,108 lines of verse are divided into four unequal parts. It is the last section, beginning at line 2,401, which concerns us.[34]

---

[30] Fürbeth, 'Zur deutschsprachigen Rezeption', 147, n. 27.

[31] Johann Seffner, 'Lehre vom Krieg', in *Deutschen Chroniken und andere Geschichtsbücher des Mittelalters*, VI, Österreichische Chronik von den 95 Herrschaften (MGH, Hanover and Leipzig, 1909), 224–30.

[32] *Ibid.* 225.

[33] R. Leng, *Ars belli. Deutsche taktische und kriegstechnische Bilderhandschriften und Traktate im 15 und 16 Jahrhundert* (2 vols., Wiesbaden, 2002), I, 80; Fürbeth, 'Die "Epitoma rei militaris"', 313.

[34] Johannes Rothe, *Der Ritterspiegel*, ed. H. Neumann (Halle and Salle, 1936).

As a highly educated man, Rothe could draw on a team of classical
or late Roman writers, not least Aristotle, Cicero ('meister Tulius'), Sallust, Seneca, Augustine and Cassiodorus ('meister Cassiodorius') and, of
course, 'Vegecius der meister' ('*the* master'), whose authority in military
matters always came first, in support of his views. More than twenty-five
passages were either directly associated with the *De re militari* or reflect
ideas and advice given in it. From Book I Rothe referred to the good
recruit's physical characteristics; to the skills, such as swimming, horse
riding and archery which he should acquire, and to the need for constant
practice.[35] What Vegetius wrote in Book I on the building of camps also
interested him. Under Book II Rothe followed Vegetius by referring to the
skills in writing and computation which the soldier should possess, and
emphasised the value of practice over strength in battle.[36] Book III provided Rothe with most advice. He underlined the dire effects of hunger
upon an army, and stressed the need always to keep sufficient stores of
food available.[37] The importance of good morale in the army was recognised, while the passages concerned with the building of camps (referred
to under Book I) were underlined by reference to the adverse effects of
choosing unfavourable sites on which to pitch camp. The responsibilities
of the commander in selecting a favourable place to confront the enemy,
and his need to receive advice before a battle, were both emphasised.[38]

Like Seffner, Rothe wrote to instruct a largely noble/knightly readership. But he distinguished between noble and knightly. Townsmen, who
had a role to play in war, could be knightly even if they were not noble.
His *ritter* was not knightly because of his nobility; it was his skill in arms
that created the honour and respect which were his due. In such a way of
thinking the regular training emphasised by Vegetius had a crucial role
to play in maintaining the fighting man's skills. Rothe also saw knights,
with these skills, as the natural leaders of armies. To fulfil this function
successfully, they should follow the teachings of the 'Meister'. It is not
surprising, therefore, that all the identifiable influences emanating from
the *De re militari* came from Books I and III. Books II and IV had little
to offer Rothe. The emphasis was upon realism, upon the actual world
in which the significance of the role traditionally played by the knight
was yielding to that devoted to the soldier.[39] The change was gradual;
none the less, it was happening. Competence, expertise, the need for
constant readiness were the qualities increasingly expected of the fighting

---

[35] 'Wol nutzce in den crigin' (*ibid.* line 2711).
[36] 'Di gewonheid zcu dem stritin/ ist beßir danne di sterke' (*ibid.* lines 2837–8).
[37] 'Der hungir is eyn scharffis swert' (*ibid.* line 3770). Cf. 'ferro saevior fames est'
(*DRM*, III, 3).
[38] See Fürbeth, 'Zur deutschsprachigen Rezeption', 152, nn. 52, 53.   [39] *Ibid.* 152–3.

man, whatever name was given him. Leadership of a highly professional quality was expected, too. Rothe referred to 'eyn wiser herzcoge'.[40] However we choose to understand 'wiser' ('experienced'?), it is clear that the amateur, the non-professional, would no longer suffice.

The manuscript,[41] dated *c*.1470, consists of a collection of ancient and humanistic texts: Cicero, *De officiis*, Johannes Hartlieb, *Kunst der Gedächtnüss*, Aeneas Piccolomini, *De curialium miseriis*, and and one entitled *De materia bellandi*, all three Latin texts being translated into German. The manuscript was formerly in the extensive library of Anton von Annenberg built up in the third quarter of the fifteenth century. It has been argued that, in this instance, the three originally Latin texts together constitute a group or collection which might be regarded as a 'Fürstenspiegel', or mirror for princes, the military text forming part of a broad didactic work on government rather than a contribution to the narrower field of strictly military literature.[42]

It soon becomes clear that the Latin text from which this translation was made, far from being a complete version of the *De re militari*, was an abridgement or adaptation made, perhaps, with its inclusion into a 'mirror'-type collection in mind. The question arises whether the abridgement was made by the translator. The answer is a negative one. The translation is, in fact, a rendering into Bavarian dialect of a tract, *Der pulcher tractatus de materia belli*, compiled probably about 1300, in all likelihood in northern Italy, which set out to advise on the preparations necessary for war, and how these might lead to a successful outcome.[43] Comprising thirty-four chapters or sections, it drew heavily on the *De re militari*, and also on the Bible, a number of classical authors, and later writers, among them John of Salisbury. Having asked why there should be wars, it centred itself on concepts underlined by Vegetius: the choice and training of soldiers; a series of practical steps to be encouraged among those setting out to war; points to be considered by the commander; and how an army's formations should stand in preparation for battle. Most of the passages cited, taken from Book III, deal with practical problems met in the course of confronting the enemy. Book III, chapter 26, which contained Vegetius' 'Rules of war', was the most quoted of all, the principles stated there constituting good summaries of points that a future leader should consider. The significance of this text is that it is a translation

---

[40] Rothe, *Der Ritterspiegel*, line 2937.
[41] Innsbruck, Bibl. Mus. Ferdinandeum, FB. 1050, fos. 178–210.
[42] F. Fürbeth, 'Eine unbekannte deutsche Übersetzung des Vegetius aus der Bibliothek des Anton von Annenberg', *Zeitschrift für deutsches Altertum und deutsche Literatur*, 124 (1995), 281, 289, 291.
[43] *Ibid.* 290–1. See Settia, *De re militari*, 78.

made for a noble patron of strong bibliophile tendencies which would satisfy both humanistic interests and those seeking to study the best ways of approaching war. Its emphasis on Book III of the *De re militari* suggests an understanding that, in the late Middle Ages, a text relating to the leadership of armies was of great importance to those concerned with the military developments of the time.

Italian

A manuscript, which carries the date 10 August 1456, consists of excerpts from various authors including Valerius Maximus, Cicero, Seneca and Paul the Deacon.[44] Vegetius, also of their number, is cited on some four occasions, most notably to the effect that the army should be the defender of the people: 'Narra Vegetio nel'libro della chavalleria che i chavalieri debbono essere guardiani de popolari',[45] an understanding of part of Vegetius' teaching which is repeated a little later: 'I chavalieri debbono guardare il popolo.' That this was the main message conveyed to the person who selected these excerpts was underlined by a note to the effect that the defeat of the 'Gran Turco' before Belgrade in July had been the subject of great public celebrations in Florence. Armies which defended their people were doing the job for which they existed. Another manuscript, partly Latin, partly Italian, dating from the sixteenth century, reveals a further significant interest in the *De re militari*.[46] Throughout the text the reader is impressed by the respect which the compiler had for the lessons which the past can teach the present. Concentration is focused on two groups of chapters, II, 14–24 and III, 11–15. Beginning 'How to make the legion useful in present times. A text regarding the ancient Roman army' ('Principio de fare la legione utile per li presenti tempi. Tracta del antica romana milicia') (note the stated link between the past and the present), it follows Vegetius through the battle order of the old legion, showing, for example, how its members should be placed, and how many feet there should be between them. Significant are the plans of the military formations found in the first folios of the manuscript, and the small diagrams added in the margins of folios 15 and 22. These are clearly classically inspired, perhaps more directly by Aelian's work, but they none the less reflect a growing preference for the visual form of something which Vegetius had described only in words: how to draw up the army, armed with particular weapons, ready to face the enemy.

---

[44] Florence, Laur. Plut. 89 inf. 54, fos. 1–12.
[45] *Ibid.* fo. 8.   [46] Florence, Laur. Plut. 89 inf. 42, fos. 12–18v.

Moving to basic principles which should be followed, the compiler emphasised the need for the commander to be well informed about the enemy's preparations, and the number and kinds of soldiers in his army. He urged that the ways of fighting adopted by the Athenians and Spartans be studied, while Vegetius would provide examples of Roman good practice. Men should continue to train for war in times of peace, so that they were always ready to fight anywhere. Leaders should read about war: Livy and Caesar were particularly recommended, and their experiences should be drawn upon. If what these men had to teach were done, the compiler stated confidently, the republic would remain unconquered ('sua republica farà invicta').[47]

Castilian

The *Tratado de la Guerra*, attributed to Alonso de Cartagena who, as archbishop of Burgos from 1435 to 1456, played a considerable diplomatic role at the Council of Basel, is little more than a collection of 161 excerpts based on the *De re militari*, and written in Castilian.[48] The choice of excerpts in this collection (to call this a 'work' would be to err on the side of generosity) reflected, in general terms, other collections considered above. There was considerable interest in many of the early chapters of Book I relating chiefly to the practical matter of the recruitment and training of soldiers. Cartagena found more to interest him in Book II than did many other readers; his selection would reflect a historical interest in the Roman army, its personnel and organisation, as well as in some of the practical lessons it had to teach regarding warfare. Book III interested him the most: he understood its contribution to the effective functioning of the army on campaign: good health, proper logistics, sensible action and decisive leadership in the face of the enemy. No excerpts went beyond III, 9; the remainder of Vegetius' text was, for all intents and purposes, ignored.

Further excerpts from the *De re militari* would also appear under another, unexpected, label, the *Dichos* of Seneca, also translated into Castilian by Cartagena. How these extracts from Vegetius became confused with the work of Seneca is not clear. It is possible that they were mistaken for others from Vegetius found in the same manuscript collection.[49] Be that as it may, it is clear that, when he wrote his own 'La question del

---

[47] The reader is reminded of the Italian translation of Modestus referred to above on p. 226.
[48] Alonso de Cartagena, *Tratados militares*, ed. N. Fallows (Madrid, 2006), 445–62.
[49] Rolan and Suarez-Somonte, 'El *Epitoma rei militaris*', 103–50.

marqués de Santallina', Cartagena cited the oath of the 'miles' given in
De re militari, II, 5, part of which he had already translated as 'Seneca'.
Whether he recognised it or not, this suggests how far Vegetius had per-
meated the culture of this important early Castilian humanist.

Scottish

The closing years of the fifteenth century were to witness the creation of
a collection of texts including 'the translacioun out of latyn in to ynglis
[i.e. Scots] de bello campestra in Veg[et]ius de rei militari', assembled in
1494 by Adam Loutfut, Kintyre Pursuivant, for Sir William Cumming of
Inverallochy, Marchemont Herald. The manuscript[50] includes nineteen
items, of which this text is the fourteenth. Almost all concern matters
which would be of practical interest to a herald, including Loutfut's
translation of William Caxton's *The Book of the Ordre of Chyualry*.[51] A
second example of the translation can be found copied (although not
to the letter and with some minor changes) a few years later by Robert
Anderson.[52]

Far from being a translation of parts of the *De re militari*, Loutfut's
compilation was done from Giles of Rome's adaptation of Vegetius' text,
perhaps, indeed, from its French version, for most of the changes and
interpolations ascribed to Loutfut were made earlier by Giles.[53] There is
a herald's natural interest in what Vegetius had written on banners and
ensigns, and on the moral and physical qualities demanded of those who
carried them. Yet there is more to Loutfut's selection than this. Discussing
the men who made the best soldiers, he turned immediately to Vegetius'
list of occupations whose practitioners were judged as suitable, or not,
as the case might be, for military service. Those regarded favourably by
Vegetius were accepted; but Loutfut extended the list of the unsuitable
with additions, some taken from Giles, including 'barbours, writaris &
talyeouris', who, in his opinion, 'ar na worth for battell', for what use
was a 'needle or razor or pen against a spear or axe'? Still concerned with
recruitment, Loutfut then emphasised both the moral qualities ('courage
and hardynes') and the physical characteristics ('manheid & strength of
body') required of men who would serve in the army. They must be
ready to experience great hardship for 'justice & common good'; they
must rely on 'use & craft' (experience and intelligence) to achieve their

---

[50] BL Harley 6149, fos. 128v–132v. It was printed by D. Bornstein, 'The Scottish prose
version of Vegetius' *De re militari*', *Studies in Scottish Literature*, 8 (1970–71), 177–83.
[51] Ed. A. T. P. Byles (EETS, London, 1926).   [52] Oxford, Queen's, 161, fos. 97v–100v.
[53] This is underlined by Sherwood, 'Studies', 346, n. 41; Reeve, 'Transmission', 344, and
n. 193.

ends; they should regard flight as a mark of dishonour. Among such, those from rural backgrounds would provide the best infantry; but noblemen constituted the best cavalry.

Loutfut then picked up a further strand of Vegetian thinking, discipline in the ranks. There must be order in the army to avoid division which would lead to defeat. Vegetius' insistence on this point was taken further when Loutfut urged that recruits be taught to run and jump for good reasons expressed by Vegetius. In a short paragraph, he summarised briefly the training recommended by Vegetius over more than half a dozen chapters in Book I, from swimming and mounting a horse to the use of a number of weapons. This was followed by a section on the building of the camp: its position, water supply, defences and openness to the air for the sake of health. In so doing, 'it mon be considerate the place, the tyme, the power & the neid', all examples of Vegetian adaptability at its best.

Loutfut then considered a list of qualities which the 'leder of the host' should possess. He should be vigilant, sober, prudent and experienced in the 'exercisioun of werris'. Such qualities would be reflected in his actions. He must be aware of the numbers available to him to command, maintaining his men's morale and looking after their material needs, although not treating them like women. Rather, he should be more concerned with his soldiers' toughness ('strength and hardynes of the body'). He must be subtle (Loutfut was describing the thinking commander), 'for the suttellar that the fichtaris be, the sonair gett thai victorye'.[54] Likewise he argued that victory was not always won by the physically strong, 'for the hardy oft & the maist couraiouse oftast getis the victorye'. Above all, the leader must remember the factors which could prove decisive in battle: horses, armour, provisions, the scene of the battle, time and reinforcements.

Focus was then placed upon matters which should occupy the commander's mind when in the presence of the enemy. He must be aware of how, in the noisy melée of battle, it was difficult to convey orders. Here, banners should play their part in keeping the army together and in passing on instructions. Loutfut, a herald, revealed his interest in the role of heraldry, and his recognition that 'the bannerman suld be strang, leill to the prince, expert in armis, and choissin with al diligence'.[55]

Following his text, Loutfut insisted that the commander be informed about the enemy's capabilities so as to protect his men; he must have knowledge of the country in which he was operating, and he should

---

[54] This had been a theme of John Barbour's *Bruce*, written more than a century earlier.
[55] Bornstein, 'Scottish prose version', 180.

engage loyal guides to help him, sending men ahead to counter any fear of ambushes. Vegetius' insistence that counsel given by those experienced in war should be heeded was underlined, as was the practical advice that plans should be known by as few people as possible. As to where to place his best troops, Loutfut followed Vegetius' advice that they be placed on that side of the advancing army on which trouble was anticipated. As to whether it was better to use infantry or cavalry, the nature of the country should resolve that dilemma.

Loutfut left his readers with a list of factors that would dictate which of two rival armies was likely to emerge victorious. To Loutfut, a united army was a strong and effective army. A well-defended place divided the enemy as it sought to overcome the obstacles of defence. Battle should be joined only when one was ready, a time which would be influenced by the position of the sun and the direction of the wind, which would cause the dust (to which Loutfut added sand) to blow into the enemy's face. The well-prepared army, which had 'forsicht', and knowledge of the enemy's approach, enjoyed a considerable advantage. It could fight with confidence and, by obliging the enemy to come to it, could fight him when he was already tired out by marching.

What is to be made of this airing of some of Vegetius' ideas and principles by a late fifteenth-century Scottish herald? His selection of topics was an interesting, personal one. His approach, which involved largely ignoring the order of the *De re militari* in favour of a series of themes, suggests an attentive mind willing and able to understand the structures around which Vegetius had built his work. We should not be surprised that no attention was paid to the contents of Book IV. Book II had never been the most quoted; that Loutfut should have used II, 14 to emphasise the qualities expected of the commander is not surprising, for what he had read there could easily be linked (as he successfully managed to link it) to the more important discussion of the commander's responsibilities contained in Book III, which provided the bulk of the material used in this selection.

Equally, however, the early emphasis on Book I, and the stress laid on the need both to select the best recruits and to train them in the use of arms and in fighting as a unit, followed a pattern which has been observed throughout this study. Books I and III consistently provided readers with the discussion of subjects which were relevant to almost any age. By selecting here and there, and bringing together points from different parts of the *De re militari*, Loutfut was able to emphasise that the work contained material which was of use to those responsible for military affairs in his own day, and that its value lay less in its totality than in certain sections which provided the attentive reader with plenty to think about. Finally, and not least, the text underlines what we have noticed before: the importance of the role played by the work of Giles of Rome in bringing Vegetian teaching and ideas regarding the 'discipline of war' to a wider readership.

10 Vegetius in print

The *De re militari* was one of the first classical texts to become available in printed form. The seven imprints (eight if Hohenwang's German translation is included) which qualify as incunables (pre-1501) leave no doubt that the work was regarded as a most marketable commodity. It is likely that the first printing was made by Nicolaus Ketelaer at Utrecht, perhaps in 1473–74. The text, referred to at the end as the 'Epitoma de re militari', was said to be the work of Flavii Vedati Renati. It is a fine edition, stark in its simplicity (it lacks any kind of title page or information about the printer and the date of printing), the black print having retained its colour to this day. Large capital letters are in blue (in the British Library copy) or in red (in the Bibliothèque nationale de France and Bodleian Library copies; the John Rylands University Library of Manchester copy has no colour); smaller letters are in red. In Book IV, chapters 38 and 40, there are gaps for Greek words; presumably the fount was not yet available. The volume lacks all illustrative material.

This edition was soon to be followed by another, the *Epithomia rei militaris*, in folio, prepared by Nicolaus Götz ('N.G'.), who worked in Cologne (where Caxton was to learn the printing trade) about 1475. Götz was active between 1474 and 1480, printing mainly theology and a Latin Bible. His *De re militari* was set in two columns, with spaces left for capital letters, which, in the copies now in Paris, are in red. Like the Ketelaer imprint, the text has no heading. The Bodleian copy has handwritten pagination/foliation, running from 357 to 394, added at the top of each folio, which suggests that this copy once formed part of a larger volume. The British Library copy is bound with the *De viris illustribus* of Jerome, which follows Vegetius' text. The Manchester copy has book and chapter headings added by hand at the top of some pages, presumably to facilitate ease of use. It is noticeable that the heading for I, 28, is printed 'De ordinacione rei militaris' rather than the correct 'De adhortatione rei militaris'.

In 1475–76 Johann Wiener, of Augsburg, printed the second complete translation of the *De re militari* recently made into German by Ludwig

Hohenwang. Hohenwang was not a member of any humanistic circle. His interests lay first of all in writing, later in printing, and the translation of the *De re militari* was an opportunity to combine both interests, since it was probably made with the intention that it should be printed, a conclusion supported by the fact that only two manuscripts survive.[1] Johann Wiener was the producer of serious works, including books of sermons, canon law and theology.[2] Printing a work such as a German translation of Vegetius could be a financial risk. What were the factors which may have helped to make this particular venture a success?

Many works from the classical age chosen for publication by the first printers were regarded as having a special resonance which they might add to the new world into which they were pitched. Hohenwang was trying to provide the wider, German-speaking public with a rendering of a work the reading of which might be greatly eased, and its classical character brought up to date, by the provision of illustrative material related to the text. It was more than a personal interest in objects and constructions of the classical world, or a serious attempt to bring home the reality of these to his less well-informed readers, that caused Hohenwang to include some sixty-three woodcuts illustrating aspects of what could be found in the work. Towers, weapons of attack and defence, ladders, bridges, boats, all these and more found themselves adorning the text with woodcuts probably made by Hohenwang himself. The strong possibility that he was influenced by the work of Konrad Kyeser and, more probably, Roberto Valturio is suggested by the presence of the drawbridge emanating from a dragon-shaped tower, which is indebted to both writers.[3] His underlying philosophy regarding the relevance of his translation to his contemporaries is suggested by the introduction of woodcuts of soldiers wearing not Roman but late fifteenth-century dress and bearing weapons of that period,[4] as was normally found in manuscript illumination of the time.

Hohenwang was a man who enjoyed writing and who was interested in the meaning and the history of words. For him, as for many others, the *De re militari* could be viewed as a historical work. The emphasis on meaning and language makes it likely that both he and his printer, each seeking a good sale for their product, were anxious to broaden the text's readership. While the contents of the *De re militari* would satisfy one clientele which

---

[1] Karlsruhe, Landesbibl. Durlach 18; Linz, Stadtbibl. 420 (a sixteenth-century copy).

[2] F. Geldner, *Die deutschen Inkunabeldrucker. Ein Handbuch der deutschen Buchdrucker des XV Jahrhunderts nach Druckorten* (Stuttgart, 1968), I, 142; Fürbeth, 'Des Vegecii', 20.

[3] Fig. 25. Woodcuts were, of course, copied at this time before copyright or intellectual law ever existed. The copy was usually not as sharp as the original had been.

[4] Figs. 3, 5, 7, 9, 21, 61, 62.

would regard the work primarily as a military text, a proper appreciation of which was made easier by the provision of a glossary and illustrations of contemporary soldiers in action, another would concentrate its attention upon the historical and philological information which the text provided. Once again, the partners were aiming at more than one group in their attempt to broaden interest in the work. It seems likely that the intention was to open up *Von der Ritterschaft* to as wide a readership as possible, using the burgeoning interest in the classics of the time for commercial advantage.

The success of Hohenwang's translation as a publishing venture relied not only on the translation but on the aids which accompanied it to help the reader.[5] It relied, too, on other factors. One was that the *De re militari* was among the most popular classical works to be read in the medieval world: a vernacular version was likely to satisfy a demand. That demand was fuelled by the fact that the translation appeared at a time not only when a printed edition of the Latin text had recently become available and the number of manuscript copies made in Germany was sharply on the increase, but also when other versions of the *De re militari*, ranging from the complete Viennese translation[6] to abridged versions, such as Annenberg's selection (dated *c.*1470), or those made earlier in the century in the works of Johann Seffner and Johannes Rothe, may have stimulated interest in Vegetius and his ideas. In short, Hohenwang and Wiener had judged the market well. Whether regarded primarily as an example of Roman history or as a practical handbook for war, the translation was likely to enjoy a certain success.

Of the next edition, possibly printed *c.*1475 by Günther Zainer, of Augsburg, who had been printing in the city since about 1468, only a few proof leaves, found in the binding of other books produced at this time, have survived. They can be seen today in Augsburg, London and Oxford. These are from different sections of the text: from a table of contents of Books III and IV, and from I, 7, 8, 15–17 and much of 18. They are probably trial sheets, some printed on one side of the paper only, some on both. The table of contents could well have been printed first, followed by Book I, but it is likely that the work was never completed.[7]

---

[5] Twenty-three examples survive, out of a possible print run of perhaps 200. I consulted copies preserved today in Berlin, Dresden, London and Manchester. This last has only the collection of woodcuts.

[6] Seitenstetten, Stiftsbibl. 65.

[7] See Geldner, *Deutschen Inkunabeldrucker*, I, 132–7; D. Rhodes, 'A note on some fragments of Vegetius from Augsburg', in *Studies in early European printing and book collecting* (London, 1983), 139.

Possibly as early as 1476, certainly before 1479, a quarto edition was printed by Pierre César and Johannes Stoll, who appear to have worked in a kind of printers' 'commune' with Louis Symonel and partners at the sign of the Soufflet Vert in the rue Saint-Jacques in Paris. Specialist scholars have doubts regarding the accuracy of parts of this statement: for instance, Jeanne Veyrin-Forres makes no mention of this edition in her list of twenty-eight editions printed there by César and Stoll.[8] Whatever the rights of the argument, this text was almost certainly the first of the *De re militari* to be printed in France, and probably the only edition to come out of that country in the fifteenth century. It contains many mistakes and inconsistencies; whether this was because the manuscript which formed the basis of the edition was faulty, or because the type-setter was unfamiliar with Latin, we cannot tell. Perhaps, in some instances, sheer carelessness was to blame.

By the 1480s the printing scene was moving to Italy. The quarto edition of the *De re militari* prepared in Rome by the German, Eucharius Silber, alias Franck, Argenteus or Argyrios (which suggests that he understood or appreciated Greek) was completed on 29 January 1487, and was notable for being the first to be published along with other military works, in this case those of Aelian (*De instruendis aciebus*), Frontinus (*Strategematicon*) and Modestus (*De re militari*). Judging from the number of copies which have survived to this day (some forty-seven, according to the ISTC), this was a popular edition, perhaps because it included three other military texts. Late in 1494 Silber, now describing himself as 'Alamanum' (as well as 'Franck') published a new volume containing the texts of Vegetius, Frontinus, Modestus and Aelian, as well as the Latin translation (out of Greek) of Onasander's *Strategicus*. As in the earlier edition of 1487, the text which Silber produced had been prepared by Johannes Sulpitius Verulanus who, in the dedicatory letter addressed to Peter Paul de Comite, emphasised the need for the acquisition of military skills, which might be achieved by reading the authors to be found in this volume. The heading to I, 28 runs 'De adoracione rei militaris' a mistake not corrected in the 1494 'reprint'.

The following year would see another, today fairly rare, edition of the *De re militari*, one which was printed on its own at Pescia by Sigismund Rodt de Bitsche, described as 'designer of the task' ('operis architectus'), from the text supplied by Sebastian and Raphael de Orlandis, the task

---

[8] J. Veyrin-Forres, 'Le deuxième atelier typographique de Paris: Cesaris et Stol', in *La lettre et le texte. Trente années de recherche sur l'histoire du livre* (Paris, 1987), pp. 189–212. I examined the copy at the John Rylands University Library, Manchester, and the two in the Bibliothèque nationale de France, Paris.

being completed on 2 April 1488. Fairly densely printed on only thirty-four pages, it lacked capital letters at the beginnings of chapters, while spaces were left for the few Greek words. A postscript, artistically printed in the form of a lozenge, stated that the Orlando brothers, unable to allow Vegetius' teaching, so worthy of praise, to remain hidden by neglect (hardly the case, it may plausibly be argued), were bringing him to the attention of Italian youth, which was finally having to rouse itself from a long period of idleness. By studying Vegetius' teachings, the best young 'tiro' could become a 'miles'; every age might become more skilful, every individual more aware, every human spirit more developed. Behind the rhetoric lay the claim that the entire generation, and not simply its military class, could benefit from reading the *De re militari*. In his turn Rodt rendered the heading to I, 28 as 'De abhortacione rei militaris'.

This edition ends with the words 'Praise be to God, the blessed virgin Mary, and those of the heavenly court' ('Laus Deo, beate Marie virgini, et celesti curie paradisi'). However, neither Vegetius nor the heavenly powers were to save Italy from French attack a few years later. Vegetius had warned of the possible adverse effects of peace.[9] Perhaps the Peace of Lodi (1454), which had opened a long period of peace in Italy, had lulled the peninsula into a state of unpreparedness which would cost it dear. In the circumstances of the French invasion of 1494, one can understand that Vegetius (and the other military authors associated with him in book form since Silber's initiative of publishing them together in 1487) may have been regarded as having relevance to those living in Italy in the closing years of the fifteenth century. The likely popularity of Silber's work is underlined by the last incunable, printed over the period July 1495 to January 1496 by Plato de Benedictis, working in Bologna. The text, consisting of the works of Frontinus, Vegetius, Aelian and Modestus, is the same as in Silber's first combined edition of 1487, although not printed in the same order. A new dedicatory note, by Philippus Berealdus, extolling the military discipline which had brought fame to Cyrus, Alexander and Caesar, and which had helped to create the Roman Empire, was added. However, the chapter heading 'De adoratione rei militaris' for I, 28 remained uncorrected. Such evident plagiarism, even a rather carefree attitude to accuracy, suggests that Silber's initiative in publishing several classical texts relating to war under one cover had been a publishing success which could be profitably imitated. It would be reprinted, with small modifications, in 1504–5.[10]

The first editions of Vegetius' Latin text were straightforward affairs, making few or no concessions to help the reader towards a full

---

[9] *DRM*, I, 7.   [10] I consulted the copy in Paris, BnF Rés. V. 616.

understanding of the text he was reading. It may be significant that it was only in the German translation that such possible difficulties as the reader might meet (What did particular words mean? What did engines look like in real life?) were addressed in a practical way through the provision of indices or, supplying a visual need, of illustrations. Most offered little assistance in understanding the text. Nor will the mistakes or deliberate improvements introduced by the print-setters have helped. The substitution of a future tense for a subjunctive might easily create 'shall' or 'will' where Vegetius had simply intended 'may' or 'should', the addition or omission of a single letter perhaps leading to a rather different sense being given to the text.

We have already seen how, in earlier days, the meaning of unfamiliar and often rather technical words had frequently created difficulties for the readers of manuscripts. The advent of the printed form did not necessarily make things easier. So we find early printed copies of the *De re militari* marked in the margins with words unfamiliar to, or not understood by, some readers, often the very same words not recognised by the readers of manuscripts. While the manuscripts of the 1458 English verse translation included an index and Wiener's edition of the German translation did the same, it was not until the appearance of the Latin edition sold by the Parisian bookseller Jean Petit in 1515 that a fuller table ('rerum et verborum') was added. Useful as it was intended to be, its value to the individual reader would have depended upon the choice of words selected for inclusion. We may note that the Petit edition finally printed the heading to I, 28, 'De adhortatione rei militaris', correctly.

With the important exception of Wiener's imprint of Hohenwang's translation, illustrations, in the form of woodcuts depicting aspects of the practice of war, did not appear until 1511 or 1512, significantly from the press of Hans Knappe in Erfurt. This is a rare volume, which lacks a written text; even the copy now in the British Library is not complete, since eight or so leaves are missing.[11] Yet more than enough survives to illustrate how castles and town walls could be attacked using a variety of scaling ladders and movable towers, how stones and other projectiles could be thrown by a number of machines, and how several forms of cannon could be conjured up by fertile minds. Very similar to the woodcuts used by Wiener some forty years earlier, some (such as numbers 49 and 90) are marked by the monogram 'HK' (Hans Knappe), while number 10 has 'M.S', that of the artist Melchior Schwarreberg.

---

[11] It was formerly in the library of the Patent Office, London. Were those who worked there interested in the military inventiveness which the woodcuts reflected?

Such illustrations raise the matter of anachronism. This was manifest in two forms. One, just mentioned, was the illustration of various forms of cannon, a weapon unknown in Vegetius' time. The other is that the figures appearing in the woodcuts are dressed not as Roman soldiers but as up-to-date (German) soldiers of the early sixteenth century, the 'knechte' as they could have been drawn in contemporary art. These two points strongly suggest that the printers/booksellers responsible for the preparation of these editions looked upon illustrations in terms of what they could teach about war both in the past and in the present. This created an opportunity to extend the readership to include those of a practical rather than a scholarly cast of mind. It is worth recalling that while manuscripts were not infrequently copied to order, involving the copyist in relatively little financial risk, the printer had to invest considerable capital in what could be a risky venture. Anxious, therefore, to secure a return on that capital, the early sixteenth-century printer/bookseller would want to make his product more attractive to the prospective buyer, a process which aids for readers, such as indices and contemporary rather than historical illustrative matter, might help achieve. Although written a whole millennium and more earlier, Vegetius' work was being presented as possessing contemporary relevance.

The appreciation of the commercial possibilities presented by the increased interest in the military literature of the ancient world is confirmed by the fact that in 1487 Eucharius Silber created a new kind of work, four texts on military affairs issued as a single volume, the number being increased to five when the market was offered an enhanced volume some seven years later. From now on, Vegetius would increasingly appear in a multi-work form, creating a specialised collection of texts in a handy format. The introduction to Silber's 1487 edition, the first of its kind, emphasised the importance in education not of poetry or history or oratory, but of an understanding of military discipline, which made it necessary to include authors other than Vegetius, authors from whose maxims much could be learned or who taught the importance of drill and precision. Aelian, along with Modestus, now joined Frontinus and Vegetius under one cover. It was these same authors whom Plato de Benedictis, exuding enthusiasm for the text he wished to sell, would describe, with a certain sense of hyperbole, as 'authors wholly divine' ('autores penitus Divinos').

None can deny Hohenwang the claim to have been the first to produce both a vernacular translation *and* a printed edition of that translation – perhaps a good illustration of how quickly things could move when translator and printer were one and the same. Germany's speed off the mark was to leave the remainder of Europe far behind. The first printed Italian translation, that of Tizzone Gaetano di Posi, would emerge half a century later; no Castilian translation would be printed in the sixteenth or seventeenth centuries; England would have to wait until 1572 for the translation of John Sadler to appear, while neither of the fifteenth-century English translations, one prose, one verse, would be printed, essentially for scholars, until the twentieth century.[12]

Only France was to accompany Germany and Italy into printing the work of Vegetius in translation in the age of the incunable. Yet even here we have to be careful not to mislead. The work printed in June 1488 by Antoine Caillau and Guy Marchand, for the up-and-coming Parisian bookseller Antoine Vérard, was not, in spite of its claim, the *De re militari* of Vegetius but a version of the *Fais d'armes* of Christine de Pisan, written in the early years of the fifteenth century. The title page to the volume proclaimed it to be *L'art de chevalerie selon Vegece*; the volume itself had ninety-six leaves, was printed in double columns, and included four woodcuts, taken from an earlier work.[13] The careful reader would soon realise that he was not reading the genuine Vegetian text: contemporary opinion holds that the side with the greater numbers will be victorious, Christine wrote, 'but the opposing view, that of Vegetius, teaches that...' ('Contre ceste opinion Vegece dit...).' This phrase, and others such as 'according to Vegetian doctrine' ('Selon Vegece et sa doctrine'), gave the game away. The reader was not being offered Vegetius' text directly, but his opinion at one remove.[14] And while the *De re militari* was prominent as a source in Book I, Vegetius was obliged to give way to Frontinus as he did, in fact, in the *Fais d'armes*.

Was this sharp practice by Vérard? By the standards of the day, probably not. The name of Vegetius would help to sell the book, and it was probably for this reason that it was attached to a volume by a well-known French author who had based much of her work on his. When, in 1527, Philippe le Noir, a Parisian bookseller with close ties to the university, reissued Vérard's 1488 edition (with alterations), he chose another title: 'The Tree of Battles, and the Flower [i.e. extracts] of Chivalry according to Vegetius... with texts from Frontinus, Valerius [Maximus] and several other authors, as you will be able to see' ('L'arbre des batailles et fleur de chevalerie selon Vegece, avecques plusieurs hystoires et utiles

---

[12] José M. Fradejas is actively preparing an edition of the Castilian translation; the text of the second Catalan translation, transcribed and edited by Antoni Alomar, may be consulted at Palma de Mallorca.
[13] J. Macfarlane, *Antoine Vérard* (Bibliographical Society, London, 1900), 3.
[14] On this problem of 'translation', see Nall, 'William Worcester reads Alain Chartier, 137.

remonstrances du fait de guerre par luy extraictes de Frontin, Valere et de plusieurs aultres aucteurs comme pourrez veoir cy apres'). Once again the bookseller was trading on Vegetius' reputation as an authority, although this time adding the names of Honoré Bouvet (author of *L'arbre des batailles*), Frontinus (now evidently increasing in reputation) and Valerius Maximus (always a popular author). Le Noir was being rather more honest regarding the book's content than Vérard had been. The appeal to the 'ancient authors' ('veteres scriptores') was quite obvious. While this was little more than a selection of Vegetius' ideas and teachings accompanying those of others, his name was prominent on the title page. Granted the standards and practices of the day, perhaps we should not blame the bookseller too much.

In the meantime Latin editions continued to appear. In May 1515 a volume containing works by Vegetius, Frontinus, Aelian and Modestus, printed by Berthold Rembolt, was published in Paris by Jean Petit, with a verse dedication to Antoine du Prat, chancellor of France.[15] One development was the inclusion of a table, described as 'a short alphabetical index of subjects and words used in Vegetius' ('rerum et verborum que in Vegetio annotantur per seriem litterarum brevis index'), including names and terms which might be unfamiliar to the reader. A further, unexpected but interesting, development was the printing of marginalia, presumably copied from the manuscript exemplar from which the printer worked, such as 'country folk are better with arms' ('aptior armis rustica plebs'),[16] the pointed finger opposite 'the science of warfare ('Scientia enim rei bellice')[17] and the noting of names of places and authors referred to in the text. Such a development takes us back to the evidence which we examined in the first part of this study. It is not clear what prompted this wish to turn the printed page into a replica of the manuscript from which it was copied. Perhaps it constituted early signs of the critical scholarship of the text which was developed later in the sixteenth century. For the moment, the answer may have been simpler and more human. Readers living in the early age of printing may have been interested to observe the spirit of enquiry regarding the text shown by their predecessors, in some cases centuries earlier. Their comments created something resembling the strata or layers of an archaeological excavation, the marginalia added to manuscripts constituting visible evidence of reactions linking

---

[15] I consulted the copy in the Bibliothèque nationale de France, Paris. Thanks to the kindness of Dr Nicholas Bennett, I was also able to examine the copy of this rare edition in the possession of Lincoln Cathedral Library.
[16] *DRM*, I, 3.   [17] *DRM*, I, 1.

several generations of men who had read the text to see what the military experience of the Roman world had to offer their own age, and, from seeing the evidence, which of Vegetius' recommendations had struck a particular chord at different times and in different circumstances during the past few centuries.

Part III

The legacy: the *De re militari* in medieval military thought and practice

11   The development of Vegetian influence

Introduction

The transmission of ideas expressed by Vegetius, ideas which, on his admission, were not necessarily his own, was achieved through the use of the written word: the copying of his text, whether in whole or in parts (excerpts); the making of translations; and, most interesting of all, the way his ideas were reflected in those of others as they discussed matters of war, government, even religious practice. Many types of people, soldiers, rulers, even clergy, were to have an interest in what Vegetius had written.

It is one thing to see ideas proposed by or attributed to Vegetius reflected in written works. It is quite another, and a much more difficult one to pinpoint or to analyse, to say precisely how such ideas either influenced or, at least, came to be reflected in military or other forms of action. In brief, what practical influence did the teachings of the man called 'el sabio' or 'der meister' have upon the way war was conducted in the Middle Ages? Although we can say that the *De re militari* had influence at an intellectual level, how far did that influence extend to the way things were actually done? While 'the hope that Roman warfare could be studied and then imitated was a common simplification among humanists', was Vegetius' legacy in any sense practical?[1]

In seeking to answer this question, we should be careful not to jump too readily to conclusions primarily through a desire to do so. The language used to describe any perceived or suggested legacy must be carefully chosen and nuanced. Classicists and ancient historians are justified in reminding students of a later age that the reputation ultimately earned by Vegetius' apparently unremarkable piece of polemic surpassed anything which could have been foreseen in the mid-fifth century. How could a work which offered solutions to the dilemma regarding the future of the

---

[1] Wakelin, *Humanism, reading and English* literature, 85. The problem of translating ideas into 'reality' has been well expressed: 'Le médiéviste manquera toujours de moyens pour mesurer avec assez d'exactitude la causalité de tel courant d'idées sur telle transformation institutionnelle' (Krynen, 'Idéologie et royauté', 613).

Roman army largely by emphasising the lasting value of past practices realistically expect to exercise much influence upon the development of military ideas and practice in centuries to come?

The answer, it is suggested, lay in a combination of factors. One was the content of the work which offered fairly generalised, but rationally argued (and therefore persuasive) recommendations applicable at very different times in different sets of circumstances. Then there was the matter of presentation. The author's style favoured the terse, easily remembered and recognisable statement, often one of summary. If combined to another factor, in this case the fondness of the Middle Ages for the 'Epitoma' (which we can render as 'The Essential . . . '), the *De re militari*, a good example of that genre, began any contest for recognition with at least a head start. Then, as the evidence of the marginalia puts it beyond much doubt, readers were attracted to Vegetius' work because it was a text about the Roman army written by a Roman in an age when interest in things Roman was always lively, and the Roman example was one to follow. Finally, we should remind ourselves that Vegetius had no rival in the field, his work being *the* military *auctoritas* for the simple reason that there was no other text to which men could turn to learn about war. With the field all to itself, how could the *De re militari* fail?

One of the text's main strengths was its openness to adaptation, allowing for it teachings and recommendations to be reinterpreted according to time and circumstances, and thus for its reputation to grow, transforming what might have remained a little-known polemical contribution to debate into a text of stature. Taken out of its original context, the *De re militari* could be made to serve many causes, to say many things and to be interpreted in ways which its author might not recognise or even agree with. For example, classical historians may justifiably ask medievalists what Vegetius would have understood by the term 'Vegetian strategy' when used by military historians of today to describe a particular approach to battle? Convenient as it may be to turn it into a distinguishing label, is there not a danger in associating his name and what he wrote too closely with thought patterns and approaches not necessarily in keeping with those of his day? The point should be taken. At the same time, however, it is precisely the openness of the *De re militari* to adaptation which allowed the benefit of ideas sown by Vegetius to be reaped by future generations for application to conditions and circumstances very different from those for which they had originally been set down. Without wishing to claim for Vegetius more than is his due, is not the recognition of his success and, therefore, of his importance the fact that his work exercised influence far beyond his own time, and that this, in itself, is the mark of a work whose influence is seen as greater in a medieval context than in a late Antique one. Indeed, some might claim that, written, as it had been, as the Roman world was nearing its end, Vegetius' real influence was to be exercised upon the military thought and practice of future centuries.

To the question of whether the *De re militari* left any legacy to the Middle Ages, the answer, however qualified, must surely be affirmative. Multiple examples of the text, copied over several centuries, frequently glossed and commented upon by generations of readers, its ideas often brought up to date and its historical relevance increased by the addition or substitution of more recent ones,[2] witness to a work which left many and varied traces of the interests of its medieval readers, in particular of those living towards the end of the period. The selected ideas and phrases of the master included in the collections of excerpts, and the many translations of his work made into several languages over a period of some two centuries, constitute further testimony of the legacy which he bequeathed to medieval Europe. In addition, as the works considered in Part II above (on the 'Transmission') suggest, Vegetian teaching, reinterpreted with the needs of a new age in mind, contributed both to men's thinking regarding military affairs and to the ever broadening discussion of how societies should be governed, in particular to the role of authority and the use of force to be exercised for the common good. The influence wielded by the *De re militari* was extensive. It cannot be limited to war alone.

In the remaining part of this study, however, the reader will be asked to consider what influences the text could have had upon certain issues and developments in military thought and practice in the medieval world. When people referred to, and quoted, Vegetius, why did they do so? Simply to show that they had read his work or consulted the collections of excerpts which emanated from it? Or was it for other reasons? Did Vegetian ideas and teaching fuel the discussion of certain military matters which arose in later centuries? What developments in the art (or science?) of war can be attributed to the *De re militari*? Should the text's importance be measured not so much by what it contributed to the practice of war on the battlefield (after all, Vegetius described war very much as he thought it had been in an already distant past) as by his insistence on certain points, above all preparation (in the widest interpretation of that word) and the qualities which he sought from those appointed to lead? Was his greatest legacy to the medieval world to be his teaching regarding the place and function of the army in society, and what society's view of the soldier (and his profession) might be? Did the *De re militari* have a part to play in *re*-forming what many understood by chivalry, and its role in

---

[2] A marginal note in Madrid, BN 6036, fo. 4, commenting on certain Roman training practices, records that they were still used by Catalonian peasants at the end of the Middle Ages: 'Isto modo armantur rustici quando contrant duellum in Cathalonia.'

the developing medieval world? An examination of a number of themes may help us to answer such questions.

Particular points regarding the successful practice of war, discussed by Vegetius, came under the scrutiny of medieval readers. It was accepted that the work of deterrence and fighting carried out by the army would achieve little if not inspired and organised by good leadership, whose characteristics and qualities, much emphasised by Vegetius, were carefully noted by his later readers. The need for proper provision of food and weapons, an essential part of effective preparation for war, was a message which medieval leaders came to understand and to act upon, particularly from the late thirteenth century onwards. The interest expressed in every reference to the need for combatants to wear adequate protective armour, and to do their training while wearing it, suggests that this was a matter discussed in the military world of the Middle Ages, and that the *De re militari* was seen to be contributing to an ongoing discussion of the matter. What impact, if any, Vegetian teaching may have had upon conflict at sea and, in particular, upon strategy and attitudes to battle, is briefly touched upon here.

The influence of Vegetian teaching upon the creation of what we shall call the 'statist' army, both a cause and a reflection of the growth of nation states, so characteristic of the late Middle Ages, is also considered. Once again, the intellectual influence of John of Salisbury and Giles of Rome and their followers, seen later in the works of such as Christine de Pisan and Jean Juvénal des Ursins, sets things in motion. Such influence, very French in origin, would certainly encourage the transformation of ideas into reality in France itself. Nor would the process stop there, for it would become the inspiration for major developments to be observed in a number of European societies from the late thirteenth century onwards.

War and reason

If we ask ourselves what kind of war was advocated in the *De re militari*, the answer is a fairly straightforward one. A dominant theme runs through the entire work: since war is fought to secure a favourable outcome, it should be pursued not haphazardly but with intelligence and skill (Vegetius used the word 'scienter' five times). The *De re militari* offered the Middle Ages a text with a strong emphasis towards the intellectualisation and rationalisation of war which stressed the cerebral qualities of the prince and his lieutenants. It was in the wake of this tendency that a corpus of political literature, notably John of Salisbury's *Policraticus*, the *Siete Partidas* of Alfonso X, Giles of Rome's *De regimine principum*, and the various works of Christine de Pisan came into being.

A list of royal attributes, probably written in France soon after 1420 when the country's fortunes in the conflict against the English had reached their lowest ebb, shows the importance attached by the writer to royal leadership in war. 'In active war, it is important to exercise prudence of a military kind, which causes enemy attacks to be repelled, and all military activity to be carried out for the sake of the common good. The pursuit of military activity depends on force, but must be guided by prudence. And, in particular, as the commander of the army is prudent, so prudence dictates the things which it is right for us to do.' ('Es choses des batailles est tresgrandement neccessaire aucune espece de prudence, la quelle est dicte militaire, par la quelle les assaulx des ennemis sont reboutez, les negoces et affaires militaires sont ordonnnez pour la tuicion et deffense de tout le bien commun. Lexecucion de chevalerie appartient a force, mais la direction ou adresce appartient a prudence. Et par especial selon ce que elle ou le gouverneur et chief de lost est prudent, prudence est la droicte raison des choses qui de nous sont afaire.')[3] Prudence, the virtue exercised by the good commander, would bring success to the side exercising it in time and conditions of war.

There were good reasons for this. War inevitably brought death and disorder in its wake. Man must learn to contain war, too often seen as a runaway force which controlled him rather than being controlled by him, to the detriment of the common good. Among the greatest of a prince's responsibilities to his people was to ensure for them a life lived in peace, although this might require the use of the instrument of war. This led to the inescapable conclusion that a prince must inform himself on how best to wage war, as he might one day be called upon to do in the fulfilment of his public responsibilities. How should he most effectively achieve this? Vegetius was in no doubt. Let the ruler look back into history; let him see how things had been done in the past, and how such observations might inform present practice. While never exactly the same, the experiences of the past took on a didactic quality which could contribute to resolving the problems of the present. Otherwise, what point was there in enquiring how the Roman army, capable of conquering the world, had functioned?

Consideration of how Vegetius used the word 'ratio' can be instructive. It might be used to translate 'way' or 'manner', as in 'the manner of doing things'. It could mean 'administration', as in the words 'legionis ratio', implying an orderly 'administration of the legion'; or a 'system', as in 'ratio defensionis', a 'system of defence'. Finally, it might be used to convey a reasoned body of knowledge, thus making 'ratio militaris'

---

[3] BnF fr. 1233, fo. 124v.

translatable as 'military science'.[4] If few translations convey the exact meaning of the original, the examples of Vegetius' use of 'ratio' (there are some thirty of them, although he never used 'rationaliter') make it clear that he was concerned to demonstrate that successful military action must be regulated and carried out according to principles and rules (or were they, perhaps, only guidelines?) which emerged from analysis and thought.[5]

Vegetius' use of different yet complementary vocabularies indicated the thoughts which influenced his choice of words. 'Peritia' was used nine times, usually to refer to 'skill' (a basic word in Vegetius' system), occasionally to 'experience'. Likewise 'peritus' appeared ten times in different forms, assuming the meaning of 'learned' or, more often, 'skilled' or 'experienced', thus backing up the use of 'peritia'. Even more indicative of the fundamental concept which Vegetius wanted to convey was his use of words with the prefix 'prae': 'praecavere'; 'praemittere'; 'praenoscere'; 'praeoccupare'; 'praeparare'.[6] If soldiers should always be ready for war, those responsible for leading them should never enter into a conflict without serious consideration of what that decision might entail. In Books II–IV, Vegetius had insisted on the need for forethought. The Prefect of Engineers, for instance, had the responsibility of having all weapons, missiles and other equipment ready in advance so that, wherever it was, an army was like 'an armed city'.[7] The establishment of a proper logistical system was presented as being reasonable and necessary. Clearly underlined, too, was the need to be well ahead of the enemy, to be armed with knowledge of his movements, plans and capabilities, to be in possession of the best positions. Information about a locality must be sought, and maps used. Forewarned, and thus doubly armed, the commander could make reasoned and unhurried decisions, so that the army which met the enemy, fully prepared materially and psychologically, was likely to emerge successful from the encounter.[8] Battles and campaigns were often won or lost before they began.

Further consideration of Vegetius' vocabulary, this time the words with the prefix 'pro', can also be instructive. The verb 'prospicere' (act with foresight) was used only once,[9] but 'providere' was influential. As a verb it appeared nine times to convey the action of taking steps to 'provide for' a particular need in the future, through anticipation of it. As an adjective, 'providus', it was used four times, three times modifying the word 'dux'

---

[4] *DRM*, II, 19; III, 6, 22.
[5] 'Scientia rei bellicae' (I, 1); 'scientia armorum' (II, 12); 'scientia dimicandi' (II, 24); 'scientia equitandi' (III, 26). Vegetius also referred to the 'ars pugnandi' (III, 10).
[6] See the 'Index verborum' in Lang's edition.
[7] *DRM*, II, 11, 25.   [8] *Ibid.* III, 3, 6.   [9] *Ibid.* III, 14.

(as in 'dux providus', conveying the sense of the resourceful commander); on the fourth, referring to those, the 'providos', who benefited from
caution, reflecting the advantageous effects of a considered approach
to action. It is significant that all the uses of the words 'providere' or
'providus' are to be found in Book III, in which the attributes and responsibilities of the commander are described and discussed. The repeated
use of the words within this part of his work underlined the importance
which Vegetius attached to the qualities which he regarded as essential
for successful leadership.

The secret of success lay not in numbers but in confidence born of
good preparation, which enabled anticipation to play its vital role. As far
as the commander was concerned this meant avoiding the hazards on the
road, such as ambushes, which it was the task of spies to discover and
flush out. To walk into an ambush was reprehensible since it implied that
a commander had given insufficient consideration to the situation around
him. Since scouts and spies ('exploratores') featured prominently in the
De re militari[10] it is possible that their appearance in many works written in the Middle Ages reflects the significant role accorded to them by
Vegetius (and, before him, by Frontinus) as the providers of information
which would give a commander an advantage over his (unsuspecting)
enemy. Philippe de Vitri would advocate the use of spies to gain information about the enemy. To Guillaume de Machaut, their role 'is the
most important that I know of . . . for a good spy who does his work well,
is worth more than a lawyer in the Parlement. Without the good work
done by spies, one cannot get the better of the enemy' ('est la chose
plus necessaire/Que je congnoisse . . . / . . . mieux vaut une bonne espie/
Qui fait son fait seurement/ C'un advocat en parlement/ Qu'on ne puet,
sans bien espier/Ses anemis bien guerrier').[11] A generation later Philippe
de Mézières, with long experience of war in the eastern Mediterranean,
would encourage the use of spies among enemies and their neighbours.
Indeed, so important did he consider them that he advocated the spend-
ing of one third of all funds available for war on espionage.[12]

Under one guise or another, the theme of preparedness made an
appearance in every book of the *De re militari*. It did so in different forms,
underlining aspects of preparation which must precede all conflict. If the
commander should be ready to anticipate the enemy's intentions, the
army, too, must always be in a state to fight, even at short notice. The

---

[10] E.g., *ibid*. III, 6, 26.
[11] *Confort d'ami, Œuvres de Guillaume de Machaut*, ed. E. Hoeffner (3 vols., SATF, Paris,
1921), III, lines 3336–44.
[12] Mézières, *Songe du vieil pèlerin*, II, 404–06; I, 511–12.

regular training which this involved was consistently noted by readers. So, in the 1330s, Philippe de Vitri could emphasise that 'work makes an army efficient; all is lost if it is inactive' ('Labeur fait l'ost proficient/ Qui par repos devient nient'),[13] a brief and simple restatement of one of Vegetius' principal and frequently reiterated messages. That same message would not be forgotten by those who came later. Writing in mid-fifteenth-century England of his recent experiences in France, William Worcester cited Vegetius regarding the Roman emphasis on 'exercitation and usage in dedis of armes, that they might be apte and redie to bataille whan necessite fille'. It was because of their commitment to training, Worcester wrote in a marginal note drawing attention to the Roman experience, that Hannibal and the Carthaginian army had been finally defeated. Lack of training, he argued in an attempt to emphasise the contemporary application of the message, led to disastrous results: 'it is to suppose that it is rather in defaute of exercising of armes' that England had lost Normandy, although other reasons played their part in that disaster.[14]

Preparation for war also involved the provision of adequate arms, and in particular armour, and proper training in the use of both, as well as the creation of a psychological background favourable to those about to go into battle.[15] As the manuscript evidence shows, these messages struck a chord with medieval readers. Vegetius had consistently drawn attention to the importance of building up morale, emphasising that the state of mind of those actively participating in war could be a crucial factor in deciding the outcome of events. Fear was one such factor to which Vegetius made reference, directly or indirectly, on several occasions.[16] Men, he argued, were not naturally brave, but might become so with training, as weapons properly used helped to inspire confidence.[17] The part to be played by morale was something which Vegetius understood very well. More than once he underlined the need for every commander to address his men before battle, a practical step to encourage confidence in their ability to defeat the enemy.[18] Over the centuries the leader's stirring address became an essential part of any description of a battle about to take place.

---

[13] A. Piaget, '"Le chapel des fleurs de lis" par Philippe de Vitri', *Romania*, 27 (1898), lines 697–8.

[14] *The boke of noblesse addressed to King Edward the Fourth on his invasion of France in 1475*, ed. J. G. Nichols (Roxburghe Club, London, 1860), 21, 26–7, 29. See also Nall, 'Perceptions of financial mismanagement', 119–35.

[15] *DRM*, I, 20.   [16] E.g., *ibid*. III, 9, 12, 18, 21, 25.

[17] *Ibid*. I, 1; III, 26.   [18] *Ibid*. I, 1; III, 26.

From the twelfth century onwards, in particular, an increasingly intellectual attitude towards waging war can be observed.[19] As we know
it today, the text of the *Song of Roland*, dating probably from the late
eleventh century, had shown, in the character of Oliver, the 'prudence'
which should characterise the knight in war. While literary scholars are
reluctant to accept as rigid the distinction made in the poem between
Oliver ('sage') and Roland (always 'preu', sometimes 'sage', too), the
distinction none the less serves to emphasise that what was required of
the fighting man at war was not only strength and courage but 'mesure'
and 'sagesse' (skill and thoughtfulness), characteristics associated with
the man endowed with greater moral and intellectual qualities than mere
physical ones, however admirable these were. So some literary battle nar-
ratives show men using strategic skill and planning, as well as personal
prowess, to achieve victory against the odds.[20]

Vegetius used the word 'prudentia' twice, at the very beginning of his
work. In so doing, he probably intended to convey the importance of the
role of intelligence in the waging of war. Some eight centuries or more
later Giles of Rome would write that 'prudence exists in the mind' ('prudentia est in intellectu').[21] As he would have understood it, prudence
dictated a particular approach which a commander should follow. First,
he should pinpoint and analyse the problem; then he should decide how
to resolve it; finally, he should act upon that decision. This considered
approach, incorporating the need to foresee and anticipate, took into
account human experience, and what could be learned from observing
actions and their consequences, an attitude which led to the drawing
up of Vegetius' 'Rules of war' which were, in fact, conclusions drawn
from careful observation. As Vegetius' use of the adverb 'doctissime'[22]
('expertly') indicates, his fighting man had the qualities and skills of one
who had been selected and then trained before being given experience in
the practice of 'real' war, thus making him a true defender of his people's
interests, a soldier in the fullest meaning of the word.

As rulers were constantly enjoined to seek and accept advice in matters
relating to government, so commanders were encouraged to do the same

---

[19] On this, see Murray, *Reason and society*, 124ff.
[20] E.g, G. S. Burgess, 'The theme of chivalry in *Ille et Galeron*', *Medioevo romanzo*, 14
(1989), 359. Planning would not be restricted to the world of the imagination. On
practical battle plans, see C. Phillpotts, 'The French plan of battle during the Agincourt
campaign' [1415], *EHR*, 99 (1984), 59–66, and J. F. Verbruggen, 'Un plan de bataille du
duc de Bourgogne (14 septembre 1417) et la tactique de l'époque', *Revue internationale
d'histoire militaire*, 20 (1959), 443–51. Does the close contemporaneity of these two
documents suggest that, in certain circles, the penny was beginning to drop?
[21] *DRP*, I, ii, 2 (p. 50).   [22] Twice in *DRM*, II, 14.

before making decisions for which they, alone, were responsible. This practice was urged upon them to allow experience to have the maximum impact and influence upon the taking of such decisions. As Jean Juvénal des Ursins would write in the mid-fifteenth century, 'when Alexander went to war, he was not accompanied by young captains, however brave they may have been; rather he took with him those of greater maturity who had frequented wars in the past . . . and was thus advised by men of experience, the youngest of whom was sixty years old. For in battle things have to be according to reason and the best advice' ('quant Alixandre se mist en armes . . . il ne print pas josnes cappitaines, supposé qu'il en y eut de bien vaillans, mais print vieulx et anciens chevaliers qui avoient frequenté la guerre . . . experimentez en fait de guerres, par lesquelz il se conseilloit a sages et discretz, dont le plus josne avoit lx ans . . . [Car] les choses qui se font par batailles se doivent conduire par raison et meur conseil').[23]

The acceptance, by the twelfth century, of so much that the *De re militari* had to teach was a sign that in that age, as political and social society was already coming under scrutiny and analysis, so war's status as a 'science' was coming to be recognised.[24] It was now developing into a 'learned' discipline, with its own texts, as was indicated by the copying of the works of Vegetius, Frontinus and others, and by the glosses entered in their margins. In the late thirteenth century a need for vernacular versions of the full text began to be felt. Jean de Vignay's reason for translating Vegetius into French was, he claimed, the fact that the Roman was one of those 'who has said certain things which should be of value to men who want to acquire the skills of war' ('[qui] ont dit aucunes choses qui m[ou]t sont profitables a savoir a ceus qui veulent estre sage et apris darmes'), ending with the remark that it was good for the soldier to be well informed, 'for in all conflict skill in arms more often brings victory than do strength or numbers, as ill-informed people think' ('car en toute bataille seulent plus doner victoire sens d'armes et usages que force ne multitude, ce est planté de gent mal enseigniee').[25] As Christine de Pisan put it in her *Livre du corps de policie*, written *c*.1407, 'there is no activity in the world in which it is more necessary to act according to good sense and order than in making war' ('il ne soit chose ou monde plus necessaire a garder mesure et ordre que ou fait des armes . . . il ne soit chose nulle ou tant soit necessaire ouvrer part art de raison').[26]

---

[23] Juvénal des Ursins, *Écrits*, II, 236.
[24] J. A. Maravall, 'Ejercito y estado en el Renacimiento', *Revista de estudos politicos* (1961), 14; Murray, *Reason and society*, p. 129.
[25] Vignay, ed. Löfstedt, 37–8.   [26] Pisan, *Corps de policie*, 125–6.

The importance of this perspective was that it could be used to oppose the commonly held view that the outcome of battle was in the hands of 'Fortune', the turning of whose wheel was notoriously difficult to predict. Although Vegetius openly recognised that the outcome of battles could not always be accurately predicted (the element played by chance caused him to argue that battle should be avoided if possible, since the consequences could be dire), his work none the less took something out of this unsatisfactory position. The influence of chance, whether expressed in terms of Dame Fortune or of the rod of punishment wielded by God, could be countered with the help of reason, which at least ensured that man could help himself by following guidelines formulated according to the teachings of experience. The element of rationality contained in the *De re militari* was bound to find favour in an age when the influence of reason upon philosophical thought was becoming more powerful.

The soldier

Whether it was Vegetius' intention or not, one effect of his work upon certain medieval thinkers was to underline the importance of the army in society, towards which it had obligations mainly concerned with defence. Seen in this light, the role of the army as an institution only served to emphasise the place to be accorded by society to those who served in it. The army's societal role and its responsibilities towards the achievement and stability of the common good showed the important part which it had to play in the preservation of an ordered world. Vegetius had also demonstrated how far the successful fulfilment of his military role depended upon the soldier's characteristics of both mind and body, characteristics to be turned into valuable professional skills which, through regular training, could be placed at the service of society. From this it was evident that not all men would make good soldiers. Vegetius' insistence on quality rather than on numbers had the effect of underlining that those who passed the selection processes aimed at admitting only the best into the army were, in some way, an elite, just as he would also stress that the best soldier was invariably a man of experience, which could only have been developed with time and practice. Hence we find the phrase '[il a] frequenté la guerre' commonly used in French to describe the experienced soldier.

The 'tiro', or young recruit, went through a preliminary form of selection based on physical characteristics. But he needed more than these to proceed successfully through the months of training which would turn him into a 'miles', or soldier. He had to show moral qualities and, if possible, intellectual ones to make him stand out from others, qualities (the 'honestas' of Vegetius) which showed that it was worth putting him through the period of training which would ensure that he would not desert at the crucial moment. What use was it, Vegetius asked, to train a man who acted in this way? Honour was therefore regarded as one of a soldier's most important assets.

This was emphasised by the oath-taking ceremony which acknowledged the recruit's attainment of the rank of 'miles'. By swearing to serve the emperor and to show, through his actions, the loyalty or reliability of a man of honour, the soldier undertook to serve any commander with the authority to demand his obedience. Since it was the emperor's responsibility to maintain peace in his dominion, by becoming an instrument of the imperial authority the soldier was assuming a public function, in effect setting the standard by which he would be assessed. His devotion to maintaining the public good was to be judged by the oath he swore to be ready to give up his life if called upon to do so.

While emphasising these elements, Vegetius had also recognised the humanity and fallibility of the soldier. Fear, inexperience, hostile conditions could all affect how a soldier reacted to a situation; together, they might lead to defeat. Training helped to increase confidence, which, in its turn, inspired the bravery which could make all the difference between victory and defeat. Vegetius' assertion that 'a knowledge of arms increases a man's courage ('scientia rei bellicae dimicandi nutrit audaciam'), much noted by readers, would be quoted by Sir John Fortescue in his *De laudibus legum Anglie*, written about 1470.[27] Given these facts, one understands the emphasis which Vegetius placed upon the personal qualities expected of those with positions of authority within the army. The good commander would not only train his men in the skills needed in battle; he would reassure them in moments of doubt, and bring out their loyalty and determination to achieve victory in situations of crisis.

Through regular training, the 'tiro' became a 'regular' soldier. Vegetius emphasised the fact that a military career was open to him. It was a career founded on the hard work needed to acquire a variety of skills and experiences in different aspects of military life. It depended, too, on formal recognition of achievement by the military authorities, acting on behalf of the emperor. It implied, too, that society as a whole benefited from the skills and experience of a trained soldier, who became a

---

[27] *DRM*, I, 1; Sir John Fortescue, *De laudibus legum Anglie*, ed. and trans. S. B. Chrimes (Cambridge, 1942), 137.

long-term servant of society which recognised the services done on its behalf through the promotions awarded and the wages paid to him.

It was several centuries after Vegetius had written his work that the place of the soldier in society was considered and described in John of Salisbury's *Policraticus*. As we have seen, that description owed much to the *De re militari*. Salisbury viewed the 'miles' not simply as a man who bore arms, but as one who, selected and trained, assumed certain public responsibilities, accepted under oath to the Godhead of the Trinity. (The training of the 'miles', ending with the taking of an oath in a ceremony involving promises of service, would have appealed to the clergy.) The *Policraticus* showed respect for the 'miles', praised the profession of arms, and acknowledged its virtues and the role for good it might play in society.

Such was the position of the soldier as set out in philosophical discourse. He was represented as having an important function, not least as the deterrent which secured society against outside threat and attack, thus enabling the ruler to achieve order from within. We should recall that Salisbury's early years had been spent against the background of the 'Anarchy' of the reign of King Stephen (1135–54), and that he wrote his work in the reign of Henry II (1154–89), a reign characterised by the development of law and the royal authority. The *Policraticus* was Salisbury's contribution to that development. In it the army became the sovereign's hand, or 'armata manus' as he termed it. Salisbury gave the soldier a potentially active role in society, approved by God, intended to help create an ordered state with the king at its head.[28]

The late thirteenth century would see a major step forward in the acceptance of military ideas indebted in different ways, and to different degrees, to the *De re militari*, a process in which the early translations of that text probably played their part. The almost simultaneous production of Giles of Rome's *De regimine principum* greatly helped to carry forward some of the more philosophical aspects of Vegetius' work. Among these were restatements regarding the contribution of armies to the defence of society's increasingly self-aware 'patriae' and their ambitious rulers. There was, too, the greater emphasis placed upon prudence as a military virtue, as well as upon victory, not glory, being the main justification of military action.[29]

The *De regimine principum* was still in its infancy when an ordinance issued by Philip IV of France in February 1295 reminded lords of their

---

[28] A. Scaglione, *Knights at court. Courtliness, chivalry and courtesy from Ottonian Germany to the Italian Renaissance* (Berkeley, Los Angeles and Oxford, 1991), 69.

[29] See Briggs, *Giles of Rome's* De regimine principum.

obligations towards the defence of the kingdom, and that their first duty was to serve the king.[30] Another, dated February 1331, while reluctantly recognising the right to private war in Aquitaine, did so only on condition that it should cease immediately the king went to war with the kingdom's enemies.[31] In 1352, however, a further ordinance was required to reiterate that wars concerning the people of France should take precedence over all (private) conflicts, since the king's wars were fought for the interest of the common good ('rei publicae').[32] In a country divided by war, as France would be for the next century, Vegetian ideas would come to have a significant influence.

These ordinances claiming priority for wars fought by the king (in effect a step towards claiming royal control over all military activity) were intended to reduce private conflicts within the kingdom. Their publication constituted a positive step, taken by the nation's leader, to secure the achievement of peace and the common good. In so acting, however, the crown had another end in view. By making itself the sole arbiter of what constituted a just war (since such a war, custom stated, had to be declared on the sovereign authority of the king), it would strengthen the monarch's claim to be the main, indeed the sole, arbiter between conflict and peace within the country's bounds, a claim which was nothing less than an attempt to increase his political power (including the power to raise taxes to pay for war) over his subjects. The ordinances referred to above were, therefore, a challenge to those who might oppose the centralisation of power through the claim to lead the country's forces against whomever the king decided presented a threat to the peace or integrity of the kingdom.

In the worst years France saw her territory overrun by armed men, who caused and accentuated political and social divisions within the kingdom.[33] They challenged the orders of the royal authority; their criminal activities, along with the all-too-apparent inability of the crown to regain the initiative which these underlined, became the subject of much discussion among observers of the contemporary French scene, and of many suggestions for reform which would restore both the crown's authority and a measure of order within the kingdom. In that process, thinking indebted to Vegetian principles would play its part.

Commentators were concerned for the return of order which, it was hoped, would result from an effective reassertion of the control of government by the king. To Eustache Deschamps the soldiery, rather than

[30] *Ordonnances des roys de France de la troisième race* (22 vols., Paris, 1723–1849), XI, 376.
[31] *Ibid.* II, 61–2.   [32] *Ibid.* II, 511–12.
[33] See K. A. Fowler, *Medieval mercenaries. I. The great companies* (Oxford and Malden, MA, 2001).

being the agent of order, was the cause of much disorder. His use of the image of 'wolves, lions, boars and leopards' ('loups, lyons, sangliers, lieppars') to describe the undisciplined soldiery of mid-fourteenth-century France in the language of animals known for their ferocity and their violent and unpredictable behaviour, speaks volumes regarding the popular view of the soldier of the time. Deschamps' poetry, and that of others, contains many images of a war-torn country. It is not difficult to find the expression of pessimistic sentiments of this kind in his work.

But there was to emerge another side to Deschamps, the royal servant who urged that public order be maintained by an army whose task it was to serve the king by helping him achieve one of his chief responsibilities, the maintenance of domestic peace and the defence of the country. The battles of Crécy and Poitiers had been occasions of defeat. Deschamps put himself forward as the champion of a different approach to fighting war. Battles should not be regarded as opportunities to win glory. More important was the defeat of the enemy: war should lead to victory ('Finis militaris est victoria'). Noteworthy actions were all very well; but it was the end, not the means, which would have a lasting effect. He advocated listening to the ideas of *clercs*, men of learning who put forward more pragmatic principles which were summed up in the notion that war was fought for the common good, not for the winning of individual reputation. The only just wars were those fought by command of the king, whose servant the soldier must become. By the dying years of the fourteenth century there had been created in French royal circles an intellectual appreciation, bearing Vegetian overtones that, in place of the individualism characteristic of chivalric warfare, men should recognise the imperative to obey orders and to be faithful to the service of the crown. Whether the nobility, in particular, was ready for such a change of tradition is doubtful.[34] The events of the three decades 1410–40 provided some sort of an answer. 'Why are you asleep, Lord? ('Quare obdormis, domine?'), Jean Juvénal des Ursins enquired of King Charles VII about 1440, suggesting that just as the English had conquered parts of France through the use of force, so the French king might reverse the process using the same means, if his subjects were willing to obey his orders, suffer adversity for his sake, and even die in his cause, the language here bearing echoes of Vegetius.[35] The theme of the recovery of France being best achieved by the royal army could also be found in the writings of

---

[34] T. Lassabatère, 'Théorie et éthique de la guerre dans l'œuvre d'Eustache Deschamps', in *La guerre, la violence et les gens au moyen âge. I. Guerre de violence*, eds. P. Contamine and O. Guyotjeannin (Paris, 1996), 41–8; P. Contamine, *Guerre, état et société à la fin du moyen âge. Études sur les armées des rois de France, 1337–1494* (Paris and The Hague, 1972), 197–204.

[35] Juvénal des Ursins, *Écrits*, I, 387, 318–19; *DRM*, II, 5.

other men of the time, such as Robert Blondel and Alain Chartier. In all of them, the army was to be the principal instrument of the revival of the French monarchy and people.

In our search in the evidence left by contemporary opinion concerning the soldier in the late Middle Ages we may look at that provided by legal records, in particular for what they tell us about views regarding the place and role of the soldier in late medieval France. Such evidence, taken in particular from the claims and statements made by lawyers on behalf of their soldier clients in the *Parlement* of Paris, can reveal something of the attitudes towards service given to society by the soldier. Since the king represented the common good ('le roy represente la chose publique'), it was wrong, an advocate argued, to pursue in the courts a soldier wounded in the royal service while he was fighting on behalf of that good ('lui estant en expedicion pour la chose publique').[36] In weighing up what such claims might reveal, we must appreciate that they were made by lawyers trying to put their clients in a favourable moral position. Service to the king clearly stood out, as did a man's presence at an important battle. Being taken prisoner should bear no implication that a man had not fought nobly. His status was not one of shame; rather the opposite.

While such snippets from legal argument should not be linked directly to Vegetian thinking, they nevertheless illustrate how soldiers wished to have themselves presented before the courts in a manner in which they and their fellows could be seen as members of a profession of honour whose purpose it was to serve the king in a public war, formally declared and fought on the king's behalf and with his authority.[37] A man taken prisoner fighting for the king should receive sympathetic consideration for his inability to appear in court in person, and should not suffer a judgment against him because he was absent for the sake of the common good ('pro causa rei publicae'). That, after all, was what a soldier's life and duty consisted of. It was an argument likely to appeal to members of the judicial profession, who, along with soldiers and their captains, were also appointed by the king to perform a difficult public function aimed at defending the public good.

It is clear that opinions regarding the soldier were very divided. To most in fourteenth- and fifteenth-century France he was a figure to be wary of, even to fear. There can be little doubt that this unfavourable reputation was frequently deserved, and that the soldier's critics were often right in their scathing remarks made about him and his antisocial

---

[36] *English suits before the Parlement of Paris, 1420–1436*, ed. C. T. Allmand and C. A. J. Armstrong (RHistS, London, 1982), 175.

[37] M. H. Keen, *The laws of war in the late Middle Ages* (London and Toronto, 1965), 68–70.

behaviour. But these very same critics knew where part of the answer to France's problems lay, and in their writings developed a blueprint of reform which involved the crown seizing the initiative by turning the skills and experience of France's soldiers to the benefit of the public good. The army thus became the means by which the crown would reassert its authority after long years of weak rule, the means by which public order and social peace would be restored. In mid-fifteenth-century England this was also to be a major theme running through the Vegetian paraphrase, *Knyghthode and bataile.*[38]

At an intellectual level, the *De re militari* helped to restore something of their good name to both army and soldier. By emphasising its association with the general welfare, Vegetius had underlined the army's power for good. The logic of his argument, that peace could best be assured by making proper preparation for war, further underlined the claim that the soldier should be an instrument of peace and harmony, not of war and violence. At the same time, Vegetius had insisted that the army must be under the firm command of the ruler, the source of all authority, to be used by him for the benefit of society. In this way the soldier became the servant of those over whom the king ruled, creating an important and significant example of the Roman ideal of public service which helped soften the otherwise rather hard image of the physical power wielded by him.

One way we can judge the respect in which the soldier was held is to see what happened to him in old age and in death. John of Salisbury had advocated proper provision for the former soldier from public funds.[39] By the fourteenth century, a readiness to fight in the king's name was coming to be regarded as an attitude worthy of respect and honour. Walter de Milemete urged that provision be made for those, the old and the wounded, who had served the king; this would encourage others to follow suit.[40] In full flush of the 'Age of Chivalry' (*c.*1348) the statutes of the English chivalric Order of the Garter provided for care and lodging for twenty-six poor knights ('milites pauperes') at Windsor.[41] In the early years of the next century the English poet Thomas Hoccleve sought greater esteem for old soldiers, in particular from their more active juniors who had forgotten what had been done in the past. Alain Chartier could refer to the 'very honourable profession of arms' ('treshonnourable

---

[38] For which see above, pp. 187–93.   [39] *Policraticus*, VI, 10.

[40] 'On the provision of the king for his fighting men', in *Political thought in early fourteenth-century England. Treatises by Walter of Milemete, William of Pagula and William of Ockham*, ed. C. J. Nederman (Tempe, Arizona and Turnhout, 2002), 49.

[41] E. Ashmole, *The institution, laws & ceremonies of the most noble Order of the Garter* (London, 1672), 158–9.

mestier d'armes'), while later in the century Jean de Bueil was to ask that provision be made for those who, having done good service, should not be left in need. Being a soldier, particularly in the service of the king, he reminded his readers, was a profession of honour.[42]

The oaths of military service emphasised fidelity towards, and respect for, authority in the public service; the soldier should obey, never desert and always be ready to die for the Roman state. The chapter[43] drew the attention of a considerable number of medieval readers. Their interest should not surprise us, since it emphasised appreciation of the virtues of loyalty and fidelity, always prized among those whose business is war. By stressing, too, that obedience to the commander and strict attention to duty were public obligations formally undertaken, those who wrote their comments were implicitly recognising that the army was becoming a public instrument through which society might be defended. As Vegetius had written, with an optimism which won much approval, the army made the state invincible.

The *De re militari* praised the soldier willing to give up his life in the service of the king and of the common good. It may have been from this that there developed the practice of praising and rewarding those willing to face the risk of death ('exposer leurs corps') for the good and 'transquilité' of their fellows, this language being developed in ordinances in 1367–68, only to serve later as the basis of according material rewards to those who had served the king in war.[44] Years later, in a long passage, Alain Chartier would recall the noble deeds of certain Romans who had voluntarily given up their lives for the common good ('qui voluntairement ont voulu perdre la vie pour recouvrer a la chose publique sa prosperité').[45] Such men were worthy of praise.

The soldier's willingness to risk his life was also important for another reason. Linked to the traditional chivalric values associated with

---

[42] *Hoccleve's works. III. The regement of princes, 1411–12*, ed. F. J. Furnivall (EETS, e.s. 72, London, 1897), 32–4; Alain Chartier, *Le quadrilogue invectif*, ed. E. Droz (2nd rev. edn, Paris, 1950), 55; *Le Jouvencel par Jean de Bueil, suivi du commentaire de Guillaume Tringant*, ed. C. Favre and L. Lecestre (2 vols., SHF, Paris, 1887–89), I, 118; C. Allmand, 'Changing views of the soldier in late medieval France', in *Guerre et société en France, en Angleterre et en Bourgogne, XIVe–XVe siècle*, ed. P. Contamine, C. Giry-Deloison and M. H. Keen (Lille, 1991), 182. In 1459–60, the author of *Knyghthode and bataile* wrote of 'That honour as to be werreourys' (*Knyghthode and bataile*, 8, line 188).

[43] *DRM*, II, 5.

[44] *Ordonnances*, III, 361; V, 66–7, 144–5. See the grant (1424) of the *comté* of Dreux to the earl of Suffolk for his services 'a la recouvrance, garde et deffense de noz royaume et seigneurie de France pour lesquelz il a exposé incessament ses personne et chevance tant au fait de guerre et autrement'. The grant (1430) of the *comté* of Clermont to John Talbot was justified in very similar language. (Paris, AN JJ 172, no. 571; JJ 175, no. 318.)

[45] *Quadrilogue invectif*, 53–4.

knighthood, it emphasised his calling as being essentially one of obedience to his lord and willingness to serve the public good. Jean de Bueil expressed this well when he wrote of the soldier as the one 'ready to defend the rights of his ruler, of his country and of those over whom he ruled' ('prest de deffendre le droit de son prince, de son pays et de ceulx qu'il a en son gouvernement').[46] The emphasis in France was by now very much on the royal army. Service of the crown, responsible for its people, came to be regarded as service in its highest form. By extension this should place those who performed it high in the public esteem. Death met in a just conflict for the public good transformed the battlefield into the field of honour.

Leadership

The theme of good leadership featured prominently in the *De re militari*. It did so primarily by emphasising the contribution of the commander to the achievement of victory by the way that he planned a campaign, prepared his troops and outmanoeuvred the enemy with both the maximum effect and the minimum loss to his side. Vegetius' 'dux' did not deliberately seek glory.

Behind it all lay the responsibility of the ruler to provide for the physical defence and public tranquility of his people and their lands, freedoms and interests. So it was that the *De re militari* was addressed to the emperor; so, too, the reason why its teachings were included in many of the books of advice written to inform princes of their responsibilities, and why both John of Salisbury and Giles of Rome included many Vegetian ideas on war in their works. All knew, however, that not every ruler either could or would take an active and personal part in war. Indeed, the author of the *De mundo*, a pseudo-Aristotelian tract popular in the thirteenth century, advised that the prince should not fight in person, but should do so through his officers.[47] Military leadership should be devolved or delegated. As the *De re militari* made clear, military authority depended for its legitimacy upon proper authorisation to act in the ruler's name, the letter of appointment, which we would call a commission, referred to by Vegetius.[48] In the Vegetian canon, no commander could act without this letter, which, once received, gave power to his command, which he exercised in the name and with the authority of the emperor. As, in Christian tradition, a man exercised authority ultimately derived from God, so a commander did the same by virtue of authority derived from

---

[46] *Jouvencel*, II, 71. See also I, 43, 56, 118.   [47] Kantorowicz, *King's two bodies*, 263.
[48] 'Tribunus per epistolam', as one reader noted (Vatican, Pal. lat. 1573, fo. 14v).

his ruler. In this way, the ruler fulfilled the function given him to protect and defend his people.

To whom should that authority to command be given? Having described the responsibilities of commanders and their immediate subordinates for the training of soldiers, Vegetius had little choice but to recommend that commanders be appointed from among those who had experience of serving in several kinds of force, who had skills to impart to those placed under their orders, and who showed qualities, such as courage, associated with leadership. In short, authority to issue commands should be given only to those who were professionally competent and suited to do so. Promotion, a concept of which Vegetius was much aware, should be awarded on merit and broad military experience, not on grounds of cronyism or birth.[49] Leadership should be what it claimed to be, acting out a responsible public role for the benefit of society.

Whether the army was successful in defending the state depended, in large measure, upon the exercise of the commander's skills. 'A good army', Aquinas wrote, 'is reflected in its good order and in the commander who has charge over it' ('Bonus exercitus est et in ipso ordine et in duce qui exercitui praesidet').[50] Receiving much emphasis was the role to be played by the commander, whose qualities, experience and skills should enable him to reach the right decision from alternatives available to him.[51] The skills required of him were varied, having been gained largely through active involvement in war, although reading about the experiences of others was certainly of value. Aquinas, if appearing a little reluctant to attribute as much to training as Aristotle and Vegetius had taught, was happy to endorse the value of experience, which made a man into a better soldier ('In rebus bellicis milites sunt fortes per experientiam').[52] Furthermore, the commander should not shun consulting other men of experience, who should give their advice honestly. This view met with the clear approval of several readers of the text: it was also to be seized upon by a number of commentators.[53] In part of *Le confort d'ami*, a form of *De regimine principum* written in 1357 for Charles II, 'the Bad', king of Navarre, Guillaume de Machaut placed the seeking of counsel at the head of a list of things any commander must be ready to do.

---

[49] We may note that it was his 'senz, loyalté et diligence', along with his 'grande experience et industrie' which won promotion as a 'sergent d'armes' for Etienne de Brandiz in January 1374 (Bessey, *Construire l'armée française*, 82–4).

[50] Quoted in Kantorowicz, *King's two bodies*, 226, n. 222.

[51] Emphasised in comments in Novara, Cap. Duomo, XCV, fos. 19v, 20.

[52] Quoted by E. A. Synan, 'St Thomas Aquinas and the profession of arms', *Medieval studies*, 50 (1988), 425, n. 86.

[53] Florence, Laur. Plut 39. 39, fo. 30v; Vatican, Borg. lat. 411, fo. 42v; Cesena, Malatestiana, S. XIX 5, fo. 188; BnF lat. 6106, fo. 174v.

But whose counsel? Only that of men ready to put their advice into practice ('Pren conseil a ceuls qui feront/ Tout ce qu'il te conseilleront').[54]
Such a view, which had a long pedigree, appeared to conflict with that,
now growing in influence at the French court, which encouraged rulers
to seek the advice of men of learning, and to act upon it. During the
reign of King Charles V (1364–80), at least, this was probably done.[55]

In the long perspective the emphasis placed on the seeking and taking of advice may be seen as a continuation of the debate involving
the classical world regarding the relative merits of strength of body and
strength (force) of character ('virtus animi') polarised in the discussion
regarding the effectiveness of 'corpus' and 'anima'. This fell into line
with Sallust, for example, who, in his *Bellum Catilinae*, had discussed
the relative importance of physical and mental power in the winning of
victory.[56] Vegetius consistently argued that a thoughtful and considered
approach to war would triumph over numbers. From this stemmed his
insistence upon flexibility and the need for preparedness; his insistence,
too, on the emphasis which both he and those who, later, appreciated his
ideas placed upon the leader, the man needed to make important decisions based on the best and latest information received. The anonymous
author of the early thirteenth-century *Li Fet des Romains* had written that
once advice had been sought and taken, action should follow ('avant que
l'en face la chose, doit l'en conseil prendre; après le conseil, doit s[u]ivre li
fez').[57]

In the final analysis, therefore, decisions had to be taken by the commander, and by him alone, for a divided or undecided command was
a bad command. Among the skills needed was an ability to look into
the future, to consider what the enemy might be planning, and so be
prepared for any eventuality. The commander must also understand his
men, maintain their health and have an appreciation of their fears and
doubts, in spite of the fact that in much medieval epic 'care of their men
[was] a foreign concept to these leaders'.[58] His own experience should

---

[54] *Confort d'ami*, III, lines 3105, 3099–3100.
[55] See the suggestive discussion in R. W. Keauper, *War, justice and public order. England and France in the later Middle Ages* (Oxford, 1988), in particular ch. 4 ('Vox
populi').
[56] Beer, *A medieval Caesar*, 20–2, 93.
[57] On the effects of failure to follow advice, see, for instance, Nall, 'William Worcester
reads Alain Chartier', 144–6. Philippe de Commynes wrote critically of Charles, the
young duke of Burgundy, who took no advice ('ne usa de conseil d'homme, mais du
sien propre'), which, the reader knew, resulted in tragic miscalculation and death in
battle. (*Mémoires*, ed. J. Calmette (3 vols., Paris, 1924–25), I, 37).
[58] P. Noble, 'Military leadership in the Old French epic', in *Reading around the epic*, ed.
M. Ailes, P. E. Bennett and K. Pratt (London, 1998), 186. See also Verbruggen, *Art of
warfare*, 54–6.

have taught him that he should treat his men for what they were, human, while remembering that confidence is infectious and that morale can be raised by word or personal example. No army should be led out to fight unless it was confident of victory. It was up to the commander to judge this, and to raise morale to the level required to defeat the enemy.[59]

An important theme running through the *De re militari* was the need to create and maintain a sense of *esprit de corps* within the army. The various formations of the Roman army, mostly described in Book II, aimed at creating such a feeling among the soldiers. Walter de Milemete described the king's subjects as his companions in war; he should endeavour to ensure that his armies comprised people who wished to serve him.[60] Alain Chartier came close to comparing an army to a family, which accepted the authority and leadership of one 'chief', its father.[61] The emphasis placed by Vegetius upon the need for soldiers to train together as formations was reflected in the military ordinances of Charles the Bold, duke of Burgundy, who ordered his commanders to lead their units into the fields and to put them through a vigorous and regular training which would enable them to act together in the face of the enemy.[62] Military training, Vegetius had stressed, should take place not only in wartime, but in peacetime, too. This was what Duke Charles intended should happen.

Conscious that on the battlefield soldiers often became separated from their fellows, the coherence and effectiveness of their formation thus being lost, Vegetius had advised a system of ensigns to help keep men together with the others from their century.[63] Was the influence of such advice reflected in a French naval ordinance which emphasised the need for ships to keep and to act together (none was to sail ahead of the squadron's leader), or in the military ordinances issued by King Richard II in 1385, which underlined a desire to create an army having a greater sense of coherence than was often the case at that time? These ordinances reflect disapproval of those lacking basic discipline, men whose actions were aimed at securing their own reputation rather than at furthering the cause of the force of which they were part. In spite of its members being contracted to individual commanders, the ordinances demanded obedience to the army's overall commander, the

---

[59] *DRM*, III, 12. See Milan, Ambros. G 83 sup., fo. 19.

[60] Nederman, *Political thought*, 23. See the statement that the king 'should regularly recall to memory that the royal person is but one . . . while triumphant victory arises from many. For this reason, you will notice that the courage of the king is constituted by the strength of the people in the army' (48).

[61] *Quadrilogue invectif*, 55–6.   [62] Allmand, 'Did the *De re militari* . . . ?', 138–9.

[63] *DRM*, III, 13, 16; Bessey, *Construire l'armée française*, 58 (1338).

king.[64] Significantly, further steps were to be taken to secure coherence and maintain order and discipline within the army's structures: banners, for instance, would be used to keep the men together; lodgings, as the *De re militari* had taught, should also be assigned on the same principle; the watch, likewise.[65]

Just as unity spelled strength, so discord and division seriously weakened the enemy. It was, Vegetius had written, the mark of the skilled commander to sow the discord which might ultimately cause the enemy's self-destruction.[66] Towns, Machaut claimed, could be lost not only by famine but by 'discention', too. To politically aware persons living in France in the first half of the fifteenth century, what Vegetius had written would have appeared tragically true. So much of the political literature of the 1410s and 1420s centred upon the theme of division or, as it was often seen, treason. In the *Quadrilogue invectif* (1422) Alain Chartier bemoaned the feuds among his countrymen which only strengthened the enemy.[67] As it was, these words expressed the feelings of many Frenchmen at the country's darkest hour, when the English political and military effort carried all before it.

The Middle Ages took over some of the principal ideas expressed by Vegetius on commanders and the leadership which they exercised, and applied them to their own time and circumstances. In France the greatest need was to rid the country of the baleful presence of the *routiers*. Such a task required leadership and determination on the part of the crown. Much of the political/polemical literature of the Hundred Years War was aimed at urging the crown to assert its authority, rally the kingdom and build up an army under its command to clear the country of the enemy. The familiar text in the *De re militari* (II, 5) in which the new 'miles' swore to obey the ruler, never to desert, and to be willing to die for the good of the (Roman) state, contained three elements which merged: obedience to the ruler; through him, service to the common good; acceptance that loyalty might result in death.

An aspect of the obedience due to the ruler was the acceptance of commanders appointed by him. In the political and social conditions of mid-fourteenth-century France this assertion of the royal authority was intended to demonstrate that the king represented the common good, and

[64] Bessey, *Construire l'armée française*, 56–8; Keen, 'Richard II's ordinances of war', 37. A comparison of French and English ordinances in these years underlines certain similarities of content and language which they shared. Not least is their sharing of Roman ideas and principles, some conveyed by the *DRM*. We may note that the issue of individual advantage versus public good would be raised in *Le Jouvencel*, II, 100.

[65] *DRM*, III, 8. On banners as rallying points, see Bessey, *Construire l'armée française*, 58.

[66] *DRM*, III, 10.   [67] *Quadrilogue invectif*, 36, lines 19–20.

that his decisions regarding its welfare must be obeyed. So the ordinance issued by John II in April 1351 placed great emphasis on the exercise of the royal authority over the army.[68] A second such ordinance, issued by his son and successor, Charles V, in 1374, emphasised that those serving in the king's army should do so only under captains formally appointed by letters issued either by the king or by one of his lieutenants.[69] The tone of both documents carried strong echoes of the *De re militari*, the second, in particular, recalling Vegetius' recommendation that commanders must be formally appointed by the emperor, who chose them, it was implied, from men of experience who had worked their way up through the ranks, and were thus worthy of the confidence placed upon them.

By the time that the second ordinance was issued, King Charles V, an enthusiast of classical literature whose library included the *De re militari*, but who was unable to lead his army personally against the English, had appointed Bertrand du Guesclin, the pre-eminent military commander of his day, to be constable of France, an appointment which met the criteria of experience while allowing the new appointee to exercise his authority by virtue of royal mandate over the heads of a number of high-ranking royal dukes, who were instructed to obey the orders of the new constable, thus emphasising obedience to the office rather than to the man. The appointment was significant mainly for two reasons. It had strong political implications, since the constableship was a public office, representing the king, who made the appointment after consultation with the royal council. The constable, therefore, exercised authority over all but the king himself, and all should obey him.[70] It also marked a notable promotion for a man who owed relatively little to birth or social advantage, and almost everything to his military skills and reputation acquired through active service. It was no coincidence that Charles V should have appointed a tough but natural leader of wide practical experience, who saw the need to keep his soldiers under close control, appreciated the importance of planning, and fought the kind of war which denied the enemy the chance of formal battle, success on the battlefield not being regarded as the necessary prerequisite of victory, which might be achieved by other means.

The tendency towards a centralised and properly authorised command structure would soon be taken up by Philippe de Mézières, who, writing

---

[68] *Ordonnances*, IV, 67–70.   [69] *Ordonnances*, V, 660.

[70] '*Primo*, le connestable est par dessus tous les autres qui sont en l'ost, excepté la personne le roy s'il y est, soient ducs, barons . . . [at autres] de quelque estat qu'ilz soient, et doivent obéir à luy' (Bessey, *Construire l'armée française*, 83). See also F. Autrand, *Charles V, le Sage* (Paris, 1994), 578.

*c.*1390, argued in favour of the independence and, above all, the authority of the king, who should enforce his monopoly of appointments to high military command. Local commanders, he wrote, should not be chosen from among the leaders ('grans seigneurs') of local society, who, however competent in arms, were too preoccupied with their estates and interests. Rather such appointments should be made from those with fewer obligations, men of lower social rank who were none the less experienced in arms and would reside with their soldiers.[71] Service of the king, the representative of the common good, demanded not only experience but commitment, too.

Thirty years later Alain Chartier would see in du Guesclin an example to be followed in his own day, when the French royal army would be manned by men loyal to the crown, their commanders would be nominated by the king, and their appointments would be made on the basis of merit and experience. Such steps should effectively put an end to the current situation in which men still refused to serve under the banner of a particular captain because 'my father did not serve under his' ('Je n'yroie pour riens soubz le panon d'ung tel, car mon pere ne fut oncques soubz le sien').[72] It should not be social rank but military skill and virtue, recognised and rewarded by the crown, which endowed commanders with their authority. In this way the number of unqualified leaders would be reduced, the power of the crown would grow, and the effectiveness of the army would increase.

We see here Vegetian influence being brought to bear upon practice in France in the fourteenth and fifteenth centuries. Commanders were increasingly regarded as men who met the qualifications recommended by Vegetius, that experience and skill should determine the appointment of the army's leaders. By the middle of the fourteenth century, two major defeats of the noble-led French army at the hands of the English created much dissatisfaction in the kingdom. Was the nobility living up to its responsibilities to the community which formed the basis for the privileges it enjoyed? It was against this background that the appointment of du Guesclin as constable of France should be seen. Half a century later, in 1422, Alain Chartier wrote that 'it is not birth which makes the military commander, but those whom God, their understanding and courage, and the authority of the prince name as such who are to be obeyed' ('les lignaiges ne font pas les chiefs de guerre, mais ceulz a qui Dieu, leurs sens ou leurs vaillances, et l'auctorité du prince en donnent la grace doivent ester pour telz obeiz'.) Chartier knew his classical authors, among them Vegetius. He admired the way that Roman leaders might

---

[71] Mézières, *Songe du vieil pèlerin*, II, 394–5.   [72] *Quadrilogue invectif*, 58, lines 20–2.

be chosen from among men who toiled in the fields,[73] and who had no special respect for any under their command who came from families of rank or position in society. Half a century later Jean de Bueil would react in much the same way. To the question whether it was necessary for leaders to be drawn from the nobility, or was command open to talent, his reply was that since appointment to command in wartime had both military and social implications, it must be given to the best qualified, irrespective of rank, a view underlined by the semi-fictional career of the young hero in *Le Jouvencel*.

The literature of the late Middle Ages brought to the surface developments in both opinion and practice regarding the role of the commander in battle, a role both symbolised and determined by the position which he took up on the field. Leadership could be exercised in two ways. A commander might choose to lead by example, usually by placing himself literally up front, encouraging his men by the bravery and 'proesce' which he showed. Leadership of this kind was important in bringing out the best in an army drawn from many directions and not trained to fight together. Emphasising, as it did, the role of the individual, it was also the image of war put forward by the romancers as late as the fifteenth century.

However, as we have seen, there were those who felt that a ruler should not risk his life (or capture) in battle. The point was brought home to the French when their king, John II, was taken prisoner by the English at Poitiers in 1356. Vegetian thinking held the solution. Commands in battle should be handed over to the professionals who were given the ruler's commission to act in his name. Furthermore, rather than lead from the front (whatever the advantages of that approach) they should do so from within the body of the army, encouraging and directing those under their command. This was not an admission of fear or cowardice but, rather, the putting into action of the commander's directive role, which could not be fulfilled by a man actively fighting at the front. As envisaged in the *De re militari*, the commander must have an overall view of the battle scene and, through his subordinates and a system of signals, be able to convey orders which would be to the advantage of the army as a whole, and its ability to achieve victory as a united force. This was particularly the case if, having managed to get the enemy to attack, the army was fighting a defensive action. Even in an attacking mode, a tactic such as that of units advancing in waves (and then retreating to rest), associated with Braccio da Montone, was one which required careful

---

[73] Vegetius had an almost identical story concerning Quintus Cincinnatus (*DRM*, I, 3).

training and close co-ordination of troop movements.[74] The tradition of Vegetian thinking saw it as the commander's task to make this happen as effectively as possible. As always, the emphasis was on action by the group rather than on the exceptional acts of individuals. With the more highly trained armies of the later Middle Ages and, not least, the mercenary companies composed of men accustomed to fighting as units, often over periods of many years, such a view of leadership could become a reality.[75]

Chivalry, nobility and the army

What did the *De re militari* and what we regard as characteristics of medieval chivalry hold in common? Both understood the importance of personal honour, both showed great respect for courage, both regarded loyalty as an essential quality of the warrior. They shared, too, the importance attributed by chivalry to the concept of service, although what kind of service, to whom and in what form may not always have been fully understood. They had in common, too, great respect for the military skills; training was an important aspect of active knighthood as it had been, too, to the 'miles' of the Roman army.

For some two centuries before John of Salisbury wrote his *Policraticus* (1159) parts of western Europe, particularly Francia, had suffered the effects of private wars to which there appeared to be no lasting solutions. Viewed retrospectively, the *Policraticus* may be seen as the first serious intellectual justification of the use of a monopoly of force, in the form of a royal army, to bring peace to society through a reduction in private wars. To those imbued with Roman ideas and accustomed to a Latin vocabulary, the concept of social peace was summed up in the term 'res publica', attained and then maintained by the central authority. This thinking signalled two important developments, both of which emerged from the revival of Roman influence which characterised much twelfth-century intellectual life.

The first was the new emphasis which Salisbury placed upon the primacy of the 'res publica', a bonding term representing the commonly held ideals and interests of a people, which placed the common good above that of the particular.[76] The second development, intended to emphasise the role to be played by legitimate force facing the test of maintaining public order, was the prominence given by Salisbury to the army, a body under the control and command of the ruler, available

---

[74] See above, p. 172.   [75] Murrin, *History and warfare*, ch. 1.
[76] M. S. Kempshall, *The common good in late medieval political thought* (Oxford, 1999), 126.

to him as a means of securing and maintaining peace and order in his lands. Its role in society was to be an instrument of peace, a means to an end, not the end itself. It was this which gave significance to the process of selection of those who were to serve, a process which, following Vegetius, attributed less importance to birth and more to the physical and moral qualities which enabled certain individuals to submit successfully to the 'armorum disciplinam'. Society needed the best to ensure its protection.

Proposing an answer to the problem of public disorder in his day, Salisbury saw the reining in of the knightly class, the cause of much trouble, as the way towards a solution. If the poachers could be turned into gamekeepers, society would benefit. At the same time, he criticised errantry and the life of luxury among the knighthood of the day. His call was for a greater sense of responsibility among a privileged group in society.

As we saw above, the *De re militari* provided Salisbury with a text containing messages to support his own argument. Encouraged by Vegetius, he proposed a model which, over time, would lead to the creation of a military profession to be employed, under the command of the ruler, in the defence of the public good. Intended as a way of reducing conflicts between private forces, which weakened the central authority, the channelling of chivalric enthusiasm and energy into the creation of a royal army would seek the defence of the 'res publica' as a whole. As Guillaume le Breton's *Phillipidos* showed, the French crown was able to discipline the latent individualism and tendency towards separatism of much of the country's nobility to bring it into royal or public service, and make the king's cause, the achievement of peace and order under the crown, its own. The policy of war pursued by Philip II (Augustus) against the disruptive influence and ambitions of the feudal nobility and the Angevin empire was presented as having been aimed at stabilising the kingdom, a major step towards the establishment by the king of the crown's pre-eminent position within French society as a whole. In his account of the battle of Bouvines, le Breton, omitting references to individual heroism, emphasised the well-ordered army which fought as one, in close formation, each group knowing who its captain was, and using banners to identify units – practices recommended in the *De re militari*. He emphasised the king's successes as victory achieved by the royal army, fighting in the name of the organised 'state', over the 'proesce' and 'hardiesce' of its individual opponents, the country's dysfunctional aristocracy anxious to resist change and to preserve its independence, interests and privileges. 'Chevalerie' now really meant the king's armed hand (the language of Salisbury), the army acting on behalf of an increasingly powerful and effective monarchy.[77] In Spain, in the next century, the *Siete Partidas* would underline the same message: war was beneficial to society when it was fought under royal authority, which claimed the monopoly of the use of force, overseeing and legitimising its use.

In the process of being created on the basis of Vegetian ideas was the royal army, its *raison d'être* being the defence of the good of the king's subjects. Less paradoxically than it may have seemed, the new army was to be founded on a redirection of martial energies and the employment, in a public role, of the successors of the very lords and knights whose self-seeking use of violence had been the cause of social and political discord in earlier centuries, now incorporated into an army, commanded by the crown, with the aim of achieving social peace at home and the defeat of those with hostile intentions against the kingdom. The process would be a long one, taking several centuries to complete. Yet it marked the start of the attempt to link one of chivalry's leading characteristics, the sense of service, to the ideal, gained from a reading of classical authors, notably (in Salisbury's case) Vegetius, of a harmonious society whose protection was assured by the army in the royal service. This made those who constituted the army into servants of the common good, and of its wellbeing, which depended on them. Military service thus came to be regarded as an honourable activity, just as the *De re militari* had described it as the fulfilment of the highest responsibility to which a man might be called.

Thus, over the coming three centuries or so, service in the royal army, particularly if the king were leading it in person, became an honour to be aspired to, above all by the traditional chivalric element in society. And not among the chivalric alone. As the text of the *Siete Partidas* and several later writers emphasised, the service of society was something to which everyone might be called. It brought together nobles and knights, men whose lives exemplified the chivalric ethic, to fight in common cause alongside their less socially advantaged compatriots, for a good which they shared. Service in the army, led by the king, whose subjects they all were, provided the way they could do this together.

From the time of John of Salisbury onwards, Vegetius' teaching was used to emphasise the need for an army to fulfil a communal role which was essentially that of the defence of society, be it city state or kingdom. Boussard argued that in the course of the twelfth century the

---

[77] G. M. Spiegel, 'Moral imagination and the rise of the bureaucratic state: images of government in the *Chronique des rois de France*, Chantilly, MS 869', *Journal of Medieval and Renaissance studies*, 18 (1988), 157–73.

importance of individual valour was giving way to the 'collective valour' of soldiers, at this time still largely mercenaries.[78] Such developments were also reflected in the increasing realism found in some literature. Readers of Wolfram von Eschenbach's *Willehalm*, probably written in the years 1210–20, are struck by elements which have a Vegetian ring about them, in particular the writer's approach to the description of battle. By giving markedly less attention to the action of individuals, he showed that he was anti-heroic. What is more, he gave correspondingly greater attention to the groups of knights and to the dynamic of formations, showing that the organisation and control of collective, rather than individual, action by the commander, who was in the thick of the fighting and from whose perspective the battles were described, was more effective than individual deeds of prowess. Nor was von Eschenbach a lone case. A few years later, Rudolf von Ems, in both his *Willehalm von Orlens* and his *Alexander*, although allowing for individual action, would also place much emphasis on group combat carried out by well-disciplined and well-led forces trained in the art of fighting in the *mêlée*.[79]

While the doctrine of the *De re militari* lent weight to the argument in favour of creating a national army under the crown, there were aspects of military practice which emphasised certain important differences of attitude, particularly to the fighting of war, between chivalric traditions and those influenced by classical views, which we may term those advocated by military humanism. Any lasting development would require certain changes of attitude from the traditional chivalric class.

One difference concerned leadership or command. Members of the nobility felt themselves to be the natural leaders of any armed group, a view supported both by tradition and by the social system of the time. But their presumption would receive a knock from Vegetian doctrine, which was essentially that of authority founded on experience, not rank, an authority, moreover, which could not be assumed but had to be conferred by the king, or in his name, for it to be effective.

Furthermore, like everybody else, the chivalric class had had to submit to discipline. Since soldiers fought because they were, in effect, licensed to do so by the king, they had to obey his orders or those of his lieutenants. For some, more accustomed to giving orders than to receiving them,

---

[78] Boussard, 'Les mercenaires', 139.
[79] See Wolfram von Eschenbach, *Willehalm*, trans. M. E. Gibbs and S. M. Johnson (Harmondsworth, 1984), and M. H. Jones, 'The depiction of battle in Wolfram von Eschenbach's *Willehalm*', in *The ideals and practice of medieval knighthood II*, ed. C. Harper-Bill and R. Harvey (Woodbridge and Wolfeboro, 1988), 46–69. The importance of men having experience of fighting in teams and formations in peacetime is underlined in Vale, *Edward III and chivalry*, ch. 4.

this was a painful lesson to accept. Yet, at risk was the discipline, and hence the safety, of any force to which they belonged. In an army drawn from all groups in society, the nobility should learn to obey orders, just as others were expected to do. That it was 'solidarity founded upon common purpose and high morale' which brought victory was coming to be widely recognised at this time.[80]

Again, without seeking to create too great a distinction between the two traditions, it may be argued that the warning issued by Vegetius[81] that 'usus' ('skill', 'practice' or, better still, 'experience') was more effective in battle than 'vires' ('strength') would indicate that he was only too aware that, in every age and society, there are those who, honouring youth, energy and strength, had paid insufficient attention to the wisdom represented by thought, planning and experience (characteristics of the elder!) leading to considered action. This would be one of Vegetius' lasting contributions to military thinking and practice. It was well understood by those whose works we considered in the second part of this study, and was summed up by Alonso de Cartagena in his *Tratado de la guerra*: it should be recognised that in battle more is achieved by experience than by force ('Saber conviene que en la pelea más aprovecha uso que fuerza'). Had such advice been heeded, the outcomes of battles such as that of Crécy might have been different.[82]

Differences such as these may have needed a conscious change in some traditional chivalric attitudes. An attempt to bring about such a change regarding the fighting of war can be found in the *Chapelle des fleurs de lis*, written by Philippe de Vitri in the early 1330s. Vitri, a servant of the French crown, was familiar with Vegetius' work. It was almost certainly this which influenced his views and which saw him make two significant points: one, that chivalry was not a monopoly of nobility but could be practised by the whole people; secondly, since they were, in effect, responsible for the defence of the territorial state, those who carried it out should do so on a basis of knowledge and experience in order to be sure of success. It is evident that Vitri (and the same can be said of some who came after him) was struck by the intellectual approach of Vegetius' work, with its emphasis that victory depended as much (if not more) on thought as it did on spontaneity and bravery in action. For him, the considered and reasoned approach to war was the one most likely to lead to success. Those whose work was fighting should be sensible and

---

[80] A. Ayton, 'Arms, armour, and horses', in *Medieval warfare*, ed. Keen, 202.

[81] *DRM*, II, 23.

[82] *Tratados militares*, ed. Fallows, 452, no. 112. See also the editor's remarks on 'humanismo militar', sometimes at odds with chivalric tradition (36–7).

well informed for, 'in time of battle, reasoned action must have priority' ('ou temps de bataille/Mestier est que sens avant aille').[83]

Vitri might have been whistling for a wind. Within a few years, at Crécy (1346), the chivalry of France, ignoring the need for discipline in battle, fell before the order and the arrows of the English army; some of its members were even said to have turned and fled. The anger expressed by the author of the *Complainte sur la bataille de Poitiers*, written a decade later after a second major defeat at Poitiers, with its stinging criticisms of the nobility's failure, underlined its author's belief that the nobility had prime responsibility for the defence of the kingdom as a whole, a duty which, through its own failings, it had not fulfilled. To the writer, at least, it was clear where the blame for defeat lay. His criticism is of some interest, since it reveals a traditional outlook; the author could only think that responsibility for such a disaster must lie with the nobility, the kingdom's natural defenders against an exterior enemy. The idea was both chivalric and feudal. The critic did not appear to regard defence as an obligation of the community as a whole. It was taking time for the idea and, above all, for its practical implications, to take root.[84]

The *De re militari* had underlined that battle was to be joined only after all alternatives had been considered, and that it should be fought as the communal effort of an army. As we have seen, it took time for this idea to become a reality. Vegetius' emphasis on the corporate identity of the legion with its identifying banner, the use of uniforms which discouraged personal identification, and even the importance attributed to communal training of men as fighting units, sat a little uneasily with aspects of traditional chivalric mentality, which often showed a preference for a more spontaneous approach to conflict and to the role to be played by the individual.[85] At Crécy, moreoever, contrary to Vegetian urging, central direction on the French side of almost every aspect of the battle appears to have been lacking.

None the less, the opinions of Eustache Deschamps, expressed over a period of years, suggest that attitudes were changing. He could accept the importance of Vegetius and the 'clercs' ('intellectuals') of more recent

---

[83] Piaget, '"Le chapel des fleurs de lis"', 82–3.

[84] 'Complainte sur la bataille de Poitiers', ed. C. de Beaurepaire, *BEC*, 3rd ser., 2 (1851), 257–63.

[85] One is reminded of the remark made of the chronicler Froissart, that he had 'a curious ... absence of a clearly felt idea of change', a failing which he may have shared with those whose 'belles chevalleries' he continued to record (P. F. Dembowski, 'Chivalry, ideal and real, in the narrative poetry of Jean Froissart', *Medievalia et humanistica*, n.s. 14 (1986), 7, 9).

times. His description of du Guesclin as 'professional and successful in all your enterprises, a supreme man of war' ('Saige en voz fais et bien entreprenant /Souverain homme de guerre') was a recognition of the considered approach which the constable had shown to the king's wars. It was also an admission that du Guesclin was the leading soldier of his day in spite of the fact that he was not a member of the great nobility which, traditionally, had claimed the highest military positions in the land. We can observe Deschamps coming to accept these new realities and their implications. He would criticise those who went to war to win renown ('pour avoir renommée').[86] War was about service to the king (for only a sovereign could legitimately declare and wage a just war) and, because of this, it was regarded as service to the community. Chivalric values were all very well at the jousts, but in war reputation should be eschewed in favour of a more pragmatic, less individual, attitude to fighting, making a favourable outcome worth more than the individual glory which might have been won. This emphasis on service to the king and state was reflected in the channelling of traditional chivalric ideas along Vegetian lines in which service to the ruler, with obedience to the leaders appointed by him, was paramount. The man who served in a loyal and disciplined manner was being truly chivalric. The knight, Deschamps would write, should serve the king in his wars because the king represented the common good of France. Such wars were to be preferred to all other causes.[87]

The French monarchy, anxious to reassert its control of the army after a period of serious defeats and difficulties, was responsive to the need for change. The imposition of the crown's authority upon captains, ordered to act with a sense of public responsibility by exercising greater discipline over their men, would increase the monarchy's prestige in the eyes of its subjects. At the same time, by emphasising that private wars were contrary to the common good (as well as being a threat to the crown's authority), an attempt was being made to stress that only wars sanctioned by the crown and fought for the good of the people could be regarded as 'just' or lawful. These were wars in which it was an honour to die. Here we witness the crown trying to secure control of the use of legitimate force, as well as the right to decide when and against whom it should be directed, thus making a positive contribution to the practical development of the theory of the just war, or 'guerre publique'.[88]

---

[86] *Œuvres complètes de Eustache Deschamps*, ed. Queux de Saint-Hilaire (11 vols., Paris, 1878–1903), I, lxiv.
[87] *Ibid.* I, cliv. See Lassabatère, 'Théorie et éthique', 43–5.
[88] *Ordonnances*, IV, 67–70; II, 511–12; V, 144–5.

Recent critical commentary has emphasised the role played by the 'wider commitment to intellectual culture and didactic writing in France during the late Middle Ages', and the part played by intellectuals in 'applying and adapting the lessons and values of the Romans to specific circumstances affecting France'. Such lessons came through Latin texts; but we should not ignore the translations of Vegetius and Giles of Rome and, after 1372, of John of Salisbury into French, all to be found in the royal library by the end of the fourteenth century. In Italy, Roman influence would be exercised through the works of Giovanni da Legnano, Leonardo Bruni and, later, Machiavelli. By contrast, in England, a country not facing the problem of errant soldiery and its challenge to authority, the debate regarding war was rather different, neither owing so much to classical inspiration or models, nor being so practical in nature. Only when the country was divided by civil conflict in the mid-fifteenth century would the *De re militari* be adapted to create a work, *Knyghthode and bataile*, with a direct bearing upon the problems of contemporary society.[89]

In France, however, through the writings of such as Philippe de Mézières and Honoré Bouvet the theme of the legitimate use of force by the army – the new 'chevalerie' – was kept before the public. In his *Arbre des batailles* (*c*.1389), Bouvet drew upon a host of writers, including 'the doctrine of a doctor called Monseigneur Vegece, in his Book of Chivalry', to emphasise the need to accept the Roman virtues of discipline and organisation, obedience to the prince and his lieutenants, and the requirement, through regular training, for men to be ready to render military service in a fully professional manner.[90] These ideas would soon influence Christine de Pisan, whose *Livre du corps de policie* (*c*.1407) endorsed many of the ideas proposed by Bouvet. Influenced by the work of Vegetius, her work was primarily aimed at encouraging the nobility to become, in language reminiscent of John of Salisbury, the arms and the hands of the 'corps de policie', that is, of the commonalty itself.[91]

But the work went further, and was consequently more important than that, since it gave men a fresh understanding of what 'chevalerie' could mean. Since an army existed to protect society, the end of war (defeat of the enemy) became more significant than the means (such as notable

---

[89] See C. D. Taylor, 'English writings on chivalry and warfare during the Hundred Years War', in *Soldiers, nobles and gentlemen*, ed. Coss and Tyerman, 64–84. See above, pp. 139–47 (Machiavelli) and 187–93 (*Knyghthode and bataile*).

[90] *L'arbre des batailles*, IV, 9, p. 97; *Tree of battles*, p. 132; N. A. R. Wright, 'The *Tree of Battles* of Honoré Bouvet and the laws of war', in *War, literature and politics in the late Middle Ages*, ed. C. T. Allmand (Liverpool, 1976), 28.

[91] Pisan, *Corps de policie*, 125, 103.

actions by its members) by which it was achieved. The result was to place less emphasis upon physical action and more upon the achievement of the result desired. So the virtues of prudence (the wise application of knowledge to a specific end) and foresight (making the best use of experience) came to be seen as contributing more towards the achievement of the desired end than did physical action, however remarkable. In his later years, Charles V found it impossible to take part in military action. Forced to defend him against accusations of cowardice, Christine explained that he won victories by acting 'sagement et prudement', thus showing that 'chevalerie' (war) was both an intellectual and a physical endeavour: 'war carried out through reasoned action is more effective and worthy of praise than that relying on the use of arms', she reported Vegetius as having written ('car dit Vegece que plus doit estre louée chevalerie menée à cause de sens que celle qui est conduitte par effett d'armes').[92]

Likewise, by portraying the king as a shepherd who had the good of his subjects at heart, Christine portrayed successful defence of their interests as an essential part of good government which any ruler owed to his people.[93] 'Chevalerie', therefore, was closely linked to good government, since it was action motivated by the desire to work towards the general benefit of society, whose achievement it was a ruler's duty to seek to bring about. She further emphasised that if an ambititon could be satisfied by negotiation rather than by conflict, then so much the better. War was a last resort; negotiation saved lives, which might otherwise have been lost. All too aware of the propensities for independent action shown by generations of French nobility, Christine emphasised that, above all in war, it was necessary to act according to what was reasonable ('o[e]uvrer par art de raison'). Finally, she wrote, the enemy should not be attacked unless there were real need for it ('autrement ne doit estre fait se necessité n'y contraint'). It was obvious whom she was addressing.[94]

In the *Quadrilogue invectif*, written as a round-table discussion on how France should confront disaster at the moment when French fortunes in the war against England were reaching rock bottom, Alain Chartier directed many of his criticisms of the current state of the country at the

---

[92] Pisan, *Charles V*, I, 132–3; D. Delogu, 'Reinventing the ideal sovereign in Christine de Pizan's *Livre des fais et bonnes meurs du sage roy Charles V*', *Medievalia et humanistica*, n.s. 31 (n.d.), 48.

[93] Delogu, 'Reinventing the ideal sovereign', 49.

[94] Pisan, *Charles V*, I, 125–7. See the opinion of Geoffroy de Charny, a defender of traditional 'chivalric' values, who could criticise those who did 'not consider the benefit or advantage for their friends or the harm done to their enemies, but, without giving or taking advice, they spur forward in a disorderly way and perform personally many feats of arms' (*The Book of Chivalry of Geoffroi de Charny. Text, context and translation*, ed. and trans. R. W. Kaeuper and E. Kennedy (Philadelphia, 1996), 151).

nobility, who regarded war as a means of self-advantage rather than as the defence of the fatherland ('commun salut du pays de vostre nativité').[95] All should be ready to fight (here he cited an example taken from the *De re militari*) since the profession of arms was 'treshonnourable'.[96] Chartier had two further points to emphasise. A strong supporter of the monarchy and its rights, he repeatedly stressed the need for loyalty to the king; those who failed to show it were, he argued, causing 'le bien publique' and the honour of the crown (clearly linked in his eyes) to suffer.[97] What was required at a time when everyone wanted to lead (a further swipe at some over-ambitious nobility) was for authority and command to be taken into the hands of a single person, a move which would bring great benefits to the 'utilité publique'.[98] It is clear that Chartier was anxious to unite the efforts of many and put them under the control of the king, whose army they would then constitute. To regard war simply in terms of an 'aventure' was bound to lead to failure. What all Frenchmen had to do was to rally behind the king, obey his orders, or those issued by commanders appointed by him, and then do their duty. This would be true chivalry in action.

Jean Juvénal des Ursins was of like mind. Obedience to the king, he argued, was paramount. If this could be achieved, the king could create a force consisting of those already 'of the profession' ('du mestier') and new recruits who would be trained in the necessary skills, although he admitted that those of knightly background would have had more experience in the use of arms. Captains ready to act on the king's behalf were also needed; these should be selected for their experience rather than their birth, so that great care was to be given to choosing only the best.[99]

By the time that Jean Juvénal wrote (in 1452) King Charles VII (1422–61) had set about creating a new royal army based on military experience and on obedience to the king. Properly structured, its members were to be regularly mustered for inspection by royal marshals. The process, begun in 1439, was advanced over the next few years with the establishment of a corps of archers, drawn from every parish in the kingdom, each one personally selected and, in return for regular training and answering the king's summons, exempted from the 'taille' and the obligation of watch ('guet'). Significantly, the king also recruited considerable numbers of nobles to replace the foreign troops who had been relied upon

---

[95] *Quadrilogue invectif*, 53, 11.   [96] *Ibid.* 55.
[97] *Ibid.* 6, 14, 30, 53.   [98] *Ibid.* 56, 54.
[99] Much the same advice can be found in the anonymous tract *Débats et appointements*, written in the reign of Charles VII. See '*L'honneur de la couronne de France*', ed. N. Pons (SHF, Paris, 1990), 76–9.

in the past. Paid regularly, these men came to form the 'grande ordonnance', consisting mainly of nobles who, with many facing difficult financial circumstances, welcomed the opportunity to serve the king and be
rewarded financially for the privilege. In the coming years thousands of
nobles found military careers in the royal service, sometimes lasting some
twenty years in the same company, following the system of promotion
which had been set up, thus ensuring that only the best reached the top
of the military tree. As inscriptions on their tombstones would indicate,
these men now regarded themselves as members of a profession. France
had witnessed the military caste become the military profession. John of
Salisbury had been justified.[100]

At much the same time, Jean de Bueil reflected with greater subtlety
the tensions motivated by those (of knightly standing) who fought mainly
for honour and those (the more humble) whose aim was the defence of
the common good.[101] An admirer of military skills, Bueil wondered what
was the best use to be made of them. Certainly not for the advancement of
personal reputation, he wrote, as he proceeded to subordinate the values
of chivalry to those of the state. If there was satisfaction to be gained
from the skilful use of arms, it must surely be that it was employed in the
defence of the common good. He had little sympathy for those who risked
death in search of vainglory, while failing to make themselves available to
fight in the king's service should their help be required. In this conflict of
attitudes, it is clear where Bueil's sympathies lay. As he was to state time
and again, the soldier's function was a public one, to provide a service
to society; in this, the importance of the collective, co-ordinated effort
could not be underestimated.[102]

The statist army

It was the prime obligation of the medieval ruler to provide peace for those
whom he governed. War entered the picture as one of the ways by which
that state might be achieved and maintained. War and peace became inex-
tricably linked, all the more so by those familiar with Vegetius' famous
dictum that a readiness to make war was the way to peace.[103] Vegetius

---

[100] Contamine, *Histoire militaire de la France*, 201–4, 220–1; *Guerre, état et société*, pls. 9,
11, 13.
[101] D. Potter, 'Chivalry and professionalism in French armies of the Renaissance', in *The
chivalric ethos and the development of military professionalism*, ed. D. J. B. Trim (Leiden
and Boston, 2003), 158.
[102] *Jouvencel*, II, 100; Allmand, 'Entre honneur et bien commun', 474; Vale, *War and
chivalry*, 170.
[103] *DRM*, III, Praef.

hoped that a society clearly prepared to fight in defence of itself, its interests and its freedoms might prove sufficient of a deterrent to make a potential aggressor think twice before attacking.[104] Who was to provide that deterrence?

The answer lay in a word: the ruler. By the end of the thirteenth century, at the latest, kings such as Alfonso X of Castile and his brother-in-law, Edward I of England, would assume command and lead their people to war. Historians have noted that it was at this time that notable changes took place in military organisation which pointed towards an appreciation of the army's function in increasingly statist terms, as these states developed their individuality and particular interests. In the *De regimine principum* (*c.*1277), Giles of Rome offered the intellectual world an important definition of what an army, or military service, represented. His description of them as 'a certain type of prudence'[105] might sound more like the language of the philosopher (or that of the life insurance broker) than that of the soldier. Yet, it reflected Vegetius' view of war fought with 'prudentia', that is, with forethought and foresight. Giles also conveyed the important view, derived from Vegetius, that, for a ruler/state, command of an army was a form of 'investment' whose 'return' would come in the form of the 'peace dividend' its presence might encourage. It is clear that Giles saw the army as a society's means of defence against those intent upon threatening its peace. In that respect, an army was a manifestation of 'prudentia'.

As described in the *De re militari*, the army existed to protect and defend the good of the 'res publica'. In the western tradition, much influenced by Roman ideas and practices, the link between the army and the defence of a society's citizens, their persons, property and freedoms (the 'bonum commune') seems clear enough. In this process, a leading role was played by the law. But the law could not achieve this on its own.[106] The fighting of war came to be regarded 'as a species of legal activity and, conversely, of legal action carried on through military means'.[107] The use of force might be needed to maintain order in a society facing the adverse effects of

---

[104] *Ibid.* I, 7; III, 10; IV, 9.   [105] *DRP*, III, iii, 1: p. 555.

[106] On this see A. Harding, *Medieval law and the foundations of the state* (Oxford, 2002). Giles of Rome emphasised how the law and the 'militia' had complementary roles in defending the common good (*DRP*, III, iii, 1). See also Whetham, *Just wars and moral victories*, ch. III.

[107] S. Morillo, 'The sword of justice: war and state formation in comparative perspective', *JMMH*, 4 (2006), 1–12. In a not dissimilar way, the duel was originally regarded as a way of resolving disputes with the use of arms, but in a formal and disciplined manner which protected the interests of both the duellists and the common good. This was a further example of the way in which 'authority', as it strove towards a monopoly of the use of violence, encouraged the use of a semi-juridical ritual to resolve disputes which might otherwise have caused harm to the general welfare (Hughes, 'Soldiers and gentlemen', 100, 115, 118, 122).

social disruption or attack from outside. Coercion, too, might be needed to make good a claim to territory unjustly withheld. In such conditions, granted that it acted in the name of the general good, the army was subject to the directive power of the state, personified in the ruler, whose authority was assumed to be legitimate.

While using the law to extend the authority of the state in protecting the common good, rulers also encouraged the idea that the coercive power of an army should become available to them, as a monopoly. At about the same time the theory of the 'just' war was being developed, giving sovereign rulers effective control over the right to declare war against a named enemy, and to initiate the use of force which could be used only in support of a 'just' cause intended to bring benefit to the common good. Rulers thus acquired the right to decide when and against whom war should be fought. The need to have command over an army to fight those wars followed logically. Exercising the army's power in the service of the common good, princes came to assume greater authority, both political and military. Gradually, there grew up a view of the army as an institution which, like the law, was being developed to help create strong central authority to the detriment of local power and jurisdiction. The political implications of the developing view of the army in society, and of its contribution to the growth of monarchical power in particular, were there for all to note.

We may ask how Vegetius' readers responded to his ideas on the place and function of the army in the body politic. It may surprise some how many manuscripts have the simple statement or question, 'What is an army?' ('Quid est exercitus') written in the margin at the point where Vegetius had defined the army as 'the name for a host of legions, "auxilia" and cavalry gathered together for the purpose of waging war'.[108] The comment appears to reflect an awareness of something new among readers interested in what Vegetius understood the function and purpose of the army in society to be, and how that understanding might be applied to their own, later, set of circumstances. Vegetius was emphasising a function for the army which was essentially defensive. It could be the instrument of a royal response to rebellion or dissent when, as the servant of the 'res publica', it fulfilled its Vegetian role as maintainer of order against internal division, as, for instance, it did in France under King Philip II.[109] Such was the view of an army's *raison d'être* which met the requirements of the medieval world as, influenced by Aristotelian ideas, it grew into a community of increasingly independent states and principalities. At the same time it emphasised the role accorded by

[108] *DRM*, III, 1.   [109] See above, pp. 92–6.

Vegetius to the soldier, depicting him as a public servant, responsible for defending a people against the forces of disorder.[110]

Painting a very positive picture of both the army and of those (the 'milites') who formed it, Vegetius placed the army high on the list of what the successful state should possess. In a number of passages he extolled the army as the state's prime agent of security: 'There is nothing more stable or more fortunate or admirable than a State which has copious supplies of soldiers who are trained.' Peace cannot be bought, he went on: 'our enemies . . . are kept down solely by fear of our arms'. 'There is no secure possession of wealth', he would declare later, 'unless it is maintained by defence of arms.'[111] Society depended upon its army for its security. 'Who can doubt that the art of war comes before everything else when it preserves our liberty and prestige, extends the provinces and saves the Empire?'[112] It should be noted, however, that Vegetius emphasised the need for the army to 'fight with strategy, not at random' ('aventure'), and that this would not be an army which relied on numerical superiority. He was recommending the creation and development of a trained, well-motivated force, drawn from the community, which, under experienced leaders appointed by the emperor and paid from public funds, would exist to defend the state, its freedoms and its interests.[113]

Other factors tell us that, following Roman tradition, Vegetius regarded the army as an instrument of the state, and the waging of war as its prerogative and monopoly. In the Christian tradition of western Europe, at least, war was regarded as an acceptable activity as long as it was carried out for the purpose of maintaining order, a task associated with the state. Thus war was seen as a means of imposing and maintaining order and the rule of law, in circumstances where disorder reigned. In this view, war was complementary to law, the guarantor of the rules by which society was regulated in a state of peace. But there were always those who wished to act contrary to those laws, undermining that peace. So when Vegetius wrote that he who desired peace should prepare for war, his statement was not as paradoxical as it might appear. In any society, force and coercion might be required to maintain order so as to give the law its chance. This view assumed the existence of a power (the state) whose legitimacy was based upon its ability to maintain its very existence, including defence of its territory against external attack, if necessary through the use of force. Law and the ability to make war were thus seen as partners in the ambitious task of bringing peace to society. For this reason, therefore,

---

[110] Allmand, 'Changing views of the soldier', 171–88; Mallett, *Mercenaries and their masters*, ch. 8.
[111] *DRM*, I, 13; III, 13.   [112] *Ibid*. III, 10.   [113] *Ibid*. II, 20, 24; IV, 9.

the waging of war was not an option open to all, however strong they might be. As the *De re militari* made abundantly clear, what Vegetius had to say about the right to make war must be seen within an intellectual context first expressed by Augustine and then, centuries later, by the neo-Aristotelians in the thirteenth century. This taught that war could be legitimately waged only under certain conditions, namely that it was declared by a sovereign ruler (the successor to the Roman emperor), that its cause was just, and that it was fought with proper intention. It was this thinking which led to the creation of national armies, ready to defend the interests of states through military means, all the while subject to their rulers' command and leadership.

So, just as the common law was an instrument intended to create justice and harmony in society, so an army, recruited from the community and placed under the command of the ruler, came to be seen as an institution whose *raison d'être* was the defence of that law. Literary critics have seen in the *Willehalm von Orlens* of Rudolf von Ems an attempt to present the fighting of wars by the army, along with the maintenance of justice and peace, as an expression of a ruler's power and authority. While war was often regarded as socially disruptive, it was also (perhaps paradoxically) the means by which the stability of the social order could be restored.[114] If men wanted to encourage their societies to develop in peace and stability, they should be willing to see armies emerge as the means, available to rulers, of countering those wishing to use force in the pursuit of individual ambition. In this way local conflict, or 'guerre privée', might be outlawed. So it was that, from the late thirteenth century onwards, men witnessed the beginnings of a long process which saw wars increasingly fought by statist armies under the command of kings and princes.

We may note further factors which encouraged the development of such armies: money, derived from state taxation, used to remunerate soldiers at regular, agreed rates; the growth in the practice of providing weapons and other equipment, often collected in advance in national armouries such as the Tower of London (England) and the Louvre (France); and the growing practice of soldiers wearing distinctive national symbols or other uniforms provided for them.[115] Significant, too, was the recognition of the crown's financial responsibility for horses, valued before a campaign, enabling their owners to receive compensation in the case of their animals' death on royal service; and the similar

---

[114] W. H. Jackson, 'Warfare in the works of Rudolf von Ems', in *Writing war*, eds. Saunders, Le Saux and Thomas, 56–7, 70.

[115] Walter de Milemete insisted that the king should provide food and dress for his soldiers (Nederman (ed.), *Political thought*, 49).

compensation paid in England, by the mid-fourteenth century, to ship owners who lost vessels serving the crown in war at sea.

A third factor in the creation of a Vegetian-type state army was the development of a designated authority and organisation to support it. Vegetius had insisted on the need to ensure that the logistical aspects of warfare be properly carried out; wars were lost by those who ignored this advice, and armies could be starved into submission.[116] But he also recognised that such problems could not be resolved unless the army were administered centrally through a proper chain of organisation and command. Historical developments in Burgundy under Charles the Bold showed what could be done. In Venice, the setting up of the means of purchasing and storing food ahead of a campaigns, and the appointment, by the Venetian state, of officers whose specific task was to maintain links between the state and the captains who led the troops, paid from public funds, are good examples of the way that the demands of war, increasingly controlled from the centre, were fulfilled by the establishment of new institutions intended to meet the growing administrative requirements of war, as these had been outlined by Vegetius.

Consideration of surviving manuscripts of the *De re militari* suggests that interest in the development of contemporary armies was at its height in the fourteenth and fifteenth centuries: no surprise here. Several texts have marginalia noting Vegetius' assertion that a state with many soldiers was a happy state, for soldiers existed to keep the enemy from attacking.[117] 'O glorious soldiers of those days' ('O milites gloriosi horum temporum'), wrote one reader perhaps carried away by his enthusiasm for things Roman, as he imagined them to have been in an idealised past.[118] Whether this reader understood the implication for his own time of what Vegetius had written remains hidden from us. None the less he appears to have grasped the significance of the contribution which the army could make towards ensuring peace in society. As the author of *Knyghthode and bataile* emphasised: 'Seyde ofte it is: the wepon bodeth peax.'[119]

Another passage, Book II, chapter 24, was also seen as important. Emphasising the rational use of preparation and training, both essential for success in war, Vegetius stressed how necessary this was for 'the soldier by whose hands the State must be preserved'; for he was the man who 'must fight for his own life (which he must be ready to sacrifice for the common good) and for the liberty of all'.[120] How else could he give the best account of himself if he did not prepare through constant

---

[116] *DRM*, III, 3, 9.   [117] *Ibid*. I, 13.   [118] Vatican, Ottob. lat. 1964, fo. 17v.
[119] *Knyghthode and bataile*, line 1692.   [120] *DRM*, II, 24.

training and practice? One reader thought this so important that he put a line down the margin of the entire chapter,[121] whilst many others drew attention to the short passage which emphasised that liberty might be assured through the employment of soldiers. It may be no coincidence that the majority of these manuscripts are probably of Italian origin? We may be noticing the comments of men living on the peninsula who were hoping for deliverance from one form of domination or another, imperial, papal or, in the case of Florence, Milanese. Regrettably, the copy of the *De re militari* which probably belonged to Coluccio Salutati, chancellor of Florence about 1400,[122] bears no comments on the passages we have been considering. Yet points raised by Vegetius may have had a very contemporary feel for other readers in Italy at this period. In the light of developments which occurred in Venice and elsewhere in the fourteenth and fifteenth centuries, it is perhaps not surprising that Italian readers (in particular) should have reacted most readily to many of the passages in the *De re militari*.

But Vegetian ideas may also have had some, although less easily defin-able, influence in areas of Europe outside Italy. In England, the twelfth century had already witnessed advances in thinking about military admin-istration, organisation and practice. In 1181, King Henry II had issued the Assize of Arms, outlining the equipment all free men were expected to possess according to a sliding social scale, and demanding from them an oath 'to bear . . . arms in his service according to his command and out of loyalty to the king and his kingdom', an oath which bears a marked resemblance to that taken by the new 'miles' as described in the *De re militari*.[123] While it has been argued that no military threat demanded such a response in 1181, it is likely that some were thinking that an armed force, with at least some rudiment of training, constituted to answer the king's call in time of danger, would be an advantage in any future emer-gency. In 1205, when levying a force to defend the kingdom, King John emphasised that those serving in it should be prepared to go wherever they were ordered by the crown, and be ready to act in defence of the kingdom, in particular against any who might invade it.[124] In 1278, with the writ for distraint of knighthood, Edward I tried to impose a yet greater sense of obligation upon those who could afford to serve the community in a military capacity, while in 1285 the Statute of Winchester brought up to date the regulations concerning military equipment to be owned

---

[121] Naples, Naz. V. A. 22, fo. 21–21v.   [122] Bologna, Com. A. 146.
[123] 'secundum praeceptum suum et ad fidem domini Regis et regni sui' (Stubbs, *Select charters*, 183); DRM, II, 5; Prestwich, *Armies and warfare*, 75, 121.
[124] Stubbs, *Select charters*, 276.

by free men, although nothing was said about the practice and training which the effective use of these arms required.[125]

In these pieces of royal legislation we appear to witness an attempt to bring to life a sense of communal responsibility working for the good of the entire community under the lead and command of the king in a manner which, *mutatis mutandis*, took Vegetian recommendations into account. To the nobleman, the joust and the tournament constituted socially acceptable ways of training in the use of knightly weapons. For the lesser born, whose weapon was usually the bow, the need to practise was no less important, as the statutes of Henry II and Edward I demonstrate. On 1 June 1363, in a period of truce in the war against the French, Edward III once again set out England's need of trained archers, who had in the past played so important a role in English successes. In recent times, however, training had been almost completely ignored in favour of vain games such as handball, football and cock-fighting, and the supply of practised archers was running out. In future every encouragement should be given to all able-bodied men to practise with bows and arrows, crossbows and bolts at the butts on all holidays, so that vital skills should not be lost. To encourage action, the games referred to (and others) were forbidden, under threat of imprisonment should regulations be ignored. A century or so later William Worcester, bemoaning the fact that the English nobility were abandoning the practice of war for other activities, underlined his plea for more active participation in warlike practices by remarking that 'if the vaillaunt Romayns had suffred theire sonnes to mysspende theire tyme in suche singuler practik... they had not conquered twyes Cartage ayenst alle the Affricans',[126] a comment strongly Vegetian in tone.

In Castile, the military system introduced by the *Siete Partidas* of Alfonso X also emphasised the obligation of the subject to serve his ruler in time of war. Since king and people were mystically one, the obligation of defence was seen as mutual: the people must defend their king, while the king had a duty to defend them.[127] All must therefore be ready to join the army at any time to defend the 'res publica'.[128] The reiteration of such ideas, however traditional, in the formality of a 'partida' (accorded the force of law by King Alfonso XI in 1348) lent weight to the orders of a ruler very conscious of communal responsibility, and of the need to translate the principle into action. In the first half of the

---

[125] *Ibid.* 448–9, 463–9.   [126] *Boke of noblesse*, 78.
[127] *SP*, II, xix, 3; L. R. García, 'Types of armies: early modern Spain', in *War and competition between states*, ed. P. Contamine (Oxford, 2000), 43.
[128] *SP*, II, xix, 4–8.

fourteenth century Alfonso XI introduced developments which considerably increased the effective authority of the crown in military matters. Noting a certain apathy for military service, he set about re-animating those who might serve. As the creation of chivalric orders in France and England was intended to do, the founding of the Order of the Band in 1332 was aimed at linking those elected to membership of it in loyal service to the crown. The greater use of the 'soldadas' system, which in a similar fashion bound those who made agreements regarding military service in return for money (the system resembled the English indenture and the French 'lettre de retenue'), was to be observed during this reign. The system lasted well, providing the basis upon which much of the army which conquered Granada in 1492 would be raised. By thus acknowledging with honour or money (or both) those who pledged it their military support, the crown was indirectly assuming greater control over them, and their standards of recruitment and preparedness, as well as over the quality of arms used by those in the royal service. It was in the common interest that this should be done.[129]

Increased intervention by the crown in the army's affairs can be seen in the appointment of a constable and a marshal (on the French model) in 1382. However, it was the period of war between 1481 and 1492 which would really lay the foundations of the Spanish army which earned such a reputation in the Italian wars of the early sixteenth century. The developments of the fourteenth century were built upon. As the crown grew stronger and the feudal nobility became progressively weaker, both politically and militarily, so the army came ever more under royal influence, its leaders being appointed by the king and made responsible to him, while taxation raised through an increasingly efficient fiscal system paid for the development of artillery, which played a significant part in Spanish successes against the Moors. In 1492 the Catholic Monarchs set out special training programmes to be followed in times of peace. In this way a national army, raised by the crown and, under King Ferdinand, led by the king himself, came to be employed for national purposes.

In Italy, the career of Francesco Sforza, duke of Milan, showed how the ambitions of the fourteenth-century *condottieri* had been tamed and civilised. The tendency was progressively towards armies founded on extended periods of service (contracts between states and *condottieri* were made for longer and longer periods as some states grew in both size and prosperity, which led them to demand greater security), while professional captains, often former *condottieri*, were made responsible for

---

[129] N. Agrait, 'Castilian military reform under the reign of Alfonso XI', *JMMH*, 3 (2005), 88–126.

training and disciplining the soldiers who served under them. Greater uniformity of company strength was to be found in different parts of the peninsula. Leaders, however, were chosen essentially from the nobility; there was little concession to leadership based on merit such as could be found elsewhere in Europe. However, the move to greater permanence had institutional implications. It helped develop loyalty both to employers (the state) and to the captains whom they appointed; the group could only benefit from the coherence which such loyalty encouraged. Captains, too, gained experience in various aspects of leadership, such as planning and organisation, and in the maintenance of morale. States were obliged to develop administrative systems to provide and distribute arms and money, and to train the personnel who had direct contact with the captains whom they employed, and to act as their paymasters. The need to provide billeting led to officials being appointed to organise this on a regular basis. From such emerged centrally controlled administrators ('collaterali') who, in Venice, formed the vital link between the state and the soldiery.[130]

In Venice, accustomed to the threat of mercenaries and the need to defend interests overseas, the tradition of military training by individuals was of long standing, stretching back into the thirteenth century. The employment of masters to conduct training in archery, the setting up of targets in the city's squares, the encouragement given to competitions, at which prizes were offered, to develop interest and enthusiasm in the use of arms, all helped to produce archers ready to fight on both land and sea. By the end of the fifteenth century, with the decline in the practical influence of the bow and the rise in that of the handgun, similar, more centrally controlled training sessions (with even the occasional manoeuvre) were organised. The Venetian armed forces were being developed through both training, greater continuity among the commanders, and the more active participation of the state in the equipping of those who fought for Venetian interests.[131]

The Venetian state was conscious of the need for civilian organisation to make the most of its military potential. Surprisingly, as in France, it was not until the fifteenth century was well advanced that centralised control of the training of soldiers was effectively introduced. Until then *condottieri* had been responsible for training men serving under them. As we know, Vegetius had strongly underlined the need for formal training; it may have been that it needed the example provided by a work such as that

---

[130] M. Mallett, 'Condottieri and captains in Renaissance Italy', in *The chivalric ethos*, ed. Trim, 72, 74, 80, 86.

[131] Mallett and Hale, *Military organization*, 142, 202–3.

of Aelian, published in 1487, to show how this should be done. Training, when it came, took on different forms: parades encouraged men to keep rank, besides helping the mustering and inspection of troops; jousting and tilting developed certain fighting skills, while competitions inspired practice in the use of the crossbow. By the 1490s manoeuvres and regular military exercises were being introduced, and these, too, increased in the early sixteenth century. By then, formal instruction was given to handgunners, who also took part in competitions, while in 1500 those wishing to be employed by the state had to seek training at the Scuola dei Bombardieri, of which they became members. In the coming years more and more gunners were to graduate in their art at this school.[132]

In fifteenth-century Germany some saw the future of a peaceful empire lying in the hands of an imperial army. Nicholas of Cusa, whose *De concordantia catholica* was written in 1433 and to whom Vegetius was no stranger, harked back to the golden, Saxon age when the emperor had commanded a paid army to defend the peace, an army which enabled him to act as 'defender of the fatherland, maintainer of liberty, reliever of the oppressed and most inflexible pursuer of the disturbers of the common good' ('defensor patriae, conservator libertatis, relevator oppressorum [et] rigidissimus exsecutor in rei publicae turbatores').[133] In Cusa's time, by contrast, things were very different. Militarily weak, Germany was a divided country requiring strong central authority to restore order. The emperor must be allowed effective means of coercion in support of the law; otherwise there would be neither peace nor order nor justice. The coercion should be provided by a professional army. To this end Cusa advocated the revival of a single, public army under imperial control to defend all Germans, a system which had the added advantage of being cheaper than the maintenance of a number of separate armies defending local interests, significantly described as 'tyrannies' to be eliminated 'per publicum exercitum'. In the prevailing historical and political situation, however, such a search for public order and effective methods of state building was none the less utopian in character. While a programme based on such ideas, backed by the proposal to raise a 'General Penny' ('gemeine Pfennig') to help pay for it, was proposed by the Elector of Mainz at the Diet of Worms in 1495, the scheme failed. Unlike in neighbouring France, no imperial standing army, such as Cusa had envisaged it, ever materialised.

---

[132] *Ibid.* 142, 85–6.
[133] M. Watanabe, *The political ideas of Nicholas of Cusa, with special reference to his* De concordantia catholica (Geneva, 1963), 136, n. 1, citing *De concordantia*, III, xxviii, 495.

Special attention should be given to France, where the development of a centralised army has been closely followed by historians. That development was not based on military factors alone, but was linked to two others. One was the growing understanding given to the political and social implications of the term 'res publica', increasingly rendered as 'bien publique'. The second consisted of the effects which the growth of the army could have upon the enhancement of the monarchy's power and position in society. This would centre upon the achievement of a royal monopoly of the use of force, greatly reducing the effects of private war upon society, while enhancing the crown's prestige as a harbinger of peace and order. Here the interests of crown and people would be shown to coincide.

What might undermine that effort? As in England under Stephen, so in France at the end of the twelfth century it was knightly power that posed a threat to the effectiveness of the royal authority. The Church, too, saw the need to control the consequences of potential disorder through the responsible use of legitimate force, a fact which may have constituted a further reason for clerical interest in the *De re militari*. This had an effect in France in the reign of King Louis VI (1108–37) and, above all, in that of Philip II (Augustus) (1180–1223). The first pursued a struggle for control of a wide area around Paris with the knightly castellans of castles who threatened the effectiveness of the royal authority. The second went further still, challenging those members of the highest aristocracy and even the king of England himself, all regarded as opposing the powers of an expanding monarchical state.[134] It was an army slowly becoming more organised which made possible the advances of the Capetian monarchy's powers under these two outstanding kings.[135]

The importance of military power was to be underlined by Giles of Rome. The impact made by his work enabled Vegetius' message to be more widely appreciated; it is hardly a coincidence that Jean de Meun's translation of the *De re militari* should have appeared at almost the same time. The intellectual climate, given strong impetus by the Aristotelian/Thomist revolution, would draw attention to the developing independent state, with its obligation, as Aristotle had taught, of ensuring the defence of its people.[136] Indeed, during the reign of Philip IV (1285–1314) the obligation of the crown to seek the public good through the banning of private wars received considerable emphasis.[137] How should

---

[134] Spiegel, 'Moral imagination', 170–3. See the section above on Guillaume le Breton.
[135] P. Contamine, 'L'armée de Philippe Auguste', in *La France de Philippe Auguste. Le temps des mutations*, ed. R.-H. Bautier (Paris, 1982), 577–93.
[136] *Politics*, IV, iv, 1291a.   [137] *Ordonnances*, I, 328–9, 376.

that responsibility be fulfilled, and by whom? Was it the task of the nobility who, as vassals of the crown, felt a personal obligation to their lord, to take a major step forward and assume the defence of a territorially defined state as well? Their record of service was mixed, with little continuity between campaigns.[138] Or should the king use the *arrière-ban*, the general obligation to serve (perhaps the more Vegetian view) to meet the country's military needs, but in so doing appear to be releasing the nobility from its historic responsibility?[139]

It was at this time that, in England, Castile and France, control of military affairs by the crown came to be increased. It was in France, however, that the most notable and large-scale development of a state-led army would be found. By the mid-fourteenth century, reforms reflecting recognisable echoes of Vegetian thought were being set in motion. The ordinance issued by John II in April 1351 proclaimed the crown's intention of bringing the army under its control. Captains were to act with a sense of public responsibility, in particular in the way that they exercised discipline over the men in their companies, whose sizes were to be regulated according to their captains' importance.[140] A sense of value for money was to be introduced: men must fulfil the service and tour of duty for which they were paid; absences would be carefully regulated, and desertion punished. The spirit of the *De re militari* hovered over these reforms, and the ideas upon which they were based. In December 1352 the king proclaimed that all royal wars were the concern of the people as a whole, in whichever part of France they lived; by contrast (it was implied) all locally based private wars militated against the collective good of the kingdom and the 'res publica'.[141]

In promulgating these ordinances French kings were trying to achieve several things, which amounted to an attempt to secure firm control over the army. First and foremost, the ordinances demonstrated the will to impose the authority of the crown upon captains and members of companies now required to banish private feuds, a step towards state control which would increase both the monarchy's power and its prestige in the sight of its people. The crown was assuming charge of the use of legitimate force, as well as the right to decide when and against whom it might

---

[138] J. R. Strayer, 'Defense of the realm amd royal power in France', in *Studi in onore di Gino Lazatto* (4 vols., Milan, 1949), IV, 289–96; Strayer, *The reign of Philip the Fair* (Princeton, 1980), 374.
[139] Housley, 'European warfare', 131.
[140] *Ordonnances*, IV, 67–70; Bessey, *Construire l'armée française*, 63–7.
[141] *Ordonnances*, II, 511. The matter had already been the subject of royal ordinances in 1296 and 1331 (*ibid*. I, 328–9, 492; II, 61–2), and would be again in 1361 when such acts of independence were presented as a denial of the crown's right to negotiate and make terms on behalf of the kingdom as a whole (*ibid*. III, 525–7).

be directed. At the same time it was making a positive contribution to the practical development of the theory of the just war by, in effect, claiming that only wars sanctioned by the crown and, again by implication, fought for the common good could be regarded as legitimate. These reforms show clearly that the idea of the army as the force available to the state was gaining ground.[142]

Reforms notwithstanding, with the death of Charles V in 1380 the French army began to slip back into its old ways, individual captains taking over again to the detriment of the 'res publica'. The outcome would be defeat and years of occupation by the English. Much effort was spent by men, many with access to royal court circles, in setting out their views on how France could recover from the setbacks suffered at English hands. Broadly speaking, the advice given was to concentrate on an increasingly centralised and royal military organisation which would give the crown authority to assert itself against those wishing to weaken its position in society. To such, reference to Vegetius was a lifeline. He had, after all, written of the need to act, under the lead of the emperor, for the common good. Rather than be satisfied with actions which brought only passing glory, men should concentrate on doing things, such as helping to preserve the 'res publica', whose effects could be long-lasting.[143]

Writing in 1420 in language which suggested knowledge of the *De re militari*, II, 5, Robert Blondel set out what he saw as being the task of the soldier at a time when his country ('patria') was occupied by the enemy. It was his duty to defend that country by refusing to desert and being ready to die without fear for its good.[144] In his *Quadrilogue invectif*, written two years later, Alain Chartier elaborated upon the theme.[145] His stated willingness to lay down life and limb for the common good was a vigorous critique of those who failed in their obligation towards their country and the good of their natural lord, the king.[146] Frenchmen should follow the example of the Romans, who erected memorials to those who had fought for the good of the state.[147] At this point Chartier recalled the story, correctly said to have been cited by Vegetius, of the Roman matrons who had cut their hair to provide ropes for the engines of war required when the Capitol was under siege.[148] Such was the example which Chartier wanted true Frenchmen to follow.

---

[142] García, 'Types of armies', 37.   [143] *DRM*, I, Praef; II, 3.
[144] 'Robert Blondel, *Desolatio regni Francie. Un poème politique de soutien au future Charles VII en 1420*', ed. N. Pons and M. Goullet, *Archives d'histoire doctrinale et littéraire du moyen âge*, 68 (2001), 316–17, lines 14–21.
[145] *Quadrilogue invectif*, 11–12.   [146] *Ibid.* 10–11, 14, 30.
[147] *Ibid.* 17.   [148] *Ibid.* 31; *DRM*, IV, 9.

In November 1439 Charles VII formally announced his intention of taking over effective control of the army. Noting that many captains had assumed their authority and had raised forces without royal permission, he asserted his right, as king, to have charge over the army by announcing that only those chosen and appointed by the crown ('nommez et esleuz par le roy, prudens et sages gens)', each in command of a specified number of men, would have authority to act, which they could do in future only with formal, written permission of the king ('congé, licence et consentement et ordonnance du roy et par ses lettres patentes'). No soldier was to serve any captain other than those appointed by the king, and then only within the number allowed to that captain.[149]

In 1445 a further reforming ordinance was issued in an attempt to create an army founded, it was claimed, not on numbers but on experience. Fundamental were two developments which had already been tried, although in different ways: the introduction of better structures in the army's formation; and the regular use of musters as a practical disciplinary method of ensuring that numbers were maintained and that the old problem, desertion, did not rear its head again. Three years later, the king created a force, the *francs-archers*, obviating the need to raise soldiers from among those who were not among his subjects ('sans ce qu'il soit besoing de nous aider d'autre que de nosdiz subjectz'). Selected from candidates according to their suitability, trained and constantly at the ready, these men constituted in theory a truly national force. Its members were to be exempt from certain taxes and would be paid, factors which emphasised that their service was recognised as being in the public interest. In return they had to provide uniform and equipment, and train on all holidays, thus making them fitter for the king's service ('afin qu'ilz soient plus habilles & usitez oudit service'), whenever they were called. Special measures were recommended to maintain those with experience of war ('bons compagnons usités de la guerre') in the king's service, even if they were poor and lacked the means to provide what could be demanded of them. Experience, it was realised, was something too precious to throw away. Three years later orders were given for the captains of the *francs-archers* to give an oath to the king. There was to be no doubt as to who was master, in whose service the men served, and whose orders were to be obeyed. The state's military servant was in the process of being born.[150]

---

[149] F. A. Isambert, A. J. L. Jourdan and Monsieur Decrusy, *Recueil général des anciennes lois françaises depuis l'an 420 jusqu'à la Révolution de 1789* (29 vols., Paris, 1822–33), IX, 59–60.
[150] *Ordonnances*, XIV, 1–5.

It is clear that this ordinance reflected Vegetian ideas regarding those who should make up the army, and what should be expected of them. Certain clauses remind the reader of points made by Vegetius: that the 'rustici' make better soldiers than those accustomed to the life of luxury in the cities; that an army should consist of men chosen for their suitability to become good soldiers; that they should train regularly; and that they should take an oath to serve and obey the king.[151] The ordinance began, however, with a statement of what were to be the characteristics of the new army. Until recently the king's subjects had been oppressed by soldiers more intent upon pillaging than the fulfilment of their proper responsibilities. It was difficult for anyone living in France in 1445 to recall a time when the army had been a force for good order in the country. The king's purpose was to create and enforce new and higher standards for the soldiers in the royal army.

By the mid-fifteenth century France was preparing to go one step further, creating a permanent army and thus completing a process which had been begun, but never finished, more than half a century earlier. To some, with memories of the past, this was a dangerous step. To Thomas Basin, formerly bishop of Lisieux, a man wary of the growing powers of the reviving monarchy, it was one step too far, no longer justified by the military requirements of the day, and very expensive to maintain. Although intended as a way of bringing about peace, a permanent army might achieve the exact opposite, the division of society. In 1484 Jean Masselin expressed his doubts about the royal army, whose military functions the nobility could fulfil just as well.[152] To many others, in spite of doubts, the creation of the *compagnies d'ordonnance* by King Charles VII in 1445, and the consequent reduction in the number of soldiers who had roamed the kingdom causing trouble, was a welcome step likely to increase the monarchy's power and the effectiveness of its rule. Not all saw until some time later that the creation of this army constituted a turning point. The king was now master, able to create and break up commands, and to claim the loyalty of the ordinary soldier at the expense of that traditionally exercised by the captains, who now had to look to the king as the source of all military power and authority.

Change had been inspired by appeal to Roman public values and institutions. The appeal had two aspects to it. First, it aimed at supporting

---

[151] See *DRM*, I, and II, 5.

[152] P. D. Solon, 'Popular response to standing military forces in fifteenth-century France', *Studies in the Renaissance*, 19 (1972), 108–10; J. R. Major, *Representative institutions in Renaissance France, 1421–1559* (Madison, 1960), 99; P. S. Lewis, *Later medieval France. The polity* (London, 1968), 101–3; Allmand, 'Changing views of the soldier', 184.

the claims to exercise authority made by increasingly centralised governments, both monarchies and republics, as the examples of France and Venice show. It aimed, too, at maintaining peace and order, the very foundations of social stability. The future of both centralised and peaceful government was, in fact, closely linked: ordered life depended upon just and effective rule. Both were to depend upon the army, which came to be seen as an institution which rulers could not do without: 'Non sine militibus regere sua regna [possunt]', one reader of the *De re militari* commented.[153] The army would remain a positive force in the polity for as long as rulers controlled it. If that control were weakened or lost, the army could then become a negative force, a danger both in and to society, the object of fear and mistrust.

Vegetius had been clear how service and breadth of experience should underpin the exercise of authority, and how these should lead to promotion and to its corollary, the career in arms. In many parts of Europe the gradual growth of the statist army was providing opportunities for such developments. In France, the reforms of the mid-fifteenth century provided a system which encouraged members of the lesser nobility to follow their traditional, noble calling, while serving for pay in the king's army. For such, there was the attraction of the regular wage. There was, too, the added lure of recognition implied in advancement to the rank of captain, based increasingly on merit and experience, as the evidence of funeral monuments of some of these men amply testifies.[154]

Elsewhere, in Brittany for example, a certain permanence of military personnel, with implications both for efficiency and for those seeking to carve out a military career for themselves, was in evidence by the mid-fifteenth century, while the duchy of Burgundy would follow suit under the rule of Duke Charles the Bold.[155] Long years in the service of the Venetian state could lead to knighthood, promotion and other signs of honour, including, for an infantry captain, command of a body of cavalry, a sign of real prestige within the army.[156] Military rank, seen as

---

[153] Naples, Naz. V. A. 21, fo. 4.

[154] For promotion on grounds of merit, skill, effort, loyalty, courage and 'leadership qualities', see *DRM*, II, 3, 7, 8, 10, 14, 21, 24. For monuments, see Contamine, *Guerre, état et société*, pls. 9, 11, 13.

[155] M. C. E. Jones, 'L'armée bretonne, 1449–1491: structures et carrières', in *La France de la fin du XVe siècle: renouveau et apogée*, ed. B. Chevalier and P. Contamine (Paris, 1985), 147–65. See above, pp. 133–6. Contamine has emphasised the model of the 'armée royale en réduction' which inspired smaller-scale developments in Foix-Béarn and Guyenne in the second half of the fifteenth century (Bessey, *Construire l'armée française*, 11).

[156] Mallett and Hale, *Military organization of a Renaissance state*, 80–1.

recompense judged by 'professional' criteria, as described in Book II of the *De re militari*, was now becoming a reality.

We have noted that the illuminations added to some manuscripts can extend our understanding of how the text of which they form part was appreciated by those who commissioned them. The presentation of a teacher (Vegetius) reading from a book to an emperor and knights emphasises the awareness, by the artist or his patron, of the ruler's responsibilities to use his knights in the defence of his people.[157] Other illuminations stress the need for those involved in such work to be practised and fit, both physically and mentally, while Vegetius' insistence that command should be exercised only by virtue of authority, here conveyed by a baton of office, underlines interlocking themes presented by pictorial evidence strongly supporting the written word: the necessity of having soldiers for defence; the need for them to be properly trained; and the emphasis on authority exercised by those to whom it has been officially delegated by the ruler, the man ultimately responsible for the defence of his people.[158]

Provisioning and logistics

A significant aspect of the emphasis placed by Vegetius on preparation and anticipation of the army's needs was the provision of food, weapons and other military equipment, without which defeat was more likely than victory. The ancients were more aware of the problems of logistics and transport in time of war than many in the Middle Ages would prove to be, a generalisation to which Charlemagne had been a notable exception. As evidence of his scientific approach to the fighting of war, Vegetius showed himself conscious of the fact that a commander should be aware of what he was up against, not only the enemy army, but the physical factors, geographical and otherwise, too. How much could his men be expected to carry as they marched, and how far could they advance in a day? Was there fodder and grazing for the horses, water for both men and beasts? The army needed weapons with which to fight; and equipment of many kinds to help it function as it was expected to do. Ever anxious to emphasise means of victory involving the maximum chances of success while avoiding direct confrontation, Vegetius underlined two things: one was the vulnerability of the enemy to starvation and hunger, and to the lack of weapons appropriate to a particular situation; secondly, the need for an army to defend itself against any enemy action which might

---

[157] Oxford, Bodl. Laud lat. 56, fo. 1.   [158] New York, Morgan, M 364.

deprive it of its men, weapons and freedom of movement. All this could be avoided by being prepared, and by planning accordingly.[159]

If there was little original about Vegetius' ideas on logistics, their urgency and the part which they played in his vision lay in their contribution to the broader message of readiness running through his work. In Books III and IV Vegetius made repeated reference to the effectiveness of hunger as a weapon in war: 'armies are more often destroyed by starvation than by battle, and hunger is more savage than the sword' or, put differently, 'hunger... fights from within, and often conquers without a blow'.[160] It is notable that his advice regarding the need to stockpile provisions – and to have access to water and salt – is to be found in Book IV, which was concerned with siege warfare. It was doubtless the growing importance of the siege, arising from the increasing effectiveness of defensive measures from the twelfth century onwards, that made Vegetius' advice to the besieger to use starvation as a weapon, and to the defender always to be well provisioned, a message high on the scale of relevance to contemporary conditions. This is reflected in references to the subject in a variety of texts of the late Middle Ages. Philippe de Vitri advocated an approach to war in which success was achieved through starvation and without the sword ('par fain et sanz espee'). It is worth noting that in a collection of excerpts from classical authors, including some from the *De re militari*, Books III and IV, drawn up by Nicholas of Cusa (1401–64), several emphasised the military dangers of the lack of provisions and starvation.[161]

Later, in Book IV, chapters 7 and 8, Vegetius returned to the paramount importance of defended sites having full stocks of food and other material needs, including access to water. At the same time every effort should be made to deny the enemy access to supplies which he needed, by burning them if necessary.[162] In order to conserve food during a siege, civilians who could play no role in war could be shut out of the gates, leaving more for those active in defence.[163] In chapter 8 Vegetius described what would be required, in terms of weapons, *matériels*

---

[159] J. H. Pryor, *Logistics of warfare in the age of the crusades* (Aldershot and Burlington, VT, 2006) esp. 275, 279–80.

[160] *DRM*, III, 9. See also III, 3, 26; IV, 10, 11, 30.

[161] Piaget, '"Le chapel des fleurs de lis"', line 744; *Ueber eine Handschrift des Nicolaus von Cues*, ed. J. Klein (Berlin, 1866), 39–40.

[162] The loss of a provision ship to the enemy by a crusading army in the last years of the twelfth century is significantly recorded in the *Itinerarium peregrinorum et gesta Regis Ricardi* (*Chronicles and memorials of the reign of Richard I*, ed. W. Stubbs (RS, London, 1864), I, 77). On this subject, see M. G. A. Vale, 'Sir John Fastolf's "Report" of 1435: a new interpretation reconsidered', *Nottingham Medieval Studies*, 17 (1973), 78–84.

[163] See *Vegetius: Epitome*, trans. Milner, 124, n. 4 and p. 93 above.

and machines, by those responsible for the defence of walls. Once again, the need to prepare for every eventuality emerged as the leading idea. In this context the concluding lines of Book II are significant: 'The legion ought to carry with it everywhere all that is necessary for any kind of warfare, so that in whatever place it pitches camp, it makes an armed city.'[164]

How are we to judge the medieval reaction to such advice? The evidence left in the manuscripts is clear. Passages, such as III, 3 and 9, for instance, which dealt with hunger and its effects, had emphasised the need to store food and equipment in advance to meet every eventuality, a recommendation whose importance was underlined by both the illuminations painted by Niccolò da Bologna[165] and the glosses in the margins of many manuscripts. What Vegetius had written was being taken seriously. It was one thing, however, to register approval of advice found in a book, quite another to give it the practical influence it deserved. As a central part of its message, Vegetius' teaching emphasised the need to make the availability of provisions, weapons and equipment an essential part of an army's normal function; it was not an optional extra which might help achieve victory or beat off an enemy attack. As John Hale once wrote, 'food was the fuel of armies';[166] without it they could not function. There were different ways of obtaining supplies. An army could carry its own, to be on hand when needed. There was a price to be paid for this convenience, which was probably why Vegetius had insisted that all ranks should train to travel carrying loads of various weights. There was the matter of food preservation to consider. Only meats and fish that could be dried or salted would last for long; even bread had to be baked from dry flour which had been properly ground. On the march in friendly territory an army might live off the land; soldiers were certainly expected to pay for the food which they bought; likewise they might be paid in food in lieu of wages. In enemy territory, however, it was regarded as legitimate (if not always politically apt) to forage and seize food from the countryside being traversed. To counter this, as Vegetius had advocated, those commanding defensive forces should order the destruction of crops and other useful materials to prevent them falling into the hands of the attacking army. It was in response to the question how best to secure provisions that late medieval Europe witnessed the growth of the system by which armies were increasingly provided with their needs by merchants who, through their commercial networks, had access to the means of

---

[164] *DRM*, II, 25.   [165] BnF Smith-Lesouëf, 13. See above, p. 206, pl. 11.
[166] J. R. Hale, *War and society in Renaissance Europe, 1450–1620* (London, 1985), 159.

collecting, transporting and selling of provisions.[167] The importance of food is underlined by the accounts of soldiers ransacking captured towns or castles for provisions, particularly fresh food, which success had brought within their grasp.[168]

In the East, where the notion of the state had survived better than in the West, the practice of generals being appointed by and owing responsibility to the emperor, commanding armies paid and organised by the state (with all that this meant for the application of 'military science') had a long history. Imperial officials supervised and controlled the supply of arms and provisions, both to garrisons and to forces on campaign, populations recognising an obligation to sell such provisions to officials and soldiers at below the market price.[169]

There is clear evidence, however, that the matter of logistics was being systematically taken in hand by rulers from the early thirteenth century onwards. In England, the expeditions of King John into France in 1205 and 1210 were accompanied by a greater degree of organised effort under the auspices of the crown aimed at providing the food and equipment required by the king's army. What enables us to gauge this slow development is the existence of a growing number of documentary sources which underline the evolution of a centrally based system which formed the basis of that used in the Welsh and Scottish wars of King Edward I at the end of the thirteenth century. This system, which included the unpopular 'prise', or purveyance, the compulsory purchase of food at a low price by the crown to supply the army, would witness the appointment of royal victuallers, responsible for the collection and distribution of food and military supplies, for the setting up of supply bases, such as that created at Chester for the campaigns into North Wales, and for the commissioning of means of transport (carts on land, ships at sea) to convey supplies to Wales, Scotland and France.[170] In England, the Edwardian wars saw a quantitative development in the centrally organised provision of the necessities of a war taken to the enemy. With armies now growing in size, and campaigns lasting longer, food, weapons and equipment were provided on a scale larger than ever before. How campaigns could

[167] See the reference (p. 72 above) to 'vytayllers' in Caxton's translation of Christine de Pisan's *Fais d'armes*.

[168] Prestwich, *Armies and warfare*, 258–60; Contamine, *Guerre, état et société*, 124; Hale, *War and society*, 160.

[169] M. C. Bartusis, *The late Byzantine army. Arms and society, 1204–1453* (Philadelphia, 1992), 247–8; J. Haldon, 'Military service, military lands and the status of soldiers: current problems and interpretations', *Dumbarton Oaks Papers*, 47 (1993), 42.

[170] Prestwich, *Armies and warfare*, 251; R. Storey, 'The Tower of London and the *garderobae armorum*', *Royal Armouries Yearbook*, 3 (1998), 176–83; Contamine, *Guerre, état et société*, 125–8.

be conducted depended on the relationship between strategies being followed and the supply of weapons and provisions needed to support them.[171] In the reign of Edward I, the king for whom the Anglo-Norman translation of the *De re militari* had probably been commissioned, a fuller appreciation of the importance of logistics was becoming apparent. The high price of failure in military terms (discontent among soldiers, bad morale leading to desertion and problems with the civilian population) was coming to be better understood and acted upon.[172]

The importance of logistics in the English army in the late thirteenth and fourteenth centuries is underlined by contrasting it with what has been regarded as the relative failure of the English monarchy to maintain the system in the fifteenth century, at the time when its political and military power in France was on the wane. Early on, at Harfleur in 1415, the death of hundreds has been attributed to a lack of proper food supplies at a siege which lasted longer than had probably been anticipated. Then, only a few months later, the English garrison, now in control of the town, had to send out foraging parties in dangerous military circumstances, suggesting that its logistical needs had not been sufficiently catered for. The ordeal of the long march endured by the English force on its way to Agincourt underlines the difficulties experienced by an army short of food on the move.[173]

Thirty years later the English would again face problems in France attributable to the failure to take proper account of the army's logistical needs in increasingly difficult circumstances. William Worcester, the compiler of the strongly Vegetian *Boke of noblesse*,[174] recalled in a gloss on the manuscript how his master, Sir John Fastolf, known to have owned a copy of the *De re militari*, provided the fortress of the Bastille, in Paris, with sufficient food for at least half a year. This was said to have 'comforted gretly the prince', Thomas, duke of Exeter, and enabled Fastolf to meet and defeat a rebellion in the city in 1421. Furthermore, documentary evidence found by Worcester in Fastolf's papers revealed how 'yn every castelle, forteresse, and cyte or towne he wolde hafe grete providence of vitaille of cornys, of larde, and beoffes, of stokphyshe and saltfyshe owt of England commyng by shyppes. And that policie was one

---

[171] Y. N. Harari, 'Strategy and supply in fourteenth-century Western European invasion campaigns', *Journal of Military History*, 64 (2000), 297–333.

[172] See Prestwich, *Armies and warfare*, 250–2; Housley, 'European warfare', 128–9; Mallett and Hale, *Military organization of a Renaissance state*, 18. On desertion, see Allmand, 'Le problème de la désertion', 31–41.

[173] A. Curry, *Agincourt. A new history* (London, 2005), chs. 6, 7.

[174] C. Allmand and M. Keen, 'History and the literature of war: the *Boke of Noblesse* of William Worcester', in *War, government and power in late medieval France*, ed. C. T. Allmand (Liverpool, 2000), 92–105.

of the grete causes that the regent of France [John, duke of Bedford] and the lordes of the kyng ys grete councelle lefft hym to hafe so many castells to kepe.'[175] Fastolf had recognised the dangers faced by fortified castles and towns if, inadequately stocked with provisions and weapons, they came under siege. It is evident, too, that Worcester, with his interest in classical authors and their ideas, understood the significance of Fastolf's actions and, above all, what may have prompted him to act as he did. Did Fastolf represent the school of thought which saw victualling as essentially a concern of government, carried out in advance of need for purely military reasons? It is noticeable that the towns provided by Fastolf were supplied with meat and fish 'owt of England commyng by shyppes'. In 1440 the instructions drawn up for Richard, duke of York, by Fastolf and others refer to the free passage to be given to provisions ('whete and othere vitailles') shipped from England to Normandy.[176] Perhaps this was an attempt to return to the system which had prevailed in earlier times, a system which would have met with Vegetius' approval. If so, the effort was not sustained. In 1450, instructions drawn up by Fastolf for the duke of Somerset, besieged in Caen, referred to the dispatch of weaponry alone. Victuals are not mentioned, and within a few months the English had been defeated, signalling the effects of the failure to provide proper logistical support upon the unfavourable outcome.[177]

In Venice, a state with an advanced, centralised military organisation, the state employed *proveditors* who helped with, among other tasks, the provisioning of the army. These men were civilians who represented the interest of the government in the administration of war. In the second half of the fifteenth century the *proveditor-general* came to assume responsibility for getting an army on to its feet in times of crisis, and for keeping relations between government and the army on an even keel. Another aspect of their work was to assume responsibility for certain arms; the light cavalry ('stradiots') and the artillery each had their *proveditor* by the 1480s. These were often men with experience of war who appreciated the contribution of their work to the well-functioning of the army. In time and in conditions of war, organisation and administration (which carried

---

[175] *Boke of noblesse*, 68.

[176] *Letters and papers illustrative of the wars of the English in France during the reign of Henry the Sixth, king of England*, ed. J. Stevenson (2 vols. in 3, RS, London, 1861–4), II, ii, 588–9.

[177] The failure to vote subsidies led to the starvation of England's army in France and, ultimately, to its defeat. So argued William Worcester (Nall, 'Perceptions of financial mismanagement', 123–35). In France there was a lack of development in French logistical systems in the fifteenth century until, under Louis XI, important developments were enacted, and certain individuals close to the king specialised in logistical matters (Contamine, *Guerre, état et société*, 323).

a strong implication of preparation and foresight) were vital in ensuring success and avoiding defeat.

There may be significance in the fact that, since society on the Italian peninsula was not 'chivalric' as it was in other parts of Europe, logistical matters assumed greater importance than they did generally in those areas of a different tradition where war was more an activity pursued by the military aristocracy. To such men, conflict was mainly about action, inspiring leadership and deeds of arms, the 'what happened' of war. They were less interested in matters concerning the management and organisation of armies, the 'how' and 'why' things turned out as they did, which was what Vegetius had sought to explain.[178] Vegetius did not forget to view war from the point of view of the administrator, which he himself was. There were factors, subsumed in the word 'logistics', which would help determine the outcome of a siege or campaign, which did not loom large in an aristocratic view of conflict. We may plausibly argue, therefore, that Vegetius' text contributed to the growing realisation of the importance of such factors in all military campaigns, wherever and by whomsoever they were fought.

Armour

If we return to the evidence of the manuscript marginalia or to the collections of excerpts, we find that, of the themes which stand out, one was the interest consistently given over the years to Vegetius' recommendations regarding the practical and psychological advantages of soldiers having adequate armour. This was particularly so in manuscripts and collections of excerpts which can be dated to the thirteenth and fourteenth centuries, a period which, this evidence suggests, witnessed growing awareness of the need to provide the soldier with proper defensive armour. It was also, we should recall, the period which saw the change from mail to plate as the chief form of such armour.

Book I, chapter 20 of the *De re militari*, which offered Vegetius' ideas on the kind of arms and armour carried by men of earlier times (the 'antiqui'), drew the attention of many medieval readers. Acknowledging that the cavalry was normally well provided for, Vegetius had turned his attention to the footsoldiers who, he asserted, did not have the protection in battle enjoyed by their predecessors. This, he claimed, was largely of

---

[178] 'We ought to be inquiring after the *military system* of the Roman people' (*DRM*, I, 8) (my italics). See E. N. Luttwak, 'Logistics and the aristocratic idea of war', in *Feeding Mars. Logistics in western warfare from the Middle Ages to the present*, ed. J. A. Lynn (Boulder, San Francisco and Oxford, 1993), 3–7.

their own making: neglect and idleness in field exercises meant that they grew unaccustomed to using armour (a further result of a long period of peace, perhaps?) and, when obliged to wear it, found it so heavy that they successfully petitioned the emperor that they might hand in the armour covering heads and chests. Since then they had suffered heavy defeats, particularly at the hands of Gothic archers. Nevertheless the restoration of defensive armour had never been ordered, with the result that, exposed and unprotected, soldiers thought less about fighting and more about fleeing. Since he could not use a bow and hold a shield at the same time (the shield being the alternative to armour worn by the soldier), what use was an archer without armour and helmet? What was a standard-bearer, facing the same predicament, to do? Encouraged to carry out daily exercises and practice wearing armour, they could achieve a great deal. Without the armour, all risked being wounded, captured or killed, with the result that some might be tempted to flee, thus betraying the good of the community. For these reasons, they should be compelled to train using all necessary equipment. As things stood, they failed to provide the 'wall' of legionaries with shining weapons and armour as those before them had done. Recruits should be equipped and protected as in the past. For the man with no fear of being wounded would approach battle with a much greater degree of courage and confidence.

This long chapter attracted much interest and, one senses, sympathetic attention. The main plea, for the restoration of defensive armour to those who, unprotected, exposed themselves to wounds and who thought about flight as a means of escape, would be marked in nearly 30 per cent of all surviving manuscripts, as was the case of the archer and standard-bearer, who could not fulfil their functions if one hand was already employed. The value of restoring regular training with arms and armour also met with a high level of interest; the state must not be betrayed by under-trained or inadequately protected soldiers. The call for all foot soldiers to be given proper armour, thus enabling them to develop a greater degree of courage, also met with the evident approval of many medieval readers.[179]

It is evident that Vegetius, deploring the situation in his own day, was only too aware of the adverse effects of lack of protection upon the morale of soldiers. Was it this which encouraged him to favour the ambush as a means of defeating the enemy without too much physical risk? He was certainly appealing for a return to the days when soldiers not only were provided with armour by the state but wore it during training, to good effect. Until quite late in the Middle Ages, artistic

---

[179] One may note, in passing, that the call for soldiers to be given adequate protection is one which has been heard in our own time.

evidence shows the foot soldier, often an archer or crossbowman, as under-protected, what protection he did have being made of cloth rather than of metal. In so saying, however, it should be recognised that a breastplate would have inhibited archers as they drew their bows, so that a jack with quilting, studs and some mail may have provided the maximum protection compatible with efficiency. Even so, during the short period of intense volleying, the temptation to discard a hot jack must sometimes have been considerable.[180]

Other evidence, that of wills for example, indicates that men went to fight in assortments of armour passed on by their forebears as people might pass on second-hand or unwanted clothes to the less well-off. It was the cost of new armour and weapons which encouraged men to do this. The contrast with the evidence, whether picture, sculpture or monumental brass, of those of lordly or knightly status, richer and socially superior, shown encased in plate armour, could not be greater.

We may ask ourselves whether the criticism expressed by Vegetius touched a raw nerve. Clearly something of what the *De re militari* had had to say reflected later concerns. A number of elements came into play at this time. One may be said to have been important developments which took place in armies, notably that of England under the rule of Edward I, in the years spanning the end of the thirteenth and the early years of the fourteenth centuries. The English army at this time was getting appreciably larger, particularly in the number of foot soldiers which it employed, but it was 'startlingly ill-equipped'.[181] This was a sure sign of the infantry's increased contribution to war in the years ahead. All this cost money, as thirteenth-century kings discovered. The result was that, during that century, those serving in the feudal levies were obliged to provide arms and armour for themselves. Generally speaking, even those in receipt of wages from the crown were expected to pay for their own armour and weapons. Ever since the Assize of Arms, issued by Henry II in 1181, men of knightly rank or with a certain level of fortune were expected to possess certain pieces of armour, but without financial assistance from the crown.[182] The writ to assemble the 'juratos ad arma' of

---

[180] Sir John Fastolf appears to have acknowledged the need to provide armour and weapons for any 'naked man' (Vegetius' 'nudi': *DRM*, I, 20) able to serve in the wars against France (*Boke of noblesse*, 68). There would be concern in late fifteenth-century England regarding the arraying of 'naked' men during the Wars of the Roses. I owe this second observation to Tony Goodman.

[181] Prestwich, *Armies and warfare*, 133. How little things appear to change can be seen in J. Gillingham, *The Wars of the Roses. Peace and conflict in fifteenth-century England* (London, 1981), 35–7.

[182] F. Lachaud, 'Armour and military dress in thirteenth- and early fourteenth-century England', in *Armies, chivalry and warfare*, ed. Strickland, 344–66.

1231 referred to the defensive armour which those summoned should possess, while the writ of watch and ward of 1242 set out the responsibilities of those involved and what arms and armour they should have, these to be determined on a sliding scale according to their social and financial position, most having to show, among other things, a helm (*capellum*) of iron. Under Edward II further attempts were made to improve the standard of defensive equipment, but initial steps taken in 1316 failed, while those of 1322 fared only a little better. At the root of the problem lay the crown's expectation that it would be the recipient of free feudal service given by men with certain specified weapons and armour. It is the high cost of these, particularly the defensive armour, reflected in gifts made by the crown to favoured persons, or in the evidence of court cases, which underlines for us the fact that the requirement to provide these free services was something which few could fulfil. Hence the impression that only the better-off could pay for the expensive defensive armour which they were expected to provide. English soldiers, wrote Dominic Mancini in 1483, 'do not wear any metal armour on their breast or any other part of the body, except for the better sort who have breastplates and suits of armour'.[183] The quantity and quality of armour owned by a man was thus a reflection of his wealth.

Other factors also came into play. One was the development of the crossbow, a potentially deadly weapon which only the new plate armour being developed in the thirteenth century might effectively counter. Another was the advance recorded by the archer (had Vegetius not admitted the effectiveness of the Gothic archer?),[184] and especially the use of massed longbowmen, so familiar in English armies in particular, from the late thirteenth century onwards; only mail made out of small, but very expensive, rings was in any way effective against the arrow, and even this was not so protective as steel plate could be. Infantry, too, also used a short sword, more effective at thrusting than slashing, against which plate armour provided some sort of protection. In this respect, necessity was the mother of invention, for the twelfth century witnessed developments in metallurgical techniques being applied to the practical science (the 'ars mecanica') of improving both arrowheads and defensive armour. Thus the helm referred to in thirteenth-century legislation came to be followed by the greatly increased use of plate which gave improved protection against the crossbow's bolt and the thrust of the sword (encouraged by

---

[183] *The usurpation of Richard the Third. Dominicus Mancinus ad Angelum Catonem De occupatione regni Anglie per Riccardum Tercium libellus*, trans. C. A. J. Armstrong (2nd edn, Oxford, 1969), 98–9.

[184] *DRM*, I, 20.

Vegetius). Bit by bit, parts of the body, trunk, arms and legs came to be protected. Yet, by the mid-fourteenth century, the best that the French foot soldier could hope for was protection of the upper parts of his body ('armés de corps, de bras et de testes'), with nothing on the legs, the armour being light but cheap, and not necessarily effective.[185] Even so, such protection was still granted mainly to those with rank and/or money who could afford the fuller protection which plate armour had to offer, if they chose to use it.[186] Protection on the battlefield provided by the latest advances in technology or design would long remain the privilege of those who could pay for it.

Strategy and battle

Turning to consider how much influence the *De re militari* may have had on strategies, tactics and ways of fighting, we encounter major difficulties. 'The evidence that tactics, operational methods or strategies learned from the written word were actually applied in war is notoriously inconclusive in most cases', concludes one modern critic, while 'it appears fair to question the influence of theoretical treatises on the actual conduct of hostilities', writes another.[187] 'La guerre se faict a l'ueil', one fifteenth-century manuscript informed its reader; the writer probably meant that there is a limit to what the book of instruction can teach about waging war before 'experience' takes over.[188] None the less, we cannot ignore a question which has aroused considerable controversy and disagreement among students of war, the influence which the *De re militari* may have had upon medieval attitudes to methods of waging war and, in particular, to whether it was better to avoid or to confront the enemy with the possibility that battle might ensue. This was a subject which Vegetius had considered with care. Although the necessary preparation for war central to his writing was set out in anticipation that armies should be ready to meet in battle, he clearly favoured less direct means of defeating the enemy. Discuss though he did the nature and advantages of different kinds of formations or types of action on the field, or the most effective use to be made of cavalry and infantry,[189] he regarded the commitment

---

[185] Contamine, *Guerre, état et société*, 24.

[186] Commynes would report that the young and 'vaillant' Philippe de Lalaing died (unnecessarily) in battle for lack of proper armour ('pour estre mal armé') (*Mémoires*, I, 24).

[187] Luttwak, 'Logistics and the aristocratic idea of war', 6; Whetham, *Just wars and moral victories*, 53.

[188] Cited by P. Contamine, 'The war literature of the late Middle Ages: the treatises of Robert de Balsac and Béraud Stuart, lord of Aubigny', in *War, literature and politics in the late Middle Ages*, ed. C. T. Allmand (Liverpool, 1976), 121.

[189] See *DRM*, II, 20, 26; III, 6, 9, 13, 26.

to open battle as the step of last resort.[190] If a commander could achieve his ends without formal battle, so much the better.

However, influenced by 'battle-oriented conceptions of post-Napoleonic military theorists and generals', historians of the nineteenth and the first part of the twentieth century, such as Hans Delbrück and Charles Oman, emphasised the importance of battles, which they regarded as potentially 'decisive' events. Since strategic success was judged by them largely in terms of the level of destruction of the enemy achieved, it is hardly surprising that the Middle Ages failed to impress historians of this persuasion as having been a period of major innovation in the development of the art of war.[191] They noted what they regarded as a 'surprising feature', the lack of decisive encounters or, to put it another way, the long periods of hostilities which failed to lead (as critics clearly felt they should) to battle.[192] More recently, however, historians have distanced themselves from the notion that military history should be primarily the study of battles (with the emphasis placed on the activities of mounted knights to the detriment of the attention paid to their men, with the implication that battles were decided by the cavalry), for an approach which considers hostilities pursued by 'other means' as equally decisive, if sometimes not more so, in achieving the victory of one side over the other. Granted that in ancient and medieval thought and practice the destruction of an enemy's army was not required for the resolution of a conflict, and that the holding of the field of battle for a period of time was regarded as sufficient for victory to be claimed, it comes as little surprise that many of the 'other means' strongly advocated by Vegetius should have been taken up by commanders in the Middle Ages, puzzling as this may appear to historians of a later age.[193]

If victory was not to be achieved in formal battle, then by what means? Many of Vegetius' fundamental lessons regarding the waging and winning of war are to be found in Book III of the *De re militari*. Having stressed, in Book I, the importance of 'quality' (which underlined the importance of selection and training) and, in Book II, the value of proper organisation, discipline and preparation, Vegetius went on to consider how one commander might get the better of another with the least risk and physical effort. This involved keeping the enemy guessing. Surprise could bring huge advantages, not least moral and psychological ones. Trickery and deception, too, should be used to wrong-foot the opponent: the

---

[190] *Ibid.* III, 9.   [191] Whetham, *Just wars and moral victories*, ch. 1.
[192] C. J. Rogers, 'The Vegetian "Science of warfare" in the Middle Ages', *JMMH*, 1 (2002), 1–2.
[193] See Whetham, *Just wars and moral victories*, ch. 3.

ambush, for which Joshua provided a convenient biblical example,[194] was cited with approval by Gratian in his *Decretum*. Following the same line of thought, spies should be used to keep the commander informed about the enemy's plans, movements and numbers. The information thus acquired could be used to good effect, for it satisfied the demands of caution while encouraging the element of surprise, both of which could be turned to advantage.[195]

As a reading of his work makes plain, Vegetius was no battle enthusiast.[196] Was it the influence of temperament, his lack of practical military experience, or the annihilation of the Roman army and the death of the emperor at Adrianople in 378, an event which probably occurred within his own lifetime, which made him into a cautious advocate of battles? All of these, perhaps. For Vegetius, open battle was a risk,[197] a situation of which men might lose control, when reason would no longer guide their actions, when mistakes which could not be rectified would spell disaster.[198] Since victory over the enemy did not demand the destruction of his army in battle (see how Vegetius encouraged a victorious army to allow the defeated enemy to escape)[199] the aim was to achieve victory through the pursuit of a war of attrition, of fewer risks to the attacker, one of whose aims was to undermine the morale of the enemy's army. For Vegetius, the direct confrontation of battle should be avoided unless the chances of victory were exceptionally high, or necessity demanded that battle was unavoidable.[200]

Much of what Vegetius had urged found new resonance in the conditions and circumstances of later times. Transferred to war conditions in the Middle Ages, such proposals required relatively few modifications. War demanded versatility of approach, something which Vegetius had placed high on the list of attributes which the army must demonstrate. Following the teaching of Julius Frontinus, one of the authors from whom he drew both inspiration and practical advice, Vegetius advocated the use of the ruse or the tactical surprise, such as feigned retreats, or the spreading of discord among the enemy as means by which military advantage

---

[194] Jos. 8, 2.   [195] Whetham, *Just wars and moral victories*, 129–33.
[196] S. Morillo, 'Battle seeking: the contexts and limits of Vegetian strategy', *JMMH*, 1 (2002), 22.
[197] 'War was wholly unpredictable. A man's prowess could be neutralised by unfavourable terrain, the work of projectile weapons or the crush of a *mêlée*' (A. Ayton, *Knights and warhorses. Military service and the English aristocracy under Edward III* (Woodbridge, 1994), 36).
[198] See Pisan, *Corps de policie*, II, 9, where, clearly reflecting Vegetius, she discusses this view. See also Juvénal des Ursins, *Écrits*, II, 236.
[199] *DRM*, III, 21.   [200] *Ibid.* III, 9, 26. See Whetham, *Just wars and moral victories*, 164.

might be achieved, and the opponent's army defeated.[201] Aware of the difficulties of achieving success in hostile territory, and ever insistent that, when possible, the enemy should be defeated by means other than by the sword, Vegetius advocated a military policy which amounted to harassment, the shadowing of the enemy's army and the creation of difficulties for his logistical and communications system, a task in which cavalry might play an important part. Tactics of this kind were to be used by Bertrand du Guesclin as he successfully harassed and, although avoiding direct confrontation, got the better of the forces defending the English interest in south-western France in the 1370s. When Charles Oman wrote of du Guesclin's 'ingenious if somewhat uninteresting proof that a successful war may be waged without accepting battles in the open',[202] he had to admit that the French constable had 'won a reputation by avoiding battles and specialising in minor operations', a verdict of condescension if ever there was one.[203] Others had used much the same tactic before him. The small-scale action, the attention paid to disrupting the enemy's logistics, paid off. Furthermore, it had the advantage of being a strategy which could be used for purposes of both defence and aggression. It was with evident approval that Alain Chartier recalled the way that Fabius Maximus (the 'Cunctator' or 'Delayer') had dealt with Hannibal in Italy by harassing his army and, little by little, wearing him down ('tint son host ensemble et costoioit ses ennemis et les dommagoit peu a peu de gens et de vivres').[204] He did this in spite of the people demanding more positive action, which he regarded as playing into the hands of Fortune. When Minucius Rufus, with whom he shared command, attacked Hannibal, he had to be saved from defeat, thus proving the wisdom of the Fabian tactic to those prepared to wait for results.

Vegetius would also have recognised (and approved) the strategy behind the raid (a characteristic form of medieval aggression) as it came to be developed in the form known as the *chevauchée* in the concluding centuries of the Middle Ages. Carried out by companies sometimes only a few dozen strong, such raids had as their purpose the demoralisation of the enemy's civilian population (the chief victim of this form of military activity), which saw its lands and sources of production ravaged, often by fire, as the soldiery brought a region to its knees by attacking the sources of wealth which both supported the population and provided it with the

---

[201] *DRM*, III, 22, 10. Whetham, *Just wars and moral victories*, 6, 44, 128–33. However, the author emphasises that 'deception was simply not something that the knights of medieval Europe practised'.

[202] C. Oman, *History of the art of war in the Middle Ages* (London, 1924), II, 201; cited by Rogers, 'The Vegetian '"Science of warfare"', 2, n. 2.

[203] Oman, *History of the art of war*, II, 202.   [204] *Quadrilogue invectif*, 35–6.

means of paying the taxes for war demanded of it. Since a ruler's ability and determination to rule a country or region could be gauged by the level of effective defence provided in such circumstances, the *chevauchée*, with its emphasis upon material destruction and the battering of civilian morale, proved to be a particularly successful way of undermining the practical authority of the ruler whose lands were under attack.

Raids could certainly bring about control of land, since few had either the means or the manpower to counter or deter raiders with well-armed forces ready, if necessary, to take matters to the point of battle. Not surprisingly the *chevauchée* became the main English strategy in France in the fourteenth century. The fact that the force normally kept on the move gave its leaders the initiative which it was difficult to counter. The physical risks for the participants were few, while the opportunities of securing booty or prisoners for ransom drew men to military service. Not surprisingly, such a method created a deep sense of insecurity among those whose lands were being attacked, weakening the political and moral authority of a ruler whose inability to protect both people and property cast doubt upon the legitimacy of his rule.[205] In desperation those being attacked might be forced to make concessions of a political or legal nature at the negotiating table in an attempt to bring back peace and stability, political, social and economic, to a society which had suffered much at the hands of the soldiery.

What was to be the response to attacks of this kind? Indicative of a (negative) reluctance to confront on the battlefield, but also an important element of a (positive) strategy aimed at defeating the threat presented by the attackers, was the large-scale building of urban defences, and the use made of existing fortified towns and castles, many of them, although seignorial, brought under royal control for the purpose of national defence in times of crisis.[206] Inside their walls soldiers and civilians sought refuge, awaiting the moment when the enemy would have to take account of their existence. For such was the relationship between the towns and the countryside (clearly reflected in the terms of surrender of important urban centres which obliged smaller places nearby to capitulate with them, a reflection of the dependence of the lesser upon the

---

[205] A good account of a *chevauchée* is to be found in H. J. Hewitt, *The Black Prince's expedition of 1355–1357* (Manchester, 1958). See also Allmand, *The Hundred Years War. England and France at war, c.1300–c.1450* (1988, rev. edn Cambridge, 2001), 54–8; Whetham, *Just wars and moral victories*, 12, 15.

[206] On the ability of castles and fortified towns to undermine the effectiveness of a *chevauchée*, see N. Savy, 'The *chevauchée* of John Chandos and Robert Knolles: early March to early June, 1369', *JMMH*, 7 (2009), 38–56; Whetham, *Just wars and moral victories*, 10–11.

greater) that proper control of rural areas was achievable only through control of the local town, often the sole properly fortified place in the region, and frequently the centre of local government and administration, both civil and ecclesiastical. The time would come which would require the attacker either to capture these places, or to abandon the campaign.[207] This, in turn, might demand a switch from an army suited to field warfare to one prepared and equipped for sieges, a transition not always easily achieved. The outcome therefore depended upon the ability of attackers to bring sieges to a rapid conclusion, since, if the besieged had armed allies to harass the besieging force and its lines of communication, a prolonged siege did not always favour the attacking force, a point reflected in the contents of the *De re militari* in which Vegetius gave consideration to measures to be taken by those defending a besieged town or fortification.[208] Such a force, it was realised, was vulnerable to attack by another which might distract its attention from the siege, possibly allowing the besieged to sally out and attack its rear. It was for this reason that commanders were encouraged to build defensive ditches around them to keep any relieving force at bay. This was probably what King Henry V decided to do when besieging Rouen, in 1418–19: as one chronicler put it, 'oure Kynge lete make an diche all withoute, Rounde a-boute the cite, and strongly stakid it, and heggid it'.[209] The king was taking sensible precautions lest he be attacked from the rear while pursuing his aims against the walls of the Norman capital.

It was the ability of cavalry to harass the enemy which, in Vegetian thinking, would prove so effective in defending territory from exterior attack. Indeed, in circumstances when those involved in harassment could create apprehension among an enemy army, and even prevent it from living off the land, while helping to ensure the security of those within the walls of town or castle, such a relatively passive procedure, described as 'the principal medieval defensive strategy',[210] would doubtless have won the approval of Vegetius. The simultaneous policies of defending strongholds and striking blows at the attacker's logistical support could only cause him difficulties and undermine the morale of his troops, while raising that of the defenders.

---

[207] It is noticeable that, appreciating the fact that the way to control the Norman countryside was through control of its castles and towns, Henry V sought to capture these as he conquered the duchy between 1417 and 1419. See Whetham, *Just wars and moral victories*, 11.

[208] See *DRM*, IV, 1–12, 18–20, 22–3, 25–9.   [209] *Brut*, II, 399.

[210] J. Gillingham, '"Up with orthodoxy!" In defense of Vegetian warfare', *JMMH*, 2 (2004), 152.

Vegetius' ideas on battle should be considered in relation to the content of Book IV. There is some agreement among historians that if Vegetius was responsible for the apparent unwillingness of medieval commanders to risk their causes in battle, this was because, since the tenth century, they had been able to rely on the walls of castles to defend them. An area with many fortified places, such as parts of northern France in the early eleventh century, encouraged the avoidance of battles in favour of a defensive policy based on harassment of the invader; an area not so well endowed might only be defended by those willing to risk battle, as King Harold II, ruler of a kingdom with few defences, was obliged to do at Hastings in the autumn of 1066.

This was particularly important because for the coming half-millennium or so those defending castles and fortified towns were, unless betrayed, likely to emerge victorious from a period of siege. There is much truth in the view that 'the besieging of fortified places is one of the strongest links connecting warfare in the ancient world with that of the Middle Ages'.[211] It would remain so until the fifteenth century, when the development of cannon, with shot able to bring down walls, would radically alter the nature of war in western Europe. Not surprisingly, therefore, much of Book IV should be read in terms of the need to resist enemy attack. The besieged must have access to food, drink and weaponry to enable them to sit out a long siege; hence Vegetius' advice that fortified places should always have these available was taken to heart and acted upon. The besieged also required the will and the means to defend themselves; walls required maintenance, ditches had to be dug and filled with water, defensive weaponry had to be made ready. Chapters underlined the effectiveness of particular methods of defence used to delay an enemy advance and create a danger so real that he might abandon his campaign altogether.

In open territory, success was more likely to come to the side defending a prepared position which compelled the enemy to attack, preferably up a slope. Recognition of this fact and of the dangers run by an attacker provoked or lured into an assault was probably the most influential factor which deterred commanders from seeking an engagement. They avoided battles both to save lives (for the defeated party usually suffered the greater loss in men) and to avoid the political consequences of defeat, for, as armies increasingly became instruments of state, so defeat brought their states one step nearer political ruin. Realising this, and appreciating the financial repercussions of defeat, the leaders of mercenary armies

---

[211] Jackson, 'Warfare in the works of Rudolf von Ems', 64.

were among those who preferred to avoid confrontational battle if they could.

Does the post-Clausewitzian world expect all too readily that conflicts should be settled on the battlefield? Was du Guesclin's achievement evidence that Vegetius' warnings against committing everything to battle had been heeded? Or were battles rare because medieval military commanders had insufficient discipline over their soldiers, who might lack 'the mood and the will' to fight (as Delbrück thought), or was it that the weaker side sought shelter behind effective defences and refused battle (as Charles Oman thought)? Or was it simply that the Middle Ages held to a strategy that had little place for battle, preferring the use of 'other means' as it sought to resolve conflicts? We should be wary of not recognising that the world did not stand still, and that time brought change. As Europe began to take shape with the growth of sovereign territorial states in the late thirteenth and early fourteenth centuries, so ways of settling disputes over territory, other than through war, were found and developed. It should not be forgotten that it was in the years around 1300 that the skills of the negotiator came to complement those of the soldier. Conflict assumed another arm, diplomacy, which complemented the battle as a means of settling a dispute, and served as a deterrent to those inclined to resort to battle as a quick means of settling discord, while encouraging those who pursued the road of resistance through harassment to give negotiation a chance to settle what, up to that time, might only have been achieved through battle.

War at sea

Earlier consideration of the manuscript evidence indicated that readers in the Middle Ages were not greatly inclined to comment on the little Vegetius had written on naval warfare.[212] No other part of the *De re militari* has such a high proportion of unmarked manuscripts, over all about 40 per cent. This may have reflected the very general nature of what Vegetius had to say on the subject. Equally, not all readers may have recognised the kind of naval war described, war carried out largely with the use of galleys in the waters of the Mediterranean, very different from that developing in the seas of northern Europe by the end of the Middle Ages. Above all, it may underline the fact that it was only in the course of the thirteenth century that growing states gradually began to appreciate the importance of a naval capability, which would take decades to develop. Finally, how many members of the traditional military class

---

[212] *DRM*, IV, 31–46.

had much interest in fighting at sea? The author of the *Débat des hérauts d'armes*, written in the mid-fifteenth century, thought that the nobility of France (at least) preferred fighting on land, a fact that may account for the lack of attention given to war at sea in the chronicle literature of the time.[213]

The confidence shown by Vegetius when discussing war on land was somewhat diminished in the final part of his work, which considered fighting at sea. The list of authorities cited was short and hardly impressive; but since he was writing what was probably the first theoretical account of war at sea in Latin, this was hardly surprising. To this subject he devoted sixteen chapters of his work's final book: on the navy (three); on shipbuilding (four); on the art of navigation (six); and, finally, on war at sea itself (three), a somewhat disappointing tally. We should, however, recognise that Vegetius admitted that in his day there was rarely any war at sea, which had long since been pacified; conflicts were fought mainly on land.[214] Unlike the situation there, which merited serious consideration, there seemed little point in trying to write at length on naval warfare.

Vegetius therefore turned to moralising. The result was the exposition of reflections on war at sea some of which, related to themes about which Vegetius felt strongly, bear close resemblance to those met by the reader in the earlier part of the work. Take, for instance, the theme of readiness, about which he had already written more than once. No enemy would attack knowing that he would meet effective opposition. The empire's two fleets, based on Misenum and Ravenna, helped to control large parts of the Mediterranean; they provided a deterrent; and they met the need for quick reaction, the reader being reminded of the need for speed if any threat were to be successfully met. In IV, 32, Vegetius wrote briefly on the office of Prefect of the Fleet (the admiral of the future); of the chain of command; and of the captains who, every day, put oarsmen and soldiers through their paces, thereby maintaining them in a high state of alert and readiness. The parallels with recommendations made in earlier books concerning war on land were striking. A good navy maintained a well-organised system of training, and was ready for immediate action.

The four chapters on the theme of ship-building also bore close resemblance to one of the more important lessons of earlier books. Just as a successful army was founded on the careful selection and training of recruits of suitable age, so ships should be built from planks taken from timber cut at a certain time of year, and then properly seasoned to avoid

---

[213] *Le débat des hérauts d'armes de France et d'Angleterre*, ed. L. Pannier (SATF, Paris, 1877), 33.

[214] *DRM*, IV, 31.

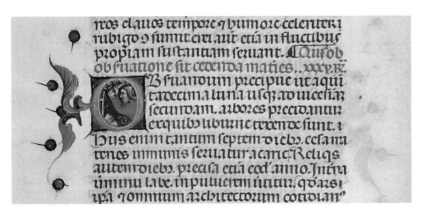

13 A man cuts wood for the building of ships. (BnF Smith-Lesouëf 13, fo. 63v)

cracking and inevitable disaster (see Figure 13). The choice and preparation of wood destined to form part of a ship from which a naval force would be built was comparable to the young man selected and trained to become a soldier, a part of the wall, or army, which would confront an enemy. As he had emphasised earlier on, Vegetius believed in careful choice and preparation.

The chapters (38–43) devoted to navigation bring us once again into the presence of a Vegetius whom we have met before. Caution is a strong theme running through this section. Vegetius showed himself well aware that the sea had to be treated with respect, its dangers being potentially greater than those posed by any human agency. These chapters consisted of a series of warnings to alert the unwary of the dangers facing the seafarer. First was the weather: winds and storms could be avoided if men read ('praenoscere') the signs and so learned when it was safe to venture out to sea.[215] In two chapters Vegetius emphasised how important it was to learn about conditions at sea before setting out.[216] The study of storms relied on experience ('usus') and reasoned study ('ratio') of the elements, while notice should also be taken of the experience of local people.[217] These chapters tell us something of the author's personality, enhancing the spirit of prudence which characterised Vegetius' approach to battle.

Only in the final three chapters did Vegetius reach the point of action itself, and then only half-heartedly. In IV, 44 he noted that war at sea could be fought with a much larger selection of weapons than war on land. For this reason it was a very dangerous business, 'so particular

---

[215] *Ibid.* IV, 38, 39, 41.   [216] *Ibid.* IV, 42, 43.   [217] *Ibid.* IV, 35, 40.

14 Soldiers sail away to fight at sea. (BnF lat. 7470, fo. 101)

care should be given to protective armour', one of the author's favourite
themes. War at sea was the cause of many deaths, the chief beneficiaries
being the fish which ate the bodies fallen into the water.

The sombre tone of this chapter was quickly abandoned when Vegetius
sprang back with a familiar idea which could be used to good effect at
sea. Just as he encouraged commanders to impose themselves upon an
unsuspecting enemy on land, so they should do the same at sea. Special spy skiffs should be used for reconnaissance to gather information
about the enemy's movements, thus enabling a commander to use the
ambush against an unwary and unprepared enemy.[218] Vegetius went on
to emphasise how advantage might be taken of nature to secure success. The enemy should be attacked when he was tired from fighting,
when he faced a head-wind or tide, or when he was confined within an
anchorage with only a single exit. The thought of being able to make
the most of such conditions even encouraged Vegetius to suggest that, in
such circumstances, the enterprising commander 'should take Fortune's
favour in [his] hands and give battle at the opportunity' ('occasio') (see
Figure 14).[219]

As for fighting the enemy, Vegetius had only limited advice to give. If
the ambush were avoided, and the enemy chose to give battle, warships
should be drawn up not in a straight line (as on land) but in a curve,

---

[218] *Ibid.* IV, 37.   [219] Cf. *DRM*, III, 18.

like a moon, thus enabling the commander, should the enemy try to break through the centre, to envelop him with the wings, where the navy's main strength had been positioned. Whatever happened, Vegetius strongly advised, the fleet should remain in deep water, where the danger from rocks was minimised, and enemy vessels could be pushed towards the shore, where they would lose speed to attack and, above all, freedom to move within an increasingly confined area.

Information regarding the main weapons to be carried and used on board ship brought the work to an end. Vegetius recommended the use of a beam, probably slung from the mast, with iron heads at either end, to be used to damage enemy vessels once they had been engaged.[220] Sickles on poles might also be used to cut the rigging of ships engaged in combat, while the steering gear of enemy ships should be attacked with sharp, double-headed axes. Ships lacking sails or rudder could only drift helplessly in the sea.

How far may one see the influence of the concluding third of Book IV reflected in later works on naval warfare or, perhaps more important still, on practical developments concerned with the development of war at sea which occurred in western Europe from the late thirteenth century onwards? Recent work on naval conflict is sceptical regarding much Vegetian influence on the practices of naval warfare, a finding which, granted the brevity of the text and the nature of the Roman fleet (largely galleys), causes little surprise. As Vegetius had emphasised, the dangers likely to be encountered by those fighting at sea were noted by the authors of the *Siete Partidas* (*c.*1270), by Christine de Pisan in her *Fais d'armes et de chevalerie* (1410), and by Jean de Bueil, former admiral of France, in his *Jouvencel* (*c.*1460). The role played by the elements, and the need to master them, was emphasised by all three authors, as it would be by Philippe de Clèves, lord of Ravenstein, in his *Instruction de toutes manieres de gurroyer . . . sur mer* (*c.*1516–19). The advice offered by Vegetius regarding the methods of securing wood in prime condition for ship-building found its way into the *Partidas*, as well as into the works of Pisan and Bueil. All accepted Vegetius' insistence on employing experienced pilots to navigate ships in difficult waters, a reflection of the Roman writer's admiration for the practical skills of those whose employment served to reassure men that they would not be caught unawares. The need for those who fought on board ship to be provided with adequate armour and weapons reappeared not only as a Vegetian preoccupation, but also as one which concerned those who recognised the relevance of his advice

---

[220] On this weapon, whose use had probably been abandoned centuries earlier, see 'Answers', *Mariner's Mirror*, 86 (2) (2000), 214–15, 218–19.

to their own day. And what could be said of armour and weapons could be said of food and water, too. In these, and in a number of other ways, it becomes evident that the concerns and advice of Vegetius would be reflected by later writers in their discussions of war at sea.[221]

A further aspect of possible Vegetian influence concerned the use of signals as the chief means of communication between the commander and those serving under him. Their use at night is advocated in an ordinance on the navy issued by the French king, Philip VI, in 1338. About 1470 Henrik van Borselen, lord of Veere, 'captain of the duke of Burgundy at sea', issued some orders intended to enable sailors to recognise friendly ships in the difficult conditions experienced at sea or in battle, and to enable the commander to convey his orders in such circumstances. Van Borselen appears to have taken up Vegetius' ideas regarding the password and signals with enthusiasm, ordering the use of the password as a method of identification. As for the trumpet, it was to serve as the means of making crews and soldiers in a number of ships act in unison. In one interesting respect, he went beyond Vegetius when he recommended a complex system of signals conveyed by lights in different forms and combinations, all planned according to a pre-arranged system. The idea of securing uniformity of effort when all knew what was expected of them lay behind these orders, which owed much to a positive implementation and development of ideas which may have owed more than a little to the *De re militari*.[222] These chapters raised other important issues reflecting what Vegetius had written in the earlier parts of his work. Ravenstein would claim that, in writing his short treatise, he would be setting down what experience had taught him, an approach which echoed that of Vegetius himself, whom he also copied by writing first on terrestrial war before turning to maritime war.[223] Ravenstein would also emphasise the importance of a naval force functioning as a unit, just as Vegetius had declared an army should do. To enable this to happen, he insisted that the admiral should have charge of everything done by a fleet. This important point had already been emphasised in the *Partidas* written more than two centuries earlier. In that text the admiral had been given the right to exercise royal power at sea and, for that reason, he must be chosen with

---

[221] See A. Jal, *Archéologie navale* (Paris, 1840), II, 289–94.
[222] Bessey, *Construire l'armée française*, 58; Vaughan, *Charles the Bold*, 227–9.
[223] *Philippe de Clèves, seigneur de Ravenstein, L'instruction de toutes manières de guerroyer . . . sur mer*, ed. J. Paviot (Paris, 1997), 38, 40. For the same author's ideas on war fought on land, see P. Contamine, 'L'art de la guerre selon Philippe de Clèves, seigneur de Ravenstein (1456–1528): innovation ou tradition?', *Bijdragen en mededelingen betreffende de Geschiedenis der Nederlanden*, 95 (1980), 363–76.

care.[224] The naming, by Pedro III of Aragon, in 1283, of Roger de Lauria as Admiral of the Crown, Catalonia, Valencia and Sicily lived up to these standards, the king appointing the best available talent to the post. That it was important is underlined by the fact that the admiral took on responsibilities which went beyond leading the fleet against the enemy. As would still be the case when Ravenstein wrote his treatise, the organisation of pay, the provision of arms and food for the sailors, and the maintenance of ships in good order were all part of the admiral's duties, which made it necessary for him to be something of an administrator as well as a strategist and tactician at sea.[225] As for the admiral's subordinate captains in the chain of command,[226] they also earned their place in the *Partidas*, where their promotion on merit and good professional reputation among their peers, rather than other factors, was emphasised.[227]

Vegetian inspiration may also be observed in the creation of the fleet. The *De re militari* had emphasised that only the best wood and other materials (brass nails, not iron ones) should be used in the building of 'liburnae', vessels built specifically for war. It said nothing, however, about where they should be built. Yet, in the Mediterranean, 'the idea of a centrally provided facility for the building and maintenance of ships mainly intended for war was well accepted' by the thirteenth century, if not before.[228] By the second half of the century, according to the chronicler, Ramon Muntaner, the growing acceptance by rulers of their responsibilities led to proposals for the creation of royal Aragonese shipyards at Tortosa and Cullera, with others possibly being established at Barcelona and Valencia.[229] In 1302 the Venetian Arsenal was accorded a monopoly of building galleys; before long, that brief would be extended to keeping twenty-five permanently ready to put to sea.[230] In the fifteenth century the Venetian senate went further by providing the source of a regular supply of wood for ship-building. Had those who showed the foresight to make such decisions, one wonders, read the *De re militari*?

In the French kingdom, which looked simultaneously to the Mediterranean, the Atlantic and the Channel, matters moved more slowly. In the mid-thirteenth century Louis IX had created the port of Aigues-Mortes

---

[224] *SP*, II, xxiv, 3.
[225] L. V. Mott, 'The battle of Malta, 1283: prelude to a disaster', in *The circle of war in the Middle Ages*, ed. D. J. Kagay and L. J. A. Villalon (Woodbridge, 1999), 149–50. The powers of the French admiral were set out in a royal ordinance issued on 7 December 1373, in which he was described as the 'chef' of all forces at sea (Bessey, *Construire l'armée française*, 68–74).
[226] *DRM*, IV, 32.   [227] *SP*, II, xxiv, 4.
[228] S. Rose, *Medieval naval warfare, 1000–1500* (London and New York, 2002), 6.
[229] *Ibid.* 125.   [230] *Ibid.* 8.

as a launching pad for the crusade. Half a century later France's developing crisis with England led to the establishment of a small royal shipyard (the 'Clos des Galées') on the River Seine at Rouen; its practical influence, however, would never be very great. When France needed galleys for its conflict with England in the fourteenth century, it was obliged to turn for help to its neighbour, Castile, with whom it set up working alliances. As for England, it was the achievement of Henry V, early in the fifteenth century, to appreciate the value of a royal fleet with which to form the nucleus of a small navy, and to provide it with a yard for further building and maintenance at Southampton. That vision was allowed to lapse, and it was for this reason that Sir John Fortescue, who probably knew of Vegetius' work, appealed to Edward IV to create a fleet which would be permanently at sea, not only to deter pirates and protect trade but also 'ffor the brekynge off an armye when any shall be made ayen hym apon the see; ffor thanne it shall be to late to do make such vessailles'.[231] The text recalls Vegetius' statement that with ships permanently ready there would be no need 'to fit out the fleet on the spur of the moment in response to the needs of some crisis, but [the Roman people] always kept it in readiness, lest they should ever be in danger', the rapid reaction force of yesteryear.[232]

Until the introduction of cannon on board ship in the second half of the fifteenth century, much naval warfare bore considerable resemblance to that all too briefly described by Vegetius. The variety and numbers of missiles used, and the fighting between soldiers and sailors on ships locked in combat, are reminiscent of the *De re militari*.[233] If the author of the *Itinerarium Hierosolymitane*, writing in the early thirteenth century, could echo Vegetius' advice for ships not to advance in a straight line,[234] but in a curve like a moon, the fleet's strength being mainly in the wings, by the century's end the common tactic in the Mediterranean appears to have been the deployment of a naval force 'in a line abreast so that there was a stronger centre flanked by a wing on each side'.[235] None the less, Vegetius would have been happy to see his prudent advice that small ships be sent forward to reconnoitre enemy movements being acted upon as a 'common tactic' in Mediterranean warfare.[236]

---

[231] Fortescue, *On the laws and governance of England*, ed. Plummer, 123.
[232] *DRM*, IV, 31. See also the concluding sentence of III, Praef.   [233] *DRM*, IV, 44, 46.
[234] 'non acies directas, sed incurvas disponant, ut si hostis tentet irrumpere, intrinsecus opprimatur conclusus', *Itinerarium peregrinorum et gesta regis Ricardi (Chronicles and memorials of the reign of Richard I*, ed. W. Stubbs I, 80*)*.
[235] Mott, 'The battle of Malta', 169; *DRM*, IV, 45.
[236] Mott, 'The battle of Malta', 156.

Let us give the last word to Ravenstein, whose work reflected basic Vegetian recommendations. One, already noted above, was the value of experience, which needed passing on in writing to later generations. Another was the need to be well prepared. Above all lay the importance, both moral and practical, reflecting Vegetius' teaching regarding the army, that a fleet should act as a body, Ravenstein's insisting (in a manner reminiscent of war on land) that ships should keep as close as they could to one another, in an orderly fashion, not touching, none going on ahead by itself ('le plus prez l'un de l'aultre que vous pourriez, en gardant toutesfoys qu'elles ne touchassent poinct, et aller plus en ordre que vous pourriez, que l'une ne passe poinct l'aultre').[237] That search for unity, both physical and moral, was personified in the admiral with overall charge (paralleled by the commander of the army), using a system of signals to convey his messages and orders,[238] which emphasised the admiral's effective control of the fleet which he commanded. This was underlined by Ravenstein's requirement that, each evening, the spy skiffs, which had never gone out of the admiral's sight, should return to the main force. The last act of the day was that every ship should signal its presence to the admiral as its commander.[239] Thus united, the fleet could sleep in peace.

Conclusion

This study has largely been about the reception and transmission of Vegetius' *De re militari*, how a text written in the fourth century AD was read, copied, received and translated into several languages, its ideas being interpreted in different ways according to time and circumstance by a variety of writers, soldiers and political leaders over a period of some 700 years (say 800 to 1500), sometimes to appear metamorphosed in contexts which their originator could scarcely have imagined. Written as the considered response of a senior imperial adviser to the question of how to meet a military crisis, it was later to be given almost iconic status as the military *auctoritas* to which men turned and which they liked to cite (sometimes incorrectly) as justifying or giving weight and respectability to their ideas and proposals. Since it was regarded essentially as a didactic work, whose purpose was to instruct, what did medieval readers expect

---

[237] *L'instruction de toutes manières de guerroyer*, 53. See *DRM*, III, 15.
[238] For Ravenstein's encouragement (perhaps following van Borselen's example) of the greater use of signals, see *L'instruction*, 57–62. Jacques Paviot, his editor, sees this as essentially a late medieval development. For examples taken from this period, see *ibid*. 76–7.
[239] *L'instruction de toutes manières de guerroyer*, 60.

to learn from the *De re militari*? Was the work primarily 'practical', 'philosophical' or both? Librarians of the period were not always certain where to shelve the text.[240] Their modern successors may still have difficulty in deciding exactly how to categorise this work, whose contents cuts across boundaries of both subject and time. Was it intended as a moral or philosophical work, or was it really a blueprint for armies and the waging of war in the future? What was Vegetius describing, and for what purpose? It is clear that opinions differed, and that even today these have not been fully resolved. Indeed, they may never be so.

What was the 'res militaris' which Vegetius had offered his readers? Early on, in I, 8, he had been at pains to distinguish his work, which was to concentrate on the military system, and on how an army should be created and made to function properly, from that of the Greeks, who had written mainly on tactics. If he lacked practical experience as a soldier, Vegetius knew much about administration, about the organisation of human resources, about how men react in a variety of situations. It was this experience which formed the background to his approach to the study of war. In the preface to Book III he denied that success in war was the result of luck and acts of courage; it was achieved, he insisted, through the study of skills and the preparation of soldiers in the techniques of war. Praising the commander who took advantage of opportunity ('occasio'), he refused to regard the use of such opportunism as luck. Nor did he place courage, however desirable, high on the list of factors which led to victory. Rather than these, he preferred a reflective and considered approach to war which might merit the label 'science'. It was, indeed, upon observation that Vegetius based the ideas of his 'disciplina militaris', as the text was sometimes called, which formed a wide-ranging study of how war should be fought to be won.

From early on, for lack of a rival, the *De re militari* spoke with authority. Why this was so was made clear by the passages, frequently marked in one way or another, in which Vegetius praised the ancient world for its willingness to learn from the past, and to set down its experiences, so that those to come might benefit from reading about them. The recourse to historical example as a pointer to good practice gave the text a sense of being one which spoke to its readers with an appreciation of accumulated

---

[240] Erfurt, Univ. CA. 2°. 5, containing the *De re militari*, was placed among 'moral philosophy' (Lehmann (ed.), *Mittelalterliche Bibliothekskataloge*, II, 45). Along with the texts of other old military writers, that of Vegetius was shelved among the 'libri philosophici' in a library in Munich in the fifteenth century (*Die Gründung der Münchener Hofbibliothek durch Albrecht V und Johann Jakob Fugger*, ed O. Hartig (Munich, 1917), 71) and, with Giles of Rome, among the 'libri morales' at St Paul, Liège, in 1460 (Thimester, 'La bibliothèque de . . . Saint Paul', 161).

wisdom based upon a genuine feeling for human experience from which those who followed could derive advantage and guidance. As Frontinus had argued, if a practice worked well, if a response to a particular situation had proved successful, and the right questions were asked of it, might it not do so again in comparable conditions? This was a fully reasoned approach to problems faced by those responsible for defending a society through the use of arms. Studying past practice, as described in what would become the subject's own handbook, transformed that practice into a science which helped men achieve success. This would diminish the influence of chance, whether expressed in terms of the fickle Dame Fortune[241] or of the rod of punishment wielded by God. If he turned to a book, man might at least learn to help himself by following the guidelines formulated according to the dictates of human reason and experience.[242]

Although written at a particular moment and in a particular set of circumstances, the nature of Vegetius' work was such that, without great difficulty, much of its advice could fairly easily be applied to many situations. It is noticeable that, from the seventh century, Vegetian teachings began to be cited in the works of others. By considering which of Vegetius' ideas were selected, for inclusion in collections of excerpts for example, and later incorporated into the writings of others, we are able to gain some insights as to how Vegetius' work was understood and what its influence may have been on aspects of medieval military thought and practice and, not least, on activity beyond the narrow military sphere. This approach, however, was not without risk. A short excerpt, taken out of context, might be misunderstood or misinterpreted by even the best intentioned of readers. Furthermore, excerpts almost inevitably reflected the interests of the person responsible for selecting them, with the result that no two collections are the same, the treatment given to particular books and chapters differing from one collection to another.

Translation, too, was not without inherent problems. Rendering a text written almost a millennium earlier in Latin into the parlance of the day could be a daunting task. Once again, the question of choice was raised, choice which might detract from or misinterpret the message conveyed by the original. Two forms of that choice are immediately apparent. One is expressed in the modern words chosen by the translator to convey his understanding of the original Latin. The risk of misleading the reader was ever present. That danger was compounded by the decision, made

---

[241] Murray, *Reason and society*, pl. III.
[242] H. R. Patch, *The goddess Fortuna in medieval literature* (Cambridge, Mass., 1927; repr. London, 1967), 107–10. See also K. DeVries, 'God and defeat in medieval warfare: some preliminary thoughts', in *The circle of war*, ed. Kagay and Villalon, 87–97.

by many translators, to consciously update their texts with references to, say, modern military equipment (the use of the words 'grete gunnes' in the 1408 English translation springs to mind), thus underlining the fact that the text could be read as a modern work, rather than as an example of a past literature with, perhaps, some contemporary relevance. Who, however, was to say that the usefulness of a work should not be perpetuated beyond its own time if there was thought to be value in it, and demand for a modern version was thought to exist?

The texts reflecting Vegetian teaching discussed above showed that seed taken from the *De re militari* was introduced into a number of different kinds of work composed in the Middle Ages, each carrying its own message for the time for which it was written. If one considers these according to their broadly defined subject matter, rather than by their date of birth (as has been done above), the kinds as well as the variety of works influenced by Vegetius become more apparent. Some have a strong military content. The influence of parts of the *De re militari* upon the *Siete Partidas* of Alfonso X was clear, whilst that which it exercised upon the military ordinances of Charles the Bold, duke of Burgundy, was even more powerful and direct. Elsewhere, ideas which helped support the works of John of Salisbury and Giles of Rome, more socio-political than overtly military, owed much to Vegetius, but in ways which required what he wrote (on the army or on the exercise of power, for example) to be accentuated and emphasised in a particular manner to support the broader arguments put forward by these writers. Furthermore, the influence of Vegetian teaching upon the thinking which led to the formation of national armies had to be related and attuned to certain historical developments, such as the growth of the state and the powers needed to make its authority effective. It was in large measure, for example, on the back of Vegetian teaching that the claim of the state to a monopoly of legitimised force was based. The wider, long-term significance of such a step is better appreciated when placed alongside the claim made on behalf of the law to be a power for order and peace in society, to the detriment of the forces of fragmentation which militated against that peace. So we observe the creation of two load-bearing pillars of the modern state. Between them, the development of the law and of the army encouraged the effectiveness of royal authority exercised for the good of the crown's subjects as a whole.

War was not always physical. There was sin, Satan and the spiritual war to consider. Already in the eighth century Alcuin of York had seen the possibilities of the *De re militari* as a text which would encourage men to prepare themselves for the great spiritual contest called Life. Other clergy, not least the monastic communities, could derive inspiration for their calling from it, in particular the need to recognise authority and the calls to obedience which it made. Vegetius' text as a spiritual allegory would persist until the end of the Middle Ages; both Denis the Carthusian and Alfonso de San Cristóbal represent a form of Christian thought and practice which showed an acute awareness of sin and its effects in the world, and the *De re militari* was a text upon which they could draw for inspiration as they battled against the forces of evil. However, the use of his work for such a purpose would, one suspects, have greatly surprised even the Christian Vegetius!

To the humanists, the *De re militari* was not only a classical text per se, but a great source of different kinds of knowledge, too. It is in this respect that the examination given to the manuscripts of the work has revealed the text as one which could satisfy many different interests in the history and culture of the Roman past. References to persons known from or encountered in other sources were often acknowledged, with that person's name being written in the manuscript's margin; the reader was meeting an old aquaintance, and reacted accordingly. References to historians and historical events met with the same response; certainly Petrarch was not averse to doing this. Curiosity regarding unfamiliar words (often military hardware) showed itself frequently in the marginalia: 'what did a word mean?' was a question often asked, as if Vegetius himself were there to provide the answer. The ownership of manuscripts of the Latin text, many of which carry emendations and corrections of badly copied or otherwise unintelligible Latin, reflects the fact that they were often possessed by persons with strong humanistic inclinations and interests, who read Vegetius and were able to derive pleasure and interest from this because his subject, war, was one which they were accustomed to reading about in the works of other Roman writers, particularly the historians. That Vegetius should be bound with, for example, texts of Frontinus, Sallust or Caesar, or with a French translation of the *Cyropaedeia* of Xenophon, a work of instruction for princes, causes no surprise. On the contrary, such works complemented one another.

The reader of the *De re militari* quickly comes to realise that much of the text's content has little bearing on the practical, everyday conduct of warfare. In this respect Vegetius differed from a number of other military writers, both before and after him, who approached the study of war with action in mind. It is possible that many modern readers, when studying his text, find it a little disappointing, as Vegetius appears to fail to provide what the title of his work, and its reputation, have caused them to expect to find.[243] The *De re militari* is not merely, even mainly, a handbook on tactics, being more concerned with the preparation for war than with

---

[243] Titles include: 'De disciplina militari', 'Epitoma/Liber institutionum rei militaris' and other variants.

its conduct.[244] To some, this may be a weakness. To others, however, it accounts for Vegetius' lasting influence, since so much of what he expressed belongs to the application of fundamental principles, making his work relevant to almost any kind of war, fought at almost any time, almost anywhere.

What were the essentials of Vegetian doctrine? Both commander and soldiers were in the army as the result of selection, the commander chosen by his ruler (king, prince), the soldier by a recruiting committee. Both occupied their positions by being able to show certain skills and aptitudes, physical, personal and intellectual. Both maintained their positions and developed their abilities through practice and preparation, emphasised as being an ongoing process. The acquisition of those skills did several things vital for success. The capability of using arms effectively gave the soldier confidence, which tended to make him brave. The manuscript evidence shows clearly that these rules, a reflection of careful observation, were among the most appreciated of Vegetius' writings. The emphasis placed by him on seven forms of fighting off enemy attacks, or on how to carry out a successful retreat, underlines, too, the importance of soldiers being able to act together, in a variety of formations, crucial in the thinking of Vegetius and many others. The important message regarding adaptability comes over loud and clear.[245]

In effect, however, the general good of any society could only be defended with confidence if there existed a force available to act, at short notice, in its defence. That force, the army commanded by the emperor, represented the 'res publica', or 'comyn profit', as opposed to the private interests of a particular class or social group. By the ninth century, paid regular armies were fast disappearing, and the use of mass force was now passing into the hands of social, hence political, elites and their followers. In much of Europe, in the coming three or four centuries, the power of royal or princely authority to control the use of force effectively was undermined by the ambition of local lords to dominate their areas of influence. This was the era when stone castles, symbols of local autonomy and power, emerged to challenge the growing authority of monarchy, signalling the need for that same monarchy, claiming to represent the 'res publica', to assert control over them. It was this need that made the army the instrument through which kings and princes tried to make effective their claim to power over particular and local interests,

---

[244] Maurice Keen twice refers to the work as a 'treatise on tactics' (Keen, *Chivalry*, 88, 111). While parts of it are undeniably so, I hope that I have shown that it is very much more than that.

[245] *DRM*, III, 20, 22; IV, 26 (Rules 18–24).

so proving themselves the dominant influence in the slow development of Europe's unitary states. Ideas taken from the *De re militari* thus made their contribution to the history of the development of individual states, republican and princely as well as monarchical, in the Europe of the centuries to come.

From the early thirteenth century onwards, armies gradually came to be regarded as instruments under princely or royal control. Alfonso X of Castile would put theory into practice in the role he accorded to the army, representing Christian Castile, in the war against the Moorish territories in the south of the country, while early fourteenth-century France would witness the development of the *arrière-ban*, or general obligation to serve when summoned by the crown to do so. Such developments were taking place against a background of development in political and social ideas founded upon those of Aristotle, now (in the years post-1250) revived and reinterpreted by Aquinas and his followers (of whom Giles of Rome was one) to meet new situations. The growth of the individual nation state would be furthered by the encouragement given it to be responsible for its own future and, hence, for its own defence. Was that responsibility to rest in the hands of the traditional (feudal) nobility, or was it to be shared by all, as clearly stated in the Castilian *Partidas*?[246] It was no coincidence that the concluding years of that same century should have witnessed the appearance of the translations of Vegetius' work into Anglo-Norman, French and Italian (Tuscan). It was in the light of such developments that the efforts of the French crown, in particular, to encourage the growth of a royal army in the fourteenth century, and a permanent one in the following century, may be seen. Nor was France alone. In northern Italy, notably in Venice, the growth of a statist army, with its accompanying organisation, would be guided by ideas and practices from which Vegetian influence was never far away.

If the *De re militari* provided historical, political and social justification for the development of armies by the growing states, it also advanced the status of the soldier, since men were once again being asked to regard service in the army, under the overall command of the ruler, as a service of responsibility and, therefore, of honour. This was particularly so in wars of defence when much was at stake. Furthermore (and again the influence of Vegetius is discernible) the army gradually came to be seen as a way of life which offered opportunities of material reward, promotion within a form of career structure and, for some, social advancement. If the late Middle Ages, in particular, were to witness a development in the way that certain sections of society viewed the soldier, recruited from

---

[246] *SP*, II, xix, 3.

within in order to defend it, it was a growing acceptance of his positive role in society, which owed much to humanist influence, exemplified by men's reading of Vegetius and the Roman historians, which encouraged that view to develop. In this matter the influence of humanism had a significant role to play.

Should it be argued, therefore, that the classic view of chivalry, traditionally knightly and equestrian, was threatened by these developments? Certainly, Vegetius recognised that cavalry could be more effective in certain conditions than in others, particularly when the terrain gave it scope and advantage. Generally, however, he appears to have preferred the infantry because of its versatility, making it less likely to be delayed or hindered by factors such as terrain. In short, infantry met Rule 11 better than did cavalry; it was more adaptable to conditions which, over time, would, and did, change.[247] Thus the growth of the well-established fortification, and later that of towns and significant urban defences, was a factor which called for the development of siege techniques, both offensive and defensive, which made fewer demands on cavalry. Not surprisingly, it was towards the end of the thirteenth century that changes in the way cavalry was used in battle manifested themselves. The ratio of cavalry to infantry grew smaller; at the same time, the willingness of knights to fight on foot, in combination with archers and crossbowmen, was encouraged. Although the chivalric class may have seen its direct influence on the outcome of battles diminished, the effectiveness of the army as a body was enhanced by such developments.

Encouraged in the *Siete Partidas*, later put into practice in the English army, and formally recognised in the Burgundian military system in the 1470s, the doctrine that, for maximum effectiveness, all parts of an army must work together came to be widely appreciated. Training in these methods taught efficiency, co-ordination and discipline: the absence of these would cause the defeat of the French army by the English at Crécy and Poitiers in the mid-fourteenth century. It was difficult to persuade the nobility, still loyal to a tradition and to obligations more personal than territorial, more local than national, to appreciate the big picture requiring that they should fight under the king for the good of society as a whole.[248] At Crécy, if one is to believe the chronicler Jean Froissart, the

---

[247] Other writers of the era felt differently; infantry fought only at close quarters, and were not as mobile as cavalry, who could (and did) dismount to fight on foot (Maurice, *Strategikon*, VII, B, 85).

[248] Strayer, 'Defense of the realm', 286–96. In the same way, French kings found it difficult to persuade assemblies of local Estates to vote taxes which might be used in an increasingly national war; money voted in a locality, it was argued, should be used for the local advantage (Allmand, *Hundred Years War*, 109–10).

French had no co-ordinated command structure. Contemporary accounts of the battle show the lack of central control or any effective way of conveying orders within the army. When the action is compared to Vegetian teaching, it is easily seen that several of his recommendations had made little impression upon French military practice of the day. The absence of an overall command is all too evident; although the French king was certainly at the battle, and probably fought bravely, there are doubts about the presence of his chief lieutenant, the constable. The ability of one group (cavalry) in an army to work alongside and in co-operation with another (crossbowmen) was conspicuously lacking on this occasion. Rivalries of class and nationality may have exacerbated this. Furthermore, for others, such as the king of Bohemia and his loyal companions, the search for honour through direct personal action had precedence over the needs of the French army as a whole. In all, this suggests a lack of awareness of the wider implications which defeat would have for both the army and the kingdom. Vegetian thinking about the place of the army, and the crucial role it was being called upon to play in French society, still had some way to go before it achieved the influence it deserved.

Yet what if the search for victory made demands which forced men to fight against their personal values, in particular against their sense of honour or fair play? Vegetius' advocacy of the use of spies to provide information of the enemy's plans upon which sound military decisions could be made troubled some, one such being Denis the Carthusian. Was this not a form of deviousness or deceit, he asked uneasily? Did the information provided not give one side an advantage? By contrast, Jean de Bueil, realising that he lived in a period of changing attitudes, tackled the issue head on in *Le Jouvencel*. Presenting the capture of a town by rebels as a threat to the public good, he argued that the most effective way to retake it would be through the use of guile, and for permission to do this he had the commander approach his king. Although the guardian of the public good, the king, a traditionalist in matters of war, was reluctant to sanction underhand methods ('entreprises de nuit'), which he regarded as dishonourable as they involved deceit ('trayson'). He would, he said, much prefer the matter to be settled by battle. However, recognising that war was fought in many ways ('il faut que la guerre se demaine en maintes manières'), he reluctantly told his commander 'I leave it to you', in effect washing his hands of the whole matter. Taking this as permission to pursue his plan, the commander went ahead, and soon recaptured the town. Whatever might be thought or said about the methods used, the aim of the exercise had been achieved, and the common good vindicated. The episode underlines the emergence of a pragmatic chivalry ready to serve the common good, within the conditions of the political and military reality of the day.[249]

Did the appearance of military professionalism lead to a decline of traditional military values and practices? Some might argue that the ethos of chivalry was the very opposite of that of the profession, and that, early on, Italy became a breeding ground for military professionalism for the reason that it had no strong chivalric tradition.[250] Yet the two were not necessarily worlds apart. Honour and courage were common to both, as were expertise or skill in arms, so that it can be argued that chivalry and professionalism were two sides of the same coin.[251] But this takes too narrow a view of professionalism. The term also implies the existence of professional structures, and of hierarchies with career paths pursued through the acquisition of competence recognised as status by other members of the profession. It implies, too, some kind of pay, even promotional structure, which rewarded such advancement.[252]

Can we say that there was a link between Vegetian ideas and the growth of a military profession? To a man, those who wrote about the desirable characteristics of the soldier and, consequently, of the army, too, referred to discipline, both on and off the field. Obedience to commands was spoken of in the same breath, for it was this which helped to create collective courage, and which made discipline (hence effectiveness) possible on the battlefield. It was, too, a characteristic of a way of fighting rather different from that which emphasised the gallantry and effort of the individual.[253] As the reader of the *De re militari* would realise, Vegetius saw the co-ordination of the effort of the entire army as crucial to victory;[254] hence the maintenance of close formations which moved and wheeled as ordered was something which professionalism, through constant training by units, working together as teams, would make possible.

This line of thought can be taken further. The decisive characteristic of a professional army was the encouragement given to long service; hence its permanence. This gave it a huge advantage over most traditional armies, which consisted of small units whose members were not known to one another and were unaccustomed to fighting as members of a

---

[249] Allmand, 'Entre honneur et bien commun', 463–81.
[250] Mallett, 'Condottieri and captains in Renaissance Italy', 67–8.
[251] Potter, 'Chivalry and professionalism', 161; Mallett, 'Condottieri and captains in Renaissance Italy', 84.
[252] See the editor's 'Introduction' to Trim (ed.), *Chivalric ethos*, 4, 6–7.
[253] *Ibid.* 29; Mallett, 'Condottieri and captains in Renaissance Italy', 86; Potter, 'Chivalry and professionalism', 178
[254] M. Bennett, 'Why chivalry? Military "professionalism" in the twelfth century: the origins and expressions of a socio-military ethos', in *Chivalric ethos*, ed. Trim, 61. In the same way, a naval force should also act as one.

larger force until brought together for a campaign or battle.[255] Beginning with Venice early in the fifteenth century, men came to be retained for periods of military service which became longer and longer; in Italy, the de facto growth of the permanent force in the service of those states which could afford it was sanctioned by the peace of Lodi in 1454. By then, France had created an institutionalised royal army, a version of which would serve the crown in the future. Yet, besides being a drain on the national finances, commentators such as Jean de Bueil saw the dangers of its permanence presenting a threat to the very liberties of Frenchmen which it was intended to preserve.[256] Nor was he alone in questioning the motives of the crown in creating such a force. Even men who had supported the army as it regained English-occupied France in the mid-fifteenth century saw these developments as a possible threat to those liberties which it had only recently helped to restore. Was the logic of Vegetian thinking, which seemed to lead inexorably towards a permanent army, going further than some deemed it wise to go?

The professional army, trained to fight as a large unit, recognised the same hierarchical structures and chains of command, developed its own interior loyalty, and benefited from the moral strengths, not least a sense of identity, gained by any group of men working together for a period of time or in a particular set of circumstances. The commander, too, knew the men serving under him, their strengths and weaknesses, what discipline he needed to impose, and how he could plan ahead with a force whose membership remained reasonably permanent and was accustomed to receiving and carrying out orders.[257] With the founding of military academies in the sixteenth century we see the beginning of formally trained and rationally oriented leadership taking over the armies of Europe.[258]

The second half of the fifteenth century would witness significant changes in the conduct of war. Armies grew in size; new formations were introduced; firearms, in their many forms, began to leave their mark both on the battlefield and on besieged towns and castles; sieges now took on an importance of their own. Accompanying these developments, and

---

[255] Vegetius had stressed the significance of the lack of familiarity between those constituting an army (*DRM*, II, 2).

[256] Allmand, 'Entre honneur et bien commun', 478.

[257] Mallet, 'Condottieri and captains in Renaissance Italy', 86; S. P. Huntington, *The soldier and the state. The theory and practice of civil–military relations* (Cambridge, Mass., 1957), 11.

[258] M. D. Feld, *The structure of violence. Armed forces in social systems* (Beverley Hills and London, 1977), 19; J. R. Hale, *Renaissance war studies* (London, 1983), chs. 8, 10.

ultimately benefiting from the recently developed techniques of printing, were a number of works on the waging of war, written in different forms by persons of different backgrounds. These compel us to ask an important question: how far were Vegetius' ideas still useful, if not valued and influential, in the period 1465 to, say, 1520?

Five texts, all written in France or Burgundy in the late fifteenth or early sixteenth centuries, may justify some observations on this question. The categorisation of Jean de Bueil's *Jouvencel* has always proved difficult. Part fact, part fiction, it is revelatory of certain military attitudes in the reign of King Louis XI. It represents the view of a man (or men) who had fought against the English in the closing stages of the Hundred Years War, and who had seen the military reforms of King Charles VII developing around them. It certainly reflects the views of someone who had experienced many years of fighting for his king and country.

The authorship of the *Rosier des guerres*, probably written in 1481–82, has long been debated, although the argument that the text represents the mature thoughts of Louis XI on a number of aspects of government is now widely accepted. In spite or, perhaps, because of the way these thoughts are expressed, they resemble, at times closely, the ideas of Vegetius on war. Indeed, the wording sometimes suggests that the author had a copy of the *De re militari*, or at least a collection of excerpts, before him as he wrote or dictated.

The dying years of the fifteenth century and the opening ones of the sixteenth would see two Frenchmen and a Burgundian, each with lengthy military experience behind him, produce works reflecting both recent developments and, at times, the influence of Vegetius upon the art of war at that period. Robert de Balsac was the author of the first of these, *La nef des princes*, which survives in both manuscript and printed form, the first compiled in the closing years of the fiftenth century, the second in 1502.[259] Born about 1435, Balsac had experienced a varied military career, serving in posts of responsibility in Italy, Gascony, Burgundy and Brittany, and finally in the service of the French crown, before dying in 1503.[260] It was thus as a soldier of long standing that he set down his ideas on the waging of war.

His work would soon be adapted by an anonymous author who both enlarged it and added matter of his own.[261] A little later, the work was taken up yet again, this time by Bérault Stuart, at that time (1508) one of France's most experienced military commanders, having served the

---

[259] Contamine, 'War literature', 106–7, 112.   [260] *Ibid.* pp. 107–11.
[261] BnF fr. 1245. See Contamine, 'War literature', 115–16; *Traité sur l'art de la guerre de Béraud Stuart, seigneur d'Aubigny*, ed. E. de Comminges (The Hague, 1976), xxxiv.

crown of Castile (he was at Granada when it was taken from the Moors in 1492) as well as that of France, fighting chiefly in Italy, where he witnessed new ways of waging war which were to influence his thinking. Significantly, he also served on occasions as a diplomat; it was while on a mission to Scotland that he died in 1508. Stuart's significance lay in his all-round view of war as it was coming to be practised in the very early sixteenth century, with its growing emphasis on the professional approach particularly to command and to the administration of armies, much as Vegetius had urged.[262]

The final text, by Philippe de Clèves, lord of Ravenstein (1456–1528), was the work of a man whose varied military and naval experience enabled him to write, about 1516, a treatise, *Instruction de toutes manieres de guerroyer* . . . , reflecting a strongly practical approach rather than an interest in classical precepts. It would be printed and published in Paris in 1558, and was deemed important enough to be translated into Dutch later in the century.

One has only to contrast these authors with the majority of those considered earlier to appreciate the difference, if not the gulf, slowly growing between them. All had much recent practical experience of war behind them, one (Louis XI, king of France) a prince who organised campaigns, four as captains at a time when both the scale of war and the means of fighting it were undergoing important and lasting changes. These were likely to be reflected in what they wrote.

Along with such developments came others which complement what has just been said. One was the growth in the number of works on practical military affairs which this group represents, a growth which would continue in the coming century over much of Europe, reflecting in some measure the increase in the number of wars between rising principalities and kingdoms which occurred in that period. Secondly, we must be aware of a tendency towards a more secular ownership and readership of texts on war in general, and of the *De re militari* in particular. Thirdly, the works on war written and now printed reflect a more pragmatic and practical approach to war. Contrast, for example, some of the fantastic illustrative matter in Roberto Valturio's *De re militari*, printed in 1472, with the stark, scientific realism of comparable matter in editions of Aelian's work printed in the mid-sixteenth century. They are worlds apart, separated by the works of Balsac, Stuart and Clèves, which serve as guides to what was going on in the development of military thought and practice, and their accompanying literature.

---

[262] Potter, 'Chivalry and professionalism', 175.

Seen from one perspective, the influence of Vegetius may appear to be on the wane by the end of the fifteenth century. Open attribution to him now appears less common than in earlier times. Seen another way, however, the influence of the *De re militari* upon fundamental matters may have been as great as ever. While it is true that the importance of selection, although emphasised in the *Rosier des guerres*, was mentioned less frequently by the sixteenth century (the rapid growth in the size of armies and formations coming into being must have been influential in bringing this about), Vegetius' insistence on adequate preparation and training remained. Such preparation could take on different forms. It might be expressed in the reminder that prudence, which demanded that careful consideration should precede action, should on no account be forgotten. In *Jouvencel*, Jean de Bueil urged the commander to prepare himself well by trying to discover the plans and dispositions of the enemy.[263] Did a prince, Bérault Stuart could none the less ask, have the resources, human and material, as well as a sufficiency of good leaders, to bring a war to a satisfactory conclusion? To Philippe de Clèves, preparation meant taking steps to raise the money necessary for war (and, to a certain extent, the measure of public support which its availability would reflect) before drawing up plans with the best advice to hand (clergy and those without experience of war were to be excluded from this process), and appointing a commander to take charge of operations.[264] Did the asking of questions about the human and financial resources available to fight a war, advocated by Stuart and Clèves, mean that the influence of intellectual culture and didactic writing on the conduct of war, often put forward by men who never had to practise what they preached, was now beginning to shrink and, with it, Vegetian influence on the conduct of war?

Whatever the case, all were agreed that good leadership was to remain high on the list of priorities when war was planned. With reason, the qualities of the commander included practical military experience, in particular at a time when so much was changing in the ways war was fought. For Jean de Bueil, experience, not social rank, made a commander worthy of his charge. It is noticeable that in both the *De re militari* and *Jouvencel* young soldiers rub shoulders with the seasoned campaigners from whom they have much to learn.[265] In spite of Vegetian warnings about the employment of mercenaries, Charles the Bold chose to employ experienced Italian soldiers in his army rather than rely on a force of

---

[263] *Le Jouvencel*, II, 92.
[264] Contamine, 'L'art de la guerre selon Philippe de Clèves', 372.
[265] Allmand, 'Entre honneur et bien commun', 467–8.

inexperienced native Burgundians, while to Bérault Stuart, too, caution (taking nothing for granted) and the use of soldiers with experience ('experimentez' or 'congnoissans la guerre') were essential factors in the achievement of victory.[266] One may recall here the Florentines' tribute to the English knight John Hawkwood, painted, in 1436, on Uccello's memorial to the old English mercenary: 'Ioannes Acutus, eques britannicus, dux aetatis suae cautissimus et rei militaris peritissimus habitus est.' Hawkwood was a man who knew a thing or two about fighting and who paused to think before he acted. His success and reputation, it was implied, stemmed from the practice of this important military virtue.

A further attribute of the successful commander was a willingness to seek and accept advice, as Vegetius had more than once recommended. Bueil urged that all aspects of a campaign should be discussed coolly ('froidement') and objectively by the commander and his staff; decisions must be taken and all differences ironed out 'à l'ostel' before the army moved off.[267] Balsac and Stuart agreed; a commander needed persons to give him advice, and he must be ready to listen to them.[268] The theme reappeared unambiguously in Stuart's work when he underlined the importance of the 'chef de guerre' having close to him men of experience ready to give him advice ('saige à la guerre . . . pour le conseiller, garder et conduire').[269] Equally, however, decisions were ultimately to be made by one person, and plans, once made, were best left in the mind of that person, a way of proceeding of which Philippe de Clèves was to approve.[270]

In Vegetian thinking one mark of the effective leader was an ability to deal sympathetically with his men, to treat them as human beings who might make mistakes. The point was not lost on some of the writers under consideration. Balsac appreciated that the time when an army had suffered a reverse could be particularly difficult for a commander. The retreat must be carefully carried out and the men given the chance to rest before resuming the attack. Here the commander must be very careful, as in eighteen out of twenty cases demoralised men, asked to resume fighting too soon, would suffer a second setback, as the obstinacy displayed by Charles the Bold clearly showed.[271] If the maintenance of morale

---

[266] *Traité sur l'art de la guerre*, lines 37, 46, 426.
[267] *DRM*, III, 6, 9, 26; Allmand, 'Entre honneur et bien commun', 470. Mézières preferred the phrase 'en chambre'.
[268] Robert de Balsat [*sic*], *La nef des princes et des batailles . . .* (Lyons, 1502), lvii[v], lxi[v].
[269] *Traité sur l'art de la guerre*, lines 247–9.
[270] *Ibid.* lines 694–700; *DRM*, III, 6; Contamine, 'L'art de la guerre selon Philippe de Clèves', 371–2.
[271] Balsac, *La nef des princes*, lviii.; *DRM*, III, 22.

was one thing, another, of which Stuart showed himself very conscious, was the need to raise men's confidence by making the best use of their different skills, which reflected the Vegetian doctrine that an army was a force of men of varied abilities, first identified, then developed before being employed as the commander built that force into a team.[272] Soldiers should be addressed by their commander, who must remind them of the importance of their individual courage as well as the good of the nation, for which they should be prepared to die.[273]

The idea that war was the ultimate public service for the defence of the state would gradually undermine the view that it could also be regarded as an opportunity for winning personal glory and reputation, as the tradition of chivalric chronicle writing had generally encouraged it. Were not men who sought personal fame and gratification through the *exploit* wrongly motivated and ready to put the wider good at risk? Such action went against everything taught by Vegetius. It threatened the sense of order and planning which he sought to instil into an army's activities. As an act of indiscipline it weakened, too, the effectiveness and authority of the commander, while undermining the sense of an army as a team. As Jean de Bueil commented tartly, such an act did nobody any good ('ne fait service à nul'). The soldier must be ready to act selflessly with others in the public service. When formations fought together, the effects were both symbolic and practical. Their unity of movement, their ability to keep close together as they advanced, wheeled (and even retreated) was a reflection both of the order which governed their movements and of the effectiveness with which they fought. Not surprisingly this theme, based upon a growing appreciation of an army's role in society, is reflected in the writings of the authors under discussion.[274]

The need to make an army an efficient organisation finally drew the attention of some writers to the Roman example of military administration found in Book II of the *De re militari*, in which readers had hitherto often shown little interest. However, what may have appeared in earlier centuries to be of rather marginal significance came to mean much more in the later Middle Ages, not only as interest in all matters Roman developed, but also for practical reasons. As armies became larger and their

---

[272] *Traité sur l'art de la guerre*, lines 389–420; *DRM*, II.
[273] *Traité sur l'art de la guerre*, lines 184–9; *DRM*, III, 12; II, 5.
[274] *Jouvencel*, II, 100; Allmand, 'Entre honneur et bien commun', 374; *Le rosier des guerres, enseignements de Louis XI roy de France pour le dauphin son fils*, ed. M. Diamantberger (Paris, 1925), chs. 4, 6; Balsac, *La nef des princes*, lv^r–lv^v; Contamine, 'L'art de la guerre selon Philippe de Clèves', 373. It may be noted that the reader who wrote marginalia in a copy of Götz's 1475 edition of the *DRM*, probably in the early sixteenth century, emphasised the importance of marching at different speeds, of manoeuvring in good order, and of preserving cohesion at all times (BL IB 3850; *DRM*, I, 9, 26, 27).

structures more complex, so the need to associate specific responsibilities with the holders of certain known offices grew. So, too, did the need to establish recognised chains of command and methods of administration to ensure the smooth functioning of the army, particularly when it was under pressure. Perhaps following Vegetius' example, Balsac urged that a commander should be aware of the nature of the terrain he must traverse, advocating that he should 'le faire metre en paincture' to bring it to life. A few years later Clèves would recommend that an officer, the 'maréchal du logis', be given a plan of the itinerary to be followed, including the bridges and paths the pioneers had to construct.[275] As the size of armies grew, and the distances they had to travel increased, so camps assumed ever-increasing importance, particularly in the sixteenth century. Vegetius had devoted several chapters in Book I to camps and to their size, shape, provisioning and defence; some of his recommendations may have influenced new practices. The emphasis upon the fortified camp as a place of refuge where an army might take shelter was certainly to be found in the *De re militari*.[276]

So it was, too, that in the military ordinances published by Charles the Bold, duke of Burgundy, between 1470 and 1474, the titles of those occupying positions of command, 'decanies' or 'centurion', may have been inspired by Vegetius' work. When Francis I of France founded a force of native infantry in 1534, he called their divisions 'legions', their number (6,000 men) being close to the legion of 6,100 men described by Vegetius. Here every hundred men were commanded by a 'centenier', clearly taken from the Latin 'centenarius' or 'centurio'. The use of modified or translated Latin titles symbolises how the army of Charles, the last Valois duke of Burgundy, was organised along the lines of the Roman model, further evidence of the pervading influence of writers from the ancient world.

Yet, writing in 1516, Philippe de Clèves showed an awareness of certain developments taking place around him which involved a lessening of Vegetian influence. The growing size of formations meant that the traditional ways of drawing up an army in three parts now had to be abandoned in favour of making the best possible use of the numbers of fighting men and the new weaponry available. It was now expected that battles would be short, so that Vegetius' advice to take advantage of the movement of the sun or the direction of the wind would no longer have the importance it had once had. Interesting, too, is that whereas Vegetius

---

[275] Contamine, 'L'art de la guerre selon Philippe de Clèves', 372.
[276] *DRM*, I, 21–5. See Mallett and Hale, *Military organization of a Renaissance state*, 92–5.

had recommended that it helped an army both physically and psychologically to occupy the higher ground, and to fight with the slope in its
favour, Clèves took the view that artillery, now assuming so influential a
role, was more effective and devastating when used up the slope ('de bas
en hault').[277]

While Vegetius taught that the commander should try to fight on his
terms, rather than on those of the enemy, war was always likely to produce
the unpredictable. For that reason Vegetius argued that the ability to
adapt to circumstances should be one of the main characteristics any
army should seek to develop. This underlined the need, emphasised
by Vegetius, for officers to be selected from those who had different
experiences of service within the army, for the men to be trained in a
variety of skills and techniques, so that all would be ready to face a
diversity of challenges. His work, however, had not been aimed at raising
the level of military proficiency among soldiers alone. In addressing it
to the Roman emperor, Vegetius had underlined the importance which
he attached to the ruler acquiring a good general knowledge of military
affairs, thus making him capable of dealing with different circumstances.
It was part of his responsibility to society to be better informed than his
subjects on matters such as war, which would bring them all advantage
through his ability to defend them properly.

It is evident that many owners of manuscripts clearly understood that
the *De re militari*, far from being mainly a guide to what should be done on
the battlefield, was a text which gave advice on a variety of subjects, thus
making it into a work to be studied before, not during, a battle.[278] The
illuminations added to some manuscripts underline this view. What the
patron or the artist regarded as being important could become the subject
of such an illumination. A sage or scribe copying a book emphasised the
importance of the tradition of conveying military ideas by means of
the written word; the bearded/robed 'philosopher'/sage/author signified
the importance of thought, not simply energy and blind action, in fighting a successful war; the ruler, often crowned, receiving advice from the
'philosopher' and his book, represented the need for the ruler to be well
informed about military affairs. It is no coincidence that a number of
the works considered in Part II of this study were books of instruction
or advice offered to princes. At the same time knights on horseback

---

[277] *DRM*, III, 13; Contamine, 'L'art de la guerre selon Philippe de Clèves', 373–4.

[278] I have seen only one manuscript of the *De re militari* which showed any signs of having
spent part of its life in somebody's pocket. But perhaps it is those copies, much used
and not confined to libraries, which have perished.

represented the active role envisaged for them as the maintainers, under the ruler, of peace and social order.

Similarly, the importance of training and preparation was underlined visually by illuminations which showed knights honing their skills with the lance; equally, the value of fitness was emphasised with pictures of infantry wrestling with each other. Particular aspects also came under the artist's microscope: scenes of men using different kinds of weapons, not least the bow and arrow; attackers and defenders in situations of siege; a variety of weapons and engines used in such conditions; and war at sea – all were the subject of illuminations intended to emphasise their importance. It was up to the patron/artist to decide what parts of the work's broad message should be drawn to the attention of the reader through the use of illumination. It is not surprising that the *De re militari* was sometimes referred to as the *De disciplina militari*, strongly suggestive that the contents were regarded as expounding the rules and principles of the *scientia militaris* which could be learned and practised by those whose responsibility it was to defend their societies through the use of legitimate and organised force.

The fact that the *De re militari* was used as the authoritative text on military affairs by a succession of writers from the ninth to the sixteenth centuries (and later) shows the esteem in which it was held during that long period. The marginalia found on surviving manuscripts constitute further evidence of that same respect accorded to Vegetian thought by readers who signalled their approval of, or interest in, the manner in which the author had based his advice on practices and experience which had brought success in the past. The authority attributed by readers to the work was underlined yet further by the number of marginalia which contained references to events, such as battles and sieges, which postdated Vegetius' era but which were used to illustrate and give life to points made by him. What such examples suggest is that readers were not surprised to find recommendations which still applied to their own time. To many, the *De re militari* was not a text of mere antiquarian interest, but one with relevance to their own day, as comments found in some manuscripts make clear.[279]

Nor can we ignore the evidence contained in the fifteenth-century translations, for these have much to tell us about the high regard in which the *De re militari* was held by the late medieval world. For a text both practical and philosophical, translation could be regarded as outstanding

---

[279] See Naples, Naz. V. A. 19, fo. 13; BL Harley 2551, fos. 10, 15, 33v, 34v, 44v, 45v, 60v, 61, 61v, 71 (for which see Reeve, 'Transmission', 296–7, 320). To these may be added Vatican, Vat. lat. 2193, fo. 112v (owned by Petrarch) and Madrid, BN 6036, fo. 4.

evidence of the authority accorded to it. Otherwise, why the need for translations into at least six western European languages before 1500? The different approaches of translators to the Latin text tell us yet more about the work's *auctoritas* as they saw it. The updating of passages of technical complexity, such as references to outmoded weapons, taxed the skills of translators who may have wished to show that the *De re militari* still possessed relevance in their own day. The practice followed by some of allowing a certain flexibility in translation may be seen as evidence of the need to maintain the enduring pre-eminence of a text which might otherwise have found itself in limbo with other works whose usefulness had passed.

The relatively early date of the first printings, in the mid-1470s, also points to the practical authority being accorded to this late classical work, which, as happened in other cases, continued to be copied even after the advent of printing. With this development, and the introduction of commercial considerations into the production of the text, various methods were used to emphasise to the prospective customer the importance and value of the work on offer. Elaborate title pages and formal dedications, wordy prefaces justifying the significance of the text, the addition of illustrative material to help readers understand what they were reading, were all part of the printers' campaign to present the *De re militari* as a work which, offering lessons regarding the fighting of war learned long ago, was still valued by men active in war in the years around 1500. In a similar fashion we may see the production of a composite volume containing works bound together by unity of theme (such was the innovation of Eucharius Silber in 1487)[280] as an important step in the large-scale production of major works on military affairs, each lending to the others something of its own *auctoritas* in the creation of a new one in which all could share. After an existence of over one thousand years, although perhaps showing signs of age, and with its virtual monopoly as the authoritative provider of advice on the waging of war being slowly eroded, Vegetius' *De re militari* still had much to offer. A 'mediocre' text? Hardly so. By 1500 its influence in a number of spheres of human activity and thought deserved more than grudging acceptance, while the story of its existence in print during the sixteenth and seventeenth centuries showed that its influence was not yet a thing of the past.[281]

---

[280] See above, p. 59.

[281] S. Anglo, 'Vegetius's "De re militari": the triumph of mediocrity', *The Antiquaries Journal*, 82 (2002), 247–67; P. Richardot, 'La tradition moderne du *De re militari* de Végèce (XVe–XVIIIe siècles)', in *Hommages à Carl Deroux. V. Christianisme et moyen âge, néo-latin et survivance de la latinité*, ed. P. Defosse (Brussels, 2003), 537–44.

Appendix I
Table of select terms used in translations
of the *De re militari*

Latin	Anglo-Norman (c.1270)	French 1 (1284)	French 2 (?mid s. xiv)	Italian 1 (c.1280)	Italian 2 (s.xv)	Catalan 1 (s.xiv (1))	Catalan 2 (c.1390)	Castilian (c.1400)	English 1 (1408)	English 2 (1458)	German (c.1475)
acies	schiera, compaignie, eschele	bataille, ost	bataille, escheles	ordine, schiera	batagla, ordine, schiera	battala, companya, escales	batalla, scala	(h)az	scheltrun	ege, frounte	spicz
adversarius	adversaire	aversaire, anemi	adversaire	nemico	adversario	enemics	adversari, enemichs	adversario	enemyes	adverser, adversaunt, foo	widersacher
aries	ariet	mouton	mouton	bolcioni, ariete	ariete	moltons	moltó, piquer	carnero	ram, tope, wetheres	ram	wider
auxilia	aide	aides	auxilia	aiuto	auxilii, subsidii	adjuda	ajudes	arudas	helperes	ayde	hilff, auxilia, zusecz
bellator	combatanz	bateilleur	combatans	combatitore	combatente	batallers	combatens	peleador, batallador	werriour, men of armes	chivaler, bellatour, werreour	krieger
bellum/proelium/pugna	bataille	bataille	bataille	battaglia (publica)	batagle, guerra	batalla	batalla, guerra	battala, hueste, pelea	bataile, oost, werre	bataile, fight	krieg, scharmuczen, veldstreit
callista	arblaste	aubaleste	arbalestes	balestri	balestre	ballestes	balestes	vallestas	springolus	crosbowys	schießzeug
castra	herbergerie	herberges	herberges	oste, campo	alogiamenti	ost	(h)ost, camp	hueste	warde	castel, bastile, fortresse	wagenburg
classicum	busigne	clasiques	chalemeour	classica	clasici	butzina	botziners	bocineros	hornes		veldgeschray

cohor(te)s	compaignies	cohortes, compaignies	compaignies	compagnie	squadre	escala, companyes	cohorts	companias, corte	warde, chors, chorte	cohors, feleshepe	haussen, cohortes
dux	prince, iuges, mestres	dus	duc	doge	duce, capitani	duc	maestre, capita	caudillo	duke, lederes, cheventeynes	duke, principal captayn	haupleutte, furst hauptman, zeug
equites	gent a chival	ceus a cheval, chevaliers	chevaliers, homes a cheval, legiere armeure	cavalieri	li cavalli, homini de cavalo	cavallers	gent a cavall, homens de cavall	los/omes de cavallo	horsmen, knights	hors, horsedmen, ryderys	der reizig zeug
exercitus	ost	olz, ost	ost, multitude de gens assemblee de faire bataille	oste	exercito	ost	host	hueste	ost, oost	oste, ooste	zeug
falx	falx	faus	faucille	falci	falce	falc	falc	fos	sithe, zykel	sekel or the sithe	sichel, falce
hasta	darz	hanste	(h)astes	hasta	hasta	lances	lança	asta, lança	lances	spere	sper
hostes	enemis	anemi, enemi	henemis	inimici	enemici, adversario	enemics	enemichs	enemigos	enemyes	foomen, the foon	vigend
lupus	lup	lou	lups	lupo	lupo	lop	leu	lobo	wolf	wulf	wolff
machina	engin	engins	engins	detti	instrumenti	armes, artificis	enginys o artificis	instruments	instrumentz, engynes	engyne	gerist

(cont.)

(cont.)

Latin	Anglo-Norman (c.1270)	French 1 (1284)	French 2 (?mid s. xiv)	Italian 1 (c.1280)	Italian 2 (s.xv)	Catalan 1 (s.xiv (1))	Catalan 2 (c.1390)	Castilian (c.1400)	English 1 (1408)	English 2 (1458)	German (c.1475)
miles, milites	chivalers	chevaliers	chevaliers, tirons, homes d'armes/de l'ost, com-paignons, gens qui doivent combatre, preux, chevetaines	cavaliere	homo d'arme, soldati	cavallers, batallers	gent armada	cavallos, cavalleros	fightares, knightes	chivaler, knyght, werreour	ritter
obsidio	sege	siege	siege	assedio	obsedio	setge	setge	cerca	sege	assege	beleger
onager	onagre	trebuché	onagres	onagro	onagri	giyns,	giny	onagros	springofs	onagir, onagre	pleydon
pedites	gent a pie	ceus/genz/ home à pié, poomiers	peons	pedoni	homini a piedi, pedoni	peons	peons	peones	footmen	footmen, men on foote	fussknecht
praefectus	prevost	prevost	proufit, prefet	prefetto	perfecto	prefeyt	prefet	mayoral	prefecte, meir	provost	vogt
res militaris	art de/ chose ke apartient a chivalerie	chose de chevalerie	art de chevalerie, doctrine des armes, maniere de l'ost, discipline d'armes	cosa/arte della cavalleria	cosa militare	art de feyt d'armes, cavalleria	mester de cavalleria/ d'armes	ordenança/ arte de la cavalleria	chivalrye, dedes of armes		ritterschaft

Latin											
res publica	la commune chose	chose commune	chose commune, le com(m)un	salute/utilita della republica	lo stato, la salute de lo stato	comunitat, conservacio de la terra, comu	comu, ciutat	comun, cosa/bien/provecho comun, comunidat, tierra	common profit, profight of the comynalte	commyn wele	gemainen nucz
tiro(nes)	chivalers, gent as armes, iovenceaus	noviaus chevaliers	iovanciaus, tirons, sergens	cavaliere	nuovi/homini, soldati	jovenes, cavaller, les novells qui son elets a feyt d'armes	tirons, jovens cavallers	tirones, mancebos	fighteris, knightis, werriours	werreoure, bacheler	neue ritter
tubicine	busigne	trompeurs	tronbeours	trombadori	tubicini	trompadors	trompadors	canares	trumpes	trumpet	trumeter
turma	banere, tourbe, turmes	tourbes ou turmes, compaignies	compaignie	turma	turme	turma, companyes dels cavallers	turmes	turba, tropel	route	tourmys	schar
vineae.. quas . . . caucias vocant	caucias	vingnes	vineis	vineae	vinee	vinyes (les quals nos apellam caucies)	gat	vinias	vynetus	vyneyerd	schneggen

Appendix II
List of manuscripts of the *De re militari*

The list of manuscripts which follows has been drawn up to include those identified since the publication of Dr Shrader's pioneering list (*Scriptorium*, 33 (1979), 280–305). The number in the final column here refers to that given to a particular manuscript in that list, to which the reader requiring more than the basic information offered here is referred.

Latin manuscripts

Location	Institution	Shelf mark	Date	Shrader
Alba Julia	Bibl. Batthyáni	III. 42, fos. 1–28	s. xiv	1
Ann Arbor	Univ. of Michigan	H. S. Smith 1, fos. 1–62	s. xii	2
Ansbach	Staatliche Bibl.	lat. 23, fos. 322v–357	s. xv	–
Antwerp	Mus. Plantin-Moretus	lat. M. 53, fos. 115–134v	s. xiii	3
Augsburg	Staats-u. Stadtbibl.	8° 161, fos. 7–101v	1435	4
Berlin	Staatsbibl.	lat. oct. 3, fos. 1–234	s. xv	6
		lat. oct. 141, fos. 55–107	s. xv	7
		theol. lat. fol. 239, fos. 321–343v	1374	9
Bern	Burgerbibl.	280	s. x	10
Bologna	Bibl. Com.	A. 146, fos. 1–26	s. xiv	13
	Bibl. Univ.	12 Busta II 2, fos. 1–22v	s. xiii/xiv	–
	Collegio di Spagna	147, fos. 67–94	1330	14
Boston (Mass.)	Public Lib.	fos. med. 22, fos. 1–69	s. xv	15
Cambridge	Fitzwilliam Mus.	Marlay Add. 1, fos. 91–151v	s. xiii	M1
	Peterhouse	75, fos. 11–16	s. xiv	17
		196, fos. 1–26v	s. xv	18
	Trinity Coll.	O. 3 29, fos. 1–47	s. xv	19
Cesena	Bibl. Malatestiana	S. XIX 5, fos. 169–203v	s. xv	20
Copenhagen	Kong. Bibl.	GKS 338, fos. 1–27v	s. xv	–
Dresden	Landes-u. Univ. Bibl.	Dc 182	(war damaged)	–

Latin manuscripts (cont.)

Location	Institution	Shelf mark	Date	Shrader
Durham (NC)	Duke Univ. Lib.	lat. 115, fos. 1–29	s. xv	–
Erfurt	Univ.	CA 2° 5, fos. 1–27v	s. xiv/xv	27
Escorial	Real Bibl.	F. iv. 28, fos. 1–161	s. xiv	24
		L. iii. 33, fos. 1–65v	s. ix/x	25
		O. iii. 9, fos. 48–81v	s. xiii	26
Eton	College Lib.	131, fos. 206–217v	s. xiv	29
Florence	Bibl. Laurenziana	Red. 151, fos. 85–105	s. xv	30
		S. Croce, Plut. 20, sin. 9, fos. 107–131	s. xiv	31
		S. Croce, Plut. 24, sin. 6, fos. 1–26	s. xiii/xiv	32
		Plut. 39. 39, fos. 1–56	s. xiv	33
		Plut. 45. 20, fos. 1–71v	s. xv	34
		Plut. 45. 21, fos. 1–75v	s. xv	35
		Plut. 53. 12, fos. 19–31	1396	36
		Plut. 89, inf. 28, fos. 82–156	s. xv	37
		Plut. 89 inf. 41, fos. 113–130	s. xiii	38
	Bibl. Moreniana	Frullani 24, fos. 5–81v	s. xv	–
	Bibl. Naz.	II. I. 75, fos. 32–49	s. xiv	40
		XIX. 72, fos. 1–43	s. xiv/xv	–
	Bibl. Riccardiana	522, fos. 1–17v	s. xiii/xiv	41
Foligno	Bibl. L. Jacobilli	C. VI. 13, fos. 48–71	s. xiv	–
Giessen	Univ. Bibl.	1256, fos. 154–201	1463	42
Göteborg	Univ. Bibl.	lat. 22, fos. 1–54	s. xv	45
Gotha	Forschungsbibl.	II 113, fos. 1–12	s. xiii	46
The Hague	Konink. Bibl.	78 F 4, fos. 137–159v	s. xv	47
Holkham	Holkham Hall	398, fos. 1–34v	s. xiv	48
Klosterneuburg	Stiftsbibl.	1094, fos. 3–42v	s. xv	50
Korčula	Op. Rizn	7	s. xv/xvi	51
Kraków	Bibl. Jagiellońska	1952, pp. 1–94	s. xv	–
		2120, pp. 473–567	s. xv	–
Lambach	Stiftsbibl.	Chart. 20, fos. 322–352v	1472	52
Laon	Bibl. Mun.	428, fos. 1–67	s. ix	53
Leiden	Univ. Bibl.	BPL 19, fos. 180–203	s. xv	54
		BPL 62, fos. 1–26	s. xiv	55
		BPL 128, fos. 1–54v	s. xv	56
		BPL 192, fos. 1–66v	s. xv	57
		Periz. F. 17, fos. 66–149	s. ix/x	61
		fos. 150–163v	s. xv	62
		Voss. lat. F. 59, fos. 53–99v	s. xiv/xv	64
		Voss. lat. Q. 59, fos. 1–53	s. xiv/xv	66

(cont.)

Latin manuscripts (cont.)

Location	Institution	Shelf mark	Date	Shrader
		Voss. lat. Q. 115, fos. 1–69v	s. xv	67
Leipzig	Univ. Bibl.	Rep. I. fol. 18, fos. 251–303v	s. xiv/xv	69
London	British Lib. [BL]	Add. Ms 11,698, fos. 2–57v	s. xiii	71
		Add. Ms 12,020, fos. 1–46v	s. xv	72
		Add. Ms 21,242, fos. 1–37v	s. xii/xiii	73
		Add. Ms 38,818, fos. 109–134v	s.xii	74
		Cotton, Cleo. D. i, fos. 83–128v	s. xi	75
		Harley 2475, fos. 219–264v	s. xv	77
		Harley 2551, fos. 1–79v	s. xv	78
		Harley 2667, fos. 2–20	s. xiv	79
		Harley 3859, fos. 1–38	s. xii	80
		Royal 5 E. xxi, fos. 127–186v	s. xiv	81
		Royal 7 C. I, fos. 281–306v	s. xiv	82
		Royal 12 B. xxi, fos. 80–120v	s. xv	83
		Royal 12 C. xxii, fos. 1–80	s. xv	84
		Royal 15 C. iv, fos. 89v–116	s. xiii	85
	Lambeth Palace Lib.	752, fos. 30–50	s. xiii	87
Lund	Univ. Bibl.	8, fos. 1–40	s. xv	89
Madrid	Bibl. Nac. [BN]	6036, fos. 1–37	s. xiv	90
		9245, fos. 1–51	1434	91
Milan	Bibl. Ambrosiana	B 91 sup. fos. 41–69	s. xiii/xiv	92
		D 2 sup. fos. 1–52	s. xii	93
		D 4 inf. fos. 1–35v	s. xiv/xv	94
		G 83 sup. fos. 1–32	s. xiv/xv	95
		I. 108 sup. fos. 1–26	s. xiv/xv	96
		R 6 sup. fos. 1–55	s. xiv	98
	Cap. S. Ambrogio	M. 37, fos. 1–16v	s. xiv	–
Monte Cassino	Bibl. dell'Abbazia	361, fos. 1–41	s. xii	100
		392, fos. 127–257	s. xiii/xiv	101
Montpellier	Bibl. interuniv./ Médecine	133, fos. 66v–97v	s. xii	102
Munich	Bayerische Staatsbibliothek	CLM 522, fos. 79–145	1468	103

Latin manuscripts (cont.)

Location	Institution	Shelf mark	Date	Shrader
		CLM 6368, fos. 1–43	s. ix/x	104
		CLM 14,331, fos. 204v–231v	s. xv	105
Naples	Bibl. Naz.	V. A. 19, fos. 1–23	s. xiv/xv	107
		V. A. 20, fos. 1–13	s. xiii/xv	108
		V. A. 21, fos. 1–36	s. xii	109
		V. A. 22, fos. 1–60	1451	110
	Bibl. Oratoriana dei Girolamini	CF. I. 7, fos. 1–113	s. xv	111
New Haven	Yale Univ. Lib.	Marston, 102, fos. 1–74	s. xv	112
New York	Pierpont Morgan Lib.	M 364, fos. 1–116	s. xv	113
Novara	Bibl. Cap. Duomo	XCV, fos. 1–34v	s. xiv/xv	114
Oxford	Balliol Coll.	146A, fos. 2–19	s. xv	127
	Bodleian Lib.	Auct. F. 3. 1, fos. 1–50v	1494	116
		Auct. F. 3. 2, fos. 125–146v	s. xiv	117
		Auct. F. 3. 3, fos. 106–130	s. xiv	118
		Auct. F. 5. 21, fos. 1–66v	s. xiv	119
		Auct. F. 5. 22, pp. 6–153	s. xv	120
		Canon. class. lat. 274, fos. 1–115	s. xv	123
		Douce 147, fos. 1–12v	s. xv	124
		Lat. class. e. 14, fos. 243–299v	1474	125
		Laud lat. 56, fos. 1–52	s. xv	126
	Lincoln Coll.	lat. 100, fos. 4–34v	s. xii	128
Padua	Accad. Papafava	2, fos. 29–124v	s. xv	–
	Bibl. Cap.	B. 47, fos. 51–99v	s. xiv	130
	Bibl. del Seminario	26, fos. 1–36v	s. xiii	131
Palma de Mallorca	Bibl. Fund. March-Servera	B96–V3–3, fos. 1–46	s. xv	–
Paris	Bibl. Mazarine	3732, fos. 36–65	s. xiii	132
	Bibl. nat. [BnF]	lat. 2454, fos. 205–237v	1472	133
		lat. 3609B, fos. 25–88v	1467	134
		lat. 5691, fos. 21–42v	s. xiv/xv	135
		lat. 5697, fos. 250–290	s. xv	136
		lat. 5719, fos. 44–65	s. xii	137
		lat. 6106, fos. 163v–185v	1435	138
		lat. 6503, fos. 5–27	s. ix	140
		lat. 7230, fos. 1–53	s. ix/x	141
		lat. 7230A, fos. 14–35	s. x	142

(*cont.*)

Latin manuscripts (cont.)

Location	Institution	Shelf mark	Date	Shrader
		lat. 7231, fos. 1–13	s. xi	143
		lat. 7232, fos. 1–79v	s. xiv	144
		lat. 7233, fos. 4–53v	s. xiv	145
		lat. 7234, fos. 1–57v	s. xv	146
		lat. 7235, fos. 1–34	s. xv	147
		lat. 7242, fos. 41–82v	s. xiv	148
		lat. 7383, fos. 1–74	s. ix	150
		lat. 7384, fos. 3–64v	s. xv	151
		lat. 7385, fos. 1–46	s. xv	152
		lat. 7386, fos. 1–51	s. xv	153
		lat. 7387, fos. 3–99	s. xv	154
		lat. 7469, fos. 1–97	1357	155
		lat. 7470, fos. 15–108	s. xv	156
		lat. 10784, fos. 23–50v	s. xv	159
		lat. 15076, fos. 103–166	s. xiv	160
		Smith-Lesouëf 13, fos. 1–68	s. xiv	162
Paris/Chicago	Les Enluminures	fos. 1–80	c.1420	–
Parma	Bibl. Palatina	253, fos. 1–82	s. xv	163
Pisa	Bibl. Univ.	723, fos. 1–14v	s. xiv	164
Prague	Nat. Lib.	2369 (XIII G. 2), fos. 64–103	s. xv	165
	Metropol. Cap. Lib.	O. LIII, fos. 28–73v	1409	–
Private coll.	formerly Phillipps Coll.	16,370, fos. 1–40	s. xii	–
Ravenna	Bibl. Classense	140, fos. 1–69v	1445	166
Rimini	Bibl. Civ. Gambalunga	SC. 33, fos. 59–115	1462	168
Rome	Bibl. Casanatense	512, fos. 1–86	s. xiv	172
		1531, fos. 1–88v	s. xv	173
St Petersburg	National Lib. of Russia	Cl. Lat. Q. 13, fos. 1–86	s. xv	–
Salamanca	Bibl. Univ.	2137, fos. 8–54	s. xv	174
Salzburg	S. Peter Stiftsbibl.	b. viii. 18, fos. 88–141	s. xv	175
San Daniele del Friuli	Bibl. Guarneriana	50, fos. 98–181	1464	176
Schaffhausen	Stadtbibl.	Gen. 27, fos. 1–73	s. xv	177
Seville	Bibl. Capit. y Colombina	7. 7. 21, fos. 157–165	s. xiv	179
Stuttgart	Württembergische Landesbibl.	Don. 81, fos. 1–88	s. xv	21
Târgu-Mureş	Bibl. Judeteana Mureş	Tq. 136 h. 43, fos. 47–111	s. xv	182

Latin manuscripts (cont.)

Location	Institution	Shelf mark	Date	Shrader
Trento	Bibl. Com.	W 3154, fos. 1–40	1437	185
Trier	Stadtbibl.	1083, fos. 119–183v	s. xv	186
Turin	Bibl. Reale	Saluzzo 3, fos. 1–26	s. xv	–
		Saluzzo 15, fos. 1–39	s. xiv	–
Udine	Bibl. Arcivesc.	17, fos. 1–39	s. xiv	187
Uppsala	Univ. Bibl.	C. III, fos. 205–240v	s. xv	–
Valladolid	Bibl. de Santa Cruz	384, fos. 1–76	s. xv	–
Vatican	Bibl. Apost. Vat.	Arch. Cap. S. Pietro, H 33, fos. 1–38v	s. xv	188
		Barb. lat. 2, fos. 1–81	s. xv	189
		Borg. lat. 411, fos. 27–55v	s. xiv	191
		Chigi. H. vii 238, fos. 54v–94v	s. xiii	192
		Ottob. lat. 1437, fos. 1–43v	s. xiv	193
		Ottob. lat. 1964, fos. 1–79	s. xv	194
		Pal. lat. 909, fos. 306–359v	s. x/xi	195
		Pal. lat. 945, fos. 63–83	s. xiv	196
		Pal. lat. 1571, fos. 1–36, 47–49v	s. xii	198
		Pal. lat. 1572, fos. 1–86v	s. ix	199
		Pal. lat. 1573, fos. 1–50v	s. xii	200
		Reg. lat. 114, fos. 90–107v	s. xiv	201
		Reg. lat. 1274, fos. 50v–56v	s. xii	203
		Reg. lat. 1286, fos. 51–77	s. xii	204
		Reg. lat. 1512, fos. 1–48	s. xiv	205
		Reg. lat. 1564, fos. 1–30v	s. xiv/xv	206
		Reg. lat. 1880, fos. 1v–64	s. xv	207
		Reg. lat. 1983, fos. 147–196	s. xv	208
		Urb. lat. 456, fos. 31–38	s. xiv	210
		Urb. lat. 939, fos. 1–38	s. xv	211
		Urb. lat. 1221, fos. 68–132v	s. xv	212
		Urb. lat. 1362, fos. 85v–130	s. xii	213
		Vat. lat. 1860, fos. 64–79v	s. xiv	215

(*cont.*)

Latin manuscripts (cont.)

Location	Institution	Shelf mark	Date	Shrader
		Vat. lat. 2193, fos. 101v–118v	s. xiv	216
		Vat. lat. 4492, fos. 1–37v	1408	217
		Vat. lat. 4493, fos. 1–41v	s. ix	218
		Vat. lat. 4494, fos. 1–46	s. xv	219
		Vat. lat. 4497, fos. 197–228	s. xiv	220
		Vat. lat. 5352, fos. 1–70	s. xv	223
		Vat. lat. 5957, fos. 1–23	s. xiii/xiv	224
		Vat. lat. 7227, fos. 2–37v	s. xiv	225
Venice	Bibl. Naz.	3347, fos. 1–42v	1462	227
	Marciana	4333, fos. 203–252v	s. xv/xvi	228
		4335, fos. 367–377	s. xv	229
		Z. lat. 463, fos. 142–212	s. xv	230
Vibo Valentia	Bibl. Capialbi	38, fos. 1–37	s. xiii–xiv	232
Vicenza	Bibl. Civ. Bertoliana	295, fos. 1–27	s. xiv	233
Vienna	Nationalbibl.	63, fos. 1–61	s. xv	235
		310, fos. 1–96	s. xv	236
		313, fos. 1–119v	s. xv	237
		3212, fos. 1–75	s. xv	238
Vyšší Brod	Stiftsbibl.	62, fos. 1–41	s. xv	234
Warsaw	Bibl. Narodowa	II 8076, fos. 76v–121v	1448	–
Wolfenbüttel	Herzog-August-Bibl.	Gud. lat. 15, fos. 1–34v	1332	239
		Gud. lat. 84, fos. 1–65v	s. ix	240
		Gud. lat. 201, fos. 1–51	s. xiv	241
		Helmst. 351, fos. 227–263	s. xv	242
Wrocław	Bibl. Uniw.	Rehd. 10, fos. 25–74v	1468	243

Latin excerpts

Location	Institution	Shelf mark	Date	Shrader
Basel	Univ. Bibl.	F. V 6, fos. 43–47v	s. xv	5
Bern	Burgerbibl.	550, fo. 188	s. xv	11
Blickling	Blickling Hall	6849, fos. 17–18v	s.xv	12
Cambridge	Clare Coll.	N. 1. 9 (ol. 18), fos. 62–62v	s. xii	16
	Univ. Lib.	Add. 4407.68	s. xiii	–
Dublin	Trinity Coll.	632, fos. 128–129v	s. xv	22
Einsiedeln	Stiftsbibl.	365, pp. 73–4	s. ix/x	23
Erfurt	Univ. Bibl.	CA 4° 393, fos. 1–20	1380	28
Fiecht	Abtei S. Georgenberg	132, fos. 62–64	s. xv	–

Latin manuscripts (cont.)

Location	Institution	Shelf mark	Date	Shrader
Florence	Bibl. Laurenziana	Redi. 151, fos. 85–105	s. xv	30
Klosterneuburg	Stiftsbibl.	740, fos. 209v–212v	s. xv	49
Leiden	Univ. Bibl.	Voss. lat. F 93, fos. 41v–45v	s. xii/xiii	65
London	British Lib. [BL]	Royal 12 E xxi, fos. 5–10v	s. xiv	–
		Harley 957, fos. 2v–8	s. xiii	76
Madrid	Bibl. Nac. [BN]	234, fos. 32–33v	s. xiii/xiv	–
Milan	Bibl. Ambrosiana	L 53 sup, fos. 17v–20v	s. xv	97
	Bibl. Naz. Braidense	AD. XVI. 20, fo. 176v	s. xv	99
Oxford	Bodleian Lib.	Add. C. 12, fos. 130–130v	s. xv	115
		Auct. F. 5. 22, pp. 1–5	s. xv	120
	St John's Coll.	98, fos. 225–226	s. xiv	129
Paris	Bibl. nat. [BnF]	lat. 3497, fos. 88–89	s. xv	–
		lat. 6476, fos. 109–112v	s. xiv	139
		lat. 7233, fos. 1–2	s. xiv	145
		lat. 7695A, fos. 132–133v	s. xiv	–
		lat. 8274, fo. 99	s. xv	157
		lat. 8314, fos. 83–86v	1171	158
		lat. 15172, fo. 133v	s. xiii	–
		nouv. acq. lat. 3074, fos. 37v–38	s. xiv	161
Rein	Stiftsbibl.	205, fo. 225	s. xv	167
Stockholm	Kungl. Bibl.	A. 215, fos. 106v–109	1472	180
Vatican	Bibl. Apost. Vat.	Barb. lat. 135, fo. 32v	s. xv	190
		Reg. lat. 358, fos. 24–26	s. xv	202
		Reg. lat. 2077, fos. 99v–100v	s. vii	209
		Vat. lat. 1494, fo. 43v	1470	214
		Vat. lat. 5114, fos. 79r–79v	s. xv	221
		Vat. lat. 5131, fos. 113–114	s. xv	222
Venice	Bibl. Naz. Marciana	lat. VI 164, fos. 48v–50	s. xiv/xv	226

Excerpts beginning 'Omnes artes'

Berlin	Staatsbibl.	lat. qu. 198, fos. 232–259	*c.*1132	8
Leiden	Univ. Bibl.	Voss. lat. O. 54, fos. 84–90v	1440	68
Oxford	Bodleian Lib.	Canon. class. lat. 268, fos. 1–9v	s. xiv	122

(*cont.*)

Excerpts beginning 'Omnes artes' (cont.)

Location	Institution	Shelf mark	Date	Shrader
Paris	Bibl. nat. [BnF]	lat. 7243, fos. 28–37	s. xiv	149
		lat. 10,784, fos. 23–45v	s. xv	159
Vatican	Bibl. Apost. Vat.	Urb. lat. 456, fos. 31–38	s. xiv	210

Vernacular translations

French translations

I. Anglo-Norman translation

Cambridge	Fitzwilliam Mus.	Marlay Add. 1, fos. 1–90	s. xiii	M1

II. Jean de Meun

Bern	Burgerbibl.	280A, fos. 1–53	s. xv	F2
Brussels	Bibl. royale	II 4847, fos. 1–104v	s. xiv	F6
Carpentras	Bibl. Inguimbertine	332, fos. 1–91	s. xiii/xiv	F11
Chantilly	Musée Condé	344, fos. 1–49	s. xv	F12
Dresden	Landes-u. Univ. Bibl.	Oc 57, fos. 1–41v	s. xiv	F13
The Hague	Konink. Bibl.	73 J 22, fos. 1–89	s. xiv	F16
London	British Lib. [BL]	Royal 20 B xi, fos. 1–95v	s. xiv	F20
		Royal 20 B xv, fos. 1–108	s. xv	F21
		Sloane 2430, fos. 1–108	s. xiii/xiv	F22
Oxford	Bodleian Lib.	Douce 149, fos. 1–111v	s. xiii/xiv	F23
Paris	Bibl. Arsenal	2551, fos. 1–103	s. xiv	F24
		2915, fos. 35–117v	s. xv	F26
		2916, fos. 1–88v	s. xv	F27
	Bibl. nat. [BnF]	fr. 1230, fos. 1–45	s. xiv	F29
		fr. 1231, fos. 1–63v	s. xiv	F30
		fr. 1232, fos. 3–41v	s. xiv	F31
		fr. 2063, fos. 1–107v	s. xiv	F36
		fr. 12,360, pp. 1–265	s. xv	F38
		fr. 19,104, fos. 1–122	s. xv	F39
Turin	Arch. di Stato	Jb II 19, fos. 1–89v	s. xv	F41
		Jb VI 11, fos. 5–85v	s. xv	F42
Vatican	Bibl. Apost. Vat.	Reg. lat. 1628, fos. 1–99	s. xiv	F44

III. Jean Priorat

Paris	Bibl. nat. [BnF]	fr. 1604, fos. 1–76	s. xiii–xiv	F35

Vernacular translations (cont.)

Location	Institution	Shelf mark	Date	Shrader
IV. Jean de Vignay				
Brussels	Bibl. royale	11,048, fos. 1–83	s. xv	F4
		11,195, fos. 1–74	s. xiv	F5
Cambridge	Gonville & Caius Coll.	424, pp. 1–78v	s. xiv	F8
	Magdalene Coll.	PL 1938, fos. 1–77v	s. xiv	F9
	Univ. Libr.	Ee II 17, fos. 3–36v	s. xv	F10
London	British Lib. [BL]	Royal 17 E v, fos. 205–274	s. xv	F18
		Royal 20 B i, fos. 1–31v	s. xiv	F19
Paris	Bibl. nat. [BnF]	fr. 1229, fos. 1–55	s. xiv	F28
Vatican	Bibl. Apost. Vat.	Rossi. 457, fos. 135–168v	s. xiv	F45
V. Anonymous (1380)				
Brussels	Bibl. royale	11,046, fos. 1–75	s. xv	F3
Turin	Bibl. Reale	Saluzzo 188, fos. 1–66	s. xv	F4
VI. Other translations				
Turin	Arch. di Stato	Jb VI 11, fos. 5–85v	s. xv	F42
Wolfenbüttel	Herzog-August-Bibl.	Blankenburg 111, fos. 1–47v	s. xiv	F46
French excerpts				
Bern	Burgerbibl.	607A, fos. 196–197v	s. xiii	–
Geneva	Bibl. publique et universitaire	fr. 83, fos. 102–102v	s. xv	F14
London	British Lib. [BL]	Add. 12028, fos. 173–185v	s. xv	F17
Paris	Bibl. Arsenal	2693, fos. 124v–133v	s. xv	F25
	Bibl. nat. [BnF]	fr. 1234, fos. 140v–141v	s. xv	F32
		fr. 1235, fos. 147–158	s. xv	F33
		fr. 1563, fos. 144v–147	s. xv	F34
		fr. 5930, fos. 6v–11	s. xv	F37
		fr. 24, 257, fos. 76v–77v	s. xv	–
Rouen	Bibl. Mun.	997, fos. 1–39	s. xiv	F40

(cont.)

Vernacular translations (cont.)

Location	Institution	Shelf mark	Date	Shrader

Italian translations

I. Bono Giamboni

Florence	Bibl. Laurenziana	Plut. 43. 20, f 1–34	s. xv	I2
	Bibl. Naz.	II ii 73, fos. 154–190	s. xiv	–
		II iv 125, fos. 1–50	s. xiv	I4
	Bibl. Riccardiana	1054, fos. 1–41v	s. xiv	–
		1396, fos. 55–76v	s. xv	I6
		1614, fos. 1–61	s. xiv	I7

II. Venanzio da Bruschino

Florence	Bibl. Naz.	nuov. acq. 291, pp. 7–173	s. xv	I5
Naples	Bibl. Oratoriana dei Girolamini	CF. II. 23, fos. 7–92	s. xv	I9

III. Other translations

Cambridge (Mass.)	Harvard Coll. Houghton Lib.	Italian 68, fos. 1–51	s. xv	I1
Florence	Bibl. Naz.	II ii 72, fos. 82v–131	s. xiv	I3
Vibo Valentia	Bibl. dei Conti Capialbi	39, fos. 1–85	s. xv	I10

Italian excerpts

Florence	Bibl. Laurenziana	Plut. 89 inf. 54, fos. 1–12	1456	39
		Plut. 89 inf. 42	s. xvi	M2
Naples	Bibl. Naz.	IX C 24, fos. 63v–69v	s. xv	–
Sant Cujat del Vallès	Bibl. Borja	Fons E, Varia	s. xv	–

Iberian translations

I. Castilian

El Escorial	Real Bibl.	&. ii. 18, fos. 1–123	s. xv	S1
		P. i. 23, fos. 1–94	s. xv	S2
Madrid	Real Bibl.	II/569, fos. 1–129	s. xv	–
Paris	Bibl. nat. [BnF]	Esp. 211, fos. 1–59	s. xv	S3
		Esp. 295, fos. 1–70	s. xv	–
Santander	Bibl. Menéndez y Pelayo	94, fos. 1–93	s. xv	–

Vernacular translations (cont.)

Location	Institution	Shelf mark	Date	Shrader
II. Catalan				
Madrid	Bibl. F. de Zabálburu	1655, fos. 1–68v	s. xiv	–
Palma de Mallorca	Bibl. Fund. March Servera	B96–V3–2, fos. 1–63v	s. xv	–
III. Castilian excerpts				
Madrid	Bibl. Nac. [BN]	8555, fos. 1–25v	s. xvi	–
		10,445, fos. 140–142v	s. xv	–
	Real Bibl.	II. 1842, fos. 256–262v	s. xv	–

English translations

I. Prose translation

Location	Institution	Shelf mark	Date	Shrader
Cambridge	Univ. Lib.	Add. 8706, fos. 1–102v	s. xv	E17
London	British Lib. [BL]	Add. 4713, fos. 4–93v	s. xv	E2
		Add. 14,408, fos. 49–66	s. xv	E3
		Harley 6761, fos. 13–57v	s. xvi	E6
		Lansdowne 285, fos. 84–138	s. xv	E7
		Royal 18 A xii, fos. 1–123	s. xv	E8
		Sloane 2027, fos. 1–36v	s. xv	E9
New York	Pierpont Morgan Lib.	M 775, fos. 25–121v	s. xv	E10
Oxford	Bodleian Lib.	Digby 233, fos. 183–227	s. xv	E12
		Douce 291, fos. 4–120v	s. xv	E13
		Laud misc 416, fos. 182–226v	1459	E14
	Magdalen Coll.	lat. 30, fos. 2–114v	s. xv	E15

II. Verse translation (Knyghthode & bataile)

Location	Institution	Shelf mark	Date	Shrader
Cambridge	Pembroke Coll.	243, fos. 1–55v	s. xv	E1
London	British Lib. [BL]	Cotton, Titus A xxiii, fos. 1–56v	s. xv	E4
Oxford	Bodleian Lib.	Ashmole 45, pp. 1–7, 18–23, 41–3, 46–56	s. xv	E11

(cont.)

Vernacular translations (cont.)

Location	Institution	Shelf mark	Date	Shrader
III. Scottish excerpts				
London	British Lib. [BL]	Harley 6149, fos. 128v–132v	s. xv	E5
Oxford	Queen's Coll.	161, fos. 97v–100v	s. xv	E16
German translations				
I. Ludwig Hohenwang				
Karlsruhe	Badische Landesbibl.	Durlach 18, fos. 1–77v	s. xv	G1
Linz	Stadtbibl.	420, fos. 1–9	s. xvi	G2
II. Anonymous				
Seitenstetten	Stiftsbibl.	65, fos. 2–146v	*c.*1438	178

Bibliography

MODERN EDITIONS OF VEGETIUS' *DE RE MILITARI*

Epitoma rei militaris, ed. C. Lang (Leipzig, 1869; second edn, Leipzig, 1885) [Particularly useful for its 'Index verborum']

ed. M. T. Callejas Bordones (Books I and II) and F. Del Barrio Vega (Books III and IV) (Madrid, 1982). [See also below, *sub* 'Modern translations: Spanish']

Epitoma rei militaris (with an English translation), ed. L. F. Stelton (New York, 1990)

Epitoma rei militaris, ed. A. Önnersfors (Stuttgart and Leipzig, 1995)

Abriss des Militärwesens (with a German translation), ed. F. L. Müller (Stuttgart, 1997)

Epitoma rei militaris, ed. M. D. Reeve (Oxford, 2004)

MEDIEVAL VERNACULAR TRANSLATIONS

CASTILIAN

An edition of the Castilian translation is being prepared by José Manuel Fradejas.

CATALAN

'La versió catalana de l'Epitoma rei militaris de Vegeci: introducció i transcripció del manuscrit del segle XIV de la Biblioteca Bartomeu March', Palma [1985] (The unpublished text of the second Catalan translation, transcribed by Antoni Alomar Canyelles, may be consulted at the Biblioteca Bartomeu March, or at the Departament de Filologia Catalana, Universitat de les Illes Balears, Palma de Mallorca)

ENGLISH

The earliest English translation of Vegetius' De re militari, ed. G. A. Lester (Heidelberg, 1988)

Knyghthode and bataile. A XVth century verse paraphrase of Flavius Vegetius Renatus' treatise 'De re militari', ed. R. Dyboski and Z. M. Arend (EETS, o.s. 221, London, 1936)

FRENCH

L'art de chevalerie. Traduction du De re militari de Végèce par Jean de Meun, ed. U. Robert (SATF, Paris, 1897)
Li abrejance de l'ordre de chevalerie, mis en vers de la traduction de Végèce de Jean de Meun par Jean Priorat, ed. U. Robert (SATF, Paris, 1897)
Li abregemenz noble honme Vegesce Flave René des establissemenz apartenanz a chevalerie, traduction par Jean de Meun de Flavii Vegeti Renati viri illustris Epitoma Institutorum Rei Militaris, ed. L. Löfstedt (Helsinki, 1977)
Li livres Flave Vegece de la chose de chevalerie par Jean de Vignay, ed. L. Löfstedt (Helsinki, 1982)
Le livre de l'art de chevalerie de Vegesce. Traduction anonyme de 1380, ed. L. Löfstedt *et al.* (Helsinki, 1989)

GERMAN

Kurcze Red von der Ritterschafft, trans. Ludwig Hohenwang (Augsburg, *c.*1475)

ITALIAN

Di Vegezio Flavio, Dell'arte della Guerra, libri IV. Volgarizzamento di Bono Giamboni, ed. F. Fontani (Florence, 1815)
L'Ars militaris di Flavio Vegezio Renato: volgarizzamento del libro primo da un codice della Nazionale di Napoli inedito ed illustrato da Giovanni Tria (Naples, 1887)

MODERN TRANSLATIONS

ENGLISH

Epitoma rei militaris, trans. L. F. Stelten (New York, 1990) [Latin and English translation]
Vegetius: Epitome of military science, trans. N. P. Milner (Liverpool, 1993; 2nd rev. edn, 1996)

GERMAN

Vegetius: Das gesamte Kriegswesen, trans. F. Wille (Aarau, Frankfurt and Salzburg, 1986)
Abriss des Militärwesens, trans. F. L. Müller (Stuttgart, 1997) [Latin and German translation]

ITALIAN

Compendio d'arte militare, trans. T. Mariotti (Treviso, 1878; Rome 1937)
Compendio delle istituzioni militari, trans. C. G. Manmana (Catania, 1997)
Vegezio, L'arte della guerra, trans. L. Canali and M. Pellegrini (Milan, 2001)

P. Flavio Vegezio Renato, L'arte della guerra romana, trans. M. Formisano (Milan, 2003)

Flavio Vegezio Renato, L'Arte militare, trans. G. Ortolani (Rome, 2009) [Latin and Italian translation]

POLISH

'*Epitoma rei militaris, Lib. I & II*', *Meander*, 28 (1973), 403–17, 485–501; '*Epitoma rei militaris, Lib. III & IV*', trans. A. Komornicka, *Meander*, 29, (1974), 198–232, 333–52

PORTUGUESE

Vegécio. Tratado de ciência militar, trans. A. de Man (Lisbon, 2006)

Vegécio. Compêndio da arte militar, trans. J. G. Monteiro and J. E. Braga (Coimbra, 2009) [Latin and Portuguese translation]

SPANISH

Flavio Vegecio Renato, *Instituciones militares*, trans. J. Belda Carreras (Madrid, 1929)

Edición crítica y traducción del 'Epitoma rei militaris' de Vegetius, libros I y II, a la luz de los manuscritos españoles y de los más antiguos testimonios europeos, ed. M. T. Callejas Bordones (Madrid, 1982)

Edición crítica y traducción del 'Epitoma rei militaris' de Vegetius, libros III y IV, a la luz de los manuscritos españoles y de los más antiguos testimonios europeos, ed. F. Del Barrio Vega (Madrid, 1982)

Flavio Vegecio Renato, *El arte de la guerra romana*, trans. A. R. Menéndez Argüin (Madrid, 2005)

Flavio Vegecio Renato, *Compendio de técnica militar*, trans. D. Paniagua Aguilar (Madrid, 2006)

PRINTED SOURCES

Aegidii Columnae Romani [Giles of Rome], *De regimine principum. Lib. III* (Rome, 1607; repr. Aalen, 1967)

Aristotle, *The Politics*

Ashmole, E., *The institution, laws and ceremonies of the most noble Order of the Garter* (London, 1672)

Balsac, Robert de, *La nef des princes et des batailles...* (Lyons, 1502)

Barbour, John, *The Bruce*, ed. W. W. Skeat (EETS, 2 vols., e.s. 55, London, 1870, 1889)

Basin, Thomas, *Histoire de Charles VII*, trans. C. Samaran (2 vols., Paris, 1933, 1944)

Baye, Nicolas de, *Journal... 1400–1417*, ed. A. Tuetey (2 vols., SHF, Paris, 1885, 1888)

Beauvais, Vincent of, *Speculum doctrinale* (Strasbourg, 1472)

Bede, *The Ecclesiastical History of the English People*, ed. B. Colgrave and R. A. B. Mynors (Oxford, 1991)

The Boke of Noblesse addressed to King Edward the Fourth on his invasion of France in 1475, ed. J. G. Nichols (Roxburghe Club, 1860; repr. New York, 1972)

Bonet, Honoré, *L'arbre des batailles*, ed. E. Nys (Brussels and Leipzig, 1883); English trans. and ed. G. W. Coopland, *The tree of battles of Honoré Bonet* (Liverpool, 1949)

Breton, Guillaume le [and Rigord], *Œuvres* ed. F. Delaborde (2 vols., SHF, Paris, 1882–85)

Bromyard, John, *Summa praedicantium* (Basel, *c.*1494)

The Brut, or the chronicles of England, ed. F. W. D. Brie (EETS, 2 vols., o.s. 131, 136, London, 1906, 1908)

Bueil, Jean de, *Le Jouvencel*, ed. L. Lecestre (2 vols., SHF, Paris, 1887–89)

Cartagena, Alonso de, *Tratados militares*, ed. N. Fallows (Madrid, 2006)

Caxton, William, *The Book of the Ordre of Chyualry*, ed. A. T. P. Byles (EETS, o.s. 168, London, 1926)

Charny, Geoffroi de, *The Book of Chivalry. Text, context, and translation*, ed. and trans. R. W. Kaeuper and E. Kennedy (Philadelphia, 1996)

Chartier, Alain, *Le quadrilogue invectif*, ed. E. Droz (2nd edn, Paris, 1950)

Chronicles and memorials of the reign of Richard I, ed. W. Stubbs (RS, London, 1864)

Clèves, Philippe de, seigneur de Ravenstein, *L'Instruction de toutes manières de guerroyer . . . sur mer*, ed. J. Paviot (Paris, 1997)

Commynes, Philippe de, *Mémoires*, ed. J. Calmette (3 vols., Paris, 1924–25)

'Complainte sur la bataille de Poitiers', ed. C. de Beaurepaire, *BEC*, 3rd ser., 2 (1851), 257–63

Le débat des hérauts d'armes de France et d'Angleterre, ed. L. Pannier (SATF, Paris, 1877)

Deschamps, Eustache, *Œuvres complètes*, ed. Q. de Saint-Hilaire (11 vols., SATF, Paris, 1878–1903)

Doctoris ecstatici D. Dionysii Cartusiani opera omnia. Opera minora, V (Tournai, 1909)

English suits before the Parlement of Paris, 1420–1436, ed. C. T. Allmand and C. A. J. Armstrong (RHistS, London, 1982)

Erasmus, Desiderius, *The Correspondence*, Letters 1 to 141, *1484–1500*, ed. W. K. Ferguson, trans. R. A. B. Mynors and D. F. S Thomson, I (Toronto, 1974)

Eschenbach, Wolfram von, *Willehalm*, trans. M. E. Gibbs and S. M. Johnson (Harmondsworth, 1984)

Fortescue, Sir John, *De laudibus legum Anglie*, ed. and trans. S. B. Chrimes (Cambridge, 1942)

   On the laws and governance of England, ed. and trans. S. Lockwood (Cambridge, 1997)

Four English political tracts of the later Middle Ages, ed. J.-P. Genet (RHistS, London, 1977)

Frechulfi Lexoviensis episcopi, opera omnia, ed. M. I. Allen (*CCCM*, Turnhout, 2002)

Frontinus, Julius, *Strategemata*, ed. R. I. Ireland (Leipzig, 1990)

Gerson, Jean, *Œuvres complètes. II. L'œuvre épistolaire*, ed. P. Glorieux (Paris, 1960)

Hoccleve, Thomas, *Works, III*, ed. F. J. Furnivall (EETS, e.s. 72, London, 1897)

'*L'Honneur de la couronne de France*', ed. N. Pons (SHF, Paris, 1990)

Juvénal des Ursins, Jean, *Écrits politiques*, ed. P. S. Lewis (3 vols., SHF, Paris, 1978–92)

Kyeser, Conrad (aus Eichstätt), *Bellifortis*, ed. G. Quarg (2 vols., Düsseldorf, 1967)

Legnano, Giovanni da, *Tractatus de bello, de represaliis et de duello*, ed. T. Holland (Washington, DC., 1917)

Letters and papers illustrative of the wars of the English in France during the reign of Henry the Sixth, King of England, ed. J. Stevenson (2 vols. in 3, RS, London, 1861–64)

El libro de la guerra, ed. L. de Torre, *Revue hispanique*, 38 (1916), 497–531; '*Libro de la guerra*'. *Compendio castigliano del 'De re militari' di Flavio Vegezio Renato*, ed. I. Scoma (Messina, 2004); 'El *Libro de la guerra* y la traducción de Vegecio por Fray Alfonso de San Cristobal', *Anuario de estudios medievales*, 37 (1) (2007), 267–304

Lucca, Ptolemy of, *On the government of rulers. De regimine principum, with portions attributed to Thomas Aquinas*, trans. J. M. Blythe (Philadelphia, 1997)

Machaut, Guillaume de, *Œuvres. III. Le confort d'ami*, ed. E. Hoepffner (SATF, Paris, 1921)

Machiavelli, Niccolò, *The Prince*, trans. Q. Skinner and R. Price (Cambridge, 1988)

Maurice [Emperor], *Strategikon. Handbook of Byzantine military strategy*, ed. G. T. Dennis (Philadelphia, 1984)

Mézières, Philippe de, *Le songe du vieil pèlerin*, ed. G. W. Coopland (2 vols., Cambridge, 1969)

Migne, J. P. (ed.) *Patrologia latina*, 199 (Paris, 1855)

Milemete, *Walter of, De nobilitatibus, sapientiis et prudentiis regum*, ed. M. R. James (Roxburghe Club, London, 1913)

Molinet, Jean, *Chronique de*, eds. G. Doutrepont and O. Jodogu (3 vols., Brussels, 1935–37)

Ordonnances des rois de France de la troisième race (22 vols., Paris, 1723–1849)

Petrarch, Francesco, *Africa*, trans. T. G. Bergin and A. S. Wilson (New Haven and London, 1977)

La Philippide, poème, par Guillaume le Breton, Collection des mémoires relatifs à l'histoire de France, ed. F. Guizot (Paris, 1825)

Pisan, Christine de, *The book of fayttes of armes and of chyualrye*, trans. W. Caxton, ed. A. T. P. Byles (EETS, o. s. 189, London, 1932)

Le livre des fais et bonnes meurs du sage roy Charles V, ed. S. Solente (2 vols., SHF, Paris, 1936–40)

Le livre du corps de policie, ed. R. H. Lucas (Geneva and Paris, 1967)

Der pulcher tractatus de material belli. Ein Beitrag zur Kriegs- und Geistesgeschichte des Mittelalters, ed. A. Pichler (Graz, Vienna and Leipzig, 1927)

Rabanus Maurus, 'De procinctu Romanae miliciae', ed. E. Dümmler, *Zeitschrift für Deutsches Altherthum*, 15 (1872), 443–51

Registrum Anglie de libris doctorum et auctorum veterum, eds. R. H. and M. A. Rouse, with R. A. B. Mynors (London, 1991)

Le rosier des guerres, enseignements de Louis XI, roy de France, pour le dauphin son fils, ed M. Diamantberger (Paris, 1925)

Rothe, Johannes, *Der Ritterspiegel*, ed. H. Neumann (Halle/Salle, 1936)

Salisbury, John of, *Policraticus*, ed. C. C. J. Webb (2 vols., Oxford, 1927). *The stateman's book of John of Salisbury. Being the fourth, fifth and sixth books of the Policraticus*, trans. J. Dickinson (New York, 1963). *Policraticus*, trans. C. J. Nederman (Cambridge, 1990)

Scottus, Sedulius, *Collectaneum miscellaneum*, ed. D. Simpson (*CCCM*, 67, Turnhout, 1988)

Seffner, Johann, 'Lehre vom Krieg', *Deutschen Chroniken und andere Geschichtsbücher des Mittelalters. VI. Österreichische Chronik von den 95 Herrschaften* (MGH, Hanover and Leipzig, 1909), 224–30

Las Siete Partidas del rey Don Alfonso el Sabio. Tomo I I. Partida segun y tercera (Madrid, 1807). *Las siete partidas. Volume 2: Medieval government. The world of kings and warriors*, ed. R. I. Burns and trans. S. P. Scott (Philadelphia, 2001)

Stuart, Bérault, seigneur d'Aubigny, *Traité sur l'art de la guerre*, ed. E. de Comminges (The Hague, 1976)

Sun Tzu, *The art of war*, trans. S. B. Griffiths (Oxford, 1963)

Testamenta Eboracensia, or wills registered at York, ed. J. Raine (Surtees Society, London, 1836)

Un texto inédito sobre la caballeria del Renacimiento español. Doctrina del arte de la cavalleria, de Juan Quijada de Reay, ed. N. Fallows (Liverpool, 1996)

The usurpation of Richard the Third. Dominicus Mancinus ad Angelum Catonem De occupatione regni Anglie per Riccardum tercium libellus, ed. and trans. C. A. J. Armstrong (2nd edn, Oxford, 1969)

Valturius, R. *De re militari* (Verona, 1472)

Venette, Jean de, *Chronicle*, ed. R. A. Newhall and trans. J. Birdsall (New York, 1953)

Vitalis, Orderic, *Historia ecclesiastica*, ed. and trans. M. Chibnall (6 vols., Oxford, 1968–80)

Wallensis, Joannis [John of Wales], *Communiloquium sive summa collationum* (1489)

Whethamstede, John, *Registra quorundam abbatum monasterii S. Albani*, ed. H. T. Riley (RS, 2 vols., London, 1872–73)

Zamora, Juan Gil de, *De preconiis Hispanie*, ed. M. de Castro y Castro (Madrid, 1955)

SECONDARY LITERATURE

Abels, R. and Morillo, S. 'A lying legacy? A preliminary discussion of images of antiquity and altered reality in medieval military history', *JMMH*, 3 (2005), 1–13

Agrait, N. 'Castilian military reform under the reign of Alfonso XI', *JMMH*, 3 (2005), 88–126

Allen, M. I. 'Flavius Vegetius Renatus. Addenda et corrigenda', in *Catalogus translationum et commentariorum. Medieval and Renaissance translations and commentaries. Annotated lists and guides*, VIII, ed. V. Brown *et al.* (Washington, DC, 2003), 336–40

Allmand, C. T. *The Hundred Years War. England and France at war, c.1300–c.1450* (1988, rev. edn, Cambridge, 2001)

'Intelligence in the Hundred Years War', in *Go spy the land. Military intelligence in history*, ed. K. Neilson and B. J. C. McKercher (Westport, Conn. and London, 1992), 31–47

'Fifteenth-century English versions of Vegetius' *De Re Militari*', in *Armies, Chivalry and Warfare*, ed. Strickland, 30–45

'War', in *The New Cambridge Medieval History. VII. c.1415–c.1500*, ed. C. Allmand (Cambridge, 1998), 161–74

'Entre honneur et bien commun: le témoignage du *Jouvencel* au XVe siècle', *RH*, 301 (1999), 463–81

'Le problème de la désertion en France, en Angleterre et en Bourgogne à la fin du moyen âge', in *Guerre, pouvoir et noblesse au moyen âge. Mélanges en l'honneur de Philippe Contamine*, ed. J. Paviot and J. Verger (Paris, 2000), 31–41

'Did the *De re militari* of Vegetius influence the military ordinances of Charles the Bold?', in *Le héros bourguignon: histoire et épopée. Publication du Centre européen d'etudes bourguignonnes (XIVe–XVIe s.) Rencontres d'Edimbourg–Glasgow, 2000*, 41 (2001), 135–43

'The *De re militari* of Vegetius. A classical text in the Middle Ages', *History Today*, 54 (6) (2004), 20–5

'The *De re militari* of Vegetius in the Middle Ages and the Renaissance', in *Writing war*, ed. Saunders, Le Saux and Thomas, 15–28

'The *De re militari* of Vegetius. How did the Middle Ages treat a late Roman text on war?', *Revista de História das Ideias*, 30 (2009), 57–73

'A Roman text on war: The *Strategemata* of Frontinus in the Middle Ages', in *Soldiers, nobles and gentlemen. Essays in honour of Maurice Keen*, ed. Coss and Tyerman, 153–68

'Des origines intellectuelles de l'armée française au moyen âge', in *Un moyen âge pour aujourd'hui. Mélanges offerts à Claude Gauvard*, ed. J. Claustre, O. Mattéoni and N. Offenstadt (Paris, 2010), 47–56

'Vegetius' *De re militari*. Military theory in medieval and modern conception', *History Compass*, 9(5), 2011, 397–409

Allmand, C. T. (ed.) *War, literature and politics in the late Middle Ages* (Liverpool, 1976)

Allmand, C. T. and Keen, M. H. 'History and the literature of war: the *Boke of Noblesse* of William Worcester', in *War, government and power in late medieval France*, ed. C. T. Allmand (Liverpool, 2000), 92–105

Alomar i Canyelles, A. I. 'La terminologia de l'armament a la versió catalana del segle XIV de l'*Epitoma rei militaris* de Flavi Vegeci Renat', *Caplletra*, 13 (1992), 53–70

Anglo, S. (ed.) *Chivalry in the Renaissance* (Woodbridge and Rochester, NY, 1990)

'Vegetius's "De re militari": the triumph of mediocrity', *The Antiquaries Journal*, 82 (2002), 247–67

Machiavelli – The first century. Studies in enthusiasm, hostility and irrelevance (Oxford, 2005)

Antonovics, A. V. 'The library of Cardinal Domenico Capranica', in *Cultural aspects of the Italian Renaissance*, ed. Clough, 141–59

Autrand, F. *Charles V, le Sage* (Paris, 1994)

Ayton, A. *Knights and warhorses. Military service and the English aristocracy under Edward III* (Woodbridge, 1994)

'Arms, armour and horses', in *Medieval warfare*, ed. Keen, 186–208

Ayton, A. and Preston, P. (eds.) *The battle of Crécy, 1346* (Woodbridge, 2005)

Baatz, D. and Bockius, R. *Vegetius und die römische Flotte* (Mainz, 1997)

Bachrach, B. S. *Armies and politics in the early medieval West* (Aldershot and Brookfield, 1993)

'The practical use of Vegetius' *De re militari* during the early Middle Ages', *The Historian*, 47 (1985), 239–55

'"A lying legacy" revisited: the Abels-Morillo defense of discontinuity', *JMMH*, 5 (2007), 153–93

Bachrach, B. S. and Bachrach, D. 'The Saxon military revolution, 912–973: myth and reality', *Early Medieval Europe*, 15 (2007), 186–222

Badia, L. 'Frontí i Vegeci, mestres de cavalleria en Català als segles XIV i XV', *Boletín de la Real Academia de Buenas Letras de Barcelona*, 39 (1983–84), 191–215

Barnes, T. D. 'The date of Vegetius', *Phoenix*, 33 (1979), 254–7

Bartusis, M. *The late Byzantine army. Arms and society, 1204–1453* (Philadelphia, 1992)

Bastin, J. 'Le traité de Théodore Paléologue dans la traduction de Jean de Vignay', in *Études romanes dédiées à Mario Roques* (Paris, 1946), 77–88

Bayley, C. C. *War and society in Renaissance Florence. The 'De militia' of Leonardo Bruni* (Toronto, 1961)

Beaujouan, G. *Les manuscrits scientifiques médiévaux de l'université de Salamanque et de ses 'colegios mayores'* (Bordeaux, 1962)

Beer, J. M. A. *A medieval Caesar* (Geneva, 1976)

'Medieval translations: Latin and the vernacular languages', in *Medieval Latin. An introduction and bibliographical guide*, ed. F. A. C. Mantello and A. G. Rigg (Washington, DC, 1996), 728–33

Bell, A. R. *War and the soldier in the fourteenth century* (Woodbridge, 2004)

Bennett, M. 'Why chivalry? Military "professionalism" in the twelfth century: the origins and expressions of a socio-military ethos', in *The chivalric ethos*, ed. Trim, 41–64

Bérier, F. 'La traduction en Français', in *La littérature française aux XIVe et XVe siècles. Grundriss der Romanischen Literaturen des Mittelalters VIII/1*, ed. D. Poirion (Heidelberg, 1988), 219–65

Bessey, V. (ed.) *Construire l'armée française. Textes fondateurs des institutions militaires. I. De la France des premiers Valois à la fin du règne de François Ier* (Turnhout, 2006)

Bischoff, B. *Manuscripts and libraries in the age of Charlemagne*, trans. M. Gorman (Cambridge, 1994)

Blanchard, J. 'Écrire la guerre au XVe siècle', *Le moyen français*, 24–25 (1989), 7–21

Bliese, J. R. E. 'Rhetoric and morale: a study of battle orations from the central Middle Ages', *Journal of Medieval History*, 15 (1989), 201–26

'The just war as concept and motive in the central Middle Ages', *Medievalia et Humanistica*, n.s. 17 (1991), 1–26

Bolgar, R. R. *The classical heritage and its beneficiaries* (Cambridge, 1954)

Born, L. K. 'Roman and modern military science. Some suggestions for teaching', *The Classical Journal*, 29 (1933–34), 13–22

Bornstein, D.'The Scottish prose version of Vegetius' *De re militari*', *Studies in Scottish Literature*, 8 (1970–71), 174–83

'Military strategy in Malory and Vegetius' *De re militari*', *Comparative Literature Studies*, 9 (1972), 123–9

'Military manuals in fifteenth-century England', *Mediaeval Studies*, 37 (1975), 469–77

Mirrors of courtesy (Hamden, Conn., 1975)

Boussard, J. 'Les mercenaires au XIIe siècle. Henri II Plantagenet et les origines de l'armée de métier', *BEC*, 106 (1945–46), 189–224

Bradbury, J. *The medieval siege* (Woodbridge, 1992)

Brault, G. J. '*Sapientia* dans la *Chanson de Roland*', *French Forum*, 1 (1976), 99–118

Briggs, C. F. 'Manuscripts of Giles of Rome's *De regimine principum* in England, 1300–1500: a handlist', *Scriptorium*, 47 (1993), 60–73

Giles of Rome's De regimine principum. *Reading and writing politics at court and university, c.1275–c.1525* (Cambridge, 1999)

Brusten, C. 'Les compagnies d'ordonnance dans l'armée bourguignonne', in *Grandson 1476. Essai d'approche pluridisciplinaire d'une action militaire du XVe siècle*, ed. D. Reichel (Lausanne, 1976), 112–69

'La fin des compagnies d'ordonnance de Charles le Téméraire', in *Cinq-centième anniversaire de la bataille de Nancy (1477)* (Nancy, 1979), 363–75

Bühler, C. F. 'The earliest appearances in print of Vegetius', *Gutenberg Jahrbuch*, 31 (1956), 91–3

Burd, J. A. 'Le fonti letterarie di Machiavelli nell "Arte della Guerra"', in *Atti della R. Accademia dei Lincei, anno CCXCIII*, Ser. 5, Classe di scienze morali, storiche e philologiche (Rome, 1897), 187–261

Burgess, G. S. 'The theme of chivalry in *Ille et Galeron*', *Medioevo romanzo*, 14 (1989), 339–62

'The term "chevalerie" in twelfth-century French', in *Medieval codicology, iconography, literature, and translation. Studies for Keith Val Sinclair*, ed. P. R. Monks and D. D. R. Owen (Leiden, New York and Cologne, 1994), 343–58

Buridant, C. 'Jean de Meun et Jean de Vignay, traducteurs de l'*Epitoma rei militaris* de Végèce. Contribution à l'histoire de la traduction au Moyen Âge', in *Études de langue et de littérature françaises offertes à André Lanly* (Nancy, 1980), 51–69

'Vers un lexique de Jean de Vignay, traducteur: contribution à l'essor de la traduction au XIVe siècle', in *The dawn of the written vernacular in western Europe*, ed. M. Goyens and W. Verbeke (Mediaevalia Lovaniensia, ser. I, 33, Louvain, 2003), 303–21

Buschinger, D. and Spiewok, W. (eds.) *Le monde des héros dans la culture médiévale* (Greifswald, 1994)

Butzmann, H. *Die Blankenburger Handschriften* (Frankfurt-am-Main, 1966)

Cambridge History of the Book in Britain. III. 1400–1557, ed. L. Hellinga and J. B. Trapp (Cambridge, 1999)

Campbell, B. 'Teach yourself how to be a general', *Journal of Roman Studies*, 77 (1987), 13–29

Camus, J. 'Notice d'une traduction française de Végèce faite en 1380', *Romania*, 25 (1896), 393–400

Cardini, F. *La culture de la guerre, Xe–XVIIIe siècle* (Paris, 1992)

Castan, A. 'Jean Priorat de Besançon, poète français de la fin du XIIIe siècle', *BEC*, 36 (1875), 124–38

Cayley, E. and Kinch, A. (eds.) *Chartier in Europe* (Cambridge, 2008)

Champion, P. *La librairie de Charles d'Orléans* (Paris, 1910)

Charles, M. B. *Vegetius in context. Establishing the date of the* Epitoma rei militaris (Stuttgart, 2007)

Chenu, M. D. 'Moines, clercs, laics au carrefour de la vie évangélique (XIIe siècle)', *Revue d'histoire ecclésiastique*, 49 (1954), 59–89

Chevalier, B. and Contamine, P. (eds.) *La France de la fin du XVe siècle. Renouveau et apogée* (Paris, 1985)

Chickering, H. and Seiler, T. H. (eds.) *The study of chivalry. Resources and approaches* (Kalamazoo, 1988)

Clements, J. 'Wielding the weapons of war: arms, armor and training manuals during the late Middle Ages', in *The Hundred Years War. A wider focus*, ed. A. Villalon and D. J. Kagnay (Leiden and Boston, 2005), 447–73

Clough, C. H. 'Chivalry and magnificence in the golden age of the Italian Renaissance', in *Chivalry in the Renaissance*, ed. Anglo, 25–47

Clough, C. H. (ed.) *Cultural aspects of the Italian Renaissance. Essays in honour of Paul Oskar Kristeller* (Manchester and New York, 1976)

Cockle, M. J. D. *A bibliography of English military books up to 1642* (London, 1900)

Cohen, D. A. 'Secular pragmatism and thinking about war in some court writings of Pere III el Ceremoniós', in *Crusaders, condottieri and cannon*, ed. Villalon and Kagay, 19–55

Contamine, P. *Guerre, état et société à la fin du moyen âge. Études sur les armées des rois de France, 1337–1494* (Paris and The Hague, 1972)

'The war literature of the late Middle Ages: the treatises of Robert de Balsac and Béraud Stuart, lord of Aubigny', in *War, literature and politics*, ed. Allmand, 102–21

'Points de vue sur la chevalerie en France à la fin du moyen âge', *Francia*, 4 (1976), 255–85

'L'art de la guerre selon Philippe de Clèves, seigneur de Ravenstein (1456–1528): innovation ou tradition', *Bijdragen en mededelingen betreffende de Geschiedenis der Nederlanden*, 95 (1980), 363–76

'L'écrit et l'oral en France à la fin du moyen âge. Note sur l'alphabétisme de l'encadrement militaire', in *Histoire comparée de l'administration (IVe–XVIIIe siècles)*, ed. W. Paravicini and K. F. Werner (Beihefte der *Francia*, 9, 1980), 102–13

'L'armée de Philippe Auguste', in *La France de Philippe Auguste. Le temps des mutations*, ed. R.-H. Bautier (Paris, 1982), 577–93

War in the Middle Ages, trans. M. Jones (Oxford, 1984)

'Mourir pour la patrie', in *Les lieux de mémoire. II (iii). La nation*, ed. P. Nora (Paris, 1986), 11–43

'Structures militaires de la France et de l'Angleterre au milieu du XVe siècle', in *Das spätmittelalterliche Königtum im Europäischen Vergleich*, ed. R. Schneider (Sigmaringen, 1987), 319–34

'Les traités de guerre, de chasse, de blason et de chevalerie', in *La littérature française aux XIVe et XVe siècles. Grundriss der Romanischen Literaturen des Mittelalters VIII/1*, ed. D. Poirion (Heidelberg, 1988), 346–67

'La musique militaire dans le fonctionnement des armées: l'exemple français (v.1330–v.1550)', in *XXII Kongress der internationalen Kommission für Militärgeschichte, Acta 22* (Vienna, 1997), 93–106

'Noblesse et service: l'idée et la réalité dans la France de la fin du Moyen Âge', in *Nobilitas. Funktion und Repräsentation des Adels in Alteuropa*, ed. O. G. Oexle and W. Paravicini (Göttingen, 1997), 299–311

'L'armée de Charles le Téméraire: expression d'un état en devenir ou instrument d'un conquérant?', in *Aux armes, citoyens! Conscription et armée de métier des Grecs à nos jours*, ed. M. Vaïsse (Paris, 1998), 61–77

'L'art de la guerre à la fin du Moyen Âge et à la Renaissance: maitrise et représentation de l'espace', in *Krieg und Frieden im Übergang vom Mittelalter zur Neuzeit/Guerre et paix du Moyen Âge aux temps modernes*, ed. H. Duchhardt and P. Veit (Mainz, 2000), 35–52

Contamine, P. (ed.) *Histoire militaire de la France. I. Des origines à 1715* (Paris, 1992)

War and competition between states (Oxford, 2000)

Coss, P. and Tyerman, C. (eds.) *Soldiers, nobles and gentlemen. Essays in honour of Maurice Keen* (Woodbridge, 2009)

Cowdrey, H. E. J. 'Pope Gregory VII and the bearing of arms', in *Montjoie. Studies in crusading history in honour of Hans Eberhard Mayer*, ed. B. Z. Kedax, J. Riley-Smith and R. Hiestand (Aldershot and Brookfield, VT, 1997), 21–35

'Christianity and the morality of warfare during the first century of crusading', in *The experience of crusading. I. Western approaches*, ed. M. Bull and N. Housley (Cambridge, 2003), 175–92

Croenen, G. and Ainsworth, P. F. (eds.) *Patrons, authors and workshops. Books and book production in Paris around 1400* (Louvain, 2006)

Curry, A. E. 'The first English standing army? – Military organisation in Lancastrian Normandy, 1420–1450', in *Patronage, pedigree and power in later medieval England*, ed. C. D. Ross (Gloucester and Totowa, 1979), 193–214

'The organisation of field armies in Lancastrian Normandy', in *Armies, chivalry and warfare*, ed. Strickland, 207–33

Agincourt. A new history (London, 2005)

Curtius, E. R. *European literature and the Latin Middle Ages* (New York, 1953)

Debae, M. *La bibliothèque de Marguerite d'Autriche. Essai de reconstruction d'après l'inventaire de 1523–1524* (Louvain and Paris, 1995)

De Ghellinck, J. *L'essor de la littérature latine au XIIe siècle* (2nd edn, Brussels, Bruges and Paris, 1954)

de la Mare, A. 'The library of Francesco Sassetti (1421–90)', in *Cultural aspects of the Italian Renaissance*, ed. Clough, 160–201

de Larrea, J. A. Fernández 'Cambios en el sistema militar Navarro en la segunda mitad del siglo XIV' (Primer congreso general de historia de Navarra 3. Comunicaciones Edad Media, Pamplona, 1988), 413–23

'Las estructuras de la guerra en la Navarra del siglo XIV. Las campañas portuguesas de 1384–1385', *Anuario de estudios medievales*, 19 (1989), 393–404

Delisle, L. *Le cabinet des manuscrits de la Bibliothèque Nationale de Paris* (3 vols., Paris, 1868–81)

Notice sur les manuscrits disparus de la bibliothèque de Tours pendant la première moitié du XIXe siècle (Paris, 1883)

Delogu, D. 'Reinventing the ideal sovereign in Christine de Pizan's *Livre des fais et bonnes meurs du sage roy Charles V*', *Medievalia et humanistica*, n.s. 31 (n.d), 41–58

Dembrowski, P. F. 'Chivalry, ideal and real, in the narrative poetry of Jean Froissart', *Medievalia et humanistica*, n.s. 14 (1986), 1–15

de Nolhac, P. *Petrarch et l'humanisme* (2nd edn, 2 vols., Paris, 1907)

Derolez, A. and Victor, B. *Corpus catalogorum Belgii. The medieval booklists of the southern Low Countries* (4 vols., Brussels, 1994–2001)

Devaux, J. 'L'alimentation en temps de guerre: l'apport des sources littéraires', in *La vie matérielle au Moyen Âge. L'apport des sources littéraires, normatives et de la pratique*, ed. E. Rassart-Eeckhout, J.-P. Sosson, C. Thiry and T. Van Hemelryck (Louvain-la-Neuve, 1997), 91–108

'L'image du chef de guerre dans les sources littéraires', in *Images et représentations princières et nobiliaires dans les Pays-Bas bourguignons et quelques régions voisines (XIVe–XVIe siècles). Publication du centre Européen d'etudes bourguignonnes (XIVe–XVIe s.). Rencontres de Nivelles-Bruxelles 1996*, 37 (1997), 115–29

'Le culte du héros chevaleresque dans les *Mémoires* d'Olivier de la Marche', in *Le héros bourguignon: histoire et épopée. Publication du Centre européen d'études bourguinonnes (XIVe–XVIe s.). Rencontres d'Edimbourg-Glasgow 2000*, 41 (2001), 53–66

'Un seigneur lettré à la cour de Bourgogne: Philippe de Croy, comte de Chimay', in *Liber amicorum Raphaël de Smedt*, ed. A. Tourneux (Louvain, 2001), vol. IV, 13–33

DeVries, K. *Infantry warfare in the early fourteenth century. Discipline, tactics and technology* (Woodbridge, 1996)

'God and defeat in medieval warfare: some preliminary thoughts', in *The circle of war*, eds. Kagay and Villalon, 87–97

Dionisotti, C. 'Tradizione classica e volgarizzamenti', *Italia medioevale e umanistica*, 1 (1958), 427–31

Donnini, M. 'Sopra alcune presenze dell' *Epitoma rei militaris* di Vegezio nel *Liber secretorum fidelium crucis* di Marino Sanudo il Vecchio', *Studi medievali*, 3rd ser., 44 (2003), 347–59

Dorjahn, A. P and Born, L. K. 'Vegetius on the decay of the Roman army', *The Classical Journal*, 30 (1934–35), 148–58

Doutrepont, G. *Jean Lemaire de Belges et la renaissance* (Brussels, 1934)

Driver, M. W. 'Medievalizing the classical past in Pierpont Morgan MS M 876', in *Middle English poetry: texts and traditions. Essays in honour of Derek Pearsall*, ed. A. J. Minnis (York, 2001), 211–39

Duggan, A. J. 'Classical quotations and allusions in the correspondence of Thomas Becket: an investigation of their sources', *Viator*, 32 (2001), 1–22

Edmunds, S. 'The medieval library of Savoy', *Scriptorium*, 24 (1970), 318–27; 25 (1971), 253–84; 26 (1972), 269–93

Ellis, R. (ed.) *The medieval translator. The theory and practice of translation in the Middle Ages* (Cambridge, 1989)

Ellis, R. and Tixier, R. (eds.) *The medieval translator. Traduire au moyen âge* (Turnhout, 1996)

Fallwell, M. L. Jr. *'De re militari. An edition of the Middle English prose translation of Vegetius' "Epitoma rei militaris"'*, PhD diss. (Vanderbilt Univ., 1973)

Feld, M. D. *The structure of violence. Armed forces in social systems* (Beverley Hills and London, 1977)

Finch, C. E. 'Codices Pal. Lat. 1571–1573 as sources for Vegetius', *Transactions and Proceedings of the American Philological Association*, 93 (1962), 22–9

Finer, S. E. 'State- and nation-building in Europe: the role of the military', in *The formation of national states in western Europe*, ed. C. Tilly (Princeton, 1975), 84–163

Flori, J. 'La chevalerie selon Jean de Salisbury', *Revue d'histoire ecclésiastique*, 77 (1982), 35–77

Forhan. K. L, *The political theory of Christine de Pizan* (Aldershot and Burlington, VT, 2002)

Fowler, K. A. *Medieval mercenaries. I. The great companies* (Oxford and Malden, MA, 2001)

Fradejas, J. M. 'Las glosas de San Cristóbal a la versión castellana de la *Epitoma rei militaris*', *Incipit*, 29 (2009), 85–100

'El modelo latino de la versión castellana medieval de *Epitoma rei militaris* de Vegecio', *Estudios humanísticos. Filología*, 32 (2010), 47–55

'Prolegómenos a una edición crítica de la versión castellana de Alfonso de San Cristóbal de la *Epitoma rei militaris* de Vegecio', *Revista de literatura medieval*, 23 (2011) (in press)

France, J. *Western warfare in the age of the Crusades, 1000–1300* (London, 1999)

'Recent writing on medieval warfare: from the Fall of Rome to 1300', *Journal of Military History*, 65 (2001), 441–73

Fürbeth, F. 'Eine unbekannte deutsche Übersetzung des Vegetius aus der Bibliothek des Anton von Annenberg', *Zeitschrift für deutsches Altertum und deutsche Literatur*, 124 (1995), 278–97

'Die spätmittelalterliche Adelsbibliothek des Anton von Annenberg. Ihr Signaturensystem als Rekonstruktionshilfe', in *Sources for the history of medieval books and libraries*, ed. R. Schlusemann, J. M. M. Hermans and M. Hoogvliet (Groningen, 2000), 61–78

'Zur deutschsprachigen Rezeption der "Epitoma rei militaris" des Vegetius im Mittelalter', in *Die Wahrnehmung und Darstellung des Krieges im Mittelalter und in der frühen Neuzeit*, ed. H. Brunner (Wiesbaden, 2000), 141–65

'Die "Epitoma rei militaris" des Vegetius. Zwischen ritterliche Ausbildung und gelehrt-humanistischer Lektüre. Zu einer weiteren unbekannten deutschen Übersetzung aus der Wiener Artistenfakultät', *Beiträge zur Geschichte der deutschen Sprache und Literatur*, 124 (2002), 302–38

'*Des Vegecii kurcze red von der Ritterschafft*. Die "Epitoma rei militaris" in der Übersetzung des Ludwig Hohenwang', in *Flavius Vegetius Renatus, Von der Ritterschaft. Aus dem Lateinischen übertragen von Ludwig Hohenwang, in der Ausgabe Augsburg, Johann Wiener, 1475/76* (Monumenta xylographica et typographica 6, Munich, 2002), 7–29 71–79 [see below: Leng]

'Vegetius, Publius Flavius', *Die deutsche Literatur des Mittelalters Verfasserlexikon*, 11(5) (2004), 1601–13

Gaier, C. 'L'opinion des chefs de guerre français du XVIe siècle sur les progès de l'art militaire', *Revue internationale d'histoire militaire*, 29 (1970), 723–46

Gallet-Guerne, D. *Vasque de Lucène et la Cyropédie à la cour de Bourgogne (1470)* (Geneva, 1974)

Gandellini, G. 'Il vocabolario della crusca e la tradizione manoscritta dell'"Epitoma rei militaris" di Vegezio nel volgarizzamento di Bono Giamboni', *Studi di lessicografia italiana*, 13 (1996), 43–121

García, L. R. 'Types of armies: early modern Spain', in *War and competition between states*, ed. Contamine, 37–68

García Fitz, F. 'La didáctica militar en la literatura castellana (segunda mitad del siglo XIII y primera del XIV), *Anuario de estudios medievales*, 19 (1989), 271–83

Geldner, F. *Die deutschen Inkunabeldrucker. Ein Handbuch der deutschen Buchdrucker des XV Jahrhunderts nach Druckorten* (Stuttgart, 1968)

Gilbert, F. 'Machiavelli: the renaissance of the art of war', in *Makers of modern strategy from Machiavelli to the nuclear age*, ed. P. Paret (Oxford, 1986), 11–31

Gillingham, J. *The Wars of the Roses. Peace and conflict in fifteenth-century England* (London, 1981)

'Richard I and the science of war in the Middle Ages', in *War and government in the Middle Ages*, ed. J. Gillingham and J. C. Holt (Woodbridge, 1984), 78–91; repr. in *Anglo-Norman warfare*, ed. Strickland, 194–207

'William the Bastard at war', in *Studies in Medieval History presented to R. Allen Brown* (Woodbridge, 1989), 141–58; repr. in *Anglo-Norman warfare*, ed. Strickland, 143–60

'"Up with orthodoxy!" In defense of Vegetian warfare', *JMMH*, 2 (2004), 149–58

Goffart, W. 'The date and purpose of Vegetius' "De re militari"', *Traditio*, 33 (1977), 65–100

'Conspicuous by absence: Heroism in the early Frankish era (6th–7th cent.)', in *La funzione dell'eroe germanico. Storicità, metafora, paradigma*, ed. T. Pàroli (Rome, 1995), 41–56

Goodman, A. E. *The Wars of the Roses. Military activity and English society, 1452–97* (London, 1981)

Goodman, J. R. 'Caxton's chivalric publications of 1480–85', in *The study of chivalry*, ed. Chickering and Seiler, 645–61

'European chivalry in the 1490s', *Comparative Civilization Review*, 26 (1992), 43–72

Gordon, C. D. 'Vegetius and his proposed reforms of the army', in *Polis and imperium. Studies in honour of Edward Togo Salmon*, ed. J. A. S. Evans (Toronto, 1974), 35–58

Guenée, B. 'La culture historique des nobles: le succès des *Faits des Romains (XIIIe–XVe siècles)*', in *La noblesse au moyen âge XIe–XVe siècles. Essais à la mémoire de Robert Boutruche*, ed. P. Contamine (Paris, 1976), 261–88

Haldon, J. 'Military service, military lands, and the status of soldiers: current problems and interpretations', *Dumbarton Oaks Papers*, 47 (1993), 1–67; repr. in his *State, army and society in Byzantium. Approaches to military, social and administrative history, 6th–12th centuries* (Aldershot, 1995), ch. VII

Hale, J. R. 'Renaissance armies and political control: the Venetian proveditorial system, 1509–1529', *Journal of Italian History*, 2 (1979), 11–31

Renaissance war studies (London, 1983)

War and society in Renaissance Europe, 1450–1620 (London, 1985)

'The soldier in Germanic graphic art of the Renaissance', *Journal of Interdisciplinary History*, 17 (1986), 85–114

Halsall, G. *Warfare and society in the Barbarian West, 450–900* (London and New York, 2003)

Hamilton, B. 'The Old French translation of William of Tyre as an historical source', in *The experience of crusading. II. Defining the crusader*, ed. P. Edbury and J. Phillips (Cambridge, 2003), 93–112

Hanley, C. *War and combat, 1150–1270. The evidence of Old French literature* (Cambridge, 2003)

Hanna, R. 'Sir Thomas Berkeley and his patronage', *Speculum*, 64 (1989), 878–916

Harari, Y. N. 'Strategy and supply in fourteenth-century Western European invasion campaigns', *Journal of Military History*, 64 (2000), 297–333

Harding, A. *Medieval law and the foundations of the state* (Oxford, 2002)

Hartig, O. (ed.) *Die Gründung der Münchener Hofbibliothek durch Albrecht V und Johann Jakob Fugger* (Munich, 1917)

Hedeman, A. D. 'Making the past present: visual translation in Jean Lebègue's "twin" manuscripts of Sallust', in *Patrons, authors and workshops*, ed. Croenen and Ainsworth, 173–96

Held, J. 'Military reform in early fifteenth-century Hungary', *East European Quarterly*, 11 (1977), 129–39

Heller, E. K. 'Ludwig Hohenwang's "Von der Ritterschaft". An evaluation, and a survey of his military and naval terms', in *In honorem Lawrence Marsden Price. Contributions by his colleagues and by his former students*, Univ. of California Publications in Modern Philology, 36, vi (1952), 173–84

Hernández González, M. I. (ed.) *En la teoría y en la práctica de la traducción. La experiencia de los traductores castellanos a la luz de sus textos (siglos XIV–XVI)* (Salamanca, 1998)

Heusch, C. 'La caballería de ayer y la de hoy. El sueño latino de algunos caballeros letrados del siglo XV', in *Modelos latinos en la castilla medieval*, ed. Mónica Castillo Lluch and Marta López Izquierdo (Madrid and Frankfurt, 2010), 289–306

Hewitt, H. J. *The Black Prince's expedition of 1355–1357* (Manchester, 1958)

The organization of war under Edward III, 1338–62 (Manchester and New York, 1966)

Heymann, F. G. *John Zizka and the Hussite revolution* (Princeton, 1955)

Hillgarth, J. N. *Readers and books in Majorca, 1229–1550* (2 vols., Paris, 1991)

Hobson, A. 'Manuscripts captured at Vitoria', in *Cultural aspects of the Italian Renaissance*, ed. Clough, 485–97

Hogan, T. L. 'The memorandum book of Henry of Eastry, prior of Christ Church, Canterbury' (unpublished PhD diss., University of London, 1966)

Hollister, C. W. *The military organization of Norman England* (Oxford, 1965)

Housley, N. 'European warfare, c.1200–1320', in *Medieval warfare. A history*, ed. Keen, 113–35

'Recent scholarship on crusading and medieval warfare, 1095–1291: convergence and divergence', in *War, government and aristocracy in the British Isles, c.1150–1500. Essays in honour of Michael Prestwich*, ed. C. Given-Wilson, A. Kettle and L. Scales (Woodbridge, 2008), 197–213

Hughes, S. C. 'Soldiers and gentlemen: the rise of the duel in Renaissance Italy', *JMMH*, 5 (2007), 99–152

Humphreys, K. W. (ed.) *The friars' libraries* (London, 1990)

Huntington, S. P. *The soldier and the state. The theory and practice of civil–military relations* (Cambridge, Mass., 1957)

Iglesias i Fonseca, J. A. 'Minima palaeographica: un codex humanístic de l'Eneida de Virgili a Sant Cugat del Vallès (Barcelona)', *Butlletí de la Reial Acadèmia de Bones Lletres de Barcelona*, 48 (2002), 569–76

Inventaire sommaire des manuscrits anciens de la bibliothèque Smith-Lesouëf à Nogent-sur Marne (Paris, 1930)

Inventari dei manoscritti delle biblioteche d'Italia, ed. G. Mazzatinti, VII (Forlì, 1897)

Isambert, F. A., Jourdan, A. J. L. and Monsieur Decrusy, *Recueil général des anciennes lois françaises depuis l'an 420 jusqu'à la Révolution de 1789* (29 vols., Paris, 1822–33), IX.

Jackson, W. H. 'Warfare in the works of Rudolf von Ems', in *Writing war*, ed. Saunders, Le Saux and Thomas, 49–75

Jal, A. *Archéologie navale* (Paris, 1840)

Jones, C. W. 'Bede and Vegetius', *The Classical Review*, 46 (1932), 248–9

Jones, M. C. E. 'L'armée bretonne 1449–1491: structures et carrières', in *La France de la fin du XVe siècle: renouveau et apogée*, ed. B. Chevalier and P. Contamine (Paris, 1985), 147–65; repr. in M. Jones, *The creation of Brittany. A late medieval state* (London and Ronceverte, 1988), 351–69

Jones, M. H. 'The depiction of battle in Wolfram von Eschenbach's *Willehalm*', in *The ideals and practice of medieval knighthood II*, ed. C. Harper-Bill and R. Harvey (Woodbridge and Wolfeboro, 1988), 46–69

Kaeuper, R. W. *War, justice and public order. England and France in the later Middle Ages* (Oxford, 1988)
Chivalry and violence in medieval Europe (Oxford, 1999)

Kagay, D. and Villalon, L. J. A. (eds.) *The circle of war in the Middle Ages* (Woodbridge, 1999)
Crusaders, condottieri, and cannon. Medieval warfare in societies around the Mediterranean (Leiden and Boston, 2003)

Kantorowicz, E. H. '*Pro patria mori* in medieval political thought', *AHR*, 56 (1951), 472–92
The king's two bodies. A study in mediaeval political theology (Princeton, 1957)

Keen, M. H. *The laws of war in the late Middle Ages* (London and Toronto, 1965)
Chivalry (New Haven and London, 1984)
'Richard II's ordinances of war of 1385', in *Rulers and ruled in late medieval England. Essays presented to Gerald Harriss*, ed. R. E. Archer and S. Walker (London and Rio Grande, 1995), 33–48

Keen, M. H. (ed.) *Medieval warfare. A history* (Oxford, 1999)

Kempshall, M. S. *The common good in late medieval political thought* (Oxford, 1999)

Ker, N. R. 'William of Malmesbury's handwriting', *EHR*, 59 (1944), 371–6

Klein, J. (ed.) *Ueber eine Handschrift des Nicolaus von Cues (1401–1464)* (Berlin, 1866)

Klein, T. 'Zur Geschichte des Codex Leiden Periz. F. 17 und zur Herkunft der Leidenen Vegetiusglossen', *Amsterdamer Beiträge zur alteren Germanistik*, 8 (1975), 1–9

Knowles, C. 'Jean de Vignay, un traducteur du XIVe siècle', *Romania*, 75 (1954), 353–83
'A 14th century imitator of Jean de Meun: Jean de Vignay's translation of the *De re militari* of Vegetius', *Studies in Philology*, 53 (1956), 452–8

Kortüm, H.-H. (ed.) *Krieg im Mittelalter* (Berlin, 2001)

Kren, T. and McKendrick, S. (eds.) *The triumph of Flemish manuscript painting in Europe* (Los Angeles, 2003)

Krynen, J. 'Idéologie et royauté', in *Saint-Denis et la royauté. Études offertes à Bernard Guenée*, ed. F. Autrand, C. Gauvard and J.-M. Moeglin (Paris, 1999), 609–20

Kunze, H. *Geschichte der Buchillutration in Deutschland. Das 15 Jahrhundert* (2 vols., Leipzig, 1975)

Lachaud, F. 'Armour and military dress in thirteenth- and early fourteenth-century England', in *Armies, chivalry and warfare*, ed. Strickland, 344–69

Lane, F. C. 'Salaires et régime alimentaire des marins au début du XIVe siècle', *Annales ESC*, 18 (1963), 133–8

Lassabatère, T. 'Théorie et éthique de la guerre dans l'œuvre d'Eustache Deschamps', in *La guerre, la violence et les gens au moyen âge. I. Guerre et violence*, ed. P. Contamine and O. Guyotjeannin (Paris, 1996), 35–48

Lawrance, J. N. H. 'Nueva luz sobre la biblioteca del conde de Haro: inventario de 1455', *El Crotalón*, 1 (1984), 1073–1111

'The spread of lay literacy in late medieval Castile', *Journal of Hispanic Studies*, 62 (1985), 79–94

Lee, A. D. 'Morale and the Roman experience of battle', in *Battle in Antiquity*, ed. A. B. Lloyd (London and Swansea, 1996), 199–217

Legge, M. D. 'The Lord Edward's Vegetius', *Scriptorium*, 7 (1953), 262–5

Lehmann, P. (ed.) *Mittelalterliche Bibliothekskataloge Deutschlands und der Schweiz. II. Bistum Mainz, Erfurt* (Munich, 1928)

Lemaire, J. 'L'homme de guerre au moyen âge finissant: le cas d'Olivier de la Marche', in *Le monde des héros*, ed. Buschinger and Spiewok, 151–60

Lendon, J. E. *Empire of honour. The art of government in the Roman world* (Oxford, 1997)

Leng, R. *Ars belli. Deutsche taktische und kriegstechnische Bilderhandschriften und Traktate im 15. und 16. Jahrhundert* (2 vols., Wiesbaden, 2002)

'Die Illustrationsfolge der deutschen Vegetius – Ausgabe von Ludwig Hohenwang', in *Flavius Vegetius Renatus, Von der Ritterschaft. Aus dem Lateinischen übertragen von Ludwig Hohenwang, in der Ausgabe Augsburg, Johann Wiener, 1475/76* (Monumenta xylographica et typographica 6, Munich, 2002), 31–79 [see above: Fürbeth]

Leonardi, C. and Munk Olsen, B. (eds.) *The classical tradition in the Middle Ages and the Renaissance. Proceedings of the first European Science Foundation workshop on 'The reception of classical texts'* (Spoleto, 1995)

Le Roux de Lincy, 'La bibliothèque de Charles d'Orléans à son château de Blois en 1427', *BEC*, 5 (1843–44), 59–82

Le Saux, F. 'War and knighthood in Christine de Pizan's *Livre des faits d'armes et de chevallerie*', in *Writing war*, ed. Saunders, Le Saux and Thomas, 93–105

Lewis, P. S. *Later medieval France. The polity* (London, 1968)

Liebeschütz, H. 'John of Salisbury and the "Pseudo-Plutarch"', *JWCI*, 6 (1943), 33–9

Mediaeval humanism in the life and writings of John of Salisbury (London, 1950)

Löfstedt, L. 'Le Végèce de Jean de Meun. Essai de classement des manuscrits', *Studia Neophilologica*, 43 (1971), 500–20

'Aucuns notables extraitz du Livre de Végèce', *Neuphilologische Mitteilungen*, 83 (1982), 297–312

'Végèce au moyen âge: motifs et modifications des traducteurs et des copistes', in *Homenaje a Alvaro Galmés de Fuentes* (Madrid, 1985), I, 493–9

Lomax, D. W. 'A medieval recruiting-poster', *Estudis històrics i documents dels arxius de protocols*, 8 (1980), 353–63

Lourie, E. 'A society organized for war: medieval Spain', *Past & Present*, 35 (1966), 54–76

Lucas, R. H. 'Medieval French translations of the Latin classics to 1500', *Speculum*, 45 (1970), 225–53

Lusignan, S. *Parler vulgairement. Les intellectuels et la langue française aux XIIIe et XIVe siècles* (Paris and Montreal, 1986)

Luttwak, E. N. 'Logistics and the aristocratic idea of war', in *Feeding Mars. Logistics in western warfare from the Middle Ages to the present*, ed. J. A. Lynn (Boulder, San Francisco and Oxford, 1993), 3–7

MacCracken, H. N. 'Vegetius in English: notes on early translations', in *Anniversary papers by colleagues and pupils of G. L. Kittredge* (Boston and London, 1913), 389–403

Macfarlane, J. *Antoine Vérard* (Bibliographical Society, London, 1900)

McKitterick, R. *The Carolingians and the written word* (Cambridge, 1989)

Maggini, F. *I primi volgarizzamenti dai classici latini* (Florence, 1952)

Major, J. R. *Representative institutions in Renaissance France, 1421–1559* (Madison, 1960)

Mallett, M. E. 'Venice and its condottieri,1404–54', in *Renaissance Venice*, ed. J. R. Hale (London, 1973), 121–45

Mercenaries and their masters. Warfare in Renaissance Italy (London, 1974)

'Some notes on a fifteenth-century *condottiere* and his library: Count Antonio da Marsciano', in *Cultural aspects of the Italian Renaissance*, ed. Clough, 202–15

'The art of war', in *Handbook of European history, 1400–1600. Late Middle Ages, Renaissance and Reformation. I. Structures and assertions*, ed. T. A. Brady, Jr, H. A. Oberman and J. D. Tracy (Leiden, New York and Cologne, 1994), 535–62

'Condottieri and captains in Renaissance Italy', in *The chivalric ethos*, ed. Trim, 67–88

Mallett, M. E. and Hale, J. R. *The military organization of a Renaissance state. Venice, c.1400–1617* (Cambridge, 1984)

Manitius, M. *Geschichte der Lateinischen Literatur des Mittelalters* (3 vols., Munich, 1911–31)

Handschriften antiker Autoren in mittelalterlichen Bibliothekskatalogen (Leipzig, 1935)

Manning, E. 'La signification de "militare – militia – miles" dans la règle de Saint Benoît', *Revue bénédictine*, 72 (1962), 135–8

Maravall, J. A. 'Ejercito y estado en el Renacimiento', *Revista de estudos politicos* (1961), 5–45

Meyer, P. 'Les anciens traducteurs français de Végèce, et en particulier Jean de Vignai', *Romania*, 25 (1896), 401–23

'Les manuscrits français de Cambridge. IV. Gonville et Caius College', *Romania*, 36 (1907), 481–542

Mitchell, R. 'Archery *versus* mail: experimental archaeology and the value of the historical context', *JMMH*, 4 (2006), 18–28

Mitre Fernández, E. and Alvira Cabrer, M. 'Ideologia y guerra en los reinos de la España medieval', *Revista de historia militar*, num. Extra. 2001, 291–334

Monfrin, J. 'Humanisme et traductions au moyen âge', in *L'humanisme médiéval dans les littératures romanes du XIIe au XIVe siècle*, ed. A. Fourrier (Paris, 1964), 217–46

'Les traducteurs et leur public en France au moyen âge', in *L'humanisme médiéval dans les littératures romanes du XIIe au XIVe siècle*, ed. A. Fourrier (Paris, 1964), 247–64

'Le goût des lettres antiques à la cour de Bourgogne au XVe siècle', *Bulletin de la Société des Antiquaires de France* (1967), 285–9

'La connaissance de l'Antiquité et le problème de l'humanisme en langue vulgaire dans la France du XVe siècle', in *The late Middle Ages and the dawn of humanism outside Italy*, ed. G. Verbeke and J. Ijsewijn (Louvain and The Hague, 1972), 131–70

Mongeau, R. G. B. 'Jean de Meun's translation of military terminology in Vegetius' "Epitoma rei militaris"', PhD diss., Fordham Univ., 1981

'The "Epitoma rei militaris" of Flavius Vegetius Renatus', *Mittellateinische Jahrbuch*, 20 (1985), 314–22

Monteiro, J. G. 'A cultura militar da nobreza na primeira metade de quatrocentos. Fontes e modelos literários', *Revista de História das Ideias*, 19 (1997/98), 195–227

A guerra em Portugal nos finais da idade média (Lisbon, 1998)

Morillo, S. *Warfare under the Anglo-Norman Kings 1066–1135* (Woodbridge, 1994)

'Battle seeking: the context and limits of Vegetian strategy', *JMMH*, 1 (2002), 21–41

'The sword of justice: war and state formation in comparative perspective', *JMMH*, 4 (2006), 1–17

Morin, D. G. 'Le catalogue des manuscrits de l'abbaye de Gorze au XIe siècle', *Revue bénédictine*, 22 (1905), 1–14

Mott, L. V. 'The battle of Malta, 1283: prelude to a disaster', in *The circle of war in the Middle Ages*, ed. Kagay and Villalon, 145–72

Murray, A. *Reason and society in the Middle Ages* (Oxford, 1978)

Murrin, M. *History and warfare in Renaissance epic* (Chicago and London, 1994)

Nall, C. 'Perceptions of financial mismanagement and the English diagnosis of defeat', in *The fifteenth century. VII. Conflicts, consequences and the crown in the late Middle Ages*, ed. L. Clark (Woodbridge and Rochester, NY, 2007), 119–35

'William Worcester reads Alain Chartier. *Le quadrilogue invectif* and its English readers', in *Chartier in Europe*, ed. Cayley and Kinch, 135–47

Nascimento, A. A. 'La réception des auteurs classiques dans l'espace culturel portugais: une question ouverte', in *The classical tradition in the Middle Ages and the Renaissance. Proceedings of the first European Science Workshop on 'The reception of classical texts'*, ed. C. Leonardi and B. Munk Olsen (Spoleto, 1995), 47–56

Nederman, C. J. (ed.), *Political thought in fourteenth-century England. Treatises by Walter of Milemete, William of Pagula, and William of Ockham* (Tempe, Arizona and Turnhout, 2002)

Newhall, R. A. *The English conquest of Normandy 1416–1424. A study of fifteenth-century warfare* (New Haven and London, 1924)

Muster and review. A problem of English military administration 1420–1440 (Cambridge, Mass., 1940)

Nicholson, H. *Medieval warfare. Theory and practice of war in Europe, 300–1500* (Basingstoke and New York, 2004)

Noble, P. 'Military leadership in the Old French epic', in *Reading around the epic. A Festschrift in honour of Professor Wolfgang van Emden*, ed. A. Ailes, P. E. Bennett and K. Pratt (London, 1998), 171–91

O'Callaghan, J. F. *The learned king. The reign of Alfonso X of Castile* (Philadelphia, 1993)

'War (and peace) in the law codes of Alfonso X', in *Crusaders, condottieri and cannon. Medieval warfare in societies around the Mediterranean*, ed. D. J. Kagay and L. J. A. Villalon (Leiden and Boston, 2003), 9–17

Oman, C. *History of the art of war in the Middle Ages* (London, 1924)

Omont, H. 'Inventaire de la bibliothèque de Ferdinand Ier d'Aragon, roi de Naples (1481)', *BEC*, 70 (1909), 456–70

Ottolenghi, M. G. A. 'La biblioteca dei Visconti e degli Sforza: gli inventari del 1488 e del 1490', *Studi Petrarcheschi*, n.s. 8 (1991), 1–238

Ouy, G. 'Simon de Plumetot (1371–1443) et sa bibliothèque', in *Miscellanea codicologica F. Masai dicata MCMLXXIX*, ed. P. Cockshaw, M.-C. Garani and P. Jodogne (Ghent, 1979), II, 353–81

'Jean le Bègue (1368–1457), auteur, copist et bibliophile', in *Patrons, authors and workshops*, ed. Croenen and Ainsworth, 143–71

Pächt, O. and Alexander, J. J. G. (eds.) *Illuminated manuscripts in the Bodleian Library*, I (Oxford, 1966)

Paravicini, A. and W. 'L'arsenal intellectuel d'un homme de pouvoir. Les livres de Guillaume Hugonet, chancelier de Bourgogne, in *Penser le pouvoir au moyen âge (VIIIe–XVe siècle). Études d'histoire et de littérature offertes à Françoise Autrand*, ed. D. Boutet and J. Verger (Paris, 2000), 261–325

Pascual-Argente, C. 'From *Invectivo* to *Inventivo*: reading Chartier's *Quadrilogue invectif* in fifteenth-century Castile', in *Chartier in Europe*, ed. Cayley and Kinch, 119–33

Patch, H. R. *The goddess Fortuna in medieval literature* (Cambridge, Mass., 1927; repr. London, 1967)

Pellegrin, E. *La bibliothèque des Visconti et des Sforza, ducs de Milan, au XVe siècle* (Paris, 1955)

Les manuscrits classiques latins de la Bibliothèque Vaticane (Paris, 1975–)

Phillpotts, C. 'The French plan of battle during the Agincourt campaign', *EHR*, 99 (1984), 59–66

Piaget, A. '"Le chapel des fleurs de lis" par Philippe de Vitri', *Romania*, 27 (1898), 55–92

Poirion, D. *La littérature française aux XIVe et XVe siècles. 1 [Grundriss des Romanischen Literaturen des Mittelalters. Band viii/1]* (Heidelberg, 1988)

Pommerol, M.-H. Jullien de and Monfrin, J. (eds.) *La bibliothèque pontificale à Avignon et à Peñiscola pendant le Grand Schisme d'Occident, et sa dispersion* (2 vols., Rome, 1991)

Bibliothèques ecclésiastiques au temps de la papauté d'Avignon, II (Paris, 2001)

Pons, N. 'Guillaume Saignet, lecteur de Gilles de Rome', *BEC*, 163 (2005), 435–80

Pons, N. and Goullet, M. (eds.) 'Robert Blondel, *Desolatio regni Francie*. Un poème politique de soutien au futur Charles VII en 1420', *Archives d'histoire doctrinale et littéraire du moyen âge*, 68 (2001), 297–374

Porter, P. 'The ways of war in medieval manuscript illumination: tracing and assessing the evidence', in *Armies, chivalry and warfare*, ed. Strickland, 100–14

Potter, D. 'Chivalry and professionalism in the French armies of the Renaissance', in *The chivalric ethos*, ed. Trim, 149–82

Prestwich, M. C. *Edward I* (New Haven and London, 1988)

Armies and warfare in the Middle Ages. The English experience (New Haven and London, 1996)

Pryor, J. H. *Logistics of warfare in the age of the crusades* (Aldershot and Burlington, VT, 2006)

Radulescu, R. *The gentry context for Malory's Morte Darthur* (Cambridge, 2003)

Radulescu, R. and A. Truelove (eds.) *Gentry culture in late medieval England* (Manchester, 2005)

Rázsó, G. 'The mercenary army of King Matthias Corvinus', in *From Hunyadi to Rácócki*, ed. J. M. Bak and B. K. Király (Brooklyn, NY, 1982), 125–40

Reeve, M. D. 'Notes on Vegetius', *Proceedings of the Cambridge Philological Society*, 44 (1998), 182–218

'The transmission of Vegetius's *Epitoma rei militaris*', *Aevum*, 74 (2000), 243–354

'Modestus, *scriptor rei militaris*', in *La tradition vive. Mélanges d'histoire des textes en l'honneur de Louis Holtz*, ed. P. Lardet, *Bibliologia*, 20 (2003), 417–32

Reynolds, L. D. (ed.) *Texts and transmission. A survey of the Latin classics* (Oxford, 1983)

Rhodes, D. 'A note on some fragments of Vegetius from Augsburg', in *Studies in early European printing and book collecting* (London, 1983), 139–40

Richardot, P. 'La réception de Végèce dans l'Italie de la Renaissance: entre humanisme et culture technique', *Studi umanistici Piceni*, 15 (1995), 195–214

'La datation du *De Re Militari de Végèce*', *Latomus*, 57 (1998), 136–47

Végèce et la culture militaire au moyen âge (Ve–XVe siècles) (Paris, 1998)

'La tradition moderne du *De re militari* de Végèce, XVe–XVIII siècles', in *Hommages à Carl Deroux. V. Christianisme et moyen âge, Néo-latin et survivance de la latinité*, ed. P. Defosse (Brussels, 2003), 537–44

Riché, P. 'Les bibliothèques de trois aristocrates laïcs carolingiens', *Le moyen âge*, 69 (1963), 87–104

Roca Barea, M. E. 'El *Libro de la guerra* y la traduccion de Vegecio por Fray Alfonso de San Cristobal', *Anuario de estudios medievales*, 37 (1) (2007), 267–304

Rogers, C. J. 'The military revolutions of the Hundred Years' War', *Journal of Military History*, 57 (1993), 241–78

'The Vegetian "Science of warfare" in the Middle Ages', *JMMH*, 1 (2002), 1–19

Rogers, R. *Latin siege warfare in the twelfth century* (Oxford, 1992)

Rolan, T. G. and Saquero Suarez-Somonte, P. (eds.) 'El *Epitoma rei militaris* de Flavio Vegecio traducido al castellano en el siglo XV. Edicion de los "Dichos de Séneca en al Acto de la Caballeria" de Alfonso de Cartagena', *Miscelanea medieval murciana*, 14 (1987–88), 103–50

Rose, S. *Medieval naval warfare, 1000–1500* (London and New York, 2002)

Ross, D. J. A. 'The prince answers back: 'Les Enseignemens de Théodore Paliologue', in *The ideals and practice of medieval knighthood*, ed. C. Harper-Bill and R. Harvey (Woodbridge and Dover, NH, 1986), 165–77

Rouse, R. and M. 'Context and reception: a crusading collection for Charles IV of France', in *Courtly arts and the art of courtliness*, ed. K. Busby and C. Kleinhenz (Cambridge, 2006), 105–78

'Early manuscripts of Jean de Meun's translation of Vegetius', in *The medieval book. Glosses from friends and colleagues of Christopher de Hamel*, ed. J. H. Marrow, R. A. Linenthal and W. Noel (Houten, 2010), 59–74

Royal Commission on Historical Manuscripts, *Eighth report* (London, 1881)

Rubio, L. 'El Ms Scorealensis L. III. 33 nuevos datos para una futura edición del Epitoma rei militaris de Vegetius', *Emirita*, 41 (1973), 209–23

Ruggieri, J. S. 'Un Vegezio "a lo divino" nel ms. escurialense & II 18', *Cultura neolatina*, 18 (1958), 207–15

Russell, F. H. *The just war in the Middle Ages* (Cambridge, 1975)

Russell, P. E. *Traducciones y traductores en la Península Ibérica (1400–1550)* (Barcelona, 1985)

'The medieval Castilian translation of Vegetius, *Epitoma de rei militaris*: an introduction', in *Spain and its literature. I. From the Middle Ages to the Siglo de Oro. Essays in memory of E. Allison Peers*, ed. A. L. Mackenzie (Liverpool, 1997), 49–63

'Terá havido uma tradução medieval portuguesa do *Epitome rei militaris* de Vegécio', *Euphrosyne. Revista de filologia clássica*, n.s. 29 (2001), 247–56

'De nuevo sobre la traduccion medieval castellana de Vegecio, *Epitoma de rei militaris*', in *Essays on medieval translation in the Iberian peninsula*, ed. T. Martinez Romero and R. Recio (Castello, 2001), 325–40

Ryder, A. *The kingdom of Naples under Alfonso the Magnanimous. The making of a modern state* (Oxford, 1976)

Sablonier, R. 'État et structures militaires dans la Confédération [suisse] autour des années 1480', in *Cinq-centième anniversaire de la bataille de Nancy [1477]*, 429–47

Santini, C. 'Le praefationes ai quattro libri della Epitoma rei militaris di Vegezio', in *Prefazioni, prologhi, proemi di opere tecnico-scientifiche latine* (Rome, 1992), II, 1001–18

Saunders, C., Le Saux, F. and Thomas, N. (eds.) *Writing war. Medieval literary responses to warfare* (Cambridge, 2004)

Savy, N. 'The *chevauchée* of John Chandos and Robert Knolles: early March to early June, 1369', *JMMH*, 7 (2009), 38–56

Scaglione, A. *Knights at court. Courtliness, chivalry and courtesy from Ottonian Germany to the Italian Renaissance* (Berkeley, Los Angeles and Oxford, 1991)

Schenk, D. *Die Quellen der Epitoma rei militaris* (Leipzig, 1930)

Schiff, M. *La bibliothèque du marquis de Santillane* (Paris, 1905)

Schnerb, B. *L'état bourguignon, 1363–1477* (Paris, 1999)

'Vassals, allies and mercenaries: the French army before and after 1346', in *The battle of Crécy*, ed. A. Ayton and P. Preston (Woodbridge, 2005), 265–72

Schryver, A. de, 'Philippe de Mazerolles: le livre d'heures noir et les manuscrits d'ordonnances militaires de Charles le Téméraire', *Revue de l'art*, 126 (1999), 50–67

Segre, C. 'Jean de Meun e Bono Giamboni traduttori di Vegezio. Saggio sui volgarizzamenti in Francia e in Italia', in *Lingua, stile e società. Studi sulla storia della prosa italiana*, ed. C. Segre (Milan, 1963), 271–300

Settia, A. A. *De re militari. Pratica e teoria nella guerra medievale* (Rome, 2008)

Sherwood, F. H. 'Studies in medieval uses of Vegetius' *Epitoma rei militaris*' (PhD diss., University of California, Los Angeles, 1980)

Shrader, C. R. 'The ownership and distribution of manuscripts of the *De re militari* of Flavius Vegetius Renatus before the year 1300' (PhD diss., Columbia University, 1976)

'A handlist of extant manuscripts containing the *De re militari* of Flavius Vegetius Renatus', *Scriptorium*, 33 (1979), 280–305

Smail, R. C. *Crusading warfare, 1077–1193* (2nd edn, Cambridge, 1972)

Smalley, B. *English friars and Antiquity in the early fourteenth century* (Oxford, 1960)

Solon, P. D. 'Popular response to standing military forces in fifteenth-century France', *Studies in the Renaissance*, 19 (1972), 78–111

Sotheby's. *Sale of the Bibliotheca Phillippica*, N.S. Medieval X (26 November 1975)

Spaulding, O. L. 'The ancient military writers', *The Classical Journal*, 28 (1932/33), 657–9

Speidel, M. P. 'Vegetius (3, 5) on trumpets', *Acta classica*, 18 (1975), 153–5

Spiegel, G. M. 'Moral imagination and the rise of the bureaucratic state: images of government in the *Chronique des rois de France*, Chantilly, MS 869', *Journal of Medieval and Renaissance Studies*, 18 (1988), 157–73

'Les débuts français de l'historiographie royale: quelques aspects inattendus', in *Saint-Denis et la royauté. Études offertes à Bernard Guenée*, ed. F. Autrand, C. Gauvard and J.-M. Moeglin (Paris, 1999), 395–404

Spiewok, W. 'Propagande pour la guerre et nostalgie de la paix dans la littérature de guerre au moyen âge', in *Le monde des héros*, ed. Buschinger and Spiewok, 279–88

Springer, M. 'Vegetius im Mittelalter', *Philo*, 123 (1979), 85–90

Stacey, R. C. 'The age of chivalry', in *The laws of war. Constraints on warfare in the western world*, ed. M. Howard, G. J. Andreopoulos and M. R. Shulman (New Haven, 1994), 27–39

Stegmann, A. '*Le rosier des guerres*: testament politique de Louis XI', in *La France de la fin du XVe siècle*, ed. Chevalier and Contamine, 313–23

Stewart, P. 'Military command and the development of the viceroyalty under Ferdinand and Isabella', *Journal of Medieval and Renaissance Studies*, 5 (1975), 223–42

Storey, R. 'The Tower of London and the *garderobe armorum*', *Royal Armouries Yearbook*, 3 (1998), 176–83

Strayer, J. R. 'Defense of the realm and royal power in France', in *Studi in onore di Gino Luzzatto* (4 vols., Milan, 1949), IV, 289–96; repr. in *Medieval statecraft and perspectives of history. Essays by Joseph R. Strayer* (Princeton, 1971), 291–9

The reign of Philip the Fair (Princeton, 1980)

Strickland, M. (ed.) *Armies, chivalry and warfare in medieval Britain and France* (Stamford, 1998)

Stubbs, W. (ed.) *Select charters and other illustrations of English constitutional history from the earliest times to the reign of Edward the First* (9th edn, Oxford, 1913)

Sutton, A. F. and Visser-Fuchs, L. 'Richard III's books: IV. Vegetius *De re militari*', *The Ricardian*, 7 (1987), 541–52

Richard III's books (Stroud, 1997)

Swanson, J. *John of Wales. A study of the works and ideas of a thirteenth-century friar* (Cambridge, 1989)

Synan, E. A. 'St Thomas Aquinas and the profession of arms', *Medieval Studies*, 50 (1988), 404–37

Taylor, C. D. 'English writings on chivalry and warfare during the Hundred Years War', in *Soldiers, nobles and gentlemen*, ed. Coss and Tyerman, 64–84

Teitler, G. *The genesis of the professional officers corps* (Beverley Hills and London, 1977)

Thimister, O. J. 'La bibliothèque de l'église collégiale de Saint Paul à Liège en 1460', *Bulletin de l'Institut archéologique liègeois*, 14 (1878), 153–68

Thomson, R. *Manuscripts from St Albans Abbey, 1066–1235* (Woodbridge, 1982)

Thorpe, L. 'Mastre Richard, a thirteenth-century translator of the "De re militari" of Vegetius', *Scriptorium*, 6 (1952), 39–50

'Mastre Richard at the skirmish of Kenilworth', *Scriptorium*, 7 (1953), 120–1

Torrents, J. Massó (ed.) 'Inventari dels bens mobles del rey Martí d'Aragó', *Revue hispanique*, 12 (1905), 413–590

Trim, D. J. B. (ed.) *The chivalric ethos and the development of military professionalism* (Leiden and Boston, 2003)

Tristano, C. 'Le postille del Petrarca nel Vaticano lat. 2193. (Apuleio, Frontino, Vegezio, Palladio)', *Italia medioevale e umanistica*, 17 (1974), 365–468

Tyerman, C. J. 'Philip V of France, the assemblies of 1319–20 and the crusade', *BIHR*, 57 (1984), 15–34

'Sed nihil fecit? The last Capetians and the recovery of the Holy Land', in *War and government in the Middle Ages*, ed. J. Gillingham and J. C. Holt (Cambridge and Totowa, 1984), 170–81

Ullmann, W. 'John of Salisbury's *Policraticus* in the later Middle Ages', in *Geschichtsschreibung und geistiges Leben im Mittelalter*, ed. K. Hauck and H. Mordek (Cologne, 1978), 519–45

Vaccaro, G. 'Glossario di un volgarizzamento di Vegezio', *Studi di lessicografia italiana*, 24 (2007), 133–63

Vale, J. *Edward III and chivalry. Chivalric society and its context 1270–1350* (Woodbridge, 1982)

Vale, M. G. A. 'Sir John Fastolf's "Report" of 1435: a new interpretation reconsidered', *Nottingham Medieval Studies*, 17 (1973), 78–84

War and chivalry. Warfare and aristocratic culture in England, France and Burgundy at the end of the Middle Ages (London, 1981)

'Warfare and the life of the French and Burgundian nobility in the late Middle Ages', in *Adelige Sachkultur des Spätmittelalters* (Österreichische Akademie der Wissenschaften. Philosophisch-Historische Klasse, Vienna, 1982), 169–94

Vaughan, R. *Charles the Bold. The last Valois duke of Burgundy* (London, 1973)

Verbruggen, J. F. 'Un plan de bataille du duc de Bourgogne (14 septembre 1417) et la tactique de l'époque', *Revue internationale d'histoire militaire*, 20 (1959), 443–51

The art of warfare in western Europe during the Middle Ages. From the eighth century to 1340 (Amsterdam, New York and Oxford, 1977)

Vernet, A. 'Autour du catalogue de la bibliothèque de Clairvaux en 1472', *BEC*, 110 (1952), 210–20

Veyrard-Cosme, C. 'Réflexion politique et pratique du pouvoir dans l'œuvre d'Alcuin', in *Penser le pouvoir au moyen âge (VIIIe–XVe siècle). Études d'histoire et de littérature offertes à Françoise Autrand*, ed. D. Boutet and J. Verger (Paris, 2000), 401–25

Veyrin-Forres, J. (ed.) 'Le deuxième atelier typographique de Paris: Cesaris et Stol', in *La lettre et le text. Trente années de recherches sur l'histoire du livre* (Paris, 1987), 189–212

Vielliard, J. (ed.) *Le registre de prêt de la bibliothèque du college de Sorbonne (1402–1536)* (Paris, 2000)

Wakelin, D. 'The occasion, author and readers of *Knyghthode and bataile*', *Medium Aevum*, 73 (2004), 260–72

Humanism, reading and English literature, 1430–1530 (Oxford, 2007)

Wallace-Hadrill, J. M. 'War and peace in the earlier Middle Ages', *Transactions of the Royal Historical Society*, 5th series, 25 (1975), 157–74

Watanabe, M. *The political ideas of Nicholas of Cusa, with special reference to his* De concordantia catholica (Geneva, 1963)

Watts, J. *Henry VI and the politics of kingship* (Cambridge, 1996)

Weichardt, H. *Ludwig Hohenwang, ein Übersetzer des 15 Jahrhunderts* (Neudamm, 1933)

Weiss, R. 'The earliest catalogues of the library of Lincoln College', *Bodleian Quarterly Record*, 8 (1937), 343–59

Welter, J.-T. *L'exemplum dans la littérature religieuse et didactique du moyen âge* (Paris and Toulouse, 1927)

Whetham, D. *Just wars and moral victories. Surprise, deception and the normative framework of European war in the later Middle Ages* (Leiden and Boston, 2009)

Willard, C. C. 'Pilfering Vegetius? Christine de Pizan's *Faits d'armes et de chevalerie*', in *Women, the book and the worldly*, ed. L. Smith and J. H. M. Taylor (Cambridge, 1995), 31–7

Williman, D. *Bibliothèques ecclésiastiques au temps de la papauté d'Avignon*, I (Paris, 1980)

Winkler, A. L. 'The Swiss and war: the impact of society on the Swiss military in the fourteenth and fifteenth centuries' (PhD diss., Brigham Young Univ., 1982)

Wisman, J. A. 'L'*Epitoma rei militaris* de Végèce et sa fortune au moyen âge', *Le moyen âge*, 85 (1979), 13–31

'Flavius Renatus Vegetius', in *Catalogus translationum et commentariorum. Medieval and Renaissance Latin translations and commentaries. Annotated lists and guides*, VI, ed. F. E. Cranz, V. Brown and P. O. Kristeller (Washington, DC, 1986), 175–84

Wood, N. 'Frontinus as a possible source for Machiavelli's method', *Journal of the History of Ideas*, 28 (1967), 243–8

Woolley, R. M. *Catalogue of the manuscripts of Lincoln cathedral chapter library* (Oxford, 1927)

Worstbrock, F. J. *Deutsche Antikerezeption, 1450–1520. I. Verzeichnis der deutschen Übersetzungen antiker Autoren. Mit einer Bibliographie der Übersetzer* (Boppard am Rhein, 1976)

Wright, N. A. R. 'The *Tree of Battles* of Honoré Bouvet and the laws of war', in *War, literature and politics*, ed. Allmand, 12–31

Index

CABRINI COLLEGE
610 KING OF PRUSSIA ROAD
RADNOR, pa 19087-3699